⊰ Mormon Thunder ⊱

Jedediah Morgan Grant, 1856. LDS Church Archives.

⇉ Mormon Thunder ⇇

A Documentary History of Jedediah Morgan Grant

by

Gene A. Sessions

GREG KOFFORD BOOKS
SALT LAKE CITY, 2008

Copyright © 2008 Gene A. Sessions
Cover design copyrighted © 2008 by Greg Kofford Books, Inc.

Published in the USA
All rights reserved. No part of this volume may be reproduced in any form without written permission from the publisher, Greg KoffordBooks. The views expressed herein are the responsibility of the author and do not necessarily represent the position ofGreg Kofford Books, Inc.

Paperback, ISBN 978-1-58958-111-1
Print-on-Demand printing, July 2020
Also available in ebook.

Greg Kofford Books
P. O. Box 1362
Draper, UT 84020
www.gregkofford.com
facebook.com/gkbooks
twitter.com/gkbooks

Library of Congress Cataloging-in-Publication Data

Sessions, Gene Allred.
  Mormon thunder :a documentary history of Jedediah Morgan Grant/ Gene A.Sessions.
     p.cm.
  Originally published: Urbana: University of Illinois Press, c1982.
  ISBN 978-1-58958-111-1
  ISBN 978-1-58958-112-8
  1. Grant, Jedediah M. 2. Mormons--United States--Biography. I. Title.
  BX8695.G72S47 2008
  289.3092--dc22
  [B]
                              2008007958

Contents

List of Illustrations — vii
Preface to Second Edition — viii
Preface to First Edition — xii
Chronology — xix

PHASE ONE: Gathering Wind (1816–47)

1 Rising Mist — 3
2 The First Rumblings — 11
3 Southern Legendry — 31
4 Crisis — 41
5 A Full-Blooded Mormon — 57
6 The Third Hundred — 71

PHASE TWO: Thunder in the East (1849–52)

7 Mountains and Brown Bread — 93
8 The Lord's Thunder — 111
9 Truth for the Mormons — 131

PHASE THREE: Raining Pitchforks (1842–56)

10 The Heavens Booming — 145
11 Second Counselor — 173
12 The Eye of the Storm — 193
13 Breaking Branches — 209
14 A Cloud of Darkness — 229
15 The Dry Moon — 243

PHASE FOUR: Wildfire (1856)

16	Arrows of the Almighty	257
17	Catechism	275
18	White Heat	289
19	Smoky Visions	307

PHASE FIVE: Rainbow (1856 and after)

20	Reverberations	321
21	Mormon Thunder: An Analysis	333

Family Afterword　345

Appendices

Appendix A　347
　　Biographical Sketches
Appendix B　383
　　"Three Letters to the *New York Herald*, from J. M. Grant, of Utah" (1852; reproduced from publisher's private collection)

Index　447

List of Illustrations

Frontispiece: Jedediah Morgan Grant, 1856. LDS Church Archives.	ii
Brigham Young, ca. 1853. LDS Church Archives.	2
Amasa M. Lyman. Publisher's private collection.	6
Bathsheba Bigler Smith. Publisher's private collection.	21
Theodore B. Lewis. Publisher's private collection	33
Nauvoo Temple with cityscape. Publisher's private collection.	42
Joseph Smith Jr., ca. 1843. LDS Church Archives.	45
Sidney Rigdon. Publisher's private collection.	54
Joseph Bates Noble. Publisher's private collection	85
Daniel H. Wells. Publisher's private collection.	95
Jedediah Morgan Grant, 1856. LDS Church Archives.	104
Joshua Grant Sr., ca. 1852. LDS Church Archives.	124
Susan Fairchild Noble Grant and Joseph Hyrum Grant, 1854. LDS Church Archives.	146
Grant's residence in West Bountiful, built 1854. LDS Church Archives.	195
Grant's second family: Susan, Joseph Hyrum, Susan Vilate, Caroline, 1856. LDS Church Archives.	224
Grant's third family: Rosetta, Jedediah Morgan Jr., Rosetta Henrietta, Caroline, 1856. Museum of Church History and Art.	225
Grant's home in Salt Lake City, ca. 1863. LDS Church Archives.	260
Six sons of Jedediah Grant: Jedediah Morgan, Joseph Hyrum, George Smith, Brigham Frederick, Heber Jeddy, Joshua Frederick, 1877. LDS Church Archives.	290
Colonel Thomas L. Kane, ca. 1862. LDS Church Archives.	328
Heber J. Grant. Publisher's private collection.	330
Two Portraits of Jedediah Grant. LDS Church Archives.	340

Images used courtesy of the Museum of Church History and Art and the Church Archives, respectively, The Church of Jesus Christ of Latter-day Saints.

Preface to Second Edition

Between the time Greg Kofford approached me about doing a second edition of *Mormon Thunder* and its present appearance, I became a founding member of the Utah War Sesquicentennial Commemoration Committee. Principal goals of that organization were the encouragement of scholarship about the conflict and a concomitant raising of awareness about it both in academic and public domains. Among other founders of the group were David L. Bigler and William P. MacKinnon, both of whom expressed an early hope that, before the sesquicentennial had passed in 2008, a much clearer picture would emerge of the forces that combined to cause that dangerous clash between the Mormons and the federal government in the late 1850s.

Recently, both Bigler and MacKinnon published their "differing, yet complementary views on the causes of the Utah War," as the editor of the *Utah Historical Quarterly* labeled them (Winter 2008, 3). Both of them provide new documents and nuanced interpretations in their accounts of the run-up to the fateful days in 1857–58 when the Mormons and the army squared off in a high-stakes game of blustery brinkmanship. Jedediah Morgan Grant appears as something of a bit player in establishing an all-or-nothing discourse that certainly heightened anxiety, fear, and hostility among Mormons during the Reformation. Missing from their accounts, however, are Grant's lengthy and well-developed descriptions in his 1852 *Three Letters to the Herald* of the problems that were developing between Mormons and Gentiles a full five years before the explosion in 1857. The chronology alone shows that the Utah War was not a storm that blew up out of a clear sky.

Historiographically speaking, defensiveness about the Mountain Meadows Massacre has slowly given way to an attempt not to justify it, but to understand, to explain, and to accommodate it—a historical and psychological effort that must precede the compassionate but difficult work of forgiving it. What is important in that effort is not just Grant's inflammatory public sermons or the enthusiasm with which, according to Bigler, he embraced Brigham Young's alleged order to begin the famous Reformation on September 14, 1856, with the highly doubtful purpose of announcing that "the time had come to throw off Washington's yoke." Rather, what is crucial to understand is the world that Jedediah Grant inhabited and which he created in his rhetoric. It was an eschatological, pre-millennial world in which every individual teetered between salvation and damnation and in which unsanitary privies and appropriating a stray cow held the same potential for eternal doom as blasphemy and adultery.

For Grant, the line between Saint and sinner, Mormon and Gentile was as straight and taut as piano wire. On one side were sinners whom Mormonism had snatched like brands from the burning but who could, at any moment, become charcoal smears of backsliding. On the other were the Saints' enemies who were also God's enemies—men who had murdered the Prophet, connived at the crime, or jeered at the suffering of the Saints. God had fixed their eternal doom; but for the first time, the Saints had the ability and the duty to protect the boundaries of their Zion. Only their vigilant righteousness would assure the Lord's strong right hand wielding the sword of vengeance in their behalf.

This world did not exist very long. Brigham Young inhabited it shoulder-to-shoulder with Jedediah Grant in the early 1850s and right up to the high point of the Reformation. By the winter of 1857–58, however, Grant was dead and Young was living in a world in which Christ had not come to save the Saints and in which the dominant question had suddenly become how to work out the terms of sharing the territory with the enemy—both literally and spiritually. An interesting question is whether Grant, had he survived into the world Brigham cannily navigated for the next twenty years, would have found himself on the sidelines and just as estranged from Brigham Young as Heber C. Kimball, another primitivist counselor.

The re-creation of that earlier world is essential to a full comprehension of the Utah War with its causes and consequences, including the Mormon Reformation and the Mountain Meadows Massacre. No one mind is more important in that effort than that of Jedediah Grant. Much of the energy behind my commitment to the second edition rests on my firm belief in the usefulness of the life of Jedediah Grant as a sharp lens through which to view Utah of the 1850s. I therefore hope this new edition will bring to Grant a bit more of the attention I believe he deserves, both as a central personality during the crisis time of the 1850s and as a focus of understanding for the nature of early Mormonism.

Jedediah's eclipse, except for his role in the Mormon Reformation, is virtually universal in historical treatments. I think there are four reasons for this comparative neglect. First, his devotion to the mission-field experience from his conversion on meant that he did not become one of Joseph Smith's inner circle, orbiting into ever-increasing esoteric and exclusive relationships. If he had been in Nauvoo, I suspect that he would have followed that trajectory because of his talents as well as his unswerving and total commitment to the Prophet. But his comparative absence means that he seems to burst on the Mormon scene only in Utah in the 1850s. Second, his spectacular preaching success shines in his Reformation sermons, even though he had obviously honed his rhetorical skills years earlier. They had not, however, enjoyed strong documentation, so there is comparatively little context for understanding the themes that held his attention and around which he built his interpretation of the gospel. Third, his equally spectacular dying came at the most dramatic of moments, with virtually "every-hour-on-the-hour" reports of his struggles against the devil (which is how he interpreted his illness) and his vision of an afterlife of complete order, flawless hierarchy, and intense busyness. Both subjects would have riveted the interest of the Saints even if Jedediah had not occupied such a prominent public position. And fourth, the fact that his son, Heber Jeddy Grant, became not only an apostle but a Church president, whose vigorous efforts to Americanize the Church and to distance it from its polygamous past, have muted the radical discontinuity between the worlds of the father and the son.

I have never been more convinced of the power of Jeddy Grant's life in explaining the Utah of the 1850s. In the preface to the first edition, I promised readers "a book that would capture the essence and meaning of early Mormonism." Having now spent these many months contemplating the history of Mormonism up through the decade of the 1850s, with one eye on the story of Jedediah Grant and the other on the developing Utah War episode, I believe even more strongly in that premise than I did when

I wrote those ambitious words more than twenty-six years ago.

The contributions of this second edition remain, primarily, those of the first: It is a re-creation of obscure aspects of Grant's life and especially a coherent, chronological presentation of his public discourses and private letters that document his thought as a Mormon. With the agile and invaluable help of Lavina Fielding Anderson, I have reshaped many a phrase and passage, both to satisfy her demanding call for clarity and literacy and to reflect my own maturing sense of what makes for good writing. For example, I have hunted out most of the passive constructions, a common bane to decent historical writing. I have also worked on eliminating mixed metaphors, weeded out typos, and corrected inadvertent inconsistencies. In every way, this version is more readable and more sensible. Many notes received updating and further explanation, and some text underwent considerable revision to bring clarity but also to reflect recent scholarship. I made the decision, however, not to attempt to add to the notes all recent scholarship that the issue at hand suggests. Instead, I have added to notes or placed new notes in material that is crucial to a textual point or that has informed a revision of the text. It is now an improved excursion into the deeply interesting life of this early Mormon leader.

It is a pleasure to thank the production crew at Greg Kofford Books, starting with Greg himself and production editor Mike Berteaux, who have worked on this edition. And it is a profound pleasure to extend thanks once again to all those who helped me to complete the first edition. My friend Bill Slaughter at the LDS Church Archives has, for a second time, earned my appreciation for helping me this time to clarify some citation issues as well as to obtain appropriate photographs and illustrations. This time around, I also thank my dear and steadfastly encouraging wife, Shantal Hiatt Sessions, and our two sons still at home, Daniel and John-Christian, for their patience. Finally, I affirm without hesitation that I alone am still responsible for whatever is right or wrong with this book.

Gene A. Sessions
February 2008
Ogden, Utah

Preface to First Edition

WHAT FOLLOWS IS A BOOK about a representative type. We banter many such types about in American history, but I have always thought that the genuine article is really quite rare. Perhaps only a few unique souls of the Andrew Jackson variety actually fit the bill. Yet I have come to believe that Jedediah Morgan Grant is an even clearer representative of the early Mormons than Jackson is of the so-called New Americans of his age. I realize at once that supporting this idea is a tall order. While I am convinced that this volume speaks for itself on that subject, I will nevertheless avail myself of this opportunity to make a few prefatory remarks that will introduce my case.

In the summer of 1975 en route to another project, I became intrigued with the life of the early Mormon leader who is the subject of this book. Completely sidetracked, I began to work on his biography with a growing enchantment. The historian's tools I wielded immediately began to uncover what seemed to me to be marvelous artifacts of the mind among the traces of his life that lay buried in the strata of Mormon history. The more I dug, the more I realized that I was excavating the early history and culture of an entire people, long extinct, by my search for the clues to this single life story. I was struck with the strange image I began to see. The current popular notions about Mormonism both from within and without were nowhere to be seen. There was no twentieth-century Mormon leader in his business suit, expounding the ideals of passive Americanism—the good life filled with material comforts and middle-class elitism. I saw instead a pious yet rambunctiously radical preacher, flogging away at his people, demanding otherworldliness and constant sacrifice. Still, I was not looking at either the popular or religious image of a Joseph Smith or a Brigham Young. I had before me, rather, one of the most enigmatic figures in the entire 150-year history of the Mormons. But I felt nevertheless that I had a crisp and remarkably significant picture of the man. I naturally wanted others to see him the same way, so I proceeded to prepare this book, in which the artifacts themselves tell the story. This is a museum on paper, a documentary history. I serve as the guide.

As a word of preliminary caution, I should add that the reader will not find retold herein the Mormon story itself. The whole craft of Mormon biography has been to retell a thousand times the same tales; only the names are changed to present a new book. I have no desire to add a volume to the dusty shelves of such a semi-useless library. This study seeks to be a real biography, one that illuminates a previously obscure life, the milieu of which inevitably comes forth as the subject moves over the paths of thousands of others who traverse the same landscape. But Grant's life requires more than just a revealing; there are considerable obstructions to a clear view of his fascinating part in the Mormon pageant. One such obstacle arises from the mixed blessing of Grant having produced a son whose own star rose subsequently higher than his own, a son who served as president of the Church of Jesus Christ of Latter-day Saints for nearly three decades during a period of the twentieth century in which Mormonism moved cautiously into the center current of American life and culture. Perhaps the most effective muddying element has developed from the common characterizations of Grant in both Mormon and non-Mormon sources produced during his lifetime and in the 124 years since his death in 1856. My task therefore must also be one of revision as well as revelation. The result, I believe, is a discovery of the genuine Jedediah Morgan Grant—an intriguing leader of ascendant qualities who called himself "Mormon Thunder," and who reflected well Mormonism's own self-image as it passed from childhood into stormy adolescence.

There has long been a belief among historians of Mormonism that virtually nothing in the form of documentary evidence was extant concerning the life of Jedediah Grant. Mary Grant Judd, who started a short biography that was published after her own death, lamented that her grandfather had left only a small missionary diary and a handful of letters from which to draw the substance of his life. She also drew upon the numerous Grant sermons preserved mostly in the *Journal of Discourses* and *Deseret News*. It seemed to me from the outset that more of Grant was contained in those sermons and the issues they broached than Mary Judd or anyone else had suspected, and that extensive analysis of his addresses to the Saints would illuminate broad facets of the man's character and worldview that had been hitherto obscure. With this goal in mind, I collected and catalogued some two dozen sermons delivered mostly during Grant's tenure as counselor to Brigham Young (1854-56). I present in this work some extensive passages from those sermons, because I believe that they provide vital insights into puzzles of the times that have consistently defied clear solution, such as the doctrine of blood atonement and the origins of the Mormon Reformation of 1856-57. I also am convinced that the key to the representative type in this case is found on the chain of his rhetoric. The reader should recognize that, as these sermons appear, they have in almost every case undergone a consistent editing process, mostly to remove repetitive passages and to present the most germane portions. This editing involved only the cutting of whole paragraphs and, in some instances, sentences alone or in groups from the middle of paragraphs. I have not noted these deletions in the book by distracting ellipses or other marking, but have carefully footnoted each quotation so that the reader, assuming some editing of each discourse, might read the unabridged sermon in its original form. In each case of such editing I have attempted diligently to preserve the preacher's intent and tone.

Having imbibed the sentiments of numerous colleagues who agreed on the importance of Grant's life but wagged their heads at the same time over the lack of extant holographic materials, I expected to find very few. To my surprise and delight, after several weeks of following leads mostly among Grant descendants, a fine collection of holographic letters and other materials emerged to be added to the sermons in the volume. I edited these items only for beginning and ending punctuation and capitalization in the case of Grant holographs. For example, a sentence in a letter from Jedediah to his wife Susan appeared in the original as follows: "you did not tell me anything about sister Loisa and Her little Children how she took or Bore the death of my Dear brother Joshua." After editing, it appeared as follows: "You did not tell me anything about Sister Loisa and her little children how she took or bore the death of my dear brother Joshua." Spelling, grammar, and intra-sentence punctuation have been preserved as in the holograph to demonstrate among other things the progressive education of Jedediah Grant, long assumed in Mormon and anti-Mormon circles to have been nearly illiterate. I have sought to reproduce handwritten materials other than those of Grant himself with virtually no editing, as I have other items that in printed form contained errors of spelling and grammar. These items and their preservation as reproduced herein are self-evident.

A book such as this would have been virtually impossible just a decade ago, but with the approach of the sesquicentennial of the Church of Jesus Christ of Latter-day Saints, the research and publication of works in Mormon history experienced a remarkable acceleration. Looking ahead to 1980, Church authorities in Salt Lake City called upon Leonard Arrington, professor of economics at Utah State University and author of the landmark *Great Basin Kingdom: An Economic History of the Latter-day Saints, 1830-1900* (Cambridge, Mass.: Harvard University Press, 1958), to create an internal research and writing enterprise that might convey both to the world and to the Saints a scholarly yet sympathetic body of Mormon history. By 1975 Arrington had established an office in the new Church Office Building tower and had filled it with more than a dozen professional historians and writers. Possessing the title of Church historian (an office previously held by apostles of the Church), he presided over something of a golden age in Mormon historiography. Previously sequestered files became open to his staff, whose writings were subject only to Arrington's own reading committee—himself, Davis Bitton, James B. Allen (the assistant historians), and a meticulous editor from Canada named Maureen Ursenbach Beecher. A rapprochement between Mormon intellectuals and those of the Reorganized Church of Jesus Christ of Latter Day Saints [now Community of Christ] flowered under Arrington's watchful eye. The two churches exchanged documents and scholars. A Mormon History Association flourished with both lay and professional members from both cultures. Annual meetings alternating between RLDS and LDS sites attracted increasing crowds as Mormon history suddenly became at the same time a very open and a very crowded field.

The first item on the Arrington agenda was the production of an ambitious and scholarly sixteen-volume history of the Church, both topically and chronologically arranged. Each volume was assigned to a specialist in the field and given the full cooperation of the Church Historical Department, its vast archives virtually wide open for the first time in history, at least to those so authorized to work on sanctioned projects. The other two priorities involved the creation of two general histories of the Church, one to replace the standard faith-supporting *Essentials in Church History*, by late Church apostle and president Joseph Fielding Smith, and the other to be a scholarly product designed for national consumption and written on a college textbook level. Auxiliary studies in subjects ranging from biography to ethnography were also to come forth as Arrington and his assistants saw fit. With these goals in hand, the Church History Division busily worked through the miles of microfilm and yards of boxed papers in the LDS Church Archives and began to produce prolifically a new Mormon history in partnership with the scores of outside scholars who flowed to the new Mecca of LDS intellect for succor and study

In 1976, the first major goal of the operation was achieved with the publication of *The Story of the Latter-day Saints* (Salt Lake City: Deseret Book, 1976), a prodigious history of Mormonism for internal consumption. Under the generalship of Arrington staffers James Allen and Glen Leonard, an army of writers and researchers (possessing everything from high school diplomas to Ph.D.'s) produced a volume of some 700 pages that tried to tell the Mormon story as a divine pageant of historical accuracy. Whatever might be the judgment as to their success in attaining that goal, there can be little doubt that they did manage to create a very fine narrative account of the Mormon story that in addition contained a splendid bibliography broken into both general and chapter divisions.

Concomitant to the effort in the division toward publication of the Allen-Leonard book, work on the scholarly analysis of Mormon history progressed under the direction of Arrington himself and assistant Davis Bitton. Again, numerous staffers and freelancers contributed research and writing to what became the critically acclaimed publication, *The Mormon Experience: A History of the Latter-day Saints* (New York: Alfred A. Knopf, 1979). Despite its shortcomings, *The Mormon Experience* stands as something of a masterpiece and as the crowning achievement of Arrington's sojourn as LDS Church historian. The text is insightful and literary, and the bibliographic quality is superb. With the Allen-Leonard volume, it creates a situation in which further general bibliographies of Mormon studies became redundant and unnecessary, except as they update and revise.

The bright decade of the 1970s produced thus a veritable galaxy of new stars in the sky of Mormon historiography. In addition to what came directly forth from Arrington's office, countless articles, papers, and monographs reached conception under its influence, adding immeasurably to the meager understanding of the Mormon movement that had existed just a few short years before. A new college-level history of Utah, for example, benefited enormously from this golden age. Under the general editorship of Richard Poll, the team of Thomas Alexander, Eugene Campbell, and the late David E. Miller collected thirty-six excellent essays on various aspects of Utah history and published them under the title of *Utah's History* (Provo, Utah: Brigham Young University Press, 1978). In this case also, perhaps the most valuable part of the book is in its bibliographic excellence. When placed on the shelf next to *The Story of the Latter-day Saints* and *The Mormon Experience*, it completes a trilogy of reference to Utah/Mormon studies that renders further general discussion of such prolix and vain.

The notes herein indicate clearly the primary sources from which this history of Jedediah Grant emerged. Citing few secondary materials, they still demonstrate my intellectual debt to all who went before. As with any volume of its length and complexity, *Mormon Thunder* has also been the beneficiary of a great wealth of time and talent drawn from among my colleagues and friends. Those who have read the manuscript and who have then provided invaluable suggestions for its improvement must lead the list of those deserving thanks. Leonard J. Arrington, James B. Allen, Davis Bitton, Maureen Ursenbach Beecher, Dean L. Jessee, and Ronald W. Walker, all of the LDS Historical Department in Salt Lake City, showed a keen interest in the progress of the work and read all or part of the manuscript at various stages. Paul Peterson, a doctoral candidate at Brigham Young University and scholar of the Mormon Reformation, also read the work and offered a comprehensive critique that improved the volume immeasurably. Another student of Mormonism, Archie Wood, read the manuscript and added his unique dimension to the criticism it needed.

Among my associates at Weber State College, the late Donald Moorman, who lent his considerable expertise on early Utah history, and Dean Lawrence Evans, who encouraged the work from the beginning, made it possible for me to proceed during some very difficult moments. As a matter of fact, Chapter 10 is really as much a product of Don's scholarship as my own. Additionally supportive in a gratifying way were two of Jedediah's great-granddaughters, Bernice Casper and Florence Jacobsen, and a great-grandson, Alvin Pack, who also read the manuscript, providing the family members' valuable perspective. Other friends who offered assistance and criticisms along the way include Ronald G. Watt, Brent Thompson, Suzanne Cottrell, Becky Johnson, John Sillito, and Roger and Laurel Barrus.

The research and writing that go into a book of this sort comprise only a part of the work required for its final production. Linda Jones Gibbs, good friend and talented artist, gave considerably of her time and substance to the graphic qualities of the book, as did Shari Lindsay, Mary Schnitker, and Bill Slaughter. Debbie Lilenquist, Francisca Vilar, Michael Krenn, Dorothy Draney, Cindy Peterson, Sue Ann Larsen, Julie Jenkins, Pat Boyer, and Corliss Speranza participated at various stages in the typing of the manuscript. Shantal Hiatt and Steve Garrett prepared the index

Additionally deserving of gratitude are the Department of History and the School of Social Sciences at Weber State College and the LDS Historical Department for the generous use of their staffs and facilities toward the success of the volume. LDS Church Historian Leonard Arrington gave generously of the support and aid at his disposal to see that this book reached completion. Richard Wentworth and his staff at the University of Illinois Press were unbelievably cooperative and patient in their efforts and deserve special recognition

After all of these, there are two people whose presence in my mind through this entire project both inspired and terrified me. Jan Shipps of Indiana-Purdue University demanded that this work be better (I am afraid) than I am capable of producing. Her suggestions nevertheless powered some very significant changes in the last revision that improved it more than I can begin to measure. William Miller of Marquette University once looked me in the eye and challenged me to write a book that would capture the essence and meaning of early Mormonism. Sensing that he had frightened me out of my senses, he added, "But don't try until you know a whole lot more than you do now." I hope I waited long enough.

In mentioning all of these people and their assistance, I have no intention of transferring blame from myself for whatever faults and errors *Mormon Thunder* contains. I can only be grateful that, during the course of this work, my friends and colleagues were as interested in the life of Jedediah Grant and its meaning as I was.

Gene A. Sessions
January 1982
Ogden, Utah

Chronology

Jedediah Morgan Grant, 1816–56

References to sermons listed below are:

DN: *Deseret News*, by date

GP: Jedediah Morgan Grant Papers, LDS Church Archives.

JD: *Journal of Discourses*

JH: Journal History of the Church of Jesus Christ of Latter day Saints (chronological scrapbook of typed entries and newspaper clippings, 1830–present)

February 21, 1816
    Born in Union in Broome County, New York, the seventh child of Joshua Grant and Athalia Howard Grant

March 2, 1833
    Baptized in Sherman's Corners, Erie County, Pennsylvania, by John F. Boynton and Evan M. Greene

March 4, 1833
    Confirmed in Sherman's Corners, by John F. Boynton and Evan M. Greene.

March 21, 1833
    Other members of Joshua Grant family baptized by Amasa M. Lyman and Orson Hyde.

Summer 1833
    Grant family moves to Chagrin, Ohio, near Kirtland, where Caroline Grant marries William Smith, Prophet's brother.

Summer 1834
: Serves as member of Zion's camp.

February 1835
: Attends series of meetings in Kirtland during which leadership of Church is restructured.

February 28, 1835
: Ordained a seventy and appointed to First Quorum of Seventy.

May–October 1835
: Undertakes missionary journey through New York with Harvey Stanley.

Winter 1835–36
: Works on Kirtland Temple.

March 1836
: Witnesses events accompanying dedication of Kirtland Temple.

April 13, 1836–March 5, 1837
: Undertakes second mission to New York, baptizing five older siblings and their families.

June 6, 1837
: Departs for third mission to New York, working with Benjamin Winchester and brother Joshua Grant.

September 1–November 12, 1837
: Travels with Joshua Grant and Benjamin Winchester on missionary journey through New York City, New Jersey, Philadelphia, Delaware, Maryland, Virginia, and on southward into North Carolina. After Winchester remains in Philadelphia and the younger Grant returns to Ohio, arrives alone in Stokes County, North Carolina.

November 12, 1837–October 9, 1838
: Carries forth missionary endeavors in southwestern Virginia and western Carolina.

November 1838
: Arrives in Missouri; visits brethren in jail in Richmond; overhears militia general order Joseph Smith and six others shot on November 12; arrives at Far West on November 12.

December 25, 1838–January 20, 1839
> Assists in movement of father's family to Knox County, Illinois, from Far West.

May 1839
> Goes to Commerce (Nauvoo), where he visits Joseph and Hyrum Smith and Sidney Rigdon.

May 12–June 1, 1839
> Goes to Quincy to stay with brother; receives call to return to North Carolina.

June 2, 1839
> Departs for second mission to South.

June 12, 1839–September 15, 1841
> Carries forth missionary endeavors in southwestern Virginia and western Carolina, most of the time in company with brother Joshua.

Winter 1842–43
> At Nauvoo.

April 7, 1843
> Called as presiding elder at Philadelphia.

May 1843
> Travels to Philadelphia.

August 1843
> Participates with visiting authorities in local conferences from Philadelphia to New York City.

Fall–Winter 1843–44
> Presides over Saints in Philadelphia.

April 24, 1844
> Arrives in Nauvoo.

May 6, 1844
> Added to Prophet's "general council."

May 9–23, 1844
> Accompanies Wilford Woodruff and George A. Smith on conference visits in Illinois, Indiana, and Michigan.

May 27, 1844
> Accompanies Joseph Smith and others on visit to Carthage.

June 23, 1844
> Carries letter from Joseph Smith to Governor Ford in Carthage; returns with orders for Prophet to surrender to authorities at Carthage.

June 27, 1844
> At Nauvoo when Smith brothers are murdered in Carthage.

July 2, 1844
> Marries Caroline Van Dyke in Nauvoo, departs for East with news of the martyrdom.

July 15, 1844
> Arrives in Philadelphia to resume position as presiding elder.

October 7, 1844
> Sustained as a member of First Council of Seventy.

Fall 1844
> Publishes pamphlet attacking Sidney Rigdon.

May 19, 1845
> Daughter Caroline ("Caddie") born in Philadelphia.

May 22, 1845
> Sister Caroline Grant Smith dies in Nauvoo.

September 1845
> Arrives with family in Nauvoo after more than a year in Philadelphia.

October 11, 1845
> Called as captain of fourteenth hundred to prepare for exodus to West.

December 12, 1845
> Receives endowments in Nauvoo Temple.

December 1845–January 1846
> Administers endowments in Nauvoo Temple; works with fourteenth hundred.

February 11, 1846
> Crosses Mississippi into Iowa among first to leave Nauvoo for West.

March–July 1846
> Leads company across Iowa to Council Bluffs.

July 17, 1846
: Called to assist in location of Winter Quarters.

August–November 1846
: Serves as envoy to Indians, escort to Thomas L. Kane, and as member of Winter Quarters municipal council.

January 25, 1847
: Appointed as captain of hundred for coming emigration.

March 1–ca. June 1, 1847
: Undertakes mission to East to confer with Kane and acquire material for large American flag.

May 19, 1847
: Second daughter, Margaret, born to Caroline in Winter Quarters.

June 17, 1847
: At head of third hundred, departs from banks of Elkhorn River, bound for Rocky Mountains.

September 2, 1847
: Margaret Grant dies of cholera on trail near Independence Rock on Sweetwater River.

September 8–10, 1847
: Brigham Young, Heber C. Kimball, and others returning east from Great Salt Lake Valley stay with third hundred.

September 26, 1847
: Caroline Van Dyke Grant dies of lingering illness compounded by cholera at encampment on Bear River.

September 29, 1847
: Arrives in Great Salt Lake City with Caroline's body after forced drive from Bear River.

September 30, 1847
: Buries Caroline, first white woman interred in Great Salt Lake Valley.

October 1, 1847
: Returns eastward with help for third hundred and to attempt recovery of Margaret's body.

October 4, 1947
: Third hundred arrives in valley.

October 1847–September 1849
: At Salt Lake City.

February 11, 1849
: Marries Susan Fairchild Noble and Rosetta Robison at home of Joseph Bates Noble.

April 28, 1849
: Elected brigadier general in Nauvoo Legion.

September 9, 1849
: Appointed agent of Perpetual Emigrating Fund.

October 19, 1849
: Leaves valley for St. Louis on PEF assignment.

ca. October 1, 1850
: Returns to valley from PEF assignment in St. Louis.

December 2, 1850
: Elected speaker of Territorial House of Representatives.

January 19, 1851
: Elected mayor of Great Salt Lake City.

Spring 1851
: Adopts (with Susan) twelve-year-old John McKeachie, renames him Lewis McKeachie Grant.

July 24, 1851
: Presides over Pioneer Day celebration at which newly arrived federal officials take offense at remarks of Daniel H. Wells and Brigham Young.

October 6, 1851
: Leaves for Washington, D.C., and Philadelphia to assist in countering charges of "runaway judges."

December 8, 1851
: Arrives in Washington, D.C., after brief stopover in Philadelphia.

December 27, 1851
: Arrives in Philadelphia with copy of runaways' report; confers with Thomas L. Kane, confirms existence of polygyny in Utah.

February 10, 1852
From Toms River, New Jersey, indicates intention of returning to Utah immediately.

March 9, 1852
First letter for *New York Herald* appears.

March 25, 1852
With John M. Bernhisel, calls on President Millard Fillmore to request that runaways' report not be submitted to Congress until rest of Mormon defense can be printed and distributed; calls on Secretary of State Daniel Webster, then leaves for Philadelphia to complete pamphlet "Truth for the Mormons."

May 1852
Publishes pamphlet containing three letters to *Herald* defending Saints' conduct in Utah.

August 20, 1852
Arrives in valley from mission to East.

August 7, 1853
Preaches sermon on uniformity, JD, 1:341–49.

October 9, 1853
Son Jedediah Morgan born to Rosetta.

October 17, 1853
Son Joseph Hyrum born to Susan.

December 15, 1853
Marries Sarah Ann Thurston.

February 17, 1854
Marries Louisa Marie Goulay Grant, widow of brother Joshua.

February 19, 1854
Preaches sermon on power of God, JD, 2:10–16.

March 11, 1854
Death of Willard Richards.

March 12, 1854
Preaches sermon on blood atonement, DN, July 27.

April 2, 1854
Preaches sermon on prophecy, JD, 2:145–49.

April 6, 1854
  Sustained as second counselor to Brigham Young in First Presidency.

April 9, 1854
  Ordained apostle and set apart as member of First Presidency.

May 1854
  Operates with notable success public works in absence of Brigham Young and Heber C. Kimball.

June 18, 1854
  Preaches sermon on apostacy, JD, 6:253–54.

August 16, 1854
  Marries Maryette Kesler.

September 14, 1854
  Preaches sermon on newcomers, JD, 3:65–69.

October 7, 1854
  Preaches sermon on immigration, JD, 2:71–74.

November 19, 1854
  Preaches sermon on righteousness, DN, December 7.

December 17, 1854
  Preaches sermon on first principles, JD, 2:225–33.

February 6, 1855
  Preaches sermon on persecutions, JH.

March 11, 1855
  Preaches sermon on faith and works, JD, 2:271–79.

April 7, 1855
  Appointed vice president and director of Deseret Theological Institute.

April 27, 1855
  Son George Smith born to Sarah Ann.

May 5, 1855
  Participates in dedication of Endowment Housze.

May 13, 1855
  Preaches sermon on missions to Indians, GP.

May 30, 1855
> Preaches sermon on Holy Spirit, JD, 3:7–12.

July 6, 1855
> Issues ultimatum from mayor's office on slothfulness in city, DN, July 11.

July 13, 1855
> Preaches sermon on reformation, JD, 3:58–61.

September 19, 1855
> Daughter Susan Vilate born to Susan.

October 6, 1855
> Preaches sermon on polygyny, JD, 3:125–27.

November 22, 1855
> Daughter Rosetta Henrietta born to Rosetta.

November 29, 1855
> Marries Rachel Ridgeway Ivins; preaches at party for group of returned missionaries, DN, December 19.

December 3, 1855–January 21, 1856
> Absent from Salt Lake City during journey to Fillmore for legislative session.

January 27, 1856
> Preaches sermon on famine, JD, 3:199–202.

March 2, 1856
> Preaches sermon on exposing wickedness, JD, 3:232–36.

March 23, 1856
> Preaches sermon on Indian policy, JH.

April 13, 1856
> Delivers Dry Moon discourse, JH, May 28.

April 19, 1856
> Son Joshua Frederick born to Louisa.

July 24, 1856
> Offers prayer at Pioneer Day celebration at Brighton (Silver Lake), JD, 4:7–9.

August 3, 1856
Preaches sermon on need for repentance, JD, 4:15–10.

Summer 1856
Opens farming operation in partnership with George and Thomas Thurston in Weber Valley.

September 12, 1856
Arrives in Kaysville with Joseph Young for conference of home mission.

September 14, 1856
Demands repentance and repetition of baptism and confirmation as sign of reform at Kaysville, commencement of the Reformation.

September 15, 1856
Members of Kaysville Ward rebaptized at Weinal's Mill.

September 16, 1856
Adjourns conference in Kaysville and carries Reformation to Farmington.

September 17, 1856
Members of Farmington Ward rebaptized in millrace north of fort wall.

September 18, 1856
Adjourns conference in Farmington and returns to Salt Lake City.

September 21, 1856
Preaches sermon on rebuking iniquity, JD, 4:49–51.

September 25, 1856
Meets with city bishops to instruct them on preparations for Reformation activities; departs for conference in Centerville.

September 26, 1856
Refuses to rebaptize Centerville Ward; goes to Farmington.

September 28, 1856
Returns to Centerville, commits ward members to reform.

September 29, 1856
Members of Centerville Ward rebaptized; missionaries carry Reformation to Bountiful.

September 30, 1856
Rejects Bountiful Saints, returns to Salt Lake City; observes entry of party of handcart emigrants, weeps openly.

October 2, 1856
Preaches sermon on cleanliness, JD, 4:188-89.

October 7, 1856
Blasts presidents of First Council of Seventy for alleged slothfulness in duties.

October 12, 1856
Preaches sermon on overcoming evil, JD, 4:150-53.

October 15, 1856
Son Brigham Frederick born to Maryette.

October 21, 1856
Places burden of Reformation program upon bishops.

October 26, 1856
Preaches sermon on unity and respect for authority, JD, 4:122-29.

November 1, 1856
Preaches sermon on handcart emigration, JD, 4:70-75.

November 9, 1856
Preaches sermon on hypocrisy, JD, 4:83-87.

November 19, 1856
Makes last visit to Historian's Office; growing increasingly ill.

November 22, 1856
Son Heber Jeddy born to Rachel. Confined to bed; receives first of several administrations from Wilford Woodruff and Franklin D. Richards.

November 23, 1856
Receives administration from Heber C. Kimball, Daniel H. Wells, Jesse C. Little, Woodruff, and Richards.

November 26, 1856
Receives one of two visions of "spirit world."

November 29, 1856
Typhoid compounded by double pneumonia; has extremely difficult night.

December 1, 1856
> Dies of typhoid pneumonia at home, 10:20 p.m.

December 4, 1856
> Funeral and burial.

PHASE ONE
Gathering Wind: 1816–47

Brigham Young, ca. 1853. LDS Church Archives.

"They looked just as I saw them in the vision."

1
Rising Mist

THIS STORY MIGHT EASILY BEGIN one day in 1848, shortly after the first Mormons had arrived in the desolate Valley of the Great Salt Lake. Brigham Young, powerful leader of this curious band of religious enthusiasts, was busily engaged in the construction of a small cabin in which to house that portion of his growing polygamous family that had arrived in Utah. As his daughter later described the scene, he was nailing shingles to the roof when he noticed a small group of men walking toward the house. Striding in front of them was a lanky man of about thirty whom Young recognized immediately as his longtime friend and fellow traveler in the faith, Jedediah Morgan Grant. Young straightened up as the group stopped in front of the house.

"Brother Brigham," said Grant, "we have some urgent public business that we need to discuss with you."

"Well," replied Brigham, "you can see that I have work here that also needs me."

Grant stood his ground: "President, we want you to quit working with tools. We need you to work with men. We have got plenty of carpenters in Zion, but there is only one Brigham Young."

The man on the roof undoubtedly bristled a bit. He had been a carpenter, glazier, and cabinetmaker before 1832, when he met a man in Ohio named Joseph Smith and decided to dedicate his life to the religious and social movement Smith had organized two years before. While he had become quickly absorbed in the Mormon ministry, Young had never forsaken his trade. He took pride in his work and enjoyed it as a respite from the weighty spiritual and temporal responsibilities that came upon him, particularly after his ascension to the Church's presidency after the death of Smith in 1844. Grant's demand was therefore a severe one, yet the

"Lion of the Lord" dropped his hammer and went with the men to a council meeting. According to Young's daughter, he "rarely worked with tools after that day."[1]

It could begin there, but to understand perhaps the only man who dared call Young off that roof, we must go back some 2,000 miles and more than three decades to an older site and to a stranger time, to the place and date of Grant's birth. Generations of New Englanders remembered the year he was born in the town of Union, Broome County, New York. But it was not because of him that they remembered it. They recalled it rather as "the year everyone froze" and the "summer without summer." Deep into the spring of 1816 and across the landscape of the northern United States, an unusual series of winter storms plunged down from Canada and the Arctic, gaining strength over the Plains and the Great Lakes before skidding through New York and Pennsylvania and then to the sea through New England and the Middle Atlantic states. Farmers of the region, dependent upon the timely arrival of spring, waited in vain that year for the sun to melt away the chill of winter.[2]

Through May and into June, the cold continued. The few who managed to get their fields planted saw seedlings emerge from the barely thawed ground only to freeze during the night. July and August of 1816 seemed more like October and November of a normal year, and by September a new winter had set in hard on the heels of an old one that had never really gone away. The result was catastrophic. Many simply starved, while others, like the Grants of Broome County, or the Smiths of Norwich, Vermont, pulled up and pushed on, always hoping for a better year in a better place. For the Smiths, their ten-year-old son Joseph Jr., and his seven siblings, that place was near Palmyra in the Finger Lakes country of New York. For the Grants, it was someplace else, but the pattern was the same.

During the years following the birth of the Republic, life in rural America was seldom easy, especially for the farmer on the fringes of the frontier. Years like 1816 were merely hard thumps to a numb body. In contrast to the opulent vision of what America would become, most lived on the razor's edge of basic survival. The dirt yielded grudging sustenance for men and their families only after fervent coaxing from behind a mule and a wooden plow. Diseases, seldom understood and constantly present, added to the harshness of the environment. Infants were particularly vulnerable, especially during a year like 1816, when famine contributed to the steady advances of typhoid, diphtheria, pneumonia, and the rest. But little "Jeddy" Grant, beginning life under the most difficult of conditions on February 21, 1816, survived.

His parents, Joshua Grant and Athalia Howard Grant, had come as children into the trans-Appalachian region seeking with their families the promises of the New World that had seemed to dry up in New England. They married in 1804 in a place called Neversink, in Sullivan County, New York. In the dozen years following, they had produced four sons and two daughters, all of whom were living, contrary to the more common experience of parenthood at the time: small wooden boxes and little mounds of dirt in the graveyard.

After the disaster of 1816, the Grants, like the Smiths and so many of their fellows, decided that the horizon held more hope than did the frozen soil of their old homestead. They had starved out. In Ontario County, near Naples, New York, where the Grants resettled in 1816, five more children came into the family. Like their siblings, they too would survive childhood.

As the twelve Grant children grew to adulthood, they participated in the family enterprise of shingle-making and managed in addition to gain the rudiments of an education at the knee of their mother and in the common schools of the district. Jeddy learned to write competently and to express himself well. He grew rapidly to a lanky stature of more than six feet. Deep-set eyes and a square jaw accentuated his long face.

Sometime during his youth, or perhaps at the time of his birth, Jedediah suffered a broken nose that healed at the bridge but bent sharply to the left. As he reached manhood, he had become a rugged-looking lad whose swarthy complexion matched well an angular frame and sinuous limbs. He was a frontier boy, and one whose hopes went no further than the wrinkled face of his father and the earthy struggle for life into which he was born.

At least once prior to 1833, when Jeddy was seventeen, the family moved again, this time to the area around Erie, Pennsylvania. There the Grant universe changed shape dramatically. Jedediah's sister Theda remembered those days well. "Mormonites" were in the area.

In the winter of 1833, when I was twelve years of age, two Mormon missionaries came to my father's farm near Erie, Pennsylvania. They were

Amasa M. Lyman, the missionary who preached to the Grant family. Publisher's private collection.

Amasa Lyman and Orson Hyde. My father was deeply interested in this new religion and invited these missionaries to hold cottage meetings in our home. My mother lay sick with rheumatism and could hardly stand to have any one touch her. I remember how tall Elder Lyman looked as he stood by the side of Mother's bed telling us of the gifts and blessings of the restored Gospel and that these blessings follow the believer, in this day, as they did in the days of the Saviour. My mother asked why she could not be blessed as she had perfect faith that God could heal her. The elders placed their hands on her head and prayed for her recovery. Later that evening my mother got up, dressed herself, went out of doors and climbed the stairs, which were on the outside of the house and, with my help, prepared a bed in which the elders slept that night.[3]

Lyman and Hyde, working in company with two other Mormons, John F. Boynton and Evan M. Greene, quickly proselytized the Grant family and many of their friends in and around Erie. The story they related had great appeal for the simple-hearted people whom they had come to save. The boy Joseph Smith, they said, had been in the area about Palmyra for just a few years when he began to have wonderful religious experiences, including visitations from heavenly personages. One of these angelic visitors had subsequently led Smith to the side of one of the numerous drumlins in the area and had delivered into his hands a marvelous book, written in curious hieroglyphics on golden plates and containing an account of ancient Americans who knew the God of the Hebrews. Smith had translated this "Book of Mormon" and published it, after which he had returned the plates to the angel and received instructions to organize again on earth the primitive church of Christ. This he did in April of 1830 near Palmyra.

Since that time he had moved the headquarters of his church to Kirtland, Ohio, as hundreds of converts joined the movement. Some, like Hyde, came to Mormonism from other current groups striving for religious purity, such as the Campbellites. Others, like Greene's uncle, Brigham Young, accepted Smith as a new prophet of God simply because he offered them hope. They had nothing; Mormonism offered everything, from spiritual refreshment to temporal dignity in a new Zion that their charismatic leader told them they would build somewhere in the West. And so it was also with the family of Joshua and Athalia Grant in the spring of 1833.

Jedediah became the first Grant to embrace the new religion, accepting baptism at the hands of Boynton and Greene at Sherman's Corners, Pennsylvania, along with two friends, on March 2, 1833.[4] Theda Grant Reeves remembered that most of the rest of her family joined the church in Erie, being baptized by Lyman and Hyde on March 21, 1833.[5] Having thus united with the Mormons, the family moved that same year to Chagrin, Ohio, some five miles from Kirtland.

Shortly after their arrival in Ohio, the Grants' nineteen-year-old daughter, Caroline, met and fell in love with the Prophet Joseph's brother William Smith. They married in Kirtland in the fall of 1833. This familial tie with the Smiths only heightened the dedication of the Grants to their new religion. In the zeal of his youth, Jedediah was especially anxious to become involved in the Prophet's cause. His chance came quickly.

Joseph Smith had announced the location of his "Zion on the American continent," a place where his followers would receive their inheritance from God. He had even begun to send settlers to this place—Jackson County, Missouri. The old settlers of the area, however, did not enjoy the coming of the Mormons, inasmuch as many of the lands God was giving to these "Latter-day Saints," as they called themselves, were already in the hands of someone else. By the early spring of 1834, the Missourians were taking matters into their own hands, making life for Smith's advance party as miserable as possible. Consequently, the Prophet put out a call for the organization of "Zion's Camp," an army to march to western Missouri to deliver it from the Gentiles. Barely eighteen, Jed Grant eagerly volunteered.

For many of the men who went with Joseph to "redeem Zion" from the hostile Missourians, the experience stretched beyond the bounds of their faith. Not only did the small army fail to accomplish its supposed mission, but the hardships and trials of the journey forced some to reevaluate their commitment to the Restoration and its youthful leader. For others, however, Zion's Camp was a spiritualizing experience that increased faith and ratified the contract with God and His prophet.[6] Among the latter group was young Grant. Twenty years later he would remember of the adventure only the positive, only a vision of the hand of God.

> In the year 1834, when Zion's Camp was moving from Kirtland to Missouri, one day I left the camp and went out to hunt in the woods of Ohio, and strayed away from the camp some 10 or 11 miles. The camp kept moving on all the time, and I entirely lost the track, and having no compass, I knew not towards what point I should travel. I kept travelling on till the after part of the day; I then concluded I would pray, but I could not get any impression where the camp was. However, I soon after received an impression from the Spirit, the same Spirit we had in Kirtland, and the same Spirit we enjoy in this place; and immediately after receiving the impression, I looked before me, and there was the camp moving on in regular order. I could see it just as clear as I did in the morning; there were the people, the wagons and horses, all in their places as I left them in the fore part of the day, and I supposed they were not more than 80 rods off. But after turning for a moment, I again looked in the same direction, but all was gone. Still the Spirit told me to travel on in the same direction I had seen the camp; I did so, and after travelling some 8 or 10 miles, came up with them, and when they first came in sight, they looked just as I saw them in the vision.[7]

After spending the better part of the season on the trek to Missouri and back, Jeddy passed the winter in Ohio, contemplating his recent experiences and deepening in his dedication to Joseph Smith and Mormonism. In February 1835 he attended a series of meetings in Kirtland at which the Prophet literally reorganized the Church of the Latter-day Saints upon the steadfast veterans of Zion's Camp. Nineteen-year-old Jed Grant saw the Twelve Apostles—Brigham Young, Heber Kimball, and the rest—chosen and ordained, and was then himself selected as one of the First Quorum of Seventy, a select cadre of missionaries called to spread ambitiously the message of Mormonism throughout the world.[8] The Prophet Joseph himself ordained his young disciple. It was a life of few comforts promised under the hands of Joseph Smith that day, but Jedediah Morgan Grant, child of 1816 and the American frontier, knew little else. What was more important to him, the familiar hard life now had purpose.

Notes

1. This story appears twice in slightly different forms in Susa Young Gates, "Life in the Lion House," typescript, n.d., Susa Young Gates Collection, Utah State Historical Society, Salt Lake City. The most complete biography of the Mormon leader is Leonard J. Arrington, *Brigham Young: American Moses* (New York: Alfred A. Knopf, 1985).

2. The unusually cool summer of 1816 probably resulted from what was perhaps the greatest volcanic eruption in recorded history at Tambora, Indonesia. University of Colorado Professor Owen B. Toon, while working at the NASA Ames Research Center, analyzed the cooling effect of that 1815 eruption and believes that it blew such tremendous amounts of sulfates into the stratosphere that enough sunlight reflected back into space during the ensuing year to create the infamous "year without summer" over North America. The *Danville* (Vermont) *North Star* reported the following on June 15, 1816: "Some account was given . . . of the unparalleled severity of the weather. It continued, without any essential amelioration, from the 6th to the 10th instant—freezing as hard as five nights in succession as it usually does in December. On the night of the 6th, water froze an inch thick—and on the night of the 7th and the morning of the 8th, a kind of sleet or exceeding cold snow fell, attended with high wind, which measured in places where it was drifted, 18 to 20 inches in depth. Saturday morning the weather was more severe than it generally is during the storms of winter." Quoted in David M. Ludlum, *The Vermont Weather Book* (Montpelier: Vermont Historical Society, 1996).

3. Reminiscence of Theda Grant Reeves, as told to Joseph Hyrum Grant Jr., November 26, 1904, Lathrop, Mo., typescript in possession of Alvin G. Pack, Salt Lake City. Such charismatic activity was sweeping across the region in a wave of revivalist excitement. The classic work on the subject is Whitney R. Cross, *The Burned-Over District: The Social and Intellectual History of Enthusiastic Religion in Western New York, 1800–1850* (Ithaca, N.Y.: Cornell University, 1950). For a balanced and scholarly assessment of the rise of early Mormonism, see Richard L. Bushman, *Joseph Smith and the Beginnings of Mormonism* (Urbana: University of Illinois Press, 1984). For a wide spectrum of views on the life of Smith himself, see also Fawn M. Brodie, *No Man Knows My History: The Life of Joseph Smith* (New York: Alfred A. Knopf, 1945), Robert V. Remini, *Joseph Smith* (New York: Viking Penguin,

2002), and Richard Lyman Bushman, *Joseph Smith: Rough Stone Rolling, a Cultural Biography of Mormonism's Founder* (New York: Alfred A. Knopf, 2005).

4. Journal History of the Church of Jesus Christ of Latter-day Saints chronological scrapbook of typed entries and newspaper clippings, (1830–present), January 15, 1833, 1–3, LDS Church Archives.

5. Reminiscence of Theda Grant Reeves.

6. For a more detailed analysis of this concept, see Thomas G. Alexander, "Wilford Woodruff and the Changing Nature of Mormon Religious Experience," *Church History* 45 (March 1976): 114.

7. Jedediah M. Grant, May 30, 1855, *Journal of Discourses*, 26 vols. (London and Liverpool: LDS Booksellers Depot, 1855–86), 3:9.

8. D. Michael Quinn, *The Mormon Hierarchy: Origins of Power* (Salt Lake City: Signature Books, 1994), 57-69, presents a historical analysis of the establishment, authority, and purposes of the Twelve and the Seventy that does not necessarily coincide with current interpretations of the original missions and responsibilities of the two groups.

"I have three calls to preach where I am not able to fill one...."

2

The First Rumblings

LATE IN MAY OF 1835, Jedediah Grant and twenty-five-year-old Harvey Stanley left Kirtland on a proselytizing mission to the state of New York. Grant, scarcely nineteen, looked forward to visiting the familiar sites of his childhood and to seeing some of his older siblings who had left home prior to the family's conversion to Mormonism and who were still living in New York. His younger brother Joshua, who was nearly seventeen, was also to spend the season in the service of the church, as a consecrated worker on the Kirtland Temple project.[1] But Jedediah, seeing himself as a traveling emissary of Christ in the latter days, had the exciting assignment; as subsequent events proved, he undertook the task with zeal.

Grant and Stanley traveled to Buffalo from Fairport on the steamer *General Porter*. From there they walked into the hinterland of New York, trying their hand at the business of itinerant preaching. The territory through which they passed was not new to Mormonite efforts. Most had heard of "Jo Smith's delusion," and the Baptist and Campbellite ministers were ready at every turn in the road to frustrate the green young men from Ohio. Stanley's journal of the mission recorded continual frustration but no diminution of dedication on the part of either companion. There were also some successes. For five months they preached the Mormon gospel in Wyoming and Genesee Counties and then through Livingston County on a rough line between Buffalo and the former Grant home at Naples, Ontario County. By the time they returned to Kirtland in October they had baptized thirteen.[2]

Through the winter of 1835-36, Jedediah worked alongside his brother Joshua on the temple, witnessing subsequently the Pentecostal events of its dedication in March 1836. But he was anxious for another mission. A few days later he was on his way back to New York, this time alone. Like dozens of other converts to the new religion, his commitment to spreading the faith was astonishing. He would be gone except for brief recesses only for the next ten years.

Behold it came to pass in 1836, on the 13 of April, that I, Jedediah Grant, left Kirtland, Geauga Co., Ohio, on a mission to the east to proclaim the everlasting Gospel of Jesus Christ. I travled east, stoped to my brothers in Jarard, staid 3 days and went on my way rejoicing. Traveled east, stoped again at Brother Curtises in Portland, held 2 meetings in that place & one in company with Elder Charles Tompson. The people was vary attentive and some of them was vary much believeing. Left here the 25 of April, traveled east until came to Bennington, Genesse Co. Thair I held 11 metings. In that place the people was vary frenly and gave me monney to bare my expenses. I staid at or made it my home at Sq. Casess and Mr. Shaws.

I left hear May the 17 and pursued my way east. Stoped at my brothers and sisters in Cowhocton. Held in this place 11 metings which ware attended by a large number of people even in somuch that the schoolhouses ware not large enoph to hold them. Thay were vary attentive and some ware vary much believeing. I did not want for wordes, for the Lord gave me his Spirit which gave me the power of uterance, and not withstanding some of the people were vary unbelieving and thair priests ware vary much sturd or aroused up, and some of them attended the metings which I held in this place and I gave liberty far objectsions if thair wure enny, but I codnt get a word out of thair heads but as soon as I wold git 3 or 4 miles off thay wold begin to go round from house to house and warn the people against goewing to hear me preach, but the honest harted wold not hear to them nor thair precepts. But thay was determend to hear the truth and obay it in spite of men or Satan, but O how the priests cride false prophets, Jo Smith, Gold Bible. I also held 3 metings in Sringwater and 3 in the townd of Naples which ware attended by a larg number of people and some of them ware believing.[3]

Grant thus traveled among friends from his youth or whom he had met during his first journey with Stanley. The brother with whom he stayed at Girard, Pennsylvania, was probably Nelson Grant, who was born in 1810 and would have been the last sibling to leave home as the family moved west. The Grants had earlier lived for some time south of the

Finger Lakes in the vicinity of Springwater and Naples. Jedediah's twenty-three-old brother, George D. Grant, was still living in the area and subsequently submitted to baptism on July 7. (See below.) The brother and sister at Cohocton in Steuben County to the south were undoubtedly his oldest brother, Joseph, born in 1805, and his sister Lois, born in 1807. That Grant had aimed his mission at his siblings had thus become obvious by the places he chose to visit

If Grant's journal to this point displayed anything it was an aura of overt confidence. Traveling alone, albeit among family and friends, did not seem to trouble the twenty-year-old missionary, so it was his successes rather than any loneliness that caused him to long for some assistance in his work.

> I laberd in this part of the vineyard 5 weaks. Thare was cry after cry saing come over and help us, thare fore I cryed unto the Lord that he wold send some of his survants to help me, and before I cryed, he herd, and while I was yet speking he did ansur me and sent unto me Elders DC Smith and SW Denton and J Grant, Jr. Thay arrived hear on the 25 of June and O what joy fild my heart when I beheld the servants of the living God whom he had led hear by his holy Spirit. What a joiful meting it was to meat with the survants of God. It was as a draft of cold water to a thursty sould. I was oer whelmed with joy and inexspresable satisfaction.
>
> I had labored in this place about 5 weaks when the brethren came. Elder D and myself commenced labring togeather. We held 4 metings togeather. We appointed a 2 days meting in the tound of Springwater in Mrs. Miner's barn. The meting was dedicated by Elder S. Thare was 3 surmons deliverd on each day. The Lord blessed us with his holy Spirit. Some of the people was vary unbelieveing.
>
> We also appointed a 2 dayes meting in the town of Naples. We left this place on Mundy the 4 of July. We held a meting the next Thusday in the tound Naples. After meting Br. George Grant and Lenard Wilson and Claricy Furington came forred for baptism. Ordinance adminstred by Elder S.
>
> On Sunday morning thare was so menny people came together that the barn codnt hold them. I deliverd discorse on the first principles of the Gospel taking the 37, 38, and 39 verses of the 2 chapter of Acts. At the intermishon Anny Wait and Mary Gordin was baptise by Elder D. In the after noon Elder D preached and Elders S and G bore testimony. We then had an intermishon

of 15 minits. As son as we had dismissed thare was a Cristian elder arose and spoke, but his voice trembled so that he did not make menny observations but he said that the Book of Mormon contradiced its self and the Bible. After he had set doun I told the peple that we wod stil have an inter mishion of 15 minits during which time Elder Parsons wold bring forred the contradictions, but he sad that he had not time now but he sad that he had red the book through. I told him that I was glad of it, for he cold find it so much the quicker, but he sad that he had not got the book. But I told him in the presenc of people that I would lend him the book or sel it to him and he mite have as long time as he wanted to find it, and I told that I wold meat him in enny place or at enny time and investigate the subject, but he refused. After intermishon I administered the sacrament and Elder S confurmed those that had ben baptised. I then dismised the people and appointed another meting for Munday. After meting Jabus Wait came forward and I baptised him. Elders S and D left hear the 12 of July. After they left hear, Br Joshua and myself commensed labring from house to house.[4]

When Don Carlos Smith and S. Wilbur Denton returned to Kirtland late in July, they reported having found Jedediah Grant in Naples. They worked with him for a time, establishing a branch there with seven members. Young Joshua Grant Jr., who had traveled to the area with them, remained behind with his brother when the others left.[5]

Grant was already employing fruitfully his obvious gifts as a forceful preacher. He took pleasure in debates with sectarians, and relished contemplating the effects of his sermons in behalf of the Restoration and the Book of Mormon. Having found his niche in life, he was interested in doing nothing else.

Sunday, the 17 of July, we held a meting at the same place whare we held our 2 days' meting in the tound of Naples. I delivered a disscorse in the forenoon of about 2 ours in length. We then had an inter mishsion of I oure. We then had a privlige of convursing with Elder Pursery, and of hearing his objectsions against the Book of Mormon. One was that he did not believe it. Another was that Joseph Smith, Jr., got a coppy right. I shoed him that that was nothing against the book. The poore man semed to be vary soraful to think that he had not enny more grounds to work upon. After intermishsion Br. Joshua delivard a disscorse. We then dismised. We held a meting about

2 miles from this place in the same tound.

July the 24, I held a meting in the tound of Cowhocton 2 miles from Blouits Corners. My meting was attended by a large number of people which ware vary attentive, and Br. Joshua held one in the tound of Naples. Sabbath, the 31 of August, we held 3 metings, 2 in the tound of Naples and 1 in the tound of Cowhocton

July 16th, Susan Punks came forward and was baptised by me. August the 3th, Mahaly Farington and Lucindia Farington and Mary Wait was baptized by me for the remishsion thair sins

Thursday, the 4 of August, I held a meting on lint hill in the Methodis meting house.[6]

Basking in the successes of numerous baptisms, Grant seemed surprised on August 9 when his eighteen-year-old brother decided he had had enough and left for home. It would have been a natural thing for Jedediah to go with him, the season being about at an end. But his work was too exciting, too much a part of him. He would linger a few more days in Naples and then push on into the East, again by himself.

August 7 we held 4 metings. August the 9 Bro Joshua left for the west!!

Sunday 14 I held 2 metings in the tound of Naples and one prayer meting, and the Lord inspired the heart of Br Leonard Barber and he came forward and was baptised!!!

Tusday 16 I Baptised Betcy Grant and went on my jurny est. Travied as far as Sinicafals [Seneca Falls], and held 2 metings. Munday, the 22, I went to Savanna, Wain Co., and held 3 metings during the week

Sunday the 28 I held 2 metings in the tound of Butler.

Monday, the 29, I pursued my way est. Arrived at my brothers in Sulivan Co., town of Falsburg, the 8 of September. Appointed a meting in the tound of Neversink for Sunday 11th and during the weak I held 3 more. On Sunday the 18 I held 2 in the same tound and the schoolhouses codnot hold more than half of the people. I maid 3 more appointments for Tusday and Wensday and Thursday and Sunday the 25 I held 2 more and 3 more during the week. I held 3 more. Sunday, October the 2, I held 2 and 3 more during this weak. October the 7 I also held 2 metings, 3 during the weak, 3 more Sundy the 16. I held 2 more during weak and I baptised Austin Grant and Jane Grant and Harris Gillet and Cally Gillet.

Sunday the 23 and during the weak I held 6 more. Sunday, the 30, held 1. November. In this mo. I held 12 which were attended by a large number of people, many of them ware believeing. John A. Ackley came forward and obaid the Gospel!!!

December. In this mo. I held 18 metings and baptized 12. Samuel and Aananet Carpender, Beny Boston and Thedy Gillet and Miles and Jane Wheatten and Robert Achley and William Brundage and wife Jothan Barlow and also wife and Betcy Ramont.

January. In this mo., from the first to the 15, I held 4 metings and baptized 6. Edward Grow and wife and John Erits and wife and Pheby Pain and Mary Edwards. I have not given a ful accoun of my labor in this and for this reson: I have ben so bissey night and day that I have not enny time to write.

I left Fallsburg on the 16th of January, 1837. During my stay at that place I held 60 c[ottage] metings which ware attended by people that ware attentive to what was said and from among those attendeded my metings I baptised 23, one of which was my brother. I left them all overwhelmed in tears. They ware all determined to ceep the commandments of the Lord in spite of all the priests of Bail; they gave me food and rament and monney to bare my expences home. I obtained subscribers for the Messenger and Advocate [a church magazine]. After I left Sulivan Co. I travled a north west corse, arived at Sisters Blackmond the 19th. Appointed a meting for Sundy the 22 but in concequence of the snow faling soe deep and drifting so tremendously that the people ware unable to get to the schoolhouse. I was calculating to start or pursue my jurny west as soon as Mundy the 23 but cannot on account of the snow. I spent my time in taulking or reding or writing. So past away the 20 and 21, 22 and 23 days of January.

January the 24. This day I also spent in reding with the exseption of going to Louisville, 3 miles distance from Sisters B[1ackmond]. I staid with E Pettingile the 25 and 26, both of which days I spent in reding and writing.[7]

Although his astounding successes in promulgating Mormonism beckoned him to stay, Jedediah Grant made his way slowly westward on his return trip to Kirtland and his family at Chagrin. There was nevertheless no rush in the journey, for his real home was in the field, striding from house to house, and from meeting to meeting, challenging a generation of vipers with the doctrines of a new creed and with the spirit of revival. And Kirtland, his destination, was to him only a way station, a place in which to regenerate and from which to leave on another mission to the East.

Saterday the 28 I held a meting in the stone schoolhouse near Sisters B. The people was vary attentive and appeared to be vary much pleased with the doctrin.

Sunday the 29 I held 2 metings in Louisville, one at 11 o'clock and one in the evening, which was attended by a larg multitude of people, some of which declard that the doctrin was true. Some seammed to be all carried away with it, and none rose in oposition to it, but all seammed to be satisfied that we had benn belied and shamfully abused by this generation.

I left Louisville the 30 and pursued my jurny west. Arived at my uncles in Catoe February the 2. I held meting the 5 and started on my jurny the 6. West to Wane Co., Savanna, and held a meeting and from thence I went to Waterloo and held 2 metings, and from thence I went to Naples and Cowhocton and held 2 metings which was attended by a larg number of people. I left my sisters house on the 22 of Feb. and pursued my way west. Arrived at Portag Church the 23 and staid there and in the regons round abought until the 6 March during which time I held 7 metings. I left there the 5 of March and arived in Kirtland the 13th whare I staid until the 6 of June 1837.[8]

Those three months that Grant spent in Kirtland could not have been very pleasant for him. The trauma through which the Church was passing that spring almost destroyed it completely. For a wide-eyed missionary, fresh from the task of preaching a glorious vision of eternal truth, the harsh realities of a frail and earthly organization that the Church had become in his absence must have caused him considerable anguish. Apostasy had become a rapidly spreading cancer, as Smith's abilities as an administrator fell far short of his mystical hold on his followers. Caught up in somewhat naive financial machinations, the young prophet had allowed the Church to tumble to the brink of economic ruin and certain social disgrace. But in spite of all the turmoil that inevitably swirled about him as he now found himself confronted with the stark humanity of his own beloved cause, Grant's enthusiasm for the work seemed undiminished. As he wrote to his friend Warren Cowdery in April, his impatience with the Kirtland troubles had caused a longing for an accelerated progress in the spreading of the gospel "until its sacred influence shall be felt by all, and the knowledge of God cover the earth as the waters do the sea."⁹ Grant had reached a point of total commitment. Even the apparent failings of his prophet-leader raised no significant doubts. The time for doubting had passed.

As soon as he could manage it, he was off again. In the face of great strife at the center of Mormonism, it was nevertheless very difficult for him to understand why others did not share his pleasure in a work that to most was intensely arduous, even under the best of circumstances. Nearly a century and a half later, Silvan S. Tomkins would suggest six stages of gradually deepening commitment through which the dedicated adherents of a movement pass to a point of no return and beyond which no other way of life seems possible or desirable.¹⁰ Grant seemed well on his way to the final stage of the Tomkins model, where he would have to continue in his commitment as a proselytizing preacher even when he was no longer among nonbelievers. The society of the Saints in Kirtland, being already converted, held little appeal.

I then left Kirtland in company with Elder Wm. Markes. We went on borde a steme bote at Fairport. We arrived at Buffalow the 7th. From thare we went to the church in Alligany Co., town of Portage. Elder Markes came thare on bisness of a temporal nature. He staid a few days and returned to the state of Ohio!! I staid in Portage and in the vicinity about 4 weekes holding metings as often as it was conveniant. After I left the church in Portage, I went into Steuben Co., the town of Bath; tarried in that place about 4 days durin which time I held 3 metings and baptised 5 pursons. I then left for Sulliven Co. While on my jurney I stoped in Broom Co., whare I held metings. I arrived in Sullivan Co. the first of August in this part of the cuntry found 2 elders, J. Grant and B. Winchester; thay had ben laboring with dilegence and had added 12 to the church. Thare was 5 more baptised after I arived.

September lst, I left the Saints in S[ullivan] and went to the sity of NY in company with J[oshua] and B[enjamin]. From NY we went to the state of NJ and so on to Phelidelpha preaching by the way. From P we went to the Chesapeke Bay. Thare we seperated after travlen some distance. I again found Br J[oshua]. We then concluded to go to the church in N.C., preaching by the way. After we arived in Harison Co., Br J staid about 2 weekes then left for the state of Ohio. I still staid in H[arrison] Co. until the first of Nov!!!

Durin my stay in H Co., baptized 2 persons

After I left that part of country, I pursued my corse south and after a jurney of 270 mi I arived in Stok's Co., NC. On the evening of the 12 of Nov. The same weeke I commenced holding metings. I soon had calls to preach in difrent places. The people became vary desirous to heare to the truth, so much so that thay came out by hundreds to heare the Word of the Lord declared in it planeness as in days of old!!! But the priests ware vary much enraged and endeverd to ceep the people from heren the truth, but with out effect.[11]

The preachers alone may not have been able to bother Jedediah Grant in the South, but in Stokes County the young missionary confronted a force within him that challenged the course of his life. Feeling alone and deserted, and worried about dissensions in the church, Grant inevitably became reflective and unsure of himself. In his mind he felt Satan vexing him with tactics reminiscent of the temptation of Christ. He wrote of the experience to a family with whom he had stayed in Harrison County, Virginia, some time before.

Stokes Co   April 12, 1838

Capt Bigler dear sir I received your letter the last of January but words wold fail to tell you the satisfaction I received when read your letter it being the first word of consolation that I received from enny frend since I left your house, save those that I have made since I left, but how shal I tell my feelings when I read the heartrending sentence: Br [Don Carlos] Smith cannot come. My God said I is all my hopes blasted? Can it be posable that I shal not mete Br Smith on the happy plaines of North Carolina. These thoughts past my mind then I beheld that all my antisapations was blasted in a moment by rude winds of disapointments but alas ses the Tempter your alone in a distante land without monney and clothes. Now said he I shoe you a butiful plan that will rase you to emanunce direcly. Now ses he you had better leeve NC and goe direcly to the Illinois and thare goe to studing law or goe to worke on a farm. By eather of these means said he you can acquare welth and honor but if you stay here you are deprived of the society of your friends [and] relations. You will receive nothing but pursecution for all the time you spend in the vineyard. Not onley this said he I intend to sowe the seed of discord in Kirtland and elswhare. This said he will disharten menny of your colleges [colleagues] and tha will forsake the vinyard and you will be left alone. These temtasions came upon me like the sweeping whirld wind upon the mountaintop, but when I contemplated for a moment I said in my heart the Tempter is a lyer and was from the beginning that he may sowe discord among the Saints. Yet said I he cannot overthrow the Word of the Lord. After beholding the cloven foot of the Tempter I arose from my seate and like a hungray lion in [the] forist in pursute of his pray I went to the grove with grate velosity and uncovered my head and prostrated myself upon the ground and pourd out my sole to the God of Iserael and the cloud was rent asunder. The tempttasion was gone and the Spirit of Lord spake peace to my sold saing fere not I am with thee. Then did I discover that I was not alone for the Lord was with me. I then arose rejoycing and commenced proclaiming the Gospel the truth of the Son of God. I have preached in 4 co since I came to this cuntry. I have 3 calls whare I amnot able to fill one and I alsos have plenty of pursecusion and some desputes with the priests both Methodist and Baptist but so far truthe has prevailed. I have not confined my labors to enny purticular place for the people have all benn ancious to have me preach thare fore I have ben in enny direction preaching the Word. I have however sta[r]ted a church or in other words I have baptised 4 since came to this cuntry and thare is a prosspect of more being baptised. I intend to stay heare until the last of August then I shal goe to seey my br in the state of NY or I shal come by your house and take the river and goe to the state of Illinois or Missouri. I want that you shold indever to have some of the elders (if enny shold come thare) come to me. Tell them that the cuntry is helthy and the people kind and hospitable. I wold be vary glad if you wold take the paines to send me some of the papers enny that has letters in regarde to Sharnge [?] or on others matters of importance. If Br Winchester is thare tell him that I wold give all my monney to seey [illegible] if it shold be along [illegible]. Write all the news you can think of about Kirtland and Missouri and the affairs in that county. I doubt exspect that this letter will be a full compensation for the much interesting news contained in your letter. Thare was good news enogh to over balance the bad!!!!! Give my love to all inquareing frends. I am as ever yours &c.

J M Grant to J G Bigler

Write as soon as you receive this and not delay as I have done. Forgive me as sorry and leave it above to mingle in the joys of infinite love which may God in mercy grant as your portion and that of our race.[12]

To the women in the Bigler household, Grant attached a note in which he waxed eloquent, and though perhaps falling somewhat short, tried his hand at a well-turned metaphor that would inspire his sisters in Christ to righteousness.

Bathsheba Bigler Smith. Publisher's private collection.

Sarah and B[athsheba]. W[ilson]. Bigler
Dear Sisters in the Bandes of Gospel Grace

I imbrace the opertunity to write a few lines to you believing that you will rede them with a degre of susfaction forgiting my fayables which with you are fundnable [?] no doght!! I have oftimes thought of the few days that I spent in that branch of the church in not only thought of the days but I have vary often thought of the kindness which I received from Cal [Colonel?] Martin and your relation[s] in general. I want that you shold give them my respects and tell them that I can never forgit them in time nor in eternity. When I read the sympathetick wordes in you letter my felings on that ocasion I shalnot attempt to desscribe!! But it sufiseth me to say that I was happy to here that you had not forgoten to wish me well while I labor in the vinyard of the Lord and that these wishes had ben made known to him that holes the desteneys of all mandkind in his own powerful hand!!! Deare sisters may the Lord God of Israel uphold you while in the morning of life!!! and thare are angel voices heard in childhood's frolic hours!! when life is but an April day of sunshine and of showers!! This season is now yours. The beams of morning shine upon you the opening scenery of life in perspective! extends the flowery [illegible] to your longing visions!! Then let pure religion be your companion. Go with him hand in hand through the jorney of life and when the frosts of age shall chill your brows and your change shall come she will be near to give you peace. She will seize the fleeting spirit in her snowy hands.[13]

As the sultry days of summer set in, Jedediah Grant had been absent from the central activities of Mormonism for more than a year. Correspondence with friends and kinsmen in Ohio and the new gathering place in Missouri in combination with local rumors made him understandably uneasy. Something had gone wrong, and now he was so far away that he could not get a clear image of conditions at home. His fears that the Church had not extricated itself from the Ohio troubles of 1837 were painful glimpses of the truth. He had left Kirtland just prior to the failure of the Safety Society, an ambitious and foolhardy economic scheme by which Smith had hoped to amortize his movement. While Grant had optimistically garnered converts to Mormonism, its leader had been forced to flee from Ohio, leaving his debts and many disillusioned followers behind him. Grant had thus begun a long career of heady optimism about the appeal of the Mormon message and, at the same time, nagging pessimism about the reality of the Mormon experience. His answer to the problem at this stage of his life was simply to remain in the mission field, where the discrepancy between the promise and the fulfillment, between the ideal and the real, could be lost in isolation. His edited letter to Moses Martin from Surry County, North Carolina, on May 18, 1838, revealed signs of all of this, but more abundantly still of his continued fervor for the missionary effort in the South.

Dear Brother in the Lord,

 Although I have been separated from you many months, I have not forgotten you; and be assured that I have often times desired your company, for I have labored alone most of the time since I left Kirtland.
 I have traveled from state to state, proclaiming the word of God; and for the last six months, I have been preaching the gospel in the counties Stokes, Surrey, Patrick and Rockingham, in this state.
 The faith of our church, never had been made known to any of the people in this part of the country, until I came here. They had heard many false reports from the mob in Missouri. The people in Jackson County having sent to their friends in this country, all the exaggerated and false stories, which they were disposed to. And by this means the minds of many have become prejudiced against our people.—And it is almost impossible, to convince this people that the stories are incorrect.
 I have one very important request to make, which is, that you would use your utmost endeavors to have some of the elders come to this country without delay. Have this request made known to the Church in Far West; tell

them, that doors are open in every direction throughout those counties, and it is altogether out of the question for me to fill half of the calls, all of which are very urgent indeed; and the prospects are very good for building up a church. But I have to go to so many places, that it is not possible for me to build up churches, unless I can have help in this great work of the Lord.

I have no doubt when I say there can be a large church built up in this country, but that you know that it is a very hard thing for one alone, to start the work, in a state where the sound had never been heard, save by false reports.

But the people are all very willing to hear: and many are very much believing in the principles that I hold forth. You well know that the state of North Carolina has been past by, by all our elders. I am the only elder I think, that has ever visited this state.

Brother Moses; I want that you should send me some of the papers containing the letters of br. Joseph on slavery. Send them to Webb's Post Office, Stokes Co. N.C. The climate in the country is healthy, and the people hospitable and kind. The elders can come to the Kanawha salt works by water, where they will be within 100 miles of Patrick court house, and when they get there they may enquire for me; and if I am not there, they may enquire for Webbs Post Office.

I have baptized 4 since I came to this country, and the prospects are flattering.

All manner of stories are in circulation here about br. Joseph, he is in jail for murder! and has run away from Kirtland to Mo!!!! How do these sayings agree? Give my love to all. Yours in the covenant of grace.

J. M. Grant.[14]

Grant naively expected missionaries from Missouri to respond eagerly to his call for help. Although he may have suspected trouble in Missouri, he obviously knew little about the gravity of the situation there in the summer of 1838 as anti-Mormon tension rose to the point of crisis. Even providing Martin with directions for new missionaries to find him, he apparently had no doubt that his glowing report of conditions in Virginia and North Carolina would bring elders to assist him very shortly.

Thomas B. Marsh, president of the Quorum of the Twelve Apostles, answered Grant's letter to Moses Martin in August 1838. His reply, written at Far West, a final bastion of the besieged Mormons in Missouri, painted a sketchy but positive picture of conditions there. It also skirted the young missionary's request for help with a nebulous promise.

Elder Grant:

    Your letter of the 18th of May, directed to Br. Moses Martin was a few days since handed to us; and we hasten to give you some information relative to our situation in this part of the land. I have used my influence to send some Elders to your assistance, and I think that one or more will be sent to that region, before long.

    Heaven seems to smile upon the saints here, in almost every respect, and surely we ought to be the more faithful to *Him* who pours out his blessings upon us. Many, very many, have emigrated to this place, this season, and we are informed that many more are on the road.

    Another town has lately been laid out for the benefit of the saints about 25 miles from Far West, called Adam ondi ahman, it is on the Grand river, surrounded by a beautiful country of land.

    Crops in this upper country, are exceedingly flourishing this season: I think that the prospects for an abundant crop of corn, were never greater. Wheat is from fifty to seventy five cents per bushel, corn meal is sold in this place for 75 cents per bushel and will probably remain as high as that until the new corn is ripe, when it will probably be much lower, as we understand that contracts are making for corn at 20 cents per bushel; good bacon is from 6 to 8 dollars per hundred, and pickled pork about the same. I think that provisions of all kinds will soon be very plenty among us

Yours with respect,
T. B. Marsh[15]

    Subsequent to his receipt of the Marsh letter, Grant decided to end his first mission to the South. Having probably received accurate accounts of the deteriorating Missouri situation from family members who had moved there in the spring, he was no doubt anxious to see to their welfare, although the South had been very good to him and his chosen career.

    I established a small branch of the church in Patrick Co., Va., which co. bounds Stokes Co. on the north. I preached in Stokes, Surry and Rockingham Co., N.C. My labors ware so exstensive that I did not baptise menny yet I lade the foundation for a grate work!! I preached in thare court houses and chapels in all parts of the cuntry. I had large congregations whare ever I held metings. I held some debates with the Methodists, all of which resulted in faver of the truth, and in the glory of God our Heavenly Father. The people in N.C. and Va. ware kind indeed to me; thay gave me a beast to ride, clothing in abundance. They also gave me monney to bare my exspenses to the Far West. I left on the 9th Oct., 1838, had a prospers journey!![16]

Unfortunately, Grant did not give the particulars in his journal of that trip to Far West, Missouri. Apparently, as he arrived in western Missouri, he learned of the arrest of several Mormon leaders, including Smith, at Far West on October 31 by elements of the state militia, acting under an infamous order from the governor that the Saints must be removed from Missouri or be "exterminated." Discovering that his brother George was among the number in custody, Jedediah went to Richmond, where the brethren were jailed temporarily. According to Hyrum Smith, testifying later in July 1843 on the Missouri troubles, Jedediah Grant stayed in the same tavern where General John B. Clark of the Missouri militia and his cadre were housed. There the returning missionary heard Clark order Joseph Smith and six others shot on November 12. He saw the men so ordered choose their rifles and two balls each for the task. Clark saluted them, saying, "Gentlemen, you shall have the honor of shooting the Mormon leaders on Monday morning at 8 o'clock!" At about that moment, according to the Prophet's brother, they discovered young Grant's presence, which saved the lives of the brethren, because Clark and his men were afraid the Mormon lad would tell what he had witnessed.[17] Whether the incident at the tavern took place as later reported is a matter for speculation, for there is little corroborating evidence. But it is clear that Grant visited the jailed Mormon leaders on his way to a reunion with his family at Far West. Parley P. Pratt, for example, sent word by him to his wife that young Grant should be given charge of his livestock until the apostle could obtain his freedom.[18] The young man was appalled at what he found at Far West.

Arived in Far West the 12 Nov., found the church in sore afflictions haven ben purcicuted by a lawless mob who have no fere of God before thair eyes. The purcicution was so grate that menny had been put to death for thare religion. Menny ware put in irons, surrounded by a strong guard, and the hole church bound to leve the state of Missouri!![19]

Grant's seventeen-year-old sister Theda would remember those days as follows:

> In the spring of 1838, with other Saints, we moved to Far West, Missouri. At this time Jedediah and Joshua Jr. were preaching the Gospel in the Southern States. My older brothers and sisters were married. Father planted crops and built a cabin. He harvested a moderate amount of food in the fall. Mob violence was now becoming worse in Missouri. In the winter my brother Jedediah came to Far West from the mission field bringing with him a company of converts from Virginia. Through Jedediah's aid the farm was exchanged for a yoke of oxen, a wagon and a horse. Jedediah was anxious to get Father and Mother away from Far West to a place of safety, as they were growing older and he could see trouble ahead. Father felt bad having to leave as he had a beautiful place, part timber and part prairie. Wild turkeys came in sight of the house. One which father shot weighed eighteen pounds after it was dressed. Deer were also plentiful.
>
> On Christmas Day we started to Illinois. At Henderson Grove, Illinois, Father found a vacant cabin and moved into it. He started to tap the trees and proceeded to make maple syrup. Jedediah left us here and went on to Virginia to continue his missionary work. Nelson, my older brother, came and persuaded my parents to come to his home. These were cabin days. Part of us slept in our wagon and we stayed with Nelson and his family the following year. In the fall of 1840, Father and Mother moved to Altona, about sixty miles northeast of Nauvoo where there was a branch of the Church.[20]

Thus, while the Saints were fleeing Missouri, eventually to resettle on a bend in the Mississippi River in Illinois, the Grants, with the assistance of their sons, were establishing themselves in the community in which they would live out their lives. But Jedediah, beginning to complain about a lifelong affliction with "sore eyes," was more interested in promulgating Mormonism than in settling.

> I, in company with my father and his family, left Far West Dec the 25 for Knox, Co., Ill. After a jurney of 21 days we arrived safly at the destined spot. I staid in Knox Co. about 4 months. I was some what afflicted duren

the time with sore eyse, tho I held meetings with the brethren and baptised 2 duren the time.

I left Knox May 12th, and went to the village of Commerce. I thair had the privilege of seing some of the brethren that ware in prison when I left Far West, namley Joseph and Hiram Smith and Sidney Rigdon. I staid in the village of Commerce about 3 days duren which time the elders of the church received much instruction from the presidents of the church. After I left Commerce I went to the village of Quincey. I had a brother living 2 miles from town.

I staid with my br until June 1th on which day thare was a conference of elders assembled in the town of Quincey, Adams Co., Ill. I was apointed by the conference to go again to the state of N.C. Elder Abraham O. Smoote was apointed to travel with me, but he not being able [to] start under 2 weekes it was thought best for me to start befor. Acordingly, the 2 day of June I went on bord the steam boat Benj Frankling.[21]

Actually, Grant had requested his return to the South himself. At a conference of seventies on June 1, he presented a letter from North Carolina asking that he renew his efforts in the South. He was happy to accept the subsequent assignment to continue his profession as a preacher of Mormonism.[22] This time he would stay for three legendary years.

⇁ Notes ⇀

1. Joseph Smith Jr., *History of the Church of Jesus Christ of Latter-day Saints*, edited by B. H. Roberts, 7 vols., 2d ed. rev. (1902-12; Salt Lake City: Deseret Book, 1964 printing), 2:205-6. This work is based largely on a lengthy manuscript compiled between 1839 and 1856 by various clerks. Although finished to appear as the work of Joseph Smith himself, in reality it was adapted from the great bulk of documents created by others as well as the Prophet during his lifetime.

2. Journal of Harvey Stanley, holograph, LDS Church Archives.

3. Jedediah Grant, Journal, holograph, LDS Church Archives, April-May 1836. Apparently, Grant had Stanley's diary in his possession after the first mission to New York, for when he undertook his second mission east, he used the back portion of the booklet to record his experiences from 1836 to 1839. Consequently, both journals are in the same volume and are filed with the Grant papers in the LDS Church Archives.

4. Ibid., June–July 1836.

5. Journal History of the Church of Jesus Christ of Latter day Saints (chronological scrapbook of typed entries and newspaper clippings, 1830–present), August 1, 1836, 1, LDS Church Archives.

6. Grant, Journal, July–August 1836.

7. Ibid., August–January 1836–37. The Blackman (or Blackmond) sisters of Sullivan County were converts of Grant's first mission to New York. See Stanley, Journal. Note the success Grant enjoyed in his 1836–37 New York mission in contrast to the slow progress of the 1835 journey into the same area.

8. Grant, Journal, January–June 1837. Note the scant attention he gave in his journal to the three months at Kirtland in 1837.

9. Jedediah Grant, Letter to Warren Cowdery, Journal History, April 11, 1837, 1.

10. Silvan S. Tomkins, "The Psychology of Commitment: The Constructive Role of Violence and Suffering for the Individual and for Society," in *The Antislavery Vanguard: New Essays on the Abolitionists*, edited by Martin Duberman (Princeton, N.J.: Princeton University Press, 1965), 170–98.

11. Grant, Journal, June–November 1837.

12. Jedediah Grant, Letter to J. G. Bigler, April 12, 1838, holograph, Jedediah M. Grant Papers, LDS Church Archives.

13. Ibid. Inasmuch as Grant addressed the Bigler women as "Sisters in the Bandes of Gospel Grace" while beginning his letter with "Capt Bigler dear sir," it is possible that the two were the persons he mentioned in his journal as having been baptized during his stay in Harrison County.

14. Jedediah Grant, Letter to Moses Martin, May 18, 1838, *Elders Journal* 1 (August 1838): 51.

15. Ibid., 51–52.

16. Grant, Journal, October 1838.

17. Journal History, July 1, 1843, 8. Historians generally accept evidence indicating that the Mormons survived the execution order because Militia General Alexander Doniphan refused to carry it out. Richard Lyman Bushman, *Joseph Smith: Rough Stone Rolling, a Cultural Biography of Mormonism's Founder* (New York: Alfred A. Knopf, 2005), 367, fails even to mention the Hyrum Smith account. Grant himself, however, tacitly verified Smith's account when he included it in the "Appendix" to his pamphlet, *Three Letters to the New York Herald, from J. M. Grant, of Utah* (Philadelphia: By the author, 1852), 61, and identified the witness, "a young man by the name of Grant," as "The present Editor." (See Appendix B in this volume.)

18. Journal History, December 1, 1838, 1.

19. Grant, Journal, November 1838.

20. Reminiscence of Theda Grant Reeves, as told to Joseph Hyrum Grant Jr., November 26, 1904, Lathrop, Mo., typescript in possession of Alvin G. Pack, Salt Lake City.

21. Grant, Journal, December–June 1838–39.

22. Journal History, June 1, 1839, 1.

"You wish me to create a sermon from nothing, for this paper is blank."

3
Southern Legendry

As JEDEDIAH GRANT PREPARED to leave Illinois in the summer of 1839 for his second mission to Virginia and North Carolina, the Mormons were already in the process of transforming the Mississippi River village of Commerce into a new city and gathering place for the Saints. They would call it Nauvoo, which Joseph Smith said was an ancient word meaning "Beautiful." The Mormons had left Missouri and Zion behind, for the time being, and were looking toward a prosperous future in western Illinois. But Grant was more concerned about his own immediate future as an itinerant preacher. When his appointed companion, Abraham O. Smoot, demonstrated some hesitancy about the mission to the South, Jedediah decided to depart without him, perhaps hoping to make connections at a later time. The young preacher went on down the river alone, leaving Quincy on June 2, 1839.

> We arived at St. Louis the next day; I thair left the boat to go and see my br in the state of Ill. 6 miles from St. Louis, but on my way I lerned that he had gone to Stark Co. I then went back to St. Louis. I thare found Br Fisher. I staid with him until the 4th; I then went acros the river again into the state of Ill. and found one of my cusons by the name of Nathan Barlow. I found him and family all well. I staid with him until Thursday. I then went to St. Louis and went on board the Georgeia for the purpus of speding my jearney to N.C.; on board the boat I found Elder John P. Green. He was on his way to the sity of Cincinatia (Ohio). I parted with him in the sity on the 10th of June and on the 12th I left the boat at the mothe of the Gyendott River in the state of Va! From thence I went up the river about 75 miles.
>
> I think stoped on Saturday evening at the house of S McGinis. He was vary desirous to have me stop and hold meting on the Sabbathe, so I gave

out word that I wold preach at 2 o clock in the evening. The people gave good attention and all appeared vary frendly. On Monday I pursued my journey. Arived at Wythe Ch[urch] the 22ct. Staid in town until Wednsday duren which time held 4 metings, one in the ch[urch] and 3 in the Presbyterian metinges house. I had menny people to all of my metings. The people ware vary frenly. Thay gave me $13 in money and clothing on my rode from Wythe to N.C. I held a meting at the house of Mr. Staford on Sabbath the 30th. I held meting at Washill Motir House Surry Co., N.C. On the 4th of July I had meting at Westfield Meting H[ouse]. After I had ben in Surry, Stokes and Patrick, Va., some 4 or 5 weekes preaching the Gospel in difrent places, hoping and looking for Elder Smoote, but in vain ware all my hopes. But on the 1 of August my hopes was realised in meting with Elders [Sylvester B.] Stoddard and [Charles] Bird. We were vary glad to mete in a strange land. We commenced laboring togather in Patrick and Surry. Tusday, August 29, we baptized two in S. Co.[1]

At this point, Grant ceased to write in this journal. Apparently, he never again saw fit to keep a journal. Perhaps, as a granddaughter claimed, "He was too busy making history to record it."[2] But she also realized that much of the history he was making was more in the realm of legend.[3] The second, unrecorded mission to the South produced some tales of mythic proportions that have thrilled subsequent generations of Saints, always anxious to learn of the supposedly ignorant Mormon missionary who confounded the learned priests and lawyers with truth and common sense. Such anecdotes have become an important part of the Mormon lexicon of faith. Mormon storyteller Theodore B. Lewis has recorded one of them as follows:

In the early part of President Grant's ministry, he gained quite a reputation as a ready speaker, frequently responding to invitations to preach from such subjects or texts as might be selected at the time of commencing his sermon, by those inviting him. In time it became a matter of wonder with many as to how and when he prepared his wonderful sermons. In reply to their queries he informed them that he never prepared his sermons as other ministers did. "Of course, I read and store my mind with a knowledge of gospel truths," said he, "but I never study up a sermon." Well, they did not believe he told the truth, for, as they thought, it was impossible for a man to preach such sermons without careful preparation. So, in order to prove it, a number of persons decided to put him to test, and asked him if he would preach at a certain time and place, and from a text selected by them. They proposed to give him the text on his arrival at the place of meeting, thus giving him no time to prepare. To gratify them he consented. The place selected was Jeffersonville, the seat of Tazewell county, at that time the home of the late John B. Floyd, who subsequently became secretary of war, and many other prominent men. The room chosen was in the court house. At the hour

Theodore B. Lewis. Publisher's private collection.

appointed the house was packed to its capacity. Mr. Floyd and a number of lawyers and ministers were present and occupied front seats. Elder Grant came in, walked to the stand and opened the meeting as usual. At the close of the second hymn, a clerk, appointed for the occasion, stepped forward and handed the paper (the text) to Elder Grant, who unfolded it and found it to be blank. Without any mark of surprise, he held the paper up before the audience, and said: "My friends, I am here today according to agreement, to preach from such a text as these gentlemen might select for me. I have it here in my hand. I don't wish you to become offended at me, for I am under promise to preach from the text selected; and if any one is to blame, you must blame those who selected it. I knew nothing of what text they would choose, but of all texts this is my favorite one. You see the paper is blank (at the same time holding it up to view). You sectarians down there believe that out of nothing God created all things, and now you wish to create a sermon from nothing, for this paper is blank. Now, you sectarians believe in a God that has neither body, parts nor passions. Such a God I conceive to be a perfect blank, just as you find my text is. You believe in a church without Prophets, Apostles, Evangelists, etc. Such a church would be a perfect blank, as compared with the Church of Christ, and this agrees with my text. You have located your heaven beyond the bounds of time and space. It exists nowhere, and consequently your heaven is blank, like unto my text." Thus he went on until he had torn to pieces all the tenets of faith professed by his hearers, and then proclaimed the principles of the gospel in great power. He wound up by asking, "Have I stuck to the text and does that satisfy you?" As soon as he sat down, Mr. Floyd jumped up and said, "Mr. Grant, if you are not a lawyer, you ought to be one." Then turning to the people, he added: "Gentlemen, you have listened to a wonderful discourse, and with amazement. Now, take a look at Mr. Grant's clothes. Look at his coat: his elbows are almost out: and his knees are almost through his pants. Let us take up a collection." As he sat down another eminent lawyer . . . arose and said: "I am good for one sleeve in a coat and one leg in a pair of pants, for Mr. Grant." The presiding elder of the M. E. Church, South, was requested to pass the hat around, but he replied that he would not take up a collection for a "Mormon" preacher. "Yes you will," said Mr. Floyd; "Pass it around," said Mr. Stras, and the cry was taken up and repeated by the audience, until, for the sake of peace, the minister had to yield. He accordingly marched around with a hat in his hands, receiving contributions, which resulted in a collection sufficient to purchase a fine suit of clothes, a horse, saddle and bridle for Brother Grant, and not one contributor a member of The Church of Jesus Christ of Latter day Saints, though some joined subsequently. And this from a sermon produced from a blank text.[4]

The certain origins of this tale, as eventually told and retold across Mormondom for the next century and a half, remain as obscure as Grant's day to day activities during this period of his life. Only one thing is certain and that is that the blank text legend, like most such stories, had some basis in fact. There were, for example, several persons at the meeting who united with the Mormons subsequently and who gave Grant's performance with the blank text all the credit for their conversions. One of these, James Jackson Howe, loved to tell his grandchildren of the shock that Grant's message sent through the courthouse that day.[5] The story survived, not only among the Mormons in the West, but also in the South itself. In 1909, Joseph Hyrum Grant, one of the famous preacher's seven sons, received a letter from James G. Wood, who had just returned from a mission to Virginia.

Inasmuch as I have just returned from a land where your dear father labored as a missionary in the cause of truth so many years ago, and still not forgotten, I feel confident that a few lines would be of interest to you. In my last letter I mentioned about a man 92 years old who bore his testimony to his children that Elder Jedediah M. Grant preached the true Gospel of Christ and he wished them to obey it. He told them that he was at the meeting of Jeffersonville, Tazewell County, Va., at the courthouse when they chose for Elder Grant a blank text to speak from and how humiliated the minister was when he was asked to pass the hat, and how cheerfully the people put in their change.[6]

So it is quite certain that it happened, but it is just as certain that the story, as told by Lewis, underwent considerable embellishment over the years. For example, if John B. Floyd attended the meeting in Tazewell County and was so impressed as to champion a collection for Grant, he strangely forgot what had happened by the time he became Secretary of War under James Buchanan. During the so-called Utah War of 1857–61, Floyd had charge of the Utah Expedition sent to the territory to "subdue" the Mormons. He showed no inclination at that time to favor the Saints nor their representatives.

In any case, apart from such tales of spiritual valor was the real world of a long mission to the South, and much of it alone. From Surry County, North Carolina, on December 15, 1840, Grant summarized his experiences in the South for the Church periodical *Times and Seasons*. Even after the editor's touch, the letter revealed a maturing confidence and an increase in knowledge that made such legends as the blank text at least plausible.

I embrace this opportunity of telling you something about the "Times & Seasons" in this part of our Masters vineyard: undoubtedly, you had concluded that the times must have been very hard with me, or I would have written to you before, giving an account of my success in the ministry; but you very well know, that it is not expedient for those who are pruning the vineyard to trouble you with a detailed report of the Times & Seasons while sowing the good seed among the Gentiles. For the last 17 months I have been laboring in the following counties: viz; Surry, Stokes, Rockingham, and Guilford, in N.C. also in Patrick, Grayson, Wythe, Smith, and Washing[ton], in southwestern Virginia. Perhaps no part of the United States has heard as many false reports from Mo. as the citizens of the before mentioned counties. During the last two years, the western breezes from Ephraim's lovely plains, have been frequently impregnated with scurilous reports, and base epithets of the foulest kind against the saints of the Most High: also, some of the upper Mo. land vermins have passed through this country, retailing slander and abuse with a lavish hand; the above, in connection with the various falsehoods from the North, which have been now vamped over by the Rev. D. Ds. and put in circulation by their deceptive Editors, who are duly blackening their columns with the most unhallowed falsehoods that ever disgraced civilized society. From the foregoing you can readily see that the enemies of truth in this region of country have been deeply supplied with weapons to fight against the great work of the last days, inhaling, as they have, the western air, pregnant with lies, and slanderous reports, a fine (stimulant you know,) for the "heaped up teachers" of the Gentiles, to assist them in saving their sinking craft from irretrievable ruin, its inevitable doom, where ever truth prevails. The priests have contended in public against the impenetrable law of God written to Ephraim, until they have become disheartened and have left the field of public investigation clear and undisturbed; they now use a private influence, threatening their members with excommunication if they listen to the doctrine of the saints. I shall not attempt to describe the course, or conduct of the priests,—a whole Encyclopedia of wit, argument, and abuse would not more than do the subjects justice. It sufficeth to say, that all their public exertions have proved abortive and insufficient to prejudice the public mind, and their *private* influence is not sufficient to keep the honest in heart from hearing the fulness of the gospel as taught in the last days by the servants of the Lord, who are unfurling the bloodstained banner among the nations of the earth.

I introduced the gospel into this country in 1838. At that time there had been no preaching (to my knowledge) by the Latter Day Saints within 200 miles of this county. You may well suppose that the people had a great curiosity to hear "the Mormon" preach, so much so, that they came out by hundreds from every direction of the country, inviting me to go east, west, north, and south, and when they found that I could not travel extensive enough on foot to satisfy them, they soon made up a hundred dollars and bought me a horse and equipage, suitable for traveling; my circuit soon become very extensive but I still had 3 requests for preaching, where I could fulfill one. I continued to sow the good seed in various parts of Carolina, and Virginia until the 9th of Oct. I then bid adieu to my hospitable friends and eight saints, with whom I was sorry to part. I bent my course for upper Missouri to visit my parents, and the saints in that region of country. I did not, however, reach upper Missouri before I met some of L. W. Boggs's mob militia returning home: from them, I learned to some faint degree, the situation of the saints. I still pursued my course onward, and arrived at Far West on the 12th day of Nov. I there saw a fertile country once rich with the blessings of peace, and industry, but suddenly blackened with the smoke of desolation; and its pure stream reddened with the blood of the saints of the Lord and a wilderness sheltering the widow and the orphan.

"In Caldwell forest the night wind was high
Fast drifted the snow through the bleak winter sky,
And trees, cliffs and mountains were hoary and cold,
The clear waves of her streams congealed as they rolled."
I heard the mother weep, I saw the children cry,
I saw the blooming youth, the tears gushed from his eye,
I saw the priests of Zion, their feet made fast in chains,
I heard her prophets groan, her Virgins sighed in vain.

You are well acquainted with the distress of those days. "To tell it all would take a thousand tongues, a throat of brass, and adamantine lungs." On the 25th of Dec. I left the land of sorrow, of anguish, pain, and wo, in company with my aged parents, and after a journey of three hundred miles, we arrived at my brothers in Knox co. Ill. where we fully realized our expectations.

I tarried in Knox co. until the 12th of May, preaching as often as my health would permit: I baptized but 2 in the co. I attended the Conference at Quincy the last day of May, it was thought best for me to return to N.C. accordingly, I started the next morning, I arrived in Carolina the last of June, and commenced preaching in Surry co. I soon found that the mind of the public had become very much prejudiced since I left in 1838, but many were yet willing to listen to the truth of heaven. I used every exertion possible to remove prejudice from the minds of the people. I had not been here long before my heart was made to rejoice by the arrival of Elders S. B. Stoddard and C. Bird, by their assistance much prejudice was removed, although they staid but a few weeks, yet I trust that much good will result from their labor. Before they left, some 6 or 8 came forward and were baptized, for the remission of their sins in the name of the Lord Jesus. After Elders S. and B. left, I continued to hold forth the fulness of the gospel in different parts of this land. In January, 1840, I had the much desired privilege of meeting with my Br. Elder J Grant Jr. We have continued to travel and preach very extensively, having more calls than we could or can possibly fill but few have, as yet, joined the saints. We have, within a few weeks past baptized 10, and 5 more have offered themselves as candidates for baptism, which will increase the number baptized to 40 and hundreds are believing in various parts of our circuit.—The prospect for harvest is at this time more flattering than it has ever been. I think that many will ere long be adopted into the kingdom and participate with the saints in the glory of the last days, which may God, in his mercy grant, through Jesus our Savior and friend.

J. M. Grant[7]

Grant's prediction of a bountiful harvest of souls proved accurate. Laboring with his brother Joshua and the others, he managed to persuade not a few denizens of northern North Carolina and southwestern Virginia to "be adopted into the kingdom." After more than three years among these people, the lanky Mormon circuit rider had become an institution. James H. Moyle, working in the Surry County area forty years later, discovered the base Grant had established so secure that two generations of missionaries had called it "the nest" and seldom ventured from it into the more hostile land around it.[8] In the legend that followed, no one could stop the dauntless preacher. To engage him in debate was to court humiliation.

Elder Grant was challenged by a very eminent Baptist preacher, named Baldwin, to a discussion. Brother Grant consented. The place chosen was the fine, large church of his proud and imperious antagonist. Mr. Baldwin was described to me, as a man, overbearing in his manner—a regular browbeater. When the time came for the discussion, the house was densely crowded. Umpires were chosen, and everything was ready to proceed, when Brother Grant arose and said: "Mr. Baldwin, I would like to ask you a question before we proceed any farther." "Certainly so," said Baldwin. "Who stands at the head of your church in south west Virginia?" Mr. Baldwin very quickly and austerely replied, "I do, sir; I do." "All right," said Brother Grant;

"I wished to know that I had a worthy foe." Mr. Baldwin looked a little confused for a moment, and then said: "Mr. Grant, I would like to ask you, who stands at the head of your church in southwest Virginia?" Brother Grant arose and with bowed head replied, "Jesus Christ, sir." The shock was electrical. This inspired answer completely disarmed the proud foe, and the humble servant of God again came off victor.[9]

It is difficult to measure in concrete terms the actual results of the Grant mission to Virginia and North Carolina. When he finally prepared to leave in the fall of 1842, he appointed a conference at Burkes Garden, in Tazewell County. No figures for total attendance at that meeting appear in the record, but sixty persons participated from the Burkes Garden congregation alone. The conference was evidently an impressive affair. Supposed to last three days, September 10–12, it carried over to September 14. Grant, now nearly twenty-seven years old, prayed and preached at every meeting. Also playing an important but secondary role in the meetings was twenty-four-year-old Joshua Grant Jr., who had been with his brother in the region for more than two years.[10]

At the key session on September 12, Jedediah preached from 2 Corinthians 4:17: "For our light affliction, which is but for a moment, worketh for us a far more exceeding and eternal weight of glory." Shortly thereafter, Grant was on his way west to weigh out his own measure of glory.

Notes

1. Jedediah Grant, Journal, June–August 1839, holograph, LDS Church Archives.

2. Mary Grant Judd, *Jedediah M. Grant: Pioneer Statesman* (Salt Lake City: Deseret News Press, 1959), xi.

3. Ibid.

4. Theodore B. Lewis, quoted in Andrew Jenson, *Latter day Saints Biographical Encyclopedia*, 4 vols. (1901; rpt., Salt Lake City: Western Epics, 1971), 1:57–58.

5. James Jackson Howe, Personal History, holograph, photocopy in possession of LuDeen Atwood, Bountiful, Utah.

6. Quoted in Judd, *Jedediah M. Grant*, 59–60.

7. Jedediah Grant, Surry County, North Carolina, December 15, 1840, Letter to the editor, *Times and Seasons*, March 15, 1841, 347–48.

8. James Henry Moyle, *Mormon Democrat: The Religious and Political Memoirs of James Henry Moyle*, edited by Gene A. Sessions (Salt Lake City: Signature Books in association with Smith Research Associates, 1998), 91–92.

9. Lewis, quoted in Jenson, *Biographical Encyclopedia*, 1:58.

10. *Times and Seasons*, January 2, 1843, 63. George M. Tibbs, clerk of the conference, reported that "when Elders J. M. and J. Grant, (at the close of the meeting) came to bid adieu to the saints and friends in Virginia, the scene was truly affecting." Joshua Grant reported that he and his brother had baptized 200 persons during their stay in the South. Journal History of the Church of Jesus Christ of Latter day Saints (chronological scrapbook of typed entries and newspaper clippings, 1830–present), April 9, 1843, 1, LDS Church Archives.

"We expect to have times, times, and the deciding of times."

⇥ 4 ⇤
Crisis

FULL OF TUGGING MEMORIES, but anxious to see friends and loved ones again in the West, Jed and Joshua Grant made their way in the early fall of 1841 to the Ohio River from Tazewell County, Virginia. From a landing near Huntington, they took a boat down the river to the Mississippi and then up to Nauvoo, the bustling city that had replaced the little village of Commerce from which they had departed. They found the new Mormon capital in a state of perpetual and sometimes painful growth as converts like their own from the East and others from England and elsewhere poured in at an amazing rate. There were certainly markings of a typical frontier community, but beyond these were the signs of the Saints striving to build a perfect city based on Joseph Smith's ideals of unity and order.

On a hill above the spreading community was the foundation of a new temple, bigger and different from the one at Kirtland. While Smith hoped that the building would spiritually empower and unify the people who followed him, the edifice was soon to have other meanings and symbolisms. As Grant surveyed the remarkable changes that had taken place in Nauvoo during his three-year absence, he could have had little knowledge and even less understanding of the complex transformation that his beloved cause had undergone. Even those Saints who watched it happen could not begin to comprehend its enormous portent, although many of them could sense a radical departure of the movement from its primitivist origins in the 1830s.

At the center of it all towered the enigmatic Joseph Smith, whose mind was ranging across the philosophies of the world to envision a certain universalization of Mormonism. He had redefined the word "Mormon," saying that it meant "more good" and that the movement would seek to include any good idea the world's diversity had to offer. The Prophet had developed in the course of all of this some rather exotic

Nauvoo Temple with cityscape. Publisher's private collection.

ideas. Because of persecutions and due to the radical nature of some of these concepts, they often developed under shrouds of secrecy that made them seem even more controversial and strange. The most startling case in point was the plurality of wives, which apparently began in earnest in 1841 among a closed cadre of Church leaders. Other expansions of doctrine had developed in this later variety of Mormonism by the time Grant arrived in Nauvoo that were challenging the perseverance of many early converts who had known the faith in a simpler form.

Dissent and defection had always plagued Mormonism, but with these new developments came new and more discordant mutinies. Although Grant was too far down the road of total commitment to forsake his intense loyalty, no matter what continuous revelation wrought, many of his friends and kinsmen had already joined those among the Saints for whom the old ways tasted far sweeter than the new. In spite of this painful reality and whatever he may or may not have known about the changes that were taking place in Mormonism, Jedediah Grant would plant himself squarely among the loyalists in any controversy that might endanger the strength of the church. Consequently, as he began to sense what was happening to Nauvoo he must have taken considerable pride in the realization that converts he had garnered in the South were joining thousands of others from the East, Canada, and Europe, replacing the defectors and assuring Nauvoo's expanding greatness. The burgeoning city on the Mississippi had become at once the impressive symbol and the political seat of the rapidly changing socio-religious phenomenon, but as the unity and strength of Nauvoo had multiplied, so also had its divisions and the seeds of its own destruction. Only the Prophet's great and mysterious magnetism could keep his movement's divisive forces from outstripping its unifying ones. Rising from the trials and failures of his past career as a leader, Smith seemed to have developed a profound ability to relate love and power, and to use both to inspire his followers. As long as he was in Nauvoo, the city and its motivating force would prosper.

Grant's activities through the winter and spring of 1843 showed nothing but continued devotion to the cause he had espoused as a boy a decade before. Responding to numerous calls to preach, he was still in his element. He spoke of his recent experiences in the South, eliciting "breathless attention" at such gatherings as the recently organized Young Men's and Young Ladies' Society at Nauvoo. By the end of March he was commonly sharing the stand with other former missionaries with exciting tales to tell, such as Brigham Young and Heber C. Kimball, recently returned from Great Britain. These were indeed days of reflective pleasure and glory.[1]

At the April conference of the Church in 1843, Grant received another mission call, this time to preside over the branch at Philadelphia. His brother Joshua received a similar assignment to Cincinnati. Jedediah's brother-in-law, Apostle William Smith, was about to take a "business trip" to Philadelphia; the Prophet was no doubt anxious to shore up his brother's efforts in the East. Jedediah, now twenty-seven years old and full of the preacher's fire, seemed the likely candidate, particularly in view of his kinship to the headstrong apostle.[2] William had been in and out of the Prophet's graces since his selection as one of the Twelve in 1835. On occasion, the animosity between the two brothers nearly led to physical violence. History is crowded with such problematic characters as William Smith, for whom there is always only speculation about motivation. In William's case, there seemed to be operating a volatile mixture of sibling rivalry and seething rebelliousness. His wavering loyalty to the Prophet became an increasingly embarrassing and disturbing flaw in the Smith family and created problems of leadership, not unlike common knots errant brothers have tied in ruling circles since the beginnings of politics.

Despite the lack of firm evidence to suggest that Grant was sent to Philadelphia principally to bolster his brother-in-law in the faith, their departure for the same place at the same time would indicate more than coincidence. In addition, the Philadelphia congregation had come into existence primarily through the efforts of Grant's boyhood friend and former missionary companion Benjamin Winchester, who was still in the area and who was demonstrating some signs of independence that must have disturbed the leadership at Nauvoo. If Grant could hold the reins on both his rambunctious brother-in-law and his headstrong friend at the same time, his assignment might prove crucial as the center of the movement at Nauvoo sought to maintain control of its fringes to the east. Besides all of this, there can be little doubt that personal reasons also influenced Grant's selection for the position in Philadelphia inasmuch as his sister Caroline Smith was in poor health and was going to Pennsylvania with her apostle husband, presumably for medical care.[3]

Shortly after the Grant brothers received their assignments to the East, there arose some question as to whether they should be ordained high priests, which was the ecclesiastical office Smith had designated for those in positions of presidency. The basis for the controversy seemed to hinge on their youth. The Prophet responded with characteristic resolve, handling the entire question in one swoop. "It is not necessary," he wrote on April 19, "that Jedediah and Joshua Grant should be ordained high priests in order to preside; they are too young."[4] Joseph was also concerned that the young brothers were copying "Zebedee Coltrin's habit of clipping half their words," or abbreviating words in the course of their sermons. "I intend to break them of it," said Smith, whose desire was that the young men be as effective in their new callings as possible. "If a high priest comes along," added Joseph, "and goes to snub either of them in their presidency, because they are seventies, let them knock the man's teeth down his throat—I mean spiritually."[5] Joseph Smith knew the sons of Joshua Grant well enough to prophesy as he closed that "you shall make a monstrous wake as you go."[6] In the storm that was coming, "a monstrous wake" would be necessary for simple survival in the faith, if for nothing else.

Joseph Smith Jr., from a daguerreotype of a portrait attributed to William Majors at Nauvoo, ca. 1843. LDS Church Archives.

A month later, Joseph took his brother William, Jedediah Grant, Ebenezer Robinson, and Horace K. Whitney in his carriage to the boat landing from which they would depart on their missions to the East.[7] The four men were soon on their way down the Mississippi and up the Ohio, destined for Philadelphia and New York. Grant took up his residence in Philadelphia, and early in August presided over his first conference there, with many of the apostles, including Brigham Young, Heber C. Kimball, Orson Pratt, George A. Smith, Wilford Woodruff, and John E. Page in attendance, as well as some 300 Saints from eastern Pennsylvania and western New Jersey.[8] At the close of the meetings, the apostles, Grant, and about half the Saints went up the Delaware River for a picnic at Gloucester Point. There, for diversion, Jedediah engaged Apostle Page in a debate over whether prosperity was an indicator of the correctness of a people's religion, Grant arguing the negative. When the contest had ended, Brother Brigham, being portentously impressed, judged the young seventy the winner.[9]

Late in the summer, the brethren moved the conference to New York City, where they rented the Columbian Hall on Grand Street for a series of meetings. In addition to the six apostles, Jedediah Grant was notably present and participating. Brigham Young keynoted the conference, calling forcefully for the continued gathering of the Saints and for support in the building of the temple at Nauvoo. Grant was to collect funds for the temple; indeed, that task would occupy the greater part of his attention during the ensuing winter as the apostles left for Pittsburgh and the West early in October.[10]

On April 24, 1844, Joseph Smith, now a candidate for president of the United States, rode to the upper steam boat landing to meet Elder Jedediah Grant, who was returning from Philadelphia with money for the temple fund and a distinguished visitor, Judge William Richards of New Jersey.[11] William Smith had returned to Nauvoo with a company of Saints from the same area, leaving his wife in Philadelphia.[12] Grant found Joseph preoccupied with a severe threat to his life and to the safety of the society of Saints. Disenchanted apostates and other enemies were fomenting serious discord in the community. Seemingly dedicated to Smith's downfall and the end of Mormon power in western Illinois, this group had set in motion a "conspiracy" that two months later would cost the Prophet his life and would precipitate a crisis in the Church that would threaten its ultimate collapse. Grant jumped inevitably into the middle of it all.

Perhaps the most intriguing evidence of the new position of strength Grant's service in Philadelphia had earned him came on May 6, when Joseph Smith added him to his "general council." This so called Council of Fifty had been established in March of 1843 to carry forth the political goals of the kingdom, which to say the least were uncertain and mysterious. Smith's candidacy for President seemed for the time to be its most important concern; but as the group operated in secrecy and contained only a select few loyalists, its very existence suggested conspiracy and a quest for temporal power that would seem to be beyond the scope of a religious order. Whatever its aims at this point, Grant's inclusion on the council, along with his joining the Masonic Lodge in Nauvoo, indicated his rising prominence in the ruling circles of Mormonism and the confidence Smith had invested in him.[13] In the ensuing days of turmoil and trial, his position of trust would become even more apparent.

Through May and into June, Grant remained close to his leader. Historians of Mormonism have charted well the storm gathering about Joseph that carried him to his death in Carthage Jail on June 27, 1844—Smith's destruction of an anti-Mormon press at Nauvoo and the order for his arrest. Young Grant, ever loyal and devoted, remained anxious to do anything he could to serve the Prophet. His final opportunity came on the night of Sunday, June 22, after Joseph and Hyrum Smith had returned to Nauvoo following a short flight across the river into the West.

> About four o'clock, p.m., Joseph, Hyrum, the Doctor, and others started back; while, walking towards the river Joseph fell behind with O. P. Rockwell; the others shouted to him to come on; Joseph replied, "it is of no use to hurry, for we are going back to be slaughtered," and continually expressed himself that he would like to get the people once more together, and talk to them to night. Rockwell said if that was his wish he would get the people together, and he could talk to them by starlight.
>
> It was the strong persuasions of Reynolds Cahoon, Lorenzo D. Wasson, and Hiram Kimball, who were carrying out Emma's instructions, that [con]cluded Joseph and Hyrum to start back to Nauvoo. They recrossed the river at half past five; when they arrived at his Mansion in Nauvoo, Joseph's family surrounded him, and he tarried there all night, giving up the idea of preaching to the Saints by starlight.
>
> He sent the letter to Governor Ford of this date by Col. Theodore Turley, and Elder Jedediah M. Grant, who carried it to Carthage, where they arrived about 9 p.m. They gave the letter to Governor Ford, who first agreed to send a posse to escort Gen. Smith in safety to Carthage; immediately afterwards Mr. Skinner came in and made a very bitter speech to the Governor, in which Wilson Law and Joseph H. Jackson joined, telling him naught but lies, which caused Elder Grant to ask if messengers to him were to be insulted in that manner. The Governor treated them coldly, and rescinded his previous promise and refused to send, or allow an escort to go with Joseph, as he said it was an honor not given to any other citizen. He would not allow the messengers to stay in Carthage through the night, but ordered them to start at 10 o'clock and return to Nauvoo with orders for Gen. Smith to be in Carthage by 10 o'clock tomorrow morning without an escort, and he threatened that if Gen. Smith did not give himself up at that time, that Nauvoo would be

destroyed, and all the men, women, and children that were in it. Messrs. Grant and Turley immediately started, but on account of their horses being wearied they did not arrive in Nauvoo until about 4 a.m. of the 24th, when they went to Gen. Smith to report to him the state of excitement in Carthage; he would not hear one word of the warning as he was determined to go to Carthage and give himself up to the Governor.[14]

Three days later, mobbers with blackened faces forced their way into the jail in Carthage, killing the Prophet and his brother Hyrum and seriously wounding future Church president John Taylor. The ensuing shock to the Mormon faithful defies description; but in spite of the final scenes in the intense drama that was the life of Joseph Smith, events in the ordinary lives of the Saints continued. For his part, Grant had found time to court Caroline Van Dyke in Nauvoo. He married her on July 2, 1844, not a week after the death of the Prophet and Patriarch at Carthage, but for such a true believer there was no time to waste on selfish indulgences. Smith's aide Dr. Willard Richards had commissioned George J. Adams to bear news of the martyrdom to the apostles campaigning in the East and particularly to Brigham Young. Adams failed to carry out his mission, and the task fell to Grant on his wedding day. As soon as the ceremony concluded, he and Caroline boarded a steamer for the East.[15]

In addition to his mission as bearer of black crepe to Brigham Young and the Twelve, Grant had another reason for haste in returning to Philadelphia. His sister Caroline had written from Pennsylvania. Her illness had worsened, and her husband, William Smith, seemed distant both physically and spiritually. Indeed, her letter bore lamentation amid courageous cheer.

Philadelphia May 5th 1844

Dear Brother I have wated with patience I will not say but with a tolarabl smothe faice until yesterday for a letter but when evening came and no letter I cold not keep a smooth faice any longer. So you may emagin the scean for I shal not write it but this morning all nature wears a smile and how can I ware a frown (in the midst of the beauties and splendurs of a May day morning) who once had such a happy heart and boyent spirits but lo the distroyer had drawn a clowd ovr my sky a frown on my brow and a veil ovr my once happy face but yet I look forward to a day not fair distent when the distroyer shall leave my horison clear of his poysonous influance and then I can injoy life with a knowledge of the injoyement a for most asuredly I understand the bitter and then why not appreciate the sweet. Well hear I have been writing all this time and have not told you one word of news. Then to comence you must know the Church one and all are vary ancious to see you. The first inquery when any of the sisters come in is when do you think Brother Grant will come? Have you had any news? What no letter yet and sutch like expresions. As for me I am about the same as when you left with the exception of a dreadful blister which has cept me in bead one or two days. I have not been any whare since you left oanly once to meating and that made me sick so I shal have to stay close at home you see in order to get well which I am determined to do if the Lord will. Dr Newel has not been down yet but sent word he was coming soon. I shall have the water drawn off when he comes. Now tell W[illiam]!!! he must keep up his spirits and do the best he can and not give himself trouble about my sufring for a want of means for I have been vary well provided for so far. Last Sabath Br Walton took up a colection for me and got two dollars and forty four cents but that is not all I have had for Br Woodbury last week gave me a v [five] and Br Rawson gave me one and half and Sister Busannett still continues to come with her basket and Bell Armstrong gave me a 1 and all the sisters are vary kind. Br Sparks and Sister Cobb arived hear last Monday. They told me all the twelve ware apointed an eastern mision so I am in hops Wm will come on with them. I think he can do better hear than thare. Br Hyde is in Wilmington and will be hear next Sunday. Tell Wm there is dredful times lo down Toms River. Annah ret [?] Mccan Ephram and I do not know how many more danced at Annahs home coming and an old Mrs. Potter aunt Sally and a number more are dying for the want of breth. O dear what can the mater be? The children are talking about theyr father evry day and asking me when he will come. Do tell him to write and tell me all the news and you—canot you find one hour to write to your sister and her little ones. Write as soon as you receive this and let me kow how fathers people are and all the news. Yesterdays paper says Joseph has turned Emma outdoors for improper conduct with other men. Tell Wm Mrs. Wikoff has sent after that coverled she gave me when we ware in Jersey. When you go home tell mother and all our people I want to see them vary much George and Betsy and there children. Tell Athalia Gorge and Wm that Mary and Caroline are wishing evry day they ware hear. What fine times they wold have. Little Cad [Caroline] wants to saive a peas of evry thing she has for Wm. J. M. I kneed not tell you I am loansom in the midst of company. You know that without my saying it. Give my love to Sisters Caroline Richards and Rawson. Br Rawson is well and wants to see his wife and litle girl the worst I ever saw a man. The church are all doing vary well I believe but they are looking for a letter from you. You wold do well I think to write a letter to the Church. Monday. Not as well as yesterday and still no letter. I hope there is one on the road. The children say give their love to Father and Uncle J. M. Two weeks a go to day I sent a letter to Wm so you see I am keeping my promas of writing evry two weeks. Tell Wm I wold like to see him an hour or two mightly well about this time. So good by. Helth peace and hapiness to you all by the bushel. Remember me to Mother Smith. And pleas excuse mistakes and blots.

Caroline G. Smith[16]

Jedediah and his new bride arrived in Philadelphia on July 15, 1844. As presiding elder, young Grant made a survey of the members and then sent a report to Nauvoo indicating that all had been "peace and quiet" in the city since the burial of the martyrs.[17] With regard to his primary mission of informing the Twelve of the tragedy of Carthage, Grant found on his arrival in Philadelphia that the brethren had already learned of the death of the Smiths by the newspapers. He consequently did not attempt to go any farther east. Indeed, within a day or two of his own arrival in Philadelphia, several of the Twelve, including Brigham Young, Heber Kimball, Orson Pratt, and Wilford Woodruff, had met in Boston, where they resolved to return at once to Nauvoo to carry on the leadership of the kingdom.[18] Two of the apostles, John Page and William Smith, apparently failed to realize the same responsibility and chose to remain in the East. A crisis of leadership had descended upon the Saints, and Grant found himself geographically and spiritually deep in the middle of it.

He immediately set himself to work trying to buttress the Church in Philadelphia and the surrounding area against the inevitable onslaught of confusion and disorder that would follow the death of the Prophet. Having again received a commission to collect money in the East for the completion of the Nauvoo Temple, he expended a great deal of his efforts in that direction. During a conference at Philadelphia on August 31 and September 1, Jedediah and his brother-in-law William Smith preached unity to the Saints, Grant using the temple fund as a rallying point and symbol of the continuation of the kingdom despite the loss of its leaders. The young seventy also chose himself to offer nearly every prayer as if he knew that the wolves were already among the flock.[19] But he could have had no idea that one of them was sitting next to him on the stand. Some of them, though old friends, were more easily identified, as were the sounds of their howling in the night.

Philadelphia Sept 4th 1844

Pres. Brigham Young

Dear Brother in Christ. We feel it our duty to inform you of the course taken by Elder B. Winchester since his return to this section of country, we feel that we should render ourselves culpable if we remain any longer silent as he is leveling his shafts at you and the Quorum over which you preside, stating, both in public and in private that you have slandered him here, and in New York, Boston and elsewhere and that your Quorum did force upon him the "Gag Law" when he had his trial in Nauvoo. The reason of this was not as you and others have asserted, because he had disobeyed your counsel, but the main reason was that you knew him to be a deadly enemy to the "spiritual wife system" and for his opposition he had received all manner of abuse from all who believed in that hellish system.

Last evening he cried out in the *poor woodchuck tone* "My God! must I now be crushed to the earth because I am a virtuous man." The question was put to him as it had previously been at the conference on Satturday last. "Did the Twelve ever either directly or indirectly teach you the doctrine that you allude to, or did you ever hear them teach it to others?["] He answered "both questions in the negative asserting at the same time that the Twelve" did believe and had taught the doctrine, and that he had witnessed the sufferings of innocent females whose characters had been traduced and ruind forever. He then spoke of what he knew; he spoke of Sarah Alley and the young lady who lived with Brother Clayton and Adam's Girl as he called her, with many comments doleful in their nature.

He generally spends his time in traveling from house to house and is always sure to introduce some topic of conversation, to excite the curiosity of all present to ask him divers questions about what he calls "the spiritual wife system." He then unbosoms his feelings freely; declaring that the "Twelve" teach the doctrine. When reprimanded for this course, he always says "I wish to remain neutral but when individuals whom I have brought into the church ask me questions I am bound to answer them." He has been to New York and taken the same course there as here; he justifies himself in so doing by saying that you have spoken against him and censured his course: he calls upon Elder McLane who testifies that you did slander Elder Winchester at the conference in N York and at his house in the fall of 1843. He makes *no bones* of saying if the Quorum of the Twelve suspend him again under circumstances similar to those under which he was before suspended that he would give no heed to their decission but ["]go ahead about his business."

After conference Elder Wm Smith left here for New York with the intention of writing you the official letter in regard to Elder B. You will also learn from the minutes of the conference held in this city that Elder B W refused to vote to sustain your quorum. He also stated at the conference that he could not go out and preach and bring females into the church to be ruined as others had been &c. The foregoing are a few of the many complaints of Elder Winchester. We have not embodied them in the form of charges, but as testimony in connection with the minutes of the conference and what Elder Wm Smith may forward to you. In conclusion we subscribe ourselves Your Brothers in the New Covenant

John P Smith, Clerk   J M. Grant, Elder

NS Brother Brigham. Will you please do me the favour to request Bro. Clayton to record and forward the deed I left in his hands which is going to George Jeffries of this city. Give my best respects to all inquiring friends and reserve the same for yourself. If you can spare time please write to me on the receipt of this and oblige me of your best friends. J. M. G.[20]

As Grant quickly discovered, the resistance of such as Benjamin Winchester to the leadership of the Twelve had far-reaching and potent effects on the operation of the Church in Philadelphia and its environs. The temple at Nauvoo had become an emblem of the Quorum's hegemony, and the presiding elder soon encountered recalcitrance among the Saints toward the temple fund. Attacks against the leadership of the Twelve commonly centered around the accusation that the apostles were at the center of the pernicious "spiritual wife system." Since the bulk of the Saints remained unaware of Joseph Smith's teachings of polygamy, such nebulous charges as those Winchester leveled struck hard at the Twelve as the quorum under Brigham Young tried to continue Smith's program, including the expansions of doctrine that had taken place during the Nauvoo period. Grant therefore found himself in the uncomfortable position of defending the Twelve against charges he probably knew to be true.

Phila. Oct. 11th 1844

Eld. Whitney,

Dear Br, in the new Covenant: Having the opportunity I imbrace it, to send you the money that I have collected, or obtained, for the building of the temple of the Lord, in Nauvoo. The amount has fallen far short of my expectation, but I have done my duty before the Lord and his people in this city. All will bear me witness that had the liberality of the Saints been eaguel to my exertion the same would have been ten fold more then what it now is. On all ocasions when the elders in this branch were going to preach, I have requested them to obtain all they could for the temple. Elder Lutz laid the subject before the Saints at Easton in this state, and in Willmington, Del. The amount given will be conveyed to you by the bareer of this. The clerk of each branch is requested to keep an account of the money obtained in the respective branches, &c. Br Lutz will send the money [he] has received to Br Kimball.

Many reasons might be assigned for the backwardness of the Saints in this city in not helping to build the temple. The spirit that you and the Twelve have had to contend with in Nauvoo has been here in full force, Eld. Benj Winchester has walked foremost in the ranks of the factions to oppose the Quorum of the Twelve and the building of the temple. When Benj comes back from Pittsburg we expect to have times, times, and the deciding of times.

Dear Br, I wish you to assure the Twelve that they as well as yourself and many others have had my prayrs and simpathy in this day of trial, long, long to be remembered, and never to be forgoton. I have been absent in body but present in spirit, but alas, I might have been otherwise, had I not known the mind of our beloved and martird Prophet on that point. I cannot be deceived. I know what he thought of the Twelve, and also what he though[t] of Eld Rigdon. Did all know this they would say with me that the Twelve stand in their propper place.

I wish to be remembered to all enquarin friends. As ever your Br &c

J M. Grant

Will you pleas write to me as soon as this comes to hand?

P.S. Br John Foreman who will be baptised this day is the one selected to bear the temple money to Nauvoo. His object in going west is to see the country and learn more of our religion. He is a worthy yong man from the state of Del. I will now give you the names of the subscribers for the temple and the amount given by each subscriber. Patience Hampton 4 dollars; Wm Bates do. 5; John Schwortz, one dollar; Christiana Read, do. one; Hanna Read one; Philop Elphry, one; Deliah Thomson, 50 cts; Wm. A Adams one dollar; John Loyle one; Wm. Milligan one; George Wiser, 50 cts; John Houskeeper 50 cts; Matilda Coock, 50 cts; Calob Reve, 25 cts; Noah Gee, 3 dollars. 31 Dollars, 25 cts.

Sidney Rigdon. Publisher's private collection.

Br Whitney my wife wishes you to tell Judge Richards and wife that there friends in this country are all well. We were sorry too that [they] went with Elder Rigdon. Yours, J M. Grant.[21]

    While Grant braced for the return of Winchester from Pittsburgh and "the deciding of times" in Philadelphia, he received word that on October 7, 1844, a conference of the Church had sustained him to replace Josiah Butterfield as a president in the First Council of Seventy,[22] a group of seven men who had the responsibility of assisting the Twelve in directing the missions of the Church. Now in a position of General Authority over the Church he had been trying so desperately to hold together in the key eastern city of Philadelphia, Jeddy Grant, about to turn twenty-eight years old, realized that the crisis and the fight to resolve it had barely begun.

⇥ Notes ⇤

1. Journal History of the Church of Jesus Christ of Latter day Saints (chronological scrapbook of typed entries and newspaper clippings, 1830-present), March 28, 1843, 1-2, LDS Church Archives.

2. Joseph Smith Jr., *History of the Church of Jesus Christ of Latter day Saints*, edited by B. H. Roberts, 7 vols., 2d ed. rev. (1902-12; Salt Lake City: Deseret Book, 1964 printing), 5:337. On William Smith, see Irene M. Bates, "William Smith, 1811-93: Problematic Patriarch," *Dialogue: A Journal of Mormon Thought* 16 (Summer 1983): 11-23, and D. Michael Quinn, *The Mormon Hierarchy: Origins of Power* (Salt Lake City: Signature Books, 1994), 594-97. For an interesting example of the rivalry between Joseph and William, see Richard Lyman Bushman, *Joseph Smith: Rough Stone Rolling, a Cultural Biography of Mormonism's Founder* (New York: Alfred A. Knopf, 2005), 299-303.

3. Smith, *History of the Church*, 5:367.

4. Ibid., 5:368.

5. Ibid.

6. Ibid.

7. Ibid., 5:385.

8. Scott G. Kenney, ed., *Wilford Woodruff's Journal, 1833-1898*, typescript, 9 vols. (Midvale, Utah: Signature Books, 1983-85), August 6, 1843.

9. Journal History, August 8, 1843, 1.

10. Smith, *History of the Church*, 5:549-53; Journal History, October 4, 1843, 1.

11. Smith, *History of the Church*, 6:343.

12. Ibid., 6:341

13. Klaus Hansen, *Quest for Empire: The Political Kingdom of God and the Council of Fifty in Mormon History* (East Lansing: Michigan State University Press, 1967); Journal History, May 6, 27, June 8, 11, 1844, all p. 1. For a list of the Council of Fifty's members appointed 1844-45, see Quinn, *Origins of Power*, 521-31. According to Quinn, Grant "apparently knew that Joseph Smith had proposed polygamous marriage to his sister," Roxcy (or Roxey), who married William Smith (1847-53) after the death of her sister, Caroline Grant Smith. Ibid., 527, 594. See also D. Michael Quinn, "The Council of Fifty and Its Members, 1844 to 1845," *BYU Studies* 20 (Winter 1980): 163-97.

14. Journal History, June 23, 1844, 2; Smith, *History of the Church*, 6:551-52.

15. Journal History, July 2, 1844, 1. See also Smith, *History of the Church*, 7:158-59. Caroline Ann Vandyke (or Van Dyke) was born January 16, 1818, in Broome County, New York. Coming from the same area as the Grants, she was probably the daughter of a family friend.

16. Caroline Grant Smith to Jedediah M. Grant, May 5, 1844, holograph in possession of Rachel Grant Alsop, Salt Lake City. According to Quinn, *Origins of Power*, 594, William had begun to participate in plural marriage as early as 1841.

17. Journal History, July 15, 1844, 2; Smith, *History of the Church*, 7:191.

18. Kenney, *Wilford Woodruff's Journal*, June 27, 1844; "History of Brigham Young," June 27, July 1, 9, 16, 17, 18, 1844, holograph, LDS Church Archives.

19. Journal History, September 1, 1844, 1; Smith, *History of the Church*, 7:266.

20. Jedediah Grant, Letter to Brigham Young, September 4, 1844, holograph, Brigham Young Collection, LDS Church Archives. Winchester's animosity toward the Twelve had deep roots and antedated the death of Joseph Smith. On May 27, 1843, for example, he had questioned the power of the apostles in relationship to the elevated status of the new Patriarch Hyrum Smith, this after Brigham Young led the fight to censure Winchester for speaking in Philadelphia against the Prophet and the Twelve. At the insistence of the Twelve, he was disfellowshipped and lost his license to preach. Smith, *History of the Church*, 5:410–12. The Twelve excommunicated Winchester and his wife on September 26, 1944. Ibid., 7:223.

21. Jedediah Grant, Letter to Newel K. Whitney, October 11, 1844, holograph, L. Tom Perry Special Collections and Manuscripts Division, Lee Library, Brigham Young University, Provo, Utah.

22. Smith, *History of the Church*, 7:297. Grant had received his appointment on March 9, 1845, was "seated" as a president on November 26, sustained by the Twelve two days later, and "ordained" a Seventies president on December 2, 1845. Quinn, *Origins of Power*, 549.

"I have had no rest for over ten years. But all is right."

⊨ 5 ⊨
A Full-Blooded Mormon

LATE IN THE FALL of 1844, Wilford Woodruff arrived in Philadelphia on his way to New York City. In his journey eastward, he had visited the branches of the church, finding them in a continuing mood of uncertainty and division. Sidney Rigdon, counselor and close adviser to the slain Prophet, and late a contender for his mantle, had been excommunicated at Nauvoo in September and was cutting a wide swath through the branches and among the Saints in the East. With his headquarters at Pittsburgh, Rigdon had launched a concerted campaign to derail the Twelve and to spread disunity in the church. In Philadelphia Woodruff found Grant sitting on an even more agitated beehive than the one he had seen at Pittsburgh. In addition to combating the influences of Sidney Rigdon, Grant was wrestling with a difficult situation involving his unruly brother-in-law William Smith (nominally his superior in the ecclesiastical structure), renegade Elder Benjamin Winchester, and the irascible Samuel Brannan.[1]

It seems that William Smith had accused Winchester of having had a hand in the killing of his brothers at Carthage. Winchester was suing Sam Brannan for printing Smith's accusation, and Grant had been arrested for violating an injunction against distributing Brannan's papers among the Saints. Woodruff unfortunately recorded few details of this highly unusual fracas in Philadelphia, but his report suggested that Grant had been caught in the middle of the Smith-Winchester imbroglio almost by accident. His being "arrested" for circulating the Brannan materials probably referred to a restraining order having been placed on him while the court handled the dispute. The entire affair must have been extremely painful for Grant, inasmuch as Smith was the husband of his increasingly ill sister Caroline, and Winchester had been a boyhood friend in Erie, Pennsylvania, a fellow member of Zion's Camp, and a missionary companion for a time in 1837.

Additionally, having baptized some five hundred persons in the area, Winchester was almost solely responsible for having raised up the branch at Philadelphia over which Grant was presiding.[2] Whatever the case, when Woodruff arrived early in December, Grant, free under a $1,000 bond, was trying to keep peace among the factionalized Saints and at the same time inspire their allegiance to the Twelve, of whom William Smith was one. As if all of this was not enough, Smith himself had stated loudly that he was not accountable to the rest of his quorum, because he was receiving his own revelations. But remarkably enough Woodruff found the church at Philadelphia to be "in the best order," as he wrote to Brigham Young on December 3, "as good as any one east of the Mountains."[3]

Woodruff was indeed impressed with what he found in Philadelphia, for despite the vexing burdens Grant had weighing upon him, he had managed to maintain a semblance of order. "I think he has saved the church in Philadelphia," wrote the traveling apostle. "I found him just right; he is with us with all his heart." The young loyalist had shown his mettle, at least to Apostle Woodruff: "Elder Grant is a man after my own heart. He is true in all things." The visiting elder advised Grant "to remain a little until the difficulties are a little more over." To Brigham, Woodruff added the following: "Give him counsel as you see fit; he will go where you say."[4]

With that letter to Nauvoo and despite his knotty problems in Philadelphia, Jedediah Grant had obtained his diploma of loyalty and devotion to the Quorum of the Twelve. But if Woodruff's endorsement was not enough, the presiding elder at Philadelphia had taken upon himself the task of publishing a polemic against Sidney Rigdon, who was probably the most serious obstacle (at least in the East) to the Twelve and their attempts to establish control and to restore order in the Church. The pamphlet was probably written and at the printer's prior to the departure of Wilford Woodruff and his party for New York and Liverpool after a short stay in Philadelphia. The apostle's detailed journal made no mention of the publication; and on the title page, Grant listed himself as "One of the Quorum of Seventies," possibly indicating that he had completed it still unaware of his appointment to the presidency of the First Quorum of Seventy. Though it bore the heavy hand of a capable editor, it was unmistakably the product of Jedediah Grant, with the concerted assistance of occasional visitors to Philadelphia through the critical fall of 1844.[5]

Some historians have doubted that Grant actually produced the pamphlet, inasmuch as he was absent from the center of Rigdon's activity most of the time and because of the polished quality of the text. Grant himself explained away the first problem in his opening "Note to the Reader," in which he carefully described the sources of any information to which he himself was not privy. In addition, throughout the text of the work, he credited still others for providing various pieces of information. Nevertheless, there can be little doubt that Grant generated the pamphlet only with considerable assistance, but it is also clear that someone else had not ghostwritten it. First, several of Grant's peculiar (though perhaps not unique) phraseologies appeared at typical points in the text. Second, the most commonly suggested author for the pamphlet, Elder Orson Hyde, delivered a similar exposé on Rigdon before the high priests' quorum in Nauvoo on April 27, 1845. But there were few similarities between the transcript of that address and the pamphlet, except in terms of general detail.[6] Obviously, Grant's work enjoyed considerable polishing before being printed to facilitate readability and to insure consistent style and grammar. Despite his nineteenth-century style and spelling habits, Jedediah Grant had certainly demonstrated, prior to 1844, a facile mind and an ability to express himself on paper at least as well as the author of the *Collection of Facts* on Sidney Rigdon.

As he closed his pamphlet, the loyal Grant sought to explain Rigdon's course with as little pain as possible to the Saints who had followed the errant counselor. It was not easy to remove a veritable pillar of the early church.

> Is not the conclusion irresistable with you, as well as with me, that the mental harmony of Mr. R's mind, is greatly impaired, I cannot reason otherwise. I would not, however, have anyone pluck a laurel from his brow, that in justice belongs to him; his eloquence has often captivated the multitude, enlisting the feelings of many in his favour; I have watched over him and his family in the days of my boyhood, when mobs were threatening their destruction, and even now I would travel over hill and dale to bring them back to the fold from which they have strayed.
>
> But, can any of the Elders of Israel set calmly down and hear Mr. Rigdon belch forth his abuse, like the burning lava from Mount Vesuvius, with the avowed design to blacken the character and reputation of the martyred prophet, who has honorably won a fame more lasting then the monuments

of Greece or Rome, or the Pyramids of Egypt, that have for centuries lifted the same point to heaven, amidst the sands and whirlwinds of the Desert. Elder Smith proved himself to be, what but few have been in any age, namely, a competent Leader of the church of Christ. From the page of history, we learn that every age has produced its Orators, Philosophers and Statesmen. Yet all admit that judicious leaders have been scarce in every age of the world. Can we then, without a reply, bear to have the tombs of the virtuous dead desecrated by the fruits of a disordered imagination. Is it not our duty to rise up and defend, by all honourable means, bleeding innocence; if we do it not, will not their blood cry against us; we owe it to their bereaved families, mother and lonely Brother and weeping sisters. We owe it to the church of God, to ourselves, our wives and children to the latest generation; by every tie that binds us to our religion, by the sacred covenants made to the fathers on this land, or in Asia; by every noble feeling in our natures; by the memory of the past and the hope of the future. May we remember to do justice to the martyred Prophet and Patriarch, lest our right hands forget their cunning, and our tongues cleave to the roof of our mouths.

We will conclude the subject in our next number.[7]

The "next number" to which Grant referred at the end of his attack on Sidney Rigdon never came forth. Perhaps his chronically sore eyes prevented another such effort; more probably the problems of Philadelphia—a dying sister whose apostle husband was in the process of forsaking the Church, combined with the overwhelming burdens attending his pastorate—kept him from further pamphleteering. In any case, he had signed his name among the loyal ones. The church, the Twelve, and Brother Brigham would have further need of him in the near and difficult future.

By the middle of January 1845, Jedediah Grant's pamphlet attacking Sidney Rigdon had reached Nauvoo and the eyes of the Twelve. Brigham Young and his associates were looking on the new year as one of consolidation and preparation. The temple must be completed so that the Saints could be endowed with what Joseph Smith had called a "crown of glory," a commitment to the future of an eternal kingdom. With their backs to the past, the leaders at Nauvoo were more anxious to urge Grant to harvest the wheat than they were to commend him for trying to blow away the chaff.

Beloved Brother Jedediah Grant

We the Twelve in council assembled in the Office of Dr. Willard Richards address a few lines to you by the hand of our beloved Brother Elijah Fordham who will in a few days take his leave of this place, for your part of the country on special business for the Church—he will have documents to show the leading principles of his mission but as there are some things that we wish to communicate to you that it would not be wisdom to commit to the Churches in general but particularly for yourself by which you may learn our private feelings and desires for the welfare of the Latter Day Saints—we have selected some forty men which are to act as agents for the Church, as you will see by the Times and Seasons and the circular that they will carry.

We have had the pleasure of seeing your little publication called J. M. Grant's Rigdon No. 1. and we are happy to say, that we feel it was written in the Spirit of meekness and Love, and our hearts bless you for the bold patriotic stand that you take in the defence of truth—but after some experience, and much reflection—and care that we have looked upon the whole scene that has transpired before our eyes, we have come to the conclusion that if we will drop them and say nothing about them, that they will soon die, for we have learned to our entire satisfaction that all the food they have to feed their minds, is a course of contradiction and slander. Therefore we will say to you and to all the Elders, preach the Gospel of Peace and good will to the children of men though we have not the least fault to find with you, neither would we find fault with others, though we apprehend that there has been an imprudent course taken by some which has created confusion among Saints in the Eastern country—

Brother Grant, all this you will understand, we would wish you to keep what ought to be kept to yourself, we would instruct the Elders through you over whom you have jurisdiction for all those who can [to] leave that part of the country and return to Nauvoo, and ordain good men that are obliged to stay there to preside over the Churches—if you find any Elders that are confirming the Doctrine that Ridgon makes his Hobby horse thinking to ride into power, cut off such Elders from the church—and send them immediately to Nauvoo, to give an account of themselves if they have any faith and let them know that you have power—

We want you as soon as you receive the necessary instruction from Brother Fordham this letter and the circular to go to, with your might in the strength of Israel's God to gather up men and means to send to Nauvoo early in the Spring—

We wish all young men that can come, and men that can leave their families to come up and stay with us this summer, to cultivate the ground, and to work on the Temple—that we may sustain ourselves here this Season, that we may finish the Temple and receive our endowments—and if the Brethren want their endowments, now is the time for them to put forth their hand, and help us, and if we are blessed, we expect that a sufficient portion of the Temple will be finished in the fore part of next Winter so that we can commence to give the brethren their long looked for blessings. If there are brethren in that country who have farms that would like to trade for farms in this Country, they had better send a description of the same to some person in this place, whom they would wish to act as an agent for them, that it may be published in the Neighbor, for our design is, if possible, to purchase all the farms in Hancock County belonging to our enemies this Season.

Fear not Brother Grant to teach the Saints the law of Tithing—the necessity of their tithing themselves one tenth of all they possess unto the Lord with an eye single to his glory that Salvation may go freely to the nations of the Earth and that they may say when they are gathered to Zion that the Prophecy is fulfilled that we have gathered together by sacrifice.

We wish the brethren who come up here this Spring forget not that this is a new country where there are wolves and dogs and where they have Wolf Hunts and we wish the brethren to come prepared to meet all emergencies—

Have no concern Brother Grant about this doctrine causing Saints to apostatize and follow after Rigdon for we say unto you in all confidence that the Wheat will be gathered into the garner of the Lord, and we do not care how soon the Chaff is blown to Pittsburg.

Say, Your tithing will all be committed into the hands of our Agents, or the Agents as the Churches abroad may appoint for their own convenience and altho' when we made out a list of names we overlooked yours, but meant to have had yours with the rest, but now we will say unto you, we will appoint you, and you must act upon the authority of this letter, until the next Times and Seasons comes out, but if the Paper is not yet gone too far, we will yet have your name in this number.

We want you to start the brethren as early as possible in the Spring, and when you are gathering tithing such as cannot pay money, clothes, dry goods all kinds of clothing, shoes, cutlery and jewelry.

Your Brother George who lives here, is well and his family—and your Father and family were well the last time he heard from him—

You will remember Brother Grant that you are appointed as one of the First Presidents of the Quorum of the Seventies, and one of the Presidents of the First Seventy—when you have an opportunity to see brother Parley P. Pratt and Wm. Smith, be ordained to that office or either of them can do it if you choose.

We think it would be well for you to tarry in that place thro' the Summer or until you hear from us again, to manage the affairs of the Church—We expect that brother Wm. Smith will return to Nauvoo as soon as the circumstances of his family will admit; therefore you will not have him to assist you—

Let the brethren who come up here, provide themselves means to sustain themselves while here, and coming here, without infringing upon the tithing—

We bless you in the name of the Lord and pray that the Spirit may attend your labors and subscribe ourselves your Brothers in the Gospel of our Lord Jesus Christ

Brigham Young President
Willard Richards Clerk[8]

Elijah Fordham delivered his messages to Grant in Philadelphia, tarried a few days while the presiding elder put together the temple collection, and then left with it in haste for Nauvoo. It was the middle of the night prior to the day of Fordham's departure before Grant finally found time to pen a short note for Elijah to carry back to Young in the City of Joseph, as the Mormons were now calling Nauvoo.

Br Brigham. My health is very bad. I have had no rest for over 10 years. But all is right. You told me to come here, and when you say come to Nauvoo, I will come. If it meets your mind, I want to go to Cape Cod, in May next and spend the summer and preach and recruit my health and then come to Nauvoo in the fall. We expect a Grant to make its appearance in our place of residence, some time near the last of April. My wife is a full blooded Mormon and we both worshop the God of Joseph and Joseph is our God the other side of the vail, and we look on you as our head and leader in this world, and ever after, and Joseph your head forever, and we want to be as near Joseph, as you and your Quorum will let us come.

It is now past 12 o'clock at night. Br. Fordham is puting up his money to start in the morning. Please remember me to Br George. Tell him Sister Caroline is worse. It is doubtful whether she ever lives to come to Nauvoo. We exersise all the faith we can for her.

You may depend on my doing all I can for the temple. Please give my love to all the brethren that enquire after me. I would give any thing if I could be at Nauvoo and talk with you and Br Kimball. Will you both write to me? Tell Br Kimball he would not be treated here as he was last year, but [with] the help of the Lord. I have got the church strait. They will I hope pay their tithing. Elder Brown is in New Jersey his wife in this city. He got married in less than two months after he came here. Br. Wm. [Smith] is in the east, doing all he can to get ready to come to Nauvoo. Please pardon me if rong: as ever yours &c

J M Grant.[9]

Though brief, this letter said a great deal. Perhaps because Grant wrote it late at night when he was obviously tired, it showed some normal human frailty that he had seemed to hide so well during a decade of trying missionary service. But in spite of his admission of bad health (probably his eyes) and weariness, Grant hastened to submit himself to the will of the brethren before asking for a sort of vacation to Cape Cod. His pleas for letters from Young and Kimball and his pessimistic assessment of his sister's chances for recovery revealed in writing for the first time an agony of soul that had surely come upon him often during the trying months of 1844 and 1845.

The next few months were typical of the past ten years that had led Jedediah Grant to admit his weariness to Brother Brigham. Full of mingled joy and pain, they presented an ironic juxtaposition of life and death as his first child, a girl named for her mother, was born on May 9 in Philadelphia, while three days later in Nauvoo, his thirty-year-old sister Caroline died at the home of her sister-in-law Emma Smith, the Prophet's widow.[10] Orson Pratt preached the funeral discourse on May 24, after which Caroline was buried "in the tomb of Joseph," a place the Prophet had prepared for himself and his family.[11] That afternoon, the widower William Smith, apparently reconciled to the Church and the Twelve, was ordained patriarch to the Church. There was afterward "a warm exchange of good feeling between William Smith and the quorum." The cordiality suffered a quick death, however, as the Prophet's brother shortly thereafter claimed that the Church depended on the Smith family for the priesthood. Following a subsequent series of clashes with the Twelve and a published attack on that group, Smith was dropped from the Quorum and from his calling as patriarch. On October 19, 1845, he was formally excommunicated.[12]

As for Grant, his hoped-for sabbatical became impossible as the requirements of building the Church in the East and of forwarding men and means to Nauvoo bore down upon him. By the middle of the summer, as he wrote to his friend Wilford Woodruff, then in England, his efforts and those of others were bearing fruit, and the energies of the Church seemed to have been restored. It was not a time for slackening endeavor.

No 353, North 3d St Philad'a.   July 12 1845

Elder W. Woodruff.

    Beloved Brother in the Kingdom of God. I hope you will forgive me for not writing to you 'ear this. You know it is impossible for me to forgit you. Though I confess my negligence in writing, yet all within me bears witness that Br Woodruff has been remembered, at the family alter and before the congregation of the Saints, when ever the hour came to offer our oblations to the Father in the name of Jesus our Elder Brother.

    Dear Brother you are greatfully remembered by the Saints in this city. We rejoice to hear of your prosperity in your almost boundless field of labour. I have received bouth of your interresting letters and also the minuts of you[r] general conference. While reading the same, my soul was filled with joy for a moment I seemed to be with you. With the velocity of lightning, my thoughts crost the briny deep and traced you in your various meanderings through England and Scotland, the land of my fore fathers nativity.

    I also viewed with much satisfaction the cource persued by all my brethren who went from the land made dear to us by the Sacred Covenants the Lord made to Brother Joseph, our martered Lawgiver and renowned Prophet, that this land should be our everlasting inheritance. I might dear brother dwell much on past sceanes you know so well. That I may comply with your request, namely to give you all the news I can either from Nauvoo, East West North or South, I leave the news from Nauvoo for the last, as that will be the beast [best] of all.

The work of the Lord had prospered in Philad'a since you was here; some twenty or thirty new members have been baptised, our congregation has greatly increased in numbers, the Spirit of the Lord is in our midst. Therefore our union is strong. We are doing all in our power to help compleate the temple and Nauvoo House. Prayers are offered without ceasing by day and night that we may have the privelige of fulfiling the commandments, that the blessings long looked for may come upon us in the house of the Lord.

In the city of New York the cause is onward. New members are joining the church. All are alive on the subject of building in Nauvoo the City of Joseph, and finishing the temple. Elders Parley P Pratt and S Brannan are going ahead with printing and circulating truth. Elder Pratt has thrued a flood of light through all this part of the vineyard to the joy of many Saints.

Boston is blessed with more Saints than any other city in the eastern states. Elder Willard Snow has charge there under the direction of Elder Pratt. That branch I think numbers between 3 and 4 hundred members. In all the eastern states the Saints are well united, beaing willing to listen to the Council of the Twelve, and pay their tithing, as the Lord has said. Many have emigrated to Nauvoo to help in all things to cary out the measures of Br. Joseph and Hyrum Smith.

Through the northern sections of the states the almost innumerable branches of the church are on the increase, not withstanding the elders in general are call[ed] to Nauvoo. The interiour of the different states are now beholding hundreds of their best citizens leaving to locate with the Saints and help build the temple of our God.

From the South the news is cheering to me and all the Saints. You are aware of my labours in south western Virginia and North Carolina. Before I left there, I organized a conference of 200 members, consisting of seven churches in seven different counties. The last account shows an increase of over 100; 50 since I left the field. The accounts received from Alabama Georgia Mississippi Louisiana and Tennessee goes to show that the South keeps not back.

The news from Cannada proves that the North is giving up also as the Prophet said. The bread will soon be ready to bake. The wood has caught fire, and the oven is heating fast.

Nauvoo the City of Joseph, last but not lest, is rising in the magasty of the God of Joseph and Hyrum. Her charter is the law of God, her officers the

Twelve Apostles, and their assistance which is all the spiritual authorities of the whole church and kingdom. Her strength is all power in heaven and on earth. Her banner is Love. The wisdom of her inhabitants re[a]ches to heaven. Before them the wecked tremble. I feel hapy Br Woodruff that I can in truth inform you that the dark cloud which hung over Nauvoo a few months ago has burst asunder. And never, no never, did the sun of peace and prosperity shine on the church as at present. The earth brings forth her strength. The Saints in Hancock County and the adjacent counties will this season rase grain enough to support half of the whole state. In many other parts of the state the frost destroyed almost the entire crop of summer grain. Many of our enemies alredy have to beg grain of the Saints. The temple I supose is nearly covered by this time. The work for the inside is in a rapid state of completion. One hundred hands are now at work on the Nauvoo House. The brick is all ready for the same. Lumber &c &c. The roof will be put on this fall. But you know they build so fast, with so little meanes, that when both houses are completed, the debt for the same will be large indeed, but the commanment will be fulfiled, and the blessings decent [descend] on the true hearted Saints of the Lord. My soul magnifies the Lord for all these precious things.

The murderers of Brs. Joseph and Hyrum have been accquited by the mob jury. They are now in the hands of the Devil for distruction in the own due time of the Lord. The last news from Nauvoo said that nine of the Twelve were there in good health and spirits. I learn that Elders B. Young H. C. Kimball J Taylor, W Richards G. A. Smith O. Pratt O. Hyde Wm Smith John E Page and A Lyman are all in Nauvoo at present, busy night and day giving council to the whole church as the Spirit directs.

Thire is thirty one quorums of seventies completely organised under their rispective presidency as the Lord directs. I hope to see you soon after our first Penticost if the Lord will. Please remember me to all the brethren who went from America. My wife joins with me in sending our love and respects to you and Sister Woodruff. Please write to me as soon as this come to hand and oblije your br in the kingdom of peace,

Jedediah M. Grant[13]

As the summer drew to a close on the Delaware River, Jed and Caroline took their four-month-old daughter "Caddie" and headed for the Mississippi and the society of the Saints in the City of Joseph. Brigham

Young had sent news at the end of August reinforcing the glowing picture of conditions in Nauvoo that Jedediah had given to Wilford Woodruff. The best word of all for the young couple was that the temple would be ready for endowments and other Mormon covenant rituals shortly after the fall conference of the Church.[14] Consequently, they hastened onward to Nauvoo with an excitement and an eye to a peaceful future in the shadows of the temple—a future that would never be.

⇸ Notes ⇷

1. Journal History of the Church of Jesus Christ of Latter day Saints (chronological scrapbook of typed entries and newspaper clippings, 1830 present), December 3, 1844, 2; Joseph Smith Jr., *History of the Church of Jesus Christ of Latter-day Saints*, edited by B. H. Roberts, 7 vols., 2d ed. rev. (1902–12; Salt Lake City: Deseret Book, 1964 printing), 7:317. For a brilliant and complex analysis of the succession crisis, see D. Michael Quinn, *The Mormon Hierarchy: Origins of Power* (Salt Lake City: Signature Books, 1994), 143–243, which argues persuasively (243) that, "With the exception of Sidney Rigdon, William Smith, Lyman Wight, and John E. Page, senior apostle Brigham Young retained the loyalty of the entire Mormon hierarchy as constituted at Joseph Smith's death."

2. Andrew Jenson, *Latter-day Saints Biographical Encyclopedia*, 4 vols. (1901; rpt., Salt Lake City: Western Epics, 1971), 4:692. See David J. Whittaker, "East of Nauvoo: Benjamin Winchester and the Early Mormon Church," *Journal of Mormon History* 21 (Fall 1995): 30–83.

3. Journal History, December 3, 1844, 3; Wilford Woodruff, Letter to Brigham Young, December 3, 1844, holograph, Brigham Young Collection, LDS Church Archives.

4. Woodruff, Letter to Young, December 3, 1844.

5. Jedediah M. Grant, *A Collection of Facts Relative to the Course Taken by Elder Sidney Rigdon, in the States of Ohio, Missouri, Illinois, and Pennsylvania* (Philadelphia: Brown, Bicking & Guilbert, Printers, 1844).

6. Orson Hyde, *Speech of Elder Orson Hyde Delivered before the High Priests Quorum in Nauvoo, April 27, 1845, upon the Course and Conduct of Mr. Sidney Rigdon, and upon the Merits of His Claim to the Presidency of the Church of Jesus Christ of Latter-day Saints* (City of Joseph [Nauvoo]: Printed by John Taylor, 1845).

7. Grant, *A Collection of Facts*, 46–48.

8. Brigham Young, Letter to Jedediah Grant, January 21, 1845, holograph, Brigham Young Collection. This letter left Nauvoo in the hands of Elijah Fordham on January 27,

1845. On January 31, and though he had been functioning as such for some time, Grant was designated as an official agent for the collection of temple funds. Journal History, January 27, 1845, 1, and January 31, 1845, 2; Smith, *History of the Church*, 7:362–69.

9. Jedediah Grant, Letter to Brigham Young, April 1845, holograph, Brigham Young Collection.

10. Journal History, May 22, 1845, 1, and May 24, 1845, 1.

11. Brigham Young, Letter to Parley P. Pratt, May 26, 1845, holograph, Brigham Young Collection. In his "History of the Life of Oliver B. Huntington also His Travels and Troubles Written by Himself" (typescript, LDS Church Archives), Huntington erroneously reported Caroline's death as having occurred on May 23 when in reality she died late in the evening of Thursday, May 22, and was buried two days later (Saturday).

12. Smith, *History of the Church*, 7:418, 458–59, 483.

13. Jedediah Grant, Letter to Wilford Woodruff, July 12, 1845, holograph, Wilford Woodruff Collection, LDS Church Archives. Note Grant's giddy spirit of optimism and his happy belief that the future of the Church was secure in an ever more prosperous Nauvoo.

14. Journal History, August 27, 1845, 1.

"This camping ground should be the saddest of all sad places to me...."

6
The Third Hundred

ARRIVING IN ST. LOUIS sometime near the end of September, the Grants learned that all was not well with the Saints on the Mississippi. On September 7, the Twelve had decided that anti-Mormon feeling rising in the area would soon force the Church to evacuate to a new gathering place.[1] In addition, the schism in the hierarchy had widened as a new and frightening animosity had developed between the Twelve, led by Brigham Young, and the surviving Smiths and their loyalists, led by the Prophet's widow. Of particular chagrin to Grant was the role in all of this of his brother-in-law William Smith. Indeed, not only had William Smith become a leading advocate of a wholesale Mormon defection from the leadership of the Twelve based upon opposition to the "damnable doctrine" of plural marriage; but during his stay in St. Louis through the late summer, he had apparently become involved in a sexual relationship with a young Catholic woman who was living in the home where he and his daughter were boarding. Grant's personal and public horror at the ex-apostle's behavior sent him into a rage matched only by Smith's own vehement denials of any improprieties. The reverberations from the meeting of the two former friends and kinsmen rattled all the way to Nauvoo, as the Grants stormed northward to inform the Church of William's shameful fall from grace.[2] For Jedediah and Caroline, the unpleasantness in St. Louis marked only the beginning of the trials that would soon beset all such "full-blooded Mormons."

Reaching Nauvoo sometime around the beginning of October 1845, Grant found the situation to be even worse than he had gathered while in St. Louis. In addition to the fear and uncertainty generated through the continuing leadership crisis, mobs roaming the countryside, burning and pillaging Mormon homes and farms, had forced hundreds of Saints into

Nauvoo for safety. The Grants could not have been in the City of Joseph long before they learned that the Twelve had determined to lead the Saints to a new place of refuge in the Rocky Mountains. Indeed, at the first session of the October conference of the Church, they heard Brother Brigham propose that all the Saints should go to the West with the Twelve. He then prophesied that the Lord would "shower down means" to accomplish his resolution "to the very letter."[3]

The prospects of leaving Nauvoo could not have bothered Grant much; he had never lived there for longer than a few months. Abandoning the temple on the hill, however, was something else. The greatest efforts of his mission to Philadelphia had been absorbed in a search for temple donations to build a house of the Lord, a monument unto Joseph. In this Grant was not alone. Abandoning the temple and the immense sacrifices it represented brought puzzled sorrow into the hearts of the Latter-day Saints at Nauvoo. Parley Pratt's answer—that God's people were always required to make great sacrifices and that they could "build a larger and better Temple in five years from this time than we now possess"[4]—was not entirely satisfying. Nevertheless, there was little time for looking back. Moving thousands of people across the wilderness in a modern exodus to the promised land would take more than words and faith.

On October 11, twenty-five men received assignments from the Twelve to take charge of a hundred families each and to supervise their preparations for the journey across the Great Plains. Grant became captain of the fourteenth hundred.[5] Through the rest of October and November, he worked with his charges, making sure they had all the items on the list that the committee on preparation had drawn up shortly before conference.[6] He was so involved in his efforts that it was not until December 2, some fourteen months after being sustained as one of the presidents of the First Quorum of Seventy, that he was finally ordained to that position along with Benjamin L. Clapp and Albert P. Rockwood.[7] Ten days later the seven presidents received their endowments in the temple along with their wives.[8] Joseph's "crown of glory" would hold firmly the frontiersman's hat or the pioneer bonnet.

Grant spent December and January working with his hundred and administering endowments in the temple. During this time, pressures from the outside continued to mount. The Saints worked strenuously to provide for themselves temporally by acquiring oxen and wagons in exchange for their homes and farms, and to gain spiritual sustenance through the endowment ceremony in the new temple. A steady stream of men and women passed through the great edifice to covenant with the God of Joseph and Brigham that He would be their God, and they would be His people.[9] On February 3, 1846, Brigham Young reported that the temple "was thronged all day, the anxiety being so great to receive, as if the brethren would have us stay here and continue the endowments until our way would be hedged up, and our enemies would intercept us." At one point Young even walked away from the temple, saying that he was getting his wagons ready to go, but when he returned the crowd was still there "to overflowing," in anxiety that they would not get their blessings before the Twelve left the city. Brigham resumed the ordinances until, on that single day, 295 persons received them.[10] Finally, in the first week of February, the Saints began to leave the City of Joseph. On February 9, the roof of the temple caught fire and burned. Young, watching in the distance, proclaimed it the will of the Lord and turned his face to the West.[11]

Jedediah and Caroline were among the first to leave Nauvoo, partly because they had been there only a short time and owned no property in the city. Along with the bulk of those who left early, they probably stopped at Sugar Creek, some seven miles from the Mississippi in Iowa Territory. There, Grant celebrated his thirtieth birthday. Still in charge of the fourteenth hundred, he busied himself gathering them together as they arrived and passing instructions to them from Brigham and the Twelve. On Monday, February 23, 1846, the Twelve met with the captains of the hundreds to chart the course across Iowa.[12] Over the next few days, the companies of the modern "Camp of Israel" began to push along the divide between the Missouri and the Des Moines rivers, bound for the Rocky Mountains.

The movement across Iowa picked up speed as the weather improved and as the Saints became conditioned to the processes of mass movement. Captain Grant had known no permanent home for a dozen years, and he seemed to enjoy being in the thick of the Mormon migration, preaching to the Saints, trading with the Indians, and joining the leadership councils held along the trail from Sugar Creek to Garden Grove and Mt. Pisgah.[13] In mid-June the marching column of Mormons arrived at Council Bluffs on the Missouri River, where the brethren decided to stop while a company of men proceeded into the Rockies to locate a suitable resting place for the Saints.[14]

By the middle of July, Grant was at Council Bluffs, participating in the councils there and taking assignments from Young and the other leaders of the encampment, including one that placed him in a party charged with locating a site for winter quarters on the west bank of the Missouri River.[15] It seemed that the U.S. government had agreed to enlist 500 Mormons in an "Army of the West" as part of its war against Mexico. This would necessitate a delay in the move across the plains, at least until the coming spring of 1847. The Latter-day Saints would have to wait a while longer to see the end of their wanderings in the wilderness.

Contrary to common belief, the Mormon Battalion enlistment did not come as a surprise to the Church at Council Bluffs. Indeed, Mormon leaders had hoped that the government would allow an enlistment of 2,000 men instead of the 500 who eventually formed the battalion. Jesse C. Little, president of the Eastern States Mission, arranged with the Polk administration for the battalion after the brethren in Iowa realized that army paychecks would be of considerable help in the coming trek to the mountains. A mythology subsequently grew up around the Mormon Battalion story that suggested the U.S. government had surprised the Saints in Iowa with their request for soldiers and that the Mormon leadership had agreed to send men into the war with Mexico in order to prove the patriotism of the Latter-day Saints in the face of persecution.[16]

As the Saints moved to the site of Winter Quarters during the first weeks of August 1846, Jedediah Grant, a member of the new municipal council, took a prominent part in the organization of the community, assuming such responsibilities as selecting twenty-four policemen for the camp village and locating newcomers and their stock. The Twelve also called on him to serve as an ambassador to the Indians in the area and to the few old settlers with whom the Saints would have to deal.[17] An additionally significant duty seemed to devolve upon him due to the presence in the Mormon camp of Colonel Thomas L. Kane, a member of one of the first families of Philadelphia and close confidant of Vice President George M. Dallas. Kane had taken an intense interest in the plight of the Mormons when fund-raising missionaries arrived on the Delaware late in 1845 seeking help for the soon-to-be exiled Saints on the Mississippi. The son of a highly regarded judge in Philadelphia, Kane's growing attachment to the cause of the Mormons had already brought them considerable benefits, and his service was just beginning. It was probably Kane's influence with Dallas that had tipped the scales in President Polk's hesitant decision to allow the Mormons to form the Battalion. When Kane then decided to visit the Saints himself (arriving at the Bluffs on July 11), Young assigned Grant to serve as a kind of liaison officer to the colonel during his stay.[18] Although it does not appear that Grant had met Kane when they must both have been in Philadelphia, by the time the Pennsylvanian left the encampment for the East on September 8 the two men had established a firm friendship, one that would prove in the near future to be of great value to the Church, as it would continue to need the favor of such an influential non-Mormon.[19]

Into the fall and winter of 1846, the Saints labored strenuously to get themselves ready for the coming spring's journey to the promised land. Grant for his part continued to move about, fulfilling assignments from Young and the Twelve who, on November 26, divided Winter Quarters into wards and called bishops to preside over them. Wanting them free "to attend to other business," Brigham Young also released Grant, Albert Rockwood, and Benjamin Clapp from the municipal council.[20] As it turned out, Brother Brigham had considerable business in mind for Elder Grant. At the end of January, the first four captains of hundreds being organized for the migration of 1847 received their assignments—Daniel Spencer, Edward Hunter, Willard Snow, and Jedediah Grant.[21]

On February 9, 1847, Grant returned from a trip to Fort Leavenworth with a letter from Colonel Kane to Brigham Young.[22] Ten days later, the Quorum of the Twelve voted to send Grant to Philadelphia and Washington to "communicate with Colonel Kane and through him to the President of the United States, in all matters pertaining to the welfare of the saints."[23] The Twelve also gave him full power to speak for the Church. The weight of this assignment to represent the Church in the East during this critical period seemed all the heavier inasmuch as Caroline was seven months pregnant with their second child. Her health, moreover, had been poor for several months. It was not a good time to be leaving home.

On the morning of March 1, Brigham Young, John D. Lee, and Jedediah Grant met with Willard Richards in the historian's office, where they prepared a packet of thirty letters for Grant to carry with him to St. Louis and the East. He also received a copy of "The Word and Will of the Lord" (Young's account of God's directions for the Mormon migration), and a letter of instructions on the purchase of materials to be used in the making of a large American flag.[24] The Mormons were going into Mexican territory, but they would carry the standard of the United States with them, inasmuch as the President had made it clear to them through Jesse C. Little that he would expect the Saints to support the American acquisition of California and New Mexico.[25] With his mission clear, Jedediah bade Caroline adieu and headed east.

Arriving in Philadelphia, Grant worked for several weeks with Thomas Kane on maintaining and improving Mormon relations with the Polk administration. Of prime concern was continuing federal permission for the Saints to remain in the Winter Quarters area, government-designated Indian land. Satisfied that all was going well between Kane and the various departments in Washington,[26] Grant hastened back to the Potawatomi country in order to take charge of his company of emigrants. Within two weeks of reaching Winter Quarters about the first of June, he had his people assembled, organized, and waiting on the southwest bank of the Elkhorn River for their leader's signal to start for the Rockies.[27]

Brigham Young's advance party had left Winter Quarters in April, and a decision had been made to keep the 1847 migration to four additional companies. They were to travel together but were to maintain their group integrity by camping a half mile apart as they moved along the Platte River. Daniel Spencer was to captain the first hundred families, Edward Hunter the second (in cooperation with John Taylor), Jedediah Grant the third, and Abraham Smoot the fourth. Willard Snow, whom the brethren had originally designated as one of the four captains, was to assist Grant as leader of his second fifty. On June 17, 1847, the "Camp of Israel" began to move westward onto the sea of grass called the Great Plains.[28]

Traveling with Grant was John Young, brother to the president of the Twelve, and on occasion also Charles C. Rich, commander of a military party in the Nauvoo Legion. Rich was in charge of an artillery company that was traveling independently but in close cooperation with the emigrating Saints. He also had charge of transporting the Nauvoo Temple bell and a small skiff to be used in water scouting. The third hundred moved very well during the first few days, so well, in fact, that it overtook and passed the second company and an irate John Taylor, who subsequently stormed into Grant's camp on horseback June 24 to accuse Grant and Young of disobeying orders and being out of place. When Parley Pratt, the ranking apostle in the emigration, arrived in the camp that evening, he listened patiently while Taylor harangued the leaders of the third company for "being disobedient and insulting to the priesthood,"[29] and then, in Rich's words, "gave us a good lecture."[30] On Pratt's advice, Grant agreed to obey counsel and to apologize to Taylor, and the incident passed.[31]

With his ebullience thus a little trimmed, the thirty-one-year-old began his tenure as a pioneer leader. But there were other, more personal problems to shackle his spirits. When he had returned from the East, he had found that Caroline had become the mother of a new daughter, born May 19, 1847, and named Margaret, but both mother and child were ailing. Caroline had been so weak that she could barely begin the journey a month later, and the infant was dangerously frail.[32] True to his status of total commitment, however, Grant had no choice but to push on, despite conditions of health or the burdens of small children. To ease the hardship, Grant kept his friend Joseph Bates Noble traveling close by so that his niece, fifteen-year-old Susan Fairchild Noble, could be near Caroline and her two children.[33] Their care undoubtedly removed a great deal of worry from the captain so that he could devote his energies to the task of running the company.

The trek was going well for the third hundred until a few miles west of Grand Island on the Platte on the night of July 12. The companies were camping all together for the first time, feasting on buffalo meat and enjoying a social respite from the grueling journey along the muddy river. During the night, the cattle and oxen in Grant's company broke out of the yard, smashing in the process several wagons and killing and maiming some of the livestock in the camp. The third company had no choice but to stay over in order to repair equipment and find the scattered stock while the other three proceeded.[34] Four days later Captain Grant still counted as missing seventy-five precious head of cattle, including twenty yokes of oxen.[35] So critical was this loss to the third hundred that the other companies slowed up while volunteers dropped back to assist in search for the cattle, but they found very few. Finally, on July 23, nearly two weeks after the breakout, Grant's party limped into view of the other companies at a place called Cedar Bluffs.[36] The next day, as Brigham Young was entering the Valley of the Great Salt Lake for the first time, Jedediah Grant and his company of Saints again fell considerably behind the rest of the trekkers still on the Platte.[37] It would be a long and difficult journey the rest of the way into the promised land.

From July 24 on into the dusty days of August, the third hundred struggled to keep up with the rest of the emigration. Realizing that the party could make better progress in somewhat smaller groups, given the shortage of livestock, Grant divided his company early in August, allowing Bates Noble and his fifty to press ahead separately. He sent his ailing wife ahead with their daughters while he remained most of the time in the rear with Willard Snow and his fifty, keeping them going and trying to ease the hardship somewhat with his presence.[38] But no matter what efforts the group expended, the third hundred continued to lag several miles behind the other three companies, while all four were yoking up cows and sometimes men to keep the wagons moving along the trail.[39]

In the middle of August, Phineas Young and four companions prepared to leave the emigrating Saints for the valley. Members of the advance party, they had returned with news and letters from Brigham Young and the others with him, and were now going back. Camped with his company some hundred miles east of Fort Laramie, Grant penned a short letter for Phineas to carry to his brother Brigham. But Jedediah was not about to complain to his leader, nor would he reveal the extent of the difficulty with which his company was grappling.[40]

Kimball Spring Aug 15/47

Prest. B. Young and Counsil.

Dear Brethren, After my best respects & c I will inform you that the brethren and sisters composing the third hundred of the camp of Israel are mostly enjoying good health and spirits and we all greatly desire to see you and those that are with you and if kind Heaven smiles on us we expect to soon enjoy that priveledge, although we [are] a little in the rear from several causes which Br Phineas the bearer of this whill explain to you. He has been with us about three weeks. He met us about one hundred and seventy five miles below Fort Larimie. He is now on the eve of returning as the brethren of the camp are senseable of your great anxiety to hear from us and your families in Winter Quarters. I will say for your satisfaction that they were all well without scarsly an exception when we left Winter Q.

We have been highly favored in our journeying cons[i]dering our late start and the numerous host that are journeying together.

In relation to our waggons, teams, and general information conserning the camp Br Phineas can relate it to you with as much correctness as though were I to write all the particulars.

I send you the communication from Colonel Kane and assure you that all things are working in Washington in the different departments about as wee would wish them. The colonel entertains no fears of our being removed from W. Quarters. His hand hart and feelings are as warm as ever and a little more so. He wished me to explain to you the meaning of the dash at the close of his letter which is "his respects to the counsil and all "his Mormon friends all around and over the Omahaw Hills."

I send you a letter from Sister C. and also from Br B[?].

Your Br John is with us and is well and of great use to the camp giving us counsil and advise.

If there are any teems sent back to assist the camp wee wish you to remember the third hundred.

Your children, Br C. Decker and wife, Ed. Ellsworth wife and children are all well. On my return from the East I found my wife very ill so much so that she was nearly unable to undertake the journy. Her health has continued very bad and is so still. She feels the need of the prayers and faith of those who have influence with the most high.

I wish you and the counsil when assembled to remember her in your prayers that she may recover her health.

Please remember me to all the brethren in your camp. As ever yours

J. M. Grant[41]

One month after the loss of so much of his livestock, Grant made camp with his company at Independence Rock, near where the Oregon Trail left the Platte to follow the Sweetwater River due west a hundred miles to South Pass.[42] Before reaching the clear relief of the Sweetwater, the Saints had passed through some of the most unpleasant country in the world. The alkaline soil produced only sparse vegetation, and much of the water found in the region was brackish and toxic. Adding to the natural forsakenness of the countryside were the signs of foolhardy migrations of white men that had gone before. The way was strewn not only with the flotsam of overburdened wagons, such as discarded furniture and broken implements, but also with the rotting carcasses of the beasts of burden that men used and then abandoned whenever a leg broke or poisoning set in from consuming foul grasses and water. Susan Noble, then fifteen years old, remembered the scene often in later years as she recounted pioneer tales to her grandchildren.

> Oh, that smell was terrible, especially when it was seasoned with the nasty water. It was enough to kill us all—man and beast. Even to this day, at the scent of carrion, I am carried backward to those days on the plains. We didn't blame the travelers ahead of us so very much, for we could do but little better for those who were to follow us, but we did, however, drag off all dead critters from the camping places.
>
> My, how we boys and girls worked day after day to keep our cows and sheep from taking too large a dose at one time of this brackish water. The weather was so hot, though, and the animals increased in their thirst by the salty country, that in spite of our poundings, and pleadings, they would gorge themselves upon the morbific, soap bubbley stuff and then almost immediately begin being sick. An epidemic of cholera had broken out, spreading first among the animals and then attacking the people, especially the children. As the days passed and the conditions grew no better, the malady increased in severity. I remember one afternoon when our best milch cow stretched out and died. This was the first of our animals to go. All through camp, oxen, horses, sheep, pigs, and even the chickens were affected alike. As the human sick list grew, greater loads were added to the weary cattle. Oh, it was just terrible! the vomiting and purging and knife like cramps that sapped the vitality in just a few hours, bringing some of the strongest to the wagons and keeping them there for days and finally leaving them pale and weak.
>
> But hope was before us; Sweet Water, they declared, was just a day or so ahead. This was a clear, sparkling river running eastward from the Rockies. As our wagon was close to Captain Grant's, I remember how worried he was and how he prayed at our evening meetings that the animals and people would be spared to reach our new home in the mountains.[43]

Grant's prayers were not just for the success of his company. Caroline's health had improved considerably, but she was still far from well. Leaving Independence Rock, Jedediah's hundred welcomed the relative pleasantness of the Sweetwater country. But by the end of August, several cattle had died of poisoning, exacerbating the already critical shortage of teams.[44] Worse still, the incidence of cholera in the camp increased dramatically, bringing suffering and death particularly to the young and ailing. Caroline Grant was among the first to contract the feared disease, but she was holding her own; then came Thursday, September 2. Susan Noble would remember the scene clearly many years later.

We were close to Captain Grant. His wife Caroline, was exceptionally kind to me, inviting me often to fix our supper with her. Then in the evening, as I helped tend Sister Grant's two little girls, Caroline, two years, and Margaret, six [actually four] months, I was regularly charmed with Brother Grant's talks, many of which were from his experiences with the Prophet Joseph. At times, as he spoke, he seemed to be so filled with the inspiration of heaven, that all present thrilled with emotions of testimony.

Sorrow now visited our Captain's wagon. As Sister Grant had not been very well for several days, little Margaret got the cholera and by sundown she was seized with violent spasms. I was so worried, I stayed close by their wagon while I took care of "Caddie," as we all called the oldest girl. As night came on, Margaret grew worse. About mid night I was sent to my bed, but later as I looked up, I could still see the parents, accompanied by Sisters [Eliza R.] Snow and [Rebecca W.] Riter and Brother and Sister Noble, working with the child by the fire on the sheltered side of their wagon.

The hot weather had brought on a thunder storm, the first for days. A terrible wind was springing up from the west, driving the loose clay dust before it. In just a few minutes the down pour was upon us. The fires sizzled briefly and were forced out; everyone hurried for shelter. The gale, resembling a hurricane, roared through the country with terrific speed, bringing sheet like columns of rain in alarming force against the wagon. Several tents were toppled over and almost blown away, while the drenched occupants in their night clothing raced to safer abodes. The storm seemed to be coming from the mountains. After a little it slackened, yet it kept up most of the night. Worried but weary, I finally went off to sleep.

The next morning when I awoke, the sun was shining brightly on my wagon cover. Margaret flashed immediately into my mind. I quickly sat up. No one else had been to bed in our wagon. I was ashamed that I had gone to sleep. Outside I could hear low voices, and I learned that we were to move on to the Sweet Water before making breakfast. Just then, from the wagon next to ours, I heard little Caddie calling, half lonesome like, for her mother. I was only half dressed but I was soon ready, and scrambling out, stood for a moment looking about from the wagon tongue. One quick glance and I read part of the sorrow the night had left behind. Over on the side of a rolling clay hill about a stone's throw away, and half surrounded by people, principally women, was a new little mound. Nearer me, the men were busy in the slippery clay, hitching up the cattle for moving. Climbing quickly into Sister Grant's wagon, I threw myself by the side of Caddie, sobbing as only a heart broken girl can. After a little, I heard the folks returning. Then, as I waited, I thought of that cold burial, and I knew there had been no material for a box of any sort—oh, it was terrible!

Brother Grant's animals were now hitched to his wagon. I then heard Brother [Levi Evans] Riter suggest quietly, "Brother Grant, Sister Riter will ride with Caroline and Caddie this morning. Caroline is not well and must be relieved from all care and further worry." As I softly climbed from the wagon, Brother and Sister Grant saw me. Sister Grant exclaimed, "Oh, Susan!" and throwing her arms around me, she gave expression to her feelings, weeping as if her heart would break.

That morning as we moved forward, the trail proved heavy and slippery. Every swale and gully was chokeful of mud and debris, forced there by the storm of the night before. The air this morning, though, was cool and invigorating. Such a wonderful change naturally revived our spirits. By noon we were on the Sweet Water. The Bad Lands, like a departing nightmare, lay grim in the distance. A much needed rest, with plenty of good feed for the animals and a river of clear, fresh water for all, revived the sick and again set us thinking of the mountains.[45]

Through the following week the weather continued to be unseasonably poor, with cold temperatures and even some snow. With the death of her baby, Caroline Grant became increasingly ill, so much so that most in the company expected her own death at any time.[46] The gloom in the third hundred deepened with each gray day, until on the morning of September 8, "like messengers from another world,"[47] Brigham Young, Heber Kimball, and others of the advance party arrived at the encampment of Bates Noble's fifty on Quakenasp Creek. The returning pioneers had left John Taylor's company some twelve miles ahead at 9 o'clock, intending to stay with Jedediah's company for a few days before continuing on back to Winter Quarters. In the middle of the afternoon, Grant arrived at the camp with Willard Snow and his fifty.[48] Upon meeting, Brigham, Heber, and Jedediah reportedly "hugged each other like youngsters."[49]

The reunion provided a needed recess from the strains of the past few days. Unfortunately, it also gave a band of Indians an opportunity to raid the stockyard while the camp's guard was down. In a lightning assault, they made off with more than forty horses and mules before the Saints could stop them and mount up for a chase. Some two hundred Mormons followed the Indians toward the Platte, but returned with only five of the stolen animals.[50] This was a heavy blow to the third hundred, repeatedly hit already with livestock shortages. Brigham consequently sent a rider to the valley requesting all the help possible for the emigrating camp and particularly for Grant's company bringing up the rear.[51] He then instructed the members of his returning party to give up their horses to the third hundred. "After seeing the whole of Jedediah M. Grant's company on their road to the Valley at 9 a.m.," Young reported, "I called on my council and all the returning brethren, except the teamsters, to take a walk with me to Winter Quarters."[52]

The third hundred families limped forward even more slowly as a result of this last reverse of their fortunes. On September 14, Grant obtained permission from Taylor and Pratt to break his company into tens so that the slower groups would not hinder those more able to keep up.[53] This seemed to liven spirits, at least for those moving ahead. Additionally, a major goal on the trail, South Pass, was just beyond the horizon. As Susan Noble recalled,

> We had heard so much of South Pass that we thought, of course, a dangerous and difficult climb was before us. One can hardly imagine our surprised feeling when we found the continental divide a long, broad, easy upland valley with spendid trails. It was hardly believable until we saw the waters of the Sandy running westward toward Green River. As our hopes were now flying high, many a teamster shouted, including the women. All felt they had a right to be happy, looking forward and not backward. As our wagons rolled easily along, all joined in singing many a trail song.
>
> > O, wife, let us go; oh, don't let us wait,
> > I long to be there and I long to be great;
> > While you, some fair lady; and who knows but I
> > May be some rich Governor long 'fore I die.

Our soaring spirits were soon to return, however, and hug the ground in silence; for joys seem to ebb and flow with sorrows ever present. In just a few days, mountain fever had confined a great number to their wagons. It was with difficulty that the sick could ride forward at all, for the roads became but trails, rough and difficult. Brigham Young had warned us that at the first sign of the mountain sickness, we were to use plenty of composition, cayenne, and vegetable pills. These were to assist in breaking the fever. Brother Young told us of his sickness, of the distressing pain that throbbed in his head, and at the same time the trouble that settled in his back and various joints of his body. When the fever ceased, cold chills were followed by hot flashes that tended to make him almost mad with pain. Brigham Young declared that he was delirious for most of two days; and that this was the reason why he had to follow into the valley two days behind the foremost of the trail breakers.

Sister Grant, full of faith and hopeful determination, fought off the first signs of the fever, but as she was weakened from the effects of cholera and deep sorrow, back it came with alarming consequences. It was with difficulty now that we could travel at all. Friday night it was decided that part of the camp was to lay over Saturday as well as Sunday, that the others should move forward and during Saturday, as they progressed, help make the roads better. By Monday we were sure all would again be on their way.

As Sister Grant's condition became rather critical Saturday, she and her bed were gently transferred to a tent that was set up near by. Sunday brought a higher fever and complete delirium. For the first Sunday on our long journey there was no singing, preaching, or music heard in the camp. These were replaced by fasting and prayer for Caroline's recovery. As your grandfather [Jedediah Grant] was a very sympathetic man, this grief, added to the worry and sorrows of the past, was almost more than he could bear. Sisters Riter and Snow and the menfolks always stayed close at hand, rendering assistance whenever possible. Brother Grant often took Caddie from me, hugging and kissing her while the tears ran down his face.

During the evening of Sunday, as I sat near the fire at the tent door with little Caddie on my lap, I watched carefully the language expressed in the eyes of the attendants. Later on when the child went to sleep, I was quietly taking her toward my wagon to tuck her away from the cool mountain air, when Sister Snow caught up to me, and as she handed me a shawl, she exclaimed a little anxiously, "No, don't take her away." Not until then did it really dawn upon me that there seemed to be no hope. Wrapping the shawl about me and the sleeping child, I sat waiting in silence. About midnight Sister Grant rallied a little and whispered, "Susan—Caddie." I sprang up so quickly when I was called that I waked the little girl, who opened her big eyes and stared about on every side. In a moment we were both by the bed, while Caddie kissed her mama and tried to huddle into the covers, Sister Grant looked at us knowingly, then as she contentedly closed her eyes again and seemed to be sinking, I heard her whisper to Jedediah, "All is well! All is well! Please take me to the valley—Jeddy. Get Margaret—bring her—to me!" Brother Grant answered tenderly and meaningly as he sobbed with sorrow, "Yes, yes, Caroline. I'll do my best. I'll do my best."[54]

Joseph Bates Noble. Publisher's private collection.

While the women of the third hundred prepared the body of their leader's young wife, the men built a box from a dismantled wagon bed. On the morning of September 27, Grant left with her remains for the promised valley, some seventy-five miles distant. Driving day and night, he made the infant settlement near the Great Salt Lake on the evening of September 29, 1847. For him, arrival at this new Mormon refuge was certainly less than joyous. Indeed, it had a leaden effect on the entire community. As Clara Decker Young wrote to her husband Brigham, "I followed [Caroline] to the grave the next morning which made me feel very lonesome."[55] They buried her a short distance from the pioneer fort then under construction. That his wife was the first white woman buried in the valley was a distinction no doubt lost on Jedediah.

The day after the burial, October 1, Grant left for the mountains with help for his company, now strung in a long line between Big Mountain and Echo Canyon.[56] After seeing to the needs of his people, he rode east with his friend Bates Noble to retrieve the body of little Margaret buried near the Sweetwater River. Noble often told of the experience:

> At Bear River, again we camped. As we sat there alone at night by our little camp fire in the very heart of the Rockies, after meditating in silence for some time, Brother Jedediah turned and requested, "Brother Bates, let's have a hymn or so." After a number had been sung, Jedediah said, "Now sing 'God moves in a mysterious way his wonders to perform.'" As we finished:
>
>> Blind unbelief is sure to err,
>> And scan his works in vain;
>> God is his own interpreter,
>> And he will make it plain.
>
> Brother Grant sat with bowed head for some time, then he looked up and, glowing with his former inspiration, which I had not seen upon him for some time, declared in a firm voice which always characterized his unwavering testimony, "Bates, God has made it plain. The joy of Paradise where my wife and baby are together, seems to be upon me tonight. For some wise purpose they have been released from the earth struggles into which you and I are plunged. They are many, many times happier than we can possibly be here. This camping ground should be the saddest of all sad places to me, but this night it seems to be close under heaven." As Jedediah spoke, there vibrated into my bosom a feeling that comes only under the inspiration of heaven. Then we knelt in prayer; Brother Grant being mouth. It seemed to me that no human soul could have listened to his words and doubted that he talked to his Father in heaven; doubted that the Gospel of Jesus Christ had been restored and that Joseph Smith was divinely chosen; doubted that Caroline and Margaret were with their Heavenly Father in celestial glory. This incident alone was enough to have converted me had I been the least bit of a "doubting Thomas."
> Early the next morning we were again on our journey. Generally we chatted, at other times we rode silently forward; in these moments I often wondered if we should find the little mound as we had left it. It was not the Indians that I feared so much as the prairie wolf. Once or twice during those long days, Jedediah dropped a word or two that also showed his anxiety. Our apprehensions were multiplied at our camp the first night on the Sweet Water.

Here two graves left by Oregon companies had been ruthlessly pilfered.

Another day or so and we were at the end of our eastward journey. As we intended making it back to Sweet Water for the night, we stopped our rig in the trail of the saleratus camping grounds where just a month previous a terrible night had been spent in a driving thunder storm. We now stepped forward, carrying the box and shovels. A few paces from the little grave we stopped hesitatingly, set down our things and stood with eyes fixed before us. Neither tried to speak. An ugly hole replaced the small mound; and so recently had the wolves departed that every sign was fresh before us. I dared not raise my eyes to look at Jedediah. From the way I felt, I could but guess his feelings. Like statues of the wilderness we stood, grown to the spot, each fully realizing that nothing more could be done. After several minutes of silent tears, we quietly withdrew, carrying away again only that which we had brought.[57]

The third hundred had entered the valley by the time Grant and Noble returned from their fruitless errand across the divide. Jeddy had done his best, just as he had promised.

Notes

1. As late as September 9, 1845, Brigham Young and the other apostles at Nauvoo believed that the Saints could stay in western Illinois. Events during the ensuing week quickly convinced them otherwise. See Joseph Smith Jr., *History of the Church of Jesus Christ of Latter-day Saints*, edited by B. H. Roberts, 7 vols., 2d ed. rev. (1902-12, Vol. 7, 1932; Salt Lake City: Deseret Book, 1964 printing), 7:439-47.

2. William Smith, Letter to Emma Smith, [October] 21, 1845, holograph, William Smith Collection, Church Archives. Linda King Newell discovered this intriguing letter while doing research for her book (coauthored with Valeen Tippetts Avery) *Mormon Enigma: Emma Hale Smith, Prophet's Wife, "Elect Lady," Polygamy's Foe* (Garden City, N.Y.: Doubleday, 1984). William's lengthy assertion of innocence in the face of Grant's charges bears some resemblance to John Caldwell Calhoun's fifty-page letter to Andrew Jackson denying that he ever spoke against the general during the Florida troubles of 1818. For a compelling investigation of William's aspirations to church leadership, see D. Michael Quinn, *The Mormon Hierarchy: Origins of Power* (Salt Lake City: Signature Books, 1994), 213-26.

3. Smith, *History of the Church*, 7:465. For a brief but thorough analysis of these events, see Leonard J. Arrington and Davis Bitton, *The Mormon Experience: A History of the Latter-day Saints* (New York: Alfred A. Knopf, 1979), 95–105.

4. Smith, *History of the Church*, 7:463–64. Pratt was also anxious to note that it was best for the Saints to leave a beautiful place "as a monument to . . . our industry, diligence and virtue," rather than "a desolate place." Ibid.

5. Ibid., 7:481–82; *Journal History*, October 11, 1845, 1. The Twelve would captain the first company.

6. On October 4 the committee presented to Young a list of "Requirements of Each Family of Five for the Journey across the Plains." Among other details, it suggested that "each family consisting of five adults, will require 1 good strong wagon, well covered. 3 good yokes of oxen between the ages of four and ten. Two or more cows. One or more good beeves, some sheep if they have them." Smith, *History of the Church*, 7:454–55. The list also provided specific recommendations for food, clothing, and implements.

7. Journal History, December 2, 1845, 1. Following the ordinations, Brigham Young spent an hour praying. Smith, *History of the Church*, 7:538.

8. Journal History, December 12, 1845, 1; Smith, *History of the Church*, 7:544. According to Young, several of those endowed that day "tarried in the Temple all night." Ibid.

9. Smith, *History of the Church*, 7:537–83.

10. Ibid., 7:579.

11. Ibid., 7:581. The fire burned about half an hour and was extinguished before doing much damage, but Young's resignation to its destruction showed clearly his attitude toward the edifice and the probability of its otherwise being "defiled by the Gentiles." Ibid.

12. Ibid., 7:595.

13. Journal History, March 8, 21, 27, 30, May 10, 1846, all p. 1, and May 21, 1846, 2.

14. Smith, *History of the Church*, 7:607.

15. Journal History, July 14, 1846, 1, and July 17, 1846, 2.

16. The general fiction about the recruitment of the Mormon Battalion continues unabated in the modern Church, despite accurate accounts of the event published in Smith, *History of the Church*, 7:611–14, and more fully in B. H. Roberts, *A Comprehensive History of The Church of Jesus Christ of Latter-day Saints, Century One*, 6 vols. (1930; rpt., Provo, Utah: BYU Press, 1965 printing), 3:60–103. An excellent compilation of documents relating to the enlistment is David L. Bigler and Will Bagley, eds., *Army of Israel: Mormon Battalion Narratives* (Logan: Utah State University Press, 2000), 31–71.

17. See Journal History, August 10, 13, 15, 17, 25, 30, September 15, 17, 1846, all p. 1.

18. See Journal History, August 31, 1846, p. 1, and September 3, 1846, p. 2.

19. Colonel Kane later referred to Jedediah as "my old friend Grant." Thomas L.

Kane, Letter to Brigham Young, October 17, 1852, holograph, Brigham Young Collection. See also Journal History, September 8, 1946, 1.

20. Journal History, November 26, 1846, p. 4; see also September 5, 8, 13, 12, November 8, 1846, and January 16, 1847, all p. 1.

17. Journal History, January 25, 1847, 1, and January 29, 1847, 2.

18. Journal History, February 9, 1847, 1. Kane warned Brigham that, unless the tide of public opinion against the Church could be turned, the Saints would probably be forced to evacuate the lands of the Pottawatomi Nation. Thomas L. Kane, Letter to Brigham Young, December 2, 1846, holograph, Brigham Young Collection.

23. Journal History, February 20 and 24, 1847, both p. 1.

24. Journal History, March 1, 1847, 1. "The Word and Will of the Lord," a revelation Brigham Young recorded at Winter Quarters on January 14, 1847, outlined the plan for the coming migration to the West and delineated rules of conduct for the Saints during the period of the exodus. The Church later canonized it as Section 136 of the Doctrine and Covenants.

25. Milton Milo Quaife, ed., *The Diary of James K. Polk during His Presidency, 1846 to 1849*, 4 vols. (Chicago, 1910), 1:444-46, 449-50. There had been some understandable reluctance on Polk's part to subsidize the movement into this territory of a people whose loyalties might go to Mexico or another power.

26. Jedediah Grant, Letter to Brigham Young, August 15, 1847, holograph, Brigham Young Collection, LDS Church Archives.

27. Journal History, June 15, 1847, 1.

28. Journal History, June 17, 1847, 4.

29. Joseph Kingsbury, Diary, June 14, 1847, holograph, LDS Church Archives.

30. Charles C. Rich, Diary, June 24, 1847, typescript, LDS Church Archives.

31. Ibid. See also Journal History, June 24, 1847, 2.

32. Grant, Letter to Young, August 15, 1847.

33. Carter E. Grant, "Robbed by Wolves: A True Story," *Relief Society Magazine* 15 (July 1928): 355-57.

34. Journal History, July 12, 1847, 2; Patty Sessions, Diary, July 13, 1847, holograph, LDS Church Archives.

35. Journal History, July 17, 1847, 1; July 18, 1847, 3; July 19, 1847, 2; and July 20, 1847, 2-3.

36. Sessions, Diary, July 23, 1847.

37. Ibid., July 24, 1847.

38. Journal History, August 12, 1847, 1; Carter Grant, "Robbed by Wolves," 355-57.

39. Journal History, August 17, 1847, 2.

40. Grant realized in addition that Phineas Young would explain the straits in which the third hundred found itself, and that John Taylor and Parley Pratt had prepared a more extensive report than he could give in a short letter that had to contain other items of information. See Journal History, July 25, 1847, 2–3.

41. Grant, Letter to Young, August 15, 1847.

42. Journal History, August 24, 1847, 1.

43. Carter Grant, "Robbed by Wolves," 357–58. Carter Grant reported his grandmother's story "as she many times told it to us children." Grant hastened to add that "Grandmother died when I was about thirty years of age, so my information is not childish memory."

44. Journal History, August 28, 1847, 1–4.

45. Carter Grant, "Robbed by Wolves," 358–60. They were actually already on the Sweetwater, where Margaret died on September 2, probably somewhere near Muddy Gap.

46. Journal History, September 2, 1847, 2.

47. Carter Grant, "Robbed by Wolves," 360.

48. Journal History, September 8, 1847, 1.

49. Carter Grant, "Robbed by Wolves," 360.

50. Ibid.; Journal History, September 8, 1847, 2.

51. Journal History, September 9, 1847, 12–13.

52. Journal History, September 10, 1847, 1.

53. Journal History, September 14, 1847, 1.

54. Carter Grant, "Robbed by Wolves," 361–62. See also Journal History, September 26, 1847, 2. Caroline's death occurred south of the present site of Evanston, Wyoming, on the upper Bear River.

55. Clara Decker Young, Letter to Brigham Young, Journal History, September 29, and October 3, 1847, 1; Carter Grant, "Robbed by Wolves," 362.

56. The first element of the third hundred arrived in the valley on October 4, 1847. Thirty-three members of the first ten families, driving fifteen wagons, reported some startling statistics: they had lost two persons, Caroline and Margaret Grant; of eleven horses that had started with them, two survived; they were missing twelve of forty-five oxen and eight of forty cows. Journal History, October 4, 1847, 1.

57. Joseph Bates Noble, quoted in Carter Grant, "Robbed by Wolves," 363–64. Unfortunately, no Noble diary for this period is extant. The dramatic experiences of the Third Hundred inspired a musical production, *The Trail of Dreams*, written by James Arrington, Marvin Payne, and Steven Kapp Perry with music and lyrics by Steven Kapp Perry. It premiered at Utah Valley State College on January 7, 1997, by the Plucky Little Production Company and was recorded by Prime Recordings.

under in the East:
PHASE TWO
Thunder in the East: 1848–52

"My home is ever dear to me. But absence makes it doubly so."

7
Mountains and Brown Bread

IN THE FIFTEEN YEARS since Jedediah Grant had joined the Mormon Church—nearly half his life—he had never really had a home. Zion's Camp, more than six years as a missionary, nearly three as presiding elder at Philadelphia, and the year and a half in the wilderness had prevented him from calling Ohio, Missouri, or Illinois "home." Moreover, the loss of Caroline as he had moved into the Rockies with the third hundred seemed to augur a continuing life of itinerancy and homelessness. More certain still was the likelihood that Brother Brigham would have future tasks in the East for him to perform, given his experience and his friendship with Thomas Kane. Yet once he was in the valley, his wanderer's stripe seemed to disappear. Perhaps it was his devotion to little Caddie, or maybe there was something in the air of the Great Basin that made even such a Mormon as Jed Grant want to stay put.

By his thirty-second birthday in February 1848, Grant had constructed two log houses on his lot in Wilford Woodruff's block just south of Brigham Young's block (present Church headquarters in downtown Salt Lake City). A census taken on February 24 showed just him and Caddie living there, owning very little besides the houses, three wagons, eight oxen, and four chickens.[1] In spite of some requests from the East that Grant come back to take care of this problem or that, it also appeared that Church leaders were willing to let the young widower take care of his little daughter and build up his inheritance in the West, at least for the time being.[2]

Through 1848 Grant worked on improving his lot in the city, an acre and a quarter (across the corner from the Temple Block) that was later to be the site of Zion's Cooperative Mercantile Institution (ZCMI). In addition, he put under cultivation a piece of acreage near the center of the new city.³ The president of seventy also fulfilled several community assignments, such as assisting in bridge building at the Jordan River and Mill Creek and participating in a week-long exploring expedition on the Great Salt Lake. In the fall, he led a relief party into the mountains to help bring in a company under the command of Willard Richards and, with Daniel H. Wells, took charge of the cattle that were to return east to pull in another migration the next summer. And being Jedediah Grant, he availed himself of numerous opportunities to preach to the Saints, often occupying the stand at the brush-covered bowery with Young and Kimball. Indeed, he generally accompanied the First Presidency in its travels, and even assisted Brigham and Heber in the ordination of John Smith, the late Prophet's uncle, as presiding patriarch of the Church on New Year's Day, 1849.⁴

The winter of 1848–49 was particularly cold; but despite the hardships the severe winter brought to the community, it had a brighter side. "The young people," wrote John L. Smith, "are getting married by the wholesale this cold weather. I think there was a wedding every night from Christmas to New Year, and one evening three couples were married."⁵ Jeddy Grant, only thirty-three years old, caught the spirit. On February 11, 1849, he married Susan Noble at the home of her Uncle Bates, with Brigham Young performing the ceremony.⁶ Susan had been mother to Caddie since Caroline's death at the Bear River. Shortly thereafter, in the manner of the Mormons' own "peculiar institution," he also married Rosetta Robison.⁷ With Susan, Rosetta, and Caddie, and the lot on East Temple (Main) Street, Jedediah Grant had a Mormon family and, for the first time, a Mormon home.

In the midst of this domestic drama, Grant had moved officially into the center of theocratic power in Great Salt Lake City as the spring of 1849 brought some new and different responsibilities from those he had taken before. The Mormons in the Great Basin needed government and Brother Brigham was determined that they should have it, especially inasmuch as the United States now had clear title to the region under the Treaty of Guadalupe Hidalgo with Mexico. The Saints had applied to Washington for statehood, but they needed officials to govern in the interim so that an orderly transition could take place. William W. Phelps and Jedediah Grant joined three apostles, Amasa Lyman, John Taylor, and Parley Pratt, to form a committee to fill the ticket for the ensuing elections.

With this activity, Grant walked to a place in the forefront of politics in the "State of Deseret" from which only death would remove him.[8]

Despite having had no military experience whatsoever, Grant also accepted a high rank in Joseph's private army, the Nauvoo Legion, transplanted to the West for the defense of the Saints. At the end of April 1849, Church leaders reorganized the legion with Daniel H. Wells as major general commanding, Jedediah Grant as brigadier general in command of the first and mounted cohort, and Horace S. Eldredge as brigadier general leading the second cohort, comprised of infantry. The next few days saw farmers, in the tradition of the Roman Cincinnatus, drilling and marching about the infant city, in preparation for some assault—perhaps from increasingly nervous Native Americans in the area, or perhaps from more dangerous enemies—the ones Brigham and Heber mentioned in the same breath with the cricket hordes from the East.[9]

Daniel H. Wells. Publisher's private collection.

As summer came on, the men of the Nauvoo Legion again became farmers, coaxing water from ditches onto the drying lands of the valley and fighting the adverse forces of nature, from crickets and grasshoppers to hailstorms and weeds. Between sweating days working the soil and building a larger home on his East Temple Street lot, Grant continued to act in his position as community leader, which in Mormondom meant acting in an ecclesiastical role. There was a decorative division of church and state after the American prescription; but as in the days of Puritan New England, the same men were responsible for the welfare of both the body and the soul of the people.

By July of 1849, the Saints in the Great Salt Lake Valley were able to see almost as clearly as Brigham himself their leader's vision of a kingdom in the midst of the mountains. Two years had passed since the first Mormons had emerged from Emigration Canyon; and despite some setbacks, a feeling of permanence had settled over the people. They held a big celebration in town on July 24, with Jed Grant as master of ceremonies.[10] The ranks of the Saints in the Rockies were swelling impressively as hundreds of families made the trek across the plains and as missionaries in England and elsewhere added to the Church men and women anxious for a new life in the New World, an American Zion. Brigham Young and his associates in the leadership of their ambitious "State of Deseret" were pushing out the boundaries of the kingdom to accommodate the newcomers. During trips out of the valley, such as one to Brownsville on the Ogden River to the north in early September, Young and those with him (on that occasion Grant, Kimball, and Thomas Bullock) were constantly on the lookout for new sites for settlement. Between preaching sermons to Mormons already in the area, they would lay out cities and plot farms. The future, as well as its land and people, seemed promising, at least for these Saints who were hoping to lay the foundation in the wilderness for a millennium of spiritual and temporal perfection.[11]

Four years after the conference at which Mormons had been asked to abandon the civilization they had built on the Mississippi, they had constructed a new one in the Rockies. Because of its setting, the new City of the Saints was perhaps even more remarkable than its predecessor to the east. For Americans still absorbing the meaning of the Mexican War and the resulting radical expansion of the map of the Unites States, the role of the Mormons in that drama may have been a mere curiosity, but newspapers in the East were nevertheless interested in the peculiar people, so recently removed from immediate proximity. A correspondent traveling with a group of forty-niners headed for California in July of that year reported on the new Mormon settlement on the frontier while remembering a prayer by "the Rev. Mr. Grant."

THE MORMON VALLEY NEAR THE GREAT SALT LAKE
(From the *New York Tribune*, October 9, 1849)

From the overland emigrants to California we have later news, which is, however, much of the same purport as that before received. A great deal of sickness is reported among them: and for 500 miles, as we are told, the road over which they pass is strewed with the bodies of dead beasts of burden. Our last letters are dated from the Great Salt Lake, where the Mormons are established. One of the correspondents of The Tribune gives a minute and curious account of this singular sect, and the results of their industry in their new home. We give it a place here, confident that our European readers will find it interesting. Our correspondent writes under the date of July 8:

"The company of gold diggers which I have the honour to command, arrived here on the third inst., and judge our feelings when, after some twelve hundred miles of travel through an uncultivated desert, and the last one hundred miles of the distance through and among lofty mountains and narrow and difficult ravines, we found ourselves suddenly, and almost unexpectedly, in a comparative paradise.

"We descended the last mountain by a passage excessively steep and abrupt, and continued our gradual descent through a narrow canon for five or six miles, when, suddenly emerging from the pass, an extensive and cultivated valley opened before us, at the same instant that we caught a glimpse of the distant bosom of the Great Salt Lake, which lay expanded before us to the westward, at the distance of some twenty miles.

"Descending the table land which bordered the valley, extensive herds of cattle, horses, and sheep, were grazing in every direction, reminding us of that home and civilization from which we had so widely departed—for as yet the fields and houses were in the distance. Passing over some miles of pasture land, we at length found ourselves in a broad and fenced street, extending westward in a straight line for several miles. Houses of wood or sun-dried brick were thickly clustered in the vale before us, some thousands in number, and occupying a spot about as large as the city of New York. They were mostly small, one story high, and perhaps not more than one occupying an acre of land. The whole space for miles, excepting the streets and houses, was in a high state of cultivation. Fields of yellow wheat stood waiting for the harvest, and Indian corn, potatoes, oats, flax, and all kinds of garden vegetables, were growing in profusion, and seemed about in the same state of forwardness as in the same latitude in the States.

"At the first sight of all these signs of cultivation in the wilderness, we were transported with wonder and pleasure. Some wept, some gave three cheers, some laughed, and some ran and fairly danced for joy—while all felt inexpressibly happy to find themselves once more amid scenes which mark the progress of advancing civilization. We passed on amid scenes like these, expecting every moment to come to some commercial centre, some business point in this great metropolis of the mountains; but we were disappointed.

No hotel, sign post, cake and beer shop, barber pole, market house, grocery, provision, dry goods, or hardware store distinguished one part of the town from another, not even a bakery or mechanic's sign was any where discernible.

"Here, then, was something new: an entire people reduced to a level, and all living by their labour—all cultivating the earth, or following some branch of physical industry. At first I thought it was an experiment, an order of things established purposely to carry out the principles of 'Socialism' or 'Mormonism.' In short, I thought it very much like Owenism personified. However, on inquiry, I found that a combination of seemingly unavoidable circumstances had produced this singular state of affairs. There were no hotels, because there had been no travel; no barbers' shops, because every one chose to shave himself, and no one had time to shave his neighbour; no stores, because they had no goods to sell nor time to traffic; no centre of business, because all were too busy to make a centre.

"There was abundance of mechanic shops, of dressmakers, milliners, and tailors, &c.; but they needed no sign, nor had they time to paint or erect one, for they were crowded with business. Beside their several trades, all must cultivate the land, or die; for the country was new, and no cultivation but their own within a thousand miles. Every one had his lot, and built on it; every one cultivated it, and perhaps a small farm in the distance.

"And the strangest of all was, that this great city, extending over several square miles, had been erected, and every house and fence made, within nine or ten months of the time of our arrival; while at the same time, good bridges were erected over the principal streams, and the country settlements extended nearly one hundred miles up and down the valley.

"This territory, state, or, as some term it, 'Mormon Empire,' may justly be considered as one of the greatest prodiges [sic] of the age, and, in comparison with its age, the most gigantic of all republics in existence, being only its second year since the first seed of cultivation was planted, or the first civilized habitation commenced. If these people were such thieves and robbers as their enemies represented them in the States, I must think they have greatly reformed in point of industry since coming to the mountains.

"I this day attended worship with them, in the open air. Some thousands of well dressed, intelligent looking people assembled; some on foot, some in carriages, and on horseback. Many were neatly, and even fashionably clad. The beauty and neatness of the ladies reminded me of some of our best congregations in New York. They had a choir of both sexes, who performed extremely well, accompanied by a band who played well on almost every instrument of modern invention. Peals of the most sweet, sacred, and solemn music filled the air, after which, a solemn prayer was offered by the Rev. Mr. Grant (a Latter day Saint), of Philadelphia. Then followed various business advertisements, read by the clerk. Among these I remember a call of the seventeenth ward, by its presiding bishop, to some business meeting; a call for a meeting of the thirty second quorum of the seventy, and a meeting of the officers of the second cohort of the military legion, &c, &c.

"After this, came a lengthy discourse from Mr. Brigham Young, president of the society, partaking somewhat of politics, much of religion and philosophy, and a little on the subject of gold, showing the wealth, strength, and glory of England, growing out of her coal mines, iron and industry; and the weakness, corruption, and degradation of Spanish America, Spain, &c., growing out of her gold, silver, &c., and her idle habits.

"Every one seemed interested and pleased with his remarks, and all appeared to be contented to stay at home and pursue a persevering industry, although mountains of gold were near them. The able speaker painted in lively colours the ruin which would be brought upon the United States by gold, and boldly predicted that they would be overthrown because they had killed the prophets, stoned and rejected those who were sent to call them to repentance, and finally plundered and driven the church of the Saints from their midst, and burned and desolated their city and temple. He said God had a reckoning with that people, and gold would be the instrument of their overthrow. The constitutions and laws were good, in fact, the best in the world, but the administrators were corrupt, and the laws and constitutions were not carried out. Therefore they must fall. He further observed, that the people here would petition to be organized into a territory under that same government, notwithstanding its abuses, and that, if granted, they would stand by the constitution and laws of the United States; while at the same time he denounced their corruption and abuses.

"But, said the speaker, we ask no odds of them, whether they grant us our petition or not! We never will ask any odds of a nation who has driven us from our homes. If they grant us our rights, well; if not, well; they can do no more than they have done. They, and ourselves, and all men, are in the hands of the great God, who will govern all things for good, and all will be right, and work together for good to them that serve God.

"Such, in part, was the discourse to which we listened in the strongholds of the mountains. The Mormons are not dead, nor is their spirit broken. And, if I mistake not, there is a noble, daring, stern, and democratic spirit swelling in their bosoms, which will people these mountains with a race of independent men, and influence the destiny of our country and the world for a hundred generations. In their religion they seem charitable, devoted, and sincere; in their politics, bold, daring, and determined; in their domestic circle, quiet, affectionate, and happy; while in industry, skill, and intelligence, they have few equals, and no superiors on the earth.

"I had many strange feelings while contemplating this new civilization growing up so suddenly in the wilderness. I almost wished I could awake from my golden dream, and find it but a dream; while I pursued my domestic duties as quiet, as happy, and contented as this strange people."[12]

While the *Tribune*'s correspondent may have longed to be immersed in the pursuit of domestic duties after the model of the Saints in the Great Basin, he undoubtedly would not have wished to have, as another part of his life, the Mormon responsibility to be willing to leave the quiet contentment of home in order to fulfill the demands of an Old Testament prophet whose desire to gather the chosen people was often all consuming. Brigham Young, realizing that many of Mormonism's converts were financially unable to migrate halfway around the world or halfway across a barren continent, established a system called the Perpetual Emigrating Fund Company that would provide travel money in a rotating fund for anyone willing to work for his passage after arriving in the Basin. It was an ingenious scheme by which the vast reaches of the Rockies would be filled with Latter-day Saints, gathered from the corners of the earth. It was a plan, however, not unlike most of Brother Brigham's: It required a good deal of hard work. Agents for the company would have to establish themselves over the long route from Liverpool through New Orleans and St. Louis to Great Salt Lake City. On September 9, 1849, Jedediah Grant became one of these agents.[13] His appointment to this position signaled the end of a two-year sabbatical as a farmer and the beginning of another period as an emissary of the Mormon Church in the East.

Two weeks after the fall conference of the Church, a large party of elders under John Taylor left Great Salt Lake City on their way eastward to fulfill their various missions. Among them was Grant, bound for St. Louis and efforts in behalf of the PEF. Among his assignments was arranging for some freighting back to the valley in the spring. This was the first time Grant had really left home, although he had traveled for the Church almost continually between 1834 and 1847. Now he was leaving two wives and a little girl whose mother he had buried. In addition, the two Grant women he kissed before he rode off were really not much more than girls themselves: Susan was seventeen and Rosetta sixteen. Notwithstanding their youthfulness, he had grown fond of their constant company and their womanly care for him and his four-year-old daughter. Consequently, when the eastbound party met George A. Smith's emigrating company on October 23, some fifty miles east of the city,[14] Jedediah wrote a quick letter back to Susan in which he revealed some of his anxieties. He then sent it back to the valley with Johann Snedaker, a member of the Smith company and the father of a young man who had been working for the Grant family.

> Ten Miles from the Weber.   Oct. 24th 1849
>
> By this I wish to say to you, that I am well, and all that are with me. We went the new rout which took us one day longer to get to the Weber then it would on the old road.
>
> In this kenyon I met John's father. He will take back Lion and Berry [oxen]. He wants John to live with him this winter. I hope you will not mourn his loss. John was to work for me until harvest for his board. After harvest I was to give him what I thought right, for five hickry shirts that I bought of Goodyer for Johon. I paid five dollars. For shoes 2 dollars. His pants—coat stockens &c I charged 6 dollars on bushel of barley 2.50 , which will make over 5 dollars a month, which I think is all he urned.
>
> Br [Richard S.] Robi[n]son will call and see you as soon has he lands in the Valley. You can get him to do your coopering: tub barrel &c. You can let him have corn or beef for pay. After the wheat is thrashed corn shucked, and barley &c sell what you do not want for seed and bread. You can also sell some beef. Save one bushel of potatoes for seed and eat the rest. Save some of the carrets for seed. See well to your health and little Caddy's. You shall have my prayers by night and day for your wellfare. I need not tell you how I feel. You know that. Yours affectionately
>
> J M. Grant.[15]

Before meeting another traveler headed west to whom he could entrust letters, Grant wrote twice more to his small family in the Valley of the Great Salt Lake.

<blockquote>

SweetWater   40 Miles West of Rock Independence
Nov 3'd 1849

My Dear Susan.

This is to let you, and Rozetta, know that we are geting along finely on our journey. Our horses and mules have done first rate. Indeed the Lord has blessed us in evry sense of the word. The weather and road has been good all the way thus far.

Soon after I left home, from cold or inaction of my liver, one of my eyes has become very much inflamed. It is some better at this time but it still hurts very much to look long on white paper. So I shall have to cut my letter short in reighteousness. By wishing you all the good luck happiness and comfort that you can reasonably expect in my absence. Kiss dear little Caddy on both cheaks for me, and believe me ever yours.

J M Grant

Fort Karney   Nov 28th

Dear Susan. When I wrote the above I expected to meet Thomas Williams and send by him. In this we have been disappointed. My health is much better then it was on the S[w]eetwater. All in camp are well and in good spirits. We have had good weather most of the way and the roads have been tolerable good. Some of our anamils have done well or stood the trip well, and some have failed altogether. My team is the best in the train doing finely.

If I could see you and Rozetta and little Caddy my heart would leap for joy. May the Lord bless you and keep you from all harm that we may meet again. I have many things to talk about when I see you. The Lord bless you. As ever your affectionate husband.

J M Grant

the last written by dim Candlelight.[16]

</blockquote>

Traveling light and fast, the band of Mormon elders made good time as it journeyed east, despite a frightening skirmish with marauding Indians somewhere along the Platte.[17] They nevertheless arrived at the Missouri unscathed and then separated to take on their various assignments. Grant made his way to St. Louis, where he settled in for a long winter away from home. In obedience to the last instructions Young had given him, he pushed himself as hard as possible, even to the point of undertaking some fairly dangerous business propositions in order to get some freighting lined up for the spring. His activities seriously curtailed through bad health, he nevertheless had accomplished his mission in St. Louis as early spring grasses began to show on the prairie. By mid-April he was ready to leave St. Louis for Council Bluffs and the West; but realizing that the freight wagons would be cumbersome and that he would have several layovers as he fulfilled his tasks for the PEF between the Mississippi and the Bluffs, he persuaded a horseman headed for the gold fields to carry two letters to Salt Lake City, one a report of his activities to Brigham Young.

St Louis Mo.   April 16th 1850

President Young,

Dear Brother I shall leave St Louis tomorrow or the 18th and prepare as soon as possible for starting on my journey over the plains. Some things strange to me have taken place since we parted at the mouth of the canyon among the many I will name a few, connected with the Carring Company.

Br John Taylor enlisted Mr. Kinkade to let him have ten tons of freight, which Mr. K. compiled [complied] with and advanced him one thousan dolls. price ten cents per lb or 200 dolls per ton.

Mr Parry Little, Br Charles Deckers br in law, took the balance at the same rates. Brothers Roundy and Smoot sent me word that they would carry for ten cents per lb.

After duly considering the matter I come to the conclusion (in as much as we could get nothing to do in line of carring passengers at our price of 300 dolls per man) that I would try my hand at it, on my own limited meanes. As you had told me the las lesson you gave, that you wanted me to go it steep, I came to the conclusion that I could not do so unless I should do some thing. So atat [at it] I went. For Col Reese I cary 16 tons. For Mr Beach five tons. Price for hauling ten cents per lb or 200 dolls per ton. I get 3 wagons on credit and one for the credit on all the balance. My casers

Jedediah Morgan Grant, 1856. LDS Church Archives.

[boxes], iron for chanes staples and rings also on credit. I have taken two small houses to build in the Valley and get 200 cash advance on them. I get all my drivers here. they have their own expenses to the Bluffs, find their own riding and I board them through. Again to increase my capital I get some of the drivers to lend me say, some 10 dolls some 15 some 20 others

25 so on to as high as seventy five dollars. I give them a due bill payable in the Salt Lake City. I borried some 300 dolls. Got my bord on credit or good will. I pay for wagons here without casers 53 dolls. Freight up the river on wagons from 7 to 8 dolls a peas. Casers double will cost 6 dol. each. Chanes 9 cents for lb. Staples and rings the same. Yokes cheep at the Bluffs. Whips and tar yarn and lead cheep tacks cheap, ten ware cheap sugar cheap coffee dear also flour and meat. But by the blessing of the Lord, I can make it all. Mr Beach through strong salisitation on my part, will take some fifty good cooking stove[s] of the best kind.

Everything is going rite. The Government will I think let us alone severely. You may look for from 7 to 8000 Saints this season and yet they are coming. My prayer is O Lord help thy people to gather by thousands and millions. Brake the oppressors port [apart?] and set the captive free.

Elder Babbitt was here some 2 weeks ago. He has the "proper fire" is jest what we all here think he should be. The Saints here number between 4 and 5000. Br Orson Pratt past through here on his way to the Bluffs. He informed me that two ship lodes were on the way coming. Elder NH Felt had done honor to the cause in this city in the midst of this great people. They all love him and he has ruld them with the septer of love. He is coming to the Valley this year.

Elder Woodruff is on his way with several hundred of the eastern Saints. Elders on their way to Europe have all been blessd and prospered. Br Bernhisel was well the last account. There has been a great change in society since I was las through the cities of the East. Crime of the species has multiplied to an alarming extent. The South is boiling over. The North is ise bound and frezing deeper every day. A split is sure and fast hastening.

I am sick of St Louis and long with great desire to be once more at my quiet home in the beautiful Valley of the mountains to enjoy the society of my family and kind friends. But all is rite. May heaven bless you all.

I will send you a few itomes from different papers of the day. Perhaps they may be of some use to the Dr. [Willard Richards] as a matter of history. Please remember me to Br Kimball also to the Doctor, Br Whitney and Squire Wells. My kind regard to yourself and family. Any favour you may show my family will be on my part duly appreciated.

Before Joseph Young went [to] England he sent a letter to you by my request informing you of the fate of three of your mules. One we had to leave at Fort John, one on the Plains the rest we got through. Those that failed had evidently been broke down by some one previously. Your [other?] mules stood the trip first rate.

If I could see you and talk one hour could tell you more than I can write. In spirit you know all about matters and things and you may rest assured that I have and will go it as steep as I can. I send this by Dr. J. T. Temple. By the same I will send a letter to my family and also to Br George. 5 to 1 of golddigers this year will pass through your Valley to what past last year. I will write you from time to time. Br. [Edwin D.] Wool[l]ey and Haywood [Joseph L. Heywood] are well. Br [Edward] Hunter was the [last] account! Br Wooley sends his respects also Col John Reese. Both are here and well and doing well. Br Hyde was well the [last] account. As ever

J M Grant[18]

In his letter to his senior wife (who was not yet eighteen), Grant displayed an intriguing and tender attitude toward his peculiarly Mormon family back home in the mountains. He here let slip that his feeling for Rosetta was still very paternal. Along with Caddie, Rosetta was one of the "children."

St Louis   April 18th 1850

Dear Wife and Children

Dr. J. T. Temple of this city is about leaving for the gold mines via Salt Lake. I send by him, why and wharefore when I come. It seems a long time since we parted. One hour with your presence would give me more pleasure than I can express with my pen. My home is ever dear to me. But absence makes it doubly so. My prayer is and shhall ever be that the Lord will keep you from all harm and comfort you in all things. Many emotions arrise within me when I think of the few days we have spent in each others society but circumstances rendered it kneedful that we should part for a few months. All for the best I hope in the end.

My Dear Susan how do you get along in my absence? Are you well? How is Rozetta and Caroline? Are they well? Tell them I will come home as soon [as] possible with my business over the Plains which will be slow. I shall not be home as soon as I expected when left.

You know I expected to return with a passenger train. In this I have been disappointed. But all is right. I will bring you and the children some things for your comfort that will please you I think firstrate. Tell Caddy she must learn to read and her Papa will bring her some fine books.[19]

Grant admitted that he had not enjoyed good health through the winter but even then refused to reveal to Susan and the others that he had spent some time in St. Louis lying dangerously close to death. In fact, he apparently felt so strongly about keeping the gravity of his past condition secret that virtually nothing about it survived in the traces of his life. He never discussed it on paper or in public. That it happened at all came through only in the sketchy reports of other Saints in the East who feared for his life. What he would say here about it was evidently an epitome of understatement.

My health has not been very good since I came to St Louis. At present it is better then it has been heretofore. City air and diet dont suit me like the mountains, and brown bread &c &c. I have been up the river to see my people. My father and mother, 2 brs and 2 sisters they were all well. Br Joshua is at the Bluffs. He is going on with me this year. I will have plenty of oxen wagons and cows and for myself family and friends some little articles of different kinds to the amount of several hundred dolls. For the merchants I will carry 21 tons of goods or freight. You may look for me the first of August if good luck attends me. Write every opportunity. Let me know how you all are getting along &c &c. Tell Rozetta that her mothers people are coming this year. I wish to secure as much grain as you well can. I have take[n] 2 houses to build and will have to hire some help and board them while buildin, and per chance build some for myself at the same time. I wish you to have the oxen sent to some good place to make them fit for beaf in the fall. I mean, Lion and Bury. If you want help of any kind get it and promis dry goods or money as soon as I arrive in the city. Get evry thing that you cant do without on the same principle but bare in mind that I am bringing jest what we want nicknacks &c. Promis as little money as possible.

You must all do the best you can till I come. I have sent you three letter[s] before this. Kiss Caddy for me. Yours affectionately

J. M. Grant

Tell Sister Chaley that her man is well all but being home sick. He is coming.

Tell those who enquire that those on their way to Europe were all well the last account.

Please remember me to Br Benson and his people also to Br Noble and his.[20]

It was a happy Jedediah Grant who emerged from the canyon as the summer of 1850 ended over Utah Territory. But surprise would probably have described better the emotions of his family when they saw him for, as he was often wont to do, he had picked up a stray. He had decided to bring home to his three girls an addition to the family, this time a small Scottish boy named John McKeatchie who had lost his parents en route to Zion. He and Susan would subsequently adopt the lad and rename him Lewis Grant.[21]

After nearly a year away from his family, Grant was ready for a more sedentary life in the shadows of the mountains, but the paths of Mormonism and their inevitable crossings with those of the Gentile government of the United States would require one more trip to the East. This time the angular frame and swarthy face of Jed Grant would be seen in the highest offices of the land.

⇒ Notes ⇐

1. Journal History of the Church of Jesus Christ of Latter day Saints (chronological scrapbook of typed entries and newspaper clippings, 1830–present), February 24, 1848, 8, LDS Church Archives.

2. George W. Bratton, for example, wrote to Brigham Young from Illinois, requesting that Jedediah and his brother George come and prevail upon William Smith and his wife, who were preaching against the Church. Journal History, February 26, 1848, 4. Following the death of his first wife Caroline, Smith had married a second Grant sister, Roxy (or Roxcy) Ann.

3. Journal History, February 24, 1848, 8.

4. See Journal History, March 6, 1848, 2; April 24, 1848, 2; August 10, 1848, 3; October 4, 19, 26, and November 26, 1848, all p. 1, December 24, 1848, 2; and January 1, 1849, 1. For an interesting history of the now-lapsed office of presiding patriarch, see Irene

M. Bates and E. Gary Smith, *Lost Legacy: The Mormon Office of Presiding Patriarch* (Urbana: University of Illinois Press, 1996).

5. Journal History, January 1, 1849, 2.

6. Family records of Bernice Grant Casper, Salt Lake City. D. Michael Quinn, *The Mormon Hierarchy: Extensions of Power* (Salt Lake City: Signature Books in association with Smith Research Associates, 1997), 182, infers some significance to the fact that Grant (among many others in the hierarchy) "delayed" his entry into polygamy "more than three years." It seems more likely that he was simply adjusting to the loss of Caroline and/or waiting for Susan and Rosetta to reach their mid-teens, an acceptable age for marriage among young women in the nineteenth century.

7. Family records of Daniel Evans Marshall, Ogden, Utah.

8. Journal History, March 4, 1849, 1.

9. The early drills of the Nauvoo Legion took place on the flats west of town near the Jordan River. Marches always ended at "the stand," where the leaders preached to the troops. See Journal History, April 18, 1849, 3, and May 5 and 26, 1849, both p. 1. An effulgent history of the legion and its successor organization is Richard C. Roberts, *Legacy: The History of the Utah National Guard from the Nauvoo Legion Era to Enduring Freedom* (Salt Lake City: The National Guard Association of Utah, 2003).

10. Journal History, July 21, 22, and 24, 1849, all p. 1. See Eugene E. Campbell, *Establishing Zion: The Mormon Church in the American West, 1847-1869* (Salt Lake City: Signature Books, 1988), 37-39, for a meaningful account of these benchmark festivities.

11. See Journal History, September 1, 1849, 2, and September 2 and 3, 1849, both p. 1.

12. Journal History, October 9, 1849, 2-3.

13. Journal History, September 9, 1849, 1. The PEF Company formally organized a year later with Brigham Young as president and Grant and seventeen others as directors.

14. *Frontier Guardian*, January 9, 1850; Journal History, October 27, 1849, 21.

15. Jedediah Grant, Letter to Susan Grant, October 14, 1849, holograph in possession of Betty Mae Nebeker Laub, Salt Lake City (hereafter Laub Collection). She is a descendant of Jedediah and Susan.

16. Jedediah Grant, Letter to Susan Grant, November 1849, holograph, Laub Collection.

17. See John Taylor's report of the journey east, October 19, 1849, holograph, LDS Church Archives; cf. Erastus Snow's account, October 19, 1859, holograph, LDS Church Archives. Grant apparently comported himself gallantly, earning Taylor's praise and that of his companions. *Frontier Guardian*, January 9, 1850.

18. Jedediah Grant, Letter to Brigham Young, April 16, 1850, holograph, Brigham Young Collection, LDS Church Archives. Note the differences with regard to home and

family in comparison to letters written in the 1830s and 1840s from the South and from Philadelphia. Grant had obviously developed an affection for the valley, in addition to his now having a family to miss and about which to worry.

19. Jedediah Grant, Letter to Susan Grant, April 18, 1850, holograph, Laub Collection.

20. Ibid. His advice to Susan about buying everything "with as little promise of money as possible" underscores his having few liquid assets after a long absence but bringing with him in return a healthy portion of goods from the East with which to pay his family's bills.

21. Jedediah Grant family group sheets, Family History Library, Church of Jesus Christ of Latter day Saints, Salt Lake City.

"I could shake all this eastern country with the sound of my voice."

8

The Lord's Thunder

GRANT ARRIVED HOME BARELY in time for the October conference of 1850. He preached at the Sunday session held in the Bowery, and then turned his attentions to his family.[1] Between his own enterprises in St. Louis and the efforts of Susan on the farm with the help of the two hands, John Snedaker and Henry Robison, the family could look forward to a winter spent in the enjoyment of relative prosperity. Public affairs, however, would continue to occupy much of his time, inasmuch as he moved inexorably toward the top echelons of the Mormon hierarchy. In the solidifying theocracy of early Utah, Brigham Young was expending increasing amounts of energy on forming a nominally civil government in anticipation of Deseret's official incorporation into the United States. The Utah Act had passed Congress on September 9 as part of the Compromise of 1850, a package of legislation designed to avert controversy over the expansion of slavery into the territories recently acquired from Mexico. Because of the larger questions involved in the compromise measures, Utah gained territorial status as a kind of afterthought. Consequently, Washington gave little thought to the factor of Mormon leadership controlling the territory, as President Millard Fillmore subsequently appointed Brigham Young himself as governor. At the time no significant voices rose in objection to this apparent union of church and state. The Saints in Utah, needless to say, were happy with the arrangement, although they had hoped for immediate statehood.

On December 2, 1850, when the general assembly of the State of Deseret organized in a session at the Council House, Jedediah Grant became speaker of the house with Thomas Bullock as clerk. The assembly continued to meet for several days to complete its organization, took a Christmas recess, and then reconvened on January 6, 1851. Three days later it passed an incorporation bill for Great Salt Lake City, at the same time nominating Speaker Grant to serve also as its mayor. On January 19, following his unanimous election to the post, the thirty-four-year-old Mormon preacher became the first mayor of the infant City of the Saints.[2]

From that date onward, there was little time for Jedediah Grant to enjoy his mountains and brown bread. Besides the consuming duties of his two political offices, Grant continued to function routinely as a General Authority of the Church, traveling and preaching from Ogden in the north through the settlements quickly spreading southward. At times simply the task of filling the quorums of seventy and ordaining new members of those groups took entire days.[3]

Notwithstanding the demands of growing ecclesiastical responsibilities in the expanding communities of the Mormon kingdom, political problems continued to take precedence through 1851 for the leadership of the Church. On March 28, the general assembly met to recognize the organization of Utah Territory and to provide land in Great Salt Lake City for the erection of public buildings. Brigham Young, who took the oath of office as governor on February 3, received authorization to draw $20,000 from the federal treasury for the construction of these government facilities. This money would come to Utah with the federal officials arriving in the summer, but coming with that money were some people and some problems that would precipitate the first serious clash between the Mormons and the federal government. Given his temperament and his position, Grant was bound to be "square up to the handle" in the middle of whatever was coming west to Utah that summer.

Most of the judges and other officers arrived in the valley on July 19. Accompanying them were Dr. John M. Bernhisel and Elder Almon W. Babbitt, who had been representing the Saints in Washington. Babbitt carried the $20,000. On July 23 he met with territorial officials, including Governor Young and Speaker Grant to deliver the money; but showing a sudden concern for the legality of the recent elections, Babbitt refused to turn over the funds. This set a nervous tone for the coming July 24 celebration, at which the federal officials were to be special guests. Mayor Grant himself presided over the festivities, apparently having no idea that the proceedings of the day would eventually comprise a prime cause for another long mission to the East. As Grant toasted the First Presidency as "the highest fountain, and first fed from the celestial kingdom, freely receiving and freely giving truth, eternal truth, to all the sons and daughters of Adam over this wide world,"[4] Daniel H. Wells sat sternly behind the pulpit steeling himself for a belligerent oration in which he would blast the United States for allowing within its borders mobocracy and barbarity. Needless to say, such "foreigners" to the Mormon situation as Territorial Secretary Broughton D. Harris of Vermont roiled with rage at "the Squire's" seemingly disloyal comments. Unaccustomed to the blunt style of Mormon oratory, they also took exception to subsequent remarks from Governor Young about President Zachary Taylor being "dead and damned."[5]

Nearly a month after the July 24 affair, Associate Justice Perry E. Brocchus of Alabama arrived in Utah. He quickly learned from Harris and the others of the words Wells and Young had so defiantly thrown into the face of the United States. Two days after his arrival, the *Deseret News* published the text of Wells's address. The printed version infuriated Brocchus. At a special conference of the Church in the second week of September, the Alabaman requested permission from Young to address the Saints. Brigham agreed, having no reason to expect what followed. Brocchus began by complimenting the Saints for their peacefulness and for their efforts toward running efficient and just courts prior to his arrival. He then took exception to portions of the Wells address, strenuously defending the Polk administration in calling for the Mormon Battalion and also defending the government in general for refusing to interfere in the Missouri and Illinois persecutions. Growing steadily in its offensiveness, the Brocchus speech finally settled on the women of Mormondom. "He directed a portion of his discourse towards the ladies," remembered Brigham Young, "and, libertine as he boasted himself, strongly recommended them to become virtuous."[6] Now it was the Saints' turn to be furious.

As Brocchus finished, Young was on his feet: "Judge Brocchus is either profoundly ignorant, or willfully wicked, one of the two." After having alluded to the Alabaman's own questionable morality, the governor repeated essentially all that he and Daniel Wells had said on July 24 and then underlined it: "I know Zachary Taylor, he is dead and damned, and I cannot help it. I am indignant at such corrupt fellows as Judge Brocchus coming here to lecture us on morality and virtue. I could buy a thousand of such men and put them into a bandbox."[7] The knot of enmity was thus inextricably tied. Despite an exchange of letters between the judge and the governor in which both men tried to clarify their positions, it was not long before Brocchus, Harris, and some of the others were on their way east to campaign against the Mormons. Harris had also had a severe clash with the Mormon leadership over the census and related matters; but the essence of the problem was polygamy, which the federal officers saw as symbolic of the degraded and rebellious condition of the Mormons in Utah. Disappointed when the Saints responded so defensively to their remonstrances against plural marriage, they decided to take the fight against Mormonism back to the States."[8]

Apart from all this, Young had in the meantime called Grant on another mission to the East, this time to work with Ezra T. Benson in encouraging the Saints in the Potawatomi country to emigrate to Utah and in superintending the migrations of 1852. Authorized on September 14 to leave shortly after the October conference, Grant's plans changed suddenly with the departure of the "runaway officials." His orders now sent him on to Philadelphia and Washington to assist Colonel Kane and Dr. Bernhisel in answering the charges of Brocchus and Harris, who were loudly venting their outrage in both official and public remonstrations. Young wanted to be certain that all of the ground was covered in the East, inasmuch as he realized that both Kane and Bernhisel were unaware of certain things that were bound to emerge with the report of the runaways—for Kane, Mormon polygamy, and for Bernhisel, the Mormon side of the Brocchus-Harris incidents in Utah. In addition, public opinion in the East would most certainly take a dramatic turn against the Saints.[9] At stake, of course, was Young's gubernatorial appointment.

Under the direction of Ezra Benson, the party of missionaries left Salt Lake City on October 6. Three weeks later they had made Fort Kearny some 200 miles up the Platte River from Council Bluffs. Having an opportunity to send a letter with some westward travelers, Grant wrote a note in which he admonished his family to righteousness. He knew that his assignment would keep him through the winter and possibly beyond,[10] so leaving home was a painful experience.

Fort Kerarney   Oct 27th 1851

Dear Susan and Family:

    I have time only to rite a line. My health is good, and my prayers are that you are all live and well enjoying your peaceful home in quiet. God my

Heavenly Father bless you and I bless you all in the name of Jesus. You have my prayers by day and night. Take care of your health. Look well to little Caroline. Keep her feet warm and dry, and send her to school. Tell how you get along if you have got your house fixed, and the furniture &c &c. Rosetta I want you to tell Henry [Robison] to sow one half acre of tomatoes. Write evry mail and I will do the same.

We are all getting along very well. Our horses are weak mine in perticular. Tell John [Snedaker] to take good care of the horses. I have a grate desire to hear from you: my home is ever dear to me, and when deprived of it, it is only more dear. I want you Susan to see that prayers are attended to. Call on John. He is an elder in grace and it is his duty to pray in my house in my absence. I will close by saying be ye blessed. As ever yours,

J M Grant[11]

The group arrived at Kanesville on the Missouri on November 14, 1851. The next morning Grant climbed into a stage for St. Louis, from which he took a steamer for the East. After a brief stopover in Philadelphia for a conference with Kane, he proceeded to Washington, arriving on the evening of December 8. Three days later he reported his situation to Susan, revealing as he wrote a high optimism concerning his mission, despite some nagging bad health and several doses of anti-Mormon propaganda.

Washington City D.C.   Dec. 11 1851

My Dear Susan and Family.

I have not been able to write to you for several weeks. You will recollect that my eyes were inflamed somewhat when I left home; they continued weak and my health poor all the way to the end of our journey over the Plains. The day we crossed the Missouri River, I took a violent cold in my head and eyes. While at Kanesville I kept [to] my room all the time, and suffered much with pain in my head and eyes. In the stage from Kanesville to Weston Mo. I also suffered in like manner; and the same while on the steam boat to St. Louis.

After this by the advice of Bro. Thomas Wrigley (presiding elder in St Louis branch) I applied green tea leaves to my eyes, which took out the inflamation and pain, and I am fast recovering, but as yet I am not able to read or write much; however Dr. Bernhisel has prepared some eye water that is helping my eyes very much indeed; my health is very much improved, and you may look for letters every mail.

After so much about my health, I will inquire after yours and Rosetta's, Johns' and Caroline's; are you all well? You must let me know every opportunity, for I feel the need of good news.

You are in heaven or one of the heavenly places, from which I am far away, battling against hellish influences that would sweep all Saints from the earth.

But he who said to the deep, "Be still," can calm the rage of man, whose puny arm is as the grass that falls to its Mother Earth. I arrived in this city on the evening of the 8th. Judges Brandenbury and Harris arrived on the evening of the 6th, 2 days in advance of myself. On their way through Missouri, they and Brockus published all the filth and slang that they could think of or write; they have commenced the same game here, crying, "Treason, Poligamy, Profanity, Abominations," (to indecent for such men as Brockus to name.) Dr. B. and Col. Kane and I will meet them with a steady nerve in the name of "The All Powerful God," on whome we rely for success and victory. Knowing the cause of the Saints to be just, we feel that we can do something for them.

When in Philadelphia I had a very pleasant visit with Col. Kane. His is as ever our warm friend; his zeal is unabated and his ambition unchecked. He thinks all will come out right.

The Doctor is quite sanguine for the interviews he has had with President Filmore that he will continue to do our people justice.

Tell Rosetta and Caroline and John that I hope they are learning fast; tell me how they get along. Remember me to Bros. Geo. and Joshua and their families. You may let Bro. Bullock see this letter, lest my letter to President Young should not come to hand. My blessing be and abide with you all forever.

J. M. Grant

P.S.—Susan you will I hope take good care of your health. See well to little Caroline. Remember me to Mrs Robinson and family, and all inquiring friends. Tell Bro. B, all the papers sent from the Valley are safe in the hands of the delegate, and he is right side up with care.

J. M. G.[12]

Some of Grant's optimism on his arrival in Washington no doubt stemmed from an expectation that he would be able to confront immediately such men as the President and the Secretary of State with the truth from Utah; but Bernhisel, caught in a delicate political situation, refused to allow the rough frontiersman even to make his presence in the city known in official circles. Profoundly frustrated and having received a copy of the runaways' report to the President, Grant left for Philadelphia and a meeting with Colonel Kane.[13] As he reported to the First Presidency a few days later, explaining some of the runaways' charges, and particularly one of them, was a difficult task.

Washington City D.C.   Dec. 30, 1851

To President Brigham Young, and Council.

Ever Dear Brethren You would have heard from me ere this, had my health been such as to have justified me in writing. Inflamation in my eyes has been the cause of my indisposition from which I have but lately recovered. Presuming that others have informed you, in relation to our trip over the Plains, my narrative will therefore be from my journal commencing at Kanesville Iowa.

Many of our brethren and sisters hailed us as messengers from a far country, sent to do them good; and did them in going to a land of health, where the ague comes not, and the fever climbeth not over the mountains. As usual we were met, by more or less pale faces, bleached by ague and fever, reminding us that it was a reality that we were again in the lower world. The general affairs here in relation to the Saints are very much as you have oftn described them. And as we expected to find them. More I need not say. "Little boats should keep near the shore. Larger ones may venture more."

I found the Saints at St Louis in good spirits, and very desirous to obay the call "Come Home." Nothing of very great importance occured on the journey to the eastern cities. While in Phila I called to see our ever to be remembered friend Thomas L. Kane. I found his hand heart and words as warm as ever, active and alive to the general wellfare of his friends in the far of[f] West.

I arrived in this city the evening of the 8th. Judge Brandebury and Secretary Harris arrived on the evening of the 6th. I found our delegate Dr.

J M Bernhisel in only tolerable health. Much labor and anxiety for his friends has worn upon his health, but his zeal is as ever only more so. You have no doubt by this time received the accounts in the newspapers published by Brandebury and his congators[?]. Their verbal statements are if papible exagerated as is also their official report to the President of the United States. Their allegations fill over 18 pages of foolscap paper blasily[?] written imbracing charges of allmost every varies [various] hue in the catalogue of crime.

On the 24th late in the afternoon our delegate received a note from the State Department informing him that the charges made by the returning officers of Utah Territory, against Gov. Young and others of said territory, had been received and would be sent on Monday the 27th instant to the House of Representatives. Responding to the call made upon the President by the House on the 15th, viz, for all the information in his possession relating to the late difficulties in Utah. Ter. The Dr was informed at the same time that if he wished to see the charges or send any accompanying documents with them he would have to do so before Monday the 27th.

On the 25th the State Department as well as other departments were closed. On Friday the 26th we called on President Fillmore to ask a delay but we were told by him that no delay could be had &c. We then called on Mr Webster, for a copy of the report which the clerk said we should have by 4 P.M. Accordingly it came to hand.

At five o clock I took the cars for Phila. At 8 the next morning I was talking with Col. Kane. He was soon looking over the charges. When he came to the one relating to our domestic relations he past it by saying it was false. I found myself therefore under the disagreeable necessity of volunteering to tell him how far it was false and how far it was true.

The following are the notes that I prepared and read them to him with verbal explanations—

Our Family or Domestic Relations, Philosophically Considered:

In the propagation of our principals and the gathering to gather of those who imbraced them, it was found after nine years experience, that the aggregate number of females was three to two males, showing that one third of our women must remain single, or marry out of the church.

Either was thought impolitic. The Prophet Joseph Smith was left therefore to inquire of the Great Alouheam who is and ever has been the disposer of this matter, granting from time to time special dispensations according to the situations and circumstances of the people to whom said dispensations were given; the dispensation given by the Lord through the Prophet, to the Church of Jesus Christ of Latter Day Saints is one limited and strict in its nature; like unto the one given unto Abraham and others in his day and not as elastic as the dispensation appears to have been in the days of David and Solomon. In relation to relatives belonging to the same family see Abrahamic Dispensation Gen 20est and 30est chapters. I will add that a mother after the death of her husband may attach herself to another family without becoming a wife to the head, or any branch of said family. See Isa 4. chap.

The rights of women among us are sacredly regarded and respected. They are kindly treated well provided for and saved in the scriptual sense of the word; see, first Tim 20nd chat and 15 ver. In reply to the complaint that our leaders have larger families than others I will say that their known good qualities had the affect to fill up their families several years ago so they have had no additions except children, which for ought I know has been equal to the prolific account given by the judges and secretary. If so it looks like ancient days, or the faith of the ancients reduced to practice. See Judges 8, c and 30 v. also 10 c and 4 v.

I will not undertake to tell you in this communication how the Col seemed to feel after my announcement of the whole matter. Let it suffice for me to say here that I am satisfied he will not fail to do all in his power to help us in the present cricis of affairs. Indeed he declares that he will never leave us when we are in trouble &c &c &c.

From all the facts we can gather and the council we have received from different sources we at present think it will be best to take issue before the Committee on Territories and have a commision sent to Utah and take depositions. This will delay the matter and give us a fare chance. In the meantime our delegate will address the President officially on the subject desiring him to stay executive procedings or action untill after the investigation. By this you will see that they intend giving them a long pull at least.

Brandebury and congators evedently are quite uneasy. After labouring for over two weaks night and day to get their report more to gather to suit them, they sent it to the President and he sent it to the Department of State, and we were furnished a copy. After all this they withdrew their report and have been for several days altering and revising.

If we see fit we will call for another copy. At presant it is said the report will be sent to the House, on the 5th of January making only a delay of 8 days from the time Mr. Webster said it would be sent. Dr. Bernhisel thinks it is a fixed fact that Governor Young is to be removed from office &c. It is urged that another gov should be appointed forthwith and sent out amediately and demand of Gover[nor] Young the 20,000 dolls, and that 2 regiments 2000 men of the army be sent out to help in force the laws of the United States &c.

I will now name the present candidates for Gov. First B. D. Harris (secretary) of Vt., Latson of N.Y. Gen. Doniphan of Mo. and others not a few. "What a long tail our Pup has got."

The Doctor will send you a copy of the charges. As far as I am concerned I feel that all will be as the Lord wants it. In the meantime we will do all in our power, keeping ourselves rite side up with care. I have written several times to Br Benson but as yet have not received his answer as it takes a long time to get news from Kanesville. I have received a letter from Br Gipson dated Oct 26. This is the last news from the Valley, and all that I have received since General Wells letter baring date Oct. 1st.

From all I can learn from different parts of the States you may look with safty for a large emigration the coming season, not only of the Saints, but of gold digers and others going to Oregon. Every body seems uneasy and unsatisfied. The Spirit of the Lord is being withdrawn from the earth more and more as the end draweth near. Do me the favor of remembering me to my friends in the Valley. I [am] believe me as ever your brother

J M Grant.[14]

Grant did not give the colonel very much detail about Joseph Smith's introduction of plural marriage. This may have been simply because he was unaware of it, as were most Mormons. At any rate, the rationale that Grant gave Kane for polygamy was essentially the same church polemic that dominated Mormon apologia for the next half century and beyond.[15] For his part, Kane was deeply disturbed by his friend's revelation. "I wish to thank you," he wrote Young, "for sending my old friend Grant the bearer to me of his tidings. I ought not to conceal from you that they gave me great pain. Independent of every other consideration, my Pride in you depends so much on your holding your position in the van of Human Progress, that I have to grieve over your favor to a custom which belongs essentially, I think, to communities in other respects behind your own." Kane presciently worried about the practice as time went on, particularly with certain men who would naturally abuse it. He also pointed to inevitable consequences of polygamy that he saw as inimical to human progress. Making no apologies for his opposition to the practice, he was nevertheless anxious to assure Young of his continuing support: "I think it my duty to give you thus distinctly my opinion that you err: I can now discharge you and myself from further notice of the subject."[16]

Following his delivery of the polygamy explanation to Colonel Kane, Grant continued to work closely with the Philadelphian, finding him to be more keen to the operations of Mormon Thunder than was Bernhisel in Washington. As soon as the runaways' report to the President appeared, Grant's impulse was to publish a rebuttal, but the Mormon delegate to Congress had resisted, hoping that careful politics would be more effective in preventing rash action on the part of the government against the Saints in Utah. In the first weeks of the new year, Grant grew increasingly impatient with "the Dr." By the middle of February, he was ready to return to Kanesville and then to Utah with an emigration in the spring. While visiting friends in eastern New Jersey, he wrote a letter to Susan that revealed his feeling that he could do little more in the East and that home was on his mind.

Thoms River N Jersey   Feb. 10: 1852

My Dear Susan,

    I have written home evry mail but as yet have not receved one word from my family. My last letter was written to John from Phila. Since then I have been to N. York. I am now on my return to Phila where I will stay one or two weeks and then start for Kanesville. My health is good, better than it has been for years. You will recolect of my telling you of my mother whiping me when a boy for rubing my belly when I would laugh. Also of a nervous weakness that I oftimes complained of after speaking the same as above aluded to, only worse. After speaking it seemed as if my bowels were tired out in sted of my loungs. By the advice of Br Israel Ivins of the place (who is an old friend of mine) I bought one of Dr Fitch's "Abdominal Supporters." From the time I commenced wairing them my health has improved very much indeed. Now I feell little or now inconvenience after speaking as heretofore.

I have now [no] special news of any importance to tell you. Our affairs in Washington are more flattering then heretofore but we cannot yet tell how they will turn out. Gov. Young is not yet turned out of offices and I have been prophesying that he will not be, but the Dr thinks he will be. The dust is setling a little and our sky looks clearer then it did when I last wrote. All things will work together for our good in spite of the judges or all hell to help them.

The winter here has been colder then it has been for fifteen or 20 years. I am very desirous to hear how you all get along this cold winter in the midst of the mountains. I received a letter while in N. York from Sister Roxcy Ann. She said that my father and mother were yet alive but my mothers health was very poor. Brs Austin and Reves was expected home every day. They had news from them, to that amount. The balance of my relatives in the country were all well.

Tell John and Henry to be on hand to trade with the emigrants for thousands are coming this year going for gold. I wish you to have Rozetta and Caroline go to school as much as possible. Tell me how John gets a long with his studdies &c.

Do not fail to remember me to Brothers George D and Joshua Grant and their families and the same to Br Bates Noble Sister Robbison and family and all who may inquaire after me.

For your health have John take you out to the farm and to as many other places as convenient. Do not lean forward when sitting or walking. Do all in your power to preserve your health. If you would make you some shoulder braces to keep back your arms and make you stand strate you would find that it would strengthen you[r] longs.

Tell Rozetta that she must send me a letter so that I can see how fast she has improved in writing. Tell Caroline that she must learn to spell and read and when her father comes home he will bring her a fine little book to write on. The Lord bless you all and preserve you in health and good spirits, as ever yours truly

J M Grant[17]

From Toms River Grant journeyed to Philadelphia, planning only a short stay prior to leaving for the West. But after conferring with Thomas L. Kane about the situation in Washington with regard to the runaway judges and the fate of the Saints in the Great Basin, he agreed to another plan. He would stay in Philadelphia, where he and the colonel would write a series of letters to the *New York Herald* in which Grant, as both civil and ecclesiastical leader among the Mormons, would refute the bulk of the runaways' charges and make light of the rest while attempting to turn public opinion in the East to the favor of Brigham Young and his followers.

With the development of this program in Philadelphia, Grant's thoughts turned quickly about. A letter home, written less than a month after his last, displayed an enthusiasm for the task at hand, in spite of some sad news from the West that might under other circumstances have hastened his return to Utah.

                                          Philada   March 7 1852

My Dear Susan

Yours of the 27th of Nov has after so long a time come to hand being the first letter from my home since I parted with you and my dear family. Your letter gave me much satisfaction to learn that you were all in good health but I will not undertake to tell you my feelings on hearing of the death of my dear brother Joshua Grant. When I parted with him he clasped both arms around my neck and gave me his last imbrace in this world. He has gone home to rest. In life he was very dear to me. We have spent years together preaching the Gospel. While he tired I believe I did all in my power for him. Peace and honor be to his memory.

In February I received a letter from Sister Roxcy Ann. She was living with my father and mother their health was as good as could be looked for under the circumstances. My mother you will recollect I have told you has a cansor on her nose. Ann says it gives her much pain and has eat very deep indeed. My father is quite well. He will be 76 this month if my memory serves me.

Brothers Austin Grant and Reves; Ann said was expected home every day, they had received late news from them. My Brothers Nelson and Howard, were well, and Austin and Reves families, also all of my relatives in that country. Dr J M Bernhisel is in tolerable good health. My health is good far better then it use to be when I lived in this country several years ago.

I am in hopes that your health and the little family that you have to see to will be good. Do your best to preserve your health. My prayers are offered for you all that you may live. You did not tell me anything about Sister Loisa

Joshua Grant Sr., ca. 1852. LDS Church Archives.

and her little children how she took or bore the death of my dear brother Joshua. Tell me in answer to this. You and Rozetta must try and comfort her all you can. Think how you would feel if I should leave for an other world.

    I am at present very busy writing during the day for the New York Herald in reply to the allegations of Brandebury Brocchus and Harris against Governor Young and all our people in Utah Territory. They have stirred up a mus in this country and I have got my reighteous indignation up to its very zenith and Col Kane is backing me and the Lord gives me his Spirit and I am in my element. I want to live fifty years yet at least to fight the devils. I have subscribed for the Herald for one year. Call at the post office for them. Do not let any of them get destroyed. Keep them all safe till I come. I will send you this mornings paper containing my first letter in reply to the runaway officers. When my next come out I will also send that and so on, till you get the whole series.

The Doctor our delegate is very lamblike, but the Col as well as myself are determined to put him through. He must stand up as the strong man armed. We will not admid to dodge the question on the all important item in this country of Mormon polygamy. We are determined to know what Congress has, can, or will do on that subject. There will be no action of Congress untill April next on or in relation [to] the territories. Governor Young is not yet removed though it is and has been rumored that he was, and that he would be. I have and keep prophesying that he will not be removed. I keep on prophesying good if it never comes to pass; as yet no judges have been appointed to fill the vacancies in Utah Ter.

Elder Benson was well the last account. Remember me to Brother George D Grant D H Wells and their families and all who may inquire after me.

Tell daughter that I have been to see her Aunt Margaret and her little cousins in New York. They want to see little Caroline very much indeed. Tell her she shall have the candy when I come if she will be a good girl and mind her book and learn and act like a lady. Tell Rozetta and John and Henry and all [the] children to do the best they can &c &c &c & &c. Tell John to be sure and see to the peach trees and fencing the forty acres &&c.

The weather has been colder this winter then for many years. All say it is the coldest winter they ever saw. Sister Ann says it has been unusual cold [in] Illinois.

You may look for thousands of Saints this season to come to the vallies of the mountains. The spirit of gathering is up on the people of the Lord. They are coming as clouds and doves to their windows.

I will say to conclude I shall be happy when my work is done in this country to step into your house and see how you all are getting along.

I want John to keep up prayers in the famaley. Do not for get this duty. Be faithful in keeping the commands of our God for all hell is against us. Where can we go if we leave our God. Be true to him and all will be right.

Tell me all the news you can think of. Direct your letter to Kanesville Iowa. I may be detained in this country longer then I could wish or you could desire but I shall not leave as long as there is so much to do. If I am not home untill August, be sure and write evry mail. I have written evry mail excep when my eyes was so that I could not write. I have written to Governor Young one long letter. I will write to him this week and to Br George.

When the judges report first came and I wanted to reply amediately but the delegate thought not best so I have all to do this late hour but by the help of the Lord I will do all I can and the delegate will do all in his power. In his way his is a good man but has but little Mormon Thunder in him not so much as I once though[t] he had, but he is worth a thousan Babbits for what he does do is good and he leave[s] no stink behind. He thinks me indescent but time will show my notions, or the Mormon notions, that are in me having been but [put] their by Joseph Brigham Heber Willard and others with a little that was always in me.

Good night. God bless you all is my prayer as ever your husband and friend

J M Grant[18]

Having reported only once to Young since his arrival in the East in December, Grant decided a few days after writing home to Susan to get off a letter to Brother Brigham. Addressing the letter to the governor alone, the absent mayor displayed some of his frustrations and deep feelings.

Philada   March 10th 1852

President Brigham Young
My Dear Brother in the Gospel.

Since my last letter to you and your council I have received yours of Dec 1st for which I feel thankfull to you and the Lord. All the items in your letter I will try and profit and comply with the same. Our affairs in Washington are much the same as when I last wrote.

The territorial bills will not be taken up in the House of Representatives until the third week in April.

The main blast is at you, as or in like maner, was it once against Brother Joseph Smith. Brother Brigham this letter is for you. You know how I feel, and God my Heavenly Father I think also knows. At any rate I am willing that all in earth or heaven should know. But why is it that when I am away from you, other good men do not think as I do. I am aluding to Winter Quarters, and the first winter in the Valley. The Carring Company, and my present situation. All is calm with me and our delegate he is one of the best men in the church, but God forgive me I have prayed and prayed to think and look at things as he does but cannot do so. On my arrival in Washington he thought it not wisdom for the President to know that I was in the city, also thought and said, it would not do for me to talk with members of Congress on the Utah difficulties. He thought it not for me to write for the press. After being in Washington over two weeks I was introduced to President Fillmore, and during near four weeks in Washington he gave me an introduction to one member of Congress Senator Dugless of Illinois. I conversed with no one but the Doctor himself. I did all in my power to infuse my spirit into him. We had not one unpleasant word, for I was determined it should not be said that I was always disagreeing with good men.

My expences being high and having nothing to do I left with the Doctors consent. Up to this date he has not thought it necessary for me to return. He has of later not altogather or fully permitted me to write for the press, but has in a degree gave his consent. I have commenced a series of letters to the New York Herald the first of which I will send you as also all my letters and doings.

Col Thomas L Kane is rite side up with care, thinks as I do in the matters of defence &c. You are not yet removed from office, though it has been rumered that you was, and that you would be &c.

Polygamy is the bone in the throat. It causes a grate deal of coughing and sneezing wind &c. But I shall give it to them as I would feed a hemloc tree to a jackass.

Donaphin of Mo is talked of as the governor of Utah. No judges are yet appointed.

If you have time please call on Susan and read my letter to her of last night. I hope and believe you all pray for us, in this land. The Lord helps us and I think and feel that all things will work together for our good. Yours forever

J M Grant[19]

It would appear that, although Grant felt quite uncomfortable in his relationship with Bernhisel, he had seen in his writing for the press with the help of Kane a clear chance to generate electricity in behalf of

Mormonism. As always before, such an opportunity was too sweet and inviting for Preacher Grant to pass by.

⇝ Notes ⇜

1. Journal History of the Church of Jesus Christ of Latter day Saints (chronological scrapbook of typed entries and newspaper clippings, 1830–present), October 6, 1850, 1, LDS Church Archives.

2. Ibid., December 2, 1850, 1, and January 6 and 9, 1851, both p. 1. For a clear outline of the "Beginnings of Civil Government" in Utah, see Eugene E. Campbell, *Establishing Zion: The Mormon Church in the American West, 1847–69* (Salt Lake City: Signature Books, 1988), 201–15. D. Michael Quinn, *The Mormon Hierarchy: Extensions of Power* (Salt Lake City: Signature Books, 1997), 235–41, describes Young's increasing disregard for the Council of Fifty as a shadow government as he moved to create a territorial theocracy in the early 1850s.

3. See, for example, Journal History, February 8, 1851, 1, where Jedediah Grant and Henry Harriman reported ordaining eighty-four new seventies in one meeting.

4. Journal History, July 23, 1851, 1, and July 24, 1851, 5.

5. For details of the entire affair, see B. H. Roberts, *A Comprehensive History of the Church of Jesus Christ of Latter-day Saints, Century One*, 6 vols. (Salt Lake City: Church of Jesus Christ of Latter-day Saints, 1930), 3:510–54.

6. "History of Brigham Young," September 8, 1851.

7. Ibid.

8. Roberts, *Comprehensive History*, 3:510–54.

9. Journal History, September 5, 8, 14, 15, 1851, all p. 1; September 22, 1851, 5; October 23, 1851, 2, 5, and October 31, 1851, 2. The news of what had happened to the runaway judges spawned a potent upsurge in anti-Mormonism, which had waned temporarily due both to the distractions of the impending crisis over slavery and the tragic scenes of the exodus across Iowa. Within days of the officials' return, publications began to multiply in a growing chorus of condemnation of Young and his "uncivilized" followers. See, for a telling example, Jotham Goodell, *A Winter with the Mormons: The 1852 Letters of Jotham Goodell*, edited by David L. Bigler (Salt Lake City: Tanner Trust Fund, Marriott Library, University of Utah, 2002).

10. Journal History, October 23, 1851, 2, 5.

11. Jedediah Grant, Letter to Susan Grant, October 27, 1851, holograph in possession of Betty Mae Nebeker Laub, Salt Lake City (hereafter Laub Collection). Note his continu-

ing concern for Caddie's health and, in addition, the longing to know even that the family members were "live."

12. Jedediah Grant, Letter to Susan Grant, December 11, 1851, holograph, Laub Collection. Two people named John surface in these letters to Susan. One is the Scottish child John McKeatchie (later renamed Lewis M. Grant) and the other farmhand John F. Snedaker. While he makes no differentiation between them, context helps identify which one he means in each case.

13. Jedediah Grant, Letter to Brigham Young, March 10, 1851, holograph, Brigham Young Collection, LDS Church Archives.

14. Jedediah Grant, Letter to Young, December 30, 1851, holograph, Brigham Young Collection. For a brief and blunt analysis of the origins of polygamy by Mormonism's founder, see Richard Lyman Bushman, *Joseph Smith: Rough Stone Rolling, a Cultural Biography of Mormonism's Founder* (New York: Alfred A. Knopf, 2005), 323–27, 437–46.

15. Common discourse in Mormondom today continues to repeat a comforting justification for plural marriage related to a mythical surplus of women in early Church demographics. Ironically, Grant contradicted his own claim to Kane of a 3:2 Mormon women-to-men ratio when, in one of his letters to the *New York Herald*, appearing just a few weeks later, he indicated that there were in Utah six men for every five women. See Appendix. Scholars investigating Mormonism's peculiar institution continue to debate the numbers, but virtually all affirm a higher percentage of men in nineteenth-century Utah than the myth would suggest. See, for example, Lowell "Ben" Bennion, "The Incidence of Mormon Polygamy in 1880: 'Dixie' versus Davis Stake," *Journal of Mormon History* 11 (1984): 27–42; Kathryn M. Daynes, *More Wives than One: Transformation of the Mormon Marriage System, 1840–1910* (Urbana: University of Illinois Press, 2001); Larry M. Logue, *A Sermon in the Desert: Belief and Behavior in Early St. George, Utah* (Urbana: University of Illinois Press, 1988); Richard S. Van Wagoner, *Mormon Polygamy: A History* (Salt Lake City: Signature Books, 1986). Similarly, Grant's assertion that Mormon leaders were not marrying new wives was more polemical than factual.

16. Thomas L. Kane, Letter to Brigham Young, October 17, 1852, holograph, Brigham Young Collection.

17. Jedediah Grant, Letter to Susan Grant, February 10, 1852, holograph, Laub Collection. "Brs Austin and Reves" referred to Grant's brother Austin and to his sister Theda's husband, William Reeves.

18. Jedediah Grant, Letter to Susan Grant, March 7, 1852, holograph, Laub Collection.

19. Jedediah Grant, Letter to Young, March 10, 1852, holograph, Brigham Young Collection.

"I have now completed my letters to the *New York Herald*. They may do some good."

9
Truth for the Mormons

A PRODUCT OF COLONEL KANE'S "long quill" and Elder Grant's "inspiration,"[1] a letter entitled "Truth for the Mormons" appeared in the *New York Herald* on March 9, 1852, over Grant's signature as mayor of Great Salt Lake City. Its opening lines were blunt and eye-catching.

JAMES GORDON BENNETT, Esq.

Sir:—I will thank you to print, as soon as you can, the substance of this letter. Considered only as news, it ought to be worth your while. There is a great curiosity everywhere to hear about the Mormons, and eagerness to know all the evil that can be spoken of them. Announce you that I am a Mormon Elder, just arrived from Utah—Mayor, in fact, of Salt Lake City, where my wife and family are still living—a preacher, brigadier of horse, and President of the Quorum of Seventies, and the like; and not one subscriber that waded over shoe tops through the slime of details you gave of the play actor's divorce trial lately, will not be greedy to read all I have to say, about the filthier accusations that have been brought against me, and my friends and brethren. This is what I have to count upon, thank Falsehood. And, if you will publish my letter entire, I will ask for no editorial help from you. I am no Writer; but, with the help of the Power of Light, am not afraid of what you can say against us. So long as I walk by the rule of my Master, you walk by the rude working of your fancies.

I must say, I have had my doubts about writing out upon these matters; my doing so not being approved by our Delegate in Congress, Dr. Bernhisel. The Doctor is one of our gentlemen at home; a real gentleman, and would not say a rough word, or do a rough thing, to hurt the feelings, or knock off the spectacles of any man, for the world. But I am no gentleman, in his sense at least, and have had slights enough put upon me, personally, since I came eastward, to entitle me to any amount of stand up self-defense. Dr. Bernhisel's official course in this matter, I suppose I am bound to who said to him, "Take up the report of the three officers criminating your constituents, when it comes from the State Department into the House; ask for a Special Committee with power to send for persons and papers, and put the false witnesses on oath; but don't stoop to wrangle upon your religion, morals, and political opinions with Mr. Webster or the Congressmen at large, whom the country considers to have enough to do to take care of their own."

This is all very well, and very high and mighty and dignified certainly; but while the grass grows the cow starves—while Congress is taking its months to do the work of a day, the verdict of the public goes against us—as the law word is, by default—and we stand substantially convicted of any thing and everything that any and every kind of blackguard can make up a lie about. And now I hear that the charges are not to be pushed—two of the officers want to come back to us as friends—they are to be virtually abandoned after doing us all the harm they can. What Mr. Webster thinks, we care a little; what is the opinion of most members of Congress, you can hardly believe, in your part of the world, how very little; but Public Opinion, that power we respect as well as recognize; and, therefore, I am now determined, on my own responsibility, to write myself, and blurt out all the truth I can. I may not be discreet, but I will be honest.[2]

For his part, Bennett attached a short review of the letter in which he tried to match wits with its authors and to editorialize on the condition of the Mormons and their current conflict with Washington.

Elder Grant's Defense of the Mormons—Curious and Interesting Letter.—

We call the attention of our readers to the defense of the Mormons, as contained in the curious and scorching letter of Jedediah M. Grant, which we publish this morning. Brother Jedediah is "a Mormon Elder, Mayor of Salt Lake City, a preacher, brigadier of horse, and President of the Quorum of Seventies, and the like." He therefore "speaks as a man having authority," and fights the enemies of the Saints "square up to the handle."

His letter has for its object the vindication of the Saints of Utah Territory against the allegations contained in the late report submitted to Congress by the United States Judges recently returned from Salt Lake City.

That report, on its first mention in the *Herald*, it will be remembered, created a sensation; and, on its subsequent presentation to Congress, certain preliminary steps were taken with a view to an investigation into the facts concerning the Mormons. The substance of the accusations brought against them by the returned Judges is, that they are a seditious set of people—that Brigham Young, in his speeches and his acts, was little better than a traitor—that he had outraged the authority and the officers of the government, and had defamed the memory of General Taylor, by declaring that he was in hell—that this same Governor Young was the supreme despot of Mormondom—that he imitated the Grand Turk in his family affairs, having from twenty to thirty wives, and a large number of children—that the other dignitaries of the church had also a plurality of wives, according to their official standing—and that polygamy, on a very liberal scale, was the distinguishing institution of the Mormon community.

His Honor the Mayor of Salt Lake City proceeds to answer his judges by discrediting them as witnesses. Judge Brandebury, it appears, gave great offence to the Saints, from neglecting the important duty of wearing a clean shirt. This offence is represented as inexcusable, from the abundance of soap and water at the Salt Lake. After being received in great state, at the city bath house, on his arrival, where he was honored with a grand ball, which was opened with prayer, it was expected that he would look to his shirts, and not forget the washerwoman. Judge Snow and lady, and Mr. and Mrs. Harris, were received in the same way, with a grand ball at the bath house, opening with prayer and closing with a benediction—Governor Young presiding on each occasion. Mrs. Harris danced with the Governor, and "with a will, too," as it appears, and seemed to be delighted with the Mormons. Affairs looked well for harmony between the officers and the people; for, notwithstanding "that shirt which the Judge had on at the 14th of July celebration," there was no trouble till the arrival of P. E. Brocchus, one of his associates.

The appearance of this gentleman in Zion seems to have been the immediate cause of a rupture. After giving a character to Judge Brocchus unsubstantiated by proofs, Elder Grant proceeds to a report of the September celebration at "the Bowery" of Salt Lake City, where the grand flareup took place between the Judge and the Governor. The Judge was put down in attempting to lecture the Mormon ladies upon morality—unquestionably a very bold undertaking. The reply of Governor Young, according to the Elder's report, must have been a clincher. But one important fact is admitted. Elder Grant testifies, substantially, that Governor Young declared that while General Jackson was among the angels in heaven, the good old General Taylor was roasting in the other place. Awful, truly terrible, when it is further declared that "Brigham Young spoke this out of his knowledge by the priesthood." This is a direct confirmation by Elder Grant of the Doctrine of spiritual manifestations. What says Greeley to that?

A few days after this affair, the offended United States Judges were missing in the New Jerusalem, having taken up their line of march for Washington. We do not discover that their report is answered by Elder Grant. A different view of the circumstances is given, and a different coloring to the same facts, which show that Judge Brocchus acted very imprudently in his address. It also appears that he or his official associates did not sufficiently respect those habits of industry, while among the Mormons, for which they are so remarkable. But the pith of the charges against Gov. Young and his community is not answered. Their love and devotion to the Union is declared to be faithful and unchanged. The only difficulty is that the organization of their society conflicts with the laws and institutions of the United States. Polygamy is admitted to exist; for Elder Grant will hardly deny that Brigham Young has at least seven wives. The Saints are, no doubt, very much attached to their very peculiar institutions. They are the practical fulfillment, on a small scale, of the "good time coming," when socialism shall be universally established. We apprehend that the government will yet have some trouble with these Latter Day Saints and angels, and that there is some truth in the reports that they have broken out into open mutiny. The Saints deserve great credit for that persevering industry which has built up a prosperous community in a desert; but they must make up their minds to submission to the federal authorities, and come down to the established arrangement of one wife at a time, or abide by the consequences of their higher law. Meantime, would it not be well for our city fathers to give a corporation dinner to the Mayor of Salt Lake City? He does not ask for intervention, or material or financial aid; but why not give him a dinner or a ball, and get his opinion on the Maine Liquor law?[3]

In the context of growing tension in the nation over the question of the rights of the South to extend its "peculiar institution" into the western territories, Mormon obedience to federal authority was an issue that transcended the nuances of the problem itself. Bennett realized this, but he was subsequently unwilling to publish anything further from the Mormon and his ally in Philadelphia, who were continuing to expound on the so-called rebellion in Utah. Despite Bennett's apt and time-conscious criticisms of the letter of March 9, however, Grant's article had an immediate impact in New York and Washington, where its charm and appeal to curiosity made it popular reading. Very shortly, the New Yorker's wry advice to his city's officials about inviting the mayor of Salt Lake City for a chat had more significant reference to men on the Potomac.

Quite to the surprise of Delegate Bernhisel, who had hoped to restrain the feisty preacher and his Philadelphian accomplice, the letter to the *Herald* opened some eyes and some doors in the capital, although their actual effectiveness defied assessment. One senator, Hannibal Hamlin of Maine, told Bernhisel that they "had confirmed in him what he believed before, that the returned officers were d——d scoundrels."[4] Discussing the 1852 crisis during the Mormon centennial three-quarters of a century later, B. H. Roberts tended to minimize their impact, agreeing with Editor Bennett that they did not answer the charges, even though the second letter addressed each allegation separately. In addition, before their publication in pamphlet form in May, President Fillmore had already decided against the runaways, as had Secretary of State Daniel Webster, who ordered them to return to their posts immediately or resign. Fillmore had also nominated Orson Hyde to a vacancy on the supreme court of Utah. Although Hyde's nomination failed in the Senate because of his lack of legal training, it was a clear indication of the president's decision to side with the Saints and, in particular, to respond favorably to the petition Grant mentioned in his May 13 letter to Brigham Young. Dated September 19, 1851, the petition called upon the president to avoid a recurrence of the runaway incident by appointing "men to fill the aforesaid vacancies who are indeed residents among us."[5]

One certain effect of the letters emerged at once. Grant's presence in the East quickly became an asset to the Mormon delegate; and by the middle of March, Jedediah was back in Washington. The tempest over the federal report was still swirling, but now a partial Mormon response had taken form in the *Herald* and could command some attention. On March 25, Bernhisel and Grant called on President Fillmore to request that the judges' report not be submitted to Congress until the rest of the Mormon defense could be printed and distributed in pamphlet form.[6] Fillmore granted the request; and after a visit with Secretary of State Webster, Grant returned to Philadelphia to assist Kane in the final work on the book, which would contain the first letter and two more. In the midst of that work, he paused to send two reports home—one to Susan and one to Brigham.

                                                                          Philada   April 15th 1852

My Dear Susan and familey,

    I am well and have prayed that you all may enjoy this blessing and all others necessary for your peace and happiness in my absence. How do you all do? Are you all well and in good spirits?

    I feel like coming home and hope it will not be long before I leave this country. I want to see you all very much indeed. Is my Caroline girl well? Does she grow fast, and learn her book and behave first rate? How are you Susan? I can not take you to Iron County this April, hence you will not get turned over on the rocks eggs and all. Rozetta how is it with you? Do you go to school? If so send me a letter and tell me now fast you learn &c. John how do you get along? Have you been to school 4 or 5 months since I left?

    Send me a line to Fort Larame, telling all about matters and things, how Henry and his people get along &c &c.

    Since my last long letter to you of five pages, I have been preparing two long letters for the New York Herald, but Bennett is not willing to publish them entire so I have concluded to put them in pamphlet form. It will detain me untill the first days of May, but I think by July 24th you may look for me coming out of the kanyon in duble quick time.

    The dust has settled in the country that the judges kicked up, and a good deal went into their own eyes and ears, and has made them speechless. I do not know but they have been winked at by blind people, and kicked a cross lots by criples, and nibled to death by young ducks and cared to hell through the keyhole by bumblebees, for they have not been seen in Washington for several weeks. I here give you my tost to the devil of percicution: May the American eagle pick out his eyes and the young ravens of the Valley eat them; may he be compeled to take the telegraph for France; the power of propulsion land him on the deserts of Arabia; may the Upas tree be planted on his grave that the poison may kill all who may attempt to reserrect him.

    I am and have been looking for an other letter but as yet none has come to hand. Give my respects and kind reguards to Br George D Grant and his family, and Br Joshua's familey. Tell them to keep up good spirits.

When I come I may bring you some few little notions, but it will take all or nearly so, that I can rase in this country to bring me home. I shall come quite different than I did 2 years agoe, but I think I will be much better sitisfied with this trip then that, though I make not one red cent. Do the best you can till [I] come and all will be right. Remember me to Sister Robbison and her familey. May the Lord Bless you all. As ever yours truly

J M Grant [7]

Philada   April 15th 1852

President Brigham Young.
My Dear Sir

Since my last to you, nothing of any great importance has taken place in Congress, in relation to Utah affairs. Soon after my letter appeared in the Herald, the Dr found it took well in Washington and did much good. His spirits revived, though at first he evidently thought that the verry Devil would be kicked up. But at present he sees that a little Mormon Thunder was what was kneeded.

In my last to you, I did not qualify how we feed jackasses hemlock trees. It did no doubt accure to you, they would only eat the twigs and little ends of the bowes, leaving the main body and limbs in our own hands unfed out as the asses cannot digest big things. My letter No. 2 Mr Bennitt was not willing to put it in his paper entire. So we have concluded to put the series in pamphlet form, and send one to every editor who is of any note, in the nation, with a polite note for them to publish such and such a part.

At present things look very favorable. We have know [sic] reason to think that you will be removed from offices. We can not yet tell who will be appointed judges for Utah.

It will be out of my power to be here untill May. I will do all in my power to set things right and help Br Bernhisel all I can. He is one of the best men in the world, but he must have his way and I some times will have mine, but all is right. The defunked officers are laughed at.

In this city you could see pasted up in many parts, a fine large woodcut, picture representing some 5 or 6,000 United States troups, lead on by generals, cols and captains, &c, aginst the people of Utah. When low theire met by a few women holding children in their arms. It then represents the leading officer commanding a retreat, say[ing] he could not with his men meet a caltry[?] like that, &c!!!

Col. T. L. Kane is doing all he can in our cause. He is you know long winded with the quill, and I give him inspiration, but his stile is long and peculiar to himself. As soon as my pamphlet is out I will start for the Bluffs, but I can not leave in time to help Br. Benson to push the emigration. Some ten, or 15 have left this city and more are going this spring. Br. Eward Pell late from the state of California, with his two sisters left in the cars this morning for Salt Lake, in company [with] Br Wm. Derr and family.

Pleas say to Br Wm Clayton that I have filled his bill for blank books, only I got more than he sent for, and as good as he wanted in every sense.

My pamphlet or book will fill near one hundred pages. I wish to be remembered to my friends.

> May the Lord my God bless you.
> As ever your brother
> to bles the good, and fight the Devils
> in hopes too save the good and dam the bad.
> I am on hand as ever

J M Grant

If you see Br E M. Sanders do me the favor of saying to him, that I have called on his relatives in this city and made enquiry in relation to the land in Ohio. They say it has all been sold for taxes and neither they nor any of the heirs will get any thing for it &c &c.

In relation to Br Wm Glover's folks I can not go to see them. I am busy all the time, and by the help of the Lord I am and will keep doing all I can. I have felt the power of God, to that extent that at times, it has seemed to me if it was necessary I could shake all this eastern country with the very sound of my voice. My health has been good and thank God I have had no fear. Your prayers have been heard and I have felt their efficucy. Our honorable judges and Day, Harris, dare not churp. If they are not dead they are as stale as death itself. I want to see you Br Brigham and your council and all of my dear friends in the Valley. I am sick of this country and want to get back to my farming again.[8]

Obviously quite anxious to get back to the mountains, Grant knew that he had much yet to do. From the beginning of his current visit to the East, he had seen his responsibility mostly in terms of swaying public opinion in favor of the Saints, while Bernhisel was to continue to handle the politicians in Washington. In spite of this, the impetuous preacher had champed at the bit when Bernhisel refused to introduce him into the highest offices in the capital. With the commencement of his work on the letters to the *Herald* with Kane, however, Grant seemed to have found a comfortable place for himself in the present difficulties. He worked contentedly into the first days of May getting the letters ready for publication. As soon as the pamphlet was ready for distribution, he prepared to leave the East for Kanesville and Utah, but first he forwarded a last report to Brigham Young in which he expressed his belief that his mission had been a success.

New York   May 13th 1852

President Young.
My Dear Sir

Soon after my last letter to you, I received two welcome communications from you, and a copy of a letter sent to Mr. Whittlesey also a copy of the Memorial of the People and Legislature to Congress &c all good and in time. In all of your letters you speak of the papers sent to me on the way to the States last fall. They all came safe to hand, and at Fort Kearney Br. S W Richards clerk of the train, for and in behalf of the camp sent you a letter in which we gave due notice of the receiving of said papers. You have ere this no doubt received my letters &c. I have written to you every month since I came east. In my first letter I gave reasons why the Bracchus, and other letters, were withheld.

Your Whittlesey letter needs no help from me or any one, it is of, and in itself, good things steaped. Your last message in this country brings a primeam over all other coin of the kind. Some articals in the Deseret News, are issues from the same mint. Indeed I may say that all the late news from the Valley has been the thing wanted to right our ship in this country. She is at this time in good trim and under full sail before a fine breze from the west, but I look for squalls. Pirates are plenty! and watching! The main crisis is yet, now pending before Congress. The President has made his nominations.

The battle will be fought in the Senate, first relating to the appointments. We look, pray and fight for victory! The enemy is on the alert. He sees if we gane in the Senate, the victory, the day will also be ours in the House.

Nominations for secretary W Richards for one of the judges O Hyde. The Doctor has not seen fit to tell me who the chief justice is to be, but I infer it will fall on the write one. Br Heber C Kimball has been spoken of &c. I have now completed and ready for circulation in pamphlet form, my letters to the New York Herald. They may do some good. I will send a copy to each member of Congress and the principal editors of the Nation. You will see on reading them, that our friend, Col Kane has had hold of them in earnest &c.

The hand of the Lord has been stretched out in our favor. Men think they do it all but they are fools, or they would see that the Lord has moved the hearts and minds of the people as the wind moves the trees of the firist. I have all the time said and felt that it would be as the Lord wanted it, whether Congress goes one way or another. All is right. Mormon Thunder is the Lords Thunder, and it knocks off the scails and horns of Gentileism. We feel in this country the affect of prayer of er you know where!!

I think Congress as near as I can learn are not willing that Utah should have any part of their God, which is Gold. Utah as heretofore may make up her mind to work for nothing and find herself. President Fillmore has acted nobly, but he has nothing to do with the appropriations &c.

I will leave on Saturday morning for Philada. and from there westward. I have been detained in the East much longer then I would, could I have had my own way, but all is right. We are looking every day for an other mail from the Valley. I wated untill this late hour in hopes of its arrival. I can not wate any longer. If I do you would not get this letter untill July. With kind regard and meayes(?). I am yours truly

J M Grant

You are safe as Governor at any rate.[9]

Young's letter "to Mr. Whittlesey" that Grant mentioned apparently did not survive either in Church or public records; but inasmuch as Elisha Whittlesey was comptroller of the Treasury in the Fillmore administration and as Governor Young was being accused of squandering the $20,000 that Almon Babbitt had brought from Washington for the erection of public buildings, the letter was probably an explanation of the way the money had been spent. The Council House had been used as headquarters for government in Utah since its construction by the Church shortly after the Mormons arrived in the Great Basin; Brigham Young therefore used the appropriation for the purchase of that building for use as a statehouse until his followers could erect new buildings for the government at the new capital in Fillmore, Millard County. In mentioning the Whittlesey letter and the other items from Utah, Grant was simply adding to his assessment that the Saints' public relations campaign in the East had been successful, or "that the Lord has moved the hearts and minds of the people as the wind moves the trees of the forest."

It is likely that, if Grant had left for the West in February as he had planned,[10] he would not have felt as positive about his mission's results. Prior to his work with Kane on the *Herald* letters, he was unable to feel that his presence in the East had had any worthy result. It was one thing to generate the sounds of Mormon Thunder, but not since he led in the publication of the anti-Rigdon pamphlet in 1844 had he seen in print the echoes of his thinking. To the bumptious preacher, the booklet entitled "Three Letters to the *New York Herald*, from J. M. Grant, of Utah" was symbolic of flashing triumph. With the help of Thomas Kane and "the Power of Light," its pages sent Grant's Mormon Thunder roaring across the eastern plain.[11]

← Notes →

1. Jedediah Grant, Letter to Young, April 15, 1852, holograph, Brigham Young Collection, LDS Church Archives. See Chapter 21 for a detailed discussion of the letter's authorship.

2. *New York Herald*, March 9, 1852. See Appendix for the three letters. Even though Grant's commission to the East included admitting to the world the existence of plural marriage among the Mormons, he refers only to his "wife" back home.

3. Ibid. The second letter answered the report's allegations item by item, except for the charge of polygamy, which he deferred to the third letter. In that missive, he nevertheless failed to answer the charge directly and instead maneuvered around it with arguments for the right of local governments to legislate their own institutions, a tacit admission at best. See Appendix.

4. Journal History of the Church of Jesus Christ of Latter day Saints (chronological

scrapbook of typed entries and newspaper clippings, 1830–present), July 17, 1851, 2, LDS Church Archives.

5. *Congressional Globe*, 25:92–93. See also B. H. Roberts, *A Comprehensive History of the Church of Jesus Christ of Latter-day Saints, Century One*, 6 vols. (Salt Lake City: Church of Jesus Christ of Latter-day Saints, 1930), 3: 517–41.

6. Journal History, March 25, 1852, 1.

7. Jedediah Grant, Letter to Susan Grant, April 25, 1852, holograph in possession of Betty Mae Nebeker Laub, Salt Lake City. A notoriously poisonous plant, the South Asian Upas tree could supposedly kill anything within fifteen meters. Its use as a literary device was quite common in the nineteenth century. See, for example, Lord Byron's *Childe Harold's Pilgrimage*, Canto 4.

8. Jedediah Grant, Letter to Brigham Young, April 25, 1852, holograph, Brigham Young Collection.

9. Jedediah Grant, Letter to Brigham Young, May 13, 1852, holograph, Brigham Young Collection.

10. Jedediah Grant, Letter to Susan Grant, February 10, 1852, holograph, Laub Collection.

11. See Chapter 21 for a detailed discussion of the letters' origin.

PHASE THREE
Raining Pitchforks: 1852–56

"The hearts of men fail them for fear of the impending storm. ..."

⇌ 10 ⇌
The Heavens Booming

B Y THE FIRST OF JULY 1852, Jedediah Grant was in Kanesville on the Missouri River, preparing to assist Ezra T. Benson with a migration to Utah of some 6,000 Saints in eighteen companies. Each company would consist of from fifty to seventy-five wagons filled with foodstuffs, clothing, furniture, squalling infants, and occasionally a pigpen or chicken coop.[1] It had been five years since Grant had first made the trip as captain of the third hundred in that 1847 cautious step of Mormons into the wilderness. The scenes would be the same this time, but the route was now well traveled and the migration several times larger. And now, even those who had never been in Utah were going home. Others, like Jed Grant, John Taylor, Erastus Snow, and Franklin D. Richards, were returning to Zion after the fulfillment of missions, and the anticipated homecoming lay sweet on their minds.[2]

As the migration of 1852 worked its way up the Platte, the Saints who had preceded them to the mountains were celebrating the fifth anniversary of the entry of the first Mormons into the valley. There was good reason to celebrate that year. After a winter of worrying about whether Brigham Young would remain as governor and whether the federal government would respond to the report of the runaway judges with action against the Saints, it appeared to all by July 24 that Truth and its emissaries had prevailed in the East. Indeed, among the toasts given that day was one by Wilford Woodruff to John M. Bernhisel and Jedediah M. Grant, "noble defenders of the Constitution, of their country, and the rights of the Beehive. Should their enemies kill their bodies, like the two Prophets in Jerusalem, they would again stand upon their feet to the fear and consternation of their enemies."[3] Among soaring Mormon heroes of the moment, Jedediah Grant flew understandably close to the front.

Susan Fairchild Noble Grant and Joseph Hyrum Grant, 1854. LDS Church Archives.

Pleased as he might have been with the results of his mission, and in particular the letters to the *Herald*, Grant's thoughts at the same time centered on the more common longings of the heart.

West of the South Fork of Platte   July 23 1852

Dear Susan,

I have written to you 4 letters but have not received one word from you. Nothing could have gave me more comfort then to have heard from my family by a letter from you. I felt disappointed when I met Br. Campbell with the mail from the Valley and not one word for me, from any friend or person. If my letters have failed to reach you, you have without doubt felt some of the same in[t]imations that I have felt. Being at St Louis last spring when the mail left Kainsville I had to sent my letters by gold diggers. I trust they have been received ere this.

It seems a long time since I left home. How is Rozetta and my little Caddy girl? After a long journey and much fatigue and anxiety and toil on the plains I long to see my familey and rest and enjoy their dear society. May my Father in heaven bless you and preserve your lives and mine that we may long live to enjoy each others society throughout all of the eternities. My love to all my friends. God bless you for ever in haste. Yours for ever

J M. Grant[4]

Despite his natural concerns for the welfare of his wives and daughter, when Grant arrived in Salt Lake City in the afternoon of August 20, he found them well and as anxious for him as he had been for them. But Grant was home from Babylon, where he had struggled valiantly to protect the rights of his idealized and pure society back home. Yet the Mormon society he had known and mostly imagined in his nearly continuous wanderings in the East and South in its behalf had gone through a series of profound transitions. The intoxicating mysticism that had permeated Mormondom during the reign of Joseph Smith in Kirtland and Nauvoo had disappeared. The Saints in the Great Basin now lived on a more terrestrial fringe of desert hardship and uncertainty. Rather than foster security, their isolation helped feed a constant fear that any sign of weakness on their part would bring violent purges and death at the hands of their enemies, whom they perceived to be nearly everyone outside the bounds of the Church. For Grant and his Jacksonian frame of reference, this meant that the Saints must be completely on the side of the cause or completely against it. There could be no middle ground.

Within two days of his arrival in the valley, the returning hero was addressing a large congregation in the tabernacle, telling of his last triumphant sortie among the Gentiles. The next day he spent in lengthy debriefing sessions with Young and other leaders of the Church. During these heady days of glory, Grant probably did not perceive the forces building in Zion that would soon lead him into battle against his own people, as they struggled to master an untamed wilderness and at the same time pay their constant devotions to an ever-demanding religion. For now it was enough to have conquered the Gentiles on their own field of conflict. The adulation and the storytelling soon ended, however, and the duties of mayor, speaker of the house, and one of the First Council of the Seventy, as well as those of militia commander and farmer, quickly had him back into his normal routine of life in Deseret.[5]

Mayor Grant seemed pleased with the progress of his city. Not only were its borders expanding as thousands of Latter-day Saints came home to Zion, but the physical appearance of the place belied its pioneer village origins. Building projects all over the city signified permanence and peace. On New Year's Day, 1853, he offered the benediction at the dedication ceremonies of the Social Hall, a gracious building a block from his home in which the Saints could meet for entertainment and enlightenment; and a month later he participated as mayor of the city and as a General Authority of the Church in the groundbreaking ceremonies of the Salt Lake Temple. On March 7, Grant could truly call it his city, inasmuch as a few days after the fête on Temple Block, he was unanimously re-elected mayor, riding a crest of success due to his forceful allegiance to the religion of Joseph and Brigham.[6]

As exciting as it was, the development of Salt Lake City as an urban oasis in the midst of a rural Deseret had begun to create friction in reality and in symbolic contrast, as the ever-growing influence of the expanding city overshadowed the immense calm, virtue, and patience that had endowed the Mormon landscape in the Great Basin with its sustaining power. The growing materialistic orientation of the city had already led some important leaders to believe that Mormon society had become too secular and to reproach it for its materialism. There were those who had always longed for the simpler gospel of Kirtland, and those who still wondered about the rambunctious and expanding dictatorship of Brigham Young. Polygamy, now a public fact, seemed to many to represent all the ills of a primitivist movement gone the way of the world. Some mumbled aloud their longings for a more esoteric faith and even a return to the old religion, with notions wrapped in the idea that a lineal descendant of Joseph Smith should be leading the Church in any case. As a matter of fact, far from the Valley of the Great Salt Lake at this very time, some Mormons who had refused to follow Brigham and the Twelve into the West were beginning to discuss ways to re-create an older form of the Restoration movement. Within a decade the Reorganized Church of Jesus Christ of Latter Day Saints (now the Community of Christ) would come into being among the ruins of the old church in the Mississippi Valley, with Joseph's eldest son at its head. Grant's commitment to the cause, however, was one dimensional. His loyalty to Brigham Young would not waver any more than had his loyalty to Smith. He would fight the enemies of Mormonism no matter who or where they were.

Grant's two prophets had taught that the family was the key to salvation and that a man who would build his kingdom in heaven should build a large household on earth. In consequence, Jedediah Grant married in 1853 a third living wife, Sarah Ann Thurston. That same year Susan and Rosetta each gave him a son—Joseph Hyrum and Jedediah Morgan Jr. In addition, Jedediah and Susan formally adopted the Scottish boy who was now twelve years old and apparently proud to be known as Lewis M. Grant, the mayor's eldest son.[7] It seemed an eternity since Grant and his orphaned daughter had come into the valley after having buried Caroline and Margaret. All had changed and yet nothing had changed. The cause was the same. There were still devils to fight and souls to save for a millennium of peace, a millennium that the leaders of the Saints preached was absolutely imminent.

It was already a splendidly peaceful scene that Grant surveyed as he reached his thirty-seventh birthday in February of 1853, but the preacher had never been in a tranquil situation before. The existence of enemies had become rather tantalizing to his spirit—the Missourians during Zion's Camp, the reverend doctors during his missions, the apostates in Philadelphia, and the runaway judges in Washington. It seemed that he had always been away, fighting for the Saints, always idealized in his mind as the best people in the world. Now they were before him and around him, growing in numbers and inevitably showing the flaws of their humanity. Jedediah Grant began to be troubled over that reality. He wanted none of their humanity, only their purity. His thunder was now upon the Mormons themselves, who had inherited, he told them in April conference, "all the good in Heaven and on earth."[8] There could be no excuse for anything short of perfection in unity and grace. "All Saints," he continued, "should see to clearing the inside of the vessels, like Moroni of old, and carry out the law of God."[9] Brigham Young listened from behind. His young friend was a fine preacher. They could use more of him. Repentance and reform were always good for a righteous people.[10]

At the 1853 celebration of the Fourth of July, Mayor Jedediah Grant, hero of the recent fight against the runaway judges, presented a long toast:

> To the Goddess of Liberty—May she be protected by the American eagle and all her brood—May a bevy of Zephyrs escort and plant her in every land; there may the tree of life vegetate and bear fruit that all her admirers may eat thereof and live forever.
>
> To the Demon of Oppression—May the America Eagle pick out his eyes, and the young ravens of the Valley eat them; may a bevy of whirlwinds escort and bury him in the great desert of North America—May the Upas tree vegetate and flourish on his grave that its poisonous breath may kill all who attempt to resurrect him.[11]

As anxious as he was in the hot days of 1853 to bless freedom and curse oppression, Grant could not ignore the signs all about him that the Mormons had been taking a bit too much liberty with their religion. Some had even seditiously suggested that, because the great charismatic events that had characterized the Pentecostal days of the Church in Ohio were no longer in evidence, Brigham's right to leadership was suspect and that perhaps there ought to be more mystical happenings among the chosen people. As a result there had arisen in Salt Lake City and in some outlying areas a rebellious attitude that suggested that somehow the practical religion of Brigham was not the charismatic faith of Joseph, so maybe Brigham did not really wear a prophet's mantle. This heresy frightened the autocracy, not only because it violated the rules and covenants of the Church but also because it flew directly in the face of Brigham Young's authority to control the course of doctrine and practice within the Church. On August 7, 1853, Grant mounted the stand in the Bowery to preach a sermon in which he would attack squarely the marshaled forces of chaos and evil as they subverted the unity and order of Mormonism. Apparently believing that the bloodstream of the body of the Saints needed purification, he openly fought dangerous notions that the Restoration had lost its way under its new leadership. The Church, he maintained, could and ought to change, but only under the laws set down upon the rule of the priesthood. That must be the unchanging order of the universe.

Talk not to me about the uniformity of nature; where is it to be found upon this earth, among men, in the mountains, among the valleys, in the ocean, or among the streams that water the land?

Before you censure my views upon this subject, look at mother earth, at the ocean, at the rocks, at the planets that bespangle the blue vault of heaven; in short, at nature in all her works, which you will find stamped with the insignia of continual change. But pass on.

You look and you see the Church driven from the earth; you see it left without a prophet, without a Seer, without Apostles, and without the voice of inspiration. You hear the professed ministers of Christ teaching the benighted multitude, that the day when angels administer to men had ceased; that the sacred Urim and Thummim is lost; that the holy Priesthood is no longer needed, and the sacred place where they offered sacrifices for Israel is gone, all are gone.

In this way, century after century passed away; nation rose against nation, and kingdom against kingdom; nations and kingdoms rose, and in their turn fell in succession, to give place to others, while nature, in her convulsive throes, shook the earth from centre to circumference. Pass on still, and do you look for uniformity?

But says one, "You Mormons tell us, that in the age in which we live there is a work commenced on the earth that will entirely eclipse every other dispensation, and usher in a day of righteousness, overcome Lucifer the arch deceiver; a day wherein he is to be bound, and thrust into the pit, and lose his power; when the earth will be redeemed, and appear in her primeval bloom and beauty, and man shall cease to war against his fellow man; when the convulsions of the earth shall cease—the earthquakes cease to bellow, the thunder cease to roar, and the lightning cease to become destructive, and to mar the face of nature, spreading terror and dismay among animated beings; when the earth and all nature shall become calm and tranquil, and the glory of God shall be among men."

"Why bless me, with the exception of a few points," say statesmen, "your society had decidedly changed from what it was in the days of Mr. Smith. Because of the peculiar traits of his character, it could not have possibly existed under his government; we are glad to see the decided improvement that has been made under the administration of Mr. Young." This is their language. They suppose that the "Mormons" have turned a somerset, have apostatized, and altered their character and creed as a people. I always take great pleasure in such honorable men, and wise men, that that which they call "Mormonism" changeth not. It is the same now as in the days of Joseph.

"And do you Mormons in the Valley believe and advocate the same doctrines that Joseph Smith did?"

Yes, sir, precisely, not one practical point of the religion has changed; we as a people may be fluctuating, but our religion changeth not.[12]

The tone of Grant's sermon made plain that he had encountered much smugness in the East relative to the "new" Mormonism under Brigham Young. This was trouble enough, but he had also become quite offended at having spent his soul in the defense of the Saints only to come among them and find them "fluctuating" in the faith and falling prey to the very same sophistries he had encountered among unsympathetic Gentiles. Taking spiritualism as an example,[13] Grant then turned his guns on those who sought to resist the power of Young and his lieutenants in the leadership of the Church. After all, maintained the preacher, it was that very hegemony that gave Mormonism its deep appeal, its power, and its consistency.

Says one, "I like it very well, if you did not gather together, and suffer Brigham Young to lead you like one man."

In that consists the beauty of our religion; and he can wield us as a people, like God does the armies of heaven. He can wield us to preach, to pray, or to fight. We have everything spiritual, temporal, and natural, as it should be. We believe it is just as much our religion to talk about wheat, plowing, sowing, and gathering in at harvest time, it is just as much our religion as anything connected with it.

"Pertaining to the Mormons away off in the Valley, they never will be much anyhow," says one. They used to tell Joseph Smith he could never accomplish anything, for he had neither money nor friends. They tell us we cannot accomplish much, "for everybody says you are crazy followers of Joe Smith, and believers in the Book of Mormon; therefore what can you do?" We will do just as Jesus Christ said the mustard seed would do. If you will read and learn what it did, you will then know something about the future history of "Mormonism." You will ascertain just what we will do.

"But do you really believe your Church is the kingdom Daniel spoke of—the stone that should be hewn out of the mountains without hands?" I suppose he might have said with hands just as well, for it is no matter whether it was hewn out with or without; suffice it to say, the result of it is what we see; no matter how it came out of the mountain. What does the historian represent by that stone? Something that would begin to roll, and smite the great image on its feet, and roll forth until it should fill the whole earth. If you want to know what "Mormonism" is, it is that which will roll forth until it fills the whole earth.

Do we expect to find uniformity at this time? No sir; but we look for mobs, and the very scum of hell to boil over. Do we look for a privilege to fold our hands and sing lullaby baby, etc.? No; we expect the rage of all hell to be aimed at us to overthrow us; we expect mobs, and troubles with the Indians. The earth will be rent by earthquakes, and a thousand thunders will utter their voices, and make the ears of mortals tingle, and their hearts to fail within them; and the voice of God will be heard, that will pierce the wicked to the very core.

Do the Latter Day Saints expect to settle in peace? MARK you, your peace has not come yet, for Lucifer is not yet bound; and while the earth is fearfully convulsed because of the wickedness on its face, the nations will gather themselves and make an effort to wrest the kingdom from the Saints, and destroy them root and branch.

We are not coping with a few people here and there, but with the world, with all the enemies of God, with all hell, and with the devil and his host. That is "Mormonism."

You need not wonder that we raise stout boys in the mountains, for we want children of the right blood; we do not want a scrubby breed here. Men of "Mormon" blood are not afraid to die. The men that tremble, and whose hearts go pit-a-pat because they have got to die, are not worth a picayune. A man that refused to walk up in the track, no matter what comes, and steadily press forward, though there should be a lion in the way, is not of "Mormon" grit. That was the grit Joseph had; and when he spoke, he spoke by the power of an endless Priesthood, which was upon him; and that is the power by which Brigham speaks. When he stood up in the majesty of his Priesthood, and rebuked the judges here, I know some of our milk and water folks thought all the fat was in the fire. "Brother Brigham has gone rather too far; he might have spoken a little milder than he did; I think it would have been much better," &c. This was the language of some hearts; and I feel to say, damn all such poor pussyism. When a man of God speaks, let him speak what he pleases, and let all Israel say, Amen.[14]

As Grant preached sermon after sermon in the following weeks, he expanded on the same themes—unity, obedience, and perfection. In this he was an echo of Brigham Young and Heber Kimball, but the electric quality of his didactic made him a separate entity, a fiery personality known as Brother Jeddy, the Sledgehammer of Brigham, Mormon Thunder. Adding to his oratorical abilities was a practical view of life and of the Saints that suggested determination and a no-nonsense approach to societal progress, at the base of which was hard work. Perhaps confusing the pioneer quest for survival and the first bloom of enthusiasm for material objects as apostasy, Grant wandered far and wide throughout Utah preaching the gospel of hard work and a moral philosophy that he believed went hand-in-hand with his sense of Mormon destiny and mission. In his mind, the whole of the struggle was not only between good and evil, but between Mormonism and an inferior morality that was bent on weakening the Church's influence in the territory. Like many other leaders of the time, Grant held the Church to be a homogeneous body that encircled known religious truth. If the people would just adhere to the gospel and work hard they would prosper both in spirit and body, but there must be a total surrender of conscience and intellect to the will of Mormon teaching. After all, said Grant as he preached his persuasive logic across the high air of the Great Basin, hard work and obedience were all the Saints had going for them. "Other communities have gold and silver to aid them," he once said, "but this people have to accomplish all they do accomplish, by the bone and sinew alone, which the Almighty has given them."[15]

Through the winter of 1853-54, Grant practiced what he preached. Besides farming a plot in Davis County to sustain his growing family, he served again as speaker of the House of Representatives in the territorial legislature, spent long days in the mayor's office governing the bulging young city, and preached nearly every week at the Sunday tabernacle meetings in the Bowery. Being involved also in ecclesiastical duties as one of the Seven Presidents of Seventy, he devoted increasing amounts of time to the organization and direction of the various quorums of seventy as the Church institutionalized itself in the valleys of the mountains.[16]

Because of his high station in the community, Grant frequently mingled with guests at social activities, where he kept an ear constantly cocked, making certain to be aware of the various currents in the stream of Salt Lake City life. Among the persistent swirls in the early days of 1854 was the nuisance of spiritualism. Grant had an answer for that phenomenon and an unequivocal one at that. "I am more or less familiar with the doings of the Spirit Rappers," he said at the beginning of a sermon on February 19, 1854, explaining that they had been in vogue the last time he had visited New York and Philadelphia.

> I am satisfied now, and was then, that they are manifestations of spirits; and startling are the sentiments, developments, and doctrines they have made known. It has been treated as a bubble upon the wave that soon would burst asunder; but I am satisfied the result of the manifestations of the spirit (wicked spirits) will be to combine their forces in as systematic an order as they are capable of, to successfully resist the Priesthood upon the earth.
>
> I am aware that even some of the Latter-day Saints are slow to believe in relation to the power of Lucifer, the son of the morning, who was thrust from the heavens to the earth; and they have been slow to believe in relation to the spirits that are associated with him; but from the first revelations of the Almighty to brother Joseph Smith, not only revelations in relation to the deep things of the kingdom of God, and the high things of heaven, and the depths of hell, but revelations showing him the power of Lucifer, the opposite to good, that he might be aware of the strength of his opponent, and the opponent of the Almighty—I say, from perusing these revelations, I have always been specially impressed with the doctrine relating to the power of Satan, as well as with the doctrines relating to the power of God.
>
> I wish to come down to our own day, for you know I am fond of rooting,

grubbing, building, fencing, and doing the things needed right here at home. Let us then confine our remarks to this dispensation, when the Prophet Joseph Smith was visited by an holy angel, clad in robes of light, who authorized him to sound the trump of the Gospel of peace, and receive the sacred records from the earth, and the Urim and Thummin, and who laid hands upon him and gave him the Holy Ghost, and authorized him to baptize for the remission of sins, and organize the kingdom of God on the earth. What do we see at this time? We see the manifestations of the power of Satan immediately after the revelations of the angel to Joseph. For instance, there were spirit mediums in Kirtland, when the Church was first organized there by brother Parley P. Pratt and others; but when Joseph went with the Priesthood, the devil had to leave, for he [Joseph] had learned the power of Lucifer; and Joseph organized the Church, established the Priesthood, and set everything right.

When Joseph Smith was alive, his declaration to me was as the voice of Almighty God. Why? Because he had the Priesthood of God on the earth; the Priesthood that is without father, without mother, without beginning of days or end of years, which is God's authority, the eternal power and right of the government of God upon the earth. I was subject to that government in the days of Joseph.

When the family organization was revealed from heaven—the patriarchal order of God, and Joseph began, on the right and on the left, to add to his family, what a quaking there was in Israel. Says one brother to another, "Joseph says all covenants are done away, and none are binding but the new covenants; now suppose Joseph should come and say he wanted your wife, what would you say to that?" "I would tell him to go to hell." This was the spirit of many in the early days of this Church.

If Joseph had a right to dictate me in relation to salvation, in relation to a hereafter, he had a right to dictate me in relation to all my earthly affairs, in relation to the treasures of the earth, and in relation to the earth itself. He had a right to dictate in relation to the cities of the earth, to the natives of the earth, and in relation to everything on land and on sea. That is what he had a right to do, if he had any right at all. If he did not have that right, he did not have the Priesthood of God, he did not have the endless Priesthood that emanates from an eternal being. A Priesthood that is clipped, and lacks length, is not the Priesthood of God; if it lacks depth, it is not the Priesthood of God; for the Priesthood in ancient times extended over the wide world, and coped with the universe, and had a right to govern and control the inhabitants thereof, to regulate them, give them laws, and execute those laws. That power looked like the Priesthood of God. This same Priesthood has been given to Joseph Smith, and has been handed down to his successors.

I do not care how many devils rap, it is no trouble to me. I say, rap away, and give as many revelations as you please, whether you are good spirits or bad ones, it does not trouble my cranium. Rap away, for I trust in the anchor of my soul that is sure and steadfast, in the Priesthood of God upon the earth.

What would a man of God say, who felt aright, when Joseph asked him for his money? He would say, "Yes, and I wish I had more to help to build up the kingdom of God." Or if he came and said, "I want your wife?" "O yes," he would say, "here she is, there are plenty more."

There is another main thread connected with this, that I have not brought out. You know in fishing with the hook and line, if you draw out suddenly on the line when you have got a large trout, you may break your line; you must therefore angle a little, and manage your prize carefully. I would ask you if Jehovah has not in all ages tried His people by the power of Lucifer and his associates; and on the other hand, has He not tried them and proved them by His Prophets? Did the Lord actually want Abraham to kill Isaac? Did the Prophet Joseph want every man's wife he asked for? He did not, but in that thing was the grand thread of the Priesthood developed. The grand object in view was to try the people of God, to see what was in them. If such a man of God should come to me and say, "I want your gold and silver, or your wives," I should say, "Here they are, I wish I had more to give you, take all I have got." A man who has got the Spirit of God, and the light of eternity in him, has no trouble about such matters.

If ever you are brought into the presence of God, and exalted to a seat in His celestial kingdom, it will be by virtue of the Holy Priesthood, therefore you have got to be proved, not only by being tempted by the devil, but the Priesthood will try you—it will try you to the core. If one thing won't try you, something else will be adopted, until you are like the passive clay in the hands of the Potter. If the Lord our God does not see fit to let the devil loose upon you, and mob you, He will employ some other means to try you as in a crucible, to prove you as gold is tried seven times in the furnace.

The world philosophizes about the "Mormons," about their leaders, and the life they are living. There are a thousand conjectures among them in relation to the "Mormons." The grand secret is told in a few words; the fact is, the Almighty God has spoken from the heavens, sent heavenly messengers, and organized His Church, restored the Holy Priesthood, established His government on the earth, and exerted His power to extend it, and send forth His word. And that Priesthood understands the principles and motives by which men are actuated, and it understands the workings of the devil on the earth; that Priesthood knows how to govern, when to strike, and when not to strike.

If this Priesthood is upon the earth, and you are controlled thereby, and listen to its counsels, you will be united as one people.

Let the devils rap, then, and let them talk, and mutter, and have their mediums; what do I care, so long as the Priesthood is upon the earth, and the Apostleship is upon the earth, and the government of God, and the light and influence of the Holy Ghost, are upon the earth? Can they shake the Saints? No. But let a man lose the Spirit of God, and depart from this Church, and from the men that hold the Priesthood of God on the earth, and I have no doubt that Lucifer will reveal a great many truths to him, and teach and advocate principles and sentiments that will agree with doctrines of this Church. And they will even imitate Joseph Smith's hand writing, and the hand writing of brother Hyrum, of Bishop Partridge, and of Bishop Whitney, and others; and they will give you flaming revelations, and the light they emit will blaze like a comet.

Now Lucifer has philosophy enough and religion enough to suffer his agents to run along with the truth hand in hand, and make himself appear like an angel of light, and teach hundreds of true principles, if he can only thereby get you to swallow one item of false doctrine. But the grand story is, the devil may rage as long as he pleases, and use all the cunning and craft that he may, yet he never can overreach those who hold the keys to the Priesthood, nor succeed in deceiving them. This Joseph taught the people, but they were slow to believe. But now the energies of the people move as one man; and if they want to build a Temple, they can build it, and whatever they want to accomplish they can do.

The Priesthood is a power we should respect, reverence, and obey, no matter in whose hands it is. Let Lucifer mix in truths with error, and work great signs and wonders to deceive the very elect, but it is not possible. Why? Because they have learned the Priesthood, and they possess the power thereof that cannot be shaken. Let the Rappers go ahead, then, for it is not possible for them to deceive the elect of God; and let the witch of Endor, and all other witches and wizards, with the prince and power of the air at their head, do their best, if we keep the commandments of God we shall continually soar far above their power and influence.

I want to have nothing to do with Satan, I desire not to shake hands with him, nor to do anything that will bring me in contact with him, for he is powerful, and if he once gets you in his grasp and shakes you, you will think you are less than a grasshopper. Let us rally around the standard of God, and when we are in the circle of truth, then let the devil and the enemies of the Church of God fire their loudest guns, and wage their war, and marshal their strength, yet, armed with the armor of righteousness, clothed with the Priesthood and generalship of the Almighty, we shall successfully resist, and triumphantly conquer Satan and all his allied forces of the earth and hell. They will then find out whether Joseph had a right to rule this earth by the power of the Priesthood. They will then find out that the "Mormons," notwithstanding their curious bumps, for they have got some curious bumps, are authorized to preach the Gospel of God, gather Israel, build up Zion, bind Lucifer with a chain, and establish the reign of peace on earth.

My prayer is that the Saints may understand that they are safe as long as they listen to the Priesthood authorized of heaven, are united in one, and not divided into clans, but become one great clan, under one head. Then let all the clanism of the world rally against us, and we are as firm as the rock of ages, that supports the throne of Jehovah.[17]

On March 11, 1854, Dr. Willard Richards, confidant of Joseph and second counselor to Brigham, died at the age of forty-nine. Though there may have been some "clans," or factions, developing among the Saints according to Grant's fears, the entire community united in its sorrow over the passing of Brother Willard. Grant undoubtedly had thoughts about his own association with the doctor, particularly during those days of trepidation in the summer of 1844 when Jedediah had gone as his messenger to the Twelve in the East. That event now seemed far in the past, and the passing of Richards seemed to have little to do with the future of Jedediah Grant.

The next day, Grant delivered another sermon. He did not mention in its course the death of the second counselor, nor did he deviate from his now-common themes of unity and repentance among the Saints. This discourse of March 12, 1854, began on level ground, discussing the power of the Spirit in effecting conversions and on the importance of keeping the Holy Ghost as a companion. But gradually and characteristically it changed. As the lean preacher began to wring white vapor from the war clouds in his mind, he moved into a subject that would make that particular sermon the most famous, the most quoted and misquoted, discourse of his career. Yet if it had not been for the death of Willard Richards, and the meaning it had for the destiny of Jedediah Grant, the March 12 address might not have taken on the degree of notoriety that it did. Apart from any other consideration, however, this address represented an intriguing response to a community much divided over what Mormonism was and what it should be. The preacher's fiery and shocking words of that cold day in March provide, as one scholar of Mormonism put it, "a revealing picture of the attitude and mind set of those whose identification of themselves as a Chosen People living in a Promised Land was overpowering."[18]

Now in relation to a passage in the Book of the Doctrine and Covenants. It is written in the Appendix of the Book of Doctrine and Covenants Paragraph 10, that the Church of Jesus Christ of Latter Day Saints "believe that all religious societies have a right to deal with their members for disorderly conduct according to the rules and regulations of such societies, provided that such dealings be for fellowship and good standing; but we do not believe that any religious society has authority to try men on the right of property or life; to take from them this world's goods, or put them in jeopardy either in life or limb; neither to inflict any physical punishment upon them. They can only excommunicate them from their society, and withdraw from their fellowship."

This was written by Oliver Cowdery. He believed it was right, and I know it was adopted when Joseph Smith was absent on a journey; but whether he sanctioned it or not I never did know. But in the ancient church, Paul refers to covenant breakers. What disposition ought the people of God to make of covenant breakers?—they who are led by the meek and quiet Spirit of God; who trust in Jehovah, and watch and pray, and partake of the sacrament of the Lord's Supper; who do right, and have kept their baptismal vow;—I say what ought such a people to do with covenant breakers? "Why," says one, "forgive them to be sure." Very good, but what else ought they to do? What does the Apostle say? He says they are worthy of death. I wonder whether he was really in earnest, or happened to get into a wild freak and advanced principles and sentiments that were incorrect? I am inclined to believe his decision was a correct one.

Then what ought this meek people, who keep the commandments of God do unto them? "Why," says one, "they ought to pray to the Lord to kill them." I want to know if you would wish the Lord to come down and do all your dirty work?—Many of the Latter Day Saints will pray, and petition, and supplicate the Lord to do a thousand things they themselves would be ashamed to do. I would like men never to ask Jesus Christ the Lamb of God, his Father, their associates, or the angels of the high heavens, to do anything they would not be willing to do themselves.

When a man prays for a thing, he ought to be willing to perform it himself. But if the Latter Day Saints should put to death the covenant breakers, it would try the faith of the very meek, just, and pious ones among them, and it would cause a great deal of whining in Israel.

In the days of Moses for certain crimes they were to bring the guilty persons before the congregation, and each man and woman were required to bring a stone to throw at the person worthy of death.

Then there was another old commandment.—The Lord God commanded them not to pity the person whom they killed; but to execute the law of God upon persons worthy of death. This should be done by the entire congregation showing no pity. I have thought there would have to be quite a revolution among the Mormons, before such a commandment could be obeyed completely by them. The Mormons have a great deal of sympathy. For instance, if they can get a man before the tribunal administering the law of the land, and succeed in getting a rope round his neck, and having him hung up like a dead dog, it is all right; but if the Church and Kingdom of God should step forth and execute the law of God, O! what a burst of Mormon sympathy it would cause. I wish we were in a situation favorable to our doing that which is justifiable before God, without any contaminating influences of Gentile amalgamation, laws, and traditions, that the people of God might lay the axe to the root of the tree, and every tree that bringeth not forth good fruit might be hewn down.

"What! do you believe that people would do right, and keep the law of God, by actually putting to death the transgressors?" Putting to death transgressors would exhibit the law of God, no difference by whom it was done;

that is my opinion.

You talk of doings of different governments, the United States if you please. What do they do with traitors?—what mode do they adopt to punish traitors? Do traitors to that Government forfeit their lives? Examine also the doings of other earthly governments upon this point, and you find the same practice universal; I am not aware that there are any exceptions. But people will look into books of theology, and argue that the people of God have a right to try people for fellowship, but they have no right to try them on property or life. That makes the devil laugh, saying, I have got them on a hook now; they can cut them off, and I will put eight or ten spirits, worse than they are, into their tabernacles, and send them back to mob them. What a fine thing it was that I got Oliver Cowdery to write that piece of law, and introduce it into the Book of Doctrine and Covenants!

But if the Government of God on earth, and Eternal Priesthood, with the sanction of High Heaven, in the midst of all his people, has passed sentence on certain sins when they appear in a person, has not the people of God a right to carry out that part of his law as well as any other portion of it? It is their right to baptize a sinner to save him, and it is also their right to kill a sinner to save him, when he commits those crimes that can only be atoned for by shedding his blood. If the Lord God forgives sins by baptism, and there is another law that certain sins cannot be atoned for by baptism, but by the shedding of the blood of the sinner, query, whether the people of God be overreaching the mark, if they should execute the law to save such? They used to do it anciently. We would not kill a man, of course, unless we killed him to save him. We would not baptize a man unless we baptized him to save him. We would not lay hands upon a man that he might receive the Holy Spirit, only for the salvation of the man. And every act of men having the priesthood upon the earth, should be for the salvation of the people.

I am aware that there are a great many strange things connected with religion. In one light they are odd, in another they are strange. For instance, Jesus at certain times was unusually meek, lowly, humble, condescending, administering to the sick, bearing the infirmities of the people, and weeping over their distresses. At another time he was whipping them out of the temple, calling them a generation of vipers, hypocrites, &c.

Br. Joseph Smith was operated upon in the same manner. At times he was mild, meek, and lowly in spirit; and at other times, when the Spirit of the Almighty rested mightily upon him, requiring him to chastise the people, or rebuke any servant of God, his words then cut to the centre.—Is not this the case with all men of God possessed of the Eternal Priesthood? Ask the best men in the world—the quorum of the Twelve if you please—how they felt when Joseph was inspired to whip them? I know how I have felt. Ask others how they have felt when Br. Brigham has considered it necessary to chastise them. Look at the power, strength, and might that is in him when the Holy Ghost is upon him, and the spirit of chastisement and reproof. Men of God under this influence have made their friends quake from the centre to the circumference of their bodies.

The gospel is adapted to the capacity of man in a state of heathenish darkness; and when he repents, and when he is baptized, and when he is confirmed, and receives the Holy Ghost; and it is adapted to his capacity when he arrives at the state of manhood, during all his progression. The ordinances of the gospel, the keys of the Holy Priesthood, the signs, covenants, and charges thereof, and all the ordinances of God, will keep a man on the stretch continually. When people become discontented, and murmur against a man of God, it is a sure sign of apostacy. They say, "O give me ancient Mormonism; give me that which I first heard, when repentance, faith, and baptism for the remission of sins, and the laying on of hands was preached, and the healing of the sick by the same process, and the gift of tongues; when this comprised the whole of the religion of Christ it was very good." This appears to be one of the finest wishes of the world; but such people are on the eve of apostasy. The laws of God keep men on the advance movement.

I know br. Orson Pratt says we shall at some time come to a dead stand, but that time is a long way off, I do assure you. I never want it to come, or to believe that it ever will come. When a man wants the first principles of Mormonism, the first things which he heard, and wants no new principles, no new revelation, no further advancement, but desires a dead stand, saying I have got enough, and I want no more, he is pretty sure to apostatize.

A man that is godlike, never can attain to too much; he never can think of too much. His mind is not able to stretch wide enough to embrace all the great things of God; but the revelations of eternity are continually opened up to him, and the hidden wisdom of God shines forth upon his intellect, enabling him to explore the heights, the depths, the lengths, and the breadths of the intelligence of the Framer of the Universe, and the Creator of all its fullness, who can give power after power, endowment after endowment, ordinance after ordinance, and priesthood after priesthood, without end. Give me the man who will advance in the line of his duty; who is filled with the Holy Ghost; who will strive to fulfil the end of his creation, and who will not say it is enough, I want no more thirsting after the knowledge of God, for the fountains that flowed from his presence is exhausted.

I do not know but br. Orson Pratt is right in his conjecture; he is a philosopher, and a great reasoner; but it is owing to my weakness perhaps, that I cannot see that we shall ever come to a dead stand. I have an idea that progression is eternal; it may be my weakness, and the narrowness of my understanding, that leads me to this conclusion. The verbal instructions we receive from time to time are good, and refreshing to the mind. We get line upon line; I live on line upon line all that time; it is just as good to me as the sayings of the Bible, Book of Mormon, or Book of Doctrine and Covenants. I would like to see better revelation from those books than President Brigham Young, Heber C. Kimball, and the Twelve, have preached from this stand. It tastes to me just as sweet as the revelations contained in those books; their teachings are as delicious to me as anything contained in any of the written revelations of God.

We have line upon line, line upon line, here a little and there a little. We are advancing and growing in grace, and in the knowledge of truth. When a man undertakes to contract and narrow in his views, he ceases to grow in grace and in the knowledge of truth. That which is narrow is not Mormonism. That which is limited is not Mormonism! Mormonism is not like the bed that a man cannot stretch himself upon, or the cover that a man cannot wrap himself in.

What have I to do with the first principles taught to me? You talk of the endowments that will make you acquainted with God. You talk of his ordinances; but as you advance, you will take upon yourselves more responsibilities, and covenants. When children first go to school, the responsibility on them is light; but as they advance, and become acquainted with principle after principle, doctrine after doctrine, precept after precept, it increases, and they are made more perfect, and prepared by their education and training to occupy an important station in their sphere.—So it is with the people of God. If you shall thus advance, and then turn and trample the holy commandments of God under your feet, and break your sacred and solemn covenants, and become traitors to the people of God, would you not be worthy of death? I think you would.[19]

The teaching of blood atonement in the stark words of Jedediah Grant, being so foreign to the American ideal of the separation of church and state, have undeniable shocking power. Moreover, the Saints were supposed to be inheritors of the earth, and were not the meek to inherit the earth? Yet here was a rising star in the Mormon hierarchy standing before a congregation calling for capital punishment against those members of his religious order who had broken their covenants. Having taken the same covenants with God, he believed explicitly in their meaning. He could not countenance the slack that was falling in the line of truth, which brought him to the point of hurling even such a thunderbolt as blood atonement into the midst of the Saints. In his mind the "restoration of all things" was literal, and the March 12 sermon was an illumination of this one idea in his conceptualization of the Restoration. Antagonists of Mormonism have gleefully used this speech to bludgeon the Church, but their renditions of it have rarely given Grant the privilege of finishing and more clearly explaining the practical meaning of his words.

> Do you think it would be any sin to kill me if I were to break my covenants? Let every man preach for himself; I am preaching my own faith to day. Do you believe you would kill me if I broke the covenants of God, and you had the Spirit of God? Yes; and the more Spirit of God I had, the more I should strive to save your soul by spilling your blood, when you had committed sin that could not be remitted by baptism.
>
> There are principles to suit every state to which we shall advance, through all the stages as we rise in the spheres of intelligence, and there are principles to govern us while in those spheres; consequently I want the Saints to understand one or two real practical points as to what they have a right to do.
>
> "But" says one, "will not Uncle Sam play the devil with you?" We are next to him; Uncle Sam is a part of us, and we are a part of Uncle Sam, and it is Uncle Sam and us together. We have a right to worship God according to the dictates of our own conscience, and have a right to carry out our religion; and there is nothing in the Constitution and laws of the United States to the contrary.
>
> May the God of Israel bless you in the name of Jesus: Amen.[20]

To the Saints who heard it, that speech was just a natural part of rambunctious Brother Jeddy. No one scrambled to protect himself from the seventy's murderous intentions, because he had none. He just wanted the Saints to be the best people in the world, to do right. The image of capital punishment for sin was Old Testament anyway, and the prophets were again walking the earth, demanding perfection and unbending allegiance to a fearsome God. Within the context of 1854 Utah, Grant's March discourse rattled windows and doors, but it probably killed no one.[21]

This sermon on the subject by no means represented the origin of the doctrine of blood atonement, although it certainly restated it in graphic phrases that would have a significant impact on the Saints. Blood atonement first emerged during the Missouri crisis, a period of religious civil war, emotional outburst, and lost dignity for the Saints. Both the Mormons and the Missourians had been convinced of each other's culpability before God. The uncompromising hostility of the struggle for the rich farmlands of Missouri left the Saints scarred and resentful of their enemies, the most dangerous of whom were their own apostates. In the time since Missouri, the complex idea of blood atonement, with its Old Testament flavorings, had become intrinsic to the pulsating energy of the Reformation. The cosmic philosophy that shaped the Mormon character encompassed a familiar theme: life is brief, fate harsh, nature ruthless, and the past a tragedy, but all are necessary for salvation. If reality holds neither joy nor peace, eternity will by some great natural law produce a converse measure of triumph. In the hands of Grant and his colleagues, the concept of blood atonement was but one of the phenomena that was to wash away the guilt feelings of those who were responsible for violating the Mormon covenant with God. Though the impact of blood atonement was shattering and provided a powerful stimulus to more violent emotions and preaching, it seldom found its own harsh reality in Mormon society. It never was a physical force that administered secular justice with a voice of fire. Rather it was a religious exaltation of words that attempted to discipline the wayward back into spiritual conformity.

A few days later, Jedediah Grant was back on the stand again, preaching at the Bowery on the afternoon of April 2. News had reached the West that war had erupted in the Crimea. Moreover, the winds blowing in from the East brought dusty images of increasing sectional strife in the United States. In Grant's millenarian hands, the tenor of the times created frightful omens, and at the same time, hopeful signs in the heavens.

The time has been, that even many of our Elders, when the sun was retiring in the west, looked for some sign in the heavens—for some flaming sword unsheathed, or some visible display of the power of the Almighty, by which they might know of the near approach of the Son of God. Others have feared greatly they would not live to see the fulfilment of the prophecies of brother Joseph, brother Brigham, and others; they have felt very anxious indeed about it. But I am convinced, that the class of Saints which have been so struck with anxiety and fearfulness, may now dismiss their fears, and dispense with all their anxiety, in relation to the predicted events that are coming upon the earth, for they are rolling in with such rapidity—they are rushing upon the astonished world with such velocity, as to exceed even our most sanguine expectations.

The things that are transpiring upon the earth are certainly as great and as momentous as any of the revelations hold forth, or as any of the predictions of the Prophet Joseph have foretold.

Notwithstanding this display of the power of God in fulfilling His word, we need not expect the eyes of the inhabitants of the earth to be opened to understand the meaning of the astounding events that are transpiring around them, for one of the marked signs of the last days is, the blindness of the people; we are told they should have eyes and see not, and ears but hear not, and hearts but understand not. If in the days of Jesus this was true of the Jews and surrounding nations, it is doubly so now in relation to the nations with which we are acquainted.

Though the fulfilment of the words of the Prophets is clear and visible to us as the noonday sun in its splendor, yet the people of the world are blinded thereto; they do not comprehend nor discern the hand of the Lord. The Saints who live in the Spirit, walk by the Spirit, and are governed by the counsels of the Almighty, can see the working of the Lord, not only in our midst—not only in Utah Territory, in the midst of the people of God who assemble in this Tabernacle—it is not only in this latter day capacity we view the work of God, but we let our minds stretch abroad to creations' utmost extent, and we can see the hand of the Lord in all the events of earth. We see it in the revolutions of our own continent; we see it in the scattering and scourging of the house of Israel; in the fading away of nations, on the right and on the left; in the present commotion in our own nation; in the broils and contentions between the South and the North; in short, we see it in all the events connected with our own and other nations living on the continent of North and

South America. And when the mind's eye stretches abroad across the mighty deep, throughout Europe, we see the hand of the Lord visibly at work there, not only in the spread of the Gospel, in the prosperity of the people of God, and in the proclamation of the eternal principles of truth through the agency of the Elders of Israel, but in the warcloud gathering black around, dyeing the ocean with human gore, and drenching the solid earth with blood.

We see it in the preparations of war, and the framing of treaties of peace among strong nations. The world is in commotion, and the hearts of men fail them for fear of the impending storm that threatens to enshroud all nations in its black mantle. Treaties of peace may be made, and war will stop for a season, but there are certain decrees of the Gods, and certain bounds fixed, and laws and edicts passed the high courts of heaven, beyond which the nations cannot pass; and when the Almighty decrees the wicked shall slay the wicked, strong nations may interfere, peace conventions may become rife in the world and exert their influence to sheath the sword of war, and make treaties of peace to calm the troubled surface of all Europe, to no effect; the war cloud is still booming o'er the heavens, darkening the earth, and threatening the world with desolation.

Why is it that the Latter day Saints are perfectly calm and serene among all the convulsions of the earth—the turmoils, strife, war, pestilence, famine, and distress of nations? It is because the spirit of prophecy has made known to us that such things would actually transpire upon the earth. We understand it, and view it in its true light. We have learned it by the visions of the Almighty—by that spirit of intelligence that searches out all things, even the deep things of God.

Can the wise men of Europe tell the result of the present war between Russia and Turkey with the allied powers? No, they cannot. If the present war should be suspended for a time, can they tell you when the next will break out, and what will be the result of it? No, they cannot. But if you will listen to the revelations of God through the spirit of prophecy, and to the servants of God, you may learn it all with certainty.

Three days before the Prophet Joseph started for Carthage, I well remember his telling us we should see the fulfilment of the words of Jesus upon the earth, where he says the father shall be against the son, and the son against the father; the mother against the daughter, and the daughter against the mother; the mother-in-law against the daughter-in-law, and the daughter-in-law against the mother-in-law; and when a man's enemies shall be those of his own household.

The Prophet stood in his own house when he told several of us of the night the visions of heaven were opened to him, in which he saw the American continent drenched in blood, and he saw nation rising up against nation. He also saw the father shed the blood of the son, and the son the blood of the father; the mother put to death the daughter, and the daughter the mother; and natural affection forsook the hearts of the wicked; for he saw that the Spirit of God should be withdrawn from the inhabitants of the earth, in consequence of which there should be blood upon the face of the whole earth, except among the people of the Most High. The Prophet gazed upon the scene his vision presented, until his heart sickened, and he besought the Lord to close it up again.

When we hear of war in foreign lands—when we hear of the revolutions among the nations afar off, we necessarily infer that distresses incident to war and the hottest of the battle will not come nigh unto us. It is natural for man to make favorable conclusions as to his own safety, when danger threatens, but the Prophet saw in the vision, that war and distress of nations will not only occur in Europe, in Asia, and in the islands of the sea, but he saw it upon the American Continent—in the region of country where he first introduced the doctrine of the Son of God; so we may look for calamity in our own borders, in our own nation, as well as in the nations of foreign climes.

Some think, because of the peculiar situation of the country of the United States—the government being so well organized, little or no difficulty will ever come upon this continent, notwithstanding the European wars. Allow me to tell you in relation to that—when the Spirit of the Lord is powerfully manifested in any of the Elders of Israel, the first thing that is presented to his mind is the shedding of the blood of the Prophet, and those who did the deed.

It is no matter how much they deal in compromised measures, or how often they try to adjust difficulties that thicken around them—it is a stern fact that the people of the United States have shed the blood of the Prophets, driven out the Saints of God, rejected the Priesthood, and set at naught the holy Gospel; and the result of rejecting the Gospel has been, in every age, a visitation from the chastening hand of the Almighty—which chastisement will be administered in proportion to the magnitude and enormity of their crimes.

Consequently I look for the Lord to use His whip on the refractory son called "Uncle Sam"; I expect to see him chastised among the first of the nations. I think Uncle Sam is one of the Lord's boys that He will take the rod to first, and make him dance nimbly to his own tune of "Oh! Oh!!" for his transgressions, for his high mindedness and loftiness, for his evil, for rejecting the Gospel, and causing the earth to drink the blood of the Saints—for this, I say, I expect he will be well switched among the first of the sons.

I do not desire thousands to lose their lives by war, and the attendant distresses; the spirit in me is different to this; but I rejoice that the reign of Satan is short upon the earth, and that the work of the Father has commenced on the face of the earth—in the north, in the south, in the east, and in the west; and it is seen in our midst by the progress of the work of apostasy; for there is half wise and half foolish, as represented by the parable of the Savior.

In the midst of this people there is faithfulness, virtue, and integrity, and they are the most righteous and the best people upon the face of the whole earth; but when the world look upon us, and upon our morals, they look through dark spectacles and goggles, which blind them, they cannot see, and they therefore think we are the blackest people in crime, and the deepest sunk in degradation. When I see that the world have eyes, but cannot see, ears, but cannot hear, hearts, but cannot understand, it speaks volumes on the end being near, when the Son of God will come in the clouds of heaven to take vengeance on the ungodly, and reign in the midst of His people, and bring to a termination the reign of Satan.

Let us hear, see, understand, obey, and serve God faithfully, that we may make our way, through changing elements and the crash of worlds, into the presence of our Father who is in heaven, for Jesus sake. Amen.[22]

Like the March 12 discourse, but for different reasons, Grant's April 2 sermon made a hard impression on the collective mind of the Saints.[23] Brigham Young heard it, but his mind was occupied with a matter less transcendent than astounding prophecy. That evening he met with the Quorum of the Twelve to request names of candidates to fill the vacancy in the First Presidency. The apostles declined, saying that it was Brother Brigham's privilege and responsibility to choose as his second counselor the man who would sit in council with him and Brother Heber, and who would carry the word and will of the Lord and His servant Brigham to the inhabitants of Israel.[24] The requirement was for Mormon Thunder.

⇜ Notes ⇝

1. *Deseret News*, August 7, 1852.

2. Journal History of the Church of Jesus Christ of Latter day Saints (chronological scrapbook of typed entries and newspaper clippings, 1830-present), August 20, 1852, 1, LDS Church Archives.

3. Scott G. Kenney, ed., *Wilford Woodruff's Journal, 1833-1898*, typescript, 9 vols. (Midvale, Utah: Signature Books, 1983-85), July 24, 1852.

4. Jedediah Grant, Letter to Susan Grant, July 23, 1852, holograph in possession of Betty Mae Nebeker Laub, Salt Lake City (hereafter Laub Collection).

5. Journal History, August 20, 1852-December 19, 1852, passim.

6. Journal History, January 1 and February 14, 1853, both p. 2, and March 7, 1853, 1.

7. Family Records of Bernice Grant Casper, Salt Lake City.

8. Journal History, April 8, 1853, 1.

9. Ibid.

10. Brigham Young, April 17, 1853, *Journal of Discourses*, 26 vols. (London and Liverpool: LDS Booksellers Depot, 1855-86), 1:121-29.

11. Journal History, July 4, 1853, 2.

12. Jedediah M. Grant, August 7, 1853, *Journal of Discourses*, 1:341-46.

13. Jedediah M. Grant, February 19, 1854, *Journal of Discourses*, 2:10-16, in which he attacked "spiritual rapping" as a product of Lucifer. The subsequent blossoming of spiritualism in Utah during the 1860s and 1870s developed partially from the same frustrations with the more placid religion of the Brigham Young era contrasted to that of Joseph Smith. Eugene E. Campbell,

(Salt Lake City: Signature Books, 1988), 322-24.

14. Jedediah M. Grant, August 7, 1853, *Journal of Discourses*, 1:346-49.

15. Ibid., 341.

16. Journal History, August 1, 1853-February 5, 1854, passim. See also Campbell, *Establishing Zion*, 147-61, for an account of the common organization of the Church in early Utah.

17. Jedediah M. Grant, February 19, 1854, *Journal of Discourses*, 2:10-16. Note Grant's views on priesthood control—that priesthood leaders have a right to give direction in every facet of life.

18. Jan Shipps, Letter to Gene A. Sessions, August 5, 1980.

19. *Deseret News*, July 17, 1854. Campbell, *Establishing Zion*, 198, erroneously suggests that the teaching of blood atonement "emerged during the reformation" of 1856 in another sermon by Grant on October 1, 1856.

20. Ibid.; emphasis mine. Anti-Mormon polemicists have failed to mention in their use of the March 12 discourse that, when it was delivered, Grant was not a member of the First Presidency.

21. To suggest that the teaching of blood atonement directly contributed to the death of anyone in early Utah is to suggest that the leaders of the Church organized capital punishment for sin. Although reputable scholars continue to debate the issue, in the absence of any substantive and incontrovertible evidence of such activity, a discussion of the doctrine as an effective agent in Mormonism becomes an exercise in shaky speculation and spectacular fodder for the anti-Mormon press. See, for example, Jon Krakauer, *Under the Banner of Heaven: A Story of Violent Faith* (New York: Doubleday, 2003). A more useful view sees it as a characteristic development of Mormon preachments designed to demand of the Saints a perfection beyond the scope of their worldly values. It is also not out of keeping with the general tone of civic discourse across the West where the rhetoric of violence was more than common. More recently, the Mormon Church issued a statement through one of its apostles completely denying that blood atonement is a part of its doctrine. "We do not believe that it is necessary for men in this day to shed their own blood to receive a remission of sins." Bruce R. McConkie, Letter to Thomas B. McAffee, October 18, 1978, photocopy in my possession. This same letter, however, skirts the historical question, although McConkie insists that "to the present there has been no single instance of so-called blood atonement under any pretext." Many historians would dispute this declaration, although most would agree that evidence for possible instances remains less than definitive. Perhaps the most likely possibilities for actual instances of blood atonement are the Parish-Potter murders near Springville in 1857. See Polly Aird, "'You Nasty Apostates, Clear Out': Reasons for Disaffection in the Late 1850s," *Journal of Mormon History* 30 (Fall 2004): 173-91. For other examples of scholarship that touches on the subject, see also Ardis E. Parshall, "'Pursue, Retake & Punish': The 1857 Santa Clara Ambush," *Utah Historical Quarterly* 73 (Winter 2005): 64-86, and William MacKinnon, "'Lonely Bones': Leadership and Utah War Violence," *Journal of Mormon History* 33 (2007): 121-78. Perhaps the best analysis of "a culture of violence" in nineteenth-century Utah is D. Michael Quinn, *The Mormon Hierarchy: Extensions of Power* (Salt Lake City: Signature Books, 1997), 241-61.

22. Jedediah M. Grant, April 1, 1854, *Journal of Discourses*, 2:145-49.

23. See, for example, John Pulsipher's reaction to this speech in his "Scrap Book Containing Some of the Phraseology—Choice and Select Instruction and Abridged Speeches of Inspired Men," holograph, LDS Church Archives.

24. Wilford Woodruff, Journal, April 2, 1854.

"They do not comprehend the light of God, towering among the clouds and smoke."

11
Second Counselor

THE BENEDICTION AT THE morning session of conference on April 6, 1854, was offered by Elder Jedediah M. Grant of the First Council of Seventy. President Brigham Young called on him again in the afternoon meeting, this time to speak. The next morning, the faithful assembled again, this time to sustain the officers of the church: Brigham Young as Prophet, Seer, Revelator, and President of the Church of Jesus Christ of Latter-day Saints, with Heber C. Kimball as his first counselor in the First Presidency and Jedediah M. Grant as second counselor.[1] With that, a new phase in the development of Mormon Thunder had reached maturity.

Early the next Sunday, April 9, the Quorum of the Twelve met with Young and Kimball to ordain Grant an apostle and to set him apart as the third member of the First Presidency.[2] At the age of thirty-eight, Jeddy Grant had risen to the top of the Mormon hierarchy, where room for the expansion of his peculiar brand of devotion to his people and his cause was in abundance. Now the words he spoke and the actions he took were incredibly potent, for rarely in the history of religion had the leaders of a people commanded more voluntary dedication and obedience as did the few men who led the Saints in the theocracy that was early Utah. It seemed that the forceful triumvirate of Young, Kimball, and Grant would wield a powerful sword of influence over the spiritual and temporal affairs of the Latter-day Saints for years and perhaps decades to come.

Not long after the conference adjourned, Young and Kimball left the city for a tour of the southern settlements, leaving the affairs of the Church and the direction of the public works in the hands of their new co-worker. In order to keep the many projects of the Church moving that spring, the prompt and abundant payment of tithes from the local units became crucial. Having to provide for the needs of between 300 and 400 church employees from the provisions of the General Tithing Office, Grant was disturbed to discover that many wards were so delinquent in forwarding "the wheat, flour, potatoes, beef, pork, butter, cheese, &cc." that a genuine emergency with regard to the continuation of the public works had set in. Consequently, he sent Hiram B. Clawson and Charles C. Decker through the local units north of the city with letters calling on bishops "in this emergency [to] deal with the Church, as they would wish the Church [to] deal with them, under like circumstances."[3] Grant made it clear in his letters to the bishops that neither he nor the other brethren could tolerate the inevitable result of a lack of "eatables" in the tithing office—a cessation of construction on the Endowment House and the outer wall around the Temple Block.

Understandably, some local leaders were reluctant to allow their tithing to be used for the sustenance of workers in Salt Lake City, when there were poor among them at home. To one such bishop, J. G. Browning of Ogden, Grant asserted unequivocally what he expected, and that he was in charge of the situation:

I would wish to be informed from what source, or by what authority you have learned that it is your privilege or right to retain 200 or 300 bushels of wheat for the demands of your ward, when an order from the General Tithing office in this city calls for the amount of wheat on hand? The Tithing office at Ogden, is only a branch of the General Tithing office here, established there, for, and in behalf of the Tithing office in this city, and to do that portion of its business in Weber County, subject to the jurisdiction or order of the presiding bishop in this city.

When President B. Young left this city on his tour south, he gave orders to have all the tithing wheat on hand, north, collected immediately and deposited in the office here, and agreeably to his instructions teams have been sent to your place, and according to your note, cannot receive but a few bushels, when you report on hand 2, or 300. The laborers on the public works are now living mostly on half rations, and potatoes at that, and let me here observe, that all the potatoes you may have on hand on receipt of this, you will please see to; employ some hands to pick them, and keep them in an airy place so as to prevent their sprouting, or otherwise being damaged, for future use, and when an opportunity presents, we will send for them, or if any teams should be coming to this city from your section, and you find it convenient, it would accommodate us greatly to have them sent by such.

At date, I have drawn on you an order for 200 bushel of wheat, which you will please deliver upon presentation thereof, and the balance you have on hand, may remain until the president returns, unless some exigency should arise sufficient to require the delivery of it previously; if so, you will have an order to that effect over my signature.

It is true, the poor and needy in your ward should be cared for, and the worthy should be supplied with needful assistance, but you have farmers, and other able men in your ward, which should, out of their abundance minister to the wants and necessities of the poor, independent of their tithing as we have to do in this city, thereby relieving us of the embarrassing circumstances under which we are placed to prosecute the public works of the kingdom, more efficiently and effectually than we otherwise could have done.[4]

Clawson and Decker returned to the city on April 19. Apparently, Grant's dose of thunder accomplished its purpose, inasmuch as the emissaries reported that they had secured a promise from the northern settlements for some 1,400 bushels of wheat and that "the brethren in that section voted unanimously, that every bushel of wheat and pound of flour that they could spare would be forthcoming to the Church."[5] Grant's subsequent accounting of the situation to Young and Kimball stressed the success of his efforts to ameliorate the public works tithing crisis, but it also recognized the stopgap nature of the current solution. "This quantity will help along for the time being," he wrote to his brethren still traveling in the south, "but I am inclined to think, that it will but little more than supply the demands until your return; in that event would it not be a good move to wake up the bishops and brethren south to this important matter, in order to effectually sustain and carry on the public works until harvest?"[6]

At the end of the month, Young and Kimball returned to Salt Lake City to find to their satisfaction "that our public works had progressed with commendable diligence under the direction of my second counselor Jedediah M. Grant, who tarried here to oversee our general business matters."[7] The new member of the First Presidency had passed his consummating trial of leadership with proverbial flying colors.

In the second week of June, the First Presidency traveled into Davis County to attend to the property affairs of Grant's predecessor, Willard Richards, and to locate city walls to be built around the village at Farmington.[8] After their return, they prepared for a conference of the Church to be held on the final weekend in June. One of the themes of the conference was to be apostasy. Grant had some interesting thoughts on the subject and, at the morning session of June 27, gave some sardonic advice to would-be apostates in Zion:

> There are some things we know by seeing, and other things we know by hearing, tasting, smelling, &cc.; but the light of the Eternal Spirit that brought us out of darkness into the Church of God, is the great abiding testimony of this people.
>
> Indeed, men have apostatized after they have seen and heard Joseph, after they have seen angels, after they have seen the sick healed, and after they have spoken in tongues and prophesied, and had the interpretation of tongues. You will recollect that long since I gave you my advice in relation to the proper time a man ought to apostatize. My advice was that he should never apostatize in a dark and cloudy day—never when he felt bad—never because he felt hard toward his brother or brethren in the Church; but when he apostatizes, he should wait for a clear day, when everything around him is prospering; and then, before he apostatizes, he should ask counsel.
>
> In relation to men's apostatizing, I recollect in the upper room of the Temple in Kirtland, Ohio, when we were assembled there, a very noted man, by the name of Sylvester Smith, bore testimony of what he had seen of the Prophet of God, of angels, &c. He said he wanted to bear testimony, and continued to say, "I have spoken by what you call the Holy Ghost; the eyes of my understanding have been touched, and I have seen convoy after convoy of angels; I have laid hands on the lame, and they have leaped like an hart; I have spoken with tongues and had the interpretation thereof; I have seen the sick healed time after time;—but let me tell you, everything I have seen and everything you have seen is the height of idiotism." This was Sylvester Smith, after he apostatized.
>
> This was the testimony of an apostate, which is conclusive proof to me that a man may see the hosts of heaven the chariots of Israel and the horsemen thereof, and gaze on the glory of God, and be filled with the Holy Ghost; and unless he retains the Spirit of God, he will apostatize. Therefore my

advice to the Saints has been, and is, and whenever I give you good advice in the future, it will be the same, that you propose in your hearts never to depart from God or from His people, only when you are filled with the Holy Ghost; and then when you do it, ask counsel of his servants.[9]

Grant expected the Saints to obey, so it was perplexing to him during his first few months in the First Presidency to learn that getting them to respond to counsel was not an easy matter, nor was it one quickly accomplished. Through the rest of the season, the Church continued to have a difficult time keeping the General Tithing Office filled with enough food and dry goods to maintain the desired pace on the public works. Being also responsible as mayor for the welfare of the people and for the various projects in Salt Lake City, Grant remained in the thick of efforts to bring in more tithing from the outlying settlements.[10] After an unusually hot summer of trying to keep things going in the city, the First Presidency decided in September to issue a general statement "To the Saints in Utah," challenging them to remember the purpose for which they had come to Zion. It was to be a theme that Grant would pick up and repeat in his own polemics again and again. It read in part:

Upon leaving your former homes to gather to these valleys at the requirements of the Lord through his servants, where you could worship the God of Israel in accordance with his commandments, your hearts glowed with gratitude for your deliverance from the wickedness and oppression which prevail in the world, and you were fully persuaded that from and after your arrival here, you would devote all your time, energies, and means every way, becoming a saint for your salvation and the salvation of the human family to the uttermost.

Well, we are in the valleys of the mountains with none but ourselves to oppose us in doing the will of the Lord; for unless listened to, evil spirits have no power over ours to turn us from the pathway of righteousness and still there is plenty of room for reformation for in the midst of all the lessons of the past the time has not yet arrived when we can say we are one in all things which time must come and our wills must be perfectly subject to the will of the father ere we are privileged to enter upon the full fruition of all righteous desires.

You reply that these are old truths, with which we are perfectly familiar and the reply is correct, then why not live more closely in accordance with your knowledge and day by day watch and chasten yourself casting aside temptations overcoming evils that unclean spirits may not find place in your tabernacles, that you may constantly grow in the knowledge of the truth and that grace may be continually multiplied to you? The answer comes booming up on every side, "the spirit indeed is willing, but the flesh is weak," but omitting the command that which immediately preceeds it, namely, viz: "watch and pray that ye enter not into temptation."

But instead of walking uprightly at all times and under all circumstances, each pursuing his particular avocation with his face steadily set Zionward, one goes to his building, fields, or stock, and becomes so absorbed in their improvements and increases that he forgets why he came here, that the hands upon the public works need food to sustain life, that after all he is only a steward at most, and at length even forgets to thank the giver of all he possesses; while another still more culpable in that he produces nothing, strives to amass wealth and build up a name by becoming a mere trader, and far too often a shaving trader, and of course he too is soon fully imbued with the ruling passion of selfishness and the purpose for which he came here is almost, if not wholly lost sight of.[11]

For Jedediah Grant there was indeed "plenty of room for reformation" among the Mormons. He had never been able to understand nor to countenance the way many of the Saints had become more interested in their "buildings, fields, or stock" than they were in their duties to the kingdom. A few days later, he mounted the stand in the Bowery in order to give some instructions to the new immigrants who had come into the valley that season. The theme of that September 24 address was graphically blunt and its message typically Jedediah Grant, booming out principles of consistency, simple faith, and utmost obedience to the call of righteousness. By now, not six months since his appointment to the First Presidency, Grant could feel the presence of an intense calling to reform the Saints.

> I am aware much instruction has been given to the people, at least to the majority of those who are here before me; and we do not wish to preach you to death, but we wish to preach so that you may enjoy life. A thousand ideas float in the minds of the people in relation to preaching; each have their standard, and their notions of what they call the sacred desk. All

"Mormon" desks are sacred. I am no more religious to day than yesterday. I am equally as religious in the kanyons hauling wood as in the pulpit; and if I were agoing to swear in either place, I should prefer the pulpit to swear in; consequently, I consider that a man should live his religion in all places, and under all circumstances and situations in life.

I am aware that some Elders who go forth and preach long and pious sermons, frequently represent Zion as one of the most delightsome places in the world, as if the people in Salt Lake City were so pure and holy that the flame of sanctity would almost singe the hair off a common man's head. Others suppose when they come here, that they are to be fed, clothed, and housed independent of their own exertions. Some of the elders have told the Saints in England that the first two weeks after they landed here all they would have to do would be to contemplate the beauties of Zion, and be furnished two weeks provisions. The imaginations of some Saints have been so exalted by the Elders who preached to them, that they suppose that all our pigs come ready cooked, with knives and forks in them, and are running round squealing to be eaten; that every tray is filled with bread, every manger with potatoes, and every man's wagon with the choice fruits of the earth. On the contrary, when the Saints from abroad come to Zion, they will find the people so busy that they can scarcely find time to speak to them, and if they have lost some of their friends on the way, the people in Zion have not time even to help them mourn.

Some come here and are astonished, for they had supposed that they should find the stereotyped editions of Zion sitting on the seats singing "hallelujah," and shouting "Glory to God" continually but when they find us all active, some rushing to the kanyons, some gathering in the crops, and others rearing houses—when they find the people all alive with business, they think that the "Mormons" are all telegraphs; and so we are, stereotyped editions of the telegraph. Every man and woman in Zion at their duty is a telegraph moving and exerting an influence, building up, fortifying, and fulfilling the words of the Prophets by building city after city. It makes no difference whether we have gold and silver, or not; we build just as fast without money as the people of the east build with it, and a little faster. A man who has faith says he has capital in himself; he is telegraph enough to build him a house. Another man has to sit down, and count "three and two are five, five and two are seven, seven and four are eleven, and eleven and six are seventeen"; and so he will calculate, and unless he has so many dimes, he has not faith enough to draw the first rock, or the first adobie, or get the first foot of lumber, or do the first thing.

But you take a man who has got in him the true "Mormon" spirit, and he considers that he can accomplish, just what he thinks ought to be accomplished. If he considers that he wants a house, he deems himself competent to go at it, and to build such a one as he wants; if he wants a small one he can build it, and if a large one he can build it. That is the "Mormon" spirit. If you Saints who have just arrived here expect a heaven, I will tell you how to get it; if you have brought a small one with you, keep it, and keep adding to it; that is, if you want a heaven, go to and make it. If you have not means enough to buy a farm, go to work and make one; if you have not means enough to buy a house, build one, and thus gather around you the comforts of life, and the means to subsist upon. But I will tell you one thing, if you neglect to pray, neglect to watch, neglect to do your duty, and to serve your God for yourselves, you will be apt to become dissatisfied, disheartened, and dispirited, and wish to go back from whence you came. But the opposite will be the result with those who keep the commandments of God, who watch and pray, who are active in their spirits and in their religion, and work out their salvation with fear and trembling, if you please, or they may work as hard as they please without fearing and trembling, if they have a mind to. Consequently, when you come here, it is essential that you keep the same religion that you embraced before you started to come here.

I am aware that a great many have so much piety in them, that they are like the Baptist priest who came to see Joseph Smith. Joseph had the discernment of spirits to read a man, and a peculiar faculty of using up the old sectarian tone to "my dee-e-er brethren." When he heard that good old tone he used to imitate it; and whenever one of the class, who are so filled with piety, and the good old tone, came to Nauvoo, Joseph used forthwith to take a course to evaporate their sanctimoniousness, a great deal of which consists in the long ass-like tone. Before the Baptist priest, I have referred to, came to Nauvoo, he had heard brother William O. Clark, who could preach a bible and a half at a sermon, and could use the fashionable old tone, the blessed old tone. This Baptist imbibed a notion that we were as much ahead of his ideas of piety, and that our tone was as much longer than his, as the strength of the arguments produced by Clark were stronger than his; and supposed that our sanctimoniousness was co-equal with what he considered the merits of our doctrine.

Under these impressions he came to Nauvoo, and was introduced to the Prophet. In the meantime some person came up that brother Joseph would have a talk with, but while doing this he kept his eye upon the stranger, on this priest. After he got through chatting, the Baptist stood before him, and folding his arms said, "Is it possible that I now flash my optics upon a Prophet, upon a man who has conversed with my Savior?" "Yes," says the Prophet, "I don't know but you do; would not you like to wrestle with me?" That, you see, brought the priest right on to the thrashing floor, and he turned a summerset right straight. After he had whirled round a few times, like a duck shot in the head, he concluded that his piety had been awfully shocked, even to the center, and went to the Prophet to learn why he had so shocked his piety. The Prophet commenced and showed him the follies of the world, and the absurdity of the long tone, and that he had a super-abundant stock of sanctimoniousness.

You Saints who have come here, if you have around you the garb of sectarianism, must calculate that the "Mormon" plow will turn that under; you must calculate that here we are a practical people; a people who believe in their religion, and are good Saints; who do their work, and attend to their prayers in the season thereof; and are not so much in a hurry in the morning, but that they can kneel down and consecrate their families, their effects, themselves, and all they have, to the Most High God.

But in the midst of this people you will find various stripes of character. The net has been cast into the sea, and, if the parable is true, it has drawn to the shore all kinds of fish, and you must not be alarmed if you find in Zion some curiosities. If I wished to find the best men in the world, I should go to Zion to find them; if I wished to find the biggest devil, I would look in Zion for him, among the people of God; there I can find the greatest scamps. I believe the words of Christ are true, that the net has gathered of every kind of fish; that it has gathered men of every class. Do not marvel if you find here goats as well as sheep, and the speckled goats and the long-haired goats, and the smooth goats and the rough goats, and goats of every grade, size and color, mixed among the sheep. Do not think you will be without your trials here, that you are to be a stereotyped edition to sit upon stools, singing glory to God, and that that is all you have to do.

I have often said to the English brethren and sisters that were I in England, for there is where the Elders preach piety, I would tell them the first things they might expect to meet in Zion, viz; to leap into the mire and help to fill up a mud hole, to make abodies [adobes] with their sleeves rolled up, and be spattered with clay from head to foot; and that some would be set to ditching in Zion, to making ditch fence ankle deep in mire; and that they might expect to eat their bread by the sweat of their brow, as in their native country.

You come here, and you *think* that we are busy and active, but only live your religion, and you will feel the power, spirit, and fulness thereof, as you have never felt it previous to this. What I mean by the spirit is the Spirit of God, the Holy Ghost, which you can feel from the crown of your heads to the soles of your feet. It is here with you if you do right, and everything you anticipate in the Holy Ghost, and in the power of the Priesthood, and in the love of God, and everything you have thought of in your own minds is here, and God is here; and if you have thought of bad, it is here also. If you approach a large furnace, the first thing you see are the black columns of smoke rising up and towering aloft, and if you approach nearer you discover piles of coal and ore, and the ashes, dust, and cinders which have been heaved out; but all this will never convince you that there is no iron there. You would say that where there is so much iron cinders there must be iron; that the iron has been taken out and dressed; that there must have been lots of iron here, and you begin to look for the iron.

If you occasionally see a dirty sheep, do not let it try you; if you do not get a bushel of wheat as quick as you want it, do not let that try your faith. If you are agoing to die of hunger, that is the time to be strong in the God of Israel. I wish to see the new comers active in their religion; I wish to see them live their religion, and not only seek to be endowed with the spirit of Zion, but to bring the spirit of Zion with them. I wish to see them come here with their countenances lit up with the love of God, and their hearts burning with the Holy Ghost, and their voices sounding like the music of sweet instruments, to join in the songs of Zion, and in the work of our God, in cultivating the earth, and in building houses. Bless your souls, if you desire an experience of this kind, in order to build up Zion, you must learn.

We may talk of making our own heaven, and of building up the city of Zion, and making it beautiful, and having it polished after the similitude of a palace, but we must have an experience in doing such a work, before we can accomplish it. The world do not comprehend all things as they should; they do not comprehend the greatest things; the light and power of God, pertaining to man in his probation, towering among the clouds and smoke, but its force is down here in the practical duties of life, in the work under the sun that we have to do.

Now when you come to Zion, you will find men standing upon their feet; but go into the world, and there, if a man wants to show himself to be a smart man, he must mount a cabbage leaf, hiccup, and jump up to spit over his shirt collar. There was a man here last winter who thought himself a smart man because his father was a smart man; and he was all the while on the strain, like a man who mounts a cabbage leaf to hiccup, or jumps up to spit over his shirt collar in trying to be smart. What do they make of it? Nothing but a bubble, and a laughing stock for men of sense.

The ore, coal, and flux are put in the tunnel head of the furnace, and iron and cinder run to the boshes below, and are separated. You see the smoke first, but you find here the true metal.—"The Mormons, a little handful of Mormons cannot accomplish much," used to be said. But we are gathering out the tough wire, it has got to come here.

I wish the Saints who come here, to be Saints. I said last spring, curse a man who will starve the poor by keeping up the price of grain, and who will not help his brethren. I know some men will say that we have fine men among us. I know that we have first rate, good mercantile houses here; I like them first rate; but it would be better for us to do our own trading, and by that means keep our money in our midst.

These are my views, and have been all the time. I like to see a "Mormon" be a "Mormon," and act like a "Mormon." A good "Mormon" will have an elastic faith, and not say, "O brother Grant, the old snag ship is in snag harbor," but be mindful that brother Brigham is cautious how he guides her. Brother Joseph had not time to be careful, and run the ship around the snags, but was under the necessity of running the ship right on to them. But when Brigham chooses to run around a snag, or across a snag, he will do so. The ship is all oak, let her slide. If we are in snag harbor, all right; we will steer the ship, and run around the snag, or over it, just as the Lord pleases. Jesus, our elder brother, is at the helm, and has a good crew aboard, who are faithful, meek, and humble. If the Saints desire to strengthen Zion, let them be humble, meek, lowly, and contrite in spirit; let them be diligent, and seek counsel through the light of the Spirit of God, and watch and pray, and they will be filled with joy, and be happy at night, and healthy in the morning; and their spirits will be buoyant, and they can shout "glory hallelujah" in reality.

May the God of heaven fill you with the Holy Ghost, and give you light and joy in His kingdom. Amen.[12]

His conference address, delivered two weeks later on October 7, was a continuation of the same theme and carried a similar flavor spiced with a bit more salt and pepper.

I have seen the time, in Kirtland, Ohio, the first gathering place I went to, when you could have crowded the whole congregation into one room sixteen feet by eighteen; and these comprised all the Saints that were there. If we had sent up to Jackson County, and brought them all down, and had a house like this, there would have been just a little belt of people in front of the stand, and reaching part way up towards the opposite side of the room.

In the mountains, though it is difficult to gather the people here, though they come from the nations, and have the Atlantic to cross, and have to come from the different parts of the United States, we have got together a considerable body of people. However, there are as yet but few, comparatively. We are looked upon as feeble in the world, but of small height; but it is a very easy thing to bring in an emigration of four or five thousand; and we can bring wagons from different settlements, and the people who have come in are swallowed right up, as it were, so that in three or four weeks we cannot tell what has become of our immigration. They can come by thousands, and be dispersed throughout the Territory among the Saints, and find comfortable homes, and it is scarcely known and felt.

You who have been brought in here, labor, and throw back into the great purse what you have received, that we may bring double the number another year.

The idea of becoming a State in two or three years, when we have only got four or five thousand of an emigration! I do not wonder that the Latter-day Saints believe in the plurality of wives. Launch out your means to help us to bring the poor; if you do not, we will raise up the mountain boys ourselves. This piecemeal business of gathering Saints! we want it upon the wholesale principle. That's the doctrine. I tell you, a few more boys breaking the crust of nations, like brother [Daniel] Garn, after a while, by driving their little wedges, will bring them over by nations.

A great many people who come here, when they do not find everything right handy—plenty of food, houses, and all other conveniences, are discouraged, and lose their energies. If you want to know something about the "Mormon" grit, remember what brother Garn said this morning; if he is whipped, he don't stay whipped. You cannot discourage a real "Mormon." It is necessary to raise up a certain stripe in the Valley, of the real "Mormon" grit, that those who come over here, and who have the whines and the grunts, may have the "Mormon" leaven among them to leaven the whole lump.

I have had one or two cases reported to me. For instance, some of our brethren who cross the plains, when they get here, are a little peevish, snappish, vexed, and quarrelsome. When the wind blowed the other day, a man got the servant girl to hold the tent pole, to keep it from falling, but she not being strong enough, down went the tent. The man then made a scourge out of rope, and began to beat the girl, and beat her most unmercifully. I do not know whether that man is converted or not; but it makes me think of an old Baptist preacher in Virginia. He came and preached in a certain place; the next time he came round, a drunken man came staggering up to him and said, "Brother Jones, when you was last in our settlement, you converted my soul." "Well," said brother Jones, "I should think I did, for I do not believe the Lord had anything to do with it." I am rather inclined to think it is possible that the girl whipper is yet unconverted. We like men here to learn how to treat their families, their cattle, and their horses, &c.

I am entirely of a lively disposition; I know not how to be low-spirited; I never knew what it was to be lonesome in my life. Some talk about being lonesome when they are alone; I know nothing about it. I never misuse a beast, and I am not inclined to misuse people; but when they are right mean, I like to work them up with my tongue once in a while. But the idea of people going to work to beat, and kick, and pound their cattle, horses, children, and everything around them, is nonsense. Good-natured feelings and good natured conduct are worth a thousand of the opposite character. Do right, be kind and gentle. You have come in the midst of the people of God; you have come to unite with us in serving the mighty God of Jacob, and endeavor to do right.

When brethren start to come here, they are anxious to be in this place, but many of them, when they get here, see no charms in Zion. You can learn their spirits directly, for they are known by their associates. We have some High Priests, &c., who have been among us for years, and others who have come in lately, who like to associate with our enemies, those who have a sneering and malicious spirit. Talk about such persons having the "Mormon" spirit in them, and the light of the Holy Ghost, and yet love the world and the things of the world, and the spirit of the world, and the glory of the world, and the wickedness of the world! Some people can associate with those who laugh at the institutions of heaven, at the principles of eternity, and laugh to scorn the ministry of the people of God; they like to converse with them, and they love to be in their society; they love to have them around them. I would rather dig thistle roots and sego roots to live upon, and eat boiled hides, and drink the broth from them, than to take such enemies into my house, and board them; and rather than rent my house to such persons to live in, I would burn it up if they have lived in it, and have a new one. That is my grit. The filthy old building should never hold my family. I wish all the "Mormons" felt as I do, there would be a flame in Zion, and a fire in Jerusalem. I say, if all the "Mormons" felt as I do about those who laugh at our distresses, and when calamities come upon us, wag their heads and say, "Ha, ha! so would we have it," they would think there was a furnace in Zion, and a flame in Jerusalem.

I want "Mormons" to feel like "Mormons," to feel like Saints. I want a man of God to feel fired up with the Holy Ghost, and not place his affections upon the world, and the things of the world; but love your God, and your brethren that are poor and in distress, and who love God. Those high-minded hypocrites, who bow and scrape to get your dimes, let them go to where they belong, they and their dimes; that is the way I feel about them. I like to see the Saints of God fired up to help the poor, and bring them in here to strengthen the reins of Israel. I like to see them exert themselves to send forth the Gospel, and bring from the nations those who are humble, contrite, pure, and holy, and who are uncontaminated by the vices of the world. Go into the circles of high life, if you please; I know about the high and the low in the United States. Talk about high life! about converting many of that class and bringing them here! What will you bring? Those who believe the truth with difficulty. But the poor and needy, who are looked upon as the dross and offscouring of all things, are the best of all creation, and we want the best, the purest, and those that are the most holy, brought to Zion. But the breath of that person who rejects my God is like the upas tree to me—it is poisonous; I do not like it. I admit that I occasionally find some who have not been baptized, in whom there is a stripe of honor and good will which I like; but I speak generally of those who knowingly persecute the people of God, who reject the truth; I do not love them. I am like the old Indian, "Though I will forgive and forget, I always remember." It is bred in my bones; I was raised up in the "Mormon" Church from my childhood; it is sweet to me, sweeter than the honey or the honeycomb; it is life and breath to me; it is eternal life, and I love it.

I do not like the person who sneers at "Mormonism," and I do not like those who associate with such; they are no brothers, no sisters, nor friends to me. I fellowship those who love the institutions of God who love the servants of God, and the truth of God, and the principles of righteousness. But that class that sneer at the principles of the Gospel, and the institutions of the kingdom of God, who like to associate with the wicked and ungodly, are not my brothers, they are not my sisters, nor friends, nor the friends of God. But the person who seeks to convert the sinner, and bring him to the truth; I like that disposition. I see people on my right and on my left who can dwell and associate with the ungodly, drink into their spirit, and fall into the same condemnation as they do. Take a man who is pure, he sees the corruption of the ungodly.

New-comers, you will find men called Saints who are "land sharks of Utah." We have all kinds of men here, and we expect to have them; and if some of you who have been brought here by the [Perpetual Emigrating] fund this year, are no better than many of those who were brought last season, you will whine; but for God's sake, when you feel like whining, bite your tongue; and if you do not like to do that, use brother H. Kimball's remedy—chew a piece of India rubber, and keep chewing it until you get the grunt out of you.

I do not wish to detain you. May the God of heaven bless you, and bless the Saints in every land and nation, that Israel may be gathered, and the Saints saved, which may God grant. Amen.[13]

Soon after the conference adjourned, the First Presidency and others of the brethren left Salt Lake City on a journey into Utah and Sanpete counties to visit the settlements, install a stake president at Manti, and treat with the Indians. On that trip, Grant had a chance to expound on his now-common theme of cheerful dedication to building Zion, and to make himself and his views visible in the regions south of his mayoralty. He preached fiery sermons at Mountainville (Alpine), Palmyra (Spanish Fork), Provo, Springville, Ephraim, and Manti, thus spreading Mormon Thunder up and down the valleys of Utah, and making a broader spectrum of the Saints acquainted with his brand of Mormonism.[14] By the time the party returned to Salt Lake City on October 18, Grant was a fully accredited prophet among prophets. His sermons all seemed to boil down to one pervasive thread of thought, an idea with which he opened his remarks at the Bowery on November 19, and one that would be his consistent calling card to the Saints during the next two years.

I would be glad to see all the people do right; no momentary excitement will induce the multitude to do right, for we might easily, by exertion, arouse within you a thousand conflicting emotions. The English language when it is well handled has been said to be a charm of itself, and the mind may be much excited by words without much sentiment being embodied in those words. In order for a community to be right, they have to be governed by a right system or government,—by the laws of God—by the Priesthood of the Almighty.

We have professedly come to this land to keep the commandments of God. We have learned the corruption of the world,—we have come from the world,—we have been baptized into Christ by yielding obedience to his ordinances, and the Holy Spirit of God has rested upon us; its influences we have felt; our minds have been enlightened, and we have been made to comprehend things pertaining to the God we serve—his institutions in the eternal world, and his institutions on the earth. But in spite of all the wisdom, and instructions that have been showered upon us through the inspiration of the Holy Ghost, and the teachings of the servants of God, we yet hear the voice saying, "Turn ye O Israel, why will ye die?"

Now it would be pleasing to me as one individual—very pleasing—very gratifying, if I could always rise up before those who call themselves saints, and dwell upon the peaceable things of the kingdom of God, and teach to them the riches of eternal life, and the glory they are marching forward to obtain. It would please me if I could sit here, and listen to my brethren and hear them pour forth the rich truths of eternity, and speak to you of the good things of the kingdom of God, and cheer up your spirits. I would be thankful if they were never under the painful necessity of almost every Sabbath alluding to, either directly or indirectly, the wickedness, foibles, imperfections, vanities, sins, and the corruptions of the people. To dwell upon these things is by no means pleasing to the servants of God. I have for years wished that the spirit of reproof, or if you please, the spirit of chastisement would leave, then when

I attempt to speak to the people I might not feel it. Sometimes I have resisted the very spirit of reproof upon me, and looked round upon the right, and upon the left in silence. So have others. It is no pleasing task to find fault with the transgressor. It is no pleasing task to harrow up the minds of the just of the pure, of those who wish to do right, by portraying before them the sins, crimes, and abominations of the transgressor.

I am aware the prophet has said "The sinners in Zion are afraid, fearfulness hath surprised the hypocrites," etc. This presupposes conclusively that there would be sinners in Zion. They could not be made afraid if there were no sinners there; fearfulness could not surprise the hypocrites if there were none there; consequently if we are in Zion we must expect we are surrounded by sinners, and hypocrites; for in Zion the sinners are afraid, and fearfulness is to surprise the hypocrites.

Now I took particular notice of our President's remarks in the morning, and I have, from time to time, noticed his feelings in relation to the citizens of this great city. He is not the only one that has invited me and the City Council to take away the licenses from those who are retailing beer and spirituous liquor. People from different sections of the city have of late been requesting the Council to take the licenses from such men. Bishops have sent in their requests for the license of such an individual to be taken away, for such an institution is no part of Zion. I said to the Council the last time they met, "Let them work, and every man who applies for a license, give him a license; every man that wants to sell liquor, or beer, let him, and let him that wants to open a tippling shop, open it." We have opened the door, and given every man license that applied, and told every man that wanted to sell beer, to sell it; that wanted to brew beer, to brew it; that wanted to distill whisky, to distill it; and every merchant that wanted a license to sell spirits, he could have one. We have knocked the cork out of every bottle; and opened every barrel we could find, and have said to the sinners, to the gentile, and to the Jew, "Go, and drink yourselves drunk, if you choose."

Why have we done this? We have done it, gentlemen, and ladies, from the fact that the people would not listen to us, but were determined that liquor and beer should be sold. The voice of the President, by night, and by day, was to keep down these shops; the voice of the Twelve, and of the Bishops, and of others was the same; but would the people listen? No. One man who wanted a license, and who is known to be a drunkard, and a notorious tippler, and has imbibed drunkenness from his mother's womb, when he could not bring force sufficient to bear upon the City Council to get a license, had a petition circulated through the Wards. Shall I tell you the names of those who signed petitions for men to get licenses from the City Council to sell beer and strong drinks, even after all the preaching there has been from this stand? Suffice it to say that men high in authority, and of goodly reputation, signed these petitions. The City Council became wearied, and we said we will give you enough if you want licenses; and you Bishops, we will give you all you want. That was the spirit of the City Council, gentlemen, and ladies.

Now if this people have seen grog drinking, and spewing enough through our streets, if the flood gates of abominations have been up, and the stream running long enough; if you have had beer, and other slop shops enough to suit you, if you have seen drunkards reeling in our streets until you have enough of it, until you will not sign petitions for the drunkards, and drunkard shops, and spewing halls, and holes full of filth, and abominations; if you will not sign petitions, and send them in like floods, and have had enough of these things, say aye. ("Aye" burst simultaneously from thousands of voices.)

As far as I am concerned; I feel as George Miller said, that these miserable holes should go hellwards the way Ward's ducks went. I never would vote for one of them in the city, I should like to have a man tell if he ever knew me to advocate the idea of having places to retail liquor. One thing I have advocated, to have a little made in our city for medical purposes.

We blame the gentiles; but I will tell you my feelings about the gentiles, that is, that part of them that persecuted us, I hate them; that is the idea. But a man that is out of our church, but is an honorable, decent fellow, and has never killed my brethren nor robbed my friends, and has never mocked at the truth, and the God I serve, I have no prejudice against him; I never did have, and I never expect to have. But when I speak of gentiles I want you to understand I mean a certain class.

We have men among us here, for instance Col. Steptoe; he is annoyed with the soldiers, but he is more annoyed with those who sell them liquor. He is not a drunkard himself, but a very temperate man, raised in Old Virginia. Don't I like the man for his peace, and good order? I do. But I do not like to see the Mormon, saying I am a Mormon, and drinking, and rolling round in the streets, swearing, and cursing, and going to the grog shops. "O yes, I am a Mormon." I would like to see a man who professes to be a

Mormon live up to his religion; and I would like to see quorums go to work and cut off men who get drunk, and swear, and act as absurdly in the midst of the people of God. Cut them off. No temporary excitement is going to do it; but let the Presidents of Quorums go to work, and call up such a man, and if he will not do right cut him off; and for God's sake stop your petitioning the City Council. The City Council are your servants to be sure, and when petition after petition comes in, with the outside pressure backing them up, and running after them with sharp sticks, saying give this man, and that man a license; stop that. And I want Patriarchs to stop it, and I want Bishops to stop it, and Presidents of Seventies, and Presidents of hundreds to stop it. I say stop pouring in your petitions for licenses here, and grog there, and beer here, and spew there, and swearing here, and filth there. I am righteously severe on those who do it, and feel like throwing hemlock trees top foremost among them, and burying them up, and then setting fire to the trees; I want to kick them out of doors; I want to rake them. I want them transported into Salt Lake, and there drowned. They ought to be salted down, for they have an itch, and if they cannot get up a thing of one kind, they will get up one of another. They are like the crows, and buzzards, they like the carrion from the gutter better than clean meat. Let not the saints have appetites like the Turkey Buzzards, but be clean in your tastes. I do not frequent any of these grog shops, but the last time I was in one, I found there was hell and the devil, spew and froth, and every vile and unclean thing you can think of; and the cups and tables appeared not to have been cleansed since the flood.

If the people want peace, it is for them to make peace; and if they want good order, let them be orderly, and if you want a man to tell you the course of the City Council, I am the man to tell it. We want the citizens to be blessed, and we want to teach you the law of God, and good order, and have you do right, and be saved, which may God grant in the name of Jesus Christ: Amen.[15]

By the end of 1854, the Mormons knew they had a unique preacher among them, and in a high place of influence. Like Cotton Mather and Solomon Stoddard of early America, not only could the new second counselor cast with ease thunderbolts of practical religion against grogshops, general apostasy, or Sabbath breaking, but he could also generate doctrinal discourses designed to convince the Saints of the correctness of their fundamental theology.[16] It was not long before every Mormon in Utah came to expect crackling oratory with an appearance of Jedediah Morgan Grant against the mountains of Zion.

⇌ Notes ⇌

1. Journal History of the Church of Jesus Christ of Latter day Saints (chronological scrapbook of typed entries and newspaper clippings, 1830–present), April 6 and 7, 1854, both p. 1, LDS Church Archives.

2. Brigham Young Office Journal, April 9, 1854, LDS Church Archives.

3. Jedediah Grant, Letter to Bishop John Stoker and other bishops north, May 15, 1854, holograph, Brigham Young Collection. Collecting tithes to the central office in Salt Lake City had been a knotty problem from the beginning. For a broader discussion, see Eugene E. Campbell, *Establishing Zion: The Mormon Church in the American West, 1847–1869* (Salt Lake City: Signature Books, 1988), 135–39.

4. Jedediah Grant, Letter to J. G. Browning, May 13, 1854, holograph, Brigham Young Collection.

5. Jedediah Grant, Letter to Brigham Young and Heber C. Kimball, May 21, 1854, holograph, Brigham Young Collection.

6. Ibid.

7. History of Brigham Young, 1854, 47.

8. Journal History, June 9 and 10, 1854, both p. 1.

9. Jedediah M. Grant, June 28, 1854, *Journal of Discourses*, 26 vols. (London and Liverpool: LDS Booksellers Depot, 1855–86), 6:253–54.

10. Journal History, July 20, August 9, August 15, 1854, all p. 1.

11. *Deseret News*, September 14, 1854.

12. Jedediah M. Grant, September 28, 1854, *Journal of Discourses*, 3:65–69.

13. Jedediah M. Grant, October 7, 1854, *Journal of Discourses*, 2:71–74.

14. Journal History, October 10, 11, 12, 15, 18, 1854, all p. 1.

15. *Deseret News*, December 7, 1854.

16. Jedediah M. Grant, December 17, 1854, *Journal of Discourses*, 2:225–33.

"I want the Saints to live in a way that they can feel happy all the time."

12

The Eye of the Storm

THE WINTER OF 1854–55 deepened gently in the month of December with soft snowfalls and mild temperatures through the valleys of Utah. By Christmas, the weather was springlike with rain showers and warm air, which in contrast with some past winter seasons in Deseret made the Saints feel comfortable and cheery. In addition, the young City of the Saints was quickly taking on the accoutrements of a modern metropolis, with respectable hotels and other places for social gatherings. Between sessions of the legislature, Jedediah Grant and other luminaries of Utah's social and political structure strolled through the pleasant weather outside to such affairs as a military ball at the Union Hotel on December 26, a party in honor of the legislators held in the Social Hall the evening of New Year's Day ($26 a couple), and a gathering sponsored by the new federal judges and the judiciary of Utah at Union Hall on January 29.[1] The pleasant days of that mild winter seemed to symbolize that Utah and the Mormons had reached a well-deserved state of peace and comfort, at harmony with society and with the elements.

Grant had never felt better. He was at the top of his world, a leader of the Saints, and a man of remarkable influence. His spacious home, which he had completed in 1853, was now filled with the noise of six children; and his health, for years subject to stomach disorders and chronic eye problems, was better than it had been in years.[2] So confident was he of the future that he had married Louisa Marie Goulay, the widow of his brother Joshua, thus taking upon himself responsibility for that family. He had also added to his household as a plural wife young Maryette Kesler, a daughter of his friend Frederick Kesler. Concomitantly, he homesteaded a large farm in the West Bountiful area of Davis County.[3] Grant thus found himself playing a satisfying role in the beehive of activity that was the essence of the modern Zion. It had been a long road from his days as a boy preacher in the hills of western Virginia.

The valleys of Utah were filling with Saints, more coming every year from the States, Britain, and other parts of Europe. Under the direction of Brigham Young, the industries and settlements of the Great Basin kingdom were growing steadily with the blessings of righteousness. It was a time of success and a time for reflection on a precarious past that now seemed as distant as a hard winter, which in the midst of a mild one was easy to forget. Into February 1855, the weather continued to be almost eerily mild and pleasant,[4] and Grant's spirits were soaring when he addressed a Mormon Battalion reunion on the sixth of that month.

> I have read many narratives of the valor of men, and the service they have rendered their country; but I here see a set of men that have stood in the defense of their country, under the most trying and heart rendering circumstances that human beings could be placed in; having their families and friends to leave on the open prairie, in an Indian country, while en route to the great interior desert of North America; and as our forefathers fought under General Washington and saved the country from the enemy, so did this Mormon Battalion save a large tract of land from being pounced upon by the militia of several states, for heartless villains had concocted plans to have all this people murdered while upon the western frontiers.[5]

Feeling very confident that the Mormons had heroically removed themselves from any such dangers, Jedediah Grant, major general of the Nauvoo Legion and mayor of Salt Lake City, was going to hurl some lightning bolts of patriotic propaganda. He would have the Saints remember their heritage, even while basking in success and security.

> You remember that I went to Washington and visited our friend, Colonel Kane, and I know from what I there learned, that the Honorable Thomas H. Benton advocated the necessity of raising troops and cutting off all the "Mormons" from the face of the earth. Notwithstanding you had rendered your services and offered your names to go and serve your country in the war with Mexico, yet while you were doing this, one of the Senators, and one of the principal men in the Senate too, did endeavor to induce the Senate, the cabinet and the House of Representatives, to raise a force sufficiently

Grant's residence in West Bountiful, built 1854. Left, with broom, Susan Noble Grant, and granddaughter Klea Muir, 1898. LDS Church Archives.

strong to go out against the poor defenceless Mormon women and children who were left on the wild prairie unprotected. Yes, Mr. Thomas H. Benton wanted to take troops and pounce upon your wives and children whom you had left upon the banks of the Missouri River and sweep them out of existence. And when Colonel Kane argued the case and said, "Supposing you cut off the men what shall be done with the women and children." "O," said Benton, "if you argue the cause and wish to know what shall be done with the women, I say wipe them off too." "Well then," said Colonel Kane, "what shall be done with the children?" "Why," said Benton, "cut them off, men, women and children for the earth ought to drink their blood." The feeling was so strong upon the question that it came within a little of magnetizing the whole nation.[6]

What should we have done if we could not have argued that we [had] 500 men upon the plains engaged in the service of their country, and their wives and children left without protection. What, I ask, would have been the consequence if we had not had this plea? Israel must have been put upon the altar, and if we could not have raised the complement of men, what would have been the fate of this people? Israel must have been put in the tomb, unless by the interference of high heaven, a ram had been found in the thicket. Yes, brethren, had it not been for this Battalion, a horrible massacre would have taken place upon the banks of the Missouri river. Then, I say, notwithstanding your hardships, and the difficulties you passed through, you rendered service to the people of God, that will ever be remembered and such service as will bring blessings upon your heads in time and in eternity. And if your friends fell by the wayside; and if any of you lost your families, your wives or your children, and you sustained the people of God, you can depend upon a reward for all that you suffered, for you are the sons of God. This is the real relationship of this battalion to the Lord almighty. Our motto is, "sustain the Constitution of the United States," and not abuse it. We intend to live by it, and this is no chimera, as some of our enemies might be pleased to call it. You have done a good work, and I say, may God bless you all and may you honor God as you have honored your country and all will go well from this time henceforth.

When Isaac went to the altar, he was called a lad, and was 25 years old (and some of you are not much older than that now), he went cheerfully, because he knew it to be right, but he had no more of a task to perform than this Battalion, for you had to live upon what you could eat; eat beast, hides, blood and all; and you had to eat your mules and walk over the scorching plains, and be days and nights without water. I would as leave have carried Isaac's burden as yours. These things are remembered by all those who see and feel in the kingdom of God; but I am fully aware that many of those who are rather careless and wild do not realize the important service that you rendered on that memorable occasion. The burthen laid upon you was hard to bear and it was harder than there was any need for it to be.

I wish I could speak better things of the great men of our country; but I tell you what I had from Colonel Kane, in his father's own room, it is not some wild chimera, but it is the truth, as I had it from headquarters. They wanted to raise forces from Missouri and Illinois, and the authorities of the nation did advocate the doctrine of putting to death all the "Mormons" and we know it.

We are friendly to our country and when we speak of the flag of our union, we love it, and we love the rights the constitution guarantees to every citizen. What did the prophet Joseph say? When the Constitution shall be tottering, we shall be the people to save it from the hand of the foe.[7]

Even though the weather was lovely, the storehouses relatively full, and the Saints secure in the mountains, Grant wanted no one to forget. He was happy himself; but even so, if persecution and trials were not immediately at hand, the Saints needed to remember that such were the essence of righteousness, and that the enemies of the chosen people were nevertheless common and ever-present.

As an early spring seemed to follow the pleasant winter, things continued to go well for the Saints in Utah, in spite of some Indian troubles in the southern counties. Grant busied himself with mayoral and ecclesiastical duties in Salt Lake City that ranged from keeping tabs on a new sugar beet processing plant to assisting Brigham Young and Heber Kimball in the ordination of Hyrum Smith's son John as patriarch of the Church.[8] But in preaching, the lanky Mormon apostle found his greatest pleasure. He seemed to be speaking his mind in every meeting and every hall in the city through February and March of 1855. Some of his sermons were pointed and aimed at particular problems among the Saints, such as too much drinking or doing business with Gentile merchants, but on occasion he chose to preach doctrinal discourses through which the Mormons came to recognize the second counselor not only as predicative but also authoritative and logical. One of the most dynamic of such sermons occurred from the stand in the Bowery on a rainy March Sunday in 1855, when Brother Jedediah expounded upon the favorite Mormon subject of faith and works. After a lengthy treatise on the Mormon doctrines encircling the principle at hand, Grant issued his typical challenge to the Saints.

> If the Saints of God actually have the faith of the ancients, let them practise the doctrine of their works. A man will tell me that he is a "Mormon," that he believes in the faith of the ancients, when at the same time he practises everything else but their religion. My rule is to practise our religion. If I want a drink of catnip tea, or a composition, or of lobelia, it is all right, but I will first practise my religion. You know that it is hardly allowable in Utah to drink any more than five gallons of lobelia at once, for the Assembly of Deseret once had the matter under consideration.
>
> I wish to see the Saints practise their religion, and carry it out, and if they cannot live by their religion, then die by it. That is the doctrine. I want

my religion if I am going to die. Most certainly that is the time I would not like to lay it by, for it would be unwise to do that, since that is the very time that one needs it the most, and is the time when he should be immersed in it. I want to see the Saints actually show by their works that they have the faith of the ancients.

If I am sick, and send for an administrator, I want him to fulfil every word of the Lord; and if there is any body there you don't like when you come to me, invite them out of the door. When devils are in the house, and you don't like them, cast them out, but be sure to administer the ordinances right. When an Elder comes to administer to the sick, and is afraid of greasing his fingers, or of dropping a little oil on his vest or pants, and says, "O never mind the oil, there is no virtue in the olive oil; you might as well drink it as anoint with it; besides, I might grease my gloves; I will dispense with it." I want such a man to walk off. If I was sick, and he came to me in that manner, I should say, "You are a poor, miserable hypocrite." That is the way I should feel and talk. Let a man, when he has the right kind of faith, practise the works thereof; and when God says, "Anoint with oil," anoint; I don't care if it runs down your beard as it ran down Aaron's, it will not hurt you. When a man complies with every requisition of heaven, his works and his faith are right. He offers up prayer for the sick, he anoints with oil, and lays on his hands. When his works are right they will correspond with his faith, and men and women will be healed.

I wish to call upon you to be faithful, to have the right kind of faith, and to exhibit it by your works. What is the testimony of the Latter-day Saints? Our religion is as different from other people's religion as our testimony is different from theirs. When Joseph Smith bore testimony, he told the people that an angel from high heaven had spoken to him, that he had been ordained by authority from Jesus Christ, and sent forth to preach the Gospel. Did you ever hear the Methodist bear such a testimony? If not, how can you expect them to have such faith as the man who believes the testimony of Joseph Smith? The Methodists have no such testimony, only as they have it from the Latter-day Saints. Joseph also said that he had seen the dark regions of Hades; did you ever hear a Methodist bear that testimony? No. Here are Elders of Israel who have seen company after company of angels, who have seen the sick healed, the ears of the deaf unstopped, the tongue of the dumb loosed, and the eyes of the blind opened. You will hear them testify that they have seen the glory of God; and that by the spirit of prophecy, then have seen war, pestilence, and famine coming upon the earth. The Methodists do not pretend to have such testimony, and of course have not such faith. You may go to any sect you please upon the earth, and their faith corresponds with their testimony, more or less.

The Latter-day Saints have testimony, and faith comes to them by hearing the word of God, but it comes to others by hearing the words of men.

It is no wonder that the Latter-day Saints believe differently from other folks, for their works are different, and their testimony is different. We believe in gathering together; the Lord God has spoken to us from the heavens and commanded us to gather. They do not believe in gathering to where the Almighty can talk to them; they do not even pray for the Lord to send an angel to speak to them. The Latter day Saints try to live their religion, that they may converse with angels, receive the administration of holy messengers from the throne of God, be sanctified in their spirits, affections, and all their desires, that the Holy Ghost may rest upon them, and their hearts be filled therewith, and become competent to bear the presence of angels.

May the Lord bless you, and wake you up upon these points of doctrine, that your faith and works may ever correspond, and that your blessings be equal with those of the ancient people of God, in the name of Jesus Christ our Lord. Amen.[9]

For Jedediah Grant, the premium in religion was consistency, and he had come to see himself as an accomplished theologian, fascinated with the writings of such Gentile thinkers as the popular Bible scholar Dr. Adam Clarke, but even more so in the words of such premier Mormon intellects as Orson Hyde, who was preaching that spring about the marriage of Jesus to Mary and Martha as well as to other women.[10] Consequently, it was natural that, when the Deseret Theological Institute was organized on April 7, 1855, as a seminary "to teach men all that is good," Grant, along with Heber Kimball and George A. Smith, was designated a vice president and director.[11]

Never in the history of the Church, with the possible exception of a few days at Nauvoo, had the Saints enjoyed such optimistic prosperity as they did in the early spring of 1855. By the end of April, most of the crops were in and growing well under a warm sun and generous rains. Even Brigham, with his normal load of ecclesiastical and territorial cares, seemed jovial and expansive.[12] The Twelfth General Epistle to the Church, which the First Presidency signed April 25, also reflected this mood of optimism.[13] Grant was spending most of his time on the farm in Davis County, enjoying his chosen avocation as a farmer.[14] Then, toward the end of the month, the weather changed suddenly. Cold winds from the northwest shook the blooms on the fruit trees along the Wasatch Front. By May 1 the days had turned increasingly cool and the nights unusually cold.

Everyone shuddered at this perhaps ominous shift in the atmosphere, but folks in Salt Lake had little time to be concerned, because the Endowment House had reached completion and was to be dedicated May 5 with live endowments and sealings to begin that day. When the long-awaited morning dawned, the anticipatory mood of the Saints sagged with the discovery that there had been a hard freeze during the night—the fruit was gone, the crops in fields bent to the earth. The dedication nevertheless went ahead as scheduled, with Grant among those administering ordinances that day and, at the end of the day, giving the prayer.[15] It was a joyous day, as well as one of nagging trepidation.

Three days after the opening of the Endowment House, the First Presidency, along with Wilford Woodruff, Truman O. Angell, and other Church dignitaries, left Salt Lake City for an extended tour of the southern settlements. Also accompanying the party were Chief Justice John F. Kinney and Indian agent Garland Hurt. Among the purposes of the trip were such ecclesiastical tasks as the ordination of Isaac C. Haight as stake president at Cedar City, the organization of a high council at Parowan, and the political responsibilities of visiting the Indians and seeing to the preparation of facilities at the new territorial capital at Fillmore.[16] On May 13 the party spent the day in Manti, where a group of missionaries was preparing to leave on a colonizing expedition southward. Grant's remarks to them dealt with the Mormon Indian policy, and more particularly with one interesting part of it—miscegenation. In this address, he revealed a fearlessness in his character both as to convention and as to the opinions of others.

> I think that the counsel to the brethren will be to go and establish a fort and farm. You have young men that are going upon this mission. You should not adopt the Indian customs any more than you can help. You should endeavor to learn their language but not to run horses with them, or do anything that will not be good for them. It will try your faith and skill to go among them and do your duty. You will have to pray much. You will have to

learn to pray if you never learned before. You want to read and understand the Book of Mormon. You will want to teach them that book and let them know that book will be a great blessing to them. Let them know that it was written by their fathers. You must have patience with them. You must not think that the nations will be born in a day at first, but the Lord works by small means. If you are faithful the Lord will bless you and give you his holy Spirit, and the gifts of healing will be with you, and they will begin to be moved upon by the Spirit of God, and their minds will be delighted by degrees.

Some may think it is a small thing to take a squaw for a wife. They almost feel it will be a disgrace and do not wish to do it, but I will tell you if I could get a good woman, a chief's daughter, I would take and marry her; this is really my feelings and the first time I can get a squaw I intend to do it, not to gratify my passion but to raise up that people, and I will say that God will bless that man that pursues this course with a single eye to the glory of God, and I will say that any of you who will do it shall be blest, and this is true. Some may say if I was to get me a squaw my wife would leave me—let her go to hell or anywhere else she pleases, if she feels disposed to leave a good man because he undertakes to do the will of God. Now no woman shall ne'r weave a web around my neck—weblah[?] like—but if a woman will do right I will do all I can for her.

Every man that goes to build up this kingdom should trust in God, and should do his duty regardless of all consequences. I will say that when O Hyde was sent to Fort Supply [in 1853], which might be called Fort Defunct, if he had done well he would have taken a squaw to wife but he scorned it, and his eyes were more on the gold than saving Israel; he did not do his duty in this thing. I will have to relate a dream. I dreamed I was among a large number of natives, and they gathered together against me and my brethren. I thought that they were armed with great clubs, and that they were going to mash my head with their clubs, and I called on the Lord and offered up the signs of the Priesthood, and their clubs fell to the ground; they could not do me any harm. I know that you will have to live by the Priesthood, and you will be preserved through it by the power of God, when you are in the path of your duty.

I will now say to you go your way and do your duty and when you have an opportunity to marry a good young squaw, and it comes right along in your way without your seeking it I want you to do it, and I will do so to[o], so help me God, and I mean what I say as I live, and if one of my wives says she will leave me for marrying a squaw, I would say go as soon as you please, you sweet tobacco posie.

Go to now and do your duty in this and every other thing and don't fail and God will bless you both in time and in eternity, and I know it and I say it in the name of Jesus Christ Amen.[17]

After pressing south through Iron County and then back north through Beaver and Scipio valleys, the party arrived home in Salt Lake City early on the morning of May 27. It was a beautiful Sunday morning in the valley, but the effects of the cold weather that had struck three weeks before were still apparent. In addition, there was a serious threat of flooding, and the grasshoppers were as bad as they had ever been. That afternoon, the members of the First Presidency addressed the Saints, reporting mainly on their trip to the southern settlements.[18] Three days later at a gathering in the Social Hall, Jedediah Grant delivered a lecture before the Deseret Theological Institute on the workings of the Holy Spirit. He stuck to his subject through the first half of his speech but by the end seemed more anxious to raise the minds of the Saints from their worries and concerns, revealing in the process some of his confidence in his oratorical skills and a bit about the processes of his remarkable self-education.

With all the study that I have exercised, with all the books I have read and the experience I have had, I never have been able to convey, with any degree of force, the ideas presented to my mind, without the Spirit of the Lord. Believing in this fact, I have never premeditated what I should say. Some suppose that, to treat upon theology, or any other science coming under the general term, a person must have a classical education.

I hope you, as well as myself, have often thought upon the science of theology, or upon other branches of science; but notwithstanding we may reflect upon them, and think upon them till we make our heads ache, yet my experience has proved to me that an Elder of Israel cannot impress any subject on the minds of the people, unless he has the Holy Spirit.

I might reason upon this point at some length; for instance, we have some among us who are good preachers, and who are considered good in language, but yet they are not able to impress their ideas upon other minds, unless they have the Spirit of the Lord. I find others who are not considered good speakers nor good in language, yet when filled with this Spirit they can convey their ideas in a clear manner to those whom they address. Therefore I reason like this, if a person address[es] you and wishes to make a suitable impression upon your mind, he must have the Spirit.

Latter-day Saints are, and have been highly favored; the channel of communication has been opened from heaven to earth in our day, and has inspired this people with the gift of the Holy Ghost, and by that gift they have proved the things of God. When I read the productions of men I am apt to forget them; I go for instance, to Elder Hyde's grammar class, and I study, and read, and commit the rules of grammar to memory, but unless I keep my mind constantly upon that subject, it will fly away from me; it is like the man's rabbit, "when he went to put his hand upon it, it was not there." On the contrary, there are certain truths brought to my mind by the aid of the Spirit of the Lord, that I have never forgotten. Truths deposited by the Holy Ghost are treasured up in the mind, and do not leave it.

One trait I have had in my character from my boyhood, and that is, not to believe every story told me to be true. I well remember that my mother used to instruct and teach me that if I was a bad boy, I should have to go to hell, and that the fire there was seven times hotter than any fire I could possibly make, even if I should make it with beech or maple wood, and there I must burn for ever and ever. I never believed this story, but I presume that my mother did; I could not, therefore I felt no trouble about it.

Still I was particular in my notions of certain ideas. I remember reflecting when very young—my brother had killed a quail, and in conversing upon the circumstances, he asked my mother if there was not a quail heaven, which caused me to reflect much upon the idea of a future state of the animal creation. And, when quite young, I read the sermons of John Wesley, who believed that the animal creation would have an eternal existence as well as man, therefore my ideas were strengthened upon this thing; but when I came to read the vision given to Joseph Smith upon a future state, as contained in the Book of Doctrine and Covenants, I believed it, although some in our neighborhood were much troubled with the doctrine it contained, but it gave me great joy and satisfaction.

From the time I began to read books, I have been particular in relation to what I would accept for doctrine. I am aware that some persons will believe almost anything, and are not particular in relation to the doctrine they receive.

I remember well, when a boy, of hearing brother Brigham speak in tongues, and the effect it produced I shall never forget; I could feel the spirit, although I did not fully understand the tongue. I have heard others speak in tongues, but it had not the same effect, and I have marked the different impressions received under different individuals.

"No man can understand the things of God, but by the Spirit of God." Ask a person who has preached for years, if he can remember what he said; I know I cannot. I can remember that I had the Spirit of God at such a time; I remember that I taught by the Holy Ghost at such a time, and the testimony that I bore to the people, and I realize the principle, I trusted in the Lord. I know no more about shaping my discourses than I did when I first commenced to preach, and no more than if I had never preached in my life; but I always speak from the impressions of the moment, as I receive them. I want to go into a meeting without anything premeditated, and speak from the impulse of the moment, for I feel well when taking this course. Whether I feel lively and energetic or dull and sleepy, I shall speak accordingly.

I have passed through various scenes up and down in the world, and never failed to accomplish anything that has been given to me. I have in my life, crossed some of the most dangerous water courses—some which no other person would attempt to cross; not that I was any more daring than they were, naturally, but by acting in accordance with the impression that I then received, and from those impressions I knew I could cross. And on different occasions, when I have carried out those impressions, it has come out just right; and when I have not done so, it has been just the reverse.

Again, whenever I have had anything that was great or important to accomplish, I have been impressed with my own weakness and inability to perform the task imposed upon me, and that of myself I was as nothing, only as I trusted in God, and under these circumstances I was certain to speak by the power and influence of the Holy Ghost. When I have trusted in books, or in my own acquirements that I had gleaned from reading the productions of different authors, (for I used to be fond of reading the works of [Scottish philosopher Thomas] Brown, [Scottish philosopher John] Abercrombie, [English philosopher John] Locke, [English clergyman Isaac] Watts, and other metaphysical writers,) I was sure to be foiled in my attempt, for all would leave me. But whenever I have trusted in the Lord, and relied upon Him for strength, it has come out right.

There is a fountain of intelligence, and the channel thereto is open, thank God for it, and the light of heaven bursts forth through this channel.

Why was it that Joseph could take the wisest Elder that ever travelled and preached, and, as it were, circumscribe his very thoughts? Simply because he had the Holy Ghost. Why can our President do the same? Is it because he has read books for years? No. But he has sought his God, and the Holy Ghost is in him, and he is enabled to search the deep things of God. Then, I say, that man knows the most who enjoys the greatest portion of the Holy Spirit. An individual who lacks this principle may be filled with the learning of the world, but can he rise up and tell it, unless he has the Holy Spirit? I answer, no. To impress the knowledge that he possesses upon the minds of others, he must have the Holy Ghost. I wish to enquire whether the channel is open between you and the heavens, and do you draw daily from that source? If so, then you are in the narrow path, and rejoicing in the truth.

A great many people feast upon imagination instead of feasting upon that which is tangible, and they will allow their minds to be led away by fancy, and will make out how great they will be at some future time, and how good they intend to be and how much of the Holy Ghost they expect to receive; but the idea is, what do you enjoy at the present time, and what are the blessings you enjoy at this present moment, right now? Am I doing right to day? Is the Holy Ghost in me now? Is God's blessing with me now—(not at some other time)? If so, then all is well.

I want the Saints to be impressed with the motto of being happy all the time; if you cannot be happy to day, how can you be happy to morrow? I speak this from what I have learned myself; though it has given me much of trouble, and a great amount of perseverance, to be happy under all circumstances. I have learned not to fret myself. It has taken me a great while to arrive at this point, but I have obtained it in a measure, and perhaps many of you have obtained the same thing, but I doubt whether a great many have learned the secret of happiness.

In order to understand the principle of happiness you must not be ever complaining, but learn not to fret yourselves. If things do not go right, let them go as they will, if they go rough, let it be so; if all hell boils over, let it boil. I thank the Lord for the bitter as well as for the sweet; I like to grapple with the opposite; I like to work and have something to oppose. I used to dread those things, but now I like to grapple with opposition, and there is plenty of it on the right hand and on the left. When trouble gets in among you, shake it off, or bid it stand out of the way. If the devil should come and say, "Brother Brigham is not doing his duty, or is not doing right," kick him right out of your way; bid him depart, do not allow him to have place in your habitation, but learn to be happy.

I remember a noted deist who said that it was a poor religion that would not make a person happy here in this life; he would not give a fig for such a religion; and I would say the same; give me a religion that will make me happy here, and that will make me happy hereafter. If you have the blues, or the greens, shake them off, and learn to be happy, and to be thankful. If you have nothing to eat but johnny cake, be thankful for that, and if you have not johnny cake, but have a roasted potatoe and buttermilk, why, be thankful; or if you have a leg of a chicken, or any other kind of food, learn to be as happy under these circumstances as if you had ten dollars.

One time in Nauvoo, some English brethren did not like to eat corn bread, and one of them says to another, just before partaking of some, "Are you going to ask a blessing? I am not going to thank God for nothing else but corn bread, potatoes, and salt." Brethren, those feelings should not be, we ought to be happy and shake off the blues, no difference what we may be called to pass through, but let us have the light of the Lord, the channel of inspiration open, that the light of truth may break in upon our understandings, that we may be rich in faith and in good works.

I used once to be troubled with dyspepsia, and had to frequently call upon the Elders to administer, and one occasion, brother Joseph Smith says to me, "Brother Grant, if I could always be with you, I could cure you." How is it that brother Brigham is able to comfort and soothe those who are depressed in spirit, and always make those with whom he associates so happy? I will tell you how he makes us feel so happy. He is happy himself, and the man who is happy himself can make others feel so, for the light of God is in him, and others feel the influence, and feel happy in his society. I want the Saints to live in a way that they can feel happy all the time, and then we shall enjoy the Holy Spirit; then we shall meet in heaven to part and meet again; and when we get through our work assigned us, then we may assist, if not to make a world as large as this, in organizing some little lump of clay.

May God bless, save and receive you into his kingdom, is the prayer and desire of my heart, for Christ's sake. Amen.[19]

So in this brief period of peace in Zion, the Saints had come to look squarely into the eye of the great didactic storm that was Jedediah Grant. Yet even as he was teaching them "the secret of happiness" that evening, swirling about them were the makings of the kind of opposition to righteousness that Grant loved to fight with his sharp tongue and the rattlings of Mormon Thunder. Few of them would ever forget the months to come.

← Notes →

1. See Journal History, December 26, 1854, 1; *St. Louis Luminary*, March 31 and April 14, 1855.

2. *St. Louis Luminary*, March 31, 1855. George A. Smith reported in a letter to the *Luminary*, a Mormon newspaper, that he had "heard brother Grant remark that he had not enjoyed such good health during any previous session [of the legislature] although there were some very protracted joint sessions."

3. Family records of Alvin G. Pack, Salt Lake City.

4. See comments on the unusual weather in Journal History, February 1 and 4, 1855, both p. 1.

5. Journal History, February 6, 1855, 1–2.

6. Ibid., 2. Sherman L. Fleek, in his excellent *History May Be Searched in Vain: A Military History of the Mormon Battalion* (Spokane, Wash.: The Arthur H. Clark Company, 2006), 113, disputes Grant's claim that Benton was attempting to raise troops to destroy the Mormons in 1846, because "there is neither record nor evidence to support any of these claims." John Yurtinius and others have suggested that Mormons leaders used such myths and legends to steel their followers against the federal government. See Yurtinius, "A Ram in the Thicket: The Mormon Battalion in the Mexican War" (Ph.D. diss., Brigham Young University, 1975).

7. Journal History, February 6, 1855, 2–4. Grant's reference to this famous pronouncement on Mormons saving the Constitution is one of the earliest extant. For a primary source reference to the notion, see Elizabeth Ann Anderson, "Howard and Martha Coray: Chroniclers of Joseph Smith's Words and Life," *Journal of Mormon History* 33 (Fall 2007): 111. According to Martha Coray's notes, Smith said, on July 19, 1840: "Even this Nation will be on the very verge of crumbling to peices [sic] and tumbling to the ground and when the constitution is upon the brink of ruin this people will be the Staff upon which the Nation shall lean and they shall bear the constitution away from the very verge

of destruction." That he said this more than once is also likely.

8. See Journal History, February 1, 1855, 1, February 7, 1855, 3, and February 18, 1855, 5.

9. Sermon by Jedediah M. Grant, March 11, 1855, *Journal of Discourses*, 26 vols. (London and Liverpool: LDS Booksellers Depot, 1855–86), 2:272–79.

10. Sermon by Orson Hyde, March 18, 1855, *Journal of Discourses*, 4:257–63.

11. Journal History, April 7, 1855, 1. Brigham Young was president of the institute. For more on this organization, see Joseph Heinerman, "Early Utah Pioneer Cultural Societies," *Utah Historical Quarterly* 47 (Winter 1979): 71, 73, 79–80.

12. On Thursday evening, April 12, Jane Blackhurst entertained Brigham Young and Jedediah Grant along with several members of the Twelve at dinner. "The president enjoyed the repast first rate and was very jocular." Journal History, April 12, 1855, 1.

13. Journal History, April 25, 1855, 4.

14. Journal History, April 19, 1855, 1.

15. Journal History, May 5, 1855, 1 2.

16. Journal History, May 8, 1855, 1; May 13, 1855, 2–3; and May 19, 20, 21, 22, 24, and 17, 1855, all p. 1.

17. "J M Grant's address to the Missionaries at Manti," holograph, Heber J. Grant Papers, LDS Church Archives. Wilford Woodruff recorded this speech, adding that "the Speaker made other remarks that were not reported but the Spirit and power of God rested mightily upon him. He was followed by TO Angell and W Woodruff who bore testimony on the same subject." Woodruff also reported that eleven missionaries were appointed at that meeting to the Elder Mountains and Las Vegas, and that seven of them were ordained seventies under his and Jedediah's hands. For an intriguing view of the social stigma attached to Mormon intermarriage with Indians, see Todd Compton, "Civilizing the Ragged Edge: Jacob Hamblin's Wives," *Journal of Mormon History* 33 (Summer 2007): 155–98.

18. "History of Brigham Young," 1855, 51, LDS Church Archives.

19. Jedediah M. Grant, May 30, 1855, *Journal of Discourses*, 3:7 12.

"I would like to see the work of the reformation commence, and continue...."

⇌ 13 ⇌
Breaking Branches

ON THE FOURTH OF JULY, 1855, the Nauvoo Brass Band played from the balcony of Major General Grant's house on Main Street as the Legion marched to the parade grounds for the day's festivities. By that time, a long heat wave had become monotonous to the citizens of Utah. Day after day dawned hot and dry, as if the destructive frosts of the spring were demanding recompense. The First Presidency had just returned from a "scientific expedition" to the north to investigate areas for future settlement,[1] and Jedediah Grant was not pleased with the condition in which he found his sweltering city. The heat and the concomitant drought had evidently affected the Saints as well as their crops adversely. The mayor immediately issued from his office a statement of his feelings toward "the sluggards and drones" in the beehive. It appeared in the *Deseret News* on July 11, an item-by-item list of grievances against those who had forgotten their calling as citizens of the City of Zion. In the midst of the barbs, there came forth in this letter some very clear evidence of the lack of separation between the secular and the sacred in mid-nineteenth-century Utah.

First:—Your fences, in what condition are they, and in what condition should they be, to be worthy of imitation by other cities? This city should be a pattern in all things for the multitude of cities now building through this wide spread territory. Heretofore you could not have been called upon to build substantial fences around your city lots, with the same propriety as you can now, for you had to build houses and raise grain for your families. At the present time, with but very few exceptions, you have comfortable houses, and more land than you can farm as it should be farmed, for if the lots of this city were properly fenced and cultivated they would yield an abundance of grain, fruits, and vegetables for all the inhabitants of this corporation, and it is confidently believed there would be a large surplus to supply the wants of others. You who have not, are hereby very respectfully called upon to go to with your mind, might, and strength, and fence in your lots with a good and substantial fence. All who will do this, may your sleep be sweet and undisturbed, and your bodies invigorated with a clear conscience. May all the sluggards and the drones who will not do this, be bit by bed bugs, and tormented by the nightmare, and have their bodies clogged with a conscience clear as mud.

Second:—Your water ditches, are they kept clean, and bridges built over them, as the ordinance of the city requires? All the city supervisors and water masters should, without delay, do their duty, calling loudly upon the people to do theirs, until every ditch is put where it should be and kept clean, with crossways and bridges placed where they are needed. The supervisors in their respective wards have all the authority they can ask or wish for to improve and keep in order the water ditches, that health and life may flow in our streets instead of filth and death. Clean your ditches, O Israel! why will you die? Work with shovel, spade, and hoe, while it is day, for when the night cometh the clean may rest, but filth I hate; the sluggard and drone deserve their fate.

Third:—What attention are you paying to setting out shade trees along the ditches, to ornament and make beautiful the side walks of this great city? Great because it is good, good because the great are here. When the angels came to visit Abraham, he could invite them to rest under the tree, until the tender and good calf was dressed and, with butter and milk, eaten by them while he and his guests enjoyed the shade. If angels wait until some men in our city raise a tree as large as the one the calf was eaten under, it will be a long time before their women laugh the laugh of Sarah. But if the tree is raised, and the angels come and deliver a similar message causing some of the daughters of Sarah to laugh, I hope they will not deny laughing.

I am pleased with the prospects in many of our streets; several thousands of fine shade trees already add much to the beauty and comfort of our city and many thousands more might be growing, to break still more the treeless monotony that did exist here, as it does now over almost this entire Territory. Many have failed in raising trees, in consequence of setting them out too late in the spring. The fall is the time for setting out pine, fir, and cedar. I think balm of Gilead, cottonwood, box elder, quaking asp, birch, sugar maple, and mahogony, will all live if set out in February or early in March. Now is the time to make your calculations and fix your ditches, and be ready for setting out trees. My experience has taught me that it is wisdom to keep the wild trees in the streets, and out of our lots, as those that are in them, cumber the ground without yielding any income of importance. If you will listen to my advice, or take Governor Young for a pattern, you will prepare your ground in a proper manner for all kinds of fruit trees adapted to this climate. To start with, set out the apple tree, the pear, plum, cherry, peach, and apricot, not forgetting the grape, gooseberry, raspberry, currant, and strawberry, and soon, very soon, all will have plenty of the best fruit ever eaten since Adam was driven out of the garden of Eden, or since the bugs and flies commenced tormenting the drones and sluggards.

Fourth:—I wish, with many others, to see our side walks kept clear of wagons, carts, carriages, wood, poles, fencing materials, and even building materials, as far as those building can do so without too great a sacrifice. The city marshal and police have been ordered to aid in enforcing the ordinance in relation to cleaning streets and side walks. The cow pens, pigsties, &c., nearer the street than 20 feet, unless they are cleaned every day, will be removed forthwith at the expense of the owner or occupant. This may make the drones and sluggards grunt and whine, and perhaps leave the hive; if so there will be more room for the industrious bees to store their honey.[2]

The demand for diligent community responsibility that the mayor here issued was no different than the demand for spiritual cleanliness that had become the watchword of Grant's tenure as a Mormon prophet. His implicit call for complete obedience to the "best code of [religious and secular] laws and the best [ecclesiastical and civil] leaders to teach us" demonstrates that Apostle/Mayor Grant, the same as Prophet/Governor Young, made absolutely no distinction between the secular/civil and the religious/spiritual realms. The kingdom of the Saints under Young might well have been the kingdom of Israel under Solomon. Even John Winthrop would have envied the situation.[3]

Whatever its significance to Utah's lack of church-state separation, Grant's letter showed one thing for certain: He had become increasingly dissatisfied with the performance of the Saints. Perhaps the torrid weather had set his teeth on edge, or maybe he was reflecting the growing concern among the brethren that the Mormons had become too much a part of the world in the midst of their lovely valleys and that the Gentiles among them were corrupting them with abominations as fast as Brothers Brigham and Heber could build fences between the two groups. But it was Brother Jeddy's business to speak plainly about the problems at hand, as on July 8, when he lambasted the non-Mormon community of Salt Lake City for its sinister influences and attempts to controvert the growth and purity of the kingdom.[4] By July 13, Grant was ready to speak even more plainly about those among the Saints who had so readily adopted the world in place of the kingdom. Speaking at a special conference in Provo that day, the angular preacher had converted his light mood of previous months into one of fire and lightning. Apparently someone within earshot had been making jokes about the teachings of the First Presidency.

> I have noticed in my travels among the Saints, from time to time, that their profession was long and loud in relation to their strength and faith in "Mormonism," and in fact they would be much offended if called weak in the faith; they will speak well of faith, repentance, baptism, the gift of the Holy Ghost by the laying on of hands, the healing of the sick by the administration of the Elders, and of some of the general views of the Church, and claim to be very strong, very devout, and very much attached to the cause, and would feel much offended indeed if any one should even suspect that they were weak in the faith; and at the same time perhaps those individuals, who make such high professions of faith and devotedness, will acknowledge that there are certain important truths revealed from heaven which they would ridicule, scoff at, and trample under their feet.
>
> Inasmuch as the Almighty God has revealed certain doctrines and sanctioned certain practices, and seeing that the Almighty has said that these revelations and practices are true and righteous, I therefore advise that you do not allow the same to be trampled under foot as salt that has no savor. Again, let no man, whether Gentile or Jew, Israelite or Greek, nor your wives or children, nor any whom you have jurisdiction over, throw out any jeers upon, nor sneer, laugh, and scoff at, any portion of the law of God. Some items of doctrine are especially obnoxious to some men and some women who have peculiar feelings respecting them, and because of such feelings they begin to laugh at those who are favorable to those items, and attempt to spoil the good leaven.
>
> My advice in all such cases is, just tell them that there is the hole which

the carpenter made, and they can go through it, for you will have the law of God reverenced by all who reside in or visit your habitation. I merely give this advice as some that might be applied to the Saints; as some of the every day and practical advice. I allude to the entire law of God, to all that the Lord our God has revealed, whether it pertains to the building of temples, or to faith, repentance, baptism, or the laying on of hands, or to the matrimonial relations, or to any doctrine or principle which relates to the salvation and glory of man.

I say as one, that I have no fellowship for that man who will permit any person, over whom he has any rightful control, to ridicule the law, or any portion of the law, of God. I have no fellowship for those who allow any such proceedings in their houses, neither have I any fellowship for those who ridicule the law of God in any respect; and I shall be glad when they take their exit to California, or to the States, for they are, in their persons, in their actions, and by their words, detrimental to their neighbors and the circles in which they move.

I wish to see those who profess to be Saints act as Saints ought to act. In the Church of the living God I believe that every man and woman that will admit evil practices, ought to be called up and dealt with for their fellowship, and if they will not reform, regulate their households and set them in order, they ought to be cut off from the Church. It is humbug to talk about first regulating a city, a county, or a territory; but start with a family at a time, and let the Bishop who presides see what is going on with every family, and when a family is found which will admit of God and His laws being ridiculed, cut them off from the Church. If any are found who will curse and swear, and break the law of the Sabbath, bring them up and deal with them for that; and if any are known to steal, deal with them for that act.

The Church needs trimming up, and if you will search, you will find in your wards certain branches which had better be cut off. The kingdom would progress much faster, and so will you individually, than it will with those branches on, for they are only dead weights to the great wheel.

First get the families united, then get the wards, the towns, the cities, and the counties regulated, and you will have every part of the Territory right; but this spirit of ridicule must not be allowed. Is a man who loves God going to have the law of the Almighty ridiculed? Many of those who profess so much, will feign publicly to acknowledge and support the very doctrines which they and their friends deride and permit to be scoffed at, and at the same time they will practise unlawfully, in secret, those things which they accuse others of.

I would like to see the work of reformation commence, and continue until every man had to walk to the line, then we should have something like union; but you might as well cast little pebbles in the air to stay the wind as to undertake to make those walk right, pray right, and do right who are full of the devil. People must be right in their works, and be brought to know and practise their duties. You have got doctrine enough and revelation enough, and perhaps one difficulty is that you are too full of them. One doctrine which you need is to make your families, your streets, and every thing about you clean, and to prepare proper outhouses. Purify yourselves, your houses, lots, farms, and every thing around you on the right and on the left, then the Spirit of the Lord can dwell with you.

Do you suppose, when I go into a house that is filthy, that I believe that Saints of God dwell there? No, I believe that they are a filthy set of beings. Saints must practise cleanliness and purity, and show by their prayers, by all their works, and in their families, that they are reforming, and forsaking all and every kind of species of filthiness and evil practice, no matter what it is, no, not though it takes the hair off from your heads; no matter if it be high, low, rough, or smooth, the Almighty has given you a law to obey and reverence; and if you practise those doctrines which you have embraced, though all hell foam against you, by the power of God you will triumph and ask no odds of any one.

Talk about the Saints coming up to the Church of the first born, to the state of perfection which Enoch attained; if men and women ever attain to this, they have got to be pure in all their habits, pure in their spirits as well as in their doctrines, for the Lord has told us what is right and required in those things.

We have the best code of laws and the best men to teach us there are upon the earth, therefore all that is wanted is for us to practise those lessons which are taught us by the servants of the living God, and to love God with all our hearts, and live continually in the fear of the Almighty. Then when you come to meeting, you will not hear chastisement and reproof, but you will hear the peaceable things of the kingdom, and you will hear men and women speak and sing the sweet things of the kingdom of God.

In conclusion, may that light which is in you increase till you are prepared to bask in the perfect light of God. May God bless and save you, is my prayer in the name of Jesus. Amen.⁵

The conference at Provo continued two more days in a special bowery that had been constructed to shade the audience, but by the third day, July 15, so many were in attendance that some of them had to remain in their carriages in order to listen to the brethren and to escape the hot sun. On that Sunday evening, the party moved north to Lake City (American Fork), where Bishop Leonard E. Harrington entertained them at dinner prior to an evening meeting in which President Grant delivered another of his excited sermons about the need for a pruning of the vineyard.⁶ For a few short days, there had been a very real feeling of revival stirring among the Saints in Utah, but the needs of the harvest season seemed to overshadow everything, particularly in light of the poor growing season that had developed out of the late frost and a subsequent heat wave and drought.

Grant spent the rest of the summer dividing his time between the farm in Davis County, his mayoral duties, and work in the Endowment House, where, along with Heber Kimball, Orson Pratt, and Samuel W. Richards, he had taken the bulk of the responsibility for administering to the Saints ordinances such as live sealings and baptisms for the living and the dead.⁷ In addition, preparations were under way to move the legislative functions of the territory to the new capital in Fillmore.⁸ But there was also time for other things, such as the courting of Rachel Ridgeway Ivins, whom he would marry that November, and various social functions—an afternoon of eating watermelons at John Pack's, dinner with President Young in honor of returning Delegate John M. Bernhisel, a soirée at the Deseret Dramatic Association, and endless speaking engagements at such gatherings as the Pomological Society in the Social Hall.⁹ There seemed to be little time for breaking dead branches from the tree of Zion.

By the time October conference convened, Grant's marriage to thirty-five-year-old Rachel, a longtime friend from New Jersey and one of several women who had been sealed to Joseph Smith, had put into his mind the subject of his conference address. She would become his sixth living wife in anticipation of a large posterity and earthly kingdom, but more important to him had always been the consequential kingdom in heaven.¹⁰ His words in the afternoon session of October 6 were brief and to the point: The Latter-day Saints must be perfect, even though a specific doctrine or practice like polygamy might seem a difficult step in the long journey to righteousness and total submission to the laws of God.

I am aware the old maxim was that men would be judged according to the death they might die, but the Latter-day Saints believe that men will be judged by the life they live, and not by the death they die. We believe that a man will be rewarded according to his works, for it is not written that he shall be rewarded according to his ordination, or the special situation or place in which he may be called to act in the Church of God; but it is written, and that law, I believe, has never been revoked by high heaven, or by any of its legates to earth; hence it stands immutable, that all men shall be rewarded according to their works.

I am aware that many suppose that we entertain some unchristian feelings to those out of the Church, but this is a mistake; we only wish that persons who have shed the blood of our Apostles may be rewarded just according to their works. And we expect that, sooner or later, they will have meted out to them that reward which the Almighty actually knows that they deserve. When speaking of governors, rulers, kings, emperors, judges, and officers of nations and states, would we wish to reverse the general law that every person shall be rewarded according to their works? No. It would not do to have some men die as soon as many might desire, for they would not meet their proportionate reward on the earth.

I like to meditate upon this doctrine, I like to see its practical workings, rewarding every man according to his works; and I expect that the day will come when all Latter-day Saints will be perfectly satisfied with it.

I am fully aware that many people have been bred and raised in poor pussyism all their days, both in America and in Europe, and when they hear doctrines and principles taught by men who speak as freedom permits them, and as freemen have a right to speak, those who are clothed with the garments of poor pussyism get the grunts; well, grunt on until you grunt it all out. The Latter-day Saints who enjoy the light of the Lord, that power which loves the intelligence of heaven and imparts it to the faithful, thank the Lord that we expect that our elder brother, Jesus Christ, will give unto us according to our works. We expect that he will be rewarded according to his works, and that his associates will be rewarded according to theirs, and if our works are not good we ask for no good reward.

"Why," says one, "bless my soul, you do not say that it is applicable to females, do you?" Yes I do. "Oh, dear, what will the FIRST wife do in that case?" Why, bless your poor soul, she will be rewarded according to her works. That is the doctrine, and, thank God, there is no other way. You cannot alter it; you cannot revoke this eternal law. If a man has fifty wives and the fiftieth is the best, does the most good, she will get the greatest reward, in spite of all the grunting on the part of the first one.

In the Church of God, if a Teacher, a Priest, or Deacon, has the best works, if his labours are the most, if his acts are the most righteous in magnifying his calling to the utmost, he is better off than any man in the Church who does not magnify his calling. Is this doctrine applicable to ordained men in the Church? Yes, to every man of God, whether he be a Priest, Teacher, Member, Elder, or Apostle; each person will be rewarded according to his works. Is it applicable in families? Yes. "Oh," says one, "that makes me feel bad; my poor wife, my dear loving wife, the wife of my youth and the companion of my toils, what will she think of this? Bless me, I tremble for her." If her works are better, if her righteousness exceeds that of the rest of your wives, if she has more philanthropy, greater charity, and deserves more then they, she will get more. But if her works are not equal to those of some of the balance, she will still be rewarded according to her works.

I like the doctrine; I can swallow it without greasing my mouth. It is a first rate doctrine, and is a goodly part of the real faith, virtue, root and marrow of "Mormonism." Yes, it is applicable to families, thank God, and in the Church of God, in quorums, in councils, and in every other organized body; it applies to the world which we inhabit, and to every thing that is in heaven.

I know that there are hundreds of thousands of men out of this Church, and do we like them? Yes. When we talk against men out of the Church do we mean to be understood as speaking against good men—men who wish to do right? No; but we mean the poor devils and the devil's poor, that's the idea.

I want the Saints to do right and be blessed, which may God grant, in the name of Jesus Christ. Amen.[11]

The days after conference passed quickly for Grant as he participated in another exploratory expedition, this time to Cache Valley and its environs in the northern reaches of the territory,[12] in addition to completing preparations for the stay at Fillmore, where he would again serve in the legislature as a representative of Great Salt Lake County and as speaker of the house. The second counselor may also have been in poor health that fall, inasmuch as his only participation in the Sunday tabernacle meetings for several weeks was the delivery of invocations and benedictions.[13] It was rare indeed for Brigham's hammer to miss opportunities to practice the art of elocution upon the Saints; but by the end of November Grant was back on the circuit again, delivering a brief sermon on the morning of the season's first snowfall (November 11) and another at a party for a group of returned missionaries on the evening of November 29.[14]

You are here in these vallies bequeathed to us by the God of our fathers, for which we should be thankful. We can go forth in the dance, and our hearts are made glad. But these are pastimes, toys for children. The primary object we have in view is to build up the kingdom of God. This should engross our thoughts continually, at home and abroad. It should engage our talents and exertions here as elsewhere. You should not bury your talents when at home, but exert yourselves to sow the seeds of righteousness and immortality in the hearts of the saints, the principles that have inspired you while you were abroad preaching the gospel, which were revealed by holy prophets, sent from heaven by angels, and preached by prophets and apostles. You should exert yourselves to throw around them that favored influence you enjoy for their growth in righteousness and sanctification, and to prepare them for the great things that await us all.

For great things await us, not merely in theory, but in reality. Have not the saints of God the kingdom of God—to grap[p]le with, not only towns, cities, and nations, but with the world?—yea more, it has to cope with the universe, and give life and light to it, as well as to this lower creation.

There can only be one Adam, and that is the ruling power—that man who holds the keys of the kingdom of God on earth—that man is the Adam of the earth, he is God's mouthpiece, his presiding officer, and the only man who has the legal right to preside, and to turn the key of power, the key of life and death, and hold forth the sceptre of righteousness to the nations.

The relationship you sustain to your brethren who preside over you, to the Church of God, to the world, to the heavens, to your God, and to all the Gods that surround him, to the prophets, and to all the saints that dwell in the eternal worlds, is the reason why we regard ourselves thus, and have so great a work to perform.

We are led to reflect, while we rejoice at your return home, that some of our missionaries who went from here at the same time you went, have been called to another field of action, they have emigrated to another world. Bro. Orson Spencer is among that number. He has departed from this life. He died in St. Louis. After the fever had left him, he gradually declined until he fell asleep. With his surviving friends—with his family we deeply sympathize; also with others who are clad in mourning. But we do not mourn for them as for those who apostatise and die without hope.

May the God of heaven bless you; may his Spirit dwell with you, and with your families, and remain with you and with them; that you may go and return, meet and part, and continually be blessed. Whatever you do, keep the Spirit of God with you, that you may be blessed. And by all the authority and right given to me under the hands of the prophet Joseph, and the ordinations I have received from under the hands of our present prophet, and from those that were ordained by Peter, James, and John; and by the light of the Holy Ghost in me, I bless you all in the name of Jesus Christ; and may the laurels you have entwined around your brows remain there untarnished forever. May your families be blessed from generation to generation; and may the increase of heaven be upon them; may they be like Ephraim and Manasseh breaking forth on the right and on the left until they cannot be numbered for multitude. And if you have not brought your thousands with you from the nations to swell the concourse of saints in Zion, may you increase until you are like the sands of the sea, and the stars in the firmament for number. May the blessings of Joseph, of Brigham and Heber, and all the priesthood of God be and abide with you from this time henceforth and forever. Amen.[15]

Grant's pleasant and tender mood on this occasion surprised a newspaper reporter in attendance. He noted the second counselor's lengthy and eloquent blessing on the missionaries as evidence of high spirits "unusual" for Brother Jeddy. "Those missionaries that cannot dance," Grant said as he ended his speech, "and do not try, we shall consider have not fulfilled their missions this evening." He then led off the first dance, "which he executed in right good earnest," said the newsman. "The whole company caught the electric spark, and 'good earnest' characterized the exercises of the evening."[16]

On December 3, Governor Young and the rest of the legislative contingent left Great Salt Lake City for Fillmore and a protracted stay in the new capital.[17] Speaker Grant took his wife Maryette with him on the cold journey south. Upon their arrival in Fillmore, Grant addressed a letter to the rest of his family at home in Salt Lake City.

Fillmore City   Dec. 8th 1855

My Dear Family.

This is to let you know that we have arrived in the city all safe and well. The Governor's health and Br Kimballs improved all the way, and my own improved as fast as theirs. We found the road first rate. We made the trip in 4 days and a half. We had no snow untill we got into this valley and then but little. Our horses and mules stud the trip first rate. Indeed they were better when we arrived then when we started. All the companey are well and in good spirits.

I wish you to tell Br [John] Lambert to see Br [Phineas W.] Cook and have him go up to the farm and fix all the doors &c &c. Tell Br Lambert that I say he must look through the city and try to get work, as I cannot yet think of any work I have for him to do. Louis can chop the wood and feed the corn &c &c. If Br Lambert ennoyes you withhold food from him and invite him to find an other place forthwith. If you need help call on Cap [Leonard W.] Hardy that is if you kneed &c &c.

Let Br [John] Jordon have one hundred lbs of flower and 3 bushels of corn for the fowels. Let no person but him have as above. Have all the flower brought into the bedroom in the old house where Sarah Ann used to sleep. Keep all the doors locked. Call on Br [James] Beck to put in the glop in the windows. Call on Br [George] Romney for fire boards and to fix what you want fixed.

I will write by every mail and hope some of you will do the same. Try and take good care of your health do not neglect familey prayr. You all shall have my prayers for your health and prosperity. I miss you all—the dear little children I hope they are well. God bless them and every member of my familey is my daily preayr.—Maryett sends her love and says she will write and send by the mail to Susan.

We have not yet got settled but hope to in a few days. As ever yours,

J M Grant[18]

The opening session of the legislature was scheduled for the morning of December 10; but on the evening of the 9th, the First Presidency met with Daniel Wells to discuss the most pressing issue before the lawmakers—that of drawing up a memorial to Congress petitioning for statehood.[19] Following that meeting, Grant was conspicuously absent from the proceedings at Fillmore, suggesting that his health had taken a turn for the worse. On December 22, however, he had returned to full activity, being able to brave an eight-inch snowfall to sup on oysters with Heber Kimball at David Candland's inn, the Astor House.[20] The next day, after a humorous accident, he stayed in all day, writing in the process an interesting letter to Susan:

I have been impacient to hear from home and learn how you git a long with sick children. For the last year you have had much to try you in sickness yourself and dear little Hyrum has had a serious time. I hope he is well over the measles and able to play as lively as ever. Kiss him and Susan Vilate for their Papa. I hope to hear by the next mail that you are all well. Tell her she must write to me and tell me what she wants.

I will tell you of some of my adventures this morning. The pail was emty, and I knew the Indian that brings water for us would not be hear in time to bring for breakfast. So I took the pail and went for water. The night having been cold the snow was very smothe in the path. In coming from the streem I had to assend a steep hill. When about half way up the hill one of the ears of the pail came off, which gave me a cant to the left. At the same time my left foot sliped and up hill I went, pail in one hand and the other in the snow. My face met very unserimoniously with an oak bush, which gave me a scratch sumthing less then 6 inches long. On coming to an upright position, the blood droped into the water in the pail rendering it unfit for use. My glove coat sleave shirt and pants were wet. My glove and sleave froze, however I went back to the Creek got some water caring it by one ear of the pail. When I come to inspect my face by the glass I concluded I did not look fit to go to meeting so I am writing.

But in spite of scratched face or hands I am invited to a wedding at 2 o,clock at Br Ruben McBrides. His son is to be married to a Miss Williams. While on matrimony I will say what Br John Eldridge, who you will remember I married to a Mrs Lillawhight, he said he under took to correct her child and she struck him with a club or stick of wood on the back of his head laid him cold for 15 or 20 minutes. From his account she is something of a Lillia [Lilith].

Uncle Peter's wife is very sorry that you and Rozetta did not come and spend the winter herre. She says you must boath come with all the children next winter &c &c.

The Indians are very friendly indeed. They do not attempt to steel any thing. Corn is left open in the crib, clothing left on the line over night all is safe.

I have got nearly over my bad cold. I hope you will try and take care of your health and the childrens. Remember me to Sister Betsy and familey Sister Noble and familey. Tell Louis I want him to learn as fast as posable. If you have an opportunity remember me to Sarah Ann Louisa and the children Benj and Anna, also to Br and Sister Lambert.

I want to see you all. You have and shall have my prayers. God my Heavenly Father bless you and yours for ever. I am in hopes of soon hearing from you again. Yours &c.

J M Grant.[21]

On January 7, 1856, Susan Grant penned a letter to her husband in Fillmore, mistakenly dating it 1855. Between news of the children and home, she gave Jedediah a glimpse of her spirits, lonesome but high nevertheless. Rosetta then filled the rest of the space on the sheet of blue paper before it left in the mails for the south. When Grant received it, he must have become a little concerned over evidence that Rachel was not getting along with the other sister wives and that perhaps her "favored" status as a spiritual wife of the martyred Prophet had begun to grate on her seniors in the Grant household.

Great Salt Lake City   Jan the 7th 1855

Haveing a little leisure time I take pleasure in writing to you knowing you are anxious to hear how we are getting along this cold winter. You speak of its friezing in your bedroom. So it has in mine after haveing a good fire all day. We have burned a great deal of wood on account of the sickness of our children haveing much of the time to keep fires nights. But thanks to our Heavenly Father they are again able to play as brisk as ever. They are not entirely rid of the canker yet, but we are in hopes they soon will be. The little girls keep well and we are in hopes they will escape the measles untill they get older. It is now three weeks last evening since Hyrum was taken sick and he was the last of the three that took them.

As for eatables we have plenty of bread and meat and sometimes potatoes but very seldom as the weather has been so cold people could not bring them to the tithing office. However I do not think we shall any of us starve to death while you are gone, or while we get this, for there are many that have not even bread. The fatted turkey we are saveing untill you return. I thought we should enjoy it full as well then. Rosetta and myself have been closely confined at home, but think if the weather continues fine, we shall try to get out some where this week. Rachel is up to Sister Vilate Kimballs today. Caroline [Caddie] is at school; she likes it very well I believe.

You tell us to try and make ourselves happy. I can only answer for one; for my part I feel firstrate, and judge by appearances that the rest do also. We spent New Years Day very much like all other days with the exception that we had a chicken and sweeten johny cake for dinner. Benjamin and Sarah Ann was here. In the afternoon we took a short sleigh ride. However I suppose that Rachel told you all this by the last mail. She writes frequently but does not see fit to read them to us.

Lewis is going to school. Br [and] Sister Lambert are well and send their respects. I like them firstrate, her as you say because she is good to little Hyly. He talkes much about his Pa and going to ride in Papa carrage when he comes home.

Give my love to Maryett and all who take the trouble to enquire after me. I will now stop and let Rosetta write some. Hopeing this will find you all enjoying the blessing of health and happiness I am as ever yours &c

Susan Grant

Tusday eyning. I due not feel much like writing as I due not feel very well. I feel rather nurvis as I have not had much rest with the childrin for the laste few knights. The baby has bin very trubilsom for the laste few knights. In fact she never dose reste very well of a knight. Morgan was sick on friday. He had a fevure all day and knight. He has the canker vary bad in his nose and mouth. He seems well to day but he looks rathar pale but him and Hyrum is a biting around as welle [as] Maye and Charley and writing to thear Pa. If you got a letter evry time they write to you you would get wone pretty ofton.

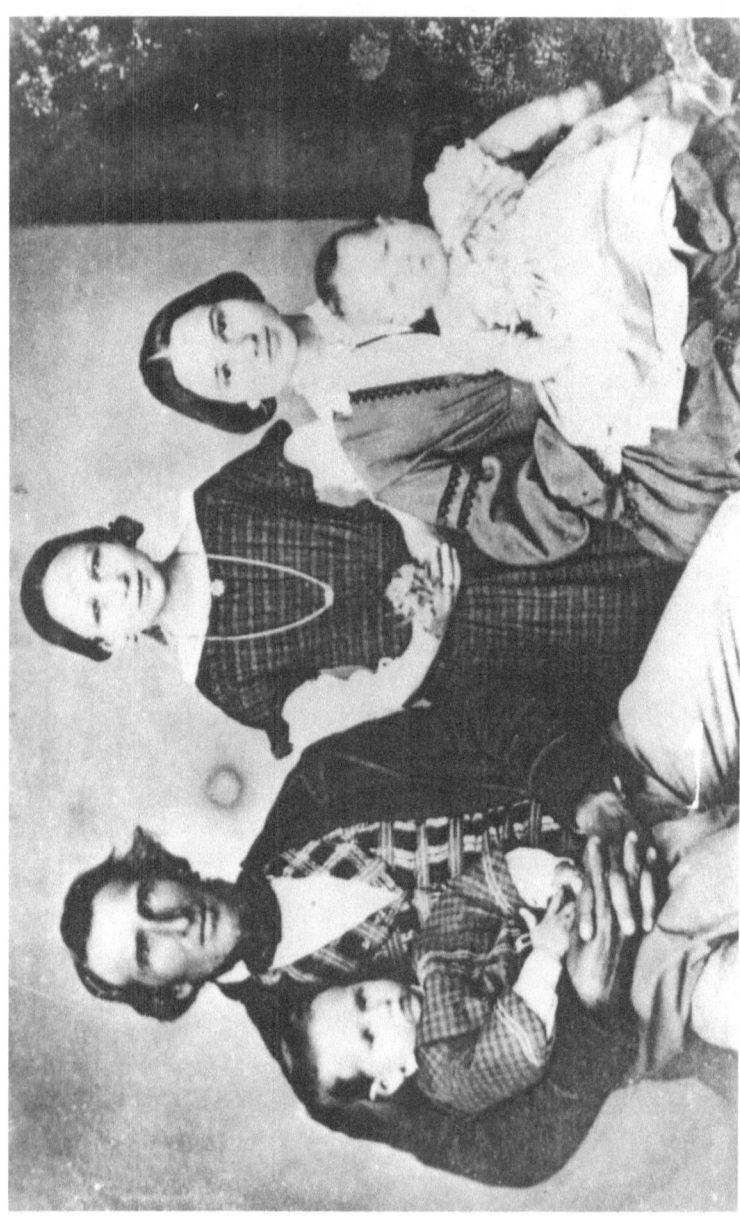

Jedediah, holding Joseph Hyrum, and second wife, Susan, holding Susan Vilate. Caroline ("Caddie"), Grant's daughter by his first wife, Caroline (deceased), standing center, 1856. LDS Church Archives.

― Breaking Branches ― 225

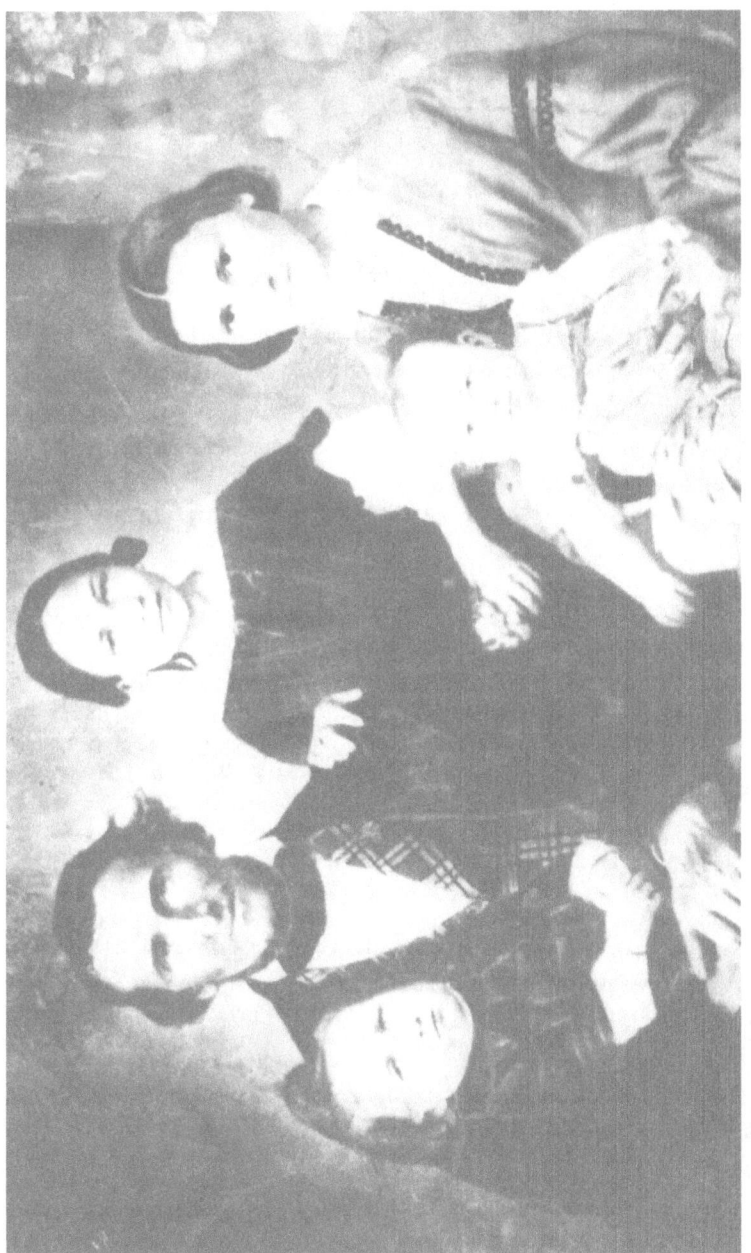

Grant, holding son Jedediah Morgan Jr.; daughter Caroline, standing center; and third wife, Rosetta, holding daughter Rosetta Henrietta, 1856, retouched. LDS Museum of Church History and Art.

Mother is with us yet. She has bin looking for Charles for the last thre weekes but he has not come yet. I expect the colde wethar has pevented him. The wethar has been so cold that it froze the milk that I took up for Morgan soled in the hour time, but it has been very plesant for a few days. The baby is criing so good knight.

Wednsday morning, I feel worse then ever this morning. I think I shal take a emetic tomarow.

The band came and ceranaided us on New Years Day and the little boys has been a cernaiding us evry cense with tin plates and spoones. We are expecting company to day so I cant write much.

Br Streper [Wilkinson Streeper] is alive yet but he is very loow. The Doctor has given him up for past cure. As for newes you cant exspect much from me as I do not go out any to hear eny newes but I exspect Rachel writes a plenty for us all so there is no use of my trying. Give my respectes to Maryett and all my friends. youres

Rosetta[22]

As Susan intimated while discussing the family food situation in her letter, this was not a time of plenty in Zion. The harvest had indeed been poor, and a famine of sorts had descended upon the Saints. It was nothing new to them, but some of its consequences would be, especially those that took shape in the mind of Jedediah Grant.

⇋ Notes ⇌

1. Journal History of the Church of Jesus Christ of Latter-day Saints, (chronological scrapbook of typed entries and newspaper clippings, 1830–present, LDS Church Archives), June 18, 25, July 1, 4, 1855, all p. 1.

2. *Deseret News*, July 11, 1855.

3. For a very critical examination of the Mormon theocracy in early Utah, see David L. Bigler, *Forgotten Kingdom: The Mormon Theocracy in the American West, 1847–1896* (Spokane, Wash.: Arthur H. Clark Company, 1998).

4. Scott G. Kenney, ed., *Wilford Woodruff's Journal, 1833–1898*, typescript, 9 vols. (Midvale, Utah: Signature Books, 1983–85), July 8, 1855. Unfortunately, no transcription of this sermon is extant. Earlier that day Judge William W. Drummond arrived in the city with a woman whom he represented as his wife but who subsequently turned out to be a "shady

lady." Whether Drummond's coming to town had anything to do with Grant's attack that day on the Gentiles is unclear in the record.

5. Jedediah M. Grant, July 13, 1855, *Journal of Discourses*, 26 vols. (London and Liverpool: LDS Booksellers Depot, 1855–86), 3:58 61. The record gives few clues as to the "items of doctrine" that some Saints found "especially obnoxious," but it is likely that leading the list at the time was plural marriage.

6. *Deseret News*, July 18, 1855.

7. Journal History, August 31, 1855, 5. Brigham Young addressed the uses of the building as follows: "We can, at the present time, go into the Endowment House and be baptized for the dead, receive our washings and anointing, etc., for there we have a font that has been erected [in 1857], dedicated expressly for baptizing people for the remission of sins, for their health and for their dead friends; in this the Saints have the privilege of being baptized for their friends. We also have the privilege of sealing women to men, without a Temple. This we can do in the Endowment House; but when we come to other sealing ordinances, ordinances pertaining to the holy Priesthood, to connect the chain of the Priesthood from father Adam until now, by sealing children to their parents, being sealed for our forefathers, etc., they cannot be done without a Temple." Brigham Young, September 4, 1973, *Journal of Discourses*, 16:185.

8. Ibid. The coming winter session of the Utah territorial legislature would be the only one held in Fillmore, after which the functions of government returned permanently to the convenience of Salt Lake City and the demographic rather than geographic center of the territory. See also *Deseret News*, July 18, 1855.

9. Rachel, the last wife, was older at thirty-five in 1855 than any of her sister wives. Jedediah married Susan Fairchild Noble, now twenty-three, and Rosetta Robison, twenty-two, on the same day in 1849. The others in order were Louisa Marie Goulay, twenty-nine (married 1851), Maryette Kesler, sixteen (married 1854), and Sarah Ann Thurston, twenty (married 1855). With the birth of a son to Rachel in November 1856, he had a son by each of the six and daughters by both Susan and Rosetta. His daughter Caroline, by his deceased wife Caroline Van Dyke, completed his living, biological posterity at the time of his death in December 1856. Adopted son Lewis (born John McKeachie in 1839) completed the family.

10. *Deseret News*, July 25, 1855; Journal History, August 30 and September 9, 13, and 30, 1855, all p. 1. Rachel R. Ivins was a member of a New Jersey family with whom Grant had had a long association. She had been sealed to Joseph Smith and married Jedediah for time.

11. Jedediah M. Grant, October 6, 1855, *Journal of Discourses*, 3:125–27. Note his emphasis on the nuances of relationships in the polygamous setting. It is possible that his own courtship of Rachel and Maryette was causing him and his other wives some conster-

nation. See below a letter from Rosetta that seemed to carry some of the adverse flavor that Grant was decrying in his October 6 sermon.

12. For an account of this trip, see Journal History, October 20, 1855, 1–2.

13. Jedediah Grant, Letter to Susan Grant and family, December 8, 1855, holograph, Bettie Mae Nebeker Laub Collection, Salt Lake City; Journal History, October 21 November 11, 1855, passim.

14. Journal History, November 11, 1855, 1, and November 29, 1855, 2.

15. *Deseret News*, December 19, 1855.

16. Ibid.

17. Journal History, December 3, 1855, 1.

18. Grant, Letter to Susan Grant and family, December 8, 1855, Laub Collection.

19. Journal History, December 9 and 10, 1855, 1.

20. See Journal History, December 10–21, 1855, passim, and December 21, 1855, 1. See also Albert Carrington, Letter to Elias Smith, *Deseret News*, December 23, 1855, which suggested nevertheless that Brothers Brigham, Heber, and Jedediah were all enjoying good health through this period. The absence of his name in the Fillmore reports may have been merely an indication of an inconspicuous role during these meetings, but that is unlikely given Grant's personality and position as speaker of the house.

21. Jedediah Grant, Letter to Susan Grant, December 23, 1855, holograph, Laub Collection. Note his reference to having just recovered from a bad cold. It is difficult to ascertain the identity of some of the persons Grant mentioned in this letter, such as "Uncle Peter."

22. Susan and Rosetta Grant, Letter to Jedediah Grant, January 7, 1856, holograph, Laub Collection.

"There is more blindness, fog, and stupidity in Israel than I had anticipated."

⇌ 14 ⇌
A Cloud of Darkness

As THE WINTER OF 1854–55 had been mild and pleasant, the one following was harsh and destructive. The members of the First Presidency, wending their way north after the adjournment of the territorial legislature in Fillmore, made it to a point about one mile south of Chicken Springs in Juab County on January 18, 1856, before the numbing cold forced them to make camp in the midst of some junipers. It was too cold for anyone to sleep that night, even though they had been up all the night before, striving to complete the work of the final session of the legislature. To keep warm as they stood in the snow discussing the future of their people, the three men and those with them burned the desert trees in great pyres that lit up the frosty hillsides.[1] The work in Fillmore had gone very well, and the brethren were proud of themselves and their associates, who had brought the greatest element of civilization to the wilderness—just and meaningful law. Also on their minds, however, was a more basic question, that of simple survival. The harvest had been poor. Between the grasshoppers, the late frosts, and a summer drought, nature had dealt a cruel blow to the kingdom of the Saints. The time ahead was going to be full of ordinary suffering, and that was always a time for extraordinary leadership.

Grant and his two companions in the presidency arrived in Salt Lake City late in the afternoon of January 21 after a day's journey from Lake City (American Fork) in Utah County. The forty-year-old mayor found his city already struggling with the problems of famine, but some important business that had begun in Fillmore momentarily overshadowed his consternation. He and his colleagues had begun to construct a plan for the organization of a freight company between Utah and the States, something that might make the Saints less susceptible to the whims of nature in the future. On Saturday evening, January 26, a mass meeting convened in the old tabernacle to discuss the feasibility of such an express and carrying company.[2] The bitter cold of that night, however, only served to remind the Saints that their problem was now. Many potato bins were already empty, and some were wondering what it all meant. Jedediah Grant, mounting the stand the next freezing morning, was not one to leave the people without answers, even if they were uncomfortable ones. He opened his remarks with praise for the legislature but moved quickly to the subject that was on the minds of his listeners—the scarcity of food and its meaning to the kingdom.

> I have seen the time, in [this] beautiful valley, when we first came here, when we had to bring enough of grain from the States to last eighteen months, that we were under the necessity of boiling and eating the hides of our cattle, and of going to the lowlands to dig thistle roots to subsist upon, that we might not die, but live on the earth.
>
> We did not all have to do this; some of us were comfortable, and had as much to live upon as we have now, for we took care to save what we brought with us. Many of those, who are now destitute of grain, are among those who were lavish with the food that the Almighty caused the earth to produce.
>
> I will here remark that I hope the Bishops in the different wards of the city will see that the poor do not go hungry, that they will keep themselves posted up as to the situation of the poor in their wards, and send round the Teachers and assistants to ascertain the condition of the people. I know that there is not grain enough to feed the people; some will have to suffer for the want of that article of food.
>
> It will necessarily be here that the Bishops and their assistants will look for the poor. Some will not go very hungry before they beg, but there are some who will actually suffer very much before they make their wants known; that class ought to be seen to and felt after, and ought to be administered to. We should feel for each other, and seek to relieve, as far as we can, the needy and distressed.
>
> I do not look for much trouble myself; I do not look for the people to suffer as they did the first winter we came here. The winter is cold and the cattle are dying, but ere long the weather will break, the people will get employment, and feel better.
>
> Do not be discouraged in a hard time, be patient until spring comes,

when you will feel pleasant and happy, and then is the time to deny the faith, if you are inclined to do so; never deny the faith in a dark day.

I for one am glad that our crops failed. Why? Because it teaches the people a lesson, it keeps the corrupt at bay, for they know that they would have to starve, or import their rations, should they come to injure us in the Territory of Utah.

With the practical lessons we have learned, and their effects upon our enemies I am glad, and I consider it one of the greatest God sends that ever happened [to] the people of the Saints, since their immigration to this land. I consider the grass hopper war one of the greatest blessings to those who see it in the light of the Lord, and who discern the hand of the Lord in It.

I hope then to see the Saints united more and more, and notwithstanding we have to be mixed with new clay, and ground over and over again, I say, come on you new recruits, I am not hide bound in my feelings, I reach out my hands to the south, to the north, and to the universe, and say, come on, we want the new recruits here.

I want to see the Territory filled up in the north and in the south, in the east and in the west, and to see the valleys flourish and blossom as a rose. I like to see the hardy men come forth from the other side of the ocean; I like to see them pouring in by tens of thousands. The new recruits, as a general thing, have stood well.

Take the Yankees in Kirtland, have they all stood the test? No. One half, at least, of the Yankee members of this Church have apostatized. Take the first quorum of the Twelve, how many of them stood by the Prophet of the living God, and kept the faith? Six only.

Then we may expect that some of our new recruits back out, depart and deny the faith, and this has been the case from the commencement. I like to see the new recruits come on, they will get ground up with the old clay and be just as good. You are only in the morning of "Mormonism," just in the commencement of it. We have no old recruits, in one sense, but we are all new recruits, enlisted under the same banner, worshipping the same God, and united under the same brotherhood of Latter-day Saints which always pertains to the Priesthood of God.

Then I like to see the English, the Scotch, Welsh, French, Danes, and men from every nation, kindred, tongue, and people, come forth and unite under the standard of truth, obey God and be one.

May the peace of God be with you; may the light of the Holy Ghost illuminate you; may the words of the Prophet be unto you as a sweet morsel; and may the leaven of the Gospel work in you; and may the God and Father of our Lord Jesus Christ bless you for ever, which may He grant, in the Redeemer's name. Amen.³

Two weeks later, the basic elements of Brother Jedediah's remarks on the food situation came forth as a statement of instruction from the First Presidency on the current crisis. Whether Grant really believed that the failure of crops had been a "good" thing, it was still a serious matter and a threat to the development and welfare of the kingdom.⁴ Spring and the new growing season were still weeks away, and in the meantime, the Saints would have to continue in their efforts to perfect their society. By the end of February the jagged facts of life under the sparse conditions of a cold winter had scuffed the edges of the people's nerves, including those of Brothers Brigham and Heber. On February 24 and again on March 2, Young blasted his followers for their wickedness. Kimball, speaking on both days, did, too. It was inconceivable to them that just because times were tough the chosen people would forget their position and covenants.⁵

On the afternoon of March 2, Grant unleashed his own brand of fury; and as Wilford Woodruff remembered it, "rained down pitchforks and forked lightning figuratively speaking upon the Gentiles who were working wickedness upon this people and defiling the females."⁶ Woodruff failed to mention that the large portion of Mormon Thunder that day crashed down on the heads of the Saints themselves. In the course of his pronouncements, Jedediah revealed a great deal about the Mormon hierarchy's view of the world of the 1850s, in both its provincial and national manifestations. The relationship of the Mormon kingdom to the nation to which it nominally belonged was becoming increasingly complicated as the peculiar ideals of the territorial theocracy clashed inevitably with the principles and agents of American democracy. The belligerency and physical threats at the heart of this sermon must certainly have frightened many in Utah who failed to fit into Grant's view of responsible citizenship.

> I have meditated considerably upon the spirit manifested through our President last Sabbath and to day, and also upon that manifested by brother Kimball, his first Counsellor.
>
> I do not know what effect their views and sayings have had upon your

minds, but I am under the impression that there is more blindness and stupidity, more fog and darkness in Israel than I had anticipated, previous to their remarks.

The President's remarks gave a very special rebuke to certain councils, and, more or less, to those who speak from this stand. He is not fond of the smoothness that some are delighted with. I am aware that the Saints come here to listen, and that many of them are fond of smooth sayings and nicely turned periods, being pleased therewith as with a beautiful song; their ears are tickled and their fancies excited, but they go away without being vitally benefitted.

We have to deal with the people of God, and we care but little about the ebbing and flowing of nations, when their ebbings and flowings do not particularly affect the Saints of the Most High. We expect to see abominations and commotions abroad on the earth, but I do hope that the time has actually come when filth will be cleansed from the midst of Israel.

As a people we are right in principle, in doctrine, and in precepts. But are we all perfectly right in practice? This is a question which we should well examine and understand.

Do all the people practise righteousness? Do they all live their religion, and the principles that they have received? In other words, do all the people act according to what they understand? Do they do the best they know how? If they were all doing the best they know how, there would be no fault with them; but I am satisfied that they are not, for if they were, the President would not stand up here and rebuke you. You are rebuked because you suffer yourselves to be led by the enemy into the fog, because the Spirit of God and the light of the Holy Ghost are not at all times upon you.

Not long ago I heard that, in a certain case, the traverse jury were eleven against one, and what is more singular, the one alone was right in his views of the case.

Several had got into the fog to suck and eat the filth of a Gentile law court, ostensibly a court of Utah, though I call it a Gentile court. Why? Because it does not magnify the laws of Utah, as provided for in the "Organic Act," by which "Act" and laws it alone exists as a court.

A brief examination will soon convince a person, of only ordinary observation, that the laws of Utah are not administered in our courts, and that the judges must know that fact, and that they have been seeking from the first, with but few exceptions, to overrule them.

Whether that course is prompted from the City of Washington, I know not. Our laws have been set at naught and walked under foot, and in lieu thereof a constant effort has been made to rule in common law, English law, and law after law totally inapplicable.

Do you suppose I respect persons who so conduct themselves? No, I do not. We have some Gentiles here whom I respect. We had a [Leonidas] Shaver whom I respected; he was a man, and a true Virginian, well represented the chivalric spirit of the South, and sought the good of his country.

But when we have a set of politicians here, who can blow hot or cold to suit their own convenience, they can officiate as constables, jurors, marshals, judges, and legislators; they can turn the law, create the law, and execute the law to suit themselves. Do I respect them? No, and I am in hopes that some of their friends present will tell them so. (Voice, I do not know that they have any.)

They act as though they took it for granted that we were a set of ignoramuses, unacquainted with the usages of courts, and unaware that they were setting aside our laws. They have sought to overthrow our laws, when there is not a law in force in Utah that will sanction their rulings, and you cannot bring an upright lawyer, one who actually understands his profession, but what will say that I am right. Every man who is conversant with the laws of the United States and of Utah, will say so.

We do not find fault with the laws of our country, they are good, but we deprecate the acts of men who strive to trample upon them; men who are filled with the Gentile leaven, and we dislike that leaven and the fog which accompanies it.

We have a few whoremasters here. Do you wish to know who they are? I can tell the first letters of their name, and I can tell where they have been practising their abominations in this City. And even some who profess to be "Mormons" are guilty of enticing and leading girls to prostitution, saying, "If you want a new dress you can get it very easily."

I have a gun and dirks in good order, and powder and lead, and am ready and able to make holes through such miserable, corrupting rascals. These characters take "Mormon" girls and debauch them, telling them that the United States will send their troops here, and that this people will be broken up and driven.

We are a part of the United States ourselves; most of us were raised in America, and we are all cradled in liberty, and if the United States desires to drench the earth with our blood, we are on hand.

Who is afraid to die? None but the wicked. If they want to send troops here let them come to those who have imported filth and whores, though we can attend to that class without so much expense to the General Government; we can wipe them out cheaply and quickly, for they are only a few in number.

They will threaten us with the U.S. troops! Why your impudence and ignorance would bring a blush to the cheeks of the veriest camp follower among them. We ask no odds of you, you rotten carcasses, and I am not going to bow one hair's breadth to your influence. I would rather be cut into inch pieces than succumb one particle to such filthiness.

I want the Gentiles to understand that we know all about their whoredoms and other abominations here. If we have not invariably killed such corrupt scoundrels, those who will seek to corrupt and pollute our community, I swear to you that we mean to, and to accomplish more in a few hours, towards clearing the atmosphere, than all your grand and traverse juries can in a year.

There are a few professed "Mormons" who, for a few dimes, wink at their iniquities, and keep the poor, mean, lazy scamps in their houses, saying, "O, they are honorable men." I admit that there are a few honorable men here who are not in the Church, some of whom I respect much.

This eternal threatening of us with the armies of the United States! I wonder what men think we are made of, when they threaten us! As if they expected that we were going to succumb to whoredom! If we were to establish a whorehouse on every corner of our streets, as in nearly all other cities outside of Utah, either by law or otherwise, we should doubtless then be considered good fellows.

If we were to allow gambling, drunkenness, and every species of wickedness, the "Mormons" would then be all right, they would not then threaten us with the armies of the United States. O no.

What is it that maddens the devils? Simply that we are determined to do right, and to set at defiance wickedness and wicked men, and to send them to hell across lots, as quick as we can.

I do not ask any odds of them myself, I never have. If they behave themselves as white men ought to behave, we will treat them as such. The armies of our nation will have plenty to do without attending to us; they will need us to help them. Yes, instead of bringing their armies to fight the people in

Utah, they will need Utah's armies to help them. They are threatening war in Kansas on the slavery question, and the General Government has already been called upon to send troops there. Well, all I have to say on that matter is, "Success to both parties."

And in relation to the election of a Speaker in the House of Representatives at Washington, the North and South, the East and West have each other by the ears; "Success to all parties," say I.

To send men here as spies to watch us! Curse the spies and those who send them, and all who sustain the system of whorehouses and the debauchery of the innocent and unsuspecting, and all who threaten that the United States are going to drive and kill the "Mormons."

Did you ever hear such a man as Judge Shaver threaten us with the United States? Did you ever hear Judge Reed [Lazarus Reid] do such a thing? No. Or Millard Fillmore, or Andrew Jackson? No, such men would scorn to threaten an innocent people with the armies of the nation.

Have we been disloyal to our country? Have we, in one instance, violated her laws? No. Have we rejected her institutions? No. We are lawful and loyal citizens of the government of the United States, and a few poor, miserable, pusilanimous, rotten, stinking rebels, come here and threaten us with the armies and those who wish to send them, are as corrupt as those who threaten us, and as vile as most of those heretofore sent here, we defy them, and the sooner we come in contact with them the better. These are my feelings every time, on that point.

As for you miserable, sleepy "Mormons," who say to those wretches, "Give us your dimes, and you shall have our wheat, and our daughters, only give us your dimes and you shall have this, that, and the other," I not only wish but pray, in the name of Israel's God, that the time was come in which to unsheath the sword, like Moroni of old, and to cleanse the inside of the platter, and we would not wait for the decision of grand or traverse juries, but we would walk into you and completely use up every curse who will not do right.

We are speaking against none who are good, they have our protection; but against those who are evil. We have many good friends who are not members of our Church, but when men come and threaten us with the armies of the United States, and under that color seek to practise every kind of debauchery, telling a young girl that "we are going to be destroyed, and for that reason she had better forsake the Mormon Church and make merchandise of her body," to serve their vile purposes, poor, miserable devils, what ought you to expect?

I wish the Saints to see and understand men and things as they are, if they have any judgment and eye sight. I could give you a list of the practices I have been speaking of, and the names of the men engaged in them. If we love salvation and liberty, and must fight for them, let us fight, and they will find that the "Mormons" are on hand to die, those who are right, and what would be the use of living, if we cannot have our rights? If we are to be driven, as we have hitherto been, the sooner we die the better; and the sooner we kill a poor set of miserable devils the better for those who remain.

I wish all the Saints to do right, and as for those who do not, my prayer is, "That they may all go hellwards, the way Ward's ducks went."

May God bless those who do right, and enable them to break in pieces wickedness and put it down, that we may be saved; I ask it in the name of Jesus Christ. Amen.[7]

Needless to say, the roaring of Jedediah Grant's thunder on March 2 caught everyone's attention.[8] No one was certain what had set it off, although it may have been as he said—that he was merely following the lead of his brethren in the First Presidency, who had indeed served up some of the same spirit in their previous discourses. Nevertheless, not since his hammering "blood atonement" sermon of March 1854 had the Saints heard and then felt to their bones the life-and-death call to righteousness that was peculiar to Brother Jeddy's blunt and often brutal rhetoric.

Through the spring of 1856, Grant became nearly as prominent a figure in the daily lives of the Saints as was Brigham Young himself. The triumvirate of Young, Kimball, and Grant had developed its full-grown power, but that power was not without its challenges. There were still those Saints in Utah who doubted whether Young really had the right to lead the Church. His style, after all, was decidedly different from that of the late Prophet Joseph Smith; and William, the last surviving brother of the Smith family, was at that moment riding a crest of popularity among some Saints who had refused to follow Young into the West and who would soon combine to form the Reorganized Church on the principle of a royal family. By the middle of March, the hardships of the famine and a concomitant rise in murmuring among its nervous victims had sent

William Smith's brother-in-law into a simmering rage. For Grant, however, his own anger was exhilarating and ultimately exciting, as it would have been for anyone who saw himself first and always as a hellfire preacher. In the course of a discourse on March 23 on Mormon Indian policy, the second counselor made clear his feelings toward the Lion of the Lord and his leadership of the Saints. Following the prophets' counsel was the only way to dispel the fog that seemed to be enveloping the people.

> I wish now to say a few words upon [general] policy. It is well known that [Joseph Smith] had a profligate brother, and there was but one broad ground of difference between the policy of Joseph and that of his profligate brother. I will first speak of the policy of Joseph, and ask what will it do? It will emancipate all who carry it out, it will break the yoke from every one who is bound, it will make all men happy, peaceable and good, save them on earth and prepare them for salvation and exaltation in the eternal worlds.
>
> It may be enquired, "did not Joseph love women?" Yes, he was a great lover of women, but his course and policy would elevate them, make them virtuous and happy, while that of his profligate brother would make them wretched and miserable, would debauch and degrade them. The one would save the world, the other would damn it. This is the difference between the policy of the Latter-day Saints and that of the world—Our policy will save the Indians, restore them to peace and bring them nigh to God, while the other policy will fight them, drive them, and kill them off from the earth. While the policy of Latter-day Saints brings men to happiness and eventually to enjoy eternal life, the other policy leads men to misery and destruction. I briefly name these cardinal points in order to lead your minds to reflection upon others that are of equal importance.
>
> I have suggested premises enough for much reflection and conversation, but I wish you most clearly to understand that the policy of our President br. Brigham, is from God. The more of the spirit the better the policy, and the better carried out. A lack of that spirit and policy will lead men to hell, while an abundance will give them heaven. If you wish your President to have good policy, you must pray that he may have an abundance of the Spirit.
>
> The greatest difficulty that this people labor under is, they do not keep up with their leaders. I have no fear that Brigham Young is not good enough for us, but my fear is that the people are not keeping up with him. If they would be as good as their leader, I should have no fear, but how many can

you find living up to the law of God? Perhaps you might find one or two hundred men and women in this community who strictly keep the celestial law. Suppose a man's family will not keep up with him, what shall he do? He has to keep with them in order to save them, in order to exalt them in the kingdom of our God, and there is the same result in a church capacity. If you have a leader who is far ahead of you, say a thousand years, of what particular benefit is his advancement to you? True, if permitted to remain in your midst, he could teach you the celestial law, and law far beyond your reach and comprehension at the present time, for you are not yet capable of receiving more than milk.

I do not think that the people, as a whole, do the best they know how. I believe that they know better than they do, for if they did the best they knew how, I think they would progress faster and have light commensurate with their day. I can perceive plenty on hand, if you would only walk in the way to receive it. Br. Brigham is full of revelations; "then why," says one, "does he not pour them out?" Because you are not yet prepared to receive them. More practice upon what we have is what we lack; practice upon the policy and teachings of br. Brigham is what we must exercise ourselves with, because they come from high heaven and will save the inhabitants of the earth; will save the tribes of Ephraim and Manasseh, will bring Judah and Israel to bow to the standard of Jesus Christ, and will cause the nations of the earth to acknowledge the government of heaven, or be cut off. Not that we are opposed to the nations of the earth, but we do not like their wickedness nor their corruptions. If they have anything good we like it, but their evil practices we do not like.

A word about the politics of the Latter Day Saints. Were we going to vote for a President of the United States, I presume our President would recommend Millard Fillmore for that office and Stephen A. Douglas for Vice-President, and then advise them to counsel together for the public good, and to counsel the democrats, the abolitionists, the pro-slavery men, the north and the south, the east and the west to all meet as brethren. Do you not see that by adopting this policy they would become good natured, and stand on an equal footing with each other? Then if they wished to adjust the slave question, they could meet in counsel and agree about it. Then they could treat that institution upon reasonable and righteous principles. Do you suppose that England, France, Russia, or any eastern nation, or the Pope of Rome, can establish a policy to govern the people? No, it will take a policy emanating from God, therefore, if this people wish any more law, doctrine, and policy, let them live to the doctrines and revelations which they have already received.

Whoever reflects for a moment will perceive that there is plenty of truth on hand for them to observe, and that more is coming continually and that too faster than we obey. The light is shining upon us direct from heaven, from the throne of light. Can good come from hell? Will light come from darkness? If light can only come from heaven, then the priesthood is the channel for it to flow through. That channel is here, and that God from whom the light comes is the being to govern the world. Then love God, the doctrines and revelations that he gives, and do the best you know how, and you shall have all that you can eat, drink, wear, understand, and make wise use of: Amen.[9]

Jedediah's meaning was implicit but clear: If the Saints wished to escape the wrath of God, which at the present time had taken the form of a famine, then they must obey counsel and cleave to righteousness. In softer terms, he was repeating his March 2 exhortation to do right or die. This was the essence of Mormon Thunder. When April conference convened in the Bowery two weeks later, 10,000 people crowded onto the Temple Block, eager as always to see and hear Brother Brigham. This time, though, they were also anxious to sense the growing spirit of revival he was fostering along with his prophet, Heber Kimball, and his sledgehammer, Jedediah Grant,[10] who was raining "pitchforks and forked lightning" through the cloud of darkness that had settled over the valleys of the kingdom. But the Saints had hardly yet felt the effects of that storm.

⊷ Notes ⊷

1. "History of Brigham Young," 1856, 66, LDS Church Archives.

2. Journal History of the Church of Jesus Christ of Latter-day Saints (chronological scrapbook of typed entries and newspaper clippings, 1830–present, LDS Church Archives), January 9, 21, and 26, 1856, all p. 1.

3. Jedediah M. Grant, January 27, 1856, *Journal of Discourses*, 26 vols. (London and Liverpool: LDS Booksellers Depot, 1855–86), 3:199–202.

4. *Deseret News*, February 13, 1856.

5. Brigham Young and Heber C. Kimball, both speaking February 14 and March 2,

1856, *Journal of Discourses*, 3:121-32, 236-43.

6. Scott G. Kenney, ed., *Wilford Woodruff's Journal, 1833-1898*, typescript, 9 vols. (Midvale, Utah: Signature Books, 1983-85), March 2, 1856.

7. Jedediah M. Grant, March 2, 1856, *Journal of Discourses*, 3:232-36. Note Grant's attack on what he saw as an unctuousness in the spirit of the believers, which has always been a prime target of the revivalist. Note also his presaging of the Utah War in the following year, when the United States indeed sent its army to subdue the Mormons. See Donald R. Moorman with Gene A. Sessions, *Camp Floyd and the Mormons: The Utah War*, 2d ed. (Salt Lake City: University of Utah Press, 2005).

8. "History of Brigham Young," 1856, 170.

9. *Deseret News*, April 2, 1856.

10. Journal History, April 6, 1856, 1.

"You who do not purify yourselves may look for the wrath of God to burn against you."

15
The Dry Moon

WHEN MOSES PRONOUNCED his blessing on the tribes of Israel prior to his leaving them for the last time, he promised Joseph (of whom the Mormons believed themselves heirs) that its land would be blessed "for the precious things of heaven, for the dew, and for the deep that coucheth beneath, and for the precious fruits brought forth by the sun, and for the precious things put forth by the moon."[1] But the modern land of Joseph was suffering in the early spring of 1856 from a sun that had brought forth only heat and drought, and a moon whose successive revolutions seemed to have put forth want and famine. The Saints in Utah could hardly afford another poor harvest after the devastated crop of 1855. The winter had been hard and cold, but substantial snowfalls had been rare, and now the spring was dawning dry and clear. Normal spring rains, essential to bring up freshly planted grains so vital to the community's quick recovery from hunger, failed to materialize well into the month of April. On Sunday, April 13, President Jedediah Grant addressed himself to the fearsome problem of drought from the stand in the Bowery. In a sermon of which no verbatim transcript survived, he discussed "the dry moon" in the heavens over the Rocky Mountains, perhaps using Deuteronomy and Moses's blessing of Joseph for his text. As he exhorted the people to exercise their faith for the moisture that would produce an abundance from the earth, it began to rain.[2]

The rains, mixed with wet snows and mild temperatures, continued every week to the end of May. Crops beneficently greened the fields, and by mid-June the Saints were realizing Grant's blessing—a bumper crop of early wheat.[3] Consequently, few Mormons who heard the "Dry Moon Discourse" soon forgot it.[4] On June 25, the First Presidency noted the bountiful crop with a directive to grain raisers instructing them to allow the poor to glean the fields so that every kernel would serve as mitigation to the famine. The enforcement clause of the letter indicated the gravity with which the brethren viewed the shortage of foodstuffs: Any grower who refused to allow the poor to glean after harvest was to be excommunicated—"let his bishop deal with him according to the law of Zion."[5] The lean time appeared to be ending, and Brothers Brigham, Heber, and Jeddy wanted recovery to be rapid and complete.

Indeed, as it came on in full maturity, the summer of 1856 bloomed with promise. Utah might yet put forth fully the bounties of the earth. For Grant, it was an expansive time, one in which the future looked bright and full of progress. His posterity was growing rapidly, with Louisa and Sarah Ann having recently borne him sons, Joshua Frederick and George Smith Grant. In addition, Rachel and Maryette were expecting children in the fall. To provide for his families, Grant was in the process of increasing his land holdings, obtaining with Thomas J. and George W. Thurston, members of Sarah Ann's family, a grant from the government for a herd ground on the south side of Weber Valley.[6] In the same area, the brethren had laid out a new village to be called Morganville (later Morgan), from the second counselor's middle name. Like his companions Brigham and Heber, he would have the privilege of having a potential city of the future named in his honor.[7]

The summer of 1856 marked nine years since the Latter-day Saints had first arrived in the Great Salt Lake Valley. In line with the fair harvest that seemed to be coming and with a feeling of having achieved permanence against even the blast of such a hungry winter as that of 1855–56, Church leaders planned in July an impressive celebration to be held at the top of Big Cottonwood Canyon on the shores of Silver Lake. About 450 people in more than seventy carriages made their way up the steep canyon on July 23. By sunset the party had made camp and assembled for prayers around a makeshift bowery. After a verse of "Come, Come Ye Saints" and a benediction from Apostle Amasa Lyman, Brigham Young had a few things to say.

> Some if they had the power, would be on the other side of these lofty peaks in ten minutes, instead of calmly meditating upon the wonderful works of God, and his kind providence that has watched over us and provided for us, more expecially during the last ten or fifteen years of our history. I could

sit here for a month and reflect on the mercies of our God, and humble myself in thankfulness because of all his favors to myself as an individual, and to all this great people.

What do you think Joseph and Hyrum would have given to have seen this day in the flesh, and to have been here instead of being taken to Carthage, like lambs to the slaughter, and butchered by their enemies? We are here hid up in the Lord's secret chambers, according to his promise, where none can molest us or make us afraid.[8]

Following the next day's dancing and merrymaking, the group assembled at dusk for toasts to the brethren and some speech-making. After being toasted as "one of the Lord's mighty chieftains" and wished a long life as "a comfort to his friends, and a terror to his enemies,"[9] Jedediah Grant rose to offer a prayer of thanksgiving and peace. Those listening would notice the marked reflectiveness and meditative quality of his oblations in contrast to his boisterous preaching of recent days. In such repose, there could be no wild flavors of fanaticism. The words of the prayer revealed instead a great deal about Grant's most human yearnings for security and continuity beneath the hovering animosity of the world.

Our Father and our God, in the name of the Lord Jesus Christ, we bow before thee, and thank thee that we have the privilege of coming to the tops of these mountains to worship thee, our God, and to celebrate the liberty of thy people and their entrance into these peaceful valleys and mountains.

We thank thee for these mountains, for the fountains of waters that flow from them, for the timber that grows upon them, and for all the blessings that thou hast vouchsafed to thy people in this land.

We thank thee that thou hast preserved this land from the eye of the wicked, that they have not desired it, that they have not coveted it, that thou hast kept it for thy people and hast brought them hither, through the instrumentality of thy servant Brigham, whom thou hast inspired by the Holy Ghost.

We thank thee that we here rest secure from our enemies, that we and our families enjoy peace and rest from the persecutions of those who hate thy chosen people.

We thank thee for this goodly inheritance which thou hast vouchsafed to thy people, and for the privilege of raising our banners and ensigns on these mountain tops. May our enemies never have power over us, and may we be blessed by doing right and keeping thy commandments, by living pure, and by being watchful and careful to do no evil, that we may multiply in our families, in our flocks and in our herds, in our fields and habitations.

We pray thee, in the name of the Lord Jesus Christ, that thou wouldst bless this valley and all the adjacent valleys; and bless the streams of water that flow from the mountains. As we are at the head of Big Cottonwood Kanyon we pray thee that thou wilt bless it, and the water that flows to the mills and to the land we cultivate. And may the timber, and grass and vegetation of every description, growing in this little valley in the tops of these mountains be blessed; and we consecrate and dedicate it to thee for the benefit of thy people, for their happiness, that they may rest here and be safe. Bless all elements that are here; may the rocks and mountains be blessed, and everything that has life.

We pray thee, in the name of the Lord Jesus, that thou wouldst bless thy servant Brigham and those associated with him, who have taken pains to prepare the way and kindly invite us to these regions. May we feel that we are blest, and that the Lord, through the dispensation of his providence, has granted to us these favors. We ask thy choicest blessings on thy servants Brigham, Heber and the Twelve, and upon all thy faithful people in every kingdom and nation. Bless our friends, and all who speak comforting words to thy people, and defend them, and may the enemies of truth and righteousness be confounded, and not have power to injure the people of God. Bless thy servant George A. Smith, and thy servant John Taylor, and thy servant John M. Bernhisel, and bless all thy servants in every land and clime. Bless those who write and defend thy people through the press, may our prayers come up before thee in their behalf, for thou knowest we have not sinned against thee in these groves—in this kanyon. We do not visit groves, as did Israel of old, to commit adultery, nor to depart from the Lord our God. But we desire to appear before thee with clean hands and hearts, to call upon thee for thy blessing and do thy will, that our inheritance may be blest and all we have, and that all the efforts we make to build up Zion and rear temples to thy name may be blest, that the people of God may flock to the mountains by tens of thousands; may the wicked be cut off, may they be taken in the snares they have spread for thy people, and fall into the pits they have dug for thy Saints, and may they not prosper on the earth.

We desire that thou wouldst fulfill the covenants made with Abraham,

Isaac and Jacob, with Lehi and Nephi, and with all the prophets that have lived on this land, that Zion may come down from above and Zion come up from beneath; that every band may be broken and all Israel be saved. O Lord, we ask thee to bless us in our efforts on the earth; may righteousness and peace spread as the light of the morning, may we rejoice in the natural fortresses of this land, and may we be the pioneers of truth, men who will break the crust of nations, gather Israel and send the truth to every clime. May we accomplish the great work thou didst commence through thy servant Joseph, that truth may reign on the earth and righteousness predominate among all people. May we have power over the wicked nations, that Zion may be the seat of government for the universe, the law of God be extended and the scepter of righteousness swayed over this wide world; and eventually with the redeemed may we be brought to celebrate thy praise, in thy kingdom and presence. These favors, and all we need to prepare us to live here, to dwell with thee and the sanctified hereafter, we humbly crave in the name of Jesus Christ. Amen.[10]

Jedediah Grant had taken keen notice of the happy spirit that seemed to have permeated the mood of the Saints that summer. As his prayer at the celebration indicated, he was feeling a generous measure of it himself, in spite of an "indisposition."[11] A few days after the party in Big Cottonwood Canyon, he arose again to speak to the people. In the course of his sermon, he demonstrated that he had given the joyfulness of the Saints some serious thought since July 24. He wanted the Saints to feel his appreciation for the summer's happiness and to recognize their good fortune in having a living God to worship, one still active in human history.

We have professedly gathered ourselves to this land to serve our God; we feel that we have found the pearl of great price. It matters but little in relation to the land that we dwell upon, or the special comforts of life that we may have found and now enjoy in this land, so we but have within us that eternal treasure that warrants us in believing that we please our God, and that He approbates our course.

I am aware that the Christians would think inasmuch as they have circulated the Bible among the nations of the earth, that they have thereby done much towards spreading the Gospel and establishing the kingdom of God on the earth. But you, as reasonable men, would consider that I reasoned very badly, were I to say that the United States by circulating the Constitution among the various governments on the earth, had thereby established so many republics.

In order for the kingdom of God to have an existence upon earth, we naturally need the radiant light of heaven, we need the divine sanction of the Almighty, and He will set a man to properly organize His people, and execute those things which He designs to have carried out. Some may ask, why the Latter-day Saints rejoice? I answer, we rejoice not alone in that we have a claim superior to the claims of others; not alone in that we have houses and lands, and power and authority, and the comforts of this city, but in the privileges given us by the Almighty, through faith and obedience, for being more happy than other people. We have not the facilities that the people of many other cities and parts of the earth possess; indeed, we are deprived of many of the comforts and luxuries which many enjoy in other climes. But suppose we are, did we come here for them? Were they the grand object of our leaving our native soil? Was this the view we had when we left Europe, the United States, or any other part of the earth, or the islands of the sea? Did we come here to obtain a better farm, to obtain the luxuries of life? If this was the object of our pursuit, we have certainly been mistaken.

It is possible that some may have been tempted, as they were in the days of Jesus, by the loaves and fishes; but those who understood the truth and comprehended and loved virtue, had no such idea. They understood that the Gospel of the Son of God proclaimed and taught by the proper officers, had been brought unto them, and that the sceptre of life had been held out to them. And may we not, as Saints of God, rejoice that we have found and received the truth, that we have tasted of its sweetness, and that it has made us happy.

It matters not whether you dwell in Great Salt Lake City, or in the different settlements of this territory, or whether you are associated with those that are following some special branch of mechanism, if you have the principles of eternal life, the gift of the Holy Ghost, the will of the Lord, the power of God within you, for then you will be contented. On the other hand, if you have not the principles that come from Heaven, though you may have rich soil to cultivate, and splendid houses to dwell in, though you may be connected with wealthy and influential families, and possess choice localities in a powerful state, you are not happy, you are not contented, for there is a vacuum where the principles of life should be, and gold and silver will not fill it and satisfy the cravings within.

If Joseph had merely sold the people the Bible and Book of Mormon, would they have received the gift of the Holy Ghost? It was, and I presume still is, a favorite theme with Mr. Alexander Campbell, of the United States, that "the word is the Spirit and the Spirit is the word," in short that there is no Spirit to be received separate from the word of God. His logic amounts virtually to this—"Simply preach the Bible, the word of God and salvation as printed in the Bible; and all who purchase the Bible thereby purchase eternal life."

Who that is rational and possessed of a disposition to scan the subject can believe such a doctrine? Doubtless Moses heard the thunder of the Almighty on Mount Sinai, and saw the lightnings, but would you say that I was reasoning correctly, if I were to say that I heard that thunder and saw those lightnings simply through reading the history thereof in the Bible? Again, would I be reasoning correctly to say, because I have read the account of what transpired on the day of Pentecost, when the Spirit was poured out upon the people and Peter spoke as he was moved upon by the Holy Ghost, that I, therefore, have seen the day of Pentecost? That because I have read the history of some of the operations of the Holy Ghost, therefore I have the Holy Ghost? Or that I heard them speak in tongues, because I have read the history of persons speaking in tongues? Certainly not.

I am aware that hundreds and thousands of different denominations disagree with Mr. Campbell, and also declare that they receive the Spirit of the Lord, what they call the new birth, a change of the heart, put off the old man and put on the new man, and at the same time the operations of their minds, their course of life and all their doings and sayings, prove that they are equally as far behind as Mr. Campbell, and that they have only the history of the light itself.

Should you light a room with gas, and should an artist take a sketch of the light, and some author write a history of the affair, and at a subsequent date some other man write a history, and should the two accounts be placed together, describing the beauty thereof and benefit thereof, would the history of the light and the benefit that had been derived therefrom, and the abundance of that light that was said to have existed, light up a hall? If it would, do not buy any more candles, but read the history of candles, and stick that history in your candlesticks; read the history of oil and wick, and stick that in your lamp, and see how much light you will get.

You may read the Book of Mormon and the Book of Doctrine and Covenants, and the word of God in its various written and printed forms, and after you have read them all, have you, by so doing, gained any rights to say that you have the light of Moses, Isaiah, Daniel, and other ancient and modern men of God? Have you any reason to say that you possess the same light, the same joy, the same spirit, as they did, in consequence of your possessing the same written word of God that they possessed? Yes, if Mr. Campbell's doctrine be correct. No doubt the followers of Mr. Campbell consider the doctrine true, and his logic and reasoning correct.

Brethren and sisters, we understand the difference between enjoying and reading of enjoyment, between the history of a feast and the feast itself; also between the history of the law of God and the law itself.

When the Prophet Joseph came among the people he did not tell them that he would sell them the word of God, but after he had established the truth in their minds and they were baptized, he then laid his hands upon them that they might receive the gift of the Holy Ghost, for he had promised this, and they received the Holy Comforter and the same light, the same Spirit, the same power of God, and the same principles of eternal life; that very gift which is the greatest gift of God, and it gave them the same joy, and the same great blessings, and this Spirit taught them the will of God.

Herein is the difference between this Church and the people of the world. They rejoice in thinking that their forefathers had such rich blessings, and that they were so happy and rejoiced so much that they saw God, His Son Jesus Christ, and Peter, James, and John; and that their forefathers received the Holy Ghost.

We rejoice that we have seen and that our Prophets have received the like blessing, and not that we read of their enjoyment. We rejoice that our God lives, that Jesus Christ His Son lives, and that the gifts and blessings are bestowed upon us.

It is generally admitted that it is natural for parents to love their young children as well as the older ones, and if there be any difference, they will love the youngest ones a little the most, for they sometimes have to be more severe with the older ones.

But the world reverse this doctrine with regard to the Almighty, for they make God love Adam, Abraham, and the ancients, but when it comes down to the present time their wonderful, peace-making religion makes them rejoice that their older brethren and sisters had rich dinners and suppers, and that they had feasted on the good things of heaven, but that our Father is so unmerciful in our day that we have to eat husks.

According to the doctrine of our religious friends, we have to rejoice that the ancients enjoyed the rich blessings of our Father, and that He will not give us anything but the history thereof.[12]

At this point in Grant's sermon, Brigham Young chimed in from behind with "and the chaff," thus reinforcing his counselor's argument that the sectarians have nothing more to offer than the memory of revelation, "the husks" of religion, as Grant had put it. This seemed to remind the preacher of how often the Saints were ungrateful for the fount of modern revelation and how readily they grumbled about anything the Lord seemed to give out that was not exactly to their liking. "I am aware," he continued, "that the Latter-day Saints require a great deal of preaching...." From that point onward the sermon was more familiarly of the Grant stripe.

Some of that, too, [is] on subjects very easy of comprehension; I will tell you what I said to one of our home missionaries a few days ago, and I said the same to one of the brethren from Grantsville, when speaking to him about the petty wrangling there.

They wanted a new local President and a new local Bishop, they wanted this, that, and the other, and wished to know what we had to say. I remarked, if you wish to know what I have to say, I will tell you.

Said I, if an angel of God should come to that village, he would say to its inhabitants, "Repent and wash your bodies, repent and clean up your door yards, repent and cleanse your out-houses," all of which I seriously think that they have very much need to do.

After they have actually cleansed themselves and commenced doing right, and have cleansed their locality, I presume that then an angel, or a man of God, might tell them what further to do.

I actually suppose that in the instructions which an angel of God would give, the very first lesson would be to teach cleanliness to the filthy, and then instruct them to keep themselves cleanly all the time. This is what our President is frequently teaching you; and yet you may go into some parts of this city, and you would actually think that [the] Provo river affords no more water than would suffice for cleansing them.

I like a place constantly kept clean, and that must be so to satisfy me, I not only want the history of a people's being clean, and of their having cleansed up their door yards, out-buildings, and grounds, but I want them to do it.

We have preached cleanliness at Fillmore, last winter; and when I went there lately I was pleased to see that they had made some little improvement.

But there is still by far too much carelessness in this matter, and some people seem to love to live amidst filth, and to snuff its nauseous and unhealthy odors, when it would be far better to apply it to enriching your soil.

You have been taught true doctrines, and the Lord God has given you the Holy Ghost which has purified your hearts, and now purify all that pertains to you.

The time will come when you will be tried in this respect; and the days of power will come, when the power of God will be more abundantly poured out upon those who are prepared for it. And you who have the truth and do not live up to it, who do not live up to that light and intelligence which is given you, who do not purify your bodies, your clothing, your buildings; your door yards, gardens, and fields, may look for the wrath of God to burn against you.[13]

Within a few days, the wrath of the Mormon God would indeed burn against the "unpure" in Zion, and a tongue of lightning from the mind of Jedediah Morgan Grant would kindle His rage.

⇌ Notes ⇌

1. Deuteronomy 33:13–14. The widely read Scott Bible commentary, published in London in 1850, elaborated upon the meaning of the passage in Deuteronomy as follows: "By the seasonable rains and refreshing dews,—those precious things which come down from above and make the earth fruitful,—and by the springs which issue from beneath, and the benign influences of the sun, all kinds of valuable productions, peculiar to each revolving moon in succession, would be abundantly afforded." Thomas Scott, *The Holy Bible . . . with Explanatory Notes*, 6 vols. (London: Seeleys, 1850), 1:419. See also Deuteronomy 33:15–17.

2. Journal History of the Church of Jesus Christ of Latter-day Saints (chronological scrapbook of typed entries and newspaper clippings, 1830–present), May 18, 1856, 1, LDS Church Archives. See also *Deseret News*, April 16, 23, 30, and May 14, 1856.

3. Journal History, May 18, 1856, 1, and June 15, 1856, 2.

4. In a letter to Orson Pratt, who had recently departed for a mission, Wilford Woodruff wrote: "We feel thankful to our Heavenly Father for His gracious mercies, in sending us a bountiful shower every week, since President J. M. Grant spoke upon 'the dry moon,' and exhorted the brethren to exercise the faith for rain—which you may remember—when it commenced raining while he was preaching." Journal History, May 28, 1856, 1.

5. *Deseret News*, June 25, 1856.

6. Journal History, July 2, 1856, 1.

7. With the Thurstons, Grant had explored the possibilities of ranching in Weber Valley in 1855, when the city and county of Morgan were organized. The scheme apparently evaporated with Grant's death in 1856, although Thomas J. Thurston was for many years a prominent resident of Morgan County. See a brief early history of the county published in the *Salt Lake Herald Republican*, June 20, 1920, and Linda H. Smith, *A History of Morgan County* (Salt Lake City: Utah State Historical Society, 1999).

8. *Millennial Star*, October 25, 1856.

9. Ibid.

10. Ibid. Note the way in which Grant's prayer linked the abundant blessings of God among the Saints with devotion to duty and righteousness.

11. Whatever condition was bothering Grant before the August 3 discourse was not debilitating, inasmuch as his activities of the preceding weeks did not noticeably diminish. Journal History, July 4, 16, and August 2, 1856, all p. 1. Nevertheless, his illness may have contributed to the closing of his speech in which he launched a frontal attack against unsanitary conditions among the Saints, a favorite subject.

12. Jedediah M. Grant, August 3, 1856, *Journal of Discourses*, 26 vols. (London and Liverpool: LDS Booksellers Depot, 1855-86), 4:15-18.

13. Ibid., 18-20.

PHASE FOUR
Wildfire: 1856

"You need to be washed clean from everything that is evil before the God of Israel."

16
Arrows of the Almighty

AS THE HARVEST SEASON progressed in early September 1856, peace and calm prevailed over the valleys of Utah Territory. Despite a dry turn in the weather as summer ended, prospects for an adequate crop promised the Saints a better lot during the coming winter than that which they had suffered during the past one. To the leaders of the Church, this happy prospect was doubly important, for on the plains at that moment were several companies of converts, mostly from Europe, pushing and pulling their few belongings toward the mountains in small handcarts. These newcomers would be virtually dependent through the winter upon the abundance of Zion's storehouses. The idea of any kind of societal upheaval in the midst of this search for economic security was as far from Deseret as were the graves of Joseph and Hyrum at Nauvoo. Prosperity and order seemed now not only pleasant but necessary to the advancement of the kingdom.

The activities of the mayor of Great Salt Lake City and second counselor in the First Presidency reflected well the mood of the Saints in Utah. Between Grant's extensive farming operations in Davis County and his attendance at various quarterly conferences with traveling groups of "home missionaries," he was enlarging his already spacious home on Main Street in the city, feeling, as the *Deseret News* reported, "that want of more dwelling room so incident to those who observe the 'peculiar institution.'"[1] Six wives and many children had a definite way of providing a man with a certain concern for material progress, and in this Grant was no different from the numerous other heads of households in 1856 Utah who were striving for the temporal blessings that would bring a comfortable existence to their families.

It was almost as if Grant had finally managed to return from the long mission that had begun twenty-three years before with his baptism and had never really ended. At least, this appeared to be the case until, with sudden intensity, a fourth phase in the process began on September 12, as Grant and his admired associate Joseph Young arrived in Kaysville, Davis County, for a local conference of the home mission. These sessions had been under way in various places since a group of home missionaries had been called in the fall of 1855. Traveling to an increasing number of outlying settlements, they were to edify the Saints and to encourage them to continue to follow counsel. Taking time from their own considerable worldly pursuits, Grant and Young, with four others, Daniel D. Hunt, Gilbert Clements, Thomas Grover, and William Willes, planned a week-long swing through the communities of Davis County, beginning at Kaysville to the north. At the same time, Patriarch John Young and others were conducting a similar tour through Utah County. As these conferences began, no one, including the principals, seemed to sense the intensity of the impending storm.

It was a warm Saturday morning about 10 o'clock when the denizens of Kaysville and the surrounding area assembled happily in anticipation of some fine sermons from the visiting brethren. Everyone seemed in fine spirits as the meeting began with a strong sermon from President Joseph Young of the Seventies on the necessity of unbending faithfulness to the kingdom. Following Young, William Willes, who had recently arrived from a mission to India, spoke on his great pleasure at being among the Saints and feeling the unity of the faith. Willes was something of a poet and singer; and at the close of his remarks, he sang an original composition to the tune of "Hope of Israel" that ended, "For Deseret is sure that all the Saints will do their duty." This was among Grant's favorite themes; and when he subsequently arose to make his remarks, he followed the last strain of Willes's hymn with a standard discourse on the subject of faith, repentance, and baptism for the remission of sins. He mingled into his words advice from Brigham Young on strengthening the Church, and then closed by counseling the Saints at Kaysville to be patient with the conference, letting it take its course, as they should also "let the things of the kingdom of God be first, and all other things in their times and seasons."[2]

Two more sessions of the conference that day, at 2:00 o'clock and at 6:00, produced again only typical sermons on such diverse subjects as irrigation, prayer, fort-building, and obedience. Grant did not speak again on

September 13, but no doubt enjoyed Willes's last hymn, "The City I Love So Well," which finished its blissful lines with an ode to the First Presidency:

> Here Brigham, Heber, and Jeddy dwell,
> And o'er the Saints preside.³

As the day's activities ended late in the evening, there was every reason to feel pleased and fulfilled. The Saints were prospering in their mountain home, the missionaries were coming home with tales of triumph, and the organization of the people had achieved the basic elements of a righteous society, being fed from the very fount of Deity itself in both temporal and spiritual affairs. All must have seemed well to the local Saints as they made their way home in the twilight in anticipation of another long day's preaching on the morrow.

As Brothers Jeddy and Joseph settled in for the evening, however, Grant noticed that his companion was troubled. As he remembered a few weeks later,

There was a dark and dull spirit there which was not very congenial to our natures, and brother Joseph Young felt life in him, he was full of the Spirit. After staying a couple of days, he said to me, "Brother Grant, they feel cold, and I guess we had better go to Farmington, preach there, and go home." After a while I said to him, "Do you know how I feel about it? In the name of the Lord Jesus Christ, I will never leave this land, until this people surrender. I will hang the flag of the Lord Jesus Christ on their doors, and there shall be a siege of forty days. Then let every man storm the castle, and rule against the bulwarks of hell, and let every Elder throw the arrows of God Almighty through the sinner, and pierce their loins, and penetrate their vitals, until the banner of Christ shall wave triumphantly over Israel. Shall we give up, and let the wicked and ungodly overcome us? No, in the name and by the power of God we will over come them. We will cleanse the inside of the platter and have Israel saved, through the name of Jesus Christ, and by the power of his word."⁴

Willes led off in the next morning's opening session with an address upon the virtues of sound education, closing with a recommendation that

Grant's home in Salt Lake City, later the site of Zion's Cooperative Mercantile Institution, with the Salt Lake Theatre in the background, ca. 1863. LDS Church Archives.

the Kaysville Saints establish Sabbath schools and literary institutions. After Willes finished, Brother Jeddy was on his feet. He began to speak in a low tone, adding to the previous address his counsel that "the Lord would not hold parents guiltless who neglected to inform the minds of their children." But from then on to the end of his sermon, there could have been no mild intonations, nor could there have been any lethargic listeners in the congregation. Willes and Gilbert Clements, who were keeping notes with which they later reported the meetings to the *Deseret News*, felt the change in the second counselor's mood and the sting in his words. Brigham Young himself had supplied the text, claimed the gaunt preacher, but "Saints, live your religion" was really more of the stripe of Jedediah Grant. He proceeded to give them a list of indicators of righteousness— "holding sacred their covenants, observing cleanliness in their persons and dwellings, setting their families in order, carefully cultivating their farms and gardens, and not to feel so anxious to have more land than they could attend to themselves."[5] These were all favorite subjects of Grant himself, but he now intended to apply more force to their total compliance. He "concluded by praying that all those who did not feel to do right might have their way opened to leave this people and Territory, and that those who did not come forward and do their first works, let them be unto you as heathen men and publicans, and not numbered among the Saints."[6]

Apparently, Grant had tired of preaching a reformation that never took hold; now he would require rebaptism and reconfirmation—outward signs of fealty to the thunderings of the Almighty through His chosen vessel. In effect, he would cut off the entire membership of the Church and require them to submit to reconversion and rededication to the principles he and his colleagues had been hurling at them for years. There would be no passive Saints in the kingdom of Jedediah's stewardship. It would be all or nothing.

Once lightning stuck, the fire quickly spread at Kaysville. By the end of the afternoon session of September 14, the Saints there had unanimously voted to renew their covenants by submitting to a rebaptism. After two more "animated" Grant harangues that afternoon, and more fiery talks that evening, the congregation adjourned to meet the next morning at John Weinal's mill for baptisms and confirmations.[7]

Willes and Clements reported the scene at the mill on the morning of September 15 for the *News*:

> Prest. Grant enjoined upon the Saints to observe the utmost decorum and reverence while the sacred ordinance of baptism was being attended to. After prayer, he proceeded to baptize Bishop Allen Taylor and his counselors, Reddick N. Allred and Dorr P. Curtis. Nearly 500 Saints were immersed under the direction of Prest. Grant, aided by Bishop Taylor, Elders Clements, Allred, Curtis, Weinel, Wm. Booth, jr., Payne, and Dinsdale; Prest. Grant baptized upwards of 80 with his own hands. After baptism the Saints repaired to the bowery, where the ordinance of confirmation was attended to by Presidents Grant and J. Young, assisted by Elders Clements, Willes, Hunt, Taylor, Allred, Curtis, [John] Ellison, T[homas] Squires, [William L.] Payne, S[amuel G.] Henderson, Dinsdale, [John] Weinel, [James R.] McPherson, and Matthews. The Spirit of God was poured out to a great degree, and peace and happiness characterised the whole assembly. Prest. Grant arose and blest the people in the name of the Lord God of Israel.[8]

It was a strange thing, indeed, these Saints bowing their heads to the revivalist cries of a lank preacher, but the time was ripe and his mood had ascended to the height of his calling to save the Saints and to damn the sinners. It was a time of wonder and of ominous portent. Probably few of the hundreds of Mormons rebaptized that day realized what was happening—that they were among the first to feel the fiery spirit of a classic revival in a closed society.

They met again in Kaysville at 6:00 in the evening. Following the sustaining of priesthood and ward officers, Grant addressed them again, counseling them in a calm and orderly fashion on ways to continue to effect the meaning of the reformation.

> Prest. Grant imparted some valuable instructions in relation to government in the branch and family circles; counseled the Bishop to call upon the brethren to follow a systematic course to sustain the home missionaries who stood in need of assistance, taking care to credit each contributor to the fund, and deliver an annual report of the same in writing to Prest. B. Young and his counsel, and to forward the contributions of the people to the houses of the home missionaries. He gave the same counsel to the Seventies in relation to Prest. Joseph Young.
> Prest. J. Young poured forth the fullness of his soul for the great manifestations of the power of God during this conference, followed on the same subject by Elder G. Clements.—Motion was made that we hold a fast on the morrow and continue the conferences.[9]

The meeting of the next morning bore all the marks of a powerful revivalist conference. The two clerks again reported "animated" addresses from the lips of Grant and Young, and even potent manifestations of the Spirit.

> The Bishop and his counselors expressed their great joy at the proceedings of this conference. During these proceedings the sick were administered to and the children blessed by Elders Willes, Clements, Curtis, Allred, Henderson, and others, in the school room adjoining the bowery.
> Father [Isaac] Allred, President of the High Priests, addressed the conference.
> Prest. Grant delivered a powerful address, at the conclusion of which he called upon all the home missionaries to arise in turn and bless the people, which they did in the name of the Lord, and by the power of the Holy Priesthood poured forth the blessing of the new and everlasting covenant on the congregation. Every heart was made glad and the people were deeply affected by the power of God.

Prest. Grant adjourned the conference . . . blessing the people in the name of the Lord.[10]

Having thus completed their expanded work in Kaysville, the party of missionaries moved on to the village of Farmington, where they called a meeting for 6:30 that evening in the upper room of the courthouse. Reminiscent of his days as an itinerant preacher in the South, Grant stood before the hastily assembled Saints to report the kindling of a reformation fire in the ward to the northwest. Although he was thrilled with the results of the four-day conference in Kaysville, he appeared reluctant to undertake the same effort in Farmington, suggesting that a similar "test" might be made of the Saints in that area during their next scheduled quarterly conference in October. Joseph Young followed with a similarly glowing report on the spiritual outpouring that had just occurred in the neighboring ward. With this, Bishop John W. Hess came to his feet, saying that a reformation was overdue, and that he wished it would begin in Farmington immediately. Brother Jeddy said nothing in response, but called on Willes and Hunt to speak. He then rose again at the podium. The Spirit, he said, had dictated his course to him. He would remain in Farmington as long as necessary to commence the revival as he had in Kaysville, and then the missionaries would continue southward to Great Salt Lake City, spreading the fires of rededication and reconsecration to the cause of Christ as they went. The great Mormon Reformation of 1856–57 had thus begun in earnest.[11]

As that crucial meeting of Tuesday evening, September 16, came to a close, Grant asked the congregation if it wished to have preaching and baptism after the order of the Kaysville revival begin the next morning in Farmington. According to the conference clerk, James Leithead, "the whole assembly rose with a sudden rush" to vote its approval.[12]

Wednesday morning at 9 o'clock, the Farmington Saints reassembled in the courthouse to hear Grant instruct them in the next phase of the Reformation—repeating the first works of baptism and confirmation. He told them that Brigham Young had sent him to Kaysville to encourage the people to live their religion, but that he had decided while there to reconvert them and to baptize them again into the Church. He assured the Farmington Saints that their attendance at the meetings of the revival would not impede their thrashing and wood-hauling efforts, after which he repeated his favorite sermons about keeping clean physically and spiritually, putting houses in order, and doing right. "If men are right," he said, "they can direct their wives and children right, and will know how to correct them in love, and how to chastize their children in mildness." The way to get right was to become sanctified by keeping the Sabbath, studying good books, and reading the scriptures. The ultimate symbol of it all was simple: "Awake," he shouted, "and be baptized for the remission of your sins, and sanctify yourselves!" At 2:00 that afternoon, the Farmington Ward met at the millrace north of the fort wall. There Jedediah Grant, with assistance from Bishop Hess and four other elders, baptized 406 persons.[13]

By this time, those traveling with the second counselor had begun to see what was happening. Gilbert Clements was amazed at the willingness of the people to confess their sinfulness and to submit to rebaptism. Listening to Grant's powerful preaching on the wickedness of the Saints had led him "to quake" and to ask, "Lord, is it I?"[14] The spirit of revival burned on.

At the evening meeting following the baptisms, Elder Thomas Grover rose to bear testimony that the Prophet Joseph himself was directing the meetings, and that the veil was about to be rent, whereupon heavenly messengers would come and minister unto the people. Brothers Willes, Hunt, and Hess added similar thoughts, Hunt stating that when Grant and Grover were speaking, he felt that Joseph and Hyrum Smith were in their midst. He further testified that the spirit of Joseph was in Brother Jeddy, making the Saints quake and tremble at his presence. Grant took the cue. He picked up a Bible and opened it to James, chapter 1. "Be ye doers of the word, and not hearers only," he thundered. If the people wanted the spirit of Joseph to be with them as well, they must keep the commandments, deal honestly one with another, and love God more than Mammon. He talked of Kirtland, and of the chariots of Israel passing over the temple, knocking men to the ground. This was the kind of power he wanted to see try the people in Utah, but doubted whether there were ten men or five women in the room who would feel the presence of angels. There was still much to be done in the work of reformation.[15]

The next day, amid blessings, fasting, and praying, the conference at Farmington continued. More persons were baptized and confirmed. When it appeared that the meetings had reached the point of fulfillment, Grant ordered the sacrament (communion) passed, after which he administered to the sick in the congregation by the laying on of hands. He called on Joseph Young to speak, then directed that the home missionaries should rise and bless the people of Farmington in the name of the Lord. When that was finished, he rose to make his final remarks. He blessed the bishopric, the teachers, the choir, and literally every person in the assembly. The home missionaries, he said, had preached by the power of God in Kaysville and Farmington. Joseph and Hyrum had spoken through them, and the spirits of the martyrs had indeed been in the courthouse at Farmington. "He blessed the whole congregation, in the name of the Lord Jesus Christ," wrote Leithead, "and prayed that the Spirit of Joseph and Hyrum and of Brigham and Heber might abide with them for ever." As he finished this final benediction, the people shouted "Hosanna, hosanna, hosanna to God," and the Farmington meetings came to an end.[16]

Returning to Salt Lake City, the elders reported the fires they had set in the north to Young and Kimball; and the next Sunday, the First Presidency, along with Joseph and John Young, addressed the Saints in the Bowery. The message was as clear as its preacher was blunt. Jedediah preached:

> If the arrows of the Almighty ought to be thrown at you we want to do it, and to make you feel and realize that we mean you. And although we talk of the old clay's being ground in the mill, we do not mean it to apply to some other place, for we have enough here who have been dried ever since their baptism, and many of them are cracked and spoiling.
>
> Some have received the Priesthood and a knowledge of the things of God, and still they dishonor the cause of truth, commit adultery, and every other abomination beneath the heavens, and then meet you here or in the street, and deny it.
>
> These are the abominable characters that we have in our midst, and they will seek unto wizards that peep, and to star-gazers and soothsayers, because they have no faith in the holy Priesthood, and then when they meet us, they want to be called Saints.
>
> The same characters will get drunk and wallow in the mire and filth, and yet they call themselves Saints, and seem to glory in their conduct, and they pride themselves in their greatness and in their abominations.
>
> They are the old hardened sinners, and are almost—if not altogether—past improvement, and are full of hell, and my prayer is that God's indignation

may rest upon them, and that He will curse them from the crown of their heads to the soles of their feet.

I say, that there are men and women that I would advise to go to the President immediately, and ask him to appoint a committee to attend to their case; and then let a place be selected, and let that committee shed their blood.

We have those amongst us that are full of all manner of abominations, those who need to have their blood shed, for water will not do, their sins are of too deep a dye.

You may think that I am not teaching you Bible doctrine, but what says the apostle Paul? I would ask how many covenant breakers there are in this city and in this kingdom. I believe that there are a great many; and if they are convenant breakers we need a place designated, where we can shed their blood.

Talk about old clay; I would rather have clay from a new bank than some that we have had clogging the wheels for the last nineteen years. They are a perfect nuisance, and I want them cut off, and the sooner it is done the better.

We have men who are incessantly finding fault, who get up a little party spirit, and criticise the conduct of men of God. They will find fault with this, that, and the other, and nothing is right for them, because they are full of all kinds of filth and wickedness.

And we have women here who like any thing but the celestial law of God; and if they could break asunder the cable of the Church of Christ, there is scarcely a mother in Israel but would do it this day. And they talk it to their husbands, to their daughters, and to their neighbors, and say they have not seen a week's happiness since they become acquainted with that law, or since their husbands took a second wife. They want to break up the Church of God, and to break it from their husbands and from their family connections.

Then, again, there are men that are used as tools by their wives, and they are just a little better in appearance and in their habits than a little black boy. They live in filth and nastiness, they eat it and drink it, and they are filthy all over.

We have Elders and High Priests that are precisely in this predicament, and yet they are wishing for more of the Holy Ghost, they wish to have it in larger doses. They want more revelation, but I tell you that you now have more than you live up to, more than you practise and make use of.

If I hurt your feelings let them be hurt. And if any of you ask, do I mean you? I answer, yes. If any woman asks, do I mean her? I answer, yes. And I want you to understand that I am throwing the arrows of God almighty among Israel; I do not excuse any.

I am speaking to you in the name of Israel's God, and you need to be baptized and washed clean from your sins, from your backslidings, from your apostacies, from your filthiness, from your lying, from your swearing, from your lusts, and from every thing that is evil before the God of Israel.

We have been trying long enough with this people, and I go in for letting the word of the Almighty be unsheathed, not only in word, but in deed. I go in for letting the wrath of the Almighty burn up the dross and the filth; and if the people will not glorify the Lord by sanctifying themselves, let the wrath of the almighty God burn against them, and the wrath of Joseph and of Brigham, and of Heber, and of high heaven.

There is nothing to prevent you from being humble and doing right, but your own little, foolish, and wicked acts and doings. I will just tell you that if an angel of God were to pass Great Salt Lake City, while you are in your present state, he would not consider you worthy of his company.

You have got to cleanse yourselves from corruption, before you are fit for the society of those beings. You may hear of people in other cities being baptized and renewing their covenants, but they are not sinners above all others; and except the inhabitants of Great Salt Lake City repent, and do their first works, they shall all likewise perish, and the wrath of God will be upon them and round about them.

You can scarcely find a place in this city that is not full of filth and abominations; and if you would search them out, they would easily be weighed in the balances, and you would then find that they do not serve their god, and purify their bodies.

But the course they are taking leads them to corrupt themselves, the soil, the waters, and the mountains, and they defile everything around them.

Brethren and sisters, we want you to repent and forsake your sins. And you who have committed sins that cannot be forgiven through baptism, let your blood be shed, and let the smoke ascend, that the incense thereof may come up before God as an atonement for your sins, and that the sinners in Zion may be afraid.

These are my feelings, and may God fulfil them. And my wishes are that

He will grant the desires of my brethren, that Zion may be purified, and the wicked purged out of her, until God shall say I will bless the rest; until He shall say I bless your flocks, your herds, your little ones, your houses, your lands, and all that you possess; and you shall be my people, and I will come and take up my abode with you, and I will bless all those that do right; which may He grant, in the name of Jesus. Amen.[17]

With that tabernacle meeting and with the actions of the brethren over the next few days, the Mormons in Great Salt Lake City became aware of a change in the mood of their leaders, similar to the change in the valley air as the summer of 1856 turned inexorably to autumn over Utah. They could not help but notice Grant's demeanor. The words he was speaking were really not any different from the ones he had always used as a preacher, but now there was certain bite to them, as if his lungs were full of fire.[18] He had somehow grown tired of waiting for the perfection among the Saints that he had always expected, and now, as a measure of secular prosperity set in on Zion, he feared that the realization of that millennial spotlessness he looked for in his people would never be. As a reformer of the same die had said before, "Faith is like wax—a little warmth and it melts."[19]

Inasmuch as the brethren had previously scheduled for the coming week other area conferences of the home mission, those who with Grant had been responsible for the opening salvos of the Reformation were soon on the road again. In addition, other home missionaries leaving at the same time had also caught the revivalist spirit, and took with them into their assigned areas the same spark as did Brother Jeddy and his assistants.[20] But at this point there seemed to be no institutionalized effort to see that a general movement took place in the Church, particularly with regard to the repetition of the first works among the Saints. Nevertheless, prior to leaving the city for meetings in Centerville and Bountiful on the morning of September 25, Grant met with the city bishops who had assembled for a conference with Presiding Bishop Edward Hunter. The second counselor's remarks to these local pastors amounted to a pointed and very brief word of warning that foreshadowed the movement to come.

The work of the reformation must commence in the wards. While I was up north I tried the people on some of the most scrutinizing questions, and found a great majority come short in most of the ordinary duties of life that the Lord requires at our hands, but you Bishops and councillors must first be right yourselves; then you are required to throw through the Ward, the arrows of the Almighty, and when you have got the people right, then pour in the oil and the wine. It is through the Bishops, that all the abominations and filth that exists in the City, is to be removed, and if this is not done, the wrath of Almighty God will burn against you, and remove you out of your places.[21]

Taking leave of what must have been a pensive set of bishops, he headed north again into Davis County, in the company of Joseph Young, William Willes, Gilbert Clements, and J. W. Johnson. The meetings of that day, Thursday, September 25, in Centerville, centered on recounting the tenets of the Reformation that had emerged during the Kaysville-Farmington conferences. Grant blasted the Saints for having their "minds set upon the things of this world" instead of seeking first and always to live their religion. In the evening meeting, he outlined the requisites of righteousness that must exist before the Lord could regenerate the earth in His millennial glory, and told them of the numerous spirits still waiting to be born, all of which suggested to the Saints in Centerville that there was still time for them to repent and come up to the standards of the Reformation. On the other hand, the second counselor made it clear that there could be no slackening of effort in keeping the commandments. As he closed, he asked all those in the congregation who were willing to repent and to live their religion to stand. All arose but one.[22]

Perhaps the one person who saw the arrows of the Almighty, but did not fear them, convinced Grant that the rapid course the reforming works had taken in Kaysville and Farmington would not do in Centerville, for in his opening remarks in the first session of Friday's meetings, Grant said that he had thought about the condition of the Saints there and that he had decided that they were not ready for the sacred ordinance of baptism. They would have to wait and to prepare themselves with more soul-searching and confessions. With this, Bishop William R. Smith rose to assure Brother Jeddy that though he recognized the poor condition of his people, he believed that he could get them ready for the saving ordinances with a fast day and other measures. Grant refused to bend. He ordered the bishop to cut off "every person that would not keep the commandments of God," and to have fellowship meetings every Sunday in which the fires of the Reformation were to be kept hot and effective. After abruptly adjourning the conference until October 16, he left Centerville for Farmington "to refresh his spirits."[23]

His strategy worked. When he returned to Centerville on Sunday, September 28, the Saints were in a completely malleable condition, having undoubtedly spent Saturday contemplating their rejection by a member of the First Presidency. Bishop Smith, having received word that Grant had decided to return after all, had called a meeting for 2:00 o'clock, and had ordered "the missionaries to rebuke sin of every kind, and those persons that were under the influence of the devil." With this preparation, the assembly that looked into the flaming eyes of the second counselor that afternoon was humble and contrite indeed—ready for arrows from the quiver of Jedediah Grant. He started with the bishop and his counselors, asking them "to covenant, in the name of God Almighty and his Son Jesus Christ, and in the presence of holy angels, the servants of God, and all men, to discharge their duties in the office and calling whereunto they were called, according to the ability God should give them." They then agreed by raising their hands. From there, he passed through the rest of the congregation, asking the same commitment, and when it was finished, adjourned to meet the next morning for baptism.[24] The pattern thus took form.

William Reeves, present during the Centerville meetings, would never forget the soul-shaking events of those few days. "The Spirit of the Almighty," he wrote, "seems to be lit up in the countenances of all; and each one seems desirous to become a brother and a friend."[25] Following such a spiritual renewal and the baptism of 231 persons at Centerville, the party of missionaries moved triumphantly southward into the community of Bountiful, where the spirit of revival clothed itself in even harsher colors than it had in the communities to the north. However unlikely it may be that the citizens in Bountiful really were more wicked than those in Kaysville, Farmington, or Centerville, to Grant and his traveling companions, the lack of the Holy Ghost in the congregation there was so palpable that the second counselor charged the people "with being as cold as the ice of the Polar regions," and of having been "in a deep sleep." He further blasted them for their slackness in attending meetings, feeling "from the unmistakable evidences around him, that the people were in a state of apostacy." The people of Bountiful had sunk into total corruption. They had to repent and to turn again to God with broken hearts and contrite spirits. After several meetings in which this theme bludgeoned the sickened souls of hundreds of people who just days before had considered themselves among the elect of God and literal Saints of the latter days, Elder Grant, breathing fire, refused to consider baptizing them in their present state; and with his cohort of holy legionnaires, he marched away, leaving a small city full of broken and fearful Mormons who could not understand the full meaning of what had happened to them.[26] They could not have known that they were witnessing the early stages of a classic revival, one of the type Richard Bushman described as literally rocking the foundations of an old society, until the structure itself threatened to crumble.[27]

Among the first to realize the kinetic scope of the new movement, Wilford Woodruff surveyed the scene on September 30 for Orson Pratt, who was in England.

> The Presidency of the Church have commenced a great reformation among this people in the valleys of the mountains. I have never heard as strong sermons delivered to the people as have been preached unto them of late. The Presidency are weighing the people in the balances, and are calling upon them to repent and be baptized for the remission of their sins.
>
> President Grant has gone into the Northern Counties, and is preaching and baptizing whole Wards, and building up Churches. I presume the same course will be pursued in the Wards in this City. The people begin to feel more then ever that they are dealing with the Spirit and power of God, and the holy Priesthood. Yes, the Latter-day Saints begin to feel that they are dealing with a Spirit that can reach the hearts, know the thoughts and intents thereof, and try the souls of men. The people are called to santify themselves before the Lord, that we may be prepared for the work of our God.[28]

Perhaps Jedediah Grant, who had read Cotton Mather, knew what was manifest among the Saints, but he never indicated such. It was to him rather the condensation of his entire career as a preacher. What he had started in the northern wards, he could not nor did he ever wish to stop. Instead, he would cast his burning arrows through the remainder of Deseret, until the very kingdom of God would burn clean and pure against the mountains of Zion.[29]

~ Notes ~

1. *Deseret News*, September 24, 1856.

2. Ibid.

3. Ibid. There was in the report no indication of any unusual excitement surrounding the meetings of the first day. They appeared to be merely typical quarterly conferences with the standard doses of discourses and counsel from the visiting authorities.

4. Jedediah M. Grant, November 2, 1856, *Journal of Discourses*, 26 vols. (London and Liverpool: LDS Booksellers Depot, 1855–86), 4:74–75. This account, combined with the calmness of the September 13 meetings, should put to rest the possibility of the "Jeddy's Mule" story that many authors have used to explain the spark that set the Reformation burning. Its original proponent, T. B. H. Stenhouse, claimed that Grant became incensed on the first day of the Kaysville meetings when he noticed that his mule, which he had lent to another elder for the journey from Salt Lake City, "seemed to be heated, sweating, and rather jaded." The second counselor supposedly waited until the end of the meeting and then flew into an uncontrolled rage, charging the elders "in the bitterest manner with cruelty to his mule and other animals, and with riding in such a manner as to nearly kill them." Stenhouse's account had Grant then advancing to more general condemnations, eventually accusing the local bishopric and Saints of "all manner of wickedness." T. B. H. Stenhouse, *Rocky Mountain Saints* (London: Ward, Lock, and Tyler, 1878), 313. Although consistent with Grant's well-established feelings against the brutal treatment of animals, the "mule" version of the Reformation's beginnings remains in several respects inconsistent with more reliable accounts of the Kaysville conference.

5. *Deseret News*, September 24, 1856. William Willes and Gilbert Clements characterized Grant's address as "soul-stirring."

6. Ibid. Grant had thus threatened his listeners with the heavy weapon of social ostracism. To be "not numbered among the Saints" in a place like 1856 Kaysville would have meant virtual isolation, in addition to political and economic disaster.

7. Ibid.

8. Ibid. Note the lack of wild fanaticism that was supposed to have accompanied Grant's Reformation preachments. In these accounts he appeared rather calm and beneficent, as opposed to the common image of the revivalist as beyond control and literally frothing at the mouth.

9. Ibid.

10. Ibid. Note the repetition in these accounts of the "blessings" Grant gave or directed upon the people. Again, this theme contradicted a persistent belief among Mormons and non-Mormons alike that the second counselor was out of control and bent

on cursing and tearing down the Saints. On the contrary, and as always, Grant's motive was to reform and then to bless abundantly the people of the covenant, that they would indeed be "deeply affected by the power of God."

    11. *Deseret News*, October 1, 1856.

    12. Ibid.

    13. Ibid. Note the manner in which Grant permitted the local leaders to set the tone of the meetings, even to allowing them to determine whether the revival would proceed or not. This again contradicts the common accounts of the Reformation that suggested a reckless bludgeoning of the people by Grant and his colleagues from Church headquarters.

    14. Ibid.

    15. Ibid.

    16. Ibid.

    17. Jedediah M. Grant, September 21, 1856, *Journal of Discourses*, 4:49-51.

    18. See the observations of Hannah Tapfield King, Diary, October 8, 1856, typescript, LDS Church Archives.

    19. Girolamo Savonarola, quoted in Roberto Ridolfi, *The Life of Girolamo Savonarola* (New York: Alfred A. Knopf, 1959), 187.

    20. See reports of other conferences beginning September 27, 1856, in *Deseret News*, October 22, 1856.

    21. Bishops' Meetings with Presiding Bishopric, Minutes, 1851-61, September 25, 1856, LDS Church Archives (hereafter cited as Bishops' Meetings).

    22. *Deseret News*, October 8, 1856.

    23. Ibid. We cannot be certain that Grant left Centerville intending to return after the Saints had spent a day suffering with their rejection; but in its effect, the move accomplished just that.

    24. Ibid.

    25. Ibid.

    26. Ibid.

    27. See Richard L. Bushman, ed., *The Great Awakening: Documents on the Revival of Religion, 1740-1745* (New York: Atheneum, 1970), xi. Bushman emphasizes the modern observer's inability to grasp the full meaning of a revival in an "old society." It was truly earthshaking, he writes, "like the civil rights demonstrations, the campus disturbances, and the urban riots of the 1960s combined."

    28. *Millennial Star*, December 13, 1856.

    29. For other scholarly accounts of the origins and course of the Reformation, see also Paul H. Peterson, "The Mormon Reformation" (Ph.D. diss., Brigham Young University, 1981); and Eugene E. Campbell, *Establishing Zion: The Mormon Church in the*

American West, 1847-1869 (Salt Lake City: Signature Books, 1988), 181-200. The late Professor Campbell paid the first edition (1982) of this work a great compliment by accepting, often word-for-word, its characterizations of Jedediah Grant.

"The reformation shall be carried into your houses...."

17
Catechism

THE SEISMIC BEGINNINGS OF THE Mormon Reformation in the early fall of 1856 would have shaken the ground in Utah much more immediately and severely than it did had it not been for the arrival at about the same time of the first parties of handcart emigrants in the valley. The Ellsworth and McArthur companies began to emerge from the canyon on September 26 while Jedediah Grant and his companions were setting fire to the souls in Centerville. Although Heber Kimball (speaking in the tabernacle two days later) tried to make a connection between the two events—that suffering was the result of sinfulness among the Saints[1]—the wretched condition of the handcart Saints as they finally pushed into the city gave nearly everyone great pains of empathy and temporarily overshadowed the portent of the coming institutionalized revival. Grant himself, after returning from Bountiful on September 30, wept openly when he saw the bony hands of an old Englishman wrapped clawlike about the bar of his handcart as he pulled it into the city.[2]

Twelve-year-old Henry Moyle, who had arrived with his family from England in the Ellsworth company, would never forget his first few days in Zion and an apparently different Grant from the one who had lambasted the quivering denizens of Bountiful a few days before.

> I remember the 2nd or 3rd day after arriving in Salt Lake City with the handcarts. My father being sick and worn out from the effects of the journey, I went up what was called Main Street hunting for a place to work for my board, calling at most all the houses, among the rest at a store, where the man let me cut wood for about one hour, when he came out and told me he guesed he would not need me, and never so much as thanked me, without giving me anything. I felt rather discouraged, but some one told me that

perhaps bishop Hunter would want a boy. So I went up to his house, and he was talking to 5 or 6 men, when I asked him if he wanted a boy to work or do choirs [chores]. When he said to me, come again tomorrow. You see I am busy now talking to all these bishops, but you come again tomorrow Bob. I was very much discouraged, and nearly worn out having started out early that morning and had no breakfast; but President Jediah M. Grant whose house was next to bishop Hunters on the North, where the ZCMI now stands, must have heard our conversation, and as I went from Hunters still thinking to turn in at President Grants not knowing who he was, he spoke to me and said good morning my boy how are you this morning, in a kind manner that it done me good, and after stating that I was looking for a place to work or do choirs: He said yes I have all the work you can do and more to, but I think you are just the boy I want, he took me in his house and questioned me as to who I was and where I was from and asked if I had had any breakfast, and when I told him no, and that a store keeper let me chop wood without giving me anything for it, he told one of his wives, who prepared me a good breakfast and they asked me to state where the store was I knew he felt surprised and angry to think I should have been so treated, after eating pres. Grant told me to rest for a while and I began to feel anxious to be doing something, but he told me I needed rest more than work.

So after I had rested for an hour or so, he gave a knife to cut the weeds in front of the door yard, and the woman let me carry in some wood, and water and other light chores, and was very kind to me, and when dinner and supper time came would have me eat with them. And after supper Pres. Grant told them to give me 8 or 10 lbs. of flour to take home to my father and mothers family which I did about 8 blocks down main street in brother Hails house, and as I was leaving bro Grant told me to come again tomorrow which I did and kept this up for a week.[3]

It was not really a different Jedediah Grant whom Moyle had encountered on Main Street, but merely a different side of an extremely complex man. On the evening of September 30, probably the same day he had made such a kind impression upon the English lad at his home, Grant attended the "bishops and lesser priesthood meeting" in the Council House to stoke the fires of the Reformation that were beginning slowly to burn in Great Salt Lake City. His tack with these local leaders was the same as it been with those at Bountiful. Having heard of the need to get their people ready for rebaptism, the bishops had been busily working with their charges to see that they would meet with Brother Jeddy's approval when he returned from the north. It would not be easy, as they soon learned. "As to getting your wards willing to be baptized, that is nothing," he told them. "The biggest devil would be willing to do that."[4] Speaking forcefully "as one having Authority and with the Power of God upon him,"[5] the second counselor began to interrogate the bishops and their counselors on such things as whether or not they were attending to prayers, in family and in secret, and whether they bathed at least once a week. Finding all of them "more or less negligent," he issued an ultimatum that combined the force both of his civil and ecclesiastical authority:

> The Bishops, councillors, and Teachers must first begin to repent and wash themselves, cleanse their premises, their Houses, back houses, and everything else about them, and then get the Holy Ghost and go from house to house and purify the whole city, and if the Bishops do not do this they shall be removed from their place, and the Marshal shall receive orders to send Policemen round to wash the Bishops and people and cleanse every house, for the wrath of God burns against us, owing to the filth and abomination that exists here, and that the Bishops etc may at once commence and assist in the work of reformation is my prayer in the name of Jesus, Amen.[6]

Within a few days, Grant had formalized the set of questions he had been asking the Saints into a kind of Reformation catechism. In its early stages, the list of queries centered on issues of cleanliness, both spiritually and physically, for in one was a manifestation of the other. Preaching in the Seventeenth Ward schoolhouse on October 2, the second counselor made it clear that the Reformation would no longer go forth merely in revival meetings, but in every house in Zion by means of the catechism, carried there by the teachers who would search the lives of the people for filth and iniquity, those interwoven symbols of apostasy and entropy.

> If there is a place on the earth where we should be faithful, it is in this city; or if there is a place where we should watch our children, it is here. Go to all the quorums in this city, and you will find some of their Presidents and Officers as corrupt as the devil. We have men that can beat the Gentiles in any mean tricks they are a mind to start up, but those who intend to serve

God should do right.

I want to see the Bishops of the Wards right, then I want to see the Teachers right; I want to see them all filled with the Holy Ghost, then they can do something. Did I ever cry peace and safety to this people, that they were ALL doing well, and that their warfare was over? No, I never did. When I know that sudden destruction awaits a people, if they do not awake to their situation, I cannot cry peace.

This people are asleep; and I will vouch that there are many of them who do not pray, or if they do, three such prayers "would freeze hell over," as a Methodist minister once said. I want you to pray with the Holy Ghost upon you.

It is your duty to keep clean. I have given the Teachers a new set of questions to ask the people. I say to them, ask the people whether they keep clean. Do you wash your bodies once in each week, when circumstances will permit? Do you keep your dwellings, outhouses, and dooryards clean? The first work of the reformation with some, should be to clean away the filth about their premises. How would some like to have President Young visit them and go through their buildings, examine their rooms, bedding, &c.?

Many houses stink so bad, that a clean man could not live in them, nor hardly breathe in them. Some men were raised in stink, and so were their fathers before them. I would not attempt to bless any body in such places. You may inquire why I talk so. Can you talk in a better style about dirt, nastiness, and filth? If you can, I cannot, and at the same time make people feel enough upon the subject to put away their filth and be clean. If you want me to speak smoother, do better and keep cleaner. Were I to talk about God, heaven, angels, or anything good, I could talk in a more refined style, but I have to talk about things as they do exist among us.

Some people wish to have me shut my mouth, and to have President Young talk. But, thank God, they cannot shut my mouth until I get through, for I never had a gag in my mouth.

There are many of the Seventies who are spiritually dead and damned, and so are many of the Elders. Many of the Presidents of Quorums are like pipe which needs to be burnt out, before it is fit to be used. It is the same with many of the High Priests and others. I pray God that this people may rise up and get the Holy Ghost, and wake up and live their religion, which I ask in the name of Jesus Christ. Amen.[7]

As he had warned in his September 21 sermon, Grant exempted no one from the searching eyes of the Reformation spirit. Before many days, the highest officers of the church found themselves submitting to the catechism at the hands of President Young himself. As John Moon Clements noted in his diary, even Brother Brigham found at least one of Grant's questions a bit difficult.

Attended a meeting of the First Presidency, The Twelve, Presidents of every Quorum, Bishops their Councillors and Teachers. Opened with singing . . . and Prayer by Franklin Richards. Afterwards Bro. Brigham arose and gave some instructions and reproof said he had some questions to put to the brethren and those that had done any of those things were to keep their seats and not hold their hands up and those who held up their hands should be cursed in the name of the Lord if they had done anything that was asked them and those who was clear to arise their right hand. Some of the questions are the following . . .

Have you ever committed murder shed innocent blood or given your consent thereto.

Have you ever committed adultery. Have you ever spoken evil of Authorities or annointed of the Lord.

Have you ever betrayed your brethren.

Have you ever stolen or taken anything that was not your own.

Have you ever took the name of God in vain.

Have you ever been drunk. Have you even taken any poles from the big field or fence or taken your brothers hay.

Have you ever picked up anything that did not belong to you and kept it without seeking to find out the owner.

Have you made promises and not performed them.

Do you pay all your Tithing.

Do you labor Faithfully and diligently for your employer.

Do you preside over your Family as a servant of God or are they subject to you.

Do you teach your children the gospel.

Do you attend your Ward meetings.

Do you pray in your families night and morning.

Do you pray in Secret. Do you wash your bodies once a week. Answered to this question himself. Said that he did not he had tried it. He was well aware that this was not for everybody. Bro. Grant said he did not suppose there was one present that some of these questions would not touch went on to say that we have need of repentance and reformation.[8]

When the fall conference of the Church convened on the Temple Block on October 5, two pervasive themes dominated the sermons—the handcart emigration and the Reformation. With more than 12,000 Saints crowded in and around the Bowery on Monday, October 6, the leaders of the Church and, most memorably, Grant urged the people to wake up from their sleep of apostasy. For most of those in attendance, this was the opening signal of a general revival. "After this conference," one woman remembered,

"the reformation" was instituted. Principally by Brother Grant's thinking the people had become adulterous, thieves, etc. It fairly raged! Every Bishop had the "cue" given to him and he rose up and lashed the people as with a cat-o-nine tails. The people shrunk, shivered, wept, groaned like whipped children. They were told to get up in meeting and confess their sins. They did so 'till it was sickening, and brought disease. The Sacrament was withdrawn, the people were pronounced unfit to partake of it, and in their souls they sat in "dust and ashes," it appeared to them, that is many of the most sensitive, and those who were desiring to do right, that they had committed the unpardonable sin! The whole people seemed to mourn for all more or less came "under the rod."[9]

In Grant's seething consciousness, all of the Saints were due for reform. He reasoned in addition that, if the people were asleep, it was because of poor leadership. Consequently, some of the second counselor's hottest fire scorched Church leaders. Meeting with the local bishops on October 7, he cited the differences between the Saints at "Kays Ward" and those at Bountiful. The reason the people in Kaysville responded so well to his preaching in September, he said, was because "the Bishop at Kays Ward had got the Holy Ghost, and the ward soon repented, and were converted, but the Bishop and his councillors at Bountiful were asleep, and as a consequence the whole ward were asleep also."[10] He ordered the bishops to purify their wards and to "infuse into them the power of God."[11] But his blasts at the lethargy of Church leaders were not always as removed as

Bountiful from the men to whom he preached. Visiting with the Seventies that same evening, he brought his thunder directly on the heads of the Seven Presidents in a demanding challenge to their worthiness to stand as leaders of the Saints. Wilford Woodruff witnessed the proceedings:

> I met at Early candle light with the Seventies and Elders in the Tabernacle. The House was nearly Full. The First Seven Presidents were present with Joseph Young presiding. President Joseph You[ng] occupied the forepart of the meeting in transacting the business of the Quorum. 70 Quorum were called upon and found to be mostly full. President J Young then called for a subscription for the Seventies. He got but Little.
>
> President J M Grant then arose and said I feel that there are some things that greeve me. President Young asked if it would not be well to send the Presidents of Seventies out. He said No they would Preach the people to sleep and then to Hell. Now this shows me that the Presidents of the Seventies the first seven Presidents are asleep and their is somthing wrong with them. If this is the case that they would preach the people to sleep and then to Hell Then this body of Counsellors are guilty of great sins either of ommission or commission and I would advise Joseph Young to cut off his council or drop them and appoint men in his stead who are full of the Holy Ghost and will act with him and assist him. Now we will take up his council and look at them. Now here is brother Levi Hancock. Why he will *fiddle diddle di fiddle diddle do fiddle diddle dum* and twaddle diddle ta. Now he might preach a month and there would be no more spirit of God in it than there would be in a Cabbage Leaf. Now If you would preach the people to sleep and to Hell you are guilty of some great hanious sins either commission or omission. You have either committed adultery or some other sins and you ought to be droped. Here is Brother Harriman might preach a month then you might put it all in the eye of a Cambrick Needle and there would be as much room in it as there would be for a bulfrog in the Atlantic ocean. Albert P. Rockwood if you would preach the people to sleep then to Hell you are asleep dead and guilty of committing Adultery or some great sins. There is no sap in you, you are as dry as an old muskrat skin and you ought to be dropped. And Zerah Pulsipher if he would preach the people to sleep and to Hell you are guilty of some abominable sins of commission or omission of committing adultery or some great sins and ought to be droped and I will say the same of Benjamin Clapp and H. S. Eldredge according to the presidents words they are asleep

and ought to be dropped. I think that Brother Joseph ought to cut them off and prune the trees around him. How can the body be kep awake and healthy when the head is asleep and dead. It has been with great reluctance that I have voted for the presidents of the seventies for a long time And I will say to these seventies if your Presidents have gone to sleep dont you go to sleep, but keep awake. If your Presidency have committed Adultry and done wrong and committed great sins that will damn them dont you do it but wake up. Is there any man that is in that council that has been ordained a counsellor to Joseph Young, if so I do not know it but each man was ordained a president and is under as much obligation as Joseph Young is to magnify his calling and do his duty but they never think of such a thing of taking any burthen upon their shoulders but leave it all for Joseph Young to do and he has to drag them along. When I vote for Rockwood, Pulsipher, Harriman and Levi Hancock I do it very reluctantly, and I have done so for years and now I want to have you to wake up and do your duty. There is no life spirit sap or Juce in Hancock, Harrimans, Pulsipher and Rockwoods preaching. No more than there is in an old mummy. These are the kind of men that are your presidents. And the seventies as a body are as dry and dead as an old chip and you are as light as the bark of a tree. It is the duty of the Seventies to sustain Brother Joseph Young to furnish him with food fuel and ramant that He may give himself to the work of the ministry[.] who has established the president [precedent] to take men who were in the battalion to be presidents. I would take men who were full of the Holy Ghost. I do not care where the Hell they come from. This is what I want. I say again the Presidents of the Seventies are asleep and if they do not wake up they should be cut off—He spoke in the power of God and the gift of the Holy Ghost.

    Levi Hancock followed him and said he had not commit[ted] Adultery he never courted any woman but his wife and she courted him. He justified himself in a measure. He was followed by Benjamin Clap who said he had not committed adultery and if he had gone to sleep he had done it since he came here for he was not asleep when he came here. He intends to serve God with all his heart and was willing to go through this territory with his pack upon his back and preach the gospel. A. P. Rockwood received the chastisement and ment to repent and go into the waters of Baptism as soon as he got a chance.

    J M Grant asked me if I had not something to say that the Seventies were under the Twelve. I told him I would like to bear testimony to what he had said. I arose and said to the people that I wish them not to trifle with the teachings of President Grant for what he had said was true. He had shot arrows of the Almighty among the people and if they did not wake up and take the warning and repent of thare sins for the day has come when it will not do to trifle with the things of God nor with his servants who hold the keys of the Kingdom and are called to lead us. I called upon the Presidents of the seventies and all the seventies to begin this hour to call upon God for the Holy Spirit and advised them to stop work and give themselves to prayer untill they could get the spirit of God. I had the spirit of God in speaking unto the people. I told them I had recorded what Elder Grant had said and I should keep it on record.

We have passed thrugh another Conference and such an won I never saw before. The spirit of God is like a flame among the Leaders of this people and they are throwing the arrows of the Almighty among the people. J M Grant is pruning with a sharp two edged sword and calling loudly upon the people to wake up and repent of their sins. The elders who have returned are full of the Holy Ghost and power of God.[12]

Perhaps the most interesting facet of this stage of the Reformation was the willingness, and even apparent anxiousness, on the part of many Mormons to confess their wickedness and to reform their lives. As one elder noted in his diary on October 8, the power of Grant's preaching brought a conference meeting of the lesser priesthood virtually to its knees.

In the evening attended the Bishops and Teachers meeting held in the Council house. Bishop E. Hunter presiding. Many and most of the Bishops from every part of the Territory or their Councillors were present[.] Bro. Hunter gave some instructions with regard to their duties as Bishops and reproved some for their neglect. and said that they should have every man to help in their wards and prove them Bro. Jedidiah then spoke in a most powerful manner and warned the Bishops to awake and wake up the people in their several Wards to repent of their sins and to turn unto the Lord that he might have mercy upon them and to be Baptized for the remission of their sins and renew their covenants before the Lord but to baptize none but those who brought forth fruit meet for repentance to give them time that there were some whose sins could not be washed away that they must atone for and be saved in another way. Great power has been manifested during the

Conference and a Spirit of reformation seems to have taken hold of many. I feel determined in my heart to seek unto the Lord and to reform in my daily walk and conversation and to work the works of righteousness the Lord being my helper. Truly I see much need of my repentance and may my heavenly father who is good and merciful and gracious aid and assist me to set my self in [order] so that my influence may prove effectual for good over my family is my prayer in the name of Jesus Christ. Amen.[13]

On October 12 Grant followed up his conference activities of the previous week with a sharp sermon in which he delivered some hard thoughts on the nature of the Reformation while speaking particularly of the handcart Saints.

Were I thirsty and could go to a spring or lake whose water was pure and clear as crystal, even the best that could be found, I should have no occasion for going to another and more distant place to procure water. And if I should find ice there, should I say it was too much trouble to break it? No, but I should labor to break that ice; and the thicker the ice, the more persevering I should labor, until I got some of the water of the crystal fountain.

While paying attention to the prayers of some persons in their family devotions, I sometimes notice that they often stop praying without breaking through the darkness and obtaining the Holy Spirit. If I found that it was necessary to pray for that length of time, or until I got the Spirit, unless I remembered that I had neglected a special duty, then I would go and attend to that duty; after which I should want to return and pray until I got the Holy Ghost; I would keep praying until I broke the ice and obtained the Holy Ghost.

Some think that they have already labored enough to obtain heaven. Such persons put me in mind of Sydney Rigdon, who said that he had suffered enough to obtain salvation. He said that the sufferings of Jesus Christ were light in comparison with what he had endured, and he would be damned to hell if he would suffer any more.

I notice that some who gather here think they have already suffered enough, and feel like saying, "I will be damned to hell if I will suffer any more."

Many of those who have come with hand carts think that they have done wonders, therefore they want every hat hoisted in deference to them, and every meal bag gratuitously opened; and they want every body to feed, clothe, and lodge them, and find them every thing they need, because they have dragged a hand-cart across the Plains.

You deserve credit for what you have done, but I make this observation that you may know that you have not yet got into the harbor of eternal life; and that you may not think that you have not anything to do now that you have come here, for, unless you keep on the armor, you will be overcome.

We want people that have come here with their Gospel armor on to keep it on, that they may shed abroad the light of God, and the gift of the Holy Ghost. We have given the same instructions to Elders that have returned, and we want every class of men and women in this Church to keep on the Gospel armor.

There is a drought and has been; the people have felt too much like putting their temporal affairs first and then attending to the spiritual at their leisure.

So much do many act upon this principle that their intellectual faculties become dark, they do not get into the light of the Lord Jesus Christ and of the gift of the Holy Ghost, of the light of eternity; but their temporal matters are first and foremost.

The temporal will keep pace as the spiritual advances. I do not believe that a man who is full of the Holy Ghost is going to live contentedly in a hog pen, in filth and in dirt, when it is in his power to prevent it. Go through our city and you will find some who are living in dirt and degradation; some who like dirt, who like to have their cow in the house and their chickens in the buttery; who like to have their pigs and children near enough for them to be fed together; and their children are as naughty and filthy as they can be. And yet such persons think they have the Spirit and power of God! This is one reason why so many people die, while journeying to this place; it is because the Holy Ghost is sick of them.

If you want the Holy Ghost, keep yourselves clean. I know that some think, when they get here, "O, we are in Zion, everything is right; there is no use in washing our children or combing their hair." I want you to understand that we wish you to be clean outside as well as inside; we want you to be clean and pure; to be good natured and possessed of every qualification requisite in a Saint of God; to have everything that can bring the light and gift of God among you.

I want the people to be pure in their words, in their deeds, in their spirits, and to be diligent in their prayers. I want men that come in from Europe, and from different parts of the United States, to purify themselves and go to with their might to work righteousness. I want the returned missionaries to know that if they have been out preaching the Gospel, we also want them to go to work now they have come home.

I want every one to understand that we have plenty of grunters, plenty of those who are made up of whining. Yes, we have more of those instruments to play upon than we have any use for.

We want you all to keep the light of our God. And we want to see the spirit of reformation in the people; we wish them to have it in practice in their houses; not only to talk about it, but to practise upon it.

The difficulty is that we cannot get the people to practise; they will listen as to a fine sermon, and we can get them to work in the kanyons and in the fields, and to do many other things; but there are too many who like intoxicating drinks, tobacco, filth, dirt, and meanness. Some like to break the Sabbath, to brand another's ox, which they find on the range, and to occasionally steal a little; there are some here who will steal, when they have an opportunity.

I wish to inform the new commers that if they want to find the finest and best men in the world, they are here; and if they want to find the meanest, most pusillanious curses that the world can produce, we have them here. We have here some of the most miserable curses that ever the Almighty frowned upon, for it takes an apostate "Mormon" to be a mean devil. We want you to have eyes to see; we do not want you to see merely what is in the books you have read, in your mathematics and your philosophy, but want you to have in you the Holy Ghost, to be full of the spirit of the Lord Jesus.

We have Elders who are fine speakers, fine orators, and who wish to talk very properly after the manner of the world. They did so in Europe, and they want to do so here; they want to preach those old sermons over, those that they have been accustomed to preach in the old world. But we want Elders to get up and preach as the Holy Ghost shall dictate; we do not want any of your long, prosy sermons; we prefer the word of life by the power of the Spirit.

I desire to see men reform in their acts, and not say "let our neighbors be converted," but let them say, in the name of Israel's God, "the reformation shall be carried into our houses, to our children, and we will take it home with us, and will gird on our armor, and go ahead in the cause of God," for this is what we are sent here for.

May God grant that you may all strive to work righteousness, in the name of Jesus. Amen.[14]

The next day, the First Presidency left the city to go into the mountains to greet another handcart company—more new clay for Young and Kimball to mold, and for Grant to try by the reformer's fire.[15]

Notes

1. Heber C. Kimball, September 28, 1856, *Journal of Discourses*, 26 vols. (London and Liverpool: LDS Booksellers Depot, 1855-86), 4:105-10.

2. "Reminiscences of Henry Moyle and Pedigree of the Moyle Family," in *Biographies and Reminiscences from the James Henry Moyle Collection*, edited by Gene A. Sessions (Salt Lake City: James Moyle Genealogical and Historical Association, 1974), 100.

3. Ibid., 104-5. Moyle's account should put to rest any notion that Grant was in some state of uncontrollable rage or frothing madness through this period.

4. Bishops' Meetings with Presiding Bishopric, Minutes, 1851-61, September 30, 1856, LDS Church Archives.

5. John Moon Clements, Diary, September 30, 1856, holograph, Church Archives.

6. Bishops' Meetings, September 30, 1856.

7. Jedediah M. Grant, October 2, 1856, *Journal of Discourses*, 4:188-89.

8. Clements, Diary, November 4, 1856. Although this event took place a month after the October 2 address, I present it here to display a common form of the catechism as it reached maturity through the fall of 1856. Compare Grant's catechism to the Book of Mormon, Alma 5.

9. Hannah Tapfield King, Diary, October 8, 1856, typescript, LDS Church Archives. In this same entry, King lamented that Grant had destroyed the Polysophical Society, a favorite of intellectuals in the city, by saying that it was a "stink in his nostrils," because it had an adulterous spirit in it.

10. Bishops' Meetings, October 7, 1856.

11. Ibid.

12. Scott G. Kenney, ed., *Wilford Woodruff's Journal, 1833-1898*, typescript, 9 vols. (Midvale, Utah: Signature Books, 1983-85), October 7, 1856.

13. Clements, Diary, October 8, 1856.

14. Jedediah M. Grant, October 12, 1856, *Journal of Discourses*, 4:150-53.

15. Journal History, October 13, 1856, 1.

"Some people talk of wildfire; I would rather have wildfire than no fire at all."

18
White Heat

ON THE SECOND MORNING of the First Presidency's journey into the mountains to meet the decimated Martin handcart emigration, Jedediah sent a letter home to his family. Likely feeling none too well himself, he was particularly concerned about Maryette and Rachel, both of whom were soon to give birth. With an expectation of traveling all the way to the Green River to meet the Martin company and to visit the Shoshone Indians in the area,[1] Grant was anxious about the welfare of his loved ones during what looked like a fairly lengthy absence from home during an early onset of winter weather.

Tusday Morning Oct 14 1856

Dear Susan and all the familey.

I will say God bless you all.

I wish you to go to Br Stewards and get 50 lbs of dried apples and if he has good peaches get 2–5 lbs. Tell Louis to bring down from the blacksmith shop some fine charcole and mix with the filth of the backhouse and clean it out this day. Tell Br Lambert to get all the lining and shealing [sheathing] for the [?] at the first mill in the kanyon.

Kiss and have kissed all the children Caddy and all for me. When Br Brundage goes up to the farm you had better go up and see that they get situated as well as they can. When we get the house finished I shall bring some of the familey from the farm to the city.

Call on Br Hill for 5 bushels of onions, 30 do [ditto] of potatoes and a load of squashes.

I have a good place to sleep. It was warm last night. Br TD Brown sleeps with me.

Six sons of Jedediah Grant: (seated left) Jedediah Morgan (Rosetta), Joseph Hyrum (Susan), George Smith (Sarah Ann); (standing left): Brigham Frederick (Maryette), Heber Jeddy (Rachel), Joshua Frederick (Louisa), 1877. LDS Church Archives.

Tell Sister Rachel not to work to hard. Tell Maryette that we will be back in 2 weeks. I think if she is quiet, she will not be sick untill we return.

God bless you all. Pray and keep the Spirit of the Lord in the house.

Yours &c

J M Grant

Tell Caroline I want her to be good girl and I will bless and get her everything she needs.

All are well in camp.

Remember me to all on the farm.[2]

Brigham Young fell ill on the morning of the next day, forcing the party to return to Great Salt Lake City without fulfilling its mission.[3] For Grant, that was just as well. Two days later, on October 17, 1856, Maryette delivered his fifth son. They named him Brigham Frederick. Each living wife had given him a son, except for Rachel, and she was ready herself to deliver at any time.[4] There were also two baby daughters, one each from Susan and Rosetta. Twelve-year-old Caddie, however, always held a special place in his affections, being the only living remembrance of his life with Caroline. His adopted son Lewis McKeachie Grant was now nearly eighteen years old and practically running the family farming operation in Davis County.

In the midst of these familial events and in spite of a growing preoccupation with the worsening plight of the handcart companies still in the mountains, Grant pushed forward with the Reformation, a time of searing self-examination for the Saints, in which they suffered not only for individual sins but also for those elements of society that were, in the minds of Grant and his colleagues, in a state of serious dysfunction. The Salt Lake City bishops seemed to get the brunt of the pressure for a sweeping spiritual regeneration in Zion. Meeting again with the presiding bishop and the local bishops on October 21, the second counselor placed the burden of carrying forth the Reformation program in the city directly on their shoulders. If every man and woman did their duty, he said, the millennial society they were trying to build would be a reality. It was as simple as that. According to the minutes of that meeting, his instructions included an order for

the Bishops to take a lively interest in the schools, you have as it were an independent sphere of action to move in, and if the President of the stake, the Bishops, Councillors and Teachers, did their duty, and would continue to do so there would be no need for a City Council, as to the reformation he wanted the Bishops to continue until it had become boiling heat, man can either be dull and sleepy, or alive and active, whichever they please, the

Bishops should occasionally go about their wards themselves at all hours, and look after the people. Know what they are about, and give instructions accordingly, don't send round any more Teachers who are governed by their wives. Do you Bishops ever reflect how many Courts have authority to cut off persons from the Church? The High Priests, Seventies, or Elders cannot cut any off, but only suspend a member, but the first presidency, High Council, and Bishops only have power to cut off from the Church, he dwelt much on the duties of the various branches of Priesthood, also on the duties of wives and mothers in Israel, and that our young men should be properly trained in the different arts of industry, referred to the duties of man and wife, especially in regard to sexual intercourse with each other, and desired the Bishops to give such instructions as accord with the Law of God and on every other subject, you Bishops are called upon to carry out a reformation [of] yourselves and the people, and he distinctly enjoined these things to be attended to by the President of the Stake and his councillors, and by the Bishops and their councillors, and that the Lord God would help them in so doing, he asked in the name of Jesus, Amen.[5]

By this time, the *Deseret News*, under its editor Albert Carrington, was ready to assess the peculiar spectacle of persons who called themselves Saints going through the processes of a hot revival.

To the world it may seem strange that reformation is needed where there are none to molest us in our religion, in a country throughout whose broad borders there is not a single brothel, grogship, or gambling hall; where murders, assassination, highway robberies, arson, husband and wife killing and other high crimes are unknown to our court records; and where even one lawyer could not make a living, at fair rates, by attending to the whole of the small amount of litigation among this numerous people. And, perhaps, some saints have deemed reform uncalled for at present, not being sufficiently faithful to at all times see afar off.

But when we are of like passions with other people, and when commodious buildings are multiplied, when numerous fields are enclosed and the comforts and luxuries of life accumulate around us, we are prone to slacken the faith and energy engaged in producing them, and to measurably forget our indebtedness for the peculiar privileges and blessings in our possession.

Prosperity and ease tempt to remissness in duty, to neglect of secret and family prayer, to unlawful indulgence of thought, word and act, to laying aside weapon after weapon and shield after shield of the gospel armor, until there is little or no defence against the assaults of the adversary. Hence the necessity for reformation, and we rejoice that the people are so zealous in a work of so much importance.[6]

The response of the people to the Reformation movement, as the *News* indicated, was indeed remarkable. Franklin D. Richards, who had recently arrived in Utah from a mission to England, noted a significant change in the Saints with the burning of revival fires in their midst.

About a week before we arrived, a work of reformation had been efficiently started, and we were just in good time to share its cheering effects with the people. As good an evidence of this as I can offer may be found in the fact, that on Sunday and Monday, at a Conference of the Territory, it required strong efforts of the Presidency and others, to raise between fifty and sixty teams to go an[d] bring in our brethren coming by the hand-carts on the Plains; whereas, on the last Sunday but one, a few remarks from brother Kimball, to a congregation of this city only, induced one hundred and fourteen to give their names to furnish teams, and one man put down fifteen yokes of cattle. The change in the feelings of the people is indeed wonderful already, and yet it has but just begun. Bishops are dropped, and their counsellors, when slothful at their duties, or when ruled by their wives, so are the Teachers, if they do not perform their duties, which are, to know every man and woman in their several districts, an[d] to live their religion themselves. Misdeeds are not only publicly denounced, but the doers of their deeds are named before the public congregations. The arrows of the Almighty are with the Presidency. The terrors of the Lord are upon them, and are coming upon the people. The high and the low are all feeling the scorching of the fire that has begun to be kindled in Zion. Already the power of the Holy Ghost has, in some instances, been so great upon them, that they have had to refrain from speaking, for the people have shrunk before them, because of the power of their words, while in other instances, congregations have been dismissed because of their darkness, and their unbelief in the word spoken. Many powers and responsibilities, heretofore retained in the hands of the Presidency, have been handed down to the Bishops. A thorough waking up has commenced, that must reach the habitation of every Saint in

Utah, and then extend to every Mission and Branch of the Church throughout the earth.

On the evening of the 6th of October, President Young kindly permitted me and my family to be baptized in the new font on the Temple Block. Oh how precious this was to us, after having first witnessed the administration of this sacred ordinance to the family of President Young, under his own hands, and those of Presidents Kimball and Grant, in like manner, each in their order. The next evening I was privileged to baptize about forty souls, the families of the returned missionaries, in the same hallowed place. I believe the Bishops have been re-baptized also, and their wards will be when the works of pruning and reformation have sufficiently appeared. I have scarcely got the run of the general items [of news] from the various parts of the Territory, further than that reformation is the leading, and is fast becoming the all-absorbing topic of the people's conversation, in the house and by the way, in their lying down as well as in their rising hours....[7]

By the end of October, Grant had settled his mind on one overriding Reformation theme. It seemed to him, in the midst of all the excitement he had started with the Davis County conferences in September, that the ultimate answer for the Saints resided in strong leadership and in an equally devoted followership, through the sanctity of priesthood authority. The root of the problem in Mormon society, he said in the Bowery on October 26, grew in the soil of disunity and disrespect for the authority of God. Before he finished this one, his fire would descend particularly hotly on the heads of women in Zion.

A great many people actually suppose that they can treat with impunity the authority of God, and the light of God, the chain that the Almighty has let down from heaven to earth, which we call the Priesthood; that they can break and insult that chain and trifle therewith, as much as they please, and when they please, that they can abuse Jehovah in His power and attributes. I reason in a differing circle, or upon a different principle; I have practised a different principle. When I offend one of God's servants, I consider it my duty to atone, to make reconciliation for my offence, no matter whether he be above or below in this Church, as the term is used; no matter whether it be President Brigham Young or my teacher, I have erred in either case.

A high Priest in the road the other day, a talented man, an important man, said, "If he could only keep the stream clear between himself and the heads of the Church, that he would consider that he was all right." I said to him, if you act upon that principle, in the same sense you have thrown it out to me, it will send you across lots to hell. The spirit of the principle to me was, that it did not matter about offending persons below him, or injuring different individuals in the Church, such as Elders, Priests, Teachers, Deacons, and Members, if he could only keep the stream pure between him and the First Presidency.

This idea a great many people entertain; they can offend their Bishops, or the Bishops' Counsellors, and the Teachers, and they can offend the President of a Branch of the Church, the President over the High Priests' Quorum, and the President over the High Council, and they can offend all the Church, so they can only have the good graces of brother Brigham and his Council, that is enough for them.

That is actually the idea of some people. Such doctrine as that, with me, is the height of nonsense. You have not their good graces, only as you treat every person right. If you are dishonest with one of those poor benighted Indians, you foul the water between me and you, and God Almighty will not give me power to bless you, until you rectify that wrong with that poor Indian, or with the least person on the footstool of God. And you should not pass by your Bishop and insult him, if you do, you will forfeit your claim to the throne of God in heaven, until you make reconciliation to that Bishop, or to any other person you have injured; and then it is time enough for you to bring your offerings, and they will be accepted in the sight of God, and in the sight of His servants.

Members of the quorum of the Twelve, when at home, ought to be right about the First President of the Church with the power of God that is in them, and communicate some of that light to brother Brigham to comfort him. Do you expect brother Brigham to put fire into the whole of this people, and no man on earth put fire in him and bless him, and give him instruction and information? Must he impart and teach, and teach, and no man tell him anything?

We have missionaries who go out to different parts of this Territory, and over the earth, gaining experience and information, but can we get them up here to tell us one single thing they know? No, unless you take them by the back of the neck, and the seat of their pantaloons and haul them in sight, making them squeal like a "possum cat," before you can get anything out of them.

We want you to impart what you know, if you have the light of God, or any information about heaven, earth, or hell. We want you to furnish your share to the fund of information, and not cry, all the day long, give, give, give, without imparting anything to the giver. We want the Twelve, when they are full of the Holy Ghost, to come up and bless us. And if any of you know how to make a good goose yoke, a hog yoke, a good jack-knife, or anything else that is valuable, do not put your hands on your mouths and cry mum.

If you know how to raise wheat, potatoes, or anything else, impart your knowledge, that the light in you may not be hid under a bushel. It is so with almost every person in the Church; if they have light they keep it under a bed, or under a bushel; they keep it locked up within their bosoms, and we cannot get it out.

If you offend your brother, you have to make reconciliation. You might as well baptize a dog, as baptize a man or woman who will not make reconciliation for the offences they have committed. Some women will say, "What is the difference, suppose I offend my husband, if I can only lie to brother Brigham, and tell him a first-rate tale, and make out that my husband is a poor curse? I will get as many blessings as I want from brother Brigham, and from others that I can make believe that I am a good woman."

I may not have used their words exactly, but those words portray their practices. That woman who offends her husband, if he has on him the power of the Priesthood and does right, I would not give a groat for all the blessings she will get from the Holy Ghost. You may as well baptize a dog, or a skunk, as such a woman, until she makes reconciliation with that man of God whom she has offended.

I do not want the old men to grow dull. Was father Adam dull in his old age, when he blessed his children, and predicted what would befall them down to the latest generation? Will a man, fired up by the fire of the Almighty, be dull? No. I do not want the old men to think that they have done enough, but to exert themselves to the last, and not to believe in a God that is lariatted out, nor be lariatted out themselves, and say, "I have worked ten, fifteen, or twenty-five years, and I do not want to work any more, my rope is long enough now."

The old men, those men who have been in the Church twenty years and more, are ready to run from the man of God that holds the keys of the kingdom of heaven. If you was full of the Holy Ghost you would not do this, but you would be round about us, instead of being all the time with your wives. It is the greatest piece of nonsense that was ever planted in a Gentile breast, for a man to tie himself down to be at home day and night with his women. Where would this kingdom go, if brother Brigham and his Council were to do so? It would go to hell, across lots, in double quick time. Do not let your wives bind you up with green withes and strong cords as Delilah did Sampson, and make you powerless. Break asunder the cords, the ropes and cables that bind you, and come forth, ye old men, out of your shells, and break your lariats and your stakes, and begin to drink of the fountain of life, with God and His servants.

I might say to the young men wake up from your sleep, that you may have the blessings of God poured out upon you. And if the women want to know what I think of many of them, let them read the 32nd chapter of Isaiah; I had better read part of it for you. "Rise up ye women that are at ease, hear my voice, ye careless daughters, give ear unto my speech. Many days and years shall ye be troubled, ye careless women; for the vintage shall fail, the gathering shall not come. Tremble, ye women that are at ease; be troubled, ye careless ones; strip you, and make you bare, and gird sackcloth upon your loins."

I want to say to many of our old women, and to hundreds and thousands of our young women, that the life of God Almighty is not in you; you are at ease, and careless, and dull, and blind, and you do not understand the rights that God Almighty wishes you to enjoy. I want such women to humble themselves in sackcloth and ashes, until they get the Holy Ghost.

I want every mother and daughter in Israel to serve their God, have the light of God in them, instead of pride, foolery, nonsense, and everything that is light and vain. Rise up, ye careless women that are asleep in Zion, and betake yourselves to mourning and lamenting before God, until the light of heaven shall shine upon you, until the light of God shall chase away your pride, and your abomination, and your sins, and be round about you, and until the eye of heaven smiles upon you and blesses you forever. I want you to be blest and saved, that your children may rise up and be blest. I want the women to understand that there is something in Zion for them to do, instead of going to sleep. There is a work upon you; you have made covenants and sacred obligations, as well as the men, and we want you not to falsify those obligations, but to keep the law of your husbands, and listen to them, and know that they are your head.

A man is a president to his family. If the Church has a head, which is Christ, then is the man the head of his family. Some men are not the heads of their families, but their wives walk on them, their daughters walk on them, and their sons walk on them, and they are as the soles of their shoes.

Talk of some men's being the heads of their families. It makes me think of the old deacon, that went to teach a man and his wife who were quarrelsome; said he, "Do you not know that you and your husband are one flesh?" "You don't say that, do you, deacon?" "Yes, the Lord has made you one." "Lord God," said she, "if you were to pass by here when me and my old man are quarreling, you would think there were fifty of us." This is often the case in Israel; instead of the men being the heads of their families, they are as sole-leather under their feet.

I want the women to understand, when they have a good husband, one that does his duty, that he is president over them, and that they have made covenants to abide the law of that husband. Talk about women leaving their husbands! I would be far from taking a woman that would leave a GOOD man. A woman that wants to climb up to Jesus Christ, and pass by the authorities between her and him, is a stink in my nostrils. I have large nostrils, and I often talk about smelling, for my olfactory nerves are very sensitive. I want women to know their places and do their duty; but there is a low, stinking pride in a woman, that wants to leave a good husband to go to another. What does it matter where you are, if you do your duty? Being in one man's family or the other man's family is not going to save you, but doing your duty before your God is what will save you.

Because I am one of the Council of the First President, will that save me? No; but if I am saved, I shall be saved because I do my duty as a man of God. Shall a man be saved because of some particular Quorum to which he belongs, or a woman be saved because she is in some particular family? No, that is foolery. Men and women are saved because they do right. It is nonsense for a woman to suppose, that because she is sealed to some particular man she will be saved, and at the same time kick up hell's delight, play the whore, and indulge in other evil acts and abominations.

Even some mothers in Israel actually suppose that if their daughters are sealed to a certain man they will be saved, no matter what they do afterwards. That is damned foolery; and I want men and women to understand that salvation is based on a better foundation, that it is made up of righteousness, joy, and peace in the Holy Ghost.

We want you to understand that the power of the Holy Ghost should be in you. We want fathers, mothers, sons, daughters, and the whole Church renovated and made one. Do you suppose that I can be saved by standing alone, or that brother Heber can, or by attempting to use our Apostleship independent of brother Brigham? We have sense enough to know that we have no power, only as we are one with him. Or can the Twelve, or any one else, have any power, only as they are one with brother Brigham? No. In the same way no woman can be right, only that woman who is one in spirit with her husband. We should then be one in understanding, in power, in gifts of God and in the light of the Gospel, and do right all the time. May God Almighty wake up the fathers, the mothers, the sons and the daughters, and bless you all and keep you in the path of your duty, and save you in the name of Jesus Christ. Amen.[8]

Although the Reformation and the "path of duty" the brethren were outlining for the Saints continued to consume the feelings and conversations in Utah during the deepening fall of 1856, news of the handcart emigrants suffering through the Wyoming wilderness in snow, ice, and starvation only served to enhance the sense of foreboding and worry with which the Reformation had infused the Mormon kingdom in the wilderness. Relief parties returning to the city reported an increasingly grim picture, as on October 31, when Gideon H. Gibbs and Horace Newell arrived in Salt Lake City "express" from the Willie Company on the Sweetwater River. They reported that twenty-six persons had died before they reached the company on October 26. "During the five days they were with them about 30 others died also, 15 of them in one day; many of the deceased pulled their carts during the day and died the same evening."[9]

Grant for one was not only deeply moved and disturbed over this incoming news from the East, but he was also ready to breathe fire over it. On November 2, after several days of combining in his mind worry over the fate of the handcart emigrants and concern for the progress of the Reformation, he had amassed all of the ingredients for another white-hot sermon. For him, the death and suffering of the hapless handcart Saints resulted from the same disobedience and sinfulness that had induced spiritual sleepiness among the people already in Zion.

As an individual I have been and am very anxious in relation to the immigration now upon the Plains. Their situation is very distressing, and several have died in brother Willie's company. Some had died before the brethren could reach them, and a few more died during the first five days after they met them. The company had encountered cold and storms, and one very stormy day which caused nearly one-third of the deaths that had happened.

They had no serious or contagious diseases, but the storms came and the air was very cold, as a matter of course some who were fatigued with the toil and anxiety of the journey sank under the inclemency of the weather; they were furnished by those that returned to them, with shoes, clothing, and food. They were not entirely destitute of provisions when the return teams met them; their rations at the outfitting were more than those of the companies in advance of them. When met they had nearly four hundred pounds of sea bread, but their last rations of flour had been dealt out on the evening previous.

Brother Willie's company was met with on the upper crossing of Sweet Water, but the whereabouts of the ox-trains and the hand-cart company in rear of brother Willie are yet unknown to us.

We have now some two hundred teams out to meet them, and some were only prepared with seven days forage for animals. It will be necessary for more teams to go to their relief, with grain and hay to sustain the animals already sent out, or they will die.

The weather had been cold enough to freeze over the Sweet Water; I mention this that you may know how the thermometer stood in that region; and some animals had been frozen to death. It is winter where they are, and they are actually in the cold and snow which was near one foot deep, and as they went east it appeared to grow deeper.

The observations made this morning, as a matter of course, would only be treasured up by those who had in them the spirit of life. We have persons that have so much death in them that they do not know the counsels that are given to the immigrating Saints, that do not know the tenor of advice contained in the general epistles of the Presidency of the Church. But I do not suppose that the thinking part of the community anticipated any censures being placed upon the First Presidency of this Church, in consequence of the sufferings of the people now upon the Plains. Still there is a certain class of people whose brains never reach above the calves of their legs, and they never will know anything about the general policy of the Church, about what is written, what is desired, counseled, or asked for.

In relation to hand-cart companies, I have said, and I say it again, that they should start by the first of May, and then they can travel leisurely according to their strength and feelings; they can then have May, June, July, and August for the accomplishment of their journey. They could not travel so leisurely this year, from the fact that there were no grain depots on the route, consequently they had to hurry through, lest their rations should fail. Were grain deposited at convenient points on the route, the trip is, in every sense of the word, a feasible one for hand-carts, for without that advantage, the present year has proved the feasibility of the undertaking.

The grand difficulty with a portion of our immigration this year has been in starting in the fore-part of September instead of the first of May, but even then it is worse with ox teams than with hand-carts, for if the cattle fail the people have no facilities for transporting their tents, bedding, clothing, and provisions. Unless I have different feelings to what I now have, I should never wish to see a train leave the Missouri river after the middle of June, or after the first day of July at the latest, until we can establish grain depots on the route, for I do not consider any train safe in starting late.

Brother Brigham has invariably advised early starts, and he gave his reasons for so doing this morning, and I do not wish to reiterate them.

I wish to see those who are directly engaged in carrying out the operations of gathering the Saints, to correctly understand the advice given and the system adopted for the gathering, and when they understand that and carry it out, as planned and given by brother Brigham, our immigration will be free from the sad results of mismanagement. But for persons, who are ignorant of the special causes and agents in any unpleasant transaction, to at once blame the head is the height of nonsense, though people in all ages have been prone to censure their leader, in times of special distress. When crickets and grasshoppers devour, when famine wastes, and when snows, storms, and accidents occur, it is natural, in that portion of the community that lack the gift of the Holy Ghost, to murmur against the leader of the people.

With Saints, what is the practical result of that murmuring? It shuts down the gate between you and heaven, between you and the Almighty, and you cannot get the Spirit of God. The murmurings and rebellions of ancient Israel prevented Moses from leading them to the land of Canaan. So soon as they had to endure hardship they began to murmur against Moses, and the result was the Lord would not give them His Spirit; the same has been the result in this dispensation.

In the days of Joseph, if a woman happened to put on her stocking wrong side out she would blame the Prophet; and if a man happened to tie his shoestring in a hard instead of a bow knot, he was angry with the Prophet for not having inspiration enough to have prevented so dire an event. The brains of that class of people never reach above the calves of their legs. I like to see the people have a little hard sense, like the mule; I like to see them understand the principles of the Son of God.

With regard to this people, I know that they are the best people on the earth, but there is more or less alloy among them which we hate. The Savior said that the Kingdom of Heaven is like unto a net that gathereth all kinds of fish; and I believe that parable holds good in our day, with regard to the gathering of the people that are caught by the Gospel of the Son of God, through the practical preaching of the Elders. I believe this, from observing the unwise sayings and doings of some who profess to be Saints.

I am aware that the world, because we are not all strictly living our religion, will imagine, as a matter of course, that we are bursting to pieces up here, and will say, "That is what we like; we told you that if you would let the 'Mormons' alone they would all burst to pieces." We can, by taking an unrighteous course, burst ourselves to pieces, but they cannot burst us to pieces, if we do right, that is certain, for they tried when there were but eight or ten in the Church, and when there were a few hundred, and when there were a few thousand, and they were unable to burst the Church. Now they flatter themselves that we shall burst under the weight of our own conduct, but I will tell you that we are after the evil doers.

If the Bishops and Teachers will go to work, together with every officer in the Church, we can soon find out those who are not disposed to do right; and let their names be written down, and let the offence and place of residence be written against the name, that we may know who are living in sin, where they live and what their offences are.

I know that a great many people are full of sympathy, and yet they talk of the celestial law that they are going to keep and abide; but let me tell you that if you violate the law, you must meet the penalty. How many have we got here that would sympathize with those who are guilty of breaking their covenants, and thereby virtually partake of their crimes? I believe it to be a correct doctrine that the sympathizer is more or less implicated. The

President enjoined it on the High Priests to expose those they knew to have committed or to be committing evil, and if they did not, hereafter the sin would be upon their heads.

Let the whole people take warning; and let every man and woman in Israel understand that the indignation of the Almighty rests upon that person who fails to expose iniquity. And let the wrath of God be upon any officer of the Church that knows of abomination, unless he comes out and makes known that abomination. I believe this ought to be, for we want the evil deeds of every person exposed.

We want to feel after the people and hunt them up; and we want the wrath of Brigham, and the wrath of Heber, and the wrath of all the men and women on earth that are right, and the wrath of Joseph, and the wrath of Michael, and the wrath of Raphael, and the wrath of the Lord Jesus Christ, and the wrath of Almighty God and of all the Gods in eternity to burn against those that will sin. And we want the indignation and fire of the Almighty to sweep through the land like the locusts of Egypt, until every nauseous weed that grows among the Saints of God is destroyed.

Words are said to be light and windy, but I tell you that talking these things foreshadows what will be literally and really. I would be glad, when I speak to the people, that the Lord would let His Holy Spirit accompany my words, for I do not want my words to go alone. We have to speak to this people often, and when we talk to them like a man reading off a sermon that is written, it takes but little effect. When words go to the people alone, they are not profited by them.

Instead of all the people being desirous and anxious, as they should, to serve their God and practise what they know to be right, many are all the time longing for some fantastical doctrine, for something to gratify their vain imaginations. If you wish to feast on the word of God and feel its realities, you must practise the revelations of Jesus Christ. You must advance and do the will of God, and then you will be blest.

I am aware, as the President said this morning, that it is of no use talking about the Holy Ghost, the power of God, the gift of God, or the light of the Almighty resting on this people, until they become morally reformed.

Some people laugh at and deride sectarian religion. I never was a sectarian; I have been in this Church from my boyhood; but in the region where I was raised, sectarian morality exceeds, in some respects, the morality of many who call themselves Latter-day Saints.

Some here keep their children too dirty for admission into a district school where I was raised; and in some houses the towels look as though they had passed Noah's ark, or had been used by some of the inhabitants of Sodom and Gomorrah, and the knives and forks have the appearance of having been rusting ever since Adam was driven from the garden of Eden.

I want to see the people wake up and reform, forsake all their evil habits and everything that is dark, loathsome and impure. I want to see them eschew all dirt, and filth, and degradation, and cease profaning the Sabbath, and the name of the Lord God of Israel; I want to see them become at least as moral and temperate as any people in the Gentile world, as we call it. I tell you that the Gentiles would be shocked at the filth and dirt of some of the sons and daughters of Israel, and feel offended to associate with them; I mean that portion of the Gentiles that are pure in their moral habits.

I want to see the people repent, as the President said this morning, and make a reformation in their lives, in their doings, and in keeping their houses, farms, and everything they have, clean and tidy.

You may talk of reform, you may preach upon a virtuous life, upon cleanliness, upon God and the Holy Ghost, but while there is filth around the house, filth in the yard, and in every part of the city, your preaching will not amount to much. Some people are never contented unless the cow yard is under their noses, the hen coop in the parlor, and the privy in the kitchen, that is if they have any privy.

I want the people to wake up to a sense of their duty, and begin to serve God and repent of their sins, repent of every improper habit.

I sometimes confess men's sins for them, and they will get up and parry off. I confessed a man's sins here lately, and he supposed that I did not know what I was talking about. If he had corrected me a little further, I would have told all his sins; I would have told the things that were in his very heart; and if he parries again, I will come out more pointedly than I did then.

In some of the wards men will rise up and confess their sins, and after a week's reflection, they will go to meeting and commence parrying, and make themselves as good as an angel. Again, some people, when they get the Spirit of God, when they actually pray fervently, are deemed by their neighbors to have sectarian religion. If God Almighty moves upon a man to pray with a loud voice and in earnest, some are ready to exclaim that he is a sectarian, and are so anxious to put away sectarianism, that they bundle the religion of Jesus Christ out of doors. In their zeal against sectarianism and doctrines they do not like, they leave God and the Lord Jesus Christ out of the question, and prayer, and keeping the Sabbath, and moral honesty, and virtue, and purity and everything that is good.

Every portion of sectarian religion that is good is my religion. If they have a precious gem it belongs to my religion; if it is purity, virtue, integrity, the gift of the Holy Ghost, fervency, and prayer, it is my religion. Some people talk of wild fire; I would rather have wild fire than no fire at all. I would like you to come up to the light of the Almighty, and if you want to pray to God, if you want to shout and make heaven and earth ring—drive the devil out of doors, chase darkness from your houses, and from your families, and raise the banner of the Lord Jesus Christ in your households, and the flag of God in your city, and say, in the name of the Lord Jesus Christ, I will do right, and root up everything that is wrong.

Those who will not repent by the preaching of the Gospel, we will bring to the standard of the Lord Jesus Christ in the right and proper way, for we are determined to save you all, if possible. In former days the Lord cut off rebellious Israel by thousands, to save them; He had no other way for saving them. He had tried every other means; He had opened the sea for them to pass over dry shod, and overthrew their enemies, the horse and his rider, in the flood; He made the mountains skip like rams, and the little hills like lambs; He spoke to the angels, saying, throw down your food to them, and the bright clouds shed down manna to sustain them; He spake to them in thunders, in lightnings, in earthquakes, and tried every means to save them, that a God could try in the plentitude of His mercy, and when He had exhausted the arrows of His wrath in chastisement, and the wells of His mercy in blessings and entreaty, He cut them off by thousands.

O Israel, hear, while the voice of entreaty is in the land, hear the voice of brother Brigham, and awake from your slumbers; forsake your sins and abominations and turn unto your God, that repentance may reach you, and remission of sins, and the gifts and blessings of God come upon you. May God bless you in the name of Jesus Christ. Amen.[10]

Jedediah Morgan Grant, having struggled upward between earth and heaven for more than forty years, had reached the pinnacle of his life. His words falling on the people with the force of lightning bolts, he had become to Brother Brigham as Aaron was to his brother Moses. Commensurate with his earliest Mormon desires, Preacher Grant had grown into a mighty orator of righteousness, tirelessly fanning into the chilling twilight a wildfire of repentance and reform.

⇒ Notes ⇐

1. Journal History of the Church of Jesus Christ of Latter-day Saints, (chronological scrapbook of typed entries and newspaper clippings, 1830–present), October 13, 1856, 1, LDS Church Archives

2. Jedediah M. Grant, Letter to Susan Grant, October 14, 1856, holograph, Betty Mae Nebeker Laub Collection, Salt Lake City.

3. Journal History, October 15, 1856, 1, and November 30, 1856, 51.

4. Alvin G. Pack, Family Records, Salt Lake City.

5. Bishops' Meetings with Presiding Bishopric, Minutes, 1851–61, October 21, 1856, LDS Church Archives.

6. *Deseret News*, October 22, 1856.

7. Willard Richards, Letter to Orson Pratt, Ezra T. Benson, and James A. Little, November 1, 1856, printed in *Millennial Star*, February 14, 1857.

8. Jedediah M. Grant, October 26, 1856, *Journal of Discourses*, 26 vols. (London and Liverpool: LDS Booksellers Depot, 1855–86), 4:122–29.

9. "History of Brigham Young," 1856, 858–59.

10. Jedediah M. Grant, November 2, 1856, *Journal of Discourses*, 4:70–75.

"Brother Heber, I have been into the spirit world two nights in succession."

19
Smoky Visions

ON THE COOL SUNDAY AFTERNOON of November 9, 1856, President Jedediah Morgan Grant stood on the stand at one end of the small building the Latter-day Saints in Great Salt Lake City would call their tabernacle until the domed edifice being planned nearby could be completed. It was a familiar sight to those pioneer Mormons—the tall, gaunt figure of Brother Jeddy looming above them for a spirited sermon on the essentials of perfection. They had grown used to his style, and to his message, although for two months or so the fire he commonly generated in his sermons had been considerably hotter as the Mormon Thunder rolled from the end of his tongue. He seemed to feel besieged, as if the burdens of preaching the Reformation had convinced him that all the evil forces in the earth's matrix had ascended upon him and his efforts. Consequently, he cast upward the tone of his thinking—love for the Saints and a desire to bless them, coupled with admiration for his companions in the First Presidency. As always, however, he spat defiance into the face of those who would impede the progress of Zion, the state of perfection, of Utopia.

I believe, with Brother Kimball, that many of this people partake of the sacrament unworthily. Some will steal their neighbour's spade, or his crowbar, or wood from his pile, or cabbages and potatoes from his garden, or hay from his stack, or go into his yard and milk his cows, and commit numerous other sins, and the next day come here and partake of the sacrament.

I seriously question, when some people are baptized, whether they do not come out of the water the same poor miserable devils as they went in.

There must be a foundation in the people, the right standard in the breast, and that must be inherent in the people more or less, or else our professions are in vain. I, therefore, want every person to leave the bread in the salvers, and the water in the cups, and not partake of the sacrament, unless they are right. I want every thief, and every unrighteous person to let the bread alone.

I am aware that we have only a few among us but what feel determined to reform; the great majority wish to live their religion, and I am glad of it.

I believe that the majority of this congregation that are here to-day, actually intend to do right. Now do not let the devil cheat you; and if the devil marshals his forces against you and beclouds your minds, tell him that you are serving the God of Israel. If you are in the dark and cannot get light, keep a firm hold on the foundation of truth, and be determined not to be jostled off it.

I believe there has been a disposition, on the part of some men and women to break the strong tie that ought to bind families together, but I do not believe they will accomplish much. I look for our relations to be permanent and the institutions of the Church to be eternal, because they are perfectly right; I now refer more particularly to our family organizations. But there is more or less discord in families, I would like it to cease altogether; and I would actually like the day to come in Israel, when the people will not only love the doctrines and revelations of the Lord Jesus Christ, but rejoice that they live in the day when the Prophet Joseph has brought them forth.

I make these remarks, not that I have had any difficulty with my own family but because there is a principle I wish to speak upon. I believe that men should lead their families, and not drive them. Some people do not understand the difference between leading and driving a flock of sheep.

Brother Willes has seen the shepherds and their flocks in the Eastern countries, and can tell you the difference in the management of flocks in those countries and America. In America the sheep are driven; in the East the shepherds lead their flocks. The American and English spirit, and also the spirit of some other nations, places the sheep in front and the shepherd must follow.

If there is any difficult place, a stream to ford, or a slippery log to walk on, the American's spirit is to try his wife first on the log, to drive his wife and children across first; he must drive. I do not like that, though some men are almost compelled to do so, because the women are determined to lead.

I have traveled with brother Heber, and I never saw a milder man in my life, when everything is right and people keep out of his track. But when they get in his path he is obliged to tread on their heels, for they cannot walk so fast as he can. He is not to blame for that; they are to blame.

In the early ages of the world there was a youth imprisoned by the ruler of the people. His parents went to the ruler and plead with him to release their son, but they could not prevail at first. They then wept and tore their reverend locks from their heads to move the ruler to pity, and when they had done this he released their son from prison. The historian remarks that it was not so much the weakness existing in the youth's parents that caused them to tear their hair, as it was the obstinacy in the ruler; they were obliged to take that course, resort to such means, to effect their purpose.

Am I to blame for scolding the people? Not at all. Is brother Heber? Not at all. Is he to blame for chastising an unruly wife? No. If she gets in his path and he steps on her heels, is he to blame? No, and if she is hurt thereby, it is the result of her own acts

What will be the result of the chastisements given to this people? I answer, if they heed them, they will bring them into the true path. It is the situation of the people that prompts the teachings they now receive from God's servants. If all the people did right, they would not be chastised at all. If a man's family conduct themselves right, do you suppose that a consistent, reasonable man will find fault with them? No. If all the people in a Ward do right, will the Bishop chastise them? No; but if they do not do right, the Bishop is placed under the necessity of coming forth, clothed in the armor and power of the Almighty, to put them right, and of calling upon the teachers to assist him in this work. And when the people repent and are found to be on the right track, the Bishop lays the rod on the shelf.

This is the case with brother Brigham. Does he chastise this, that, and the other man, because he likes the job? No. You know that he is mild, and is a father to this people; and were I to take any exception to his course, it would be on account of his being so merciful. Why? Because he is more merciful than I am. When he extends mercy to the people, he deals it out more lavishly than I would, unless the Lord should lead me as he does him. I have not so much mercy, so much of God and eternal life in me as brother Brigham has in him; it does not belong to me to have so much, for he stands at the fountain of life; he descends below all things and ascends above all things to this dispensation.

I hear men undertake to laugh and joke in their familiar chat with each other, and say that they heard brother Brigham say this or that, and that they saw brother Brigham do this, that, or the other, and strive to justify themselves on that account. But brother Brigham commands an influence that you do not command, and cannot be thrown off the line of propriety and truth, as easily as you and I. When men do not know the power that constrains them, they ought to be cautious how they speak and how they act.

Brother Brigham is a father to the Quorums of this Church; and when the people are right, has he a disposition to chastise them? No, he has a fatherly feeling to bless them, and so has brother Heber. I do not know whether I have as much of that feeling as either of them, with regard to the Church, but I do not suppose that there is a man on the earth that is fonder of children than I am. If I do not like old people so well as some do, I like children well enough to balance the difficiency.

I would be glad to see more peace, mercy, truth, equity, justice, and righteousness made manifest in the midst of this people. We want the hay, the straw, the wood, the stubble, the dross, and every impure principle burnt up. When a man is wrong and will turn round and do right, I love him better than I did before. We do not feel like casting you off, like casting you into the mire, and saying "God Almighty damn you." "Get out of the mud and may the Lord God bless you" is what we say. I had rather bless ten men than curse one. I am not led to curse, but I am led to chastise iniquity, to bring out the alloy, expose sins and bring to light that which is wrong among the people; but I do not want to curse them.

I tell you that the devil is working against us, and Lucifer is in the land.

Did you know that he had come to this country? Let me tell you the news to-day, if you have not heard it; he has come to this country and has been seen, the real old fellow himself, the same Lucifer that was cast down from heaven.

Another thing; did you know that all hell is let out for noon? The master is in the school-house, therefore. When we talk of hell we mean uncle Jim, uncle Bill, uncle Sam, and all our uncles and cousins over the wide world.

We mean old Babylon, the confusion that is over the wide world.

Some men say that they feel sick and faint, and weary, when they see so much darkness among the people. I feel as though I could say to the mountains and to all hell, get out of my way, or I will kick you out; I am not going to surrender. I want no poor pussyism around me; hang not your sickle on the tree to rust, but make it still sharper, and cut more grain in one day than you have ever done; and tell the devil that you are ahead of him. You old men, that let your sickles rust, take them down and sharpen them up, and walk into the fields and reap down the grain, that there may be wheat in the house of our God, for the harvest is great and the reapers are few.

I had rather fight the devils that are out of tabernacles, than those that are embodied. The grand difficulty we have to encounter is from devils that enter into you; they take possession of your houses, and then we have to fight devils in tabernacles. We want the devils cast out of you, and the power of God and the light of the Almighty to shine in you as a lamp.

The result of the teachings we are receiving, if practised, will reform the whole community. When you are right we will cease to chastise, we will cease to rebuke; we will cease throwing the arrows of the Almighty through you, we will cease telling you to surrender, to repent of all your sins. But until you do this, we will continue to throw the arrows of God through you, to hurl the darts of heaven upon you and the power of God in your midst; and we will storm the bulwarks of hell, and we will march against you in the strength of the God of Israel. And by the power of the Priesthood restored by the Prophet Joseph, by the light of heaven shed forth by brother Brigham and his associates, we expect to triumph; and in the name of Jesus Christ, we do not mean to surrender to evil. Amen.[1]

At about this time, Heber C. Kimball had a strange and foreboding dream about Brother Jeddy to which he was unable at the time to attach meaning—

I dreamed that we were travelling, and we came to a beautiful stream of water. I thought I was going to cross it with him, and with the expectation and understanding that he would guard me across. He crossed the stream unobserved by me, and then I saw him running up the hill as fast as he could, and he got away from me and passed out of my sight. The stream kept rising and becoming more boisterous and apparently more dangerous; and so it continued until I awoke.[2]

Within a few days, Kimball began to realize a meaning for his dream. On November 22, Rachel Ivins Grant gave birth to a son whom his parents named Heber Jeddy, for Brigham Young's two counselors. The delivery had been particularly difficult for thirty-five-year-old Rachel, being somewhat advanced in years to begin childbearing. Grant's telling labors in the Reformation and his attendance to his sixth living wife during the last days of her pregnancy had taken their toll.³ On the day she delivered, Wilford Woodruff left his desk at the Historian's Office to visit the Grants along with Franklin D. Richards. Arriving there, the two found their friend "very sick" and laid hands upon him.⁴ Unbeknownst to them, Grant had contracted typhoid, a common and "fearful sickness" of the times.⁵ The following day, he was again too ill to leave his house, and Woodruff again administered to him, this time in company with Heber Kimball, Daniel Wells, Jesse Little, and Franklin Richards.⁶ Repeatedly on the five succeeding days (November 24–28), Jeddy's close friend Wilford went to the Grant home to visit and to bless the ailing apostle, but to little avail.⁷ By November 29 Grant's dire condition deepened with the onset of double pneumonia. Woodruff and some others had spent the night at his bedside.

> President Grant had a very sick night, the worst that he has since he had been sick. The Devil worked hard all night to kill his body. The brethren laid hands upon him many times and rebuked the devil. The devil would lay upon him a strong hand from his feet to his head all through his limbs and stomach and a rib at a time and it seemed as though he would crush his body. Brother Grant though very weak would rebuke him for an hour at a time from limb to limb and rib to rib and it was a perfect warfare all night. He is easier this morning.⁸

In a near comatose condition and in a state of delirium most of the time, Jedediah Grant seemed to be at the point of death, but his friends and family members refused to believe that he might die. He was too strong, they reasoned, and he had said himself that he would never surrender. As Heber Kimball said a few days later,

> During brother Grant's brief sickness I would not believe, for one moment, that he was going to die, though my feelings would at times incline me to doubt as to his recovery; but I would not give way to them.
>
> I went to see him one day last week, and he reached out his hand and shook hands with me; he could not speak, but he shook hands warmly with me. I felt for him, and wanted to raise him up, and to have him stay and help us whip the devils and bring to pass righteousness. Why? Because he was

valiant, and I loved him. He was a great help to us, and you would be, if you were as valiant as he was, which you can be through faithfulness and obedience.

I laid my hands upon him and blessed him, and asked God to strengthen his lungs that he might be easier, and in two or three minutes he raised himself up and talked for about an hour as busily as he could, telling me what he had seen and what he understood, until I was afraid he would weary himself, when I arose and left him.

He said to me, brother Heber, I have been into the spirit world two nights in succession, and, of all the dreads that ever came across me, the worst was to have to again return to my body, though I had to do it. But O, says he, the order and government that were there! When in the spirit world, I saw the order of righteous men and women; beheld them organized in their several grades, and there appeared to be no obstruction to my vision; I could see every man and woman in their grade and order. I looked to see whether there was any disorder there, but there was none; neither could I see any death nor any darkness, disorder or confusion. He said that the people he there saw were organized in family capacities; and when he looked at them he saw grade after grade, and all were organized and in perfect harmony. He would mention one item after another and say, "Why, it is just as brother Brigham says it is; it is just as he has told us many a time." That is a testimony as to the truth of what brother Brigham teaches us, and I know it is true, from what little light I have.

He saw the righteous gathered together in the spirit world, and there were no wicked spirits among them. He saw his wife; she was the first person that came to him. He saw many that he knew, but did not have conversation with any except his wife Caroline. She came to him, and he said that she looked beautiful and had their little child, that died on the Plains, in her arms, and said, "Mr. Grant, here is little Margaret; you know that the wolves ate her up, but it did not hurt her; here she is all right." "To my astonishment," he said, "when I looked at families there was a deficiency in some, there was a lack, for I saw families that would not be permitted to come and dwell together, because they had not honored their calling here."

He asked his wife Caroline where Joseph and Hyrum and Father Smith and others were; she replied, "they have gone away ahead, to perform and transact business for us." The same as when brother Brigham and his brethren left Winter Quarters and came here to search out a home; they came to find a location for their brethren.

He also spoke of the buildings he saw there, remarking that the Lord gave Solomon wisdom and poured gold and silver into his hands that he might display his skill and ability, and said that the temple erected by Solomon was much inferior to the most ordinary buildings he saw in the spirit world.

In regard to gardens, says brother Grant, "I have seen good gardens on this earth, but I never saw any to compare with those that were there. I saw flowers of numerous kinds, and some with from fifty to a hundred different colored flowers growing upon one stalk." We have many kinds of flowers on the earth, and I suppose those very articles came from heaven, or they would not be here. After mentioning the things that he had seen, he spoke of how much he disliked to return and resume his body, after having seen the beauty and glory of the spirit world, where the righteous spirits are gathered together.

Some may marvel at my speaking about these things, for many profess to believe that we have no spiritual existence. But do you not believe that my spirit was organized before it came to my body here? And do you not think there can be houses and gardens, fruit trees, and every other good thing there? The spirits of those things were made, as well as our spirits, and it follows that they can exist upon the same principle.

After speaking of the gardens and the beauty of every thing there, brother Grant said that he felt extremely sorrowful at having to leave so beautiful a place and come back to earth, for he looked upon his body with loathing, but was obliged to enter it again.

He said that after he came back he could look upon his family and see the spirit that was in them, and the darkness that was in them; and that he conversed with them about the Gospel, and what they should do.[9]

So impressed was Grant with his vision of a perfect society in the "spirit world" that in the midst of his delirium he repeated the experience to several others who came to see him during the last days of November. Leonard W. Hardy's account differed in some interesting particulars from Kimball's. According to Hardy, Grant was most impressed with the industry and cleanliness of the spirits he saw. If the Saints would not do what he asked in the flesh, perhaps they would do it in the spirit.

He saw many of the Saints and found them pure and clean. They were clothed in pure white linen. There was not dirt or filth in the Spirit World, or darkness. Everything was in perfect order. He saw many mothers learning their little girls to work, and they appeared to be drawing out the finest threads from spindles, like the finest silk. He was told that he must come back to this world, and fight the Devils a little longer and set his family in order. The idea of his having to come back to this world was very painful to him. This was the first time that he had ever welcomed death, but he could not welcome it to himself and to his friends. He rejoiced much in the beauty and order of the Spirit World, and the beautiful gardens, walks, fruits, etc. He saw a vast number in the spirit world; they extended a great distance, but distance did not obstruct or hinder a perfect view of the vision in that world of light. There was not a particle of confusion, and no one was in each other's way.[10]

Grant had seen at last the world he wanted. At one point, after returning from such a misty excursion into the netherworld of his yearning soul, he called his wives and children to him one at a time and gave them each a blessing and told them of the reality of the great beyond. They wanted it to be so, but in the frailty of their humanity they looked at each other and said, "Perhaps it is so and perhaps it is not."[11] Whether it was so or not, the order, the beauty, and the flawlessness of his utopian imagery of the hereafter fit precisely the blueprint he and his brethren had drawn for the kingdom of God and for which he had finally exhausted himself. And whether he could subsequently have recovered from the killing effects of typhoid-pneumonia no longer mattered. Death had become the doorway to victory over the enemies of his life—filth, chaos, and imperfection. Triumph waited just beyond the end of life. His will to live on simply evaporated in the heat and the smoke of his own dreams.

On the crisp morning of December 1, 1856, Brigham Young walked the short block from his home to that of his second counselor. After administering to his longtime friend and associate, Young returned to the President's Office, believing that Grant "could not live but a short time unless there was a change soon for the better."[12] So congested were his lungs that he could not speak. At about noon, Young took heart at word that Grant was asking for something to eat, "an apple, some grapes or wine upon his stomach." Young immediately sent these things over to

Grant's home. After eating a roasted apple, Jedediah "also drank some buttermilk which he relished well, but it seemed to be something like a death appetite."[13]

That evening Young attended a meeting of some missionaries in the Historian's Office that subsequently adjourned at about 10:00 o'clock. Wilford Woodruff and Franklin Richards quickly excused themselves and started for Grant's. But as they walked onto the street, they met Dr. L. L. Sprague, who informed them that their old friend was dead, having just "breathed his last." They "went immediately into the house and found his wives and children weeping bitterly."[14] His last words, they said, were these: "Diffuse the spirit under the earth, and through the earth, and over the earth."[15] And the last faint rumble of Mormon Thunder faded into the long winter night.

Grant's death on the evening of December 1, 1856, had a profound effect on the community of the Saints. It was always a traumatic event when they lost one of their leaders; but because of the Reformation, the passing of Brother Jeddy took on additional meanings. Most Mormons who lived through those fiery days could not remember the Reformation without attaching to it their memories of its late preacher, zealously giving his life for the righteousness of the Saints. It mattered little that typhoid and pneumonia had struck him down. To most Mormons, he died a martyr.[16] Perhaps the experience of David M. Stewart, a young missionary preaching Mormonism through Yolo County, California, best summarized that imagery. When word of Grant's death reached Stewart some days later, he recorded the following in his history:

> On December the first, I preached at Auburn, and felt grieved in spirit. I could not account for it, and that night I dreamed that I saw Jedediah Grant on the top of a high mountain tower driving off the enemies of souls singlehanded. He was assailed on every hand by the legions of the Evil One; they assailed him with their teeth like mobbers who have surrounded their prey. I saw Elder Grant beat them back with superhuman power again, and again, until his strength failed him, and he fell overpowered, a martyr for righteousness.
>
> After that dream I mourned in spirit for days feeling some great calamity had fallen on the Church, the same as I had mourned in spirit when the Prophet and Patriarch were murdered in cold blood. Till the news finally

came that Jedediah M. Grant was dead. I then told my companions, "He died a martyr, for he had used every ounce of his vitality in defense of the truth."[17]

But perhaps as he did so often, Wilford Woodruff said it best of all. "His voice," he wrote in his journal, "has been like the trump of the Angel of God; he has shot the arrows of the Almighty with great power among the people. . . . A mighty man in Zion is laid low; a valiant man in Israel has fallen."[18]

⇠ Notes ⇢

1. Jedediah M. Grant, November 9, 1856, *Journal of Discourses*, 26 vols. (London and Liverpool: LDS Booksellers Depot, 1855–86), 4:83–87.

2. Heber C. Kimball, June 3, 1860, *Journal of Discourses*, 8:88.

3. Family lore has Grant becoming increasingly ill while attending to Rachel during the last days of her pregnancy and while tending little Heber at night as she recovered from the aftereffects of childbirth. Inasmuch as his household was polygynous, however, this story may be somewhat overdramatized, inasmuch as he was already very ill by the time she delivered. Sister wives would have assumed such responsibilities.

4. Scott G. Kenney, ed., *Wilford Woodruff's Journal, 1833–1898*, typescript, 9 vols. (Midvale, Utah: Signature Books, 1983–85), November 22, 1856.

5. Hannah Tapfield King, Diary, typescript, 142, LDS Church Archives. Insurance policies in the Heber J. Grant Collection, LDS Church Archives, indicate that Jedediah Grant died of "typhoid pneumonia," although at the time his physicians listed only "lung fever" as the cause of death. Given the fact that Grant had spent long hours waist-deep in the cold and unsanitary waters of baptism during the October–November period of the Reformation, his falling victim to either or both of these afflictions is at least likely.

6. Woodruff, *Journal*, November 13, 1856.

7. Ibid., November 14, 25, 16, 27, 28, 1856. "Evil spirits seemed to be let loose upon him and had the mastery," one woman remembered of those days. "The Priesthood seemed powerless when they administered to him. He raved, had visions, etc." King, Diary, 142 43.

8. Woodruff, *Journal*, November 29, 1856.

9. Heber C. Kimball, December 4, 1856, *Journal of Discourses*, 4:135–37.

10. Woodruff, *Journal*, November 26, 1856. See also Gibson Condie, Journal, 40–42,

holograph, LDS Church Archives. Compare Grant's experience with those outlined in Raymond A. Moody Jr., *Life after Life* (Covington, Ga.: Mockingbird Books, 1975).

11. Heber C. Kimball, December 4, 1856, *Journal of Discourses*, 4:137.

12. Woodruff, *Journal*, December 1, 1856.

13. Ibid.

14. Ibid. With Grant at the time of his death (in addition to family members) were L. L. Sprague, Dr. Israel Ivins, a third unidentified physician, Daniel H. Wells (who would succeed Grant in the First Presidency), Jesse C. Little, and Leonard W. Hardy. Ibid., December 2, 1856.

15. Ibid.

16. See, for example, George Laub, Diary, typescript, 95, LDS Church Archives; William Gibson, Diary, typescript, 43, Library of Congress Collection of Mormon Diaries; Warren Foote, Journal, holograph, 139, LDS Church Archives.

17. David M. Stewart, Autobiography, typescript, 32-34, LDS Church Archives.

18. Woodruff, *Journal*, December 1, 1856.

PHASE FIVE
Rainbow: 1856 and after

"Weep not for me, but weep for your own sins."

⇌ 20 ⇌
Reverberations

FROM THE GREATEST TO THE LEAST among them, the residents of 1856 Utah felt deeply the sense of Grant's death, for he had been not only a powerful political leader but also in their minds a mighty prophet. His activities in the days and weeks preceding his collapse added to the shock and wonderment that would in any event have accompanied the passing of one of the First Presidency. The December 3 edition of the *Deseret News* devoted itself to a lengthy obituary of this fourth member of the young Church's ruling triumvirate to have died in office. The *News*'s report of "deep gloom" in the City of the Saints reflected more than obligatory rhetoric. Grant's youth (forty years and nine months) combined with the relative suddenness of his decline to provide his death with an aura of tragedy that the Saints had not felt since the martyrdom of Joseph and Hyrum at Carthage.[1] The emaciated handcart emigrants passing into the city as the gloom of winter descended added to the sense of loss and foreboding that perhaps Grant himself had fomented during the early stages of the Reformation. The Saints would give immediate credit themselves to that movement for having taxed the second counselor "beyond his physical endurance,"[2] bringing him to his knees under the burden of their sins. But as Albert Carrington portentously observed, though Grant's body could not withstand the strain of carrying forth the work of God, his spirit would carry on into infinity.

Br. Grant needs no eulogy, and least of all such an one as our language could portray, for his whole life was one of noble and diligent action upon the side of truth, of high toned and correct example to all who desire to be saved in the kingdom of our God. As a citizen, as a friend, a son, a husband, a father, and above all as a Saint, and in every station and circumstance of life, whether military, civil, or religious, he everywhere and at all times shed forth the steady and brilliant light of lofty and correct example, and died, as he lived and counseled, with his "armor on and burnished," and though all Saints deeply feel his departure, yet they can fully realize that it redounds to his and our "infinite gain."[3]

That Grant lived on beyond the veil the Mormons were sure, but that the effects of his life would survive was up to those still in the flesh. So on the cold morning of Thursday, December 4, 1856, elements of the Nauvoo Legion under the personal command of General Daniel H. Wells assembled in front of Grant's expansive home on East Temple Street. The farmer-soldiers of the legion then formed in open lines from there to the tabernacle a few hundred feet away on Temple Block. With somber pageantry, a large cortège moved slowly north, a black carriage bearing the body of the fallen preacher.[4] So complex were the proceedings outside the building that the funeral service began more than an hour late. Brigham Young, who had been quite ill himself, began his address to the congregation shortly before noon. He would not again appear in public for several weeks, and he wanted the Saints to know clearly his feelings. Grant had given his life for their failings. They must now live up to his sacrifice and memory by fulfilling the goals of the Reformation. He began by refusing to succumb to emotion and then assured the Saints that Grant lived on both in the spirit and in the sermon his life itself had been. Although Young consciously avoided eulogizing his departed comrade, his sermon was full of poignant clues to his respect and reverence for Jedediah Grant as a man of God.

Some people would have to live to be a hundred years of age, in order to be as ripe in the things of God as was brother Grant, whose body now lies lifeless before us; to be as ripe as was the spirit which lately inhabited this deserted earthly tabernacle.

There are but few that can ripen for the glory, the immortality that is prepared for the faithful; for receiving all that was purchased for them by the Son of God; but very few can receive what brother Grant has received in his lifetime. He has been in the Church upwards of twenty-four years, and was a man that would live, comparatively speaking, a hundred years in that time. The storehouse that was prepared in him to receive the truth, was capable of receiving as much in twenty-five years as most of men can in one hundred. So why do we mourn? Suppose brother Grant could speak to us this day, he would deprecate to the lowest degree the fuss and parade we are making. He would say, "Away with you; stop your blowing of horns, beating of drums, and hoisting of colors. Give my body a place to lay and rest, and do not consider me better than other men. Take my body and bury it deep enough, so that it can rest where the floods cannot wash it out, where it can remain until the trumpet sounds, when I may awake up and help you again."[5]

Brigham wanted the Saints to stop worrying over the loss of Jedediah Grant, although it became very apparent to everyone present that Young himself felt it most keenly. Quickly becoming aware of his listeners' recognition of that fact, he continued:

True, brother Grant was a great help to me; he stood by me, and was willing to come and go, and do whatever was requested of him, in order to take the burden from me; but I tell you that we will have not only four, but an hundred fold for him, just as good, and so we will for every good man that lies down; I promise you that. Brother Grant we call a great man, a giant, a lion; but let me tell you that the young whelps are growing up here who will roar louder than ever he dare, and instead of there being two, or three, or four, there are hundreds of them.

Perhaps many of you will think I am not correct in my views, that I am enthusiastic, that I am mistaken; but let me tell you that the very sons of these women that sit here will rise up and be as great as any man that ever lived, and as far beyond Jedediah, or myself, and brother Heber, as we are in the Gospel beyond our little children. I am not going to gather the lions of the forest from the sectarian world, that is not where I am going to get them, but the mothers in Israel are going to rear them. They will raise hundreds and thousands that will know more about the things of God in twenty years than Jedediah did in his lifetime, which was forty years. Will they know more than I do? Yes.[6]

It became even more obvious through the rest of Young's address that he wanted Grant to live on, not only in heaven but on earth, and that the work of the Reformation would continue until all the devils had surrendered. The Church would grow and flourish on the lives of such as Jeddy

Grant. "I hope you will remember what I have said," concluded the prophet, "for it is true; and if you do not, I hope it will be told to you until you do."[7] He invoked God's blessings on the congregation and sat down. His message had been clear: The end of Grant did not mean the end of the Reformation. Nor could it.

Heber Kimball, in addition to recounting Grant's idyllic vision of the spirit world,[8] added his approbation to the words of Brigham. Mormon Thunder had not ceased; it was just rumbling somewhere else. He also admonished the Saints not to mourn Grant's death.

> I feel well, and I do not feel to condescend to a spirit of mourning. If I do weep, I will weep for my own sins and not for Jedediah. If he could speak he would say, "Weep not for me, but weep for your own sins."
>
> Before brother Grant was taken sick, he said that he had unsheathed his sword, and that it never should be sheathed again until the enemies of righteousness were subdued; and he fought the devil up to the last, and used to proclaim that he should not prevail on this earth. I can say that he left us with his sword unsheathed, and he will help Joseph and Hyrum and Willard.[9]

Kimball also hastened to remind the Saints that the work of the Reformation would go on and that they had better get used to the idea.

> Why do you not all listen to brother Brigham and Jedediah and Heber and many others? They have had the spirit of reformation all the time.
>
> Then wake up ye Saints of Latter Days, and cleanse your platters inside and out, and God Almighty will rescue us from our enemies. He will slay them; He will hurl kings from their thrones and unrighteous rulers from their places of authority and they will drop faster than you saw the stars drop from heaven, at the time that the Saints were driven out of Jackson county Missouri.
>
> I want to stir you up to faith, obedience, integrity, and everything that is good. I am preaching to you; not to Jedediah. What remains here of him goes back to mother earth, and let us strive to honor our tabernacles as did brother Grant his.
>
> My body has got to return to dust, and I will honor it, then I will take it again. I am as sure of that, as I am that I am standing here before you.
>
> God bless you forever: Amen.[10]

For two months following the death and burial of his second counselor, President Brigham Young remained in relative seclusion. He did not attend the weekly tabernacle meetings, leaving to his remaining counselor, Heber Kimball, the task of carrying forth the Reformation from the First Presidency.[11] Past December and into the new year, the Mormon Thunder of Jedediah Grant continued to echo from the hills of Zion through the medium of the ongoing revival he had fostered just prior to his death. In his own style of exuberance, Kimball pressed the movement forward with an increasing vigor that he attributed to the lingering influence of Grant.

"The Spirit and power that rested upon the First Presidency when brother Jedediah was in the flesh," he told the Saints on December 21, "are with brother Brigham and me, and you cannot get them away from us. We have the keys of the kingdom of God, and they will be on this earth, even though there should be but one left of those who hold them."[12] Other Mormon leaders, such as Wilford Woodruff, also used Grant's name and memory to inspire the Saints to reform their lives. Perhaps it was a proverbial case of a man being able to accomplish his objectives better dead than alive. Woodruff followed Kimball on December 21 with a strong appeal for renewed efforts toward reformation, and the center of his sermon rested squarely upon the tarrying image of the "martyred" Grant.

> Brother Grant is gone; the load he undertook to draw killed him, the same load that was pressing the President of this Church to the earth, when Jedediah rose up to bear it off; his spirit was strong enough, but his mortal body was not strong enough to bear its weight.
>
> Although Jedediah has been taken from us, that load, which in a measure has been removed from the Presidency of this Church, has not returned unto them, and I pray it never may. When Jedediah M. Grant went forth among the people through the north country and this city to carry out the views of President Young, and lifted up his voice like the trump of the angel of God, and called upon the people to awake out of their deep sleep and repent of their sins and turn unto God, the people were so sound asleep that they did not realize the importance of his mission; many felt that his labors and reproofs were unnecessary and uncalled for, the people did not know what he was doing. Had the vision of their minds been open as was brother Grant's, and those who sent him, they would have seen and felt the importance of that mission.

We cannot sleep any longer with the Priesthood of Almighty God resting upon us, and the work that is required at our hands. WE CANNOT SLEEP. I do not wonder that calling upon the people to wake up has killed one man, and it will kill more if we do not respond to the call; mortality cannot endure the vision of eternity that rests on them when they look on the Priesthood and see the position they are in; it has nearly laid brother Young in the grave; he felt he could not live until some man rose up and started the work of reformation.[13]

By early spring, the full excitement of the great Mormon Reformation of 1856–57 had about run its natural course. In Deseret thousands of Saints had submitted to the catechism, had openly confessed their sins of commission and omission, and had then gone again into the waters of baptism for a renewal of their covenants with the God of Israel and of Joseph and Brigham. As the movement was in progress and even as it was ending, it was difficult to assess the effects it had upon the Saints. Some, like Hannah Tapfield King, viewed its cessation with relief, having long since wearied of the confessions and the sufferings of people striving to gain perfection under the flogging commands of their beloved leaders.[14] Others, like Wilford Woodruff, saw the revival in early retrospect only in positive terms. "We have had a great reformation this winter," he wrote to George A. Smith in St. Louis; "some of the fruits are, all have confessed their sins either great or small, restored their stolen property; all have been baptized from the Presidency down; all are trying to pay their tithing."[15] Woodruff also witnessed another interesting result of the Reformation: "Nearly all are trying to get wives, until there is hardly a girl 14 years old in Utah, but what is married, or just going to be. President Young has hardly time to eat, drink, or sleep, in consequence of marrying people and attending to endowments."[16] Whatever the final result in general terms, the Reformation for those who lived through it was an experience never to be forgotten, as were all such general revivals in "old" societies.

The final work and enormous climax to the career of the Mormon preacher Jedediah Grant went ultimately far beyond the time and space of his own existence. Even as the Reformation was fading under the spring sun in the Rockies, it caught hold in such places as Great Britain, where the Saints felt the heat from Brother Jeddy's wildfire across a continent and an ocean. "President E. T. Benson is going about like a two-edged sword," wrote missionary Matthias Cowley from England, "cutting on all sides everything that is impure, and those who don't live their religion as far as they know it,— He is in this country as Jedediah was in that, in bringing about the Reformation."[17] Surprisingly, Cowley also found that the British Saints had not only sensed the heat of the fire but also the quenching of the spark that set it: "The loss of President Grant was greatly felt in this land; the affection of this people for him (although not personally known to them) could not be realized by those who are not with them."[18] But others who did know the second counselor and who heard of his death from a distance responded with more poignant feelings.

Thomas L. Kane, writing to Brigham Young from Philadelphia on May 21, 1857, found himself reminded of the meaning of friendship, and of another whose fellowship he cherished.

> I thank you for writing to me. I am growing old enough to prize the friends whom time has left me. Jedediah Grant—I had rough talks with him over Deseret matters; and have to think with bitterness that I parted from him without saying in so many words that in my soul I did him justice. Noble fellow; I could give years of my life to have written him before he died one natural and outspoken brother's letter. Yet this writing, my friend Young; does it keep down the miles of waste which seem to be growing up between us every year? I wish I had your hand to grasp.[19]

Even as he wrote that dolorous letter, a situation was developing in Washington that would dispel any fears the Philadelphian might have had that his bonds of fraternity with Brigham Young and the Mormons would break from disuse. The allegiance to the Saints of Colonel Kane, which his "gallant friend Grant"[20] had so fervently helped to secure and maintain, was to become a crucial factor in the prevention of a bloody and disastrous war between the Mormons and the U.S. government. The coming of the Utah Expedition to the Rocky Mountains in the fall of 1857 to establish firmly federal hegemony over Utah Territory ironically negated in a wave of fear and indignation many positive results of the last efforts of Kane's friend Grant, but the Mormon preacher would have been pleased to be on hand to welcome the good colonel to Utah in the spring of 1858, as he arrived on the scene to act as an intermediary between the besieged Saints and the army in the mountains. So ended finally the Mormon

Colonel Thomas L. Kane, ca. 1862. LDS Church Archives

Reformation of 1856–57, and hence also the last loud echoes of the fiery preachments of Jedediah Grant.[21]

Although the sounds of Mormon Thunder seemed to dissipate quickly against the clatter of the Utah War, they were too loud and forceful to disappear completely. Scholars of Mormon history agree that the peaceful settlement of that "war" had a great deal to do with the willingness of the Saints to burn their communities along the Wasatch Front and move south rather than submit to the Gentile army. Surely the Reformation played a significant role in preparing the Mormons for such a great and sacrificial gesture in the face of federal power. Grant would have undoubtedly enjoyed that effect of his preachings; but if the same cast of mind also contributed to the infamous Mountain Meadows Massacre of late 1857, as some have suggested, then perhaps the judgment of history upon the workings of Mormon Thunder must add to its verdict a clause of tragedy.[22]

Beyond the Reformation, the memory of Jedediah Grant continued among the Mormons in more direct manifestations. In the South, for example, his legendary mission of the late 1830s continued for decades to regenerate stories of the astounding ministry of the Mormon firebrand from the West. Among the first Mormon missionaries into the region after the Civil War were Henry G. Boyle and Howard K. Coray. They discovered as they arrived in Tazewell County, Virginia, and Surry County, North Carolina, that even thirty years later, Grant's "name and works are household words, in North Carolina and Virginia, where he labored and organized branches of the Church."[23] In the close society of southern Saints the stories went on and on, refurbishing themselves as they went, until young Grant had confounded all the preachers in the region with "blank text" sermons and razor-sharp responses to trick questions. The tales as they thus grew became an immortal part of Mormon folklore, as did Grant himself. Given his style and calculated image, it was inevitably so.

A second and perhaps more important part of the heritage of Jedediah M. Grant among the Mormons developed through his posterity. His last son, Heber Jeddy, though he never knew his father, thought of him in terms not of his ministry as a Mormon preacher but of his service as a noble father whose memory and influence in behalf of his children was eternal.[24] When Heber J. Grant acceded to the presidency of the Mormon Church in 1918, the life of his father came to mean something in the minds of the Saints that had nothing to do with the man himself. That he was the father of Heber J. Grant was all most of them knew or cared to know.

In that event, ironically, his life's meaning became heavily obscure. Yet if in no other way, through his famous son the work and desires of Jedediah Grant reached a measure of fulfillment in another world and in another century than those in which he delivered his last sermon to the Latter-day Saints. During nearly three decades as president of the Church (1918–45), Heber Grant carried the religion of his father into the mainstream of American life, far beyond the limiting reaches of its mountain province. From there its message went out to the world, clothed in a new respectability and compatibility that would have been ultimately foreign to the radical fire-eater from the year without summer, as in November 1856, when he delivered his last instructions to the Saints in Utah Territory.

Thanks be to our God, and to high heaven, the light of God is here and the truth of God is here, and we have waged a war with Lucifer, under the banner of the Lord Jesus Christ. May we be able to stand in the contest and overcome. We bring no railing accusation against our common enemy, but we tell him and his host that they must surrender. We say to the sinners in Zion, be afraid, you must surrender to the Lord Jesus Christ. We say to you, Saints, rub up your armor, gird on the sword of the Almighty and walk forth to battle, and never yield the ground.

Heber J. Grant. Publisher's private collection.

I am not of that class that believes in shrinking; if there is a fight on hand, give me a share of it. I am naturally good natured, but when the indignation of the Almighty is in me I say to all hell, stand aside and let the Lord Jesus Christ come in here; He shall be heir of the earth; the truth shall triumph, the Priesthood and Christ shall reign.[25]

Notes

1. *Deseret News*, December 3, 1856. See also "Reminiscences of Henry Moyle and Pedigree of the Moyle Family," in *Biographies and Reminiscences from the James Henry Moyle Collection*, edited by Gene A. Sessions (Salt Lake City: James Moyle Genealogical and Historical Association, 1974), 105–6, for a poignant description of the common feeling.

2. *Deseret News*, December 10, 1856.

3. Ibid.

4. The procession consisted of the following: "1. An advanced guard; 2. band of music; 3. lieutenant general and staff; 4. cavalry escort; 5. lancers; 6. First Presidency, the Twelve, and the presiding bishop; 7. eight bearers; 8. hearse conveying the body covered by General Grant's staff; 9. the general's horse, fully caparisoned and led by his groom; 10. family and relatives; 11. band of music; 12. city council; 13. president of the stake and council; 14. high council; 15. bishops; 16. members of the legislative assembly; 17. members of the Masonic fraternity; 18. friends and citizens in carriages; 19. band of music; 20. rear of the escort composed of cavalry and infantry units; 21. persons on foot. Colonels J. C. Little and L. W. Hardy of the Nauvoo Legion were in charge of the day's proceedings."

Deseret News, December 10, 1856.

5. Brigham Young, December 4, 1856, *Journal of Discourses*, 26 vols. (London and Liverpool: LDS Booksellers Depot, 1855–86), 4:130–31.

6. Ibid., 4:131.

7. Ibid., 4:134.

8. Heber C. Kimball, December 4, 1856, *Journal of Discourses*, 4:135–36.

9. Ibid., 4:137. Willard Richards, the former second counselor, had died in March 1854.

10. Ibid., 4:137–38.

11. Wilford Woodruff, Letter to editor, February 4, 1857, printed in the Church's New York City paper, *The Mormon*, May 2, 1857. Young subsequently named Daniel H. Wells to succeed Grant in the First Presidency. Wells also became the next mayor of Salt Lake City.

12. Heber C. Kimball, December 21, 1856, *Journal of Discourses*, 4:140.

13. Wilford Woodruff, December 21, 1856, *Journal of Discourses*, 4:146–47.

14. Hannah Tapfield King, Diary, typescript, 143.

15. Wilford Woodruff, Letter to George A. Smith, April 1, 1857, "History of the British Mission," holograph, LDS Church Archives.

16. Ibid.

17. Matthias Cowley, Letter to James McKnight, April 4, 1857, "History of the British Mission."

18. Ibid.

19. Thomas L. Kane, Letter to Brigham Young, May 21, 1857, holograph, Brigham Young Collection.

20. Thomas L. Kane, Letter to Brigham Young, January 5, 1855, holograph, Brigham Young Collection.

21. For a balanced account of Kane's role in the mediation of the Utah War, see Donald R. Moorman and Gene A. Sessions, *Camp Floyd and the Mormons: The Utah War* (Salt Lake City: University of Utah Press, 1992), 33–39. See also Norman Furniss, *The Mormon Conflict, 1850–1859* (New Haven, Conn.: Yale University Press, 1960).

22. Ronald W. Walker, Richard E. Turley Jr., and Glen M. Leonard, *Massacre at Mountain Meadows* (New York: Oxford University Press, 2008), is the most complete and balanced account of the event. It replaces the classic Juanita Brooks, *The Mountain Meadows Massacre* (Palo Alto, Calif.: Stanford University Press, 1950), as the most reliable version of the complicated tragedy. More polemical in tone, Will Bagley, *Blood of the Prophets: Brigham Young and the Massacre at Mountain Meadows* (Norman: University of Oklahoma Press, 2002), presents a starkly divergent opinion about the causes of the atrocity. All of these studies agree, however, that the Reformation and, more significantly, the teaching of blood atone-

ment played important roles in fostering first the mood and then the willingness of Mormon militiamen in southern Utah on the afternoon of September 11, 1857, to murder some 120 emigrants on their way to California.

23. *Deseret News*, May 5, 1869.

24. Heber J. Grant, Letter to Joseph Hyrum Grant Jr., December 3, 1917, typescript in possession of Bernice Grant Casper, Midvale, Utah.

25. Jedediah M. Grant, November 9, 1856, *Journal of Discourses*, 4:86–87.

21

Mormon Thunder: An Analysis

JEDEDIAH GRANT DREW FOR HIMSELF the image of Mormon Thunder. As it was inextricably tied to his religion, his life was very much like a great thunderstorm in the desert, with all its crackling noise, bright flashes of light, and pungent atmosphere. The similarities endured to the very end. With a final burst of thunder and lightning, the Mormon Reformation of 1856, the storm was over. Afterward, the vastness of Mormon history quickly absorbed the fading echoes of his life until he became one of the most obscure leaders of the early Latter-day Saints. But perhaps his obscurity is more within the realm of understanding than are the inaccuracies and faulty impressions that survived his death and endured until no one, not even his children, knew the man except in myth and legend.

Perhaps the best example of this among the many has to do with the publication of *Truth for the Mormons* in 1852. Mormon and anti-Mormon authors alike have consistently doubted that Jedediah Grant actually wrote the letters to the *New York Herald*. Mormon ecclesiast and historian B. H. Roberts, for example, called them "the Grant-signed letters" after concluding that "the internal evidence is overwhelming against his authorship of them."[1] The assumption here, of course, is that Grant was too illiterate and unimaginative to create such pithy phraseology as the letters contained. This denigrating assumption, perhaps more than any other, pervades the general set of distortions.

One detractor of Mormonism was so certain of Grant's inadequacies that even Kane's assistance on the project did not seem to be enough. T. B. H. Stenhouse expressed his belief that former Vice President George

M. Dallas, then residing in Philadelphia, also had a hand in preparing the letters to the *Herald*: "In after years it was really painful to the Author to learn that two of Pennsylvania's honoured sons, already alluded to in this work—one no less than an ex-Vice-President of the United States, and the other enjoying a military title—were the inspiration and authors of the famous letters."[2] Unfortunately, Stenhouse failed to substantiate what he had so "painfully learned," nor has any evidence surfaced that would support his revelation of Dallas's complicity. A close associate of Colonel Kane, Dallas had been of assistance to the Saints during the Mormon Battalion arrangements in the Polk administration, but neither Grant nor Kane subsequently made any reference to Dallas as a participant in the 1852 effort. The question of Kane's authorship nevertheless remained in the path of any revisionist conclusion on the matter.

In the mid-1970s, at the suggestion of Church Historian Leonard J. Arrington, the noted writing-style analyst Elinore Partridge examined three numbered items, the first a Jedediah Grant holograph, the second an excerpt from a Thomas Kane letter, and the third a portion of the first letter to the *Herald*. In what she emphasized as a "very tentative judgment," Partridge concluded that "the evidence of these three samples seems to indicate ... that you could make a good argument for author 1's [Grant's] having written, or at least greatly influenced, letter 3 [to the *Herald*]." In addition, based on various studies of the three samples, she found such things as organization, humor content, and construction to be much more similar in Grant's letter and the *Herald* letter than in Kane's letter and the *Herald* letter. This ought to suggest that Grant's ability to write up to the quality of the *Herald* letters (with considerable copy-editing, to be sure) deserves considerable reevaluation. There can be little question that Kane had a heavy hand in the production of the letters, but it is also likely that the Mormon collaborated word by word in their writing and that Grant had far greater intellectual abilities and discipline than the myth has ever allowed him.

The controversy surrounding the authorship of the letters to the *Herald* serves as an archetypal expression of the misconceptions that have encircled the image of Jeddy Grant since before his death 150 years ago. The Mormons of early Utah called him "the sledgehammer of Brigham," and yet his letters show a deep tenderness of feeling and a supremely gentle touch, particularly when he contemplated his children. His enemies declared that he was of an "utterly undisciplined nature,"[3] while he delivered sermons without notes that were carefully progressive in their development of ideas and demonstrated the workings of an organized and purposeful mind. An anti-Mormon exposé published in 1874 characterized him as "a man without education or mental discipline of any description."[4] A similar book, published after the turn of the century, described him as "an ignorant Cotton Mather,"[5] despite abundant evidence that he read voraciously the works of such thinkers as Wesley, Locke, Rousseau, Watts, Abercrombie, and Mather himself. He religiously attended Orson Hyde's grammar classes. He required an illiterate wife to attend school and worried constantly over the education of his children. Another writer said he was "a frothing fanatic, whom it is only charity to judge as of diseased mind,"[6] ignoring the sentient spirituality of the man that led him to weep publicly over the sufferings of the 1856 handcart companies and to adjure his family and followers to prayer as a constant source of comfort. Even his controversial teachings, of which there were many, he couched in terms of humility and deferment, begging the Saints to conform to the principles of righteousness. In short, his enemies never understood Jedediah M. Grant, and many of his admirers were just as incapable of fathoming the meaning of his existence.

Perhaps the most accurate impression of Grant that has survived the mists of time is one Frank J. Cannon voiced in 1913: "He was incapable of doubt and insensible to fear. That he was sincere is beyond question."[7] This image of fearlessness and unswerving devotion to Joseph Smith and his teachings—and then to Brigham Young—is probably faultless. He never wavered in his loyalty to Mormonism. Converted in his adolescence, he reached manhood while preaching the new religion through the farms and cities of the eastern seaboard. In the course of this experience, he developed forensic abilities that often confounded friend and foe alike. These skills, combined with a mind that could tolerate no vacillation when it came to the cause at hand, produced the phenomenal force that carried Jedediah Grant to the pinnacles of Mormon Church leadership and cast him in the role he played in the early history of the Restoration. Moreover, his dedication to Mormonism radiated from him until his pleas in its behalf seemed to come from the Almighty Himself. By the end of his life, his preachments were bringing a whole people to its knees.

The remarkable difference between the Jedediah Grant of myth and the real man that has thus emerged in the pages of this volume submits, in the final analysis, to an accounting only after contemplation of the pre-Utah period of his life, when both he and his religion were but youngsters. Unmarried until the age of twenty-eight due to extensive and continual missions for the Church, Grant knew no home until he reached the Salt Lake Valley in 1847. Although he was converted to Mormonism in 1833, he never lived in Kirtland, nor in Missouri, nor in Nauvoo, except for short periods between missionary journeys in the East from New York in the north to North Carolina in the south. He became, during those crucial years of personal development, a permanent and perpetual preacher who saw through the preacher's eyeglass a world full of imperfection, a world in dire need of repentance. By the time he had risen to the top of the Mormon ecclesiastical and political hierarchy in the 1850s, Grant was incapable of seeing a society, whether Mormon or Gentile, except in terms of its need for improvement. He had absorbed for twenty years the millennial visions of Brigham Young and Joseph Smith. Having believed them completely and having thus sacrificed two decades of his youth to their fulfillment, Grant suffered greatly in Zion over the human frailties of the Saints, among whom he was living for the first time. His dream, as it so clearly revealed itself in the throes of his death, was of a kingdom of the righteous in which cleanliness, purity, and order prevailed against all the base impulses of humanity. Grant was thus the perfect disciple of Joseph Smith, an ultimate believer in the reality of the Mormon promise: a physical world of union and crystal beauty, a celestial kingdom of glory.

Hence, the key to understanding the significance of Grant's life to the whole of Mormon history turns within the essence of early Mormonism itself. Though he lived such a short time in the limelight of history and while he was so busy trying to overcome the set of devils that he believed were threatening his people, a basic comprehension of this worldview reveals itself in the documents his life generated. In return, it sheds considerable light on the nature of Mormonism during its first struggling years of life as a nascent social force. Joseph Smith and Brigham Young taught in their own dynamic and evolutionary manners the concepts of perfection and total dedication that motivated such loyal disciples as Jedediah Grant. The universe they constructed about their followers rested upon an expansion of the meaning of humankind and its perpetual development in a unity of temporal and spiritual aspiration for which the organized Church was the channeling medium. Young Grant partook hungrily during his developing years of these Mormon ideals, shining brightly against the sometimes bleak and unpromising realities of the frontier American struggle for mere existence. But the promise for mankind under the maxims of Mormonism washed down thoroughly only with a healthy grog of sacrifice in behalf of the kingdom. In the case of Jeddy Grant, the milk of the meal was probably more nourishing than the meat. He was a true believer for whom the accomplishment of the cause was sometimes secondary to its pursuit.

Almost from the moment he joined the Mormon Church, Grant involved himself in a consuming crusade. There could be no life for him outside Mormonism and its purposes. Consequently, as he rose to the ruling councils of the young church, religion encompassed all in his world, from keeping ditches and bodies clean to attending to prayers and obeying counsel. He was in every sense a professional Mormon. For him, the Latter-day Saints had no excuse for anything short of the same total commitment to the success of the institution. They had perfection at their fingertips; they had simply to grasp it through the exercise of self-denial and devotion. As Brigham Young wanted his people separated from the world geographically and culturally, Jedediah Grant sought to have them deny the world completely, for only then, in his mind, could eternity open itself to them. In this respect, he was a curiously Mormon version of the primitive Christian ascetic, but one who would build an earthly kingdom because it would inevitably transmute itself into a spiritual dominion. This was the hard core of nineteenth-century Mormonism, and Jeddy Grant was its epitome.

Other men and women came through the experiences of early Mormonism with the same impressions of the universe and its ultimate meaning as did Grant, but in his being the doctrines of Smith and Young bubbled through a matrix of intensity and vitality that brought forth great yearnings for an immediate realization of Utopia—Zion, where purity and virtue encompassed all. As with revivalist preachers of another age—Jonathan Edwards, William Tennant, George Whitefield—Jedediah Grant believed that a lack of enthusiasm in religion (manifest in poor preaching) was the cause of much spiritual sickness among the people. He therefore dedicated himself to the art of religious discourse, something that added considerably to his role as a minister of reform among the Latter-day Saints. In his mind, the Spirit of God and successful preaching were interconnected. Where one was missing, so also was the other. He sincerely believed that his abilities as a sermonizer arose supernaturally and often began his discourses with words such as these: "I wish to have your prayers, and by the aid thereof to speak by the Spirit of the Lord, for I have found that without that Spirit I never could command language sufficient to convey my ideas."[8] For Grant and many other Mormon leaders, this idea led to a measure of freewheeling exhortation that produced an assurance in preacher and listener alike that God himself sanctioned everything said. Even when on the spikes of a Grant tirade, most Saints therefore accepted his words and, in surprising displays of humility, emotionally promised to overcome their sins, of most of which they were unaware before the second counselor mounted the stand for a fiery sermon.

Preaching had even more significance in Mormonism than in other frontier religions because of the Saints' conception of their leaders as modern prophets after the Old Testament pattern. Written words— scriptures—were important, but they could not compare to the living counsel of a prophet or apostle of the Lord. Jedediah Grant bathed himself in this belief, making even his pronouncements as mayor of Salt Lake City shouts from Sinai, commandments to Israel from the mouthpiece of God. He believed that successful preaching was the key to fruitful leadership, and that the words he spoke were veritably true because of the priesthood of God that was upon him. Realizing that only through effective charisma could the Saints "follow counsel" into righteousness, he paid great attention to the details of acquiring and developing those characteristics conducive to dynamic leadership. "There is an influence and impression which you receive listening to the discourses when delivered in this house. Here there is a substance communicated, impressions are made, for you have the man before you; you can discern the intent of his heart; the spirit, the ideas, the whole soul of the man are thrown open in his discourse, and his appearance makes an impression that the written word cannot convey."[9]

His sermons thus provide more than just a glimpse into the mind of Preacher Grant. They constitute a body of evidence suggesting that he understood the basic elements of behavioral objectives. It appears that he designed his lessons carefully to engender reform, carrying as they did a universal theme. Regardless of the subject to which he addressed himself, he seldom failed to insert in almost the same terms each time a call to perfection. His typical admonition was for "the people to wake up to a sense of their duty, and begin to serve God and repent of their sins, repent of every improper habit."[10] The theme of his sermons was always the same: "I want the Saints to do right and be blessed."[11]

Despite his use of positive motivation to obtain his objectives, Grant could tolerate no slack in the line. More than his companions in the First Presidency, Brigham Young and Heber Kimball, he believed in the free use of the lash. He would drive the money changers from the temple of Mormonism. Once caught up in the fervor of passionate evangelism during his early missions, he could never leave it. It was a way of life. If he could not chastise the corrupt world, he would pillory the Saints for their attachments to it. In the final analysis, Grant demanded the millennium. He harkened, not to a dim past of better, more righteous days as did Mather, but to a near future in which the pure dreams of the sacred were real. That measured the depth of his purpose. And through it emerged a symbolic apogee of the quickening Mormon vision of the nineteenth century.

The theme of Grant's leadership among the Saints seemed to develop shortly after his calling as second counselor to Brigham Young. Prior to that time, and although he had held influential political positions in Utah, he appeared to be only one of the many stars in the Deseret sky. Young's selection of the bumptious young seventy in the spring of 1854 to fill the chair of the revered Dr. Willard Richards must have come as somewhat of a surprise to many in Zion. Despite Grant's proven dedication to Mormonism, other men on the scene would seem in retrospect to have been more logical choices for the vacancy. But there was a certain immeasurable affinity between Young and Grant. They had been close allies in the rise of Mormonism for two decades, from Zion's Camp through the succession crisis when Grant's loyalty to the Twelve served as a high wall in Philadelphia against the assaults of such schismatics as Sidney Rigdon, Benjamin Winchester, and even Grant's brother-in-law William Smith. In addition, Brigham appreciated men of practical grit and realized further that the tall preacher possessed certain charismatic qualities that would demand the fealty of bishops, seventies, and even apostles. The unquestioning admiration of such high-minded elders as Wilford Woodruff proved the fulfillment of Young's expectation.

The relationship between Jedediah Grant and Brigham Young came through most clearly during the Reformation of 1856–57. Though this remarkable and enigmatic movement was in many ways a standard frontier

Two portraits of Jedediah Grant. LDS Church Archives.

revival with all the earmarks of such sweeping religious movements as the Great Awakening of the 1740s, it was, in another fashion, the manifestation of the idealized universe of Jedediah Grant. There can be little question that it began with a spark in his mind, in spite of his subsequent deferment to the leadership of Brigham Young. Some evidence suggests that Young had been suffering over the secularization of his charges for some time, and he would continue to do so until his death twenty years later. Such attempts at otherworldliness as the United Order demonstrated his weighty concern for the economic, political, and social separation of the Saints from the world, a clear inheritance from Joseph Smith. Without doubt, however, the actual form and function of the Reformation came from within the psyche of Jedediah Grant. From the start his superior allowed him to take the lead in the movement, from preaching the key sermons to writing the catechism of reform. This was not necessarily a sign that Grant was "the one man in the valley whom Brigham Young could not manage,"[12] as one writer suggested, but rather an indication of the president's approbation of his counselor's course, an accurate representation of the affinity of minds that existed between the two men.

After a long look at Jedediah Grant's life and views, the goals and directions of the Reformation emerge as magnified images of the Grant assessment of the body politic, its illnesses and its possibilities. He sensed instinctively but could not accept what scholars would later call the second law of thermodynamics, that in all closed systems chaos and disorder—entropy—must prevail sooner or later. The Reformation grew out of Grant's terror of this construct. So his dream of the spirit world that occurred late in November of 1856 portrayed graphically the physical world he would have had the movement create for reality—clean, orderly, perfect. These elemental concepts of his utopian ideal came from his mind in sermon and letter long before the revival fires of 1856 brought them to the forefront of the Mormon movement. The physical cleanliness theme, for example, was clearly Grant's; Young himself suffered under its requirements. Additionally instructive to this point was the continuing use of Grant's name and image to carry the movement forth after his death. There was more involved in this than the simple use of a martyr figure to fan the flames of religious enthusiasm. Grant was so much a part of the movement that it could go forth only under his name and in his words. It is even possible that his naturally fading memory in the early spring of 1857 contributed significantly to the revival's gradual decline thereafter. In many ways, therefore, the movement could grow and flourish only upon his name and upon the ideals he had forcefully injected into the Mormon gospel of human affairs. The catechism of reform that teachers and bishops read intensely to their charges was a clear product of Grant's mind and reflected all the concerns he had preached since the beginning of the Utah period of Mormon history. Surprisingly, even the most controversial of Reformation doctrines were commonly a part of his pre-1856 system of dogma.

His character stamped indelibly on the movement itself, the Reformation was then at once the end result of Jedediah Grant's career and the very substance of his role in Mormon history. He was undeniably the quintessence of frontier Mormonism. In another age and another milieu, he might have been a Savonarola or a Cotton Mather, but he was instead a unique and fascinating example of the Mormon product—a man who would confront and conquer the profane in order to realize eternity. As a Mormon apostle and president, his battle inevitably engulfed those around him. The Reformation was simply the flashing of his last call to arms; but as a significant point in the biography of Mormonism itself, it amounted to an attack of growing pains. When it ended and the artificial world it created crumbled beneath the realities of secular invasion, Mormonism underwent a dramatic change; and with that change, childhood ended.

Jedediah Morgan Grant might well have lived another four decades—to 1896, when his domain purposefully moved into the modern world as a state in a Gentile nation. Instead, in the carefully preserved echoes of Mormon mythology, he died a thundering martyr, ground down upon the very movement of righteousness he had fomented, until from his deathbed he told of visiting eternity, and then passed quietly into it in order to find an elusive peace and to fight on for the cause of Joseph. Behind him he left a people who would soon forget who he really was as they confronted irruption, first by an army of soldiers and bureaucrats and then by the world itself. Mormon resistance, like Grant's Mormon Thunder, was strong but ultimately futile. The early grave that swallowed Brother Jedediah was consequently a compassionate haven for such a boisterous amplification of what Mormonism really was, and would never be again.

⇥ Notes ⇤

1. B. H. Roberts, *A Comprehensive History of the Church of Jesus Christ of Latter-day Saints, Century One*, 6 vols. (Salt Lake City: Church of Jesus Christ of Latter-day Saints, 1930), 3:528.

2. T. B. H. Stenhouse, *Rocky Mountain Saints* (London: Ward, Lock, and Tyler, 1878), 278.

3. Frank J. Cannon and George L. Knapp, *Brigham Young and His Mormon Empire* (New York: Fleming H. Revell Co., 1913), 202.

4. Fanny Stenhouse, *"Tell It All": The Story of a Life's Experience in Mormonism* (Hartford, Conn.: A. D. Worthington, 1874), 313.

5. Cannon and Knapp, *Brigham Young*, 203. A common misapprehension among observers of early Utah is that it was a place largely devoid of culture and its accoutrements, namely a ready access to literature. Such mythology fed much of the bigotry that afflicted Mormonism in the nineteenth century. Mormons and their leaders were supposedly profoundly illiterate and deluded. A reading of the sermons Grant delivered in the 1850s puts such notions quickly to rest, but so does a look at such documents as *Catalogue of the Utah Territorial Library, October 1852* (Great Salt Lake City: Brigham H. Young Printer, 1852), that

contain evidence of the ready availability in Utah Territory of the works Grant and other leaders talked about reading and studying.

6. John Hanson Beadle, *Polygamy: or, The Mysteries and Crimes of Mormonism* (Philadelphia: National Publishing Co., 1882), 140.

7. Cannon and Knapp, *Brigham Young*, 203.

8. Jedediah M. Grant, May 30, 1885, *Journal of Discourses*, 26 vols. (London and Liverpool: LDS Booksellers Depot, 1855–86), 3:7.

9. *Deseret News*, April 2, 1856, quoting Grant discourse.

10. Jedediah M. Grant, November 2, 1856, *Journal of Discourses*, 4:74.

11. Jedediah M. Grant, October 6, 1855, *Journal of Discourses*, 3:127.

12. Cannon and Knapp, *Brigham Young*, 203. For a standard and common scholarly assessment of Grant, see Norman Furniss, *The Mormon Conflict, 1850–1859* (New Haven, Conn.: Yale University Press, 1960), 17, 30, 81, 92–94, 128. The adjectives Furniss chose to describe Grant illustrate clearly the then-prevalent view of the second counselor's personality: "uncontrollable," "bombastic," "fearless," "brawling," "loose-tongued," "excitable," "fiery," "reckless," and "unrestrained." There is some evidence that this study, first published in 1982, has had a revisionist effect on that view. For example, Eugene E. Campbell, *Establishing Zion: The Mormon Church in the American West, 1847–1869* (Salt Lake City: Signature Books, 1988), 182–83, agrees with this work's more balanced analysis of Grant.

Family Afterword

No clear picture of the living arrangements among Grant's families emerged in the historical record, although it is apparent from letters that Susan and Rosetta usually lived together and later spent most of their time at the farm in West Bountiful. The others probably inhabited the house on the lot that became the site of ZCMI. In the 1970s, well-informed great-granddaughters Florence Smith Jacobsen (Rachel's descendant) and Bernice Casper (Susan's) knew of no family lore about how well the sister-wives got along; neither one had heard anything negative or at least would say anything negative. Part of the problem here is that Jeddy died so soon after becoming a many-wived husband, after which the wives mostly went their separate ways.

Three of the six widows (Susan, Rosetta, and Rachel) married Jedediah's brother George, then divorced him. Rosetta married again, but Susan and Rachel did not. Rachel's story as nineteenth-century Salt Lake City's most famous single mother became well known because of her prominent son Heber. Susan lived out her life in West Bountiful, caring for her three children (one by George) and many grandchildren and being a ward and stake Relief Society president. After Grant's death, Sarah Ann married the family's twenty-five-year-old farmhand John Snedaker and had seven more children. Maryette abandoned her son and left for California. Details of what happened to Louisa, who lived for another twenty years after Jeddy's death, are obscure.

Appendix A
Biographical Sketches

THE INFORMATION BELOW, THOUGH by no means exhaustive, will aid the reader in identifying persons who played a part in the Grant story. Some details on Church leaders came from D. Michael Quinn, *The Mormon Hierarchy: Origins of Power* (Salt Lake City: Signature Books, 1994), 533-613, and *The Mormon Hierarchy: Extensions of Power* (Salt Lake City: Signature Books, 1997), 641-725. Biographical facts came primarily from the following sources:

AJ   Andrew Jenson, *Latter-day Saints Biographical Encyclopedia*, 4 vols. (Salt Lake City: Deseret News, 1901-30).
AU   Diaries and autobiographies of the named individual.
DAB   Allen Johnson, ed., *Dictionary of American Biography*, 11 vols. (New York: Charles Scribner's Sons, 1964).
DN   Obituaries in the *Deseret News*.
EN   Encyclopedia entries on prominent national figures.
FE   Frank Esshom, *Pioneers and Prominent Men of Utah* (Salt Lake City: Utah Pioneers Book Publishing, 1913).
FHL   Materials in the Family History Department of the Church of Jesus Christ of Latter-day Saints, Salt Lake City.
JH   Journal History of the Church of Jesus Christ of Latter-day Saints. Chronological scrapbook of typed entries and newspaper clippings, 1830-present. LDS Church Archives.
OW   Orson F. Whitney, *History of Utah*, 4 vols. (Salt Lake City: George Q. Cannon and Sons, 1892-1904).

ABEL, ELIJAH (1810-84), a free black born in Maryland, joined the Church in 1831. He was ordained an elder in 1836 and a seventy in 1841. A close friend of Joseph Smith, he was an undertaker by profession in Nauvoo. In Utah he managed a hotel prior to a mission to Canada (1883–84), during which he fell victim to an illness from which he never recovered. He died two weeks after his return to Salt Lake City. (AJ)

ADAMS, GEORGE J. (1810–80), a member of the First Quorum of Seventy and an accomplished actor, was a close confidant of Joseph Smith. Although never a member of the Twelve, he was ordained an apostle in June 1844. Following the martyrdom of the Prophet, Adams was called to carry the news to Brigham Young in the East, but he refused the assignment. Consequently falling out of grace with the brethren, he eventually affiliated with the Strangite movement. (JH)

ALLRED, ISAAC (1788–1870), a native of Georgia, came to Utah in 1847 as a member of Brigham Young's advance party. Among Mormonism's early converts, he was always known as Father Allred. After living for a time with his son Reddick Newton Allred in Kaysville, he joined his brother James in Sanpete County, where he lived until his death. (FHL)

ALLRED, JAMES (1784–1876), a native of North Carolina, was a member of Zion's Camp, one of Joseph Smith's bodyguards, and a member of the Nauvoo City Council. He came to Utah in 1851 and was one of the first settlers of Sanpete County, becoming presiding elder at Spring City. (FHL)

ALLRED, REDDICK NEWTON (1811–1905), was born in Tennessee and was baptized with most of his father's family in 1833. He was subsequently a member of the Mormon Battalion and arrived in Utah in 1849. After a mission to Hawaii (1852–55) he settled in Kaysville, where he served in the bishopric for two years. He then moved to Sanpete County, becoming bishop of the Chester Ward (1867) and then patriarch (1898). A colonel in the Nauvoo Legion, he served a term in the penitentiary in 1888 for practicing polygamy. (AJ)

ANGELL, TRUMAN O. (1810–87), was the chief architect on the Salt Lake Temple and other important Utah structures. Born in Rhode Island, he was the brother of Mary Ann Angell Young, Brigham Young's second wife. (AJ)

BABBITT, ALMON W. (1813–56), a native of Massachusetts, was a member of Zion's Camp and served subsequently as president of the Kirtland Stake (1841–43). He was in and out of favor with the brethren until the martyrdom of the Prophet, after which he remained loyal to the Twelve. Coming to Utah in 1848, he traveled to Washington, D.C., to convey a memorial petitioning for statehood and returned to the valley with federal funds for the construction of territorial buildings. In 1853 he became secretary of the territory, in which position he remained until killed by Indians while returning from another trip to Washington. (AJ)

BECK, JAMES (b. 1812), a glazier in early Salt Lake City, left a meandering journal (1859-65) that provides some curious views of life in early Utah. (AU)

BEMAN, MARY. See NOBLE.

BENNETT, JAMES GORDON (1800-55), founder and proprietor of the *New York Herald*, immigrated to the United States via Nova Scotia in 1822. Becoming involved in journalism first as a columnist, Bennett established himself as a firm friend of the Democratic Party in New York and, by 1835, had issued the first number of the *New York Herald*, a paper that for many years was a premier journal of the American political scene. DAB

BENNETT, JOHN COOK (1804-67), was born in Massachusetts. A physician by trade, he became something of a soldier of fortune in the West before joining the Church in Nauvoo in 1840. Attracting the friendship and trust of Joseph Smith, he was presented to the Church in April 1841 as an assistant president in the First Presidency. After a stormy association of about a year, Bennett launched a harsh attack in on the Prophet and the Mormon religion, primarily over polygamy, and was excommunicated in 1842. He died in Polk City, Iowa, after spending the latter years of his life raising poultry. (Andrew F. Smith, *The Saintly Scoundrel: The Life and Times of Dr. John Cook Bennett* [Urbana: University of Illinois Press, 1997])

BENSON, EZRA T. (1811-69), was baptized in Illinois in 1840. He was ordained an apostle in 1846 after several missions in the East, then accompanied Brigham Young to the Salt Lake Valley in 1847. After more missions, he was called to preside in Cache Valley, where he served until his death. He also held various territorial posts including a seat in several terms of the legislature. (AJ)

BENT, SAMUEL (1778-1846), was a colonel in the Massachusetts militia prior to moving to New York, where he saw a copy of the Book of Mormon. Baptized in 1833, he was subsequently a member of Zion's Camp and a prominent figure in the Church during the Missouri and Nauvoo periods. He was a colonel in the Nauvoo Legion, a member of the high council, and senior member of the Council of Fifty when the Saints fled into Iowa. He was there called as presiding elder of the Garden Grove Branch and was serving as such at the time of his death. (AJ)

BENTON, THOMAS HART (1782-1858), served as U.S. Senator from Missouri for thirty years. A devoted follower of Andrew Jackson, he brought valuable western support to Jackson's party. His fight for gold and silver currency won him the nickname of "Old Bullion." Benton had little regard for the Mormons or their causes but gave Grant an audience in 1852. (DAB)

BERNHISEL, JOHN M. (1799-1881), born in Pennsylvania, presided over the New York branch after his baptism and then moved to Nauvoo in 1843. In 1851 he came to Utah, where he was subsequently elected territorial delegate to Congress. During his eight years in Washington, the Church came under severe attack several times, forcing him to use considerable diplomatic skill in attempting to preserve the rights of the people in Utah. A physician by profession, in 1859 he retired to Utah, where he lived out his life in relative obscurity. (AJ)

BIRD, CHARLES (1803-84), a native of New Jersey, was an early convert to Mormonism. During the late 1830s he served a mission to the southern states, where he worked for a time with Grant. In Nauvoo he served as a bodyguard to the Prophet. Bird came to Utah in 1850, settling first at Cottonwood and then in Cache Valley. He farmed and operated a clothing business at Mendon until his death. (FE)

BOGGS, LILBURN W. (1792-1860), came to Missouri from the East in 1816. From a career as a merchant and storekeeper at St. Louis, he entered politics and was elected governor of the state in 1836, in time to preside over the removal of the Mormons. A prime villain in Mormon history, Boggs issued the infamous "extermination order" only recently rescinded in the Missouri legislature. In 1846 Boggs went to California, where he served for a time as an alcalde prior to the establishment of the state government in 1850. (DAB)

BOYLE, HENRY G. (1824-1908), joined the Church in Virginia in 1843. Following service in the Mormon Battalion, Boyle arrived in Utah in 1847. He served seven missions to the southern states and was president of the mission from 1875 to 1878. (AJ)

BOYNTON, JOHN FARNHAM (1811-90), converted Grant to the Church in 1833. Born in Massachusetts, he was among the first members of the Mormon movement and was called as an apostle in 1835. He was excommunicated two years later for apostasy. (AJ)

BRANNAN, SAMUEL (1819-89), born in Maine, became a Mormon in 1833 and served a lengthy mission in the eastern states where he published a Church newspaper called the *Messenger* in New York in the 1840s. He also led a party of Saints by sea to California departing in 1846 on the ship *Brooklyn*. The following year, he tried unsuccessfully to convince Brigham Young to move the main body of the Saints to the coast. He then returned to California, where he played a prominent role in early San Francisco history. After making and losing a fortune, mostly through land speculation, he died a pauper in San Diego. (AJ)

BROWNING, JAMES GREENE (1808-78), a native of Tennessee, came to Utah in 1850. He was the second bishop called in Weber County, where he also sat on the Ogden City Council and served several terms in the legislature. Browning also served a brief mission to England in the 1860s. (FE)

BULLOCK, THOMAS (1816-85), joined the Mormons in England in 1841 and came to America two years later. Skilled as a clerk, he held numerous important Church and civic positions in Nauvoo and Salt Lake City, serving as clerk of the 1847 pioneer company and of the territorial house of representatives, as Salt

Lake County recorder, and as chief clerk of the Church Historian's Office. (AJ)

BUTTERFIELD, JOSIAH (1795-1871), born in Maine, was one of the early converts to Mormonism. He was ordained a seventy and set apart as one of its first seven presidents in 1837 (First Council of the Seventy). Following his excommunication in 1844 for apostacy, Butterfield was rebaptized in 1845, came to Utah, but then moved to California, where he affiliated with the RLDS movement. Grant took his place on the First Council of Seventy. (AJ)

CAHOON, REYNOLDS (1790-1861), a native of New York and a veteran of the War of 1812, was among the earliest settlers of northern Ohio where he was baptized in 1830. Associated with the building of the temples in Kirtland and Nauvoo, he reached Utah in 1848 and worked on the building committee of the Salt Lake Temple. Cahoon was living in the South Cottonwood Ward at the time of his death. From the beginnings of Mormonism, he was close to its prominent leaders and served on various important councils of Church governance. (DN)

CAMPBELL, ALEXANDER (1786-1868), came to the United States from Great Britain in 1800 and settled in Washington, D.C. After spending time in the Presbyterian and Baptist churches, Campbell formed his own sect with some 100,000 adherents known as Campbellites or Disciples of Christ. A primitivist, Campbell converted many men and women who would subsequently unite with the Mormons, among them Sidney Rigdon and Orson Hyde. (DAB)

CANDLAND, DAVID (1819-1901), an early British convert, settled at Fillmore, Utah, shortly after its founding. His inn there, the Astor House, prospered until the seat of territorial government moved to Salt Lake City in 1856. Candland later settled in Sanpete County, where he was residing at the time of his death. (FE)

CANNON, FRANK J. (1859-1933), a son of George Q. Cannon, became an outspoken apostate. A journalist, Cannon worked on several newspapers in Utah and California before entering politics in 1892. He was elected to Congress from Utah in 1894 and then to the Senate in 1896 but was defeated for reelection in 1899 after switching political parties during the silver controversy. After a term as state Democratic Party chairman, Cannon returned to his writing career, gaining some national notoriety for his anti-Mormon polemics aimed primarily at the interference of Church leadership in politics. (OW)

CARRINGTON, ALBERT (1813-89), a native of Vermont and a graduate of Dartmouth, taught school and studied law prior to his conversion to Mormonism in 1841. In addition to serving as Brigham Young's secretary for two decades, he edited the *Deseret News* and presided over the European Mission on four occasions. He was ordained an apostle in 1870 and served briefly in the First Presidency under Brigham Young. He was excommunicated in 1885, but was rebaptized shortly before his death. (AJ)

CLAPP, BENJAMIN L. (1814-65), a native of Alabama, became a seventy in 1844 and one of the first seven presidents (First Council of the Seventy) a year later along with Grant. Coming to Utah among the first emigrants, he was excommunicated in 1859 after which he moved to California. (AJ)

CLARK, JOHN B. (1801-61), a Missouri lawyer, served as commander of a mounted regiment in Black Hawk War (fought in 1832 in Illinois and Michigan Territory) and was afterward a major general of militia. As a member of the state legislature in the 1830s and as a militia leader, Clark played a leading role in the expulsion of the Mormons from Missouri. (DAB)

CLAWSON, HIRAM B. (1816-1912), was born in New York, where he accepted Mormonism and moved to Nauvoo in 1841. After coming to Utah, he managed Brigham Young's office and business affairs. He was instrumental in the organization and construction of the Salt Lake Theatre and acted on its stage. Manager of Zion's Cooperative Mercantile Institution, he also served as bishop of the Salt Lake City Twelfth Ward and as financial agent of the Church. (AJ)

CLAYTON, WILLIAM (1814-79), was among the first converts to Mormonism in England in 1837. After serving a mission in his native land, he immigrated in 1840 to Nauvoo, where he became a clerk to Joseph Smith. Clayton was accomplished in music, composing for the Camp of Israel the classic hymn "Come, Come Ye Saints." He also designed the "roadometer," which calculated the distance traveled on the trek to Utah. (AJ)

CLEMENTS, GILBERT, a noted orator in early Utah, was among the home missionaries who with Grant fomented the Reformation of 1856-57. He was later a member of the Board of Regents of the University of Deseret, and served for some time as a member of the Salt Lake Stake high council. (DN)

CLEMENTS, JOHN MOON (1813-97), came from England to the United States around 1850. He converted to Mormonism in 1851 in New Orleans and immediately emigrated to Utah, where he eventually settled in Utah Valley. There he served for a time on the Spanish Fork City Council. (AU)

COLTRIN, ZEBEDEE (1804-87), born in New York, became one of the original members of the First Council of Seventy in 1835, but was released in 1837, having previously been ordained a high priest. He emigrated subsequently to Utah, where he settled eventually at Spanish Fork. (AJ)

COOK, PHINEAS W. (1819-1900), a native of Connecticut, was baptized in 1845 and came to Utah five years later. He was a well-known carpenter and cabinetmaker in early Utah, and built much of the early furniture produced in the territory. Cook built the farmhouse in Davis County that remained in the Grant family for several decades and still stands in West Bountiful. Later moving to Utah County, he founded the community of Goshen and was its bishop for three years prior to a colonizing mission to Bear Lake in 1863. At the time of his death, Cook was living in Afton, Wyoming. (AJ)

CORAY, HOWARD K. (1841-1928), born in Iowa, was one of the first missionaries to the southern states following the Civil War, serving in Virginia and the Carolinas from 1867 to 1869. He was later a bishop's counselor in Salt Lake City. (FE)

COWDERY, OLIVER (1806-50), one of the three witnesses to the Book of Mormon, was "Second Elder" in the Church and associate president with Joseph Smith. After several and prolonged disagreements with Smith, Cowdery was excommunicated in 1838 but rejoined the Church ten years later. Just prior to his death in 1850, he visited David Whitmer in Missouri and restated his testimony of the Book of Mormon. (AJ)

COWDERY, WARREN A. (1788-1851), a brother to Oliver, was for some time the presiding elder at Freedom, New York. He served as scribe at the dedication of the Kirtland Temple and for a short time as editor of the *Messenger and Advocate*. Following the Kirtland period, he dropped out of the Church, remaining in the East until his death. (JH)

COWLEY, MATTHIAS (1819-64) was born on the Isle of Man and joined the Mormons in 1843. Between missions to Great Britain, he lived in Salt Lake City. His son Matthias Foss Cowley and grandson Matthew subsequently served as apostles of the Church. (FHL)

CURTIS, DORR P. (1819-1904), was born in New York, where he was baptized in 1841. Following service in the Mormon Battalion, he arrived in Utah in 1847, married, and settled in Kaysville. He went on a mission to England (1851-54) and was then called as a counselor in the Kaysville Ward bishopric. A colonel in the Nauvoo Legion, Curtis also lived in Springville, Utah, and Oakley, Idaho. (AJ)

CUTLER, ALPHEUS (1784-1864), an early 1830s convert to Mormonism, played an important role in Nauvoo after the martyrdom, as a member of the high council and during the exodus into Iowa, where he later led a splinter movement away from the Saints moving to the Rockies. Excommunicated in 1851, he died in Fremont County, Iowa, after founding a church with headquarters in Minnesota. (JH)

DECKER, CLARA. See YOUNG.

DILWORTH, REBECCA WOLLERTON. See RITER.

DONIPHAN, ALEXANDER W. (1808-87), a native of Kentucky, came to Lexington, Missouri, in 1830 and subsequently moved to Liberty, where during the Mormon troubles of 1838 he served as commander of a brigade of the state militia. His refusal to execute Joseph Smith and other Mormon leaders made him something of a hero among the Saints. Following service in the Mexican War, Doniphan was widely discussed as a possible governor of Utah Territory to succeed Brigham Young. (DAB)

DOUGLAS, STEPHEN A. (1813-61), rose rapidly in Illinois politics after arriving there from New York at the age of twenty. After two terms in the House of Representatives, he was elected to the Senate in 1847 and served there until his death. Douglas saw himself as a great compromiser during the uneasy period of national politics prior to the Civil War, and was defeated by Abraham Lincoln for the presidency in 1860. He was perhaps the most influential man in Illinois public life during the Nauvoo period of Mormonism, particularly during his term on the state supreme court. (EN)

EDWARDS, JONATHAN (1703-58), initiated a religious revival in New England known as the Great Awakening. A graduate of Yale, he was pastor of the Congregational Church at Northampton, Massachusetts, where he attacked the secularization and liberalization of New England society. Eventually dismissed in controversy from Northampton, he moved to Stockbridge, where he wrote his most important treatises. Just prior to his death, he was appointed president of Princeton College, but died before taking office. (EN)

EGAN, HOWARD (1815-78), born in Ireland, immigrated to Canada with his family and there converted to Mormonism in 1842. He then moved to Nauvoo, where he was a member of the police force and a major in the Nauvoo Legion. Subsequently a member of the original 1847 pioneers, he was then an agent for the Pony Express and the overland mail and also served as a missionary and intermediary among the Indians. His greatest notoriety came when he shot and killed James Monroe in 1851 for seducing Egan's wife while he was absent on business. He was exonerated in a jury trial. (AJ)

ELDREDGE, HORACE S. (1816-88), was born in New York and joined the Church in 1836. In 1848 he came to Utah, where he served as marshal, assessor and collector of taxes, and brigadier general in the militia. In 1852 he became general Church immigration agent and, in 1854, a member of the First Council of Seventy. Regarded as one of Utah's ablest businessmen, he helped establish Zion's Cooperative Mercantile Institution and became one of its directors. He also became involved in banking, serving on the boards of two large financial institutions in Utah. (AJ)

ELLISON, JOHN (1818-1903), was one of the original settlers of Kaysville, Utah. Born in England, he came to Utah in 1852 and arrived in the Kaysville area a year later. He served there at various times as a high councilman, Davis County selectman, and stake patriarch. (AJ)

ELLSWORTH, EDMUND (1819-93), a native of New York, became a Mormon in 1840. He was a member of the original band of pioneers in 1847 and was also a son-in-law of Brigham Young. Following a mission to England (1854-56), Ellsworth led a handcart company across the plains. He later moved to

Arizona, where he died. (AJ)

EVANS, DAVID (1804-83), was born in Maryland and joined the Church in 1833 in Ohio. A member of Zion's Camp, he was subsequently a survivor of the Haun's Mill Massacre of 1838 and later served as a bishop in Nauvoo. In 1850 he came to Utah, where he settled in Lehi and was appointed bishop. In addition to holding the rank of colonel in the Nauvoo Legion, he was mayor of Lehi for several years and also served several terms in the legislature. (AJ)

FILLMORE, MILLARD (1800-74), was admitted to the New York bar in 1823. A protégé of Thurlow Weed, he became a member of the Whig party while serving in Congress in 1834. After a fruitless attempt to capture the governorship of New York, Fillmore ran for vice president on the successful Whig ticket in 1848. Acceding to the presidency upon the death of Zachary Taylor in 1850, Fillmore signed Utah's territorial act and appointed Brigham Young governor. For this support, the Mormons named their erstwhile capital for him—Fillmore, located in Millard County in central Utah. (EN)

FOOTE, WARREN (1817-1903), came into contact with Mormonism in his native state of New York in 1830 but did not join the Church until 1842. After four years in Kanesville, he came in 1850 to Utah, where he settled in the South Cottonwood Ward. He was a major in the Nauvoo Legion and postmaster in Union before colonizing in Dixie in 1864. Foote became a patriarch in 1889 after holding several high-level positions in the stakes and wards of southern Utah. (AJ)

FORD, THOMAS (1800-1850), lawyer, jurist, and Democratic governor of Illinois from 1842 to 1846, gained his place in Illinois history when he saved the state's credit by avoiding debt repudiation. He also earned the lasting damnation of the Mormons for his apparent betrayal of Joseph Smith in 1844 during mob action in Carthage leading to the Prophet's death. Ford wrote a careful memoir of his role in the removal of the Mormons from the state that he included in his *History of Illinois*. It would appear in retrospect that Mormon writers have greatly exaggerated Ford's villainy in the affair. (DAB)

FORDHAM, ELIJAH (1789-1879), was born in New York City and was an early convert to Mormonism. He assisted in the construction of the temples at Kirtland and Nauvoo, in addition to service in the Nauvoo Legion. In 1850 Fordham came to Utah, where he lived in Salt Lake City and then in Cache Valley. (AJ)

FULLMER, DAVID (1803-79), was born in Pennsylvania and joined the Church in Ohio in 1836. He was a member of the Nauvoo High Council and subsequently served as first counselor to Salt Lake Stake president Daniel Spencer. Fullmer also filled various civil offices in Utah, including being elected for several terms to the legislature. (AJ)

GARN, DANIEL (1802-71), filled a mission to Germany from 1852 to

1854. A native of Pennsylvania, he served for two years as bishop pro tem of the Salt Lake City Ninth Ward. (AJ)

GIBBS, GIDEON H. (1821-1901), a native of Vermont, was an early proselyte of Mormonism. After service as a bodyguard to Joseph Smith, he came to Utah in 1847, settled in Salt Lake City, and lived there until his death. He was a member of the Nauvoo Legion and participated in the rescue of the handcart emigrants in 1856. (DN)

GIBSON, WILLIAM (1809-75), was baptized in Scotland in 1840. After several years of Church work in his homeland he came to Utah, where he was a wood and iron turner. Devoted to the spreading of the gospel, Gibson had served several missions by the time of his death in Salt Lake Twentieth Ward. (DN)

GLOVER, WILLIAM (1831-91), came to Utah by way of Samuel Brannan's *Brooklyn* voyage to California. He arrived in Salt Lake City in September 1849. (AU)

GOULAY, LOUISA MARIA. See GRANT.

GRANT, ATHALIA HOWARD (1786-1853), Jedediah's mother, was born in Connecticut and married Joshua Grant in New York at the age of eighteen. She bore three daughters and nine sons, all of whom survived to adulthood. She died at Altona, Illinois, at the age of sixty-seven. (FHL)

GRANT, AUSTIN (1808-95), was the third oldest among Jedediah's eleven siblings. Born in Windsor, New York, Austin was baptized by Jedediah in 1836 during the latter's second mission to New York. He came to Utah in 1848 but later returned to Illinois, where he died. (FHL)

GRANT, BRIGHAM FREDERICK (1856-1936), was born a month and a half before the death of his father, Jedediah, to Maryette Kesler Grant, whom Jedediah had married in 1854. Abandoned by his mother as a child, he grew up out of Mormonism, but was finally baptized at the age of forty after traveling through the West as a miner and cowboy. He was later a member of the Salt Lake Stake High Council, a Young Men's Mutual Improvement Association missionary, and father of a large family. Involved in mining, insurance, and merchandizing, B. F. also served a term as Salt Lake City chief of police and at different times managed the LDS Hospital and the *Deseret News*. (DN)

GRANT, CAROLINE (1844-63), was born in Philadelphia during Jedediah's sojourn there as presiding elder. After the death of her mother when she was two years old, she was raised by Susan Noble Grant. Always known as Caddie, she died at the age of eighteen in West Bountiful. (FHL)

GRANT, CAROLINE AMANDA. See SMITH.

GRANT, CAROLINE ANN VAN DYKE (1818-47), born in New York, married Jedediah shortly after the martyrdom in 1844. She went with him to Philadelphia that year and then across the plains in 1847. She was ill before leaving the Missouri and died after a bout of cholera at the Bear River. She bore two daughters, one of whom preceded her in death by a few weeks. (FHL)

GRANT, GEORGE D. (1812-76), Jedediah's older brother, was a member of the advance party of pioneers in 1847. He settled in the Bountiful area of Davis County, where he lived until his death. Following his brother's death in 1856, George married three of Jedediah's widows, Susan, Rosetta, and Rachel. All subsequently divorced him, although Susan had a son by him named Franklin. (FHL)

GRANT, GEORGE SMITH (1855-85), one of Jedediah's six biological sons, never enjoyed good health and consequently lived in relative obscurity. (DN)

GRANT, HEBER JEDDY (1856-1945), was born to Jedediah and Rachel nine days before the second counselor's death. An early success in business, he became president of the Tooele Stake at the age of twenty-four and an apostle in 1882. He acceded to the presidency of the Church in 1918 and presided over Mormonism through nearly three decades of change in both the Church and the world. The emphasis of his administration was upon financial stability. Like his father, he was also concerned about the Saints keeping the Word of Wisdom. (DN)

GRANT, HOWARD (1817-59), born in New York, was Jedediah's youngest brother. He was baptized at the age of eight in Kirtland. After passing through the persecutions, he remained in Illinois until his death at the age of thirty-two. (FHL)

GRANT, JEDEDIAH MORGAN, JR. (1853-1933), known as Morgan, was the first child of Jedediah by Rosetta Robison. He married in 1876 and moved from Bountiful to Rich County, where he lived for two decades, after which he pioneered in the Big Horn Basin of Wyoming. There he held numerous Church positions including that of patriarch. He retired to Salt Lake City in 1925. (DN)

GRANT, JOSEPH (1805-98), the oldest of Jedediah's siblings, was born in Neversink, New York. He may have been baptized during one of Jedediah's first missions into New York, but he was never afterwards connected with the Church. (FHL)

GRANT, JOSEPH HYRUM (1853-1917), was a son of Jedediah Grant and Susan Noble Grant. He grew up in Davis County, where he farmed and raised stock on the original Grant estate. Following a term as bishop of the West Bountiful Ward (1885-90), he served for fourteen years as a counselor in the Davis Stake presidency before being called as its president in 1904. With his wife Eliza Evaeletta Eldredge, he left a large posterity, having fathered ten children. (AJ)

GRANT, JOSEPH HYRUM, JR. (1876-1929), a grandson of Jedediah, was a dentist by profession. He served a mission to Colorado (1897-99) and was bishop of the Salt Lake City Thirty-third Ward (1926–28). (AJ)

GRANT, JOSHUA (1778–1865), born in Stonington, Connecticut, joined the Mormons early in 1833 with most of his large family, including his son, Jedediah. He moved from Pennsylvania to Kirtland, and subsequently to western Missouri with the body of the Saints. He eventually settled in Altona, Illinois, about sixty miles northeast of Nauvoo. Joshua and his wife never came to Utah and possibly associated with the Reorganized Church through the influence of their son-in-law William Smith, who was married at different times to two of their daughters. (FHL)

GRANT, JOSHUA, JR. (1818–51), Jedediah's just-younger brother, was born in Naples, New York. Baptized in 1833, he became one of the youngest seventies in the Church in 1835. He served numerous missions, often traveling with his brother. He came to Utah in 1847, settling first in Vevey and then in Salt Lake City, where he died unexpectedly at the age of thirty-three. (DN)

GRANT, JOSHUA FREDERICK (1856–1907), son of Jedediah M. Grant and Louisa Goulay Grant, was a merchant in Frisco, Utah, when he became a founder of the Consolidated Wagon and Machine Company in Salt Lake City. He then became manager in Utah of the American Steel and Wire Company. He was buried in Salt Lake City after funeral ceremonies conducted by the Wasatch Masonic Lodge, of which he was a member. (DN)

GRANT, LEWIS MCKEACHIE (1839–1902), was born John McKeachie in Scotland, where he was baptized as a youngster. He was orphaned in 1850 in St. Louis while en route to Utah with his father. Jedediah brought him into the valley and adopted him into the Susan Noble Grant family. Managing the Grant estate in Bountiful, Lewis became a prominent citizen in Davis County, serving as justice of the peace, county selectman, and city judge. After a term as a member of the West Bountiful Ward bishopric, he was called as the bishop and served in that position until his death. He also served a mission to Europe (1868–70). (DN)

GRANT, LOIS. See WELCH.

GRANT, LOUISA MARIE GOULAY (1826–76), born in Indiana, married Jedediah's younger brother Joshua in 1843 and subsequently bore him two daughters. Following Joshua's death, she married Jedediah, by whom she had one son, Joshua Frederick, born in April 1856. She spent the remaining years of her life in relative obscurity. (DN)

GRANT, MARGARET (1847), Jedediah's second daughter by Caroline Van Dyke, was born in Winter Quarters while her father was on his mission to the East. She caught cholera during the trek across the plains and died on September 2 at the age of four months. Jedediah returned for her body later that fall but discovered that wolves had raided her grave. (FHL)

GRANT, MARYETTE KESLER (1839–ca. 1890), born in Des Moines

County, Iowa, was the daughter of Jedediah's longtime friend from Pennsylvania, Frederick Kesler. She married Grant in 1854. Following his death, she left her son B. F. with friends in northern Utah and went to California, where she died in obscurity. (FHL)

GRANT, NELSON (1819-99), the fourth Grant sibling, was baptized by Jedediah in 1836 during the latter's second mission into New York. Nelson later moved to Illinois, where he had settled near Quincy prior to the exodus of the Saints from Missouri. He did not come to Utah and was, in his later years, affiliated with the Reorganized Church. (FHL)

GRANT, RACHEL RIDGEWAY IVINS (1811-1909), joined the Church in her native state of New Jersey along with several members of her family. After living in Nauvoo for several years, she returned to New Jersey, eventually coming to Utah in 1853. In 1855 she married Jedediah, a longtime family friend, although she was at the same time sealed to the Prophet Joseph. She bore one son, Heber Jeddy, prior to Jedediah's death. She married George D. Grant and then divorced him, leaving her single again with the responsibility for a small son. For thirty-five years, she was president of the Thirteenth Ward Relief Society and was one of Utah's most influential women. Suffering in her later years from deafness, she died of pneumonia at the home of a granddaughter in Salt Lake City. (AJ)

GRANT, ROSETTA HENRIETTA. See MARSHALL.

GRANT, ROSETTA ROBISON (1833-73), was born in Onandaga County, New York. At the age of sixteen, she became a plural wife of Jedediah, subsequently bearing him a son and a daughter. Following his death, she married George D. Grant, divorced him, then married Horace Sunderlin. Three years later she died in Salt Lake City. (FHL)

GRANT, Rocxy ANN. See SMITH.

GRANT, SARAH ANN THURSTON (1835-1909), came to Utah at the age of twelve in Jedediah's company and married him six years later. She bore him a son, George Smith Grant, in 1855. After Jedediah's death, she married John F. Snedaker and had seven more children. (FHL)

GRANT, SUSAN FAIRCHILD NOBLE (1831-1914), was born in New York to Eunice Noble and Charles Fairchild Noble, but was adopted as a child by her grandparents, Ezekiel Noble and Theodocia Bates Noble. She joined the Church as a youngster and came to Utah with her uncle Joseph Bates Noble in Jedediah's company in 1847. After marrying Jedediah in 1849, she bore him two children in addition to raising his daughter Caroline by his first marriage and an adopted son, John McKeachie (renamed Lewis McKeachie Grant). Following Jedediah's death, she married his brother, George D. Grant, and bore him a son named Franklin Davis Grant. They were later divorced. Susan lived out her life in West Bountiful, where she was president of the ward Relief Society (1878-85) and then stake Relief Society president (1886-92), after which she was called to the general board. (FHL)

GRANT, SUSAN VILATE. See MUIR.

GRANT, THEDA. See REEVES.

GRANT, THOMAS JEFFERSON (1823-99), was ten years old when his family joined the Mormons in Pennsylvania. The tenth child in the family of Joshua and Athalia Grant, Thomas was baptized as a child but was not associated with the Church in his later years. (FHL)

GREELEY, HORACE (1811-71), a New England journalist, founded the *New York Tribune* in 1841. He used the *Tribune* over the next several years to spread his social philosophy, including abolitionism, temperance, women's rights, and Fourierism. He was among the founders of the Republican Party, but later led a defection and ran poorly as the Liberal Republican candidate for president in 1872 against Ulysses S. Grant. (EN)

GREENE, EVAN M. (1814-82), a nephew of Brigham Young, was born in New York and joined the Church in 1832. He did extensive missionary work through the eastern states during the Kirtland and Nauvoo periods and came to Utah in 1852. Settling initially in Provo, he taught school, kept the post office, served in the legislature, and compiled a book of territorial laws. He was also a high councilor and patriarch. Greene later colonized in Sevier County, where he died. (FE)

GREENE, JOHN P. (1793-1844), a brother-in-law of Brigham Young, was baptized in New York in 1832 after a career as a Methodist preacher. He served several missions in the States and in Canada prior to his appointment as Nauvoo city marshal. Greene led the force that destroyed the *Nauvoo Expositor*, an act that led directly to the arrest and murder of Joseph and Hyrum Smith. Following the martyrdom, he was in the official Church delegation that visited Emma Smith to offer condolences. He died in Nauvoo a short time later. (AJ)

GROVER, THOMAS (1807-86), a former steamboat captain from New York, attached himself to the Mormons in 1834 and subsequently became a bodyguard to the Prophet. He accompanied Charles C. Rich to Utah in 1847, but later returned to Iowa with his family in 1850 to buy cattle. He remained there until 1853, when he again came to Utah, settling at Farmington. Grover served three terms in the legislature and was a probate judge in Davis County. (AJ)

HAIGHT, ISAAC C. (1813-86), a native of New York, was baptized in 1839. He was for many years a presiding officer in Cedar City, where he was involved in ordering the infamous Mountain Meadows Massacre in 1857. Later moving to the Mormon settlements in Arizona, he died in Thatcher. (FHL)

HALE, EMMA. See SMITH.

HALES, STEPHEN (1810-81), joined the Church in Canada in the early

1830s and moved to Missouri, then Nauvoo. After working on the Nauvoo Temple, he came to Utah in 1851. He was employed on the construction of the Salt Lake Temple as a stonecutter and later served a mission to England (1864–65). (DN)

HANCOCK, LEVI WARD (1803–81), originally from Massachusetts, was an early convert to Mormonism. He was ordained a seventy and set apart as one of the first seven presidents (First Council of the Seventy) in 1835. Released two years later because it was thought that he had been previously ordained a high priest, he was restored to his former place in the First Council when it was determined that he was not a high priest. He was a member of the Mormon Battalion and spent the latter years of his life in southern Utah. (AJ)

HANKS, EPHRAIM K. (1817–96), an Ohio veteran of the U.S. Navy, joined the Mormons in 1845. After service in the Mormon Battalion, he arrived in 1847 in Utah, where he hired out to carry mail over the plains. Following service in the Utah War, Hanks became something of a permanent Indian fighter and frontiersman among the Saints, operating a trading post in Parley's Canyon. He eventually settled in Grass Valley in southern Utah. (AJ)

HARDY, LEONARD WILFORD (1805–84), born in Massachusetts, became first counselor to Presiding Bishop Edward Hunter in 1856. He was baptized in 1832, served a mission to England in the 1840s, and came to Utah in 1850. A close associate of Grant, Bishop Hardy spent several days beside the second counselor's deathbed and was with him at his death. (AJ)

HARRIMAN, HENRY (1804–91), was born in Essex County, Massachusetts. He was one of the original seventies chosen in February 1835. Set apart as a member of the First Council of Seventy in 1838, he came to Utah in an early emigration and eventually settled in southern Utah. (AJ)

HARRINGTON, LEONARD E. (1816–83), was born in New York. After joining the Church and moving to Nauvoo, he became a justice of the peace and a close associate of several Church leaders. Arriving in Utah in 1847, he subsequently settled in American Fork, where for three decades he served as bishop, mayor, and postmaster. (AJ)

HARRIS, GEORGE W. (1780–1860), baptized in Indiana in 1833, became a member of the high council at Far West in 1838 and assumed the same position in Nauvoo the following year. Between missions to the East during the Nauvoo period, he also served as city alderman and justice, and acted for some time as president of the Nauvoo City Council. Later an influential leader in Mormon settlements on the Missouri, he was president of the Kanesville high council in 1849, when Oliver Cowdery was received back into the Church. Harris was excommunicated in 1860 for refusing an order to come to Utah. (JH)

HENDERSON, SAMUEL G. (1820–1904), born in Missouri, joined the

Church in 1838. After coming to Utah, he lived first in Davis County and was in Kaysville during the first meetings of the Reformation in September 1856. He later lived in Brigham City, Cache Valley, and Star Valley, Wyoming, where he died. (FHL)

HESS, JOHN W. (1824–1903), born in Pennsylvania, became a Mormon in 1834, after which he moved with his family to Missouri. Ordained a seventy in 1841 in Nauvoo, he served in the Nauvoo Legion and then in the Mormon Battalion. He reached the Salt Lake Valley in 1847 and was called as bishop of the Farmington Ward in 1855. He served in that position until 1882, when he became a counselor in the Davis Stake presidency, then in 1894 the stake president. (AJ)

HEYWOOD, JOSEPH L. (1815–1910), a native of Massachusetts, joined the Church in 1842 after moving to Quincy, Illinois, and hearing Joseph Smith preach. In 1848 he came to Utah, where he became the first bishop of the Seventeenth Ward in Salt Lake City (1849). In the fall of 1849, he and Edwin D. Woolley went east on a procurement mission and met Grant in St. Louis in the spring of 1850. In 1855 Heywood accompanied Orson Hyde on a colonization mission to the Carson Valley, after which he was appointed U.S. marshal for Utah. He was later a colonizer in Dixie. (AJ)

HIGBEE, ELIAS (1795–1843), moved from New Jersey to Ohio as a child. In 1831 he joined the Mormons and moved to Missouri the following year. He became Church historian with John Corrill in 1838 and was serving on the Nauvoo Temple committee at the time of his death. (AJ)

HOWARD, ATHALIA. See GRANT.

HUNT, DANIEL D. (1797–1866), of North Carolina, was converted to Mormonism in 1841. He was one of the home missionaries accompanying Grant on his September 1856 swing through Davis County. Hunt eventually settled at Bear Lake, where he died in St. Charles, Idaho. (FHL)

HUNTER, EDWARD, JR. (1793–1883), a native of Pennsylvania, joined the Church in 1840 and moved to Nauvoo. There he became a bishop, a university regent and a member of the City Council. Coming to Utah in 1847, he became Presiding Bishop in 1851 and served in that position until his death. (AJ)

HURT, GARLAND, came to Utah as Indian agent in 1855. A physician and native of Kentucky, Hurt became suspicious of Mormon missionary activities among the Indians and sent protests about them to his superiors, an act that may have helped to precipitate the Utah War. He escaped to Fort Bridger in October 1857 where he reported on the Mountain Meadows Massacre to the approaching Utah Expedition and then returned to the States with the U.S. Army in 1858. (DN)

HYDE, ORSON (1805–78), was a Campbellite pastor who converted to Mormonism in 1830. He became one of the first apostles of the Church in 1835 and traveled extensively as a missionary. Dropped from the Quorum for a time in 1839, he lost the seniority that would ultimately have made him head of the Church in place of John Taylor. He spent most of his Utah years in Sanpete County and was known for his forceful oratory. (AJ)

IVINS, ISRAEL (1815-97), a native of New Jersey, was Grant's brother-in-law and close friend who came to Utah in 1853. Ivins lived in northern Utah until 1861, when he moved to Utah's Dixie, where he surveyed the city of St. George and subsequently practiced medicine. His son Anthony W. Ivins became an apostle and then counselor in the First Presidency to his cousin Heber J. Grant. (DN)

IVINS, RACHEL RIDGEWAY. See GRANT.

JACKSON, ANDREW (1767-1845), seventh president of the United States, became the symbol of an age during which Mormonism and "Americanism" grew as unlikely bedfellows. Noted for his bumptious personality and charismatic strength, Jackson expanded the powers of the presidency radically during eight years in the White House (1829-37). Mormon leaders tended to admire Jackson for his forthright policies and for his adherence to ideals of social and cultural freedom. There is little evidence to suggest, however, that Jackson looked with much favor upon Mormonism. (EN)

JACKSON, JOSEPH H. (b. 1810), visited Nauvoo in 1842, after which he became an anti-Mormon activist. In 1844 he published a pamphlet in which he railed against Joseph Smith. He alleged numerous Mormon crimes, including several perhaps paranoid notions about his own peril at the murderous hands of the Saints. (AU)

JOHNSON, AARON (1806-77), was an early Connecticut convert to the Church. He served on the high council at Nauvoo, participating in the trial of Sidney Rigdon in 1844. Arriving in Utah in 1850, he was among the founders of Springville and served as its first bishop. (AJ)

JOHNSON, JOSEPH W. (d. 1887), came to Utah in 1848. During the 1856 home mission operation, Johnson played a significant role, particularly in Centerville. (JH)

JOHNSTON, ALBERT SIDNEY (1803-61), a graduate of West Point, served as commander of the 1857 Utah Expedition against the Mormons as a brevet brigadier general. Remaining in Utah until just before the onset of the Civil War, he was afterward among the highest-ranking generals in the Confederate Army. He suffered fatal wounds at Shiloh following a series of military reverses. (DAB)

JORDAN, JOHN (b. 1812), joined the Church in England and came to Utah in 1851. He lived in Salt Lake City until 1859, then resettled in Heber City. A veteran militiaman, he took part in the Utah, Walker, and Black Hawk wars. (FE)

KANE, THOMAS L. (1811-83), the son of a prominent Philadelphia judge, befriended the Mormons in 1846 as they were being driven from Illinois. He assisted in the arrangements for the recruitment of the Mormon Battalion and visited the Saints on the Missouri River. Becoming a close friend to Grant, he and Grant worked together in 1851-52 to dampen the allegations of the "runaway judges." Kane was subsequently instrumental in the negotiations that ended the Utah War in 1858. He became a general in the Union Army during the Civil War and served gallantly until illness forced his resignation in 1863. He later visited Utah with his wife, Elizabeth, and two sons (1872-73). (EN)

KESLER, FREDERICK (1816-99), a close associate of Grant, was born in Pennsylvania. An accomplished mill builder, he joined the Church in 1840 after meeting the Prophet in Illinois. After a mission to the eastern states and the exodus from Nauvoo, Kesler built a flour mill at Winter Quarters. He remained there until 1851, when he came to Utah, building numerous mills around the territory. Ordained bishop of the Salt Lake Sixteenth Ward in 1856, he served in that capacity for forty-three years. Grant married his daughter Maryette in 1854. (AJ)

KESLER, MARYETTE. See GRANT.

KIMBALL, DAVID PATTEN (1839-83), born to Heber and Vilate Kimball shortly after the Mormon exodus from Missouri, came to Utah in 1848 at the age of nine. In 1856 he became something of a hero after participating in the rescue of the Martin handcart company on the Sweetwater River. He later served a mission to England, colonized in the Bear Lake Valley and the Salt River Valley (Star Valley), and then in the Salt River Valley of Arizona. At the time of his death, he was a member of the St. Joseph Stake presidency. (AJ)

KIMBALL, HEBER CHASE (1801-68), born in Vermont, joined the Church in 1831. A member of Zion's Camp and one of the first missionaries to England, Heber was called to the Quorum of the Twelve in 1835 as one of its original members. He was first counselor to Brigham Young from 1848 until his death in 1868. (AJ)

KIMBALL, VILATE MURRAY (1806-67), born in New York, was Heber Kimball's first wife. She joined the Church in 1832 and saw him marry forty-four other women before her death at the age of sixty-one. She was a powerful force among Mormon women in early Utah, serving as a literate and consistent defender of the faith. (DN)

KING, HANNAH TAPFIELD (b. 1807), was a very literate English woman who converted to Mormonism in 1850, after which she came to Utah. The excesses of the Reformation caused her considerable pain. Her sensitive observations of life in early Salt Lake City display a unique outlook for a Mormon woman of her time. (AU)

KINNEY, JOHN F. (1816-1901), was born in New York and practiced law in Ohio and Iowa. He served as chief justice of Utah Territory from 1854 to 1857 and from 1860 to 1863, when he became Utah's third delegate to Congress. (OW)

LAMBERT, JOHN (1820-93), became a Mormon in England and immigrated to Utah in 1850. He first settled in Salt Lake City, where he worked for the Grant family, but later moved to Kamas (1861). He was by profession a brickmason and also served in the Nauvoo Legion. (AJ)

LANEY, ISAAC (1815-73), severely wounded at Haun's Mill, survived to come to Utah in 1847. Years after the massacre, he coughed up a bullet that he had carried in his lungs since he was shot numerous times during the raid on the mill in 1838. He was a native of Kentucky. (FE)

LAUB, GEORGE (1814-80), born in Pennsylvania, emigrated in 1852 to Utah, where he became a successful contractor and carpenter. He kept a detailed diary of his experiences, including his move in 1862 to settle in Dixie. (FE)

LAW, WILLIAM (1809-91), became Joseph Smith's second counselor in 1841, but grew embittered toward the Prophet and was excommunicated in the spring of 1844. He subsequently joined in the conspiracy that led to the assassinations of Joseph and Hyrum Smith. (AJ)

LEE, JOHN DOYLE (1812-77), a longtime stalwart in the Church, took a prominent part in the murder of an Arkansas emigrant train at Mountain Meadows in southern Utah in 1857. He was subsequently excommunicated and was later tried and executed for his role in the famous massacre. His part in the Mountain Meadows atrocity unfortunately overshadowed a dedicated career of service to the Church. See Juanita Brooks, *John Doyle Lee: Zealot, Pioneer Builder, Scapegoat* (Glendale, Calif.: Arthur H. Clark, 1964).

LEITHEAD, JAMES (b. 1816), emigrated from Scotland to Canada, where he joined the Church in 1837. He came to Utah in 1850 and settled at Farmington, becoming second counselor to Bishop John W. Hess. In 1866 he was called to settle on the Muddy in Arizona Territory. He was subsequently a bishop and patriarch in the Kanab Stake. (DN)

LEWIS, BENJAMIN (1803-38), was killed at the Haun's Mill Massacre. Born in South Carolina, he was baptized in 1835, after which he gathered with the body of the Saints. Lewis was in the blacksmith shop and caught a bullet in the chest, but managed to reach his house, where he died an hour later. (AJ)

LEWIS, DAVID (1814-54), present at Haun's Mill, came in 1850 to Utah, where he worked as a cooper and farmer in addition to doing pioneer photography. He was among the first settlers of Iron County and died at Parowan. He was a native of Kentucky. (FE)

LEWIS, TARLTON (1805-90), was wounded at Haun's Mill but survived to become a bishop in Nauvoo. He then crossed the plains in the advance party of pioneers in 1847, was appointed immediately to act as the first bishop of the infant community, and later served in the same position in several southern Utah settlements. Born in South Carolina, he was baptized by his brother Benjamin in 1836. (AJ)

LEWIS, THEODORE B. (1843-99), was a veteran of the Confederate Army who came to Utah in 1865 to teach school. Converted to Mormonism a year later, he returned to the South on a mission (1868-70), and upon his return became a teacher at Brigham Young Academy in Provo. After teaching in several other Utah communities, he completed a study of law and was appointed territorial superintendent of public schools in 1894. He perpetuated in his writings the tales of Grant's missionary prowess in the South. (AJ)

LITTLE, JESSE C. (1815-93), was born in Maine and joined the Church in the East. In 1846, while serving as president of the Eastern States Mission, he befriended Thomas L. Kane, who subsequently attached himself to the Mormon cause and helped Little in the negotiations that led to the recruitment of the Mormon Battalion. Little came to Utah in 1852 after a prolonged mission in the East, and was subsequently called as second counselor to the presiding bishop (1856-74). He was a colonel in the Nauvoo Legion and a close friend of Grant. (AJ)

LYMAN, AMASA MASON (1813-77), became an apostle in 1842. He later associated with the Godbeite movement and preached unorthodox doctrine on the atonement. Subsequently dropped from the Quorum of the Twelve (1867), he was eventually excommunicated (1870). (AJ)

MARKS, WILLIAM (1791-1872), born in Vermont, identified with Mormonism early in the 1830s. Following dedicated service to the Prophet in Missouri, he was called as president of the Nauvoo Stake in 1839. He served in that position until October 1844, when he was dropped by the high council because of his sympathies with Sidney Rigdon. He later affiliated with James J. Strang, serving as his counselor for several years. In 1859, Marks became one of the original promoters of the Reorganized Church of Jesus Christ of Latter Day Saints and served until his death as first counselor to Joseph Smith III. (AJ)

MARSH, THOMAS BALDWIN (1799-1866), was the first president of the Quorum of the Twelve. A native of Massachusetts, he was one of the first converts to Mormonism following its organization in 1830. He became disaffected in 1838 and was excommunicated the following year. He was rebaptized in Nebraska in 1857 and came to Utah, where he died at Ogden. (AJ)

MARSHALL, ROSETTA HENRIETTA GRANT (1855-1915), daughter of Jedediah and Rosetta Robison Grant, married Daniel S. Marshall and lived in West Bountiful until her death. (DN)

MARTIN, JESSE BIGLER (1825-1908), was the leader of the 1856 handcart company that bore his name. This tragedy came at the end of a very successful mission to Great Britain that began in 1853. (JH)

MARTIN, MOSES (1812-99), loyal to Mormonism during the Ohio period, kept a journal of the Zion's Camp march. An original member of the First Quorum of Seventy before being dropped in 1843, he drifted in and out of fellowship with the Church before his death in San Bernardino. (JH)

McBRIDE, REUBEN (1803-91), a native of New York, came into the Church in 1834, after which he joined Zion's Camp. He remained in Kirtland until 1850, when he came to Utah, settling first in Springville and then in Fillmore, where he lived until his death. McBride also served two missions to England and for many years on the Millard Stake high council. (AJ)

McBRIDE, THOMAS (1776-1838), was a native of Virginia who converted to Mormonism in 1831 and moved to Missouri. He died at Haun's Mill, hacked to death with a corn cutter on the banks of Shoal Creek about seventy-five yards behind the mill. He was inaccurately identified years later as a Revolutionary War veteran. (AJ)

McKEACHIE, JOHN. See GRANT, LEWIS MCKEACHIE.

McPHERSON, JAMES R. (1831-1920), joined the Church in Great Britain, came to Utah in 1853, and settled in Kaysville. He later colonized in Juab and Sevier Counties, serving at various times as city councilman, member of the board of education (Nephi), and as a director of a cooperative and an irrigation company. He also served a mission to England (1884-85). (FE)

MERRILL, MARRINER W. (1831-1906), was born in New Brunswick, Canada. He was baptized in 1852 and came to Utah the following year. Ordained an apostle in 1889, he served for several years as president of Cache Stake (1899-1906). (AJ)

MONROE, JAMES M. (d. 1851), a New Yorker, joined the Church in Nauvoo in 1841. After a brief mission, he opened a school that attracted adults as well as children. His qualifications were such that he was later named to the Board of Regents of Nauvoo University. After coming to Utah, he became involved with the wife of Howard Egan and fathered a child by her. When Egan returned from a business trip in the East, he killed Monroe with a pistol but was acquitted of murder in a celebrated court case. (JH)

MOYLE, ELIZABETH. See WEBB.

MOYLE, HENRY (1844-1925), was born in England and came to Utah in 1856 in the Ellsworth handcart company. His father's large family stayed for a time in Salt Lake City but later moved to what is now Alpine, Utah. Following a mission to Great Britain in the 1890s, Moyle became patriarch of the Alpine Stake. (FHL)

MUIR, SUSAN VILATE GRANT (1855-96), Jedediah's daughter by Susan Noble Grant, married William S. Muir Jr. of Bountiful. In 1888 the couple moved to Rich County, where she died at the age of forty-one just after giving birth to her tenth child. (DN)

MURRAY, VILATE. See KIMBALL.

NAISBITT, HENRY W. (1826-1908), joined the Church in England. He came to Utah in 1854 and subsequently served a mission in his homeland (1876-78), presiding for part of that time over the European Mission. For many years, Naisbitt worked at Zion's Cooperative Mercantile Institution. (AJ)

NOBLE, JOSEPH BATES (1810-1900), became associated with Grant during Zion's Camp and as a member of the First Quorum of Seventy. From Massachusetts, he converted to Mormonism in 1832 and was subsequently a bodyguard to the Prophet, a bishop in Nauvoo and Winter Quarters, and captain of fifty in Grant's company in 1847. He served for a time in the bishopric of the Salt Lake Thirteenth Ward before moving to Bountiful in 1862. (AJ)

NOBLE, MARY ADELINE BEMAN (1810-51), born in New York, was the wife of Joseph Bates Noble, whom she married in 1834. The family eventually settled in Bountiful, after coming to Utah in the Grant company in 1847. (FE)

NOBLE, SUSAN FAIRCHILD. See GRANT.

PACK, JOHN (1809-85), was born in Canada but moved to New York, where he was baptized in 1836. After several short missions to the East, he became a member of the 1847 advance party of trekkers. He lived out his life in Salt Lake's Seventeenth Ward, with the exception of his participation in the settlement of the Carson Valley (1856-57). (AJ)

PAGE, JOHN EDWARD (1799-1867), was born in New York and was baptized in Ohio in 1833. Following a mission to Canada, he was ordained an apostle in 1838. Two years later, he was appointed to accompany Orson Hyde on a mission to Jerusalem, but he stopped in Pennsylvania, where he gained considerable influence over the Church there. He remained in the East until 1846, when he was disfellowshipped for apostasy. Joining the Strangite movement, he was excommunicated later that year. (AJ)

PARTRIDGE, EDWARD (1793-1840), was the first presiding bishop of the Church. He was born in Massachusetts and was converted to Mormonism in 1830 along with his Campbellite pastor, Sidney Rigdon. He was shortly thereafter called as presiding bishop. Following severe hardships in the Missouri persecutions, he died of pleurisy in Nauvoo. (AJ)

PATTEN, DAVID W. (1800-1838), an original member of the Quorum of the Twelve organized in 1835, was born in New York and baptized in Indiana (1832). He was killed at the Battle of Crooked River in Missouri during the Mormon War and was regarded by the Saints as a martyr to the cause. (AJ)

PAYNE, WILLIAM L. (1816-92), born in England, arrived in Nauvoo in 1843 following his conversion to Mormonism. After coming to Utah in 1850, he settled in Kaysville, where he lived until his death. (DN)

PHELPS, WILLIAM W. (1792-1872), born in New Jersey, joined the Mormons in 1831 at Kirtland and was sent to Missouri to work as a printer for the Church. He subsequently served Joseph Smith as a scribe and was appointed to the presidency of the stake of Zion. He assisted Emma Smith in the compilation of the first book of hymns for use in the Church, and served on the committee charged with the production of the Book of Doctrine and Covenants in 1835. Excommunicated in 1839 for rebellion, he was reinstated in 1841. After the martyrdom, Brigham Young employed Phelps to assist Willard Richards in the writing of the history of the Church. In 1848 he came to Utah, where he was prominent in the organization of the territory, the establishment of Deseret University, and in the territorial legislature for many years. (AJ)

POLK, JAMES KNOX (1795-1849), rose through the ranks of the Democratic Party in Tennessee to the presidency in 1845. A powerful executive, Polk achieved all of his goals as president, including the settlement of the Oregon question, tariff reduction, the establishment of an independent treasury, and the acquisition by war of half of Mexico. He did not seek reelection and died shortly after retiring from the White House. (EN)

PRATT, ORSON, (1811-81), an apostle from 1835 until his death, had a wealth of missionary experience and was considered one of the finest speakers and writers in the Church—also, apparently, a sometime unrepentant intellectual. He served as Church historian from 1874 to 1881. (AJ)

PRATT, PARLEY PARKER (1807-57), read a copy of the Book of Mormon in 1830 and sought baptism. Ordained an apostle in 1835, he wrote profusely in defense of the Church and quickly became known for his intellectual acumen. Pratt served several missions and, after coming to Utah, took a leading role in the territorial government. He was murdered in Arkansas while returning from a mission to the East. (AJ)

PULSIPHER, ZERA (1789-1872,), a native of Vermont, was converted to Mormonism in 1832, after which he became an avid missionary. One of his proselytes was Wilford Woodruff. Set apart as a member of the First Council of Seventy in 1838, he arrived in Utah with the first companies of pioneers. Following his release from the First Council in 1862, he colonized in southern Utah with his sons, who had been called to Dixie in 1861. (AJ)

REESE, JOHN D. (1815-80), a native of Wales, was baptized in 1846. Prior to coming to Utah, where he settled in Brigham City, Reese lived in St. Louis. Grant visited him there in 1850. (FHL)

REEVES, THEDA GRANT (1821-ca. 1910), received Joseph Hyrum Grant Jr. as a visitor at her home in Lathrop, Missouri, in 1904. From her, much of the early history of the Joshua and Athalia Grant family thus came into the Utah Grant family. She was the ninth Grant sibling and was baptized in Kirtland by her brother-in-law William Smith in 1833. She never came to Utah. (FHL)

REEVES, WILLIAM (1813-1902), came to Utah from England. After living in Centerville, where he was present at the Reformation meeting in September 1856, he moved to Cache Valley, where he died in Wellsville. (FHL)

RICH, CHARLES COULSON (1809-83), was baptized in 1832 and quickly distinguished himself as a military leader among the Saints. In 1844 he took command of the Nauvoo Legion with the rank of major general. After coming to Utah in 1847, he served briefly as president of the Salt Lake Stake and then became an apostle in 1849. In 1863 Brigham Young called him to settle the Bear Lake Valley, where he died in Paris, Idaho, at the age of eighty-one. (AJ)

RICHARDS, FRANKLIN D. (1811-99), was converted by Brigham Young in 1836. He became a member of the Quorum of the Twelve in 1849 and served two terms as president of the British Mission in the 1850s. He was a prominent figure in Utah politics in addition to his Church work, serving at various times in the legislature and as regent of the University of Deseret, general in the militia, and judge in Weber County. He was also Church historian for many years. (AJ)

RICHARDS, SAMUEL W. (1824-1909), was born in Massachusetts. He served as clerk to the train of missionaries that went east in the fall of 1851. A brother of Franklin D. Richards, he served as president of the British Mission from 1852 to 1854. (AJ)

RICHARDS, WILLARD (1804-54), a native of Massachusetts, was baptized in 1836 after a lengthy investigation of Mormonism. A physician, he was known as "the doctor," although after coming to Nauvoo at the end of a mission to England, he became an invaluable assistant in clerical affairs to Joseph and then Brigham. Appointed as Church historian in 1842, he carefully preserved the writings and works of Joseph Smith and was with him constantly until his death. Brigham Young chose him as his second counselor in 1847. (AJ)

RIGDON, SIDNEY (1783-1876), was a Campbellite preacher who converted to Mormonism in Ohio. He served as Joseph Smith's first counselor (1833-44) and exerted a powerful influence on the Prophet until their estrangement and Rigdon's removal to Pittsburgh. After the martyrdom. Rigdon came to Nauvoo, claiming the presidency of the Church but was rejected by the membership. He then returned to Pennsylvania, where he established his own church, drawing to his standard many former Saints disaffected from the leadership of the Twelve. (AJ)

RITER, LEVI EVANS (1805-77), was a millwright from Pennsylvania who was baptized in 1846 after investigating Mormonism for nearly a decade. Arriving in Iowa, he was ordained a bishop to preside over several families of Mormon Battalionists. He came to Utah in the Grant company in 1847, went to California for a short time, and then settled in Salt Lake City. Riter was among the Carson

Valley missionaries and also served a brief mission to Britain in the 1850s. (DN)

RITER, REBECCA WOLLERTON DILWORTH (1815-94), of Pennsylvania, was (with her husband Levi Evans Riter) a member of Grant's hundred in the 1847 migration. She was of notable assistance during the illnesses and deaths in Grant's family during the trip to Utah. She and her husband lived out their lives in Salt Lake City, after a brief sojourn in California. (FHL)

ROBINSON, EBENEZER (d. 1891), a printer from New York, joined the Church in 1835 after going to work for the Mormon printing office in Kirtland. His career thereafter led him through stormy periods of disagreement with Church leadership. Finally, deeply troubled by polygamy, he disassociated himself from the main body of the Church. Later in life, he affiliated with the Reorganized Church of Jesus Christ of Latter Day Saints. (AU)

ROBINSON, RICHARD S. (1830-1902), was baptized in England as a youngster and came to Utah in 1849 after living for three years in Iowa. After a few years as a miner in California, he settled in Utah County and then colonized in southern Utah. (AJ)

ROBISON, ELIZABETH SQUIRES (b. 1802), was a native of New York and the mother of Rosetta, Grant's third wife. After being widowed in Winter Quarters in 1846, she was an object of considerable care and concern to Grant. (FHL)

ROBISON, JAMES HENRY (1830-87), Rosetta's brother, worked for the Grants for some time as a young man. His remaining years were spent in relative obscurity. (FHL)

ROBISON, ROSETTA. See GRANT.

ROCKWELL, ORRIN PORTER (1815-78), joined the Mormons in 1830. He served as personal bodyguard to Joseph Smith and then as a hunter and scout for Orson Pratt's advance company that entered the Salt Lake Valley in 1847 ahead of Brigham Young. He operated a mail station south of the city and also served for many years as a deputy marshal. Rockwell's exploits as a gunfighter became legendary among the Saints. (AJ)

ROCKWOOD, ALBERT P. (1805-79), was set apart as one of the first seven presidents (First Council of the Seventy) in 1845. A native of Massachusetts, he was a member of the advance company of pioneers in 1847. Having been a bodyguard to Joseph Smith, he became warden of the Utah territorial penitentiary and was a member of the legislature at the time of his death. (AJ)

ROMNEY, GEORGE (1831-1920), joined the Church with his parents in England in 1839 and immigrated to Nauvoo in 1841. After arriving in Utah in 1850, Romney worked as a carpenter on the public works, becoming building foreman in 1856. He later formed a contracting firm and eventually moved into wider business circles. In addition to service as bishop of Salt Lake's Twentieth Ward, he served two terms on the city council. He was later among Mormon colonists in Mexico. (AJ)

ROUNDY, SHADRACK (1789–1872), was born in Vermont and moved to New York, where he joined the Church in 1831. After serving for several years as a bodyguard to Joseph Smith, he came to Utah in 1847 in the advance company and was appointed bishop of Salt Lake's Sixteenth Ward (1849–56). (AJ)

SANDERS, ELLIS M. (1808–73), a native of Delaware and an early convert to Mormonism, came to Utah in 1848. After living for a time in Salt Lake City, he colonized in Dixie. He was at various times a farmer, tax collector, and city water master. (FE)

SHAVER, LEONIDAS (d. 1855), of Virginia, seemed to get along well with the Mormons during his term as U.S. judge in Utah (1852–55). Unlike his predecessors, Shaver managed to maintain cordial relations with Brigham Young and other Mormon leaders, despite a growing coolness toward them just prior to his death. (JH)

SHERWOOD, HENRY G. (d. 1862), was a member of the high council at Nauvoo that excommunicated Sidney Rigdon and was subsequently one of the original 1847 pioneers. After serving on the first Salt Lake Stake high council, he went to San Bernardino in 1852, came back to Utah in 1857, but eventually returned to southern California, where he died. (AJ)

SMITH, ASAHEL, JR. (1773–1848), the Prophet's uncle, joined the Church in 1835 in New York. He subsequently served on high councils in Kirtland and in Lee County, Iowa, and was then ordained patriarch to the Church upon the apostacy of William Smith in 1845. Due to failing health, he never functioned in his office. (AJ)

SMITH, CAROLINE AMANDA GRANT (1814–45), an older sister of Jedediah, married the Prophet's brother William shortly after her family's arrival in Kirtland in 1833. With increasingly failing health, she spent the last years of her life in physical suffering. She died in Nauvoo at the age of thirty-one. (FHL)

SMITH, DON CARLOS (1816–41), the Prophet's younger brother, served numerous missions to the East and South through the 1830s. He died of pneumonia at the age of twenty-five. He was the same age as Grant, so the two were close friends through familial ties and numerous missionary experiences together. (JH)

SMITH, EMMA HALE (1804–79), born in Pennsylvania, married Joseph Smith Jr. in 1827 and was baptized in June 1830. She became the first general president of the Relief Society in 1842, but chose to remain in Nauvoo with her children when the Saints who followed Brigham Young left for the West. She remarried in 1847 and became a member of the Reorganized Church of Jesus

Christ of Latter Day Saints when it was organized with her oldest son, Joseph III, as president. (AJ)

SMITH, GEORGE A. (1817-75), a cousin of the Prophet, joined the Church in 1831 and became an apostle in 1839. He served in the Nauvoo Legion, in the territorial legislature, and as Church historian. In 1868 he succeeded Heber Kimball as Brigham Young's counselor. (AJ)

SMITH, HYRUM (1800-1844), brother of the Prophet, was among the earliest converts to Mormonism, being baptized in June 1829. One of the eight witnesses to the Book of Mormon plates, he became second counselor in the First Presidency in 1837 shortly after the death of his first wife. In 1841, he succeeded his father as patriarch to the Church and as prophet, seer, and revelator. He was martyred with his brother in June 1844. (AJ)

SMITH, JOHN (1781-1854), was an uncle of the Prophet. After a term as assistant counselor in the First Presidency, he was ordained a patriarch early in 1844 by Joseph Smith and subsequently as patriarch to the Church by Brigham Young in 1849. (AJ)

SMITH, JOHN (1832-1911), was the fourth presiding patriarch of the Church. A son of the martyred Hyrum Smith, he came to Utah in 1848, and was ordained patriarch to the Church in 1855 at the age of twenty-two. (AJ)

SMITH, JOHN L. (1828-98), born in New York, was a cousin of the Prophet. He came to Utah in 1847, after which he became president of the Swiss and Italian Mission (1856-57). He later filled two additional missions to Europe and colonized in southern Utah, where he died. (AJ)

SMITH, JOHN P. (1812-85), a native of Pennsylvania, served as Grant's clerk in Philadelphia in 1844. In 1851 he came to Utah, where he settled in Salt Lake City and sired a large family. (AJ)

SMITH, JOSEPH, JR. (1805-44), founder and first president of the Church, began his ministry reporting a series of visions that culminated in the translation from ancient records of the Book of Mormon. With a few associates, he organized a new religion in New York in 1830 that subsequently became the Church of Jesus Christ of Latter-day Saints. Persecuted severely, he and his growing body of followers moved from New York to Ohio, and from there to Missouri and Illinois, where the Prophet was murdered in June of 1844. (AJ)

SMITH, LOT (1830-92), was born in New York and was baptized as a youngster. After service in the Mormon Battalion, he settled in Davis County. He served a mission to England (1869-71) and then colonized in Dixie. Most famous among the Saints for his guerrilla exploits in the Utah War, Smith was also a dedicated missionary among the Indians, although he was killed by Indians near Tuba City, Arizona, during a Navajo uprising. (AJ)

SMITH, ROXCY ANN GRANT (1825-1900), was Jedediah's youngest sister. Following the death of Caroline Grant Smith, she married William, brother of the martyred Prophet. Although she divorced Smith in 1853, she did not unite with the Utah church but maintained cordial contacts with Jedediah, conveying family news from Illinois to him on a regular basis. She eventually affiliated with the Reorganized Church of Jesus Christ of Latter Day Saints. (FHL)

SMITH, SYLVESTER (1806–80), was one of the first members of the Church. He was a member of Zion's Camp and the Kirtland High Council. Among the original members of the First Council of Seventy, he was released in 1837, having been previously ordained a high priest. He reported having had a magnificent vision in the Kirtland Temple but later apostatized. (AJ)

SMITH, WILLIAM (1811–93), a brother of the Prophet, was born in Vermont. He married Caroline Grant, Jedediah's older sister, in 1833, and was a member of Zion's Camp. One of the original Quorum of the Twelve called in 1835, he quarreled repeatedly with his brother and other Church leaders. Disfellowshipped in 1839, he was shortly restored and served Nauvoo as a representative to the Illinois legislature (1842–43). He spent considerable time after that in Philadelphia on business. After the martyrdom, William became patriarch to the Church but soon rebelled against the leadership of the Twelve. Following his excommunication for apostasy in 1845, he joined the Strangite movement and married another of Grant's sisters, Roxcy Ann. He eventually associated with the Reorganized Church of Jesus Christ of Latter Day Saints. (AJ)

SMITH, WILLIAM R. (1826–94), a native of Ontario, joined the Church in 1841, after moving to Illinois with his adopted family. In 1850 he went to California, where he made considerable money in stock and mining. He then came to Utah and settled in Centerville, where he was ordained bishop in 1855. After participating in the Carson Valley mission in 1857, he resumed his duties as bishop of Centerville, in which capacity he served until called as president of the Davis Stake in 1877. He was also a probate judge and member of the legislature for several terms. (AJ)

SMOOT, ABRAHAM OWEN (1815–95), was an erstwhile missionary companion to Grant in 1839. After coming to Utah, he became a prominent citizen of the territory, serving terms as mayor of both Salt Lake City and Provo, and as president of the Utah Stake (1868–95). In Provo he became president of the Provo Woollen Mills, a trustee of Brigham Young Academy, and a successful banker. (AJ)

SNEDAKER, JOHN FREDERICK (1831–90), was born in Germany, immigrated to the United States, and came to Utah in the Grant company in 1847 at the age of sixteen. He subsequently lived with the Grant family until undertaking a mission to the German-speaking region of Pennsylvania in 1855. Returning to Utah after Grant's death, he married one of Jedediah's widows, Sarah Ann, and settled in the Mill Creek Ward. A farmer and dairyman, he later worked on the Union Pacific Railroad. (FE)

SNOW, ELIZA R. (1804–87), became a plural wife to Joseph Smith in 1842 and was later sealed to Brigham Young. She wrote prolifically and became Utah's first literary star. Her Church service was also extensive, culminating in her general presidency of the Relief Society from 1867 to her death. (AJ)

SNOW, ERASTUS (1818–88), born in Vermont, was a member of the Council of the Twelve from 1849 to his death. He was a dedicated missionary, serving several missions in the East and doing pioneering work in Scandinavia. He also spent a number of years in St. Louis, where he directed Church immigration and published the *Luminary*. He later presided over the Saints in southern Utah. (AJ)

SNOW, WILLARD (1811–53), a brother of Erastus Snow, was born in Vermont and joined the Church in 1833. A member of Zion's Camp, he was ordained to the First Quorum of Seventy in 1835 and filled several missions, including one as president of the Scandinavian Mission (1852–53). He died on the North Sea en route from Denmark to England. He was originally designated as a captain of a hundred in 1847 but crossed the plains that year as a captain of fifty in the Grant company. (AJ)

SNOW, ZERUBBABEL (1809–88), was baptized in Vermont in 1832. A member of Zion's Camp, he nevertheless remained in Ohio until the exodus of the Church to the Great Basin. In 1851 he came to Utah as a federal judge. In 1869 he was elected as territorial attorney general. (AJ)

SPENCER, DANIEL (1794–1868), came of Massachusetts Puritan stock and was the son of a Revolutionary War veteran. Well-educated and aggressive, he became wealthy as a merchant in Georgia and the Carolinas before his conversion to Mormonism. Coming to Nauvoo, he served a term as mayor and was bishop of a Winter Quarters ward. In Utah he was a member of the first Salt Lake Stake high council and in 1849 became stake president, serving in that position until his death. He was also an associate justice of the State of Deseret supreme court and served several terms in the territorial legislature. (AJ)

SPENCER, ORSON (1801–55), was a graduate of Union College in New York. Born in Massachusetts, he taught school in Georgia and then entered the Baptist ministry in his home state and in Connecticut. He converted to Mormonism in 1841 and moved to Nauvoo, where he became a city alderman. During the expulsion, he was called to preside over the British Mission, editing the *Millennial Star* for two years. After coming to Utah in 1849, he became the first chancellor of Deseret University. Following another mission to Europe, he traveled extensively in the United States and was eventually appointed president of the St. Louis Stake and editor of the *Luminary*. He became ill during a brief mission to the Cherokees and died in St. Louis in Oct. 1855. (AJ)

SQUIRES, ELIZABETH. See ROBISON.

SQUIRES, THOMAS, a Welshman who joined the Church in the mid-1840s, was living in Kaysville during the beginning of the Reformation. (DN)

STANLEY, HARVEY (b. 1810), Grant's companion during his first mission, remained in the Church through the Nauvoo period. He worked as a stonecutter on the Nauvoo Temple, but thereafter played no notable role in Mormon history. (JH)

STENHOUSE, THOMAS B. H. (1814–81), assisted Lorenzo Snow in establishing the Swiss and Italian Mission in 1850. He later associated with the Godbeites and was excommunicated. He then undertook a career of publishing against the Church. (AJ)

STEPTOE, EDWARD J. (1816–65), U.S. Army colonel, arrived in Utah in 1854 at the head of a 200-man expedition sent to examine a route from Salt Lake City to California and to investigate the Gunnison massacre. Grant respected Steptoe for his control over his men and for his temperance. (JH)

STEWART, DAVID M. (1826–98), joined the Church in Scotland in 1842. He came to Utah in 1847 but spent several years on Church missions to California, Oregon, and his native land. Eventually settling in Weber County, Stewart served as bishop of the Uintah Ward, high councilman, and patriarch. He served several more missions in his later years and at his death was said to have spent more years on missions than any other man in Utah. An accomplished writer, he kept a detailed journal of his experiences. (DN)

STODDARD, Solomon (1643–1719), laid important groundwork in colonial Connecticut for the intense religious revival that swept New England in the 1740s. Preaching at Northampton, Stoddard was a firm advocate of spirited oratory as a cure for spiritual sluggishness. Like Jedediah Grant in Mormon history, Stoddard openly resorted to fear as a means of arousing his communicants. (EN)

STRANG, JAMES J. (1813–56), a lawyer converted to Mormonism in Wisconsin in 1844, claimed the leadership of the Church based on a letter he allegedly received from Joseph Smith. He subsequently established a church with headquarters on Beaver Island, on Lake Michigan, where he proclaimed himself king. He was assassinated by disgruntled followers after he began practicing polygamy. (JH)

STREEPER, WILKINSON (1809–56), was converted in Philadelphia in 1840 and was living there during Grant's first term as presiding elder. Streeper remained a close friend of the Grants after he settled in Salt Lake City, where he died of a lingering illness. (FHL)

TAYLOR, ALLEN (1814–91), bishop in Kaysville during the Reformation, was born in Kentucky and came to Utah in 1849 at the head of his own company.

In 1862 he moved to St. George, and from there twenty years later to Loa in Wayne County, where he died. (FE)

TAYLOR, JOHN (1808-87), was born in England and joined the Church in Canada. He became an apostle in 1838 and was seriously wounded in Carthage Jail during the martyrdom of Joseph and Hyrum Smith. Coming to Utah, he published extensively for the Church and served missions in England and France. A staunch advocate of the continuance of polygamy in the face of government persecution, he became president of the Church at Brigham Young's death. (AJ)

TAYLOR, STEPHEN W. (1835-1920), became a Mormon in England, after which he emigrated to Utah in 1848. In 1856 he was one of the several young men sent into the mountains to aid the Martin handcart company. He later became known as a professional Indian fighter and became a close associate in military affairs of Robert T. Burton. He also served as sheriff of Summit County, as a Salt Lake City policeman, and as a missionary to England from 1869 to 1871. (FE)

TAYLOR, ZACHARY (1784-1850), Mexican War hero and twelfth president of the United States, incurred the wrath of Brigham Young and the Saints by refusing to move ahead on their appeal for statehood. Taylor was born in Virginia but grew up in Kentucky, where he joined the U.S. Army. During a career of forty years in the military, he rose to the rank of major general. In 1848 he was the Whig candidate for president and was elected easily. His death in the middle of his term was proof to the Mormons of his damnation. (EN)

TEASDALE, GEORGE (1831-1907), joined the Church in England in 1852. After coming to Utah, he managed the tithing store and became involved in Zion's Cooperative Mercantile Institution. He became an apostle in 1882 at the same time as Heber J. Grant. (AJ)

TENNANT, WILLIAM (1673-1746), an immigrant from Ireland, taught the fine art of preaching at his "Log College" in Pennsylvania. Several of his students, steeped in deep piety, argumentation, and a passion for lively preaching, were among the mainstays of the Great Awakening in American religion that occurred in the 1740s. (EN)

THURSTON, GEORGE W. (1830-1903), was a brother-in-law of Grant who became involved in the Thurston-Grant plan for the agricultural settlement of Morgan County. (FE)

THURSTON, SARAH ANN. See GRANT.

THURSTON, THOMAS J. (1805-85), was the first bishop of Morgan, Utah. A native of Vermont, he came to Utah in Grant's company in 1847 and was thereafter his close associate. He settled first in Davis County but in the early 1850s moved into the Weber River Valley in connection with Grant and Charles S. Peterson. He later colonized in southern Utah, where he lived until his death. Grant married Thurston's daughter Sarah Ann in 1853. (AJ)

TURLEY, THEODORE (1800–1872), was at Nauvoo at the time of the martyrdom and with Grant carried a message from the Prophet to Governor Ford. In 1849 he came to Utah, where he eventually colonized in Beaver County. (FE)

VAN DYKE, CAROLINE ANN. See GRANT.

WATT, GEORGE D. (1815–81), was the first convert to the Church in England (1837). He later taught phonography (shorthand) in Nauvoo and Salt Lake City, where he worked for Brigham Young as reporter and secretary for sixteen years. He was excommunicated in 1874 for his associations with the Godbeite movement. (Ronald G. Watt, "George D. Watt," *BYU Studies* 18 [Fall 1977]: 48–65.)

WEBB, ELIZABETH MOYLE (1837–61), joined the Church in England with her parents and emigrated to Utah in 1856 in the Ellsworth handcart company. She worked for the Grant family prior to her marriage to Chauncey G. Webb. (FHL)

WEBSTER, DANIEL (1781–1851), a shining light in the national legislature during the first half of the nineteenth century, came from New Hampshire but later represented Massachusetts. Webster was possibly the greatest orator in nineteenth-century America. He served twice as U.S. Secretary of State, first from 1841 to 1843 and then under Fillmore from 1850 to 1852. It was during this latter term that he dealt with the Mormons over the "runaway judges" affair. "The godlike Daniel" is best remembered for his championship of nationalism and his efforts in the Senate and through his oratory to preserve the Union against the threat of secession in the antebellum period. (EN)

WELCH, LOIS GRANT (1807–68), was the second of the Grant siblings. Jedediah visited her in 1836 during a mission to New York, where she may have been baptized, although she was not later associated with the Church. (FHL)

WELLS, DANIEL HANMER (1814–91), was living in Commerce, Illinois, in 1839 when the Mormons moved there and built the city of Nauvoo. Though he did not join the Church until 1846, he served as Nauvoo City councilman, alderman, university regent, and general in the Nauvoo Legion. In Utah he took command of the legion in addition to serving in numerous other civic capacities until 1857, when he succeeded Grant as second counselor in the First Presidency and as mayor of Salt Lake City. Following the death of Brigham Young in 1877, Wells became a counselor to the Quorum of the Twelve and also served for many years as president of the Manti Temple. (AJ)

WHITEFIELD, GEORGE (1714–70), played a prominent role in the Great Awakening in colonial America that established a pattern for American religious revivals. He studied at Oxford, where he associated with John and Charles Wesley and became a Methodist enthusiast. After coming to Philadelphia in 1739, he became something of a traveling evangelist, rebuking the people for their lethargy. He eventually returned to England, but revisited the colonies numerous times, dying in Newburyport, Mass. (EN)

WHITMER, PETER, JR. (1773-1854), one of the eight witnesses to the Book of Mormon plates. The Church was organized in his father's house in Fayette, New York, Whitmer became disaffected in Missouri in 1838. (AJ)

WHITNEY, HORACE K. (1823-84), a son of Newel K. Whitney, was for many years a bookkeeper in the office of Brigham Young. Well-educated and articulate, yet perhaps overly modest, he married Helen Mar Kimball, a daughter of Heber C. Kimball; he was the father of Orson F. Whitney and Horace G. Whitney. (AJ)

WHITNEY, NEWEL K. (1795-1850), a veteran of the War of 1812, was born in Vermont and joined the Church in Kirtland. After serving as bishop in Kirtland and Nauvoo, he became presiding bishop in Winter Quarters. He came to Utah in 1848. (AJ)

WIGHT, LYMAN (1796-1858), born in New York, was a veteran of the War of 1812. He was baptized in 1830 and stood by the Prophet through the persecutions, including the incarceration in Missouri. After his arrival in Illinois, Wight became an apostle in 1841 and became a major general in the militia. After Joseph Smith's death, he and George Miller led a small group of Saints to Texas where he was excommunicated in 1848. He remained in Texas until his death. (AJ)

WILLES, WILLIAM (1814-90), joined the Church in England, where he was a schoolteacher. He went to India as a missionary and then came to Utah in 1856, participating in the opening of the Reformation. Willes was a poet who contributed the lyrics for several popular nineteenth-century Mormon hymns. Following service as a home missionary and as a Sunday School worker, he undertook another mission to India in the 1880s. (JH)

WILLIE, JAMES GREY (1814-95), emigrated to the United States from England in 1836 and joined the Church in 1842. He came to Utah in Grant's company in 1847 and then returned to England for a mission. In 1856 he was the leader of one of the hardest-hit handcart companies, losing many of his people to starvation and exposure. He subsequently served for a few years as bishop of the Seventh Ward in Salt Lake City and then moved to Cache Valley, where he was ordained a patriarch. (AJ)

WINCHESTER, BENJAMIN (1817-1901), born in Erie County, Pennsylvania, was baptized there in 1833 at the same time as Grant. They were longtime friends and associates, serving together in Zion's Camp, on missions, and as presiding elders in Philadelphia. Winchester broke with the Church over polygamy in 1844 and was subsequently excommunicated, after drawing away many of the Saints whom he had converted in the Philadelphia area. (AJ)

WOOD, JAMES G. (1853–1918), grew up in Davis County, where he knew members of the Grant family. During a mission to Virginia in 1909, he reported meeting a man who was present at the famous "blank page" sermon of Grant's 1839–41 mission in the region. He lived most of his life in Syracuse, Utah, where he died. (FHL)

WOODRUFF, WILFORD (1807–98), was the fourth president of the Church. Joining the Mormons in New York in 1833, he quickly became known for his missionary zeal and was ordained an apostle in 1839. His journals and other writings have become invaluable to the understanding of Mormon history in the nineteenth century. He seemed to have a special relationship with Grant, admiring his dedication and loyalty to the cause of Zion. (AJ)

WOOLLEY, EDWIN D. (1807–81), a native of Pennsylvania, became a Mormon in 1837. He moved to Nauvoo in 1840, filled a mission to the East, and subsequently became close to Joseph and Hyrum Smith. In 1848 he arrived in Utah, where he became a member of the Salt Lake Stake high council and then second bishop of the Thirteenth Ward. He undertook a procurement mission to the East with Joseph Heywood and Edward Hunter in 1849 and encountered Grant in St. Louis in the spring of 1850. (AJ)

WRIGLEY, THOMAS (1816–73), joined the Mormons in England in 1842 and arrived in Nauvoo a year later. In 1844 he was called to preside over the Saints in St. Louis, holding that position until coming to Utah in 1852. Following an assignment to participate in the building of Fort Supply, he settled in 1854 at American Fork, where he was clerk of the cooperative store. (DN)

YOUNG, BRIGHAM (1801–77), was the second president of the Church. Acknowledged as one of America's great colonizers, he led the Mormons from 1844 until his death and was the dominating presence in early Utah history. He joined the Church in 1832 and became an apostle in 1835. In addition to his ecclesiastical duties, he was also governor of Utah Territory (1850–58), a founder of some 350 communities in the far West, and founder of several score business enterprises. (AJ)

YOUNG, CLARA DECKER (1828–89), was one of three women in the original 1847 party of pioneers. Married to Brigham Young in 1843, she was from New York, where her parents had joined the Church in the early 1830s. Remaining in the valley the first winter while Brigham returned to Winter Quarters, she witnessed Jedediah Grant's arrival with the body of his wife, Caroline, in September 1847. (AJ)

YOUNG, ELIZA R. SNOW. See SNOW.

YOUNG, JOHN, JR. (1791–1870), a brother of Brigham Young, joined the Church with his father and family in 1832 in New York. He was for a time president of the Kirtland Stake and also served several missions for the Church. He came to Utah in 1847 with Grant, after which he lived in Salt Lake City until his death. (AJ)

YOUNG, JOSEPH (1797–1881), a brother of Brigham Young, joined the Church in 1831. After service in Zion's Camp, he became the second of the original presidents of the Seventy in 1835. Persevering through the early trials of the Church, he became first in seniority in the First Council of the Seventy and in 1850 came to Utah, where he presided over the quorums of Seventy until his death. With Jedediah, he spearheaded the Reformation of 1856–57. The two men appeared to be very close. (AJ)

YOUNG, JOSEPH ANGELL (1834–75), a son of Brigham Young, was born in Kirtland and spent his young adulthood on missions for the Church, including participating in the heroic task of rescuing stranded handcart companies in the fall of 1856. He later operated a lumber business, took subcontracts on the Union Pacific Railroad, and supervised construction of the Utah Central Railroad. Serving several colonizing missions, he organized the United Order in Sevier County. (AJ)

YOUNG, PHINEAS H. (1799–1879), a brother of Brigham Young, joined the Church in 1832 and came to Utah in 1847. He served in the Salt Lake Stake presidency prior to being ordained bishop of the Salt Lake City Second Ward in 1864. (JH)

THREE LETTERS

TO THE

NEW YORK HERALD,

FROM J. M. GRANT, OF UTAH.

LETTER I.

[FROM THE HERALD OF MARCH 9, 1852.]

Letter from the Mayor of Great Salt Lake City.

Mormonism by a Mormon—Polygamy—Murder—Jackson in Heaven—Taylor in Limbo—Stiff Necks and Superstition—Astounding Developments, &c.

JAMES GORDON BENNETT, ESQ.

SIR:—I will thank you to print, as soon as you can, the substance of this letter. Considered only as news, it ought to be worth your while. There is a great curiosity everywhere to hear about the Mormons, and eagerness to know all the evil that can be spoken of them. Announce you that I am a Mormon Elder, just arrived from Utah—Mayor, in fact, of Salt Lake City, where my wife and family are still living—a preacher, brigadier of horse, and President of the Quorum of Seventies, and the like; and not one subscriber that waded over shoe-tops through the slime of details you gave of the play-actor's divorce trial lately, will not be greedy to read all I have to say, about the filthier accusations that have been brought against me, and my friends and brethren. This is what I have to count upon, thank Falsehood. And, if you will publish my letter entire, I will ask for no editorial help from you. I am no Writer; but, with the help

---

The Backslider in heart shall be filled with his own ways.

[2]

The fear of the Lord is the instruction of wisdom.

of the Power of Light, am not afraid of what you can say against us. So long as I walk by the rule of my Master, you walk by the rude working of your fancies.

I must say, I have had my doubts about writing out upon these matters; my doing so not being approved by our Delegate in Congress, Dr. Bernhisel. The Doctor is one of our gentlemen at home; a real gentleman, and would not say a rough word, or do a rough thing, to hurt the feelings, or knock off the spectacles of any man, for the world. But I am no gentleman, in his sense at least, and have had slights enough put upon me, personally, since I came eastward, to entitle me to any amount of stand up self-defence. Dr. Bernhisel's official course in this matter, I suppose I am bound to accept; for I have understood that he had the advice of experienced men who said to him, "Take up the report of the three officers criminating your constituents, when it comes from the State Department into the House; ask for a Special Committee with power to send for persons and papers, and put the false witnesses on oath; but don't stoop to wrangle upon your religion, morals, and political opinions with Mr. Webster or the Congressmen at large, whom the country considers to have enough to do to take care of their own."

This is all very well, and very high and mighty and dignified certainly; but while the grass grows the cow starves—while Congress is taking its months to do the work of a day, the verdict of the public goes against us—as the law-word is, by default —and we stand substantially convicted of any thing and everything that any and every kind of blackguard can make up a lie about. And now I hear that the charges are not to be pushed— two of the officers want to come back to us *as friends*—they are to be virtually abandoned after doing us all the harm they can. What Mr. Webster thinks, we care a little; what is the opinion of most members of Congress, you can hardly believe, in your part of the world, how very little; but Public Opinion, that power we respect as well as recognize; and, therefore, I am now determined, on my own responsibility, to write myself, and blurt out all the truth I can. I may not be discreet, but I will be honest.

I have written, to begin with, an examination into the causes

How long shall they utter and speak hard things.

Their Nobles shall be of themselves.

that induced the three officers to leave Utah; but find it grown on my hands too long for publication. As I must confine myself, therefore, to plain and unargued narrative, I will best begin with the original and beginning of our troubles, found, to my mind, in the notion that, unlike other populous communities, we are not fit, or have not the right, to furnish our own rulers. I doubt if the contrary ever once occurred to Mr. Fillmore, who, I am persuaded, had quite a wish to deal justly with us. What was the consequence? At the very outset of our national career, we had to have strangers sent to govern us. Who of worth and standing at home would venture out to our distant and undescribed country? Accordingly, the offices went begging among all the small-fry politicians who could be suspected of being fit to fill them. And (as I have heard, after sundry nominations were refused) the following were picked up:—

No. 1.—A Mr. Brandebury, who brought his recommendation, saying he had studied law in the office of a Pennsylvania county-court lawyer renowned for successful high and lofty tumbling in the support of the United States Bank through a bloodless civil war, but who, in every other respect, exaggerated the recommendation of a Presidential candidate, of being perfectly and entirely unknown.

No. 2.—Zerubbabel Snow, of Ohio, a lawyer practicing in the interior of that State—qualifications rather ahead of the others—willing to come out probably, having kinsfolk among us.

No. 3.—Mr. P. E. Broccus, of Alabama, of whom I have again to speak—character unknown, I hope, to the President—in the lower purlieus of the District of Columbia by no means entitled to that recommendation.

No. 4.—B. D. Harris, a smart youngster—from a Vermont printing office, I think—for Secretary.

And for Indian Agent, No. 5, a lazy little fellow named Day—with half the head of a Yankee, for he was all the time thinking of a "trade," and half the heart of a woman, for he would have run from a squaw.

"Fry stones with butter," says the proverb, "the broth will be good." I don't know what manner of appearance these men pre-

Their Governor shall proceed from the midst of them.

[4]

As the evil Figs which cannot be eaten they are so evil.

sent, now that they have taken their titles at our expense, and drawn some of Uncle Sam's money for it; but, as they came among us, the bevy was just such as you will find keeping tavern together at a railway water station. Zerub. the active partner—Lemuel, rather slow; but his uncle, superintendent of the road to secure the trains stopping there at breakfast and dinner times; with Harris, the bar-keeper to fly round spry, and Day to black boots, pump tank, and lift trunks. To our misfortune they were not kept in their proper spheres.

The first we knew of our becoming a Territory was the account of the passage, September, 1850, of the law organizing Utah, which reached us before the year was out. Nothing could exceed the clamorous joy of our citizens at learning that they were thus invited into the family party by their brethren of the Union. Our national flags went up, hailed by huzzas, all over the settlement, and when we hoisted our large one on the liberty pole at Temple Block, in Great Salt Lake city, the artillery saluted it with one hundred rounds, rammed home.

The first actual appearance among us, by personal representative, of the government majesty of the United States, was the arrival of No. 1, as above, which came as much as half a year after (the 7th of June, I think), with a limited amount of personal luggage, including one remarkably large black umbrella, and put up at a boarding house on the outskirts of the town, resorted to by traders and carriers passing through the settlement. We welcomed this from our hearts. We did not fire the cannon at it, having saved this honor for our country's standard, or its enemies. Nor did we attend to appearances as well as the French, who made ready for their king by putting white kid gloves on the guide-posts' fingers, and a clean cambric ruffled shirt and silk stockings on the body of a criminal hanging in irons. Our means, after all, were limited; but we cordially did our best. As it was the Chief Justice, numbers of us paid him our respects; and, though our calls were not returned, proceeded to get up, after our custom, a Ball in his honor. A paragraph or two, descriptive of this entertainment, will not be out of place here, if it gives you an idea of our humble but hearty fashions.

He brought me to the Banqueting House.

[5]

He sendeth springs into the Valleys which run down among the Hills.

About two and a half miles from the site of our future Temple, out of the base of what we call Ensign Mountain, a big toe of the Wahsatch range, gush up a number of hot springs, various in quality and temperature; of which one, in particular, has a constant head, strong enough to work a fulling mill. This we have conducted in pine logs to a large house in the city suburbs, and provided there the tubs and other requirements for the most luxurious artificial bathing. Though at the charge of $1 a month per family, it has become a place of frequent resort for our whole population; and as, with Mormons, society and festivity go hand in hand, this concourse has led to the erection of additional buildings, including, besides a ball-room, two parlors for club and party suppers, &c., and a famous big double-kitchen to cook up the good things in.

To this Bath House we invited Judge Brandebury. Our hours being early at Salt Lake, we sent the Governor's carriage for him at three in the afternoon; but dressing or something else detained him till five, shortly after which he arrived. The guests were then sometime assembled. Tickets had only been issued to our nicest people; and I will say it, a prettier company no honest man, not a fop, would have asked to meet. After an orchestral symphony, Brother Spencer, by his office, President of the Stake, opened with an appropriate prayer, and quadrilles commenced. Judge Brandebury took to the corner at first; but some of our ladies, making true woman's account of the Miss Nancyism of a drawed up old bachelor, that showed he had sat a good deal in the shade, took pains with him, and, though a little peaked at first, we soon got him up, and made him excited. He danced with Mrs. —— and Mrs. ——, again with Mrs. —— and Mrs. ——, and finally left them all, real old bachelor fashion, to pay his exclusive attentions to "that sweet young lady with the wreath of roses round her head"—thus describing little Miss Sarah Badlam, aged, perhaps, thirteen, be the same more or less. Supper was announced at seven. The ladies and gentlemen sat down together—Governor Young at the head of one of the tables, with Judge Brandebury opposite him. Our leading confectionery consisted of roast beef, roast mutton, chickens, roast and boiled veal, roast pig, wild fowl,

Eat, O Friends, drink, yea drink abundantly, O beloved.

[6]

As Vinegar to the Teeth and as Smoke to the Eyes,

bear meat, and game pie, helped through with garden truck and sauce, pies, puddings, preserves, pumpkin butter, and other home dainties not so well known in these parts, and oysters and sardines in cans, from the East. For drink, we had our own brew of porter and ale—which I could not recommend, as it tastes like one part of the lager article to three of water—and for Brandebury's special use, Champagne wine from the grocery. From supper we went into the dancing again, and kept it up with spirit until near two o'clock in the morning, the handing round, at twelve, of refreshments (consisting of ice creams, cake, pie, nuts, and beverages), being the only interruption till the benediction and final dismissal home.

A similar reception was given to Judge Snow and his lady (No. 2), and Mr. and Mrs. Harris (No. 4), who arrived out together, I think, the 19th of July; and they were equally pleased with our bath-house balls. Mrs. Harris, who danced with the Governor once, I recollect—and with a will too—always being anxious to be heard saying: "Strange, people East know so little of the Mormons:" "To think of their being so refined, and so peaceful, and enjoying themselves so well," &c.—" Fair and softly goes far in a day;" perhaps, though, if called upon after this, we might have said that we had not unmixed cause to be pleased with our new officials. Their speech and conduct, somehow, from the first, created and spread the impression that they wanted to get extra advantage out of us. They complained, not without reason, of the lowness of their salaries; and it was intimated to some that a vote, by ourselves, of a certain increase would be agreeable. They would not organize court, or go to work, but—an ill example to our youth—lived indolent together in their boarding houses, day after day—the only utterly idle persons in our whole community. Yet, at the same time, they assumed airs and graces, and various manners of condescension and superiority; in which, rest assured, they made a very great mistake. It is an error, the prevalent opinion that we all cleanse the nasal orifice with the big toe, and make tea with holy water. We have among us women who play on the piano and mix French with their talk, and men who like tight boots, and who think more of the grammar than the meaning of what

So is the Sluggard to them that send him.

[7]

Though thou wash thee with Nitre and take thee

they are saying; and who would ask nothing better than to be fed by other people for squaring circles and writing dead languages all their lives—albeit we would not give one good gunsmith's apprentice for the whole of them. And, though we are all out-and-out democrats, in spirit and in substance, we have plenty of the hard-to-comb curly-pates of people, of whom the saying is true, that we "have seen better days;" so that if there is any thing we can do, it is to take the measure of sham, half-cut pretensions, and write down their true figures. There was one personal infirmity of Judge Brandebury, I am sure, was as much remarked upon with us as it could be anywhere—even the boarding-house folks were not content with it.

> Affect in things about thee cleanliness,
> That all may gladly board thee as a flower.

May I hope your readers understand ? You see, with our score of spring streams rushing through the city plat, our fresh water lakes, our hot springs, baths and Jordan river, more cleansing than Abana and Pharphar rivers of Damascus—we think so much of washing—And soap is not very dear with us either ! And we read the scriptures, including Zechariah iii., 3 and 4, where we are taught that the angel would not speak with Joshua before he changed his linen.—And ;—whistle! that shirt the Judge had on at our 24th of July celebration, where we did our best to make a dignity figure of him, was the greatest—it came about as near to being *the* great unwashed—considering there were ladies present, it was on the whole, I may say, the most Disrespectful Shirt, ever was seen at a celebration. The Judge never stirred out without his big umbrella, not so much to keep the sun off, as to hide out people, no account of his being shy ; but, after, this, whenever he was seen dragging about under it, it used to be the joke that he was afraid of rain water getting in on to that shirt. But, of course, no notice was taken of such trifles ; and everything went on smooth and glassy as the pool of indolence itself, till after the 17th day of August.— This day, arrived out from the States, Mr. P. E. Brocchus, and in one short six weeks after that this man staid among us, he was the

Much soap, yet thine Iniquity is marked before me.

[8]

Haman, the son of Hannedatha the Agagite,

means of stirring up all the evil report that we have had since to encounter.

Brocchus, as far as I have been able to find any thing about him, I make out to be one of those characters that it would be difficult to examine or educate anywhere out of the District of Columbia. Their description is that of the Washington maid of all work—that is, dirty work. Having the Directory of the cellars and garrets by heart—being the very men to show new "M. C.'s" the *fashions*, after dark—quick-smell feasts—long-suffering chamberers—knowing all the "convenient" people—lobbying as only those men can who have nothing else to do—always ready to hold big men's horses, and willing to blow their noses all day in the waiting room for the chance—they live on the broken victuals of big and little kitchen cabinets, till they come at last by their chance of boneing the mutton joint, which they devour in the face of the poor they have defrauded of it.

Of such came out to us from Alabama, via Washington, nearly one year after we were made a territory by law, our second Associate Judge. To our people at Kanesville, where he stopped for other purposes than outfitting, he proclaimed his intention of running as delegate to Congress. He provided intoxicating liquors gratuitously to those in his company who would listen to his discourse on this subject. He said it was his only purpose in going out to Utah; and that, his election secured, he should return at once. He alluded darkly to dangers impending over us at Washington that only he could avert, and declared that he had come out to enable him to be our saviour. Thus he spoke and electioneered with the people of the train till he met a return company, who conveyed intelligence to the States of the election of Dr. John M. Bernhisel. His tone then changed! As soon as he arrived, he announced his intention of returning to the States. He said he was sick, and supported the character in the eyes of his fellow-lodgers by eating enormously, without taking any out-door exercise. He was hale and busy enough, to our cost. He must have obtained his influence over the others almost immediately after his arrival. They soon removed to the boarding house in which he was quartered; and there evidently, as we think we can see now, con-

He hath conceived Mischief and brought forth Falsehood.

[9]

Doth the wild Ass bray when he hath grass?

certed their schemes and courses of molestation and mischief. We heard now distinctly more of discontent and dissatisfaction, and more of the insufficient compensation and the rest.

We could do nothing ourselves; but a petition to Congress having been drawn up, asking an increase of their salaries, the Governor headed it, and sent it off by Dr. Bernhisel, on the 1st of September. Of much avail was it! Within the week after, there followed the proceedings I am now going to describe. They had not their connected appearance at the time, but we have been at no loss to understand their bearing since.

One day Brocchus reminded the Governor that he was going away very soon, and asked him to do him the favor of procuring him as large an audience of the people as possible, as he was very anxious to set before them in style the claims of the Washington monument fund. I do not know how he made out his case; but, as he was always specious and smiling, the Governor, willing to show him a pleasure, said, "I will invite you, sir, to speak at our approaching conference. It is a religious meeting, I suppose you are aware; but I wish well to your cause." One of the first buildings we ever raised at Salt Lake, was our Bowery, or gallery of rough timber and wattles, for public assemblies. Around it then was all naked ground, though it now stands in the heart of the business part of the city. Our semi-annual conferences have always met in it; and our Fall one assembling here by stated appointment, September the 6th; at its opening day, a handsome representation of the people from all quarters being in attendance, Governor Young took the first opportunity of fulfilling his promise. "I was respectfully and honorably introduced," says the published statement of Judge Brocchus.

This individual, I take it, is one of those who, by reason of a certain fluency and custom of easy rambling from subject to subject, spreading themselves out over all they have ever had a thought upon, are able to acquit themselves quite creditably in a conversation or brief friendly letter; while they break down miserably if called on for a speech or essay upon a continuous subject, which exposes in them the defects of their early education, their habitually loose texture of thought, and their want of

Their eyes did fail because there was no grass.

[10]

Stand not in the place of great men.

connected views and consistent principles of any kind. Such creatures frequently pass through the world without being voted ignoramus or lack-wit, and so with some yet may this unsteady creature Brocchus.

I make this remark because I am certain no one of his acquaintance at Salt Lake city, was prepared for such a speech as he made on this occasion. In its way it beat Brandebury's Shirt. I would give a hundred dollars for the sake of our cause, to have had a phonographer to take down the stupendous effort. I can only now profess to remember a few points of it, recalled to my memory by the use that has been made of them since. He began by stating that he had read our history with deep interest, particularly that part relating to our sufferings in winter quarters, on the Missouri River, during the severe winter of '47. I intended to have visited winter quarters, he said, but, alas, was not able. A friend of mine brought me these flowers; here they are; it is all I can present you of that sainted place! At this sympathetic display he forced a tear, and, the careless observer would have said, wiped it from his cheek, but Deseret eyes saw the handkerchief pass to the right and left, while the tear remained on the cheek by an overcast of the head. His reception was next referred to. I was a stranger and you took me in; sick, and you visited me, &c. Even a kind lady brushed the flies from my forehead; her kindness I can never forget.—Another tear was forthcoming, and wiped as before. Twenty minutes of this sort of thing quite naturally introduced the consideration of his personal merits. In the course of an able and flattering autobiography, he displayed all his advantages of experience and public service in important imaginary capacities. His appointment by his Excellency the President of the United States, was enough to show what kind of a man he was! The President being a virtuous man, could appoint none but a virtuous man like himself; he (Brocchus) being virtuous, therefore, like the President, received his appointment. By this argument he refuted any *vile calumnies* from the States that he said might have pursued his private character! After this, in a style half school-book, half 4th of July, came up Anthony (!) Putnam, the Revolutionary

Let another man praise thee and not thine own mouth.

[11]

Burning lips and a wicked heart are like

War, and Gen. Washington, who was declared a greater man than Napoleon and all his generals, and only to be compared to President Taylor. Putnam he got at Bunker Hill, but Washington at Burgoyne's, probably Braddock's, defeat. Behold him! he cried, on his white horse at the battle of Yorktown, proudly careering on his white charger over the prostrate bodies of his country's enemies. This sort of thing took up an hour more, by which the patience of the company was pretty nearly worn out, though they remained quiet. "For more than two hours," he writes, "I was favored with the unwavering attention of my audience." But a changed tone then came on him, with a change of subject. He began a studied assault upon his introducer, Governor Young, and an argument to the people against allowing the man so much influence as he possessed, the sum of it being that so long as this continued we could have no party divisions, and without party divisions we could not be a worthy object of the notice or favor of politicians. Soon, however, he found he could do nothing on this head. "Oh ladies, sweet ladies," he cried, "why do you 'go in' for such a man? Your smiles should be turned on the contemplation of men who can handle the sword— George Washington, and Zachary Taylor, the second Washington. Oh, Governor Young can't handle the sword!" Even such soft appeals as this were thrown away. From bad to worse, disapprobation rose till the orator was groaned. He tried a few insinuations more, and was groaned again, groaned with a will. At this, instead of taking his seat, he changed his ground, and made a direct and undisguised attack upon the audience itself, men and women, without distinction, accusing them of want of patriotism and attachment to the laws, and reproaching and insulting them to their face. General D. H. Wells, of Illinois, and impulsive and hot spoken man, but I am bound to say one of our most liberal and public spirited citizens, had delivered an oration on the 24th of July, severely condemning the course of the federal government towards us. Producing an imperfect report of this speech and commenting on it, Brocchus proceeded to attribute its sentiments to the people, and make them answerable for it, thereupon threatening them with destruction by the whole army

A Potsherd covered with silver dross.

[12]

It is sport to a Fool to do mischief.

and navy of the United States. In the same way he brought up ramarks of Governor Young upon General Taylor, threatening the people with destruction for them also, and declaring that his (Brocchus's) influence should break him from office, the instant he arrived in Washington. Finally, the women hissing him here, he mentioned Washington, for the first time, in connection with the monument, and as if merely incidentally. "It reminds me, *by the way*," he said, "that I have a commission from the Washington Monument Association, to ask of you (the ladies) a block of marble, as the test of your citizenship and loyalty to the government of the United States. But in order for you to do it acceptably, you must become virtuous, and teach your daughters to become virtuous, or your offering had better remain in the bosom of your native mountains."

At this climax of insult, the meeting rose as one man, and their cries and uproar compelled the speaker to take his seat. The tumult continuing, we looked to the other officers of the United States, who had been invited to the stand, to reply; but, as they failed to do so, the Governor being loudly called for, rose and spoke in substance (for I cannot imitate or remember successfully his peculiar style), as follows:—"But for this man's personalities, I would be ashamed not to leave him to be answered by some of our small spouters—sticks of his own timber. Such an orator, I should suppose, might be made by down-east patent, with Comstock's phonetics and elocution primers; but, I ask you all; have we ever before listened to such trash and nonsense from this stand? Are you a Judge, (he said, turning to him), and can't even talk like a lawyer, or a politician, and hav'nt read an American school history? Be ashamed, you illiterate ranter, (said he), not to know your Washington better than to praise him for being a mere brutal warrior. George Washington was called first in war; but he was first in peace, and first in the hearts of his countrymen. He had a big head and a great heart. Of course, he could fight. But, Lord! what man can't? What man here will dare to say, with women standing by, that he is a bit more a coward than Washington was? Handle the sword! I can handle a sword as well as George Washington. I'd be ashamed

Is this man Coniah a despised and broken Idol?

[13]

Answer a Fool according to his Folly.

to say I couldn't. But you, standing there, white and shaking now, at the hornets'-nest you have stirred up yourself—you are a coward; and that is why you have cause to praise men that are not; and why you praise Zachary Taylor. President Taylor you can't praise—you find nothing in him. Old General Taylor! what was he?—a mere soldier, with regular army-buttons on; no better to go at the head of brave troops than a dozen I could pick up between Leavenworth and Laramie. And, for one, I'll not have Washington insulted by having him compared to Taylor, for a single breath of speech. No, nor what is more, President and General Andrew Jackson crowed down and forgotten, while I am with this people—even if I did not know that one is in one place (of punishment), and the other in another (of reward). Brigham Young spoke this out of his knowledge by the priesthood.

"What's the meaning," continued the Governor, but more at large than I can give it here, "what's the meaning of this insult upon our patriotism? Is it the place of miserable vermin that feed upon its sacred body, to teach us the value of the Union? Sense enough you have to see we are bound to be its best friends. But you shall not go home to say you were never told so. Against the Union, are we? We want to have Saint Francisco on one side of us, and Saint Louis on the other, fighting and scratching like any other two saints of different denominations, do we? And the tax on the foreign goods we use isn't enough, to be sure, but we must want to pay one set of duties at a custom-house in New York or New Orleans, and then another at Jefferson City, may be, and another set again at Council Bluffs! That will help us, wont it? No, sir; we're not nailed to North or South, or any other point of the compass, here. We have come out from the North and South as well as East and West, and we want our old States to stick together, because we intend to stick to the whole of them. And we are just the very people to know what tomfool's nonsense it is, the notion of a minority that expects to get into a tight place, going off for safety into close partnership with its next neighbors. Who does not know that there is more bother with a quarrelsome neighbor than with a dozen that live further off. And what is a man's chance if, with a neighbor on each side

Should thy lies make men hold their peace.

[14]

How forcible are right words.

of him, bent upon mischief, he has no other neighbors to help him keep them straight? It is just the same with States. Let the devil of persecution get abroad against any single one of them, as it did against us at home, and let it be Georgia or Illinois on one side, and North Carolina and Tennessee, or Missouri and Iowa on the other, all ready to join, if one is not enough, to put Charleston or Nauvoo down—and where is Charleston, or South Carolina either, going to be, if she hasn't then one outsider to help her? Now, tell all this, when you return, to some of your folks in Alabama, where you say you belong;—though, if you tell them instead, the Mormons want to get up a union with Selkirk's Settlement, or the Hudson Fur Company, or be annexed by the Mexican half-breeds, or the Indians, (say the Crows, or the Blackfeet, or the Snakes), I know they'd rather believe it.—Snake stories are about all they will believe of Mormons!" After defining very fully his views after this wise, the Governor concluded, I remember, about as follows:—" What you have not been afraid to intimate about our morals, I will not stoop to notice, except to make my particular personal request of every brother and husband present, not to give your back what such impudence deserves. You talk of things 'you have on hearsay,' since your coming among us. I'll talk of hearsay then—the hearsay that you are discontented and will go home, because we cannot make it worth your while to stay. What it would satisfy you to get out of us I think it would be hard to tell; but I am sure it is more than you'll get. If you or any one else is such a baby-calf, we must sugar your soap to coax you to wash yourself of Saturday nights: go home to mammy straight away, and the sooner the better!"

This is the whole of Governor Young's speech, of which so much to-do has been made. What to make of the strange speech of Brocchus, to this day I am not clear. Had it, after all, no more meaning in it than a capon's crow? or did the man, under the impression that we were a divided people, think he could raise up a party out of those opposed to Brigham Young—and was he the two hours sweetening his preface before trying it?—or was he, again, as others think, drunk, or partially so?—or was he so unused to public speaking, and was he so scared when he came to

Can'st thou draw out Leviathan with a hook?

[15]

Is there any taste in the white of an egg?

his words of work in earnest, as to get into a sort of college lad's flurry, and say more than he ever meant to say, to extricate himself from his bashful floundering? Any of these suppositions may be true in part; but I am satisfied it was a concerted thing, although, as I have intimated, it did not strike us in that light at the time, or, in fact, in any other, much beyond its breaking up our conference. This it did. We could not go on with the church business after the disgraceful occurrence, and our meeting had to be dismissed and dispersed.

After the Brocchus outrage, the story of the misconduct of the other officers is soon related. First, we found out, to our astonishment, that neither Brandebury nor Harris were at pains to condemn or disavow his course. Soon we were threatened that Harris would return with Brocchus; not long after we heard the same ill of Brandebury, and soon after this (I am not here in the spirit of a jest; but just four days before little Sally Badlam had left Utah and its judiciary, for the mines!) their purpose of doing so was formally announced to us. The Governor, upon this, fearing they might be as good as their word, and leave the territory to legal anarchy, called a special session of the Legislature to consider of the exigency. There was a rupture at once. They would not communicate with that body or notice its existence. The Assembly passed a joint resolution directing the United States Marshal to take into his custody the papers, seals, and funds of the Secretary, as about to abscond. He disregarded it, and applying to Judge Brandebury, who, for this special purpose, constituted a United States Court for the first time, obtained an injunction on the marshal against interfering with him. The two houses passing also a resolution directing an order to be drawn for $500 on account of mileage, stationery, &c., out of the $24,000 placed in the Secretary's hands for such expenses; he refused to accept it, and on the contrary, wrote them back an insulting letter, in which he pronounced his (the Secretary's) opinion that they were illegally elected and constituted. This letter, dated September, 25, came to the Assembly next day, or Friday, Sept., 26. What they would have done, or what would have been the course of their debates it would be hard to say. But the officers, as if they feared

They conceive Mischief and bring forth Vanity.

[16]

He that diggeth a pit shall fall therein.

the Assembly really might take the Secretary's objections for more than they were worth, and resign and be reconstituted, which could have been done in a week—the next thing we knew, they were off—Sunday morning, bright and early, September, 28, A. D., 1851.

And so quiet as they kept about it all! Though the Legislature had their muss with Harris about not paying them and the rest, which figures so largely *now* on paper, the very week I left, there was nothing about it had hardly come up for as much as talk, except how Brocchus insulted the Conference on the 6th of September. Yet all this time, it turns out, they were hedging and hatching, and laying traps, playing sly attorney's tricks, giving advice, and getting crooked law papers out of honest, straightforward citizens, that suspected no offence, but looked up to them in such matters for what they professed to be, their legal protectors, advisers, and guardians. And to crown all, they have the face to talk, in the documents they have got up, of the "hostile and seditious feelings and sentiments" of the people,—our poor people! that then and now and all the time have been minding their own business, sowing, and reaping, and digging, and building, and manufacturing, as careless of the doings of the men in Rhodes' boarding-house, as you would be of goings on at the Swedish consul's in Varick street! Though, if the wiles of the Diabolonians prosper, be they ever so unwitting of guilt they will be punished indeed, by having sent them pro-consul, with rapacious legions (of relations), some "most excellent Governor Felix," or Porcius Festus, of the last hungriest of the first families of Virginia, who has missed his middy's warrant when he was young, and can't get a pursership after he has gone to seed.

I have concluded my narrative. How far it contains cause of offence, perhaps, I am unable to see; but I am sure it will surprise every one that has perused it, to know that, wretched stitching together of trivialities as it appears, it covers the whole ground of the charges made against us in the many score pages of the returned officers, and contains the true statement of every transaction in which they were concerned, by perver-

Wo be to fearful hearts and faint hands,

[17]
And the sinner that goeth two ways.

sion, made obnoxious to censure. Above, and outside of all the admissions I have been so careful to make, the reader will see that room remains for me to offer comments on our part, explaining our course, and condemning our antagonists. I refrain. I shall take my chance of doing this, when I take up, in form, the charges as they have drawn them. Though I can't expect it will please them much better than did the woman the emetic, when she told the doctor there was no good giving her any more, for she couldn't keep it in her stomach five minutes. Still, their complaint shan't be, their Physic is not done up in style.

I am your very obedient servant,

JEDEDIAH M. GRANT.

LETTER II.

More Secrets of the Temple—Polecats in Mare's nests—Bogus Coiners—Squatters without Titles—The Mormon Pope—A Bowie Knife—Pawnee Politeness—Davy Crocket a Mormon—General Taylor be (is) damned.

April 8, 1852.

"He that pricketh the eye will make tears to fall, and he that pricketh the heart maketh it to show her knowledge."—Ecclesiasticus xxii., 19.

THE Accusation of the delinquent officers contains the following passage : " Upon the following Sunday, the mayor of the City, Jedediah M. Grant, in eulogizing the strength of the Mormons, exultingly declared from the pulpit, in presence of one of the undersigned (Mr. Harris), that now the United States could not conquer them (the Mormons) by arms."

A CARD.

Mr. Jedediah M. Grant's compliments to Messrs. B. Harris, L. Brandebery, and P. E. Brocchus, late officials of the Territory of Utah, and will regret if he restores in some degree relations suspended between them, through the necessity he is under of informing the public that the above statement is a deliberate and dishonest falsehood.

You may thank yourself, Mr. Bennett, for not having this time, an interesting letter. "Well lathered is half shaved."—When I had so fully narrated the proceedings of the Returned Officers, I thought I was quit of further call to notice what I was sure the sound judgment of any man of experience would then know, could

Go out for Wool—Come home shorn.

[19]

Fools reflect sometimes, but always after their folly.

be only the attempted Extenuation or Excuse of such shameful Misbehavior. But, in your Editorial accompanying my Letter of last month, you are at pains to say; "the pith of the charges against Governor Young and his community is not answered." I must therefore accept the reproach of shirking or dodging these, if I do not bestow upon them a consideration above their deserts. I had in my mind, to regale your readers, a variety of entertaining topics; as the Dead City of the Gulf, a pastoral Love Match, an Indian Hunt, &c. &c.,; to which I thought to add some Choice Evidences of Modern Prophecy, Healing and Inspiration by the Laying on of Hands, and a neat though brief Summary of other Gifts and Blessings, under our new Covenant, which I trusted would feelingly persuade the followers of Religions among you, that theirs are but as the ancient and thirsty Structures for Fountains to be seen in Eastern Countries, through which no Water any longer runs. But all these pleasant subjects, I must now postpone to the consideration of the Charges, only invoking the God of Twaddle that he will keep me steadily to them.

Before going on, I lay before my countrymen a Difficulty I labor under in this matter. I have to take up, not to explain away but to directly contradict, all the Allegations of any account the Fugitive Officers bring against us. The Charges they first circulated—more outrageous, but therefore easier of refutation, one, for instance, that we had been Embezzling the Public Moneys—are now withdrawn; Three successive versions of what is called the Report, have been given to the Public, each less boldly criminatory than the one that went before it: but the paper that remains before Congress as their Latest Edition, and by which they must stand, for it is in Brandebery's handwriting, and is signed by him and Brocchus and Harris, contains offensive allegations more than enough, considered only as Skunk Sprinklings, to put us deservedly in ill odor with the country. I declare it false. I give the Foulmarts the Lie in their Teeth.— But they count Three, and I am but One. And I am a stranger, and our relative worth of character does not appear. And who is to decide between us, or how? Even under the rule of the Devil from Hell living in the doomed body of Louis Napoleon,

As listed on Abaddon's side, they mangle their own Flesh and slay.

[20]

And the faulty scent is picked up by the hound.

it is said to call for the Pole Cat Report of, at least, *four* police spies, before they can ruin a man for holding unpopular opinions. MY DEMAND IS THEN, THAT OUR ACCUSERS BE PUT TO THEIR OATHS! Upon their oaths at least, I insist : let them swear away the liberties of freemen. And so, if they cannot be purged of the truth, or if the voices of our noble and far distant people cannot be heard in time to prevail against them ; yet thus, when the Day comes for them to stand before the Tribunal of the Nation, which shall compel true justice to be measured them, we will have the legal pains and penalties of PERJURY at hand, with which to precede upon Earth those direr punishments reserved for False Swearers at the Great Assize of the Last Day. The full circumstantial narrative I have already published, covers, as I have remarked, nearly all I thought worth noticing in the Report. It is next to impossible for me to pick out all the wicked Insinuations and Poison Pinsticks with which it is interspersed. "He has a slid-grip that has an Eel by the tail" :—But for a fortunate leading Paragraph, in which various heads of offense are associated together (though no effort is made afterward to sustain them, unless by innuendo), I should be at a loss how to get hold of any of them pinchingly enough to mash them by my denials. I shall therefore quote it in full, numbering (not to say branding) as I go on.

" We found upon our arrival," says the Report or Information : (1) "That almost the entire population consisted of a people " called Mormons ; (2) and The Mormon Church overshadowing " and controlling the opinions, the actions, the property, and even " the lives of its members ; (3) Usurping and exercising the func- " tions of legislation and the judicial business of the Territory. (4) " Organizing and commanding the military. (5) Disposing of the " public lands upon its own terms ; (6) Coining money stamped " Holiness to the Lord ; and forcing its circulation at a standard " fifteen or twenty per centum above its real value ; (7) Openly " sanctioning and defending the practice of Polygamy or Plurality " of Wives ; (8) Exacting the tenth part of *every thing* from its " members, under the name of tithing, (9) and enormous taxes ·" from citizens not members ; (10) penetrating and supervising the

And the fact turns up like a worm from the ground.

[21]

And the sow that ought By the ear is caught.

" social and business circles, and inculcating and requiring as an " article of religious faith, implicit obedience to the counsels of " 'The Church,' as paramount to all the obligations of morality, " society, of allegiance, and of law."

To these Charges I proceed to reply in the order in which I have numbered them.

1. This is true. " Find a mare's nest—laugh at the eggs." Three Thousand miles was far to go to hunt up this one.

2. This is False, as I shall particularly explain. I call for its trial under oath : Trial !

3. False : Smack the calfskin for this too : Trial !

4. False again : Trial !

5. Trial ! This is so baseless a lie that, not " the Mormon Church," but not even one of the Mormon People, nor single citizen of Utah has claimed the right of " disposing of the public lands upon his own terms." What any of us individually have first settled upon, we have, by Law—as Squatters simply—earned a certain right of preëmption in for our Improvements. But nothing more ; and it might be a well-grounded cause of Complaint with our People that, owing to the delay of Congress in legislating for us, we to this hour remain without Titles to our Homes.

6. We did coin the Money stamped Holiness to the Lord, and what's more with a Date upon it, and what's worse a Denomination ; and, God forgive us too, a Hand in Hand thereon with opposite mystic emblems. The dies we cut ourselves, and very creditably well too, I thought ; but, reading from a Book (the only book of reference of the kind we had with us in the wilderness) the number of parts of Alloy that should go to aliquot parts of Gold, we mixed these by the recipe with the pure Virgin Gold that came to us from the Mines, and not with the Gold technically called Pure and considered to be such at the U. S. Mint. Of course our coin was below Standard, and it fell to its actual or intrinsic Value as soon as the fact was discovered. Where better money is not on hand to serve exchanges, ours is offered and taken for as much as it is worth, and no more. To deny the charge of our *forcing* it into circulation, except to Simpletons, is absurd. I don't believe the power of the Tsar of Muscovy can

And the sin to the sinful door is brought.

[22]

Set Dead Man's Bell a ringing for joy.

make his subjects think black is white, or give gold dollars in even change for gilt-washed five cent pieces.

7. This, with the no less grave charge of Murder, made in the body of the Report, and to which our whole community are accused of being accessories, I shall consider by itself and at length. Meantime, asking to be found " NOT GUILTY in manner and form as in the indictment is alleged against us :"—Trial!

8. Trial, I say, Trial! The Episcopalians in England and Ireland, the *genteelest* religionists in the world—particularly in the dry goods line—levy and forcibly collect their Tithe Tax from the people of all denominations, carting the sheaf and driving off of the pig to be sold. I don't think, however, it can be the particular Decimal Ratio Brocchus objects to, since he put one of our citizens under contribution for a much larger proportion of his annual profits of business, having borrowed the same, and come away without remembering to return it. I have in my possession two nice little notes of hand of his to Mr. J. W. Coolidge of Kanesville, which I will give the Congressional Committee on Claims their ' Tithing ' or Ten per cent. to collect for me.—In the United States, the Quakers and many other sects manage the thing, by making up statedly their Budget of expenses for the current year, and assessing each of their members his share, according to his seeming means. Then a collecting Committee visits each one, to say, " Brother Nathan, or Obadiah, Friends have computed thy yearly rate to be—so much ; which we will now receive of thee "—and if Brother Nathan or Obadiah, as the case may be, does not poney up, without discount for cash payment, promptly—he had better join some other meeting—that's all.—Mormons do not go so far. They declare as much as a tenth part of the annual increase or income of their members to be the Due of the Church, but they do not exact it. It is a Free Will Offering purely, to be estimated by the giver, and is not accepted from those who are not in full communion. Yet, by its being appropriated to the erection of Public buildings and similar purposes, the citizens of Utah who do not contribute to the Tithe Fund are participators in its benefits. So far is the impression sought to be conveyed by this charge, from being true. I would

For in Fig leaves I appeared.

[23]

He loved mutton well, that licked where the ewe lay.

like to be able to set down more to Fun than to Malice, the charge associated with it (9) of our levying "*enormous* taxes from citizens not members." The meaning of this is, that, being practical Temperance Men, we have been imposing a sort of Old European Town Gate duty on Ardent Spirits brought into Salt Lake City for sale. It makes Inebriety pay dear there, and no mistake ; but then "citizens not members," from Brocchus to bully Billy Smith inclusive, are free to go forth a day's march into the Commonwealth of our neighbours the Diggers, those "free men not fanatics" who eat slugs and grubs and, spurning other attire, pomatum their independent heads with mud ; and get drunk among them as cheap as they please. If our Law is unconstitutional, depends on his Honor Chief Justice Taney and the Supreme Court of the United States ; may it please Judge Brandebery, whose aversion to cold Water I regret to have recorded to posterity. But I wonder, (seeing that Mr. Man's Invention is Captain Anything's special standard-bearer,) Brocchus did not fish up something in this line more to the purpose, against Governor Young. I can give him a hint, for his next *Official Document furnished the papers in advance*. The "Well Regulated License System" playing the very devil among the Wigwams, the Maine Liquor Law is the Law of the United States I believe over our whole Indian Territory. It is the duty of Indian Agents to see this Law enforced. Governor Young is, under his appointment, one of these. Hearken, O Great Soul of Brocchus! I have seen more than one Cask of Whiskey, "*sacrilegeously*," as thou wouldst say, staved in, and its fire-water set running out upon the ground. Hot butter beans. Ahem !

(10.) This, Lie the last, being as groundless as the others, makes up the contingent of each of the three officers—Three lies apiece. "Almost, and very nigh, saves many and many a lie ;" but the last and least of compliments I am forced to withhold ;— they are not even ingenious lies !—Again, for the last time, I call for Trial, and dare the officers to back their words by Perjury !

The Paragraph disposed of, I can now scatter my fire. But I must first of all advert to a shade of speciousness that there is in the charges branded by me, Nos. 2, 3, 4, 10, and the rest,

He should sit close, that has riven breeks.

[24]

Rush bellowing and breathing fire and smoke.

where the standing nominative, "the Mormon Church" is made so largely answerable for the doings of its members.

It is the old Trick of the enemies of Religious Liberty, persuading the ignorant to confound the two notions of *Spiritual* or strictly Religious influence, and *Material* or Political influence. They often go hand in hand, but they are two things entirely distinct and independent of each other. The Sun gives Heat and gives Light both, often; but a candle may light a room that is below Zero, and a lamp black Stove heat it in perfect darkness as hot as a summer's day. Or, take another illustration. Upon a hint from our (not *Native*) American Cardinal Go Bragh, the old Pope's Managers send a Block of Marble to the Managers of the Washington Monument. To think as I do, that the consequence of this neighborly compliment will be to produce a certain amount of good feeling responsive to it, is to believe in the *Spiritual Influence* of this Block of Marble; to think that it is charged with percussion caps, rockets, and poisonous projectiles, that, when the block of marble is hoisted to its place, will explode like the Princeton's gun, or an old Gunpowder Plot, killing the Monument Committee, and an assortment of Members of Congress, an equally irreparable loss to their country, this is to believe in its *Material Influence*. Some people—though chiefly, to be sure, infirm females advanced in years,—do, I know, believe the Pope is a particular style of Guy Fawkes. Still, it remains another thing for him to combine *ex-officio* the powers of this worthy with those of, say Dr. Samuel Watts.

This false Notion about Churches, extends, too, to the influence of the Members of Churches. Men will rise out of all sects, fitted to exercise power outside their sects ; and, for this reason, having the greater influence inside their sect. And this cannot be avoided. But what a silly thing to scream out against that sect for its Good Fortune : "Beware of the Congregationalists : the rule of their Primate, Timothy Dwight, is Supreme." "Beware of the Unitarians : they unite under Cardinal Channing." "That Scotch Pope, Chalmers, sends his orders over to American Presbyterian General Assemblies ; away with him !" I have named at random here three notable Reverends, who were men of substance, ruling

At crippled Papistry to butt and poke,

[25]

Exactly as a skittish Scottish bull.

in their own right. Maybe they conspired: Maybe they did n't. They are all dead now—and what's the odds?—Or what odds more would it have been if they had had in Fact the sham Titles I have given them. I am called Brigadier; Mr. Benton is not seldom now dubbed the Lieutenant General. Are we, is the Country, any the better or the worse for that? I can tell you, simple W. E. Channing was, all his life, twenty times as much a real Bishop as your titular Onderdonk. And what's more, whether a recent public lecturer appears before his audience " in a clerical habit of brown cloth reaching to the feet and bedecked with a profusion of small red buttons, and on his breast, a large crucifix of gold, pendent from a chain around his neck," or whether he prefers a garb less Irish and dramatic, and more genteel, Pius the IX., the Ferretti Pope, will have just as much influence in New York as it suits the real Pope, John Hughes, to let him; and no more.—When will men learn to look beneath the surface of things!

I shall not argue this question. I am ashamed to need to argue it in this Country. But I can see, the Wrong View of it is like to make Trouble enough for our Confederacy. On our road to Universal Empire, we have to pass through Catholic countries; Canadas, Cubas, and Mexicos, with their whole regiments of titled Bishops, Abbots, Priests, Jesuits, and Friars. And sooner or later, as we swallow them down we will find this bone of Bigotry sticking in our gullet. The Point must be met and settled. And perhaps, We are as well able to meet it as others;—but, meantime, the Song may be " Hardest fend off, and look out for splinters!"

Eight years ago, I remember, I was in the Ministry at Philadelphia, when the Native party was got up; and there was nothing people wouldn't credit of the *Material* Influence of the Pope; the Romans were going to be down on us so soon! And what issued of it? Our Protestanters burnt two of the Catholic churches, and I don't know how many of their dwellings! *The Dog it was that died.* A word to the wise, Dr. Ryder, and discreet Society of Jesus!

There is a great deal in the Report, about the influence of Brigham Young—unbounded influence of Brigham Young, &c. &c.;

Hunts an old woman in a scarlet cloak.

[26]

That led as through the wilderness, through a land of deserts and of pits

and we are told: "he rules as he pleases without a rival or opposition, for no man dares question his authority." This, you observe is quite good abuse, provided you will confound the Governor's Personal or Political with his Church or Religious authority. Now, a word about this BRIGHAM YOUNG. When Joseph Smith lived, a man about whose real character and pretensions we differ, JOSEPH was often and almost invariably imposed upon by those in whom he placed his trust. There was One Man, almost only that One of his early adherents, he could always rely upon to stick closer to him than a Brother, steadfast in Faith, clear in Counsel, and foremost in Fight. He seemed a plain man to us in those days, of a wonderful talent for business and hundred horse power of industry, but least of any thing affecting Cleverness or Quickness. "Honest Brigham Young," or "hardworking Brother Brigham" was nearly as much as you would ever hear him called, though he was the almost universal executor and trustee of men's wills and troubled estates, and the confidential manager of our most intricate church affairs. We had a piebald sort of luck in those days. At last the fullness of time was come for JOSEPH to obey his own Prophecy and be slain, and his body with his brother Hiram's was brought to us one afternoon from Carthage Prison, bleeding all the way upon the wagon in which they were laid and against the boughs and hay placed under and over them to dead the jolting and keep off the flies. Brigham Young was not in Illinois at that time ; but, when our foes, grown fierce by their tasting of blood, rose in packs that became Armies to hunt us down; when the Nauvoo sky was reddened after sundown by the firing of the outfarm Settlements, and white-necked women, gathering their nightclothes about them as they ran came flying to us for shelter, and stray children appeared in the streets hungry and asking for their parents; in that hour of trial, and doubt, the worst of trial, the hopes of all who still hoped for the Human race and loved their God, were turned on him. Many who pretended to much Higher Gifts were put aside though offered. By the unanimous vote of the People in Great Council assembled, BRIGHAM was called to take the place of JOSEPH. Then first were made manifest his admirable Gifts. He rallied the hearts of the wa-

Through a land of drought, and of the shadow of death

[27]

Through a land that no man passed through, and where no man dwelt

vering, and inspired them with a portion of the Courage that was in him. He led us through the perils of the wilderness to the Canaan we inhabit, and, called to the duty it was denied Moses and Joshua to unite, he planted us also hopefully in the wonderful peace and prosperity we there enjoy. And will we desert him now? Yes! when we can find an equal man to take his place, any Man or son of Man as wise a Thinker, as good a Ruler of other men.—I can't undertake to explain Brigham Young to your Atlantic citizens, or expect you to put him at his value. Your great men Eastward are to me like your ivory and pearl handled table knives, balance handles, more shining than the inside of my watch case; but, with only edge enough to slice bread and cheese or help spoon victuals, and all alike by the dozen one with another. Brigham is the article sells out West with us, between a Roman cutlass and a beef butcher knife, the thing to cut up a deer or cut down an enemy, and that will save your life or carve your dinner every bit as well, though the handpiece is buck horn and the case a hogskin hanging in the breech of your pantaloons. You, that judge men by the handle and sheath, how can I make you know a good *Blade?*

If I were going to make one point for Brigham more than another, it would be his likeness in character to the great Man of Old, of whom it was said, that whatever you saw him once take up, you would have said it was the occupation of his life. Brigham naturally can judge between right and wrong quicker than any mortal I ever saw. He is nice in his person, and must have every thing "just so" about him; his pride, moreover, is in his affectionate and joyous temper, and a humanity that makes the dogs and cattle know him to love him. For all social harmonies, too, it is true of him by figure as it is besides in fact, that "he loves all the best *music* that heart can invent." But he has no mind for some kinds of niffy naffy finical whilly whaing. He has *never tried* to make himself a Lamb, or a Dandy, or a Lawyer; and therefore neither can I try here to make him out such. And, if men don't treat him well, and rather make up their minds to be his enemies, I go out of my way here to say what I think to his credit: it is 54° 40' then or fight: he has no manners to spend

Like Meg Wood of Elie, who liked all things well, and good things best.

[28]

No solemn, sanctimonious face I pull,

on them at all. He can't smile and stab in the same wink, as they learn to do in Washington.

When he led the Van of our Pioneers, seventy strong, pushing for the Great Basin for the first time, we were met by the Pawnee Warriors, in force say eight hundred mounted men, demanding that we, and all who followed us, should pay tribute for passing through their country. Brigham gave us our orders beforehand quietly, and we halted still till they were crowded close upon us, threatening, and off their guard. Suddenly, at the word, down went our rifles to the sights, and covered all the Head men and Chiefs individually, and *then* Brigham spoke up his answer: "Now down off your horses this instant or you Front Rank are dead in a snap!" This was all the answer he gave. Themselves then asked pardon: And no more trouble from the Pawnees have we had since!—Our saying hence is, Brigham treats his unfriends *Pawnee fashion*. After they have once proved their ill will, good bye to compliments: he shows what a proud man he was born; and, if his scorn is quiet, it is the harder to bear. Here is the explanation, if any were needed, of a scene particularly attested by Boy Harris, who, coming into the Governor's Room at a time when he was administering a rebuke to an unfaithful public servant of our own sect, was so ignorant of the first rudiments of politeness as to sit out their whole interview.—Brigham Young can mix up devotion and drollery, eloquence and old English, quaintness and magnanimity, with a variety that only the most highly educated order of perception can fully appreciate. How then, in the name of Grace, could such common-place feckless flunkies as our forlorn snobs of Officers, be expected to understand the man? You might as well have brought together old Oliver Cromwell and the turnspits of Charles Stuart's kitchen. His demeanor quizzed them, his jests puzzled them, his religion scared them, and his acts confounded them. There is one Fact shines out in Brocchus's letter. "Had he (Gov. Young) pointed his finger at me," says the "*defender of his country*," "had he pointed his finger at me, in that instant, I should have been a dead man." I shall not deny that Brocchus really did think so!

To cross back to my argument. Briefly: We Mormons may

Nor think I'm pious, when I'm only bilious.

[29]

First, the work gives credit to the workman,

value Brigham Young most for his Spiritual Endowments, and we may believe we owe him *most* for his guidance of us on our *Heavenly* pilgrimage. In the Good Old cause of God's Rule and Man's Happiness, *we know* he is the Champion who will bite the Firebrand that stands in his way, and who if hacked to pieces, will stand up in every piece to fight on for the right. In the great cause of Redemption and its Holy War, *we have seen* in him combined the virtues of the four Captains Shaddai sent to regain Man-Soul, those "rough hewn men that were fit to break the ice and make their way by dint of sword." We may *think*, besides, he can go down into the Black Den and drag forth Devils thence like Putnam's wolves: I *may* choose to say even we believe he is Greatheart himself, incarnate to slay the Giants Grim, Maul, Slaygood, and Despair, and conduct safe our pilgrims to the land of Beulah and the gate called Beautiful. What matters it; so long as outside and above all this—which to you is within the realm of Superstition, to us within the sphere of Heaven—there is that more than enough which makes Brigham Young stand up like Saul the King, a head and shoulders above all other men?—And So be it ever!

As for Mr. Young's personal opinions on subjects at large: for men so much his inferiors as these or any others to call him to account for them, is sheer Impertinence. Out of the range of his official duties, he has as much Right to think what he pleases, and say what he thinks, as any other Citizen of the United States, Mormon, Methodist, or Presbyterian. Is he to be outlawed because he holds unpopular opinions of Zachary Taylor? I will give mine then to be pilloried, as they accord with his. Taylor is not to be compared with Washington, no, nor with Jackson; and never justly will be, so long as a General's greatness is measured by the lives he *saves* and not the lives he *sacrifices*. Do you want to try the two together? Look at Taylor at Monterey, and our poor fellows' blood running there by Gutters full, through his obstinate ignorance; and then look at Jackson after the Battle of New Orleans, urged to gain renown by attacking the British in retreat, but saying: "No, Sir; by God, I am bound to the Father and Mother of every Boy that's followed me from Tennessee to bring

Then the workman gives credit to the work.

[30]

Laws catch flies, and let hornets go free.

him back safe and sound!" When Brigham Young looks into the Future, does he see Old Greyhead Jackson at the Judgment seat of God? The bodies of his (six and seven) thirteen men killed at New Orleans, come up at the Trial and stand by to grasp his hand, while they thank him for saving their beloved country. But, when they call up Zachary Taylor, thousands of Widows and Orphans, wailing, flock to lay their complaints before the Eternal Throne; and, at their head, their spokesman, appears an earthly orator the Death Angel is now just calling for—and he demands vengeance for the slaughter of his gallant son—and this is Henry Clay! When *I* lay my head down to die, I want no weight upon it like the Glory of Buena Vista.

And, as for the Governor's language—his " vehemence," and " vulgarity," and " obscenity," as the Pole Kittens Editor characterizes it—and, as for the language of Mormons in general, (see " language profane," " bitter exclamations," " invectives of great bitterness," &c., &c.,) it is our Boast, that, as we have manners and customs growing up in our Basin, differing from those of the people lying across the Beaten Tracks of Travel; so we have already, a style of speaking all our own. My Theory is, this Nation has not been pushing round the globe Westward till it has come to the East again, without becoming fitter to enter the Eastern World than it was when it started. My word for it, you'll see our Jonathan American's Sombreros from San Francisco, walk into Japan and China, just where the Old Bull Englishmen's Gaiters behind them have failed entirely. People don't note the progress of The Preparation. But it has been going on in Speech just as it has in habits and fashions. I don't ask you to believe as I do, that Mormonism is going to be the great entering wedge of new civilization into Asia. But what I have to say now, and do say, is that the people of Utah, in their Manners evince more of this adaptation, as you would call it, more of the CHARACTERISTIC WAYS of Western men; and in their Speech also bring out more forcibly those Hyperbolic Fancies which, though you style them SCREAMERISMS, are the earnest of future Splendors in Oriental diction, than the Citizens of any other part of the Union. If the Territory of Utah is to be called to account for

With irregular verbs for irregular jobs.

[31]

Picking possessive pronouns' fobs.

the sayings of its citizens of their Ex-Presidents, I offer myself again for condign punishment. At one of our public celebrations, the name of a late chief Magistrate being proposed for a Groan, it was received with such spirit that the chair called upon me to couple it with an *impromptu* sentiment; and, glasses being fresh filled for the purpose with the whitest water, I gave:

"MATTY AND MOBOCRATS : May they be winked at by blind people, kicked across lots by cripples, nibbled to death by young ducks, and carried to Hell through the key hole by bumble bees!" —(Signed Chesterfield.)

The Report or Information, assumes to give Select Expressions of other prominent members of the Church,—all of them, with the exception of those of Wells already noticed, utterly false or garbled. With regard to Mr. Wells', they are his sentiments, and good or bad taste, as they can't set the Capitol Library on fire again, nor blow up the new earthquake-proof foundations, he has a right to them, I think. But if he hasn't, tell me, is it any wonder that some of those who have gone through what we have in Illinois should extend their reproaches to the Government of that State, to the Federal Government even? Believe the operation by which we were cut out from Missouri with the knife, ever so wholesome Surgery—will you not pardon the Hospital Patient one fretful groan? Sprinkle salt on the Worms cut in sunder by your Ploughshare, and shall they not *once* turn? In the name of all that is sacred, too, if it be English Law or American Right to disfranchise a whole Commonwealth for the misdeeds of a few of its inhabitants, into what Taboo of Degradation too great, can be consigned the State of Illinois? I am most amazed at the Effrontery that is not abashed, in this connection, to remind the country of our past distressing History! It was not necessary to the success of our Enemies' Evil Scheming that they should call upon me to enter into the discussion of a matter so discreditable to the people of two of our most powerful States. I will give them a lesson in National and Patriotic Pride when I refuse to do so.—God, who saw it, knows it bears no glossing.—It is a simple story of impudent, unblushing Outrage, of religious persecution by irreligious scoundrels, backed by timorous and

And dee dashing elderly gentlemen's nobs.

[32]

O Lord, how long!

time serving politicians, traitors to every true and honest principle. My narrative would find reluctant credence were I to recount at length the atrocious details of the Mormon War in Missouri, and that in Illinois which was its continuation and conclusion. During its prevalence, every crime in the statute book was violated with impunity. Robbery! they robbed our poor sufferers of every thing, despoiling us of property to the amount of millions of dollars. Murder! Murder was rife, at every time, of every shape : murder in the field, where the body was buried for the hogs to find it; murder in the home, the blood washing the hearth stone. Neither age nor sex was spared; they murdered the frightened crying little child; the gray haired grandsire of Revolutionary times, whose blood flowed scantily from his death wound; the mother, with her babe upon her breast; the father, whose death was known to give his orphans to starvation. And all this shamelessly, and in open day. The family looking on, they murdered the father : by torture; by beating, maybe, till the wretch's bowels gushed asunder, or till death came on, after the bones, by the lashing, stood out white from the shredded flesh. Worse! the family looking on, they violated the mother, the virgin sister, whose blushing limbs were made the mark of stripes and blows, even after they had been subject to the violence that leaves the deeper brand of shame. Worse still! I must believe those awful crimes were committed that we read of with loathing and horror in tales of the sack and storm of fortress cities, but which the tongue of Christian man righteously refuses to name. Aye, before God, worse still. But let me not dare to be the feeble recorder of crimes written in their awful black on high!

—My readers who are American citizens, will gladly excuse me the printing so blotted a page of our National History.

I am, sir, till you hear from me again,
Your obedient servant,
JEDEDIAH M. GRANT.

And so I saw the wicked buried,

LETTER III.

" Who is it then whose scorn I dread,
Whose wrath or hate makes Me afraid ?
A Man! An heir to death! A slave
To sin! a bubble on the wave!

Mr. Bennett,—

Before going on with my letter, I must avail myself of a piece of good Fortune opened to me. It would be a Great Thing for some poor little children, if when in the night-time they are told the bugaboo is at the foot of their bed, the daylight could be straightway let in on it, and made to expose its true character of pillow-case, bolster, or cast off smock of the lying child's-nurse. Such opportunities to undeceive should never be lost, and I therefore call attention to the late news from Utah, that we have declared our Independence, and, to the number of 40,000 in arms, as some make it, have fortified our settlement to resist invasion from the United States. In your Editorial perverting my letter you announce your belief in this : it has been specially accredited by letters to the Intelligencer and other papers : it has been the theme of any quantity of sage discoursing at our expense; I may say, that on the whole no ill report about us yet has been presented in a form better entitling it to general acceptance. Now, hold it fast, Reader, I say : don't let this go out of your mind or memory; I stake upon it my credibility against that of my opponents in this issue. If it be proven true, believe all I have stated to be Falsehood, unworthy of an honorable man; but if it prove false, then remember that it has been proved false, and when, *the next time,* the fly swallower asks you to take up his Cry of Wolf against us, have the grace to respond : Once does me

Who had come and gone from the place of the Holy,

[34]

And they were forgotten in the City where they had so done.

---

with the same raw head and bloody bones : Any thing more about that 40.000, my friend, I must henceforth beg to refer to the Committee on the Enlightenment of the Marines!

Suppose a lad has played Truant; has begun by that first and foremost. What account does the master make of his excuses afterwards ? " On the road I met a boy, a-and he wouldn't let me a-come-a." " I don't believe it was any boy at all," says the Schoolmaster. " Oh, yes Sir, Indeed ; It was Billy Slate Pencil." And the schoolmaster knows good Billy has been in his form ever since school let in. What more does he care to ask, before he gives the truant his good trouncing, unless, maybe, what it really was put him up to his bad behavior.—These scape-grace men *have begun* by running away from School. Their excuses, thought to afterwards, are nothing here nor there. But a sensible man may still enquire ; What did they run away for? This is a fitting place to bring in some explanation of it.

It would be hard to persuade some of our people that the three were not in a plot together, to stir up troubles, and bring us to meet such another brunt in Utah, as in Illinois ended in our being driven from our garden homes there. But I take a more simple view of the case. What men who are not conscience driven, go out to new countries for, I take it, is to Seek their Fortunes, more or less like the younger sons in the Story books. Sam. Brannan, formerly of our Church, goes out to Saint Francisco to make his pile of a Million ; or Jacky Badboy leaves his poor folks in Vermont, to be returned the Honorable John Longlegs of Sicklynoy. Money or Political Honors, one or other, men expect to get; or else they stay at home.

Now, Utah is no place for ease in either of these pursuits. In the first place, though we have no gold mines among us, they are near enough to give us California prices for what we consume. In California, the State Judges complain at getting, in the District Court, only $6,500, and in the Supreme Court, $10,000 a year; the United States give our Judges and Secretary but $1,800 a year. No fortunes to be saved out of these ; with flour often as high as $12 a barrel; six cent sugar at $37\frac{1}{2}$ to 45 cents, and ten cent coffee at 40 to 50 cents ; in other words, with freight charges

---

Naked came I out of my Mother's womb, naked shall I return thither.

[35]

He that earneth wages, earneth wages into a bag with holes.

alone from the place of first import of 14 cents a pound on every thing, from a bar of soap to a bar of iron!

And, as for politics, it is still worse. We burnt our fingers once with hot politics. We hate politics—hate them,—and thank our fortune most that we have so little call to meddle in them. We have only one delegate to elect, and to that one delegate give but one precept; that he is to leave party questions alone. Yet our views of our own interests and the merits of our public servants are clear and decided enough. The confidence we place in the men we have approved through our trying perils, is, in my sight, beautiful. It shows itself in the smallest as well as the greatest public affairs; and a stranger could not be a week in our country without making up his mind that his words and influence could not weigh a feather in the scale against the counsel of the men thus tried and trusted. And so found out on his arrival P. Brocchus, who thought to climb on to the Quarterdeck through our hawse hole. And if *they* looked for it too, so found out the others.

Now it is enough everyway for my reasoning, to know that the run-away officers were disappointed and discontented with their Prospects. So far would *I* be from accusing them of being men of the mould at all to contrive or carry out a conspiracy of moment, that I should rather say, that being the feeble natures that they were, and not controlled by ruling convictions of honor or duty, they were just the more likely to be influenced by transitory and inconsiderable causes. To their main disappointment, they were perhaps able to add each his little special cause of discontent. BROCHY, as he avows, only came out to us to be sent back Delegate. Unhappy BRANDY sucked the Julep of May and December; and boy HARRIS found his gray mare the better horse. It is all sober truth that I have printed of Brandy. We did our best, as I have stated, to bring him acquainted with the dames and ripe damsels that were of the place; but he was ashamed to make himself much for wholesome or equal company, and liked too much to be alone to benefit himself or them. So, what was Heaven's judgment on the untimely gallant but to prick him to make up to the little girl I have mentioned? Had he only fancied

Who so findeth a wife findeth a good thing.

[36]

<small>Who art thou, O great Mountain? before ZERUBBABEL thou shalt become PLAIN.</small>

some elderly lady *like himself;* after some mutual carriages of love, "Brandy would have become the Latin for Goose," the turtle doves would have soon got under pie crust, and flocks of little carrier pigeons would have flown forth to the United States bearing no tidings but the praises of Utah and all big and little Mormons under their happy wings. Harris, for his part, was affected the opposite. He had not been long married; and his wife, they said, who was weakly and kept him pretty close, was *notiony* besides; so thought she would have a particular call to go to her Mother after the winter had set in to interrupt the travel. But I rather liked the looks of the little fellow, myself, and should be sorry if the Governor offended him. According to a story, he took the notion the Secretary was *his Clerk,* and accosted him soon after they met, producing a written paper, and saying, "I want it copied from here to here," (showing him) " and be sure you have it done to bring it to me to-morrow morning early;" which I think it quite natural for a young man to be chafed at, who was holding Office for the first time.

Though thus perhaps, quite early discontented, I think they were without original or settled definite purpose. Their endeavoring to cozen us out of more than the law gave them, I look upon as merely incidental. But they were afterward led, I apprehend, from step to step and circumstance to circumstance, as weak men generally are. This of course gave Brocchus with his fixed purpose of going home, a great advantage over the two others. He virtually committed them, the moment he was able to keep them from disavowing his misconduct at the Conference. What little notions they may have had of self respect or official duty being soon after sacrificed, he could have had small difficulty in persuading them finally to join his sort of moonlight flitting for the East. Once run off, of course they came home to public notoriety.—

> "Hodge speaks of the fair,
> By the profit he had there."

—To justify himself, each made up his story, and each had to support one grown by telling. Their united fables, in conclave la-

<small>Her judges are evening wolves, they gnaw not the bones till the morrow.</small>

[37]

They only consult to cast him down from his Excellency.

bored into concordance, and done into English by a Washington pen, form THE REPORT.

"From being a beggar among kings, you shall be a king among beggars."—I know I am right in rating among the substantial disappointments of the officers, the non-fulfilment of this prophecy in their not finding themselves out to be the great men and Cæsars of the village they came out to rule. I read in an old book sometime ago the Story of I remember not what royal child, I think though a son of the King of Naples, who, being more than half an idiot, was confined in apartments by himself, with attendants who, in a gentle and flattering way, watched him like the keepers of a mad house. Poor Prince Philip had sense enough to know his condition, though not enough, literally, as the phrase is, to keep his head out of the fire. One morning at breakfast, after he had poured out the contents of the tea pot over the back of his hand and scalded it dreadfully, "Ugh!" he exclaimed, "Ugh! I don't remember; tell me what it was happened to me last night." "My Lord the Natural, you gave us call to have the bed clothes changed." "Ugh! no, ugh! What else?" "Also, my Lord, upon your attaining your twenty-fifth year, the Royal Philosophical Society of Learned Men elected your highness to be one of their body." "Can't be," he responded, sobbing, "can't be; Philip is as big a fool as ever!" —I honestly believe the weakness of these vain fellows was such, that, by dint of turkey-gobblerish bloatings up over the notion of their magnificent titles and appointments, they expected, on or before being sworn in, to undergo, as it were, a grand palingenetic change—thought in fact to wake up and see themselves the morning after, Brocchus an orator, Brandebury knowing something about law, and Harris a six footer of stately port and dignified demeanor. Bad enough to wake up from such a pleasant dream; but, how much worse to be shaken by the shoulders out of it by that dreadful Brigham Young, a quoter of such thoughts as, "Why is dust and ashes proud?" "An ass is an ass if you call him a lion," "Death only discovers how little the small bodies of men are," &c., &c.; a man who casts off all kinds of titles as frippery only fit for understrappers, and insists, maybe,

Then answered Amos; I was no Prophet, neither a Prophet's son.

[38]

But I was an herdsman, and a gatherer of Sycamore fruit.

upon wearing the plain clothes at the very time he should be waited upon by the splendid liveries. What burdens in our Earthly Servant's Hall, are the born Masters of men! Since the Governor received his appointment, they tell a story, that an English snob having to address a communication to him, superscribed it, "To his Excellency, Brigham Young, Governor of Utah, Indian Agent for the Territory, and President of the Church of Jesus Christ of Latter Day Saints." "I see," says Brigham, "you have given me my Titles." "Yes," says the writer, smoothing himself down satisfied, " yes, Governor, I think they are all there." "No sir," says the Governor, " they are not; you have left out a most important one, the first I was ever honestly entitled to in my life, and which I have done nothing to be cashiered of since." " You mean the Generalship, Governor; beg pardon, allow me to add it, Sir," says the snob. "No, Squire Eglon," says Brigham; (he called him this jocosely, because, like Eglon king of Moab, in the Scripture, he was " a very fat man,") " no matter now, Squire, but next time you shall put it in by itself, without the others. It will read then right sprucely:

   ' For his Excellency, Brigham Young,
           Painter and Glazier.'"

The Excuse pays the highest possible tribute it can, in my judgment, when it attempts to authenticate its cock and bull stories, to account for the Governor's extraordinary sway and authority and influence. It is in History that a clever French woman, named Dancre, was executed for her sorcery in governing the Queen after her own desires. "By what witchcraft," said her enemies to her on her way to death, "by what witchcraft have you obtained such an ascendency?" "By that," answered she, "that a strong nature will always have over a weak one." It is so with men; it is so with the wild horses on the Prairie where one Lord Stallion leads the line; and it is so with the Mormons. Young, Mr. Young, Mr. B. Young, Elder Young, President Young, or Governor Young, call him what you please, is the one appointed Ruler and Leader of our people. The President may call another Man Governor even, and it won't be different. It can't be helped. It is the old story of MacDonald, the Lord

It hath no stalk, the bud shall yield no meal.

[39]

THE BEE is little among such as fly,

of the Isles. Coming in late to the Lord Mayor's dinner, and taking his place at the foot of the board, the Mayor sent him a message to come higher up, and repeated it, saying, " Come, take a seat near me *at the head of the Table*. To which McDonald returned answer by the servant, "Tell your Master that where McDonald is, *there is* the head of the Table." " Where the King is there is the Court," runs the adage. Where Brigham Young is, there *is* the head of the Table. And it will be as long as he lives. And it can't be helped.

If you want to see what grade of politicians these men or their prompters are; look at the care they take to convey the impression we are bold and sturdy, and knowing of our deserts. When the Governor asked them *to dine* (!), for instance, they "*believed* it was to show how brave and independent he could be in his declarations," &c., &c. Throughout these letters, I have refused to bow to any popular prejudice, and I will not now uncover my head to one so low as this. I do not believe either, that any American citizen, not of the lowest black-neb riff-raff and rabble of the cities, thinks less of any man, or set of men, for a proper sense of self-respect and consciousness of merit. A just Pride, not Vanity, tells as much for Communities as Individuals. It is our praise that we are proud. I go again in the stocks for this. Yes! Earthly Heaven of our stormy voyaging! Deseret! fair blushing cloud that tells the morning of the splendors of the day star to rise! rosy shadow of things hoped for, golden evidence of things not elsewhere seen ! and thou, too, blest youthful City,

"The New Hierusalem that God has built
For those to dwell in that are chosen his,
His chosen people purged from sinful guilt,
With precious blood that cruelly was spilt.

" The blessed angels to and fro descend
From highest Heaven's gladsome company,
And with great joy unto that city wend,
As commonly as friend does with his friend,"

Sweet Home ! Dear Utah !—As I look out from my little fourth

But her fruit is the chief of sweet things.

[40]

Art thou better than populous, No that was situate among the Rivers?

___

story window here, upon its landscape of dark back-yards and stinking alleys, does not my heart faint now, to dwell among thy saints! Yes, Sir, you whose pride it is to dissect every high affection to the skeleton, and sneer at every unworldly sentiment— Yes Sir, proud I am, and proud we all are of our Utah Home, through all the shame that is cast upon it here.—Not proud of its mountains, its rivers, lakes, woods and fields, for we think these are no more part of us than of any other of God's children. Nor proud of its wealth :—

> "Were this the charter of our State,
> On pain of hell, be rich and great,
> Damnation then would be our fate
>   Beyond remeed ;
> But, thanks to Heaven, That's no the gate
>   We learn our creed."

—You are rich in New York Town, you raise your yearly crops of Merchant Princes and Millioners, with pike-eat-pickerel overgrown-fortunes who build their chateaus so high they can look clean over the Five Points. But what's all this for glory, when it has on and over it the runnings and rotmarks of Sin that is Shame? What, Sir, I ask you, are whole dreadful columns of advertisements in your Paper, but the image of a state of society so radically corrupt, diseased, and wretched, that the charlatans of science are paid fortunes for pretending to palliate a fraction of its sufferings? In *our* country, we don't see what you look at every day. We don't see old men in the highway picking up manure with their fingers, or children in cotton-factories dwarfing their backs before their milk teeth are shed. We don't wear pantaloons sewed at ten cents a pair, and French nose-rags brocaded at one hundred dollars apiece. We don't have churches laid out in Sunday opera-boxes, for fashionable hiring. We don't see men hire other white men to wait on them at table, with bands round their hats, and cockades and uniforms to set off and proclaim their miserable subjections. Our men don't see their own species put out their hands to them for alms in the streets; and, Sir, my Lord, they don't see what's worse, able-bodied young women for money asking the favor God has made Man to beg of Woman, and that even the Dog asks of his Female! What is

___

Buying the poor for silver and the naked for a pair of shoes.

[41]

O God! that Bread should be so dear, And Flesh and blood so cheap!

---

quoted for our ancestors and forerunners of Plymouth is true of their descendants of Utah: "As Ireland will not brook venemous beasts, so will not that land vile livers." Heaven be praised! there is not yet, a brothel or a beggar, or a dram-shop or a drunkard, or a thief or a tavern keeper, or a palace or a prostitute; no, thank God! not one of them yet, in all our settlement.

And this is why we have a right to grow up proud. The Boys hear stories that come up to them through the South Pass; about their brethren being of no account in the States; that they aren't any of them asked to Dinner parties, or called out at Public Meetings or invited to lecture on Chastity and French China, or give their opinions for publication on the Right of Intervention, and whether Saltpetre will explode; and, on the contrary, are nearly everywhere, insulted by hideaway newspaper writers, preached over by parsons, pointed at even by politicians, and, generally, are treated about as shabbily as the first Christians were by the last Jews. But they—do *they* mind this, any more than any other Tales that are told? They whose lungs breath a sky air darker blue than your Atlantic out of soundings, who point their deer-tracks hunting by Mountain Peaks that are never out of sight or naked of perpetual snow, who drink the ice-water of glacier cascades, and cut timber in passes and topple it down canyon chasms near three times as high as your Niagara Falls, or Trinity Church steeple? Ask *them* is it better to hear the lark sing or the mouse squeak!

"Where the Eye sees the Spirit speeds."—We have, if I am correct, the finest firmament for astronomical observations in the world. It puzzles all computations of distance. I have been told that new-come Emigrants have been known, by paces measured, to shoot at deer a third of a mile off; and I am sure that if a man from the sea-board could alight from a balloon at my house in the afternoon, I could persuade him after he had taken tea to walk with me to West Mountain and back, though it is 23 miles off. I remember, the day we first raised the American Flag on our big Liberty Pole, we found it could be seen from every part of Salt Lake County without a glass: where it seemed small as your head, the red stripes glowed as bright as on a piece of mint stick

---

O ye, to dwell in ceiled houses and this House to lie waste!

[42]

The Mountains and the Hills shall break forth before you into singing.

in your hand. Think of it, how our boys' eyes fastened on it there, flaunting and flapping as if to dare the whole Earth to spit at it, in our breezy South West Wind! That's the way in highland atmospheres men learn to look at the rights they have. I mean mountaineers, men that shoot with rifles, not shot guns, Sir; be good enough to comprehend. And one thing once for all, I may as well have distinctly understood. We Mormons ask no favors of any man. We are no Helots, here in our own Republic. No taunting yet, has made us reply to the accusations of our want of Patriotism. They say, we are English; we are English this far, that we are no French Gumboes, to jabber on after the chip has been knocked off our hats. I know my own right, too, to stand upon this soil. My Father's paternal Grandfather, or *luckie daddie* as he liked to call him, was from Scotland; but the rest of my ancestors were New Englanders of the oldest stocks. Two of them fought for Independence in the Revolution. My brothers and myself, six footers all, with our own arms and axes have cleared the wood off more acres than we this day own. I have worked hard for my living, now thirty odd years even on. I owe no man a cent. I have never dodged a Tax Collector. I have stood up for my Country in more ways than one, that I dont condescend to mention. Also I have read the Constitution of the United States, Article IV., Section II., Clause 1st. And he that wants me to answer whether I am not as good an American as he is, shall step out like a man and insult me to my face.

I have spoken of the injustice that would have a whole community answerable for the doings of a few individuals in it. This makes me a good Lawyer's defence for the two cases of Murder brought up against our people.

In the first case, John Vaughan—John M. Vaughan of Vermont, though the officers and their report give him the name and points of a Dr. J. R. Vaughan of Indiana or Virginia, who is thought to have been assassinated (by Former Day Saints!) in the Sacramento country—John Vaughan, I say, a Doctor, on his way, it was said, to California, stopped in Utah to try the practice of his profession, and succeeding very well, determined to take up his abode among us permanently. He became a convert to our Re-

Come, let us take our fill of love till the morning.

[43]

For the good man is not at home, he is gone on a long journey.

ligion; as we hoped, a sincere one, and was baptized, to our considerable satisfaction. It was not a great while, however, before he was found abusing the facilities his medical character afforded him, and at length was detected in open delict with the wife of a respectable citizen of Iron County. The husband was the more incensed at finding the intimacy of the parties had been of long standing, and with difficulty was restrained from violence by the entreaties of his friends. Vaughan now received a solemn warning, and promised reformation. But his evil habits were too strong for him. He was guilty of Adultery under circumstances which added to the enormity of the offence; and, this time, the husband could not be withheld from taking vengeance upon the man who had fouled the milk of his children's Mother. It was in one of our frontier settlements, and as the people were coming out after service from the log school house in which church was held, that the Cuckold walked up to Vaughan and there blew his brains out. They tried the culprit, but he was acquitted.

Howard Egan's case was also one of grievous wrong. Egan was a man who, after a strange career of romantic adventure, found his first peace in the bosom of our Church. Next to his attachment to this representative of the Deity on earth, was that he bore his wife, in body a woman of the rarest beauty, and the mother to him of three children. His love partook of the nature of sinful adoration, and was punished accordingly. Affairs of importance called him to the Gold Country; he was gone over a year; when he returned, bearing the reward of his success, he found his wife had been unfaithful. She met him heavy with the fruit of her sin. Every one knew the paramour, James Monroe, merchant, the friend of William Smith the wayward brother of JOSEPH, and from his youth upward a member of the Church. He was Egan's friend too, therefore a Traitor. Egan did not remain long to be pointed at. He learned that Monroe was on his road out from the States, with a train carrying merchandise. He set out alone, nor did any know whither he had gone when he went forth to meet them. He came upon the party in the night time. It has been said that he had with him his old house dog, as knowing its nose would scent out the frequent lifter of his door

He hath taken a bag of money with him.

[44]

And will come home on the day appointed.

latch. This is not true; he found his way, by himself, to the wagon in which his betrayer was, and rising upon the tongue ward looked in upon him as he lay sleeping. He was minded then to have his life; but there was light enough to show his human face; and something in the expression of it which persuaded Egan that the sinner's dreams might be indulging him in pleasant guilt, withheld his hand. He left the ill-guarded camp for the grass in which he had picketed his horse, and upon his bear skin there slept until another morning. The horses of the train had not pastured; the men were getting breakfast ready round the fire, when he again appeared among them. Tapping Monroe on the shoulder; James, he said aloud, you must die! then beckoning him apart sat down with him a few rods off to one side. Thirty minutes he assigned him to live, during which he exhorted him to contrition and preparation for his change. At the twenty-fifth minute, he showed by his watch that but five minutes remained of the time in which, if the criminal were so minded, he could assail his executioner. At the expiration of the thirtieth, as he did not move, Egan rose and despatched him, putting a bullet through his brain. Then, sorrowing, returned home.

These crimes, I should remark, date of a time, before any legislation had noticed our existence, and when we were as much without law as any part of California at any time. But, clear of this, what particle of countenance is there for the suspicion that Our People committed them; that they aided or abetted their perpetrators, or were guilty of them art or part?

Now, let me take up the charge of Polygamy, and Governor Young with his score of wives, and a sucking baby a-piece, airing in one omnibus. This is the only specification of the charge. I pronounce it false, and call for the proofs. Who are the other Polygamists? Our Delegate and Myself? We are here, and we brand it as a lie. Who else? Speak out. The Census says our inhabitants stand in the proportion of about 6 males to 5 females. If Polygamy be general among us, every wife must have more husbands than every husband has wives, and this our *qui tam* informers have abstained from charging. Is there any intelligent visitor of our settlements then, who has seen the thing among us?

Mine anger was kindled against the Shepherds, and I punished the Goats.

[45]

They shall move out of their holes like worms of the Earth.

The otherwise abundantly Itinerant officers visited nowhere outside their boarding-house. If they saw any thing impure there, weren't they the men to shift their lodgings? What was to hinder their being mercilessly hoaxed, too, with what they showed they wanted so much to hear? " Greediest Swallow bolts most gnats." It was Willard Snow, not Professor Orson Spencer, I heard the boys say, stuffed "Brandy Without" with a story that he had two wives, "one at home and one over in the Lot." His defence being, that his first wife was too sound a sleeper for him; and the *great unmixed* did not take the joke that "The Lot" was our Grave-yard, and that the first wife had been snoozing there, for a couple of years! But, as to this charge of Polygamy again : Suppose I should admit it at once ; whose business is it? Does the Constitution forbid it? Is there any thing in the Act for the Government of the Territory, forbidding it? And where else are we to find it written down as a crime? Was either Brocchus or Brandebery sent out to hold an Ecclesiastical Court, and to discipline sinners against the Seventh Commandment, for the Good of their Souls? Couldn't their Commission be extended then, while they are living in the District of Columbia on full pay for doing nothing (except writing lies for the newspapers), so as to reform morals *there?* Or, is it true that the concerns of the bed chamber lose their national interest as they approach the shadows of the Capitol? And this leads me again to the Murder charge. Both of the cases spoken of were of Death inflicted on an Adulterer by the hand of the husband who was wronged. I say, the Murder was right; and whatever others of our people may say to the contrary, I for one stand up for the defence! Power of Truth! How I would like to do it here in good, bold, burning words, that would make the groundlings ears tingle, denouncing our whole present system of laws as good for nothing to afford protection to anything but Property, and appealing from them to the Great God's Law, the Law of Principles, that lasts from Hundred years to Hundred years, and ever will last, because it is the simple Logic of Human Right and Duty, the perfect science of all Reason put in practice.

"Shall I for fear of feeble man,
The Spirit's course in me restrain !"

For the Bed is shorter than a Man can stretch himself in it,

[46]

And the Covering narrower than he can wrap himself in it.

—Alas! to speak thus, would be Mormonism, and I dare not. But I ask my countrymen, floundering as they are in every State, among the double and triple reformed Constitutions, and Revised and re-revised Revised Statutes, does any amount of *translating* yet seem to fit the Present English Law for Our brave Country? When the Lords of Great Britain could meet their dues from their own Peers, giving verdicts upon Honor, it was all well enough for the rest of the people that had their rights to Bed Board and Wages, but had nothing to do with Honor, Chivalry and Fine Sentiments. But, with the progress of these LATTER DAYS, every American is going to be born a nobleman and a gentleman, and will claim the rights and feel the wrongs of nobleman and a gentleman. And if our Laws do not offer an *honorable* redress to the American citizen, he'll have it outside of the law; because he will seek it by the Duello of the old nobility. The open duels of the West, that pap-fed people make so much fuss over, are one of the greatest signs of civilization of the times. I *have* seen a Duellist protect Virtue and restore Honor.—I never heard of the Law doing it yet. Try it by a case. I have in my house one Flower, a wife or only daughter, through and for whom alone the light of life is dear to me. And a miscreant, not content with robbing me of this, tramples it under foot, defiles it with his filth, and then loading my head with it as a shame turns me—turns us—out on the highway, a jeer and a hissing for the passers by. And am I to be the low Englishman to hire an attorney to sue him in the Courts for a trespass *quia servitium* to get back the Hire I have lost?—the *hire* of my rose-bud, my song bird, my beauty, my darling,—the angel sent me by God, sent down by him to hell! No, by the Lord; but I will spill his blood!

And if I do will they hang me? No, he was on his way again this man, sowing his Rot among the pet lambs, when I met and slew him; and they know it is *they* owe *me* a Bounty for the scalp of his cursed wolf's head.—But I have committed what they must *call* Murder; and for this they must try me, and then hold their own Laws up for a laughing stock, to show how easily they admit a mockery of justice!

If I go on in this strain, I shall be called a fanatic, and discredit

But the poor man had nothing, save one little Ewe lamb.

[47]

It did eat of his own meat and drank of his own cup and lay in his bosom,

the highest truth that it is in me. But do I speak wild of the facts? Here is a slip I cut from that moral paper the Tribune since you published my other letter:

"Near St. Albans, Vt., the only daughter of a blind mother and decrepit father, rushed before a train of cars, was run over and killed. Cause, seduction under an unfulfilled promise of marriage. How much better than a murderer is the villain who ruined this girl?"

This is the public sentiment. And you can't get a man punished for murder who carries it out; though every once a week about, there is a paragraph runs through the papers of some infanticide or suicide by a girl that has been betrayed. In the New Jersey cases, of Mercer at Camden, and the Irish girl at Jersey City, all the powers on earth could not prevent the Juries from breaking their oaths, to find the assassins insane; and numerous are the cases everywhere, in which, as in that of Dr. Wilson in Maryland, the Governor speaks for the community, when he says as he exercises the right of pardon that "he is ashamed to have to do it." Is this right—to break the law outright, or to evade it, or to have to do a wrong? Shall a whole community—a sovereign people having the right to make their own laws, consent to a confederated hypocrisy, a common juggle? No! swear the Mormons. This is no forefather's law, or law of Ancestors of ours. It is Charles the Second's law; law, the modern fountain of which was that dirty, Scotch-fiddling lecher, foul with all disorders. Two generations nearly before that Kingling came back from the Stews of France, our ancestors had declared the first AMERICAN LAW, the Law of Massachusetts Bay and Plymouth Rock, that no English Restoration could disturb. This was the Law of the Bible; that law we now affirm. And by it Adultery is punished with Death. Mark this. Read Bancroft if you want to see if "this penalty was inexorably enforced," and, Spouters for Buncombe, only a little too hastily crammed! read the other Yankee Historians, or else be a little careful what you say. Read them, if you only want to see how many other things that you object against the Mormons, from the Jewish masquerade of Rhode Island to the Seven Pillars of Connecticut, were characteristics of the pilgrims before us. Why? Because, as Norton, one of Bancroft's own

And (David) said—the man that hath done this thing shall surely die.

[48]

He that hasteneth to be rich shall not be innocent.

authorities, says, "New England [like Utah,] New England was a religious plantation, not a plantation for Trade."

I hope it will not be long before an Act of our Territorial Legislature making Death the punishment of Adultery, will be up before Congress for its approval or rescission. We will stand there upon the broad question of State Rights. There is room for doubt if a Handful in a territory have a right to decide for themselves a question like that of Slavery, affecting the settlement of Lands, and therefore important to the interests of the United States as the proprietor and Administrator of the Public Domain; but I defy any one, strict constructionist or not, to strike a difference between the right of a fully organized society in a Territory, and one in a State, to decide for itself what shall be its *Domestic Institutions.*

This is not my opinion, but that of eminent men, whose law opinions I have taken. And if the principle of Right is to be violated in our case, hot blood will come of it that I could wish the country spared, in others. Had we had Judges—hemp twisters, not gallows apples—to attend to us, we would have had all these questions, important to our peace, on their road now to the Supreme Court for settlement. But these Forlornities—what a come down it is, to return to their feebleness!—will it be believed —what they *did* do?—They put it in their Report to the President, (who hasn't enough to attend to of his own; oh, no!) that they saw a Murderer running at large! Whose fault was it then? Why didn't they catch him? Why didn't they try him? Whose business was it if not theirs? What else were they appointed for? Maybe there were other criminals at large. If their word is good, adulterers for instance, riding in omnibuses. Then, in God's name, why did they not try *them*, too? What, my masters, suspect this, believe it too, and not think it worth while to empanel a jury, not even summon one, nay, not even open a court! You would persuade us now you were afraid to. What true American really in such a plight would have dared to come back but in a sausage? And what is the word worth of a man not above the shame of saying so? I admit Brocky was scared in the row at the Conference, though certainly " he was scant of news—told his father was

Thine own mouth condemneth thee; not I; thine own lips testify against thee.

[49]

The measure you meted out shall be measured to you again,

hanged,"—and it is rather queer he should admit it. That disturbance was shocking to us, to be sure, breaking up as it did our religious assembly, and we are entitled to speak of it as a scandal in terms of the strongest condemnation. But as far as it affected Brocchus, looked at merely as a disorderly meeting, hardly one old politician hasn't gone through a dozen such. It is not equal by odds to a divided meeting in Old Tammany. And not one itinerant Abolitionist Lecturer would have been ashamed to face twice the music, with eggs and turnips thrown in. No, my fellow citizens, do the best they may to show that they were cowards and fools, these men were only knaves.

My next and last letter I reserve to review the action of the Committee of Congress. When they have done their duty, examined the officers on oath, and heard the witnesses for our defense, no words of mine will be needed to expose the infamy of our treatment. But what delays the Committee ? Can they forget that they are leaving a Territory which is alleged to be disaffected —in open revolt, even, against the United States—nearly as free from all Government influence and authority as it was at the termination of the war with Mexico ? May not the President plead fairly that a respectful deference constrains him to wait for their Report before taking his own measures ? For it is said, that at least two of the runaways now are waiting to go back, and that one of these, a Judicial officer, will refuse to resign, under the notion that he cannot be removed from office except by impeachment. A word to these persons, who, if they were men, would have hunted me up before this : it will reach them in this public way. Are they sure, now ; are you so sure, gentlemen, if you return, you *will* " be safe ?" Not, from the cutting of throats and pulling of hair by " a desperate and murderous set," but from the process of the Law of the land, according to the Constitution and organic Act, to wit : Lemuel G. Brandebery, if the President and Congress don't break you by impeachment, you shall be tried in your own Court,—for Libel, Judge Brandebery ! You must have learning enough at least to know what that means. For Libel; and, if a Mormon Jury is such a horror to you, what sort of dam-

Pressed down and running over.

[50]

While I mused the fire burned.

ages do you think one will give for slanders as base and false as ever invited a false and indignant verdict?

> " Contented, now upon my thigh,
> I halt,"———

Your obedient servant,
J. M. GRANT.

New York, April 25, 1852.

Renvoy.

OF the brave, the impartial, and the gentle-minded who have honored my pages with their perusal, I ask pardon for the style and language I have needed to employ for the cruel, the craven, the bigoted, and the vulgar. If I have not allowed the Beauty of Truth herself to speak but with the words and gesture of the Market and the Ring : if, as I may say, I have needed a Coarse Voice, indeed, to be heard of the prejudiced multitude to whom I have been speaking,—I pray you believe, my friends, this is not natural to me, nor has it been assumed without a sacrifice of feeling. And I make bold to assure you, upon my honor, that, such as it has been hitherto maintained, a Proud Reserve upon all matters affecting us, become the subject of popular clamor, is the characteristic of the Mormon People, if not my own.

J. M. G.

May 2, 1852.

APPENDIX.

I

LETTER TO THE PRESIDENT.

NEW YORK, May 1, 1852.

SIR,

I send you copies of my letters to the New York Herald, and request for them your perusal.

Though they are written in a loose and popular style, you will see that I tender issues involving bold decisions in questions of high importance. We claim, in their broadest sense, the Rights of,—

1. Religious Liberty, including the right of Individuals to establish and maintain, as well as to bestow ecclesiastical titles upon, a Church Hierarchy, as far as themselves judge proper.—Upon which, our stand is with the ROMAN CATHOLICS.

2. Political Liberty, admitting the largest possible power of Self Government in the Community, and the entire Independence of its Domestic Institutions.—Upon which we stand with the opponents of Centralization and advocates of States Rights, and, at the present time, with THE SOUTH.

And, for all beyond this, we contradict every single statement of the Delinquent officers, and by wage of law or battel will equally rejoice to be brought to prove their falsehood.—We call for the Examination under oath.—Of this we put ourselves upon the Country.—Our last cry is Trial!

Sir, you will be rewarded for all the good you may have it in your heart to do us: I would I could say you will not be punished if you do us wrong; For I am, with sincere respect for the finer features of your character,

Your true wellwisher,

JEDEDIAH M. GRANT.

MILLARD FILLMORE,
President of the United States.

[52]

II.

THE BROCCHUS LETTER, See Page 28.

"Extract of a Letter from a Judicial Officer of the Government, at Great Salt Lake City, dated September 20, 1851.

"I shall leave for the States on the 1st October, and most gladly will I go, for I am sick and tired of this place—of the fanaticism of the people, followed by their violence of feeling towards the ' *Gentiles*,' as they style all persons not belonging to their Church. I have had a feeling and personal proof of their fanatical intolerance within the last few days. I will give you a cursory view of the circumstances and the scene.

"As soon after my arrival here as my illness would permit, I heard from Judge B. and Mr. Secretary H. accounts of the intolerant sentiments of the community towards Government officers and the Government itself, which filled me with surprise. I learned that not only were the officers sent here treated with coolness and disrespect, but that the Government of the United States, on all public occasions, whether festive or religious, was denounced in the most disrespectful terms, and often with invectives of great bitterness. I will mention a few instances. The 24th July is the anniversary of the arrival of the Mormons in this valley. It was on that day of this year that they assembled to commemorate that interesting event. The orator of the day, on that occasion, spoke bitterly of the course of the United States toward the Church of ' *Latter Day Saints*,' in taking a battalion of their men from them for the war with Mexico, while on the banks of the Missouri river, in their flight from the mob at Nauvoo. He said the Government of the United States had devised the most wanton, cruel, and dastardly means for the accomplishment of their ruin, overthrow, and utter extermination.

"His Excellency, Governor Young, on the same occasion, denounced, in the most sacrilegious terms, the memory of the illustrious and lamented General and President of the United States, who has lately gone to the grave, and over whose tomb a nation's tears have scarcely ceased to flow. He exclaimed, ' *Zachary Taylor is dead and gone to hell, and I am glad of it !*' and his sentiments were echoed by a loud amen from all parts of the assembly. Then, rising in the excess of his passion to his tiptoes, he vociferated, ' *I prophesy, in the name of Jesus Christ, by the power of the priesthood that is upon me, that any other President of the United States who shall lift his finger against this people, will die an untimely death, and go to hell.*' This kind of feeling I found pervading the whole community, in some individuals more marked than in others.

"You may remember that I was authorized by the managers of the Washington National Monument Society to say to the people of the Territory of Utah, that they would be pleased to receive from them a block of marble, or other stone, to be deposited in the monument ' *as an offering at*

[53]

the shrine of patriotism.' I accordingly called on Governor Young, and apprised him of the trust committed to my hands, and expressed a desire to address the people upon the subject, when assembled in their greatest number. He replied that on the following Monday the very best opportunity would be presented. Monday came, and I found myself at their Bowery, in the midst of at least three thousand people. I was respectfully and honorably introduced by '*His Excellency*' to the vast assemblage. I made a speech, though so feeble that I could scarcely stand, and staggered in my debility several times on the platform.

"I spoke for two hours, during which time I was favored with the unwavering attention of my audience. Having made some remarks in reference to the judiciary, I presented the subject of the National Monument, and *incidently thereto* (as the Mormons supposed), I expressed my opinions in a full, free, unreserved, yet respectful and dignified manner, in regard to the defection of the people here from the Government of the United States. I endeavored to show the injustice of their feelings towards the Government, and alluded boldly and feelingly to the '*sacrilegious remarks* of Governor Young towards the memory of the lamented Taylor.' I defended, as well as my feeble powers would allow, the name and character of the departed hero from the unjust aspersions cast upon them, and remarked that, in the latter part of the assailant's bitter exclamation that he '*was glad that General Taylor was in hell,*' he did not exhibit a Christian spirit, and that if the author did not early repent of the cruel declaration, he *would perform that task with keen remorse upon his dying pillow.* I then alluded to my nativity; to my citizenship; to my love of country; to my duty to defend my country from unjust aspersions wherever I met them, and trusted that when I failed to defend her, my tongue, then employed in her advocacy and praise, might cling to the roof of my mouth, and that my arm, ever ready to be raised in her defense, might fall palsied at my side. I then told the audience if they could not offer a block of marble in a feeling of full fellowship with the people of the United States, as brethren and fellow-citizens, they had better not offer it at all, but leave it unquarried in the bosom of its native mountain. At the close of my speech, the Governor arose, and denounced me and the Government in the most brutal and unmeasured terms.

"The ferment created by his remarks was truly fearful. It seemed as if the people (I mean a large portion of them) were ready to spring upon me, like hyenas, and destroy me. The Governor, while speaking, said that some persons might get their hair pulled, or *their throats cut, on that occasion.* His manner was boisterous, passionate, infuriated in the extreme; and if he had not been afraid of final vengeance, he would have pointed his finger at me, and I should *in an instant* have been a dead man. Ever since then the community has been in a state of intense excitement, and murmurs of personal violence and assassination towards me have been freely uttered by the *lower order of the populace.* How it will end I do not know. I have just learned that I have been denounced, together with the Government and officers, in the Bowery again to-day by Governor Young. 'I hope I shall get off safely. God only knows. I am in the power of a *desperate and murderous set.* I, however, feel no great fear. *So much for defending my country.*'

"I expect all the officers of the Territory, at least Chief Justice B., Secretary Harris, and Captain Day, Indian Agent, will return with me, *to return here no more.*"

[54]

III.

THE MURDER OF JOSEPH SMITH.

Repeated attempts against the man's person having failed, owing to the devotion of his adherents, the Anti-Mormons, as they were named, succeeded by a recourse to stratagem.

One of their enemies, the commander of a volunteer corps at a town called Carthage, 20 miles distant from Nauvoo, and a sort of Head Quarters of the Anti-Mormons, issued a warrant of arrest against Smith and others, on a charge of riotously *abating a nuisance as municipal officers of the City* of Nauvoo. Smith, his brother named Hyram, and two other companions went to Carthage with an escort to enter bail, but, on arriving, were arrested by another warrant from the same magistrate on a charge of *High Treason*, and, without being brought up on any preliminary hearing or examination, were committed by him to the town jail, on the alleged ground of " an absence of material witnesses for the Prosecution."

Their lives being menaced, Governor Ford had called out a Militia force for thier protection; but, by the 4th day of their incarceration, this all dispersed, with the exception of a company called the Carthage Grays, commanded by the Justice who had lent his judicial process to the original arrest.

The Grays served to prevent the escape of the Prisoners till the time fixed upon for Smith's execution, they then gave him up or to the keeping of an armed band of from 100 to 150 volunteers with blackened faces, who set upon him and his companions, a little after five o'clock in the afternoon of Thursday, June 27th, 1844.

The Prisoners were unprepared for their fate. At the dinner table of that day, they augured evil from the eye of fixed interest with which the Jailer seemed to regard them while eating; and this officer heard Smith urge his companions to provide for their safety by separating themselves from him, as far at least as the Prison bounds allowed. They had probably refused to do so, however, and when they were assailed, were seated with him watching the slow passage of a very sultry summer's afternoon, in a little upper story room which had a window looking out upon the open air. They heard almost simultaneously, the forcing the Prison doors, the rushing tramp of feet, and the report of a heavy volley of musketry discharged up the stairway leading to the 2d story, in which they were; and then, immediately after, an Indian yell which the Anti-Mormon troops gave as they charged up the stairway which they thus securely cleared. By a common instinct, the three Mormons sprang to their chamber door. It had no lock or bolt, nor latch that would fasten; but, by pressing against it they thought they would keep it closed. The passage or landing leading to the door was not wide, and they were athletic men, and had the strong instinct of self-preservation which nerves men to exertion on occasions when reasonable hope is vain. Had it been a contest of relative physical force

[55]

merely, they might therefore, perhaps, have stood out for some time. But the troops formed at the other end of the landing and fired against the door, which they easily riddled. One of the first shots hit Hyram Smith between nose and eyes and entered his brain. He said deliberately, I am a dead man, and according to the Mormon statements, " like a tree felled and without moving his feet," measured his length lifeless upon the floor. The weapons of the two Mormons, were two walking sticks and a revolving pocket pistol, the worthless one with six barrels, which is the most unsure of all weapons with which a man can be provided in an emergency. As soon as he saw his brother fall, Jo. Smith took this pistol, and pulling open the door himself, commenced firing upon his assailants. The affair was then soon decided. It took a few moments for Smith to discharge three shots from this revolver, and a few more to finish repeated snappings of three barrels that would not go off. This drove back the troops for a little, when they advanced again, also, and thrusting their muskets through the partly opened door, kept up an irregular fire into the chamber. The Mormons maintained their ground sometime longer with their walking sticks, striking down and parrying the direction of the musket barrels. They were thus able to respite their deaths a few moments more. It was some time too, before the Troops entered the room, continuing to fire into it from without. One of the Mormons named Taylor here sprang for the open window, but staggering in the window-sill from the effect of a musket shot in the leg which hit him as he rose, a ball from without struck him in the breast and threw him back upon the floor. Then Smith followed. But the Blackened Faces were in greater force in the Jail yard than the troops inside the Prison. They gave him a volley as soon as he showed himself in the window. Probably at almost the instant he first saw them he was pierced by their balls. He fell reeling some 15 or 20 feet down to the ground under the window, where an end was made of him. He only said as he expired : "My God! My God!" or "Oh Lord My God!" or words to that effect : but they were not content to leave his body unmutilated, stabbing and shooting into it for some time.

Another account of this transaction, also by one not a member of our church, Henry Mayhew, Esquire, of London, will be found in his work recently published, entitled " The Mormons," London, 1851.

IV.

THE MORMON WAR IN MISSOURI, See Page 32.

My forbearance has not prevented persons from objecting to my language, as too strong. I will not suffer it to stand on my own unsupported statement. After our expulsion from Missouri, various bootless attempts were made to institute legal proceedings for the recovery of property, etc. ; in some of which the evidence is before me.* I extract from various statements under oath, of eye witnesses, enough particulars to give a notion of the manner in which our different settlements were broken up. I confine

* See, also, Memorial to the Legislature of Missouri, Sess. 1838-9, and the Proceedings had thereon.

[56]

myself to two alone, strictly: HAWN'S MILLS, which was one of the most exposed, and FAR WEST, which was by much the largest of our settlements. Our people were scattered all through Caldwell, Ray, Davis, Clay, Clinton, and Corrill Counties, along the streams, and wherever the prairie was suitably drained and timbered, having paid on account of their lands there, and principally into the Treasury of the United States, over 200,000 dollars. The most shocking outrages were, as might be expected, committed upon the families of solitary or scattered settlers. But these two cases will suffice me. Let the witnesses speak for themselves.

HAWN'S MILLS.

Says one witness, David Lewis:

Accordingly, about twenty-eight of our men armed themselves, and were in constant readiness for an attack of any small body of men that might come upon them. The same evening, for some cause best known to themselves, the mob sent one of their number, to enter into a treaty with our friends; which was accepted of, on the condition of mutual forbearance on both sides, and that each party, as far as their influence extended, should exert themselves to prevent any further hostilities upon either party.

More than three-fourths of the day had passed in tranquillity, as composed as the preceding one. On the banks of the creek, on either side, were the children sporting and playing, their mothers were engaged in domestic employments, and their fathers were employed in attending to the mills and other property, or in gathering in their crops for their winter consumption. The weather was very pleasant; the sun shone clear; all was tranquil, and no one expressed any apprehensions of the crisis near us. It was about 4 o'clock, while sitting in my cabin, with my baby in my arms, and my wife standing by my side, the door being open, I cast my eyes on the opposite bank of Shoal Creek, and saw a large company of armed men, on horses, directing their course towards the mills, with all possible speed. As they advanced through the scattering trees, that stood on the edge of the prairie, they seemed to form themselves into a three-square position, forming a vanguard in front. At this moment, David Evans, seeing the superiority of their numbers (there being two hundred and forty of them, according to their own account), swung his hat, and cried for peace. This not being heeded, they continued to advance, and their leader, Mr. Comstock, fired a gun, which was followed by a solemn pause of ten or twelve seconds, or more, when, all at once, they discharged about one hundred rifles, aiming at a blacksmith's shop, into which our friends had, by this time, fled for safety, and charging up to the shop, the cracks of which, between the logs, were sufficiently large to enable them to aim directly at the bodies of those who had fled for refuge there. The several families tented in rear of the shop, whose lives were thus exposed, amidst a shower of bullets, fled to the woods in different directions. After standing and gazing on this bloody scene for a few minutes, and finding myself in the utmost danger, the bullets reaching the house where I was living, I committed my family to the protection of heaven, and leaving the house on the opposite side, took a path which led up the hill, following in the trail of three of my brethren that had fled from the shop. While ascending the hill, we were discovered by the mob, who immediately fired at us, and continued so to do till we reached the summit. In descending the

[57]

hill, I secreted myself in a thicket of bushes, where I lay till eight o'clock in the evening, at which time I heard a female voice calling my name, with others, in an under tone, telling me that the mob had gone, and there was no danger. I immediately left the thicket, and went to the house of Benjamin Lewis, where I found my family (who had fled there) in safety, and two of my friends, mortally wounded, one of whom died before morning. Here we passed that awful night. After daylight appeared, some four or five men, with myself, who only had escaped with our lives from the massacre, repaired, as soon as possible, to the mills, to learn the condition of our friends, whose fate we had truly anticipated. When we arrived at the house of Mr. Hawn, we found Mr. Merrick's body lying in the rear of the house, Mr. McBride's in front, literally mangled from head to foot. We were informed by Miss Rebecca Jud, who was an eye witness, that he was shot with his own gun, after he had given it up, and then was cut to pieces with an old corn-cutter, by a Mr. Rogers of Davies county, who keeps the ferry on Grand River, and who has since, repeatedly boasted of this act of savage barbarity. Mr. York's body we found in the house; and after viewing these corpses, we immediately went to the blacksmith's shop, where we found nine of our friends, eight of whom were already dead; the other, Mr. Cox of Indiana, struggling in the agonies of death, and soon expired. We immediately prepared, and carried them to a place of interment.

This last office of kindness due to the relics of departed friends was not attended with the customary ceremonies nor decency : for we were in jeopardy, every moment expecting to be fired on by the mob, whom we supposed were lying in ambush, waiting for the first opportunity to dispatch the remaining few, who were providentially preserved from the slaughter of the preceding day. However, we accomplished without molestation this painful task. The place of burying was a vault in the ground, formerly intended for a well, into which we threw the bodies of our friends promiscuously. Among those slain, I will mention Sardius Smith, son of Warren Smith, about nine years old, who, through fear, had crawled under the bellows, where he remained until the massacre was over, when he was discovered by Glaze, of Corrill county, who presented his rifle near the boy's head, and literally blowed the upper part of it off. Mr. Stanley of Corrill told me afterwards that Glaze boasted of this deed all over the country. The number killed and mortally wounded in this wanton slaughter was eighteen or nineteen, whose names, as far as I can recollect, were as follows : Thomas M'Bride, Levi Merreck, Elias Benner, Josiah Fullor, Benjamin Lewis, Alexander Campbell, Warren Smith, Sardius Smith, George Richards, Mr. Napier, Mr. Harmer, Mr. Cox, Mr. Abbot, Mr. York, William Merreck, a boy eight or nine years old, and three or four more whose names I do not recollect, as they were strangers to me. Among the wounded who recovered, were Isaac Laney, who had six balls shot through him—two through his body, one through each arm, and the other two through his hips; Nathan K. Knight, shot through the body; Mr. Yokum, who was severely wounded, besides being shot through the head; Jacob Myers, A. Myers, Tarlton Lewis, Mr. Hawn, and several others. Miss Mary Stedwell, while fleeing, was shot through the hand, and fainting, fell over a log, into which they shot upwards of twenty balls.

Says another witness:

" We were forced to take shelter under cover of an old log building, used as a blacksmith's shop, which was neither chinked or mudded. When

[58]

men ran out and called for peace, they were shot down; when they held up their hats and handkerchiefs and crying for mercy, they were shot down; when they attempted to run, they were cut down by the fire of guns; and when they stood still, they were shot down by putting the guns through the cracks of the building. One woman, by the name of Mary Stedwell, was shot through the hand while holding it up in the attitude of defence As she ran from the mob, others pierced her clothes: after running as far as she could, she threw herself behind a log, whilst a volley of balls poured after her, filling the log where she lay, twelve or fourteen of which were taken out and preserved. Many other women had balls shot through their clothes, while fleeing into the woods with their children in their arms; others were brutally abused. One small boy was killed, having his brains blown out; and during the affray, two other boys, belonging to Warren Smith (who was also killed at the time), hid themselves under the bellows; and, when the murderers came into the shop, after killing all within except two men (one wounded and the other not), who lay concealed from them by being covered with dead bodies of the slain, the elder of the boys, crying for mercy from his hiding place, was immediately put to death, by putting the muzzle of a gun to the lad's ear, and blowing off the top of his head. One of these savages who participated in this transaction, accosted his comrade (while committing this horrid deed) thus: 'It is a damned pity to kill boys;' to which the other said, in reply, that 'little sprouts became large trees,' and if these boys were suffered to live, they, like their father, would be Mormons. The other lad was supposed to have been killed, but they did not quite accomplish their object, the younger receiving a wound in his hip, which carried off his hip-bone. While the mob were in the shop, if they perceived life remaining in any of the wounded, while struggling in the agonies of death, they were immediately dispatched, at the same time plundering the pockets of the dead, stripping off their boots, shoes, and clothing. After the mob had learned that two men escaped with their lives, they declared publicly, that if they got into another such affair they would inspect more closely by sticking their knives in their toes. This massacre took place about sun an hour high, on Tuesday, and continued until seventeen were killed and fifteen were wounded, that I know of, the remaining few escaping. * * * * Among those who attempted to escape was a man by the name of Thomas M'Bride, a soldier and patriot of the revolution and a justice of the peace. While making the best use of his tottering limbs and worn-out frame for escape, he was met in his retreat by a young man from Davies county, by the name of Jacob Rogers, who immediately demanded the old man's gun, which was delivered up, and was then shot down by Rogers. This not killing the old man, he lifted his hands in the attitude of supplication and begged for mercy, at the same time appealing to his silvery locks as adding still more force and credit to his cries, and tales of his actions while in the defence of his country. But the young man, deaf to every thing, regarded not the old man, but, seizing an old corn-cutter or piece of a scythe, commenced first to hew off the old man's fingers while holding them up for mercy, and next cutting his hands from his arms, and then severing his arms from his body, and last of all laying open the skull and beheading the body of him who had fought and spilt his blood for the privileges enjoyed by his murderer. There not being any men left, or not enough to bury the dead, the women were compelled to bury their husbands, by throwing them into a well close to the blacksmith shop. The next day after the massacre a large company

[59]

of them came back, blowing their bugle and firing their guns in an exulting manner. They carried off goods of all descriptions, horses, waggons, and harnesses, stripping the horses and moving waggons of all the goods, furniture, and clothing of any value, leaving the widows and orphans to suffer in that inclement season of the year. Cows, hogs, and horses, were driven off in droves. They robbed the families of all their beds and bedding. * * * * A short time after this, at Hawn's mill, Captain Nehemiah Comstock, the same who commanded at the massacre, with forty or fifty others, took possession of the mill for two or three weeks, and thus cut off the resources of the widows and orphans who had survived. During this time they lived on the best that the neighborhood could afford, plundering and stealing all the palatable food which had by the industry and prudence of murdered husbands, been laid in store for themselves and families. * * * * They burned all the books that they could find, they shot the hogs and cattle, it seemed for pleasure of shooting game, as they did not consume all they killed." * * * * * *

Another witness :

"For while the Saints were engaged in solemn prayer to God,* these lawless desperadoes came upon them with the fury of demons, and commenced firing upon them while they were thus solemnly engaged ; the Saints cried for quarters, but in vain, they then endeavored to escape by flight, but were surrounded ;—the Missourians continued to shoot them ; they would even place their guns to the heads of their victims, and thus barbarously take their lives. After the firing had partially subsided, one of Comstock's men found an old Revolutionary soldier, by the name of McBride, under the bank of the creek: commanding him, he exclaimed, 'You old grey-headed Mormon, I will fix you.' The old man got on his knees, and begged for his life ; but his age afforded no protection ; he was inhumanly butchered and thrown into the creek. During the slaughter, a small boy endeavored to conceal himself in the Blacksmith shop under a bellows, but one of the assassins seeing him, was in the act of shooting him when one of the company cried out, 'Do not shoot the boy ;' another said, 'Shoot him, d—m him, he will make a big Mormon some day ;' so he put the gun to the child's head, and blew out his brains. There were in this slaughter eighteen of the Saints killed, and thirteen wounded."

FAR WEST.

(Current Selections from the Evidence here. Some of the Witnesses, Men of Education, and standing.)

* * * * This only increased their distress ; for many thousands who were driven there, had no habitations or houses to shelter them, and were huddled together, some in tents and others under blankets, while others had no shelter from the inclemency of the weather. Nearly two months the Mormons had been in this state of consternation ; many of them had been killed, whilst others had been whipped until they had to swathe up their bowels to prevent them from falling out ; * * * * * * and whilst the people were waiting anxiously for deliverance—men, women

* Upon the alarm, those in the Smithy united in Prayer.

[60]

and children frightened, praying and weeping—we beheld at a distance, crossing the prairies and approaching the town, a large army in military array, brandishing their glittering swords in the sunshine; and we could not but feel joyful for a moment, thinking that probably the governor had sent an armed force to our relief. But to our great surprise, when the army arrived, they came up and formed a line in double file in one half mile on the east of the city of Far West; they demanded three persons to be brought out of the city before they should massacre the rest.

The army arrived at Far West, the sun about a half an hour high. In a few moments afterwards, Cornelius Gillum arrived with his army, and formed a junction. Gillum had been stationed at Hunter's Mills for about two months previous to that time—committing depredations upon the inhabitants—capturing men, women, and children, and carrying them off as prisoners, lacerating their bodies with hickory withes. The army of " Gillum" were painted like Indians, some of them were more conspicuous than were others, designated by red spots; and he, also, was painted in a similar manner, with red spots marked on his face, and styled himself the "Delaware Chief." They would hoop, and hollow, and yell as nearly as Indians as they could, and continued to do so all that night. In the morning early, the Colonel of Militia sent a messenger into the camp with a white flag, to have another interview with Gen. Doniphan. On his return, he informed us that the governor's order had arrived. General Doniphan said that "the order of the Governor was, to exterminate the Mormons, but he would be damned if he obeyed that order, Gen. Lucas might do what he pleased."

* * * After this, the town was surrounded with a strong guard, and no man, woman or child, was permitted to go out or come in under the penalty of death. Many of the citizens were shot in attempting to go out to obtain sustenance for themselves and families.

* * * * *

On the next day, the soldiers were permitted to patrol the streets, to abuse and insult the people at their leisure, and enter into houses and pillage them and ravish the women.

* * * The chief men among the Mormons were marched down through their lines with a strong guard in front, and the cannon in the rear, to the camp, amidst the whooping, hollowing, yellings, and shoutings of the army, which was so horrid and terrific that it frightened the inhabitants.

One of these testifies:

"He said they were determined to shoot us on the next morning in the public square in Far West. I made him no reply; On the next morning about sunrise, General Doniphan ordered his brigade to take up the line of march and leave the camp. He came to us where we were under guard, to shake hands with us, and bid us farewell. His first salutation was: 'You have been sentenced by the court martial to be shot this morning; but I will be damned if I will have any of the honor of it, or any of the disgrace of it; therefore, I have ordered my brigade to take up the line of march and leave the camp, for I consider it to be cold-blooded murder, and I bid you farewell;' and he went away.

* * * *

"In a few moments the guard was relieved with a new set; one of the new guards said that the damned Mormons would not be shot this time, for the movement of General Doniphan had frustrated the whole plan.

[61]

"While we were in this situation, a young man by the name of Grant,* came to see us, and put up at the tavern where General Clark made his quarters. He happened to come in time to see General Clark make choice of his men to shoot us on Monday morning the 12th day of November. He saw them make choice of their rifles, and load them with two balls in each, and after they had prepared their guns, General Clark saluted them, saying : ' Gentlemen, you shall have the honor of shooting the Mormon leaders on Monday morning at eight o'clock !' "

The same witness continues :

"Some time in April, we were taken to Davies county, as they said, to have a trial ; but when we arrived at that place, instead of finding a court or a jury, we found another inquisition, and Birch, the same man who was one of the court-martial when we were sentenced to death, was now the Circuit Judge of that pretended court ; and the grand jury that was empannelled, were all at the massacre at Hawn's Mill, and lively actors in that awful, cool-blooded murder, and all the pretence they made of excuse, was, they had done it because the governor had ordered them to do it. The same jury sat as a jury in the day time, and were placed over us as a guard in the night time. They tantalized and boasted over us, of their great achievements at Hawn's Mills, and at other places, telling us how many houses they had burned, and how many sheep, cattle and hogs they had driven off, belonging to the Mormons, and how many rapes they had committed, and what squealing and kicking there was among the damned bitches ; saying that they lashed one woman upon one of the damned Mormon meeting benches, tying her hands and her feet fast, and sixteen of them abused her as much as they had a mind to, and then left her bound and exposed in that horrible condition. These fiends of the lower region, boasted of these acts of barbarity, and tantalized our feelings with them for ten days. * * * The lady who was the subject of their brutality, did not recover her health to be able to help herself for more than three months afterwards."

Elsewhere, another witness deposes on this head :

"I heard a party of them one night telling about a female whose person they had violated, and this language was used by one of them : ' The damn bitch, how she squealed !' Who this person was, I did not know ; but before I got out of prison I heard that a widow, whose husband had died some few months before with consumption, had been brutally violated by a gang of them, and died in their hands, leaving three little children, in whose presence the scene of brutality took place. After I got out of prison, and had arrived in Quincy, Illinois, I met a strange man in the street who was inquiring, and inquired of me, respecting a circumstance of this kind—saying he had heard of it, and was on his way going to Missouri to get the children if he could find them. He said the woman thus murdered was his sister, or his wife's sister, I am not positive which. The man was in great agitation. * * * * * This grand jury constantly celebrated their achievements with grog and glass in hand, like the Indian warriors at their war-dances, singing and telling each other of their exploits in murdering the Mormons, in plundering their houses, and carrying off their property. At the end of every song, they would bring in the chorus : ' God damn, God damn, God damn the Presbyterians, God damn the Bap-

* The present Editor.

[62]

tists, God damn the Methodists;' reiterating one sect after another in the same manner, until they came to the Mormons. To them it was, ' God damn the God-damn Mormons; we have sent them to hell!' Then they would slap their hands, and shout ' Hosanna, Hosanna, Glory to God!' and fall down on their backs, and kick with their feet a few moments; then they would pretend to have swooned away into a glorious trance, in order to imitate some of the transactions at camp meetings. Then they would pretend to come out of their trance, and would shout and again slap their hands and jump up, while one would take a bottle of whiskey and a tumbler, and turn it out full of whiskey, and pour it down each other's necks, crying, ' damn it, take it, you must take it;' and if any one refused to drink the whiskey, others would clinch him, whilst another poured it down his neck; and what did not go down the inside, went down the outside. This is a part of the farce acted out by the Grand Jury (!) of Davies county, whilst they stood over us as guards, for ten nights successively; and all this in the presence of Judge Birch, who had previously said in our hearing that there was no law for the Mormons in the State of Missouri. His brother was then acting as District Attorney in that circuit, and, if any thing, was a greater cannibal than the Judge. After all these ten days of drunkenness, we were informed that we were indicted for Treason, Murder, Arson, Larceny, Theft, and Stealing."

Another of the captured elders :

"We had supposed, on their first appearance, that they were friendly troops, sent for our protection; but on receiving this alarming information of their wicked intentions, we were much surprised, and sent a messenger with a white flag to enquire of them who they were, and what they wanted of us, and by whose authority they came. This flag was fired upon by Captain Bogard, who afterwards told me the same with his own mouth. * * * * After several attempts at us, they set up the most hideous yells, that might have been supposed to have proceeded from the mouths of demons, and marched us, as prisoners, to their lines. There we were detained for two days and nights, and had to sleep on the ground in the cold month of November, in the midst of rain and mud. We were continually surrounded with a strong guard, whose mouths were filled with cursing and bitterness, blackguardism and blasphemy; who offered us every abuse and insult in their power, both by night and day; and many individuals of the army cocked their rifles, and taking deadly aim at our heads, swore they would shoot us. While under these circumstances, our ears were continually shocked with the relation of the horrid deeds they had committed, and which they boasted of. They related the circumstances in detail of having, the previous day, disarmed a certain man in his own house and took him prisoner, and afterwards beat out his brains with his own gun in presence of their officer. They told of other individuals who lay here and there in the brush, whom they had shot down without resistance, and who were laying, unburied, for the hogs to feed upon. They also named individual females of our society, whom they had forcibly bound, and twenty or thirty, one after another, committed rape upon. One of these females was a daughter of a respectable family, with whom I have been long acquainted, and with whom I have since conversed, and learned that it was truly the case. Delicacy at present forbids my mentioning the names. I also heard several of the soldiers acknowledge and boast of having stolen money in one place, clothing and bedding in another, and horses in another, whilst corn, pork, and beef, were taken by the whole army to support the men and horses; and in many cases cattle, hogs, and sheep were shot down, and only a small portion of them used, the rest left to waste. Of these crimes, of which the soldiers boasted, the general officers freely conversed, and corroborated the same.

"Maj. General Lucas and his ravaging army being now in assured possession * * * even burning the houses and fences for fuel, he insisted that every man, woman and child of the Mormon Society should leave the State, except such as he detained as prisoners; stating that the Governor had sent him to exterminate them, but that he would, as a mercy, spare their lives and give them until the first of April following, to get out of the State. He also compelled them, at the point of the bayonet, to sign a deed of trust of all their real estate, to defray the expenses of what he called the 'The Mormon War.' After arranging all these matters to his satisfaction, he returned to Richmond, thirty miles distant, taking about sixty heads of families with him, and marching them through a severe snow storm, on foot as prisoners, leaving their families in a perishing condition."

These captives were then submitted to a mock trial. Birch, the judge, told them from the bench:

"'If you once think to plant crops, or to occupy your lands any longer than the first of April, the citizens will be upon you; they will kill you, every one—men, women, and children—and leave you to manure the ground without a burial.'"

And put then interrogatories; as—

"'*Secondly.* Do the Mormons believe a certain passage in the Book of Daniel?' naming the passage, which reads as follows: 'And the kingdom and dominion, and the greatness of the kingdom under the whole heaven, shall be given to the people of the saints of the Most High, whose kingdom is an everlasting kingdom, and all dominions shall serve and obey him.' Dan. vii. 27. On being answered in the affirmative, the judge ordered the scribe to put it down as a strong point for treason. But this was too much for even a Missouri lawyer to bear: he (an attorney) remonstrated against such a course of procedure. Said he, 'Judge, you had better make the Bible treason.' After an examination of this kind, for many days, some were set at liberty, others admittted out on bail, and themselves and bail expelled from the State forthwith, with the Mormon citizens. And Joseph Smith, Hyram Smith, Sidney Rigdon, Lyman Wight, and others, were committed to the Clay county jail for further trial. Two or three others, and myself, were put into the jail at Ray county for the same purpose."

Was the State of Missouri to answer for this?

"*Testimony.*—A part of these mobs were painted like Indians, and 'Gillum,' their leader, was also painted in a similar manner, and styled himself the 'Delaware Chief;' and afterwards he, and the rest of the mob claimed and *obtained pay* as militia, from the State, for all the time they were engaged *as mob*, as will be seen by reference to the Acts of the Legislature."

Major General Clark, being sent by the Governor to take the chief command, made us a speech:

[64]

REPORT OF GEN. CLARK'S SPEECH.

"It now devolves upon you to fulfil the treaty that you have entered into, the leading items of which I shall now lay before you. The first requires that your leading men be given up, to be tried according to law; this you have complied with. The second is, that you deliver up your arms; this has also been attended to. The third stipulation is, that you sign over your properties to defray the expenses that have been incurred on your account; this you have also done. Another article yet remains for you to comply with, and that is, that you leave the State forthwith. And whatever may be your feelings concerning this, or whatever your innocence is, it is nothing to me. General Lucas (whose military rank is equal with mine) has made this treaty with you; I approve of it. I should have done the same had I been here, and am therefore determined to see it executed. The character of this State has suffered almost beyond redemption from the character, conduct, and influence that you have exerted; and we deem it an act of justice to restore her character by every proper means. The order of the Governor to me was, that you should be exterminated, and not allowed to remain in the State. And had not your leaders been given up, and the terms of the treaty complied with before this time, you and your families would have been destroyed, and your houses in ashes. There is a discretionary power vested in my hands, which, considering your circumstances, I shall exercise for a season. You are indebted to me for this clemency. I do not say that you shall go now, but you must not think of staying here another season, or of putting in crops; for the moment you do this, the citizens will be upon you; and if I am called here again, in case of non-compliance with the treaty made, do not think that I shall act as I have done now. You need not expect any mercy, but extermination, for I am determined the *Governor's order shall be executed. As for your leaders, do not think, do not imagine for a moment, do not let it enter your minds, that they will be delivered and restored to you again. For their fate is fixed, the die is cast, their doom is sealed.* I am sorry, gentlemen, to see so many apparently intelligent men found in the situation that you are; and oh! if I could invoke the great spirit of the unknown God to rest upon and deliver you from that awful chain of superstition, and liberate you from those fetters of fanaticism with which you are bound—that you no longer do homage to man. I would advise you to scatter abroad, and never again organize yourselves with Bishops, Priests, &c., lest you excite the jealousies of the people, and subject yourselves to the same calamities that have now come upon you. You have always been the aggressors—you have brought upon yourselves these difficulties by being disaffected, and not being subject to rule. And my advice is, that you become as other citizens, lest, by a recurrence of these events, you bring upon yourselves irretrievable ruin."

After this, THE EXPULSION was effected. Loss of life of Mormons estimated at about 300.

THE END.

Index

Abel, Elijah, 347–48
Achley, Robert, 16
Ackley, John A., 16
Adam-ondi-Ahman, 24
Adams, George J., 48, 348
Adams, William A., 54
aged, role of, 296–97
Alabama, Mormonism in, 66
Allegany County, N.Y., 18
Alley, Sarah, 51
Allred, Isaac, 262, 348
Allred, James, 348
Allred, Reddick N., 261, 262, 348
Alpine, Utah, 187
Altona, Ill., 26
American Fork, Utah, 215, 229
Angell, Truman O., 200, 348
anti-Mormons: Grant attacks, 184–87; in Illinois (1845): 71–73; in Missouri, 7–8; in New York, 11–15; in the South, 18–23, 35–39; plot of, to kill Saints (1846): 194, 196; mentioned, 165
apostasy: Grant's 1854 sermon on, 176–77; in Kirtland, 231
Armstrong, Belle, 49
Arrington, Leonard J., 334
Astor House, 221

Authority: Grant's 1854 sermon on, 294–99; Grant's views on, 308–11

Baal, priests of, 16
Babbitt, Almon W., 98, 105, 112, 140, 348
Baldwin, Rev., 38–39
Baptist ministers: persecution by, 11, 20, 180, 185
Barber, Leonard, 15
Barlow, Jothan, 15
Barlow, Nathan, 31
Bates, William, 54
Bath, N.Y., 16
Beach, Mr., 103, 105
Bear River, 86, 90
Beaver, Utah, 202
Beck, James, 220, 348–49
Bennett, James Gordon: biography of, 349; Grant's 1852 letter to, 131–32; refuses to print second Grant letter, 134; response of, 132–34
Bennett, John Cook, 349
Bennington, N.Y., 12
Benson, Ezra T., 108, 114, 125, 145, 326–27, 349
Bent, Samuel, 349
Benton, Thomas H., 194–96, 349
Bernhisel, John M.: arrives in Utah, 112; Grant assists in East, 114–128;

Woodruff's toast to (1852): 145; mentioned, 105, 246, 349–50

Big Cottonwood Canyon: celebration at, 244; Grant mentions, in prayer, 246; 247

Bigler, Bathsheba Wilson, *21*

Bigler, Jacob G.: Grant's 1838 letter to, 19–21

Bigler sisters: Grant's 1838 letter to, 21

Big Mountain, 85

Bird, Charles, 32, 37, 350

Blackhurst, Jane, 208

Blackman sisters, 16

blank-text legend, 32–35

blood atonement: analysis of doctrine of, 165–66, 172; Grants's 1854 discourse on, 160–66, 189; mentioned, 266, 267

Blouits Corners, N.Y., 15

Boggs, Lilburn W.: biography of, 350; extermination order of, 25; Grant meets militia of, 36

Book of Mormon: Grant's assessment of 201; translation of, 6; mentioned, 14, 153, 164, 250

Booth, William, Jr., 261

Boston, Mass.: apostles meet in, 50; Grant reports on church at, 66

Boston, Beny, 16

Bountiful, Utah: Reformation meetings in, 268, 270–71, 275 ; mentioned, 276, 280

Boyle, Henry G., 329, 350

Boynton, John F., 6, 350

Brandebury, Lemuel H., 116–18

Brannan, Samuel, 57, 66, 350

Bratton, George W., 108

Brocchus, Perry E., 113–14, 116, 139

Broome County, N.Y., 4, 18

Brown, Elder, 64

Brown, T. D., 289

Brown, Thomas 204

Browning, James G., 174, 350

Brownsville, Utah. *See* Ogden, Utah.

Brundage, John, 289

Brundage, William, 16

Buchanan, James, 35

Buffalo, N.Y., 11, 18

Bullock, Thomas: appointed clerk of Council House, 111; mentioned, 96, 116, 350–51

Busannett, Sister, 49

Bushman, Richard L., 271

Butterfield, Josiah, 54, 351

Cache Valley, Utah, 217

Cahoon, Reynolds, 47, 351

Caldwell County, Mo., 37

California: Maryette Grant leaves for, 344; Mormonism in, 316–17; mentioned, 76, 213

Camp of Israel, 74, 76

Campbell, Brother, 147

Campbell, Alexander, 249–50, 351

Campbellites, 7, 11

Canada: Mormonism in, 66

Candland, David, 221, 351

Cannon, Frank J., 335, 351

Cape Cod: Grant requests vacation to, 63

Carpenter, Aananet, 16

Carpenter, Samuel, 16

Carrington, Albert, 292, 322, 351

Carrying Company, 103, 127

Casper, Bernice Grant, 344

Carthage, Ill.: martyrdom at, 47–48, 322; mentioned, 168, 245

Casess, Squire, 12

catechism, Reformation, 277, 279–80, 341

Catoe, N.Y., 17

Cedar Bluffs, 77

Cedar City, Utah, 200

Centerville, Utah: Reformation meetings in, 268–70, 275

Chagrin, Ohio: Grant family settles in, 7; Grant returns to, 16

chastisement: Grants's 1856 sermon on, 307–11

Chesapeake Bay, 18

Chicken Springs, 229

cholera: strikes Grant company, 80–82

Church of Jesus Christ of Latter-day Saints. *See* Mormonism; Mormons.

Cincinnati, Ohio, 31

Cincinnatus: Nauvoo Legion in tradition of, 95

Civil War: coming of, 105, 167–70, 235–36, 239–40

Clapp, Benjamin L., 72, 75, 281, 282, 352

Clark, John B., 25, 352

Clark, William O., 180

Clarke, Adam, 199

Clawson, Hiram B., 174–75, 352

Clayton, William, 51, 52, 138, 352

cleanliness: Grant's ideas on, 214, 251–52, 285, 304, 341; Grant's 1856 sermon on, 277–78; Mayor Grant orders, in city, 209–11, 277

Clements, Gilbert: assists in Reformation, 258–269 passim, *353*

Clements, John Moon, 279, 352

Cobb, Sister, 49

Coltrin, Zebedee, 44, 352

Commerce, Ill.: Mormons settle in, 26–27. *See also* Nauvoo, Ill.

commitment: Tomkins model of, 18

Community of Christ. *See* Reorganized Church of Jesus Christ of Latter Day Saints.

Common Law: Grant's opinion of, 233–34

Compromise of 1850, 111

Constitution, U.S., 165, 196–97

Coock, Matilda, 54

Cook, Phineas W., 220, 352–53

Coray, Howard K., 329, 353

Council Bluffs, Iowa: Kane arrives at, 74; Saints arrive at, 73; mentioned, 103, 114

Council House: Grant attends meetings in, 276, 283; Utah Territory organizes in, 111–12, 141

Council of Fifty: Grant appointed to, 46

courts, church, 291–93

Covenant, New and Everlasting. *See* polygyny.

Cowdery, Oliver, 160, 161, 353

Cowdery, Warren: biography of, 353; Grant's 1837 letter to, 17–18

Cowhocton, N.Y., 12, 15

Cowley, Matthias, 326–27, 353

Crimean War, 166, 168

Curtis, Brother, 12

Curtis, Dorr P., 261, 262, 353

Cutler, Alpheus, 353

Dallas, George M., 74, 333–34

Davis County, Utah: Grant farms in, 193, 200, 215, 257, 291, 344; Reformation events in, 258–65, 268–71

Day, Judge, 138

Decker, Charles C., 79, 103, 174, 175

deism, 206

Delaware River, 45–46, 67

Denmark: Mormons in, 231

Denton, S. W., 13

Derr, William, 138

Des Moines River, 73

Deseret, State of, 93–96

Deseret Dramatic Association, 215

Deseret News: Grant's obituary in, 321–22; report on Reformation in, 261, 292–93; statement on polygyny in, 257; Wells's oration in, 113; mentioned, 139, 209

Deseret Theological Institute: Grant addresses (1855): 202; organized, 199

Dinsdale, Brother, 261

ditches: in Salt Lake City, 210

Doctrine and Covenants, Book of, 160, 162, 203, 250

Doniphan, Alexander, 120, 127, 353–54

Douglas, Stephen A., 127, 139, 354

Drummond, William W., 226–27

Dry Moon Discourse (1856), 243, 252

Danish Mormons, 231

dyspepsia: Grant suffers from, 206

Easton, Pa., 53

Echo Canyon, 85

Education: in early America, 5

Edwards, Jonathan, 337, 354

Edwards, Mary, 16

Egan, Howard, 354, 425–26

Elder Mountains, 208

Eldredge, Horace S., 95, 281, 354

Eldridge, John, 221

Elkhorn River, 76

Ellison, John, 261, 354

Ellsworth, Edmund, 79, 275, 354–55

Elphry, Philip, 54

Evans, David, 355

Emigration Canyon, 95

Endowment House: dedication of, 200; under construction, 174; uses of, 227

endurance: Grant's 1856 sermon on, 284–87

England: Cowley in (1856–57), 326–27; Pratt (Orson) in (1856), 271; Richards (Franklin) returns from, 293; Woodruff in (1845), 65; Young (Joseph) in (1850), 105; mentioned, 239

English Mormons: 41, 179, 181, 194, 231

Ephraim, Utah, 187

Erie, Pa.: Grant family converted in, 5–7; mentioned, 57

Erits, John, 16

Europe: converts from, 43; war in (1854): 166–69

Evanston, Wyo., 90

Fairport, Ohio, 11, 18

faith and works: Grant's 1855 sermon on, 197–99

Fallsburg, N.Y., 15

family: Grant on the, 297–99

famine: Grant's 1856 sermon on, 230–32

Far West, Mo.: conditions in, 22–26; Grant visits, 37

Farington, Claricy, 13

Farington, Lucindia, 15

Farington, Mahaly, 15

farm in West Bountiful, 193, 200, 215, 257, 291, 344

Farmington, Utah: Reformation meetings in, 263–65, 269, 270; mentioned, 176

Felt, N. H., 105

fencing: in Salt Lake City, 209–11

Fillmore, Millard: decides against runaway judges, 135; Grant calls on, 135–36; mentioned, 111–28 passim, 236, 239, 355

Fillmore, Utah: Grant's illness in (1855), 228; Grant preaches cleanliness in, 252; Presidency returns from, 229; territorial government in, 219–26, 227 passim.

First Presidency: attacked for handcart disaster, 301–2; Grant appointed to (1854), 173; teaching ridiculed, 212; vacancy in, 170; Willes's ode to, 259; works on statehood, 221; mentioned, 229

— messages of: Apr. 1855, 199–200; May 1855, 202; on famine, 232; on gleaning, 243–44

First Quorum of Seventy: Grant appointed to, 8–9

Fisher, Brother, 31

Floyd, John B., 33–35

Foote, Warren, 355

Ford, Thomas, 47–48, 355

Fordham, Elijah, 61, 63, 64, 355

Foreman, John, 54

Ft. Defunct, 201

Ft. John, 105

Ft. Kearny, 114, 139

Ft. Laramie, 78

Ft. Leavenworth, 75

Ft. Supply, 201

France: Mormons in, 231

Fullmer, David, 355

Furniss, Norman F., 343

Garden Grove, Iowa, 73

Garn, Daniel, 184, 185, 355–56

Gates, Susa Young: story of, about Grant and Young, 3–4

gathering. *See* Zion.

Geauga County, Ohio, 12

Gee, Noah, 54

General Tithing Office, 174, 177

Genesee County, N.Y., 11, 12

Gentiles (non-Mormons): Grant attacks, 212, 233–37; Grant's ideas on, 190, 304–5; Grant's 1856 sermon on law of, 232–37

Georgia: Mormonism in, 66

Gibbs, Gideon H., 299, 356

Gibson, William, 120, 356

Gillet, Cally, 15

Gillet, Harris, 15

Gillet, Thedy, 16

Gloucester Point, 45

Glover, William, 138, 356

Goodyear, Miles, 101

Gordin, Mary, 13

Grand Island, 77

Grand River: Adam-ondi-Ahman, 24

Grant, Anna, 222

Grant, Athalia Howard: biography of, 356; Grant visits, 107; marriage of, 5; moves to Illinois, 26; mentioned, 49, 122, 123

Grant, Austin, 15, 123, 356

Grant, Benjamin, 222, 223

Grant, Betsy, 15, 49

Grant, Brigham Frederick, *290*, 291, 356

Grant, Caroline (Caddie): biography of, 356; birth of, 64; Grant's concern for, 101–7 passim; Susan as mother of,

94; mentioned, 80–85 passim, 93, 223, *224*, *225*, 22, 289–90

Grant, Caroline Ann Van Dyke: appears to Grant, 313; biography of, 356–57; death and burial of, 85, 90, 149; endowment of, 72; illness of, 77–85 passim; marriage of, 48; with Grant in East, 50–68 passim; mentioned, 71, 227, 291

Grant, Carter E., 90

Grant, George D.: baptism of, 13; biography of, 357; Grant's regards to, 64, 116, 122, 125; in custody at Far West, 25; marriage of, to widows, 344; mentioned, 49, 63

Grant, George Smith, 244, *290*, 357

Grant, Heber Jeddy: biography of, 357; birth of, 311, 317; role of, 329; mentioned, *290*, *330*, 344

Grant, Howard, 123, 357

Grant, Jane, 15

Grant, Jedediah Morgan: administers endowments, 72–73, 215; arrivals in Utah, 85, 87, 147–48, 229; assists family from Missouri, 25–27; at Kanesville (1852): 145; at Nauvoo (1842–43): 41–44, (1844): 46–48, (1845–46): 71–73; at Kirtland (1837): 17–18; baptism of, 7; birth of, 4–5; called reverend, 96, 99; characteristics of, 5, 14, 38–39, 127–28, 188, 207, 335–42; common assessment of, 343; Smith's criticism of, 44; death of, 316, 317, 344; deathbed visions of, 241–42, 312–15; debates Page, 45; education of, 5, 204–5; endowment of, 72; families of, *224*, *225*, 227, *290*, 344; funeral of, 321–24; health of, 206, 221, 253; homelessness of, 93; imagery of, 333; in Indian skirmish, 103, 109; in Smith-Winchester feud, 57–58; initiates Reformation, 259–63; journal of, 12–19, 24–25; Kane's regard for, 237; loses livestock, 77; loyalty to Twelve of, 51–53; ordained president of Seventy, 72; ordains new seventies, 112; ordains patriarchs, 94, 197; orders tithing sent to city, 173–75; pamphlet against Rigdon, 58–60; perceptions on Mormonism, 236–38; prayer of (1856): 245–47; preaching style of, 25–27, 180, 191–92; prominence of, 237–38; relationship with Young, 3, 4, 150, 240, 339–40; Rosetta's 1856 letter to, 223, 226; Susan's 1856 letter to, 222–23, 226; toast by (1853): 150; total commitment of, 18–20; witnesses apostles ordained (1835): 8–9; Woodruff's 1852 toast to, 145; works on Kirtland Temple, 11

— appointments of: as captain of third hundred, 75, 76; as church spokesman, 75; to Council of Fifty, 46; as director of Deseret Theological Institute, 199; as director of Perpetual Emigrating Fund Company, 109; as emigration agent, 100; as emigration captain, 72; to First Presidency, 173; to First Council of Seventy, 54, 72; to First Quorum of Seventy, 8–9; as general in Nauvoo Legion, 95; as liaison to Kane and Indians in Iowa, 74–75, 76; to Masonic Lodge, 46; as mayor and speaker, 111–12; as messenger to Ford, 47; as presiding elder at Philadelphia, 43–44; to statehood committee, 94–95; as temple fund agent, 69

— letters of, to: Biglers (1838): 19–21; Browning (1854): 174–75; family (1855): 220; Moses Martin (1838): 22–23; *New York Herald* (1852): 131–32, 383–446; Susan (1849): 101, 102, (1852): 121–22, 123–26, (1855): 221–22; Susan and Children (1850): 106–8; Susan and Family (1851): 114–15, 115–17, (1852): 136–37, (1856): 289–91; *Times and Seasons* (1840): 35–38; Whitney (1844):

53–54; Woodruff (1845): 65–67; Young (1844): 51–52, (1845): 63–64, (1847): 78–79, (1850): 103–6, (1851): 117–20, (1852): 126–27, 137–38, 139–40

— missions of, to: East (1835–37): 12–16, 18; New York (1835): 11; Philadelphia (1844–45): 43–46, 48–67; South (1837–42): 18–25, 31–39; St. Louis and East (1849–50): 100–8; Washington and Philadelphia (1847): 75–76, (1851–52): 114–47

— sermons of, on: apostates (1854): 176–77; authority (1856): 294–99; bishops (1856): 291–92; blank text (1839): 32–35; blood atonement (1854): 160–65; chastisement (1856): 307–11; cleanliness (1856): 277–78; dry moon (1856): 243, 252; endurance (1856): 284–87; evil in Zion (1854): 188–91; faith and works (1855): 197–99; famine (1856): 230–32; filthiness (1855): 212–15; Gentile law (1856): 232–37; handcarts (1856): 300–5; history and light of truth (1856): 247–52; Holy Spirit (1855): 202–6; immigration (1854): 184–87; Indian policy (1855): 200–2; iniquity (1856): 265–68; justice (1855): 216–17; Mormon Battalion (1855): 194–97; newcomers (1854): 178–84; polygyny (1855): 216–17; power of God (1854): 155–59; prophecy (1854): 166–70; reformation (1855): 216–17, (1856): 268–69; returned missionaries (1855): 218–19; seventies (1856): 281–83; uniformity (1853): 151–54

Grant, Jedediah Morgan, Jr.: biography of, 357; birth of, 149; mentioned, 223, *225*, *226*, *290*

Grant, Joseph, 13, 357

Grant, Joseph Hyrum: biography of, 357; birth of, 149; letter on Grant to, 34–35; mentioned, *146*, 221, 223, *290*

Grant, Joseph Hyrum, Jr., 357–58

Grant, Joshua (father of Jedediah G.): biography of, 358; Grant visits, 107; marriage of, 5; mentioned, 44, 122, 123, *124*

Grant, Joshua (brother of Jedediah G.): biography of, 358; calling of, to Cincinnati, 43; death of, 123–24; Grant marries widow of, 193; labors with brother, 37–41; Smith's criticism of, 44; works on temple, 11; mentioned, 13–17 passim, 40, 116, 137, 122

Grant, Joshua Frederick, 244, *290*, 358

Grant, Lewis M.: adoption of, 149, 291; arrives in Utah, 108; biography of, 358; mentioned, 222, 223, 227, 289, 358

Grant, Lois, 13

Grant, Louisa Marie Goulay: bears son, 244; biography of, 358; marriage of, 193; mentioned, 123–24, 227, 344

Grant, Margaret: appears in vision, 313; biography of, 358; birth of, 77; Grant seeks body of, 85–87; illness and death of, 81–82; mentioned, 149

Grant, Maryette Kesler: biography of, 358–59; Grant's concerns for, 289; marriage of, 193; pregnancy of, 244; mentioned, 220, 223, 227, 344

Grant, Nelson, 12, 123, 359

Grant, Rachel Ridgeway Ivins: bears son, 311–12; biography of, 359; Grant's concerns for, 289; marriage of, 215; pregnancy of, 244; sealed to Smith, 227; mentioned, 222, 223, 226, 317, 227, 344

Grant, Rosetta Henrietta. *See* Marshall.

Grant, Rosetta Robison: bears son, 149; biography of, 359; letter to Grant (1856), 222, 223, 226; marriage of, 94; relatives to visit, 107; mentioned,

103–107 passim, 116, 125, 147, *225*, 227, 344

Grant, Sarah Ann Thurston: bears son, 244; biography of, 359; family of, 244; marriage of, 149; mentioned, 220, 222, 223, 227, 344

Grant, Susan Fairchild Noble: account of 1847 trek, 80–85; assists Grant family (1847), 77, 80–85; bears son, 149; biography of, 359–60; Grant's letters to, 101, 102, 121–22, 123–26, 221–22; Grant's letters to, and children, 106–8; Grant's letter to, and family, 114–15, 115–17, 136–37, 289–91; letter to Grant (1856), 222–23; marriage of, 94; mentioned, 101, 127, *195*, *224*, 227, 344

Grant, Roxcy Ann. *See* Smith.

Grant, Susan Vilate. *See* Muir.

Grant, Theda. *See* Reeves.

Grant, Thomas Jefferson, 360

Grantsville, Utah, 251

Grayson County, Va., 35

Great Awakening, 240

Great Basin Kingdom, 93, 194

Great Britain. *See* England.

Great Salt Lake: exploration of, 94

Great Salt Lake Valley. *See* Salt Lake Valley.

Greeley, Horace, 134, 360

Green River (Wyo.), 83, 289

Greene, Evan M., 6, 360

Greene, John P., 31, 360

Grover, Thomas, 258, 264, 360

Grow, Edward, 16

Guadalupe Hidalgo, Treaty of, 94

Guilford County, N.C., 35

Gyendott River, 31

Haight, Isaac C., 200, 360

Hales, Stephen, 360–61

Hamlin, Hannibal, 135

Hampton, Patience, 54

Hancock County, Ill.: farms in, 62; progress in (1845), 67

Hancock, Levi, 281, 282, 361

Handcart pioneers: brethren to assist, 289; Grant's 1856 sermon on, 300–5; mentioned, 257, 275, 289–90, 321, 335

Hanks, Ephraim, 361

happiness: Grant's admonition to, 205–6

Hardy, Leonard Wilford (Cap): account by, of Grant's vision, 314–15; biography of, 361; mentioned, 220

Harriman, Henry, 128, 282, 361

Harrington, Leonard E., 215, 361

Harris, Broughton D.: campaign of, against Mormons, 113–14, 117; enraged at Wells's remarks, 113; mentioned, 116, 120, 133

Harris, George W., 361

Harris, Mrs., 133

Harrison County, Va., 18–19

Henderson, Samuel G., 261, 262, 361–62

Henderson Grove, Ill., 26

Hess, John W., 263, 264, 362

Heywood, Joseph L., 106, 362

Higbee, Elias, 362

Hill, Brother, 289

Historian's Office, 312, 316

history: Grant's 1856 sermon on, 147–52

Holy Spirit: Grant's 1855 sermon on, 202–6

home missions, 257–58, 265

Housekeeper, John, 54

Howe, James Jackson: account by, of blank-text sermon, 34–35

Hunt, Daniel: assists in Reformation, 258, 261, 264; biography of, 362

Hunter, Edward, 76, 106, 268, 276, 283

Huntington, Va. (W. Va.), 41

Hurt, Garland, 200, 362

Hyde, Orson: attack of, on Rigdon, 59; biography of, 362–63; grammar class of, 203, 335; missionary to Grant family, 6; nomination of, as judge, 135, 140; mentioned, 49, 67, 199, 201

Illinois: anti-Mormonism in, 71–73, 113, 196; not considered home by Grant, 93; Grant tells Bigler to go to, 19; Mormons look for future in, 31; unusual cold in, 126

Immigration: Grant's 1854 sermon on, 184–87

Independence Rock, 79, 102

India: Willes returns from, 258

Indian policy, 187, 200–2, 238, 289

Indians: Grant called as liason to, 73–74; in Fillmore, 121–22; raid on Grant camp (1847): 83; skirmish with, 103, 109; troubles with (1855): 197; mentioned, 295

iniquity: Grant's 1856 sermon on, 265–68

Iowa Territory: Saints' exodus through, 73–74

Iron County, Utah: Grant preaches in, 112; mentioned, 202

Ivins, Israel, 121, 318, 363

Ivins, Rachel Ridgeway. *See* Grant.

Jackson, Andrew, 134, 236

Jackson, Joseph H., 47

Jackson County, Mo., 7, 22, 184, 324. *See also* Zion.

Jacksonianism, 148

Jeddy's mule, legend of, 272

Jeffersonville, Va., 25–27

Jeffries, George, 52

Johnson, J. W., 269

Jordan, John, 220

Jordan River, 94

Joseph, City of. *See* Nauvoo, Ill.

Juab County, Utah, 229

Judd, Mary Grant: statement about Grant's journal, 25

justice, eternal: Grant's ideas on, 216–17

Kanawha, Va. (W. Va.), 23

Kane, Thomas L.: assists Grant in East, 75, 114–28 passim; biography of, 363–64; letter of, to Young (1857): 327; receives polygyny explanation, 117–20; relationship of, with Grant, 74–75, 93; reports 1846 anti-Mormon plot, 194–95, 196; role of, in *Herald* letters, 333–35; mentioned, 38, 79, 139

Kanesville, Iowa: 115, 121, 139, 145

Kansas: slavery question in, 236

Kaysville (Kays Ward), Utah: Reformation in, 258–63, 265, 269, 270

Kesler, Frederick, 193, 364

Kesler, Maryette. *See* Grant.

Kimball, Heber C.: account of, of Grant's vision, 312–14; administers endowments, 215; becomes apostle, 8; biography of, 264; blesses Grant, 312; called Brigham's prophet, 240; dream of, concerning Grant, 311; in East, 45, 50; ordains patriarchs, 94, 197; preaching of, 43, 94, 164, 232–33, 265, 275, 293; relationship of, with Grant, 64, 82–83, 154, 221, 246; sees famine ending, 244; spirit of, 187,

237, 265, 266; to receive temple funds, 53; mentioned, 173, 308–09, 339

Kimball, Vilate Murray, 223, 364

King, Hannah Tapfield, 280, 287, 326, 364

Kinkade, Mr., 103

Kinney, John F., 200, 364–65

Kirtland, Ohio: apostasy in, 19, 231; Grant and Stanley depart from, 11; Grant requests news of, 20; Grant returns to, 16; simple Mormonism of, 7, 148–49, 184; spiritualism in, 156; mentioned, 147, 236

Kirtland Safety Society, 17–18, 22

Kirtland Temple: compared to Nauvoo, 41; construction of, 11; manifestations in, 176, 264

Knox County, Ill., 37

Lake City, Utah. *See* American Fork, Utah.

Lambert, John, 220, 222, 223, 289, 365

Laney, Isaac, 365

Las Vegas Springs, 208

Latter-day Saints. *See* Mormons.

Laub, George, 365

Law, William, 365

Law, Wilson, 47

Lee, John D., 75, 365

Leithead, James, 262, 263, 365

letters, Grant. *See* Grant, Jedediah Morgan — letters of.

Lewis, Benjamin, 365

Lewis, David, 365

Lewis, Tarlton, 365–66

Lewis, Theodore B., 32, *33*, 366

Lillawhite, Mrs., 221

Lion of the Lord. *See* Young, Brigham.

liquor: Grant attacks sellers of (1854): 189–91

Little, Jesse C., 74, 76, 312, 366

Little, Parry, 103

Liverpool, England, 58, 100

Livingston County, N.Y., 11

Locke, John, 204, 335

Lord's Thunder, 140

Louisiana: Mormonism in, 66

Louisville, N.Y., 16, 17

Loyle, John, 54

Lutz, Elder, 53

Lyman, Amasa M.: biography of, 366; mission of, to Grant family, 6; mentioned, 6, 67, 94, 244

McAffee, Thomas B.: letter to, on blood atonement, 172

McArthur handcart company, 275

McBride, Reuben, 221, 367

McConkie, Bruce R., 172

McGinis, S., 31

McKeatchie, John. *See* Grant, Lewis M.

McLane, Elder, 52

McPherson, James R., 261, 367

magic, 11, 145

Maine Liquor Law, 134

Manti, Utah: Grant's 1855 sermon at, 200–2; mentioned, 187

Marks, William, 18, 366

Marsh, Thomas B., 24, 366

Marshall, Rosetta Henrietta Grant, 222, 225, 366

Martin, Cal, 21

Martin, Jesse Bigler, 366

Martin, Moses: biography of, 367; letter to, 22–23; mentioned, 24

Martin handcart company, 289

Mather, Cotton: Grant reads from, 271, 335; mentioned, 191, 339, 341

Matthews, Brother, 261

Medicine: Grant's ideas on, 197-98

Merrill, Marriner W., 367

Messenger and Advocate (church magazine), 16

Methodists: persecutions by, 14-15; mentioned, 25, 34, 198-99

Mexican War: Mormons in, 74, 194-97; treaty ending, 94, 96

Mill Creek, 94

millennialism, 167, 268, 335-42 passim

Miller, George, 190

Milligan, William, 54

Miner, Mrs., 13

missionaries: Grant's 1855 blessing upon, 218-19

Mississippi: Mormonism in, 66

Mississippi River: travel upon, 31, 41, 46

Mississippi Valley: RLDS church rises in, 149

Missouri: anti Mormon plot in (1846): 194-95, 196; Grant absent from, 93, 336; Mormons expelled from, 25-27, 31; persecutions in, 7-9, 37, 113, 130; rumors of trouble in, 22

Monroe, James M., 367, 425-26

Morgan, Utah, 244, 253, 257

Mormon Battalion: Grant's 1855 address to, 194-97; recruitment of, 74-75, 113, 334

Mormon Thunder: Grant calls self, 140, 333; need for, 137; mentioned, 154, 307, 342

Mormonism: association of Grant and Young in, 3, 4, 150, 240, 339-40; blood atonement doctrine of, 165-66, 172; destiny of, 41, 151-54, 328-29; dissent and defection plague Early, 41-42; government of, reorganized (1835): 8-9; Grant as essence of, 335-37, 341-42; Grant's conversion to, 7; opposition to, 12-15, 234-36; nature of Early, 97-99, 162-64, 181-83, 336-37, 342

Mormons: characteristics of early, 179-80,197-99; effect of Grant upon, 321-22, 325-26; friction and apostasy among, 148-49; Grant's criticisms of, 154, 190-91, 211-14, 259-62 ; Indian policy of, 187, 200-2, 238, 289; Illinois troubles of, 71-72; missionaries misinform, 179; patriotism of, 194-97, 234-37; significance of preaching among, 338-39; westward movement of, 31, 71-87

Mt. Pisgah, Iowa, 73

mountain fever, 84

Mountain Meadows Massacre, 328

Mountainville, Utah. *See* Alpine, Utah.

Moyle, Henry, 275-76, 367

Moyle, James H., 38

Muir, Klea, *195*

Muir, Susan Vilate Grant, 222, *224*, 267-68

Murray, Vilate. *See* Kimball.

Naisbitt, Henry W., 368

Naples, N.Y., Grant family settles in, 5; Grant preaches in, 11, 12, 13

Nauvoo, Ill.: events in (1843-44), 41-48; exodus from,72-73; growth of, 41-42, 67-68; Grants' marriage at, 48; Grant sends men and money to, 62-63, 66-67; Grant travels to (1845): 68, 71; Mormons settle in, 25-27; Rigdon excommunicated at, 57; Smith graves at, 257; mentioned, 146, 180, 199, 335

Nauvoo Brass Band, 209

Nauvoo House, 66

Nauvoo Legion: at Grant funeral, 322; nature of, 95; third hundred contingent of, 76; mentioned, 194, 330-31

Nauvoo Temple: as emblem of Twelve's hegemony, 52; Grant collects funds for, 50, 64-68 passim; ordinances in, 72-73; Young seeks to finish, 62

Neighbor (Nauvoo newspaper), 62

Neversink, N.Y.: Grant holds meetings in, 15; Grant's parents marry in, 5

New and Everlasting Covenant. *See* polygyny.

New England: in 1816, 4

New Jersey, 18, 46, 49, 121-22, 215

New Mexico, 76

New Orleans, 100

New York: conference in, 45; Grant reports on church in, 66; missions to, 11-16, 336; Woodruff arrives in (1844), 57; mentioned, 120, 122

New York Herald: letters to, 131-32, 135, 141, 333-34, 383-446

New York Tribune: article on Mormonism (1849), 96-100

newcomers: Grant's 1854 sermon on, 178-84

Newel, Dr., 49

Newell, Horace, 299

Noble, Joseph Bates: account of, of wolves story, 86-87; biography of, 368; marriages in home of, 94; travels of, with third hundred, 77-87 passim; mentioned, *85*, 108, 122

Noble, Mary Adeline Beman, 177, 368

Noble, Susan Fairchild. *See* Grant.

North Carolina: Grant reports on church in (1845), 66; missions to, 19-25, 31-39; mentioned, 329, 336

Norwich, Vt.: Smiths depart from, 4

obedience: Grant's 1856 sermon on, 238-40

Ogden, Utah, 96, 112, 174

Ogden River, 96

Ohio: Grant absent from, 93, 336; Grant lost in, 8; Mormonism in, 7, 150; rumors of trouble in 22; Young and Smith meet in, 7

Ohio River, 41

Omaha Hills, 79

Ontario County, N.Y., 5, 11

opposition: Grant's views on, 205-6

Oregon Trail, 79

Owenism, 98

Pack, John, 215, 368

Page, John E.: biography of, 368, debates with Grant, 45-46; remains in East (1844): 50; mentioned, 67

Pain, Pheby, 16

Palmyra, N.Y., 4, 6

Palmyra, Utah. *See* Spanish Fork, Utah.

Parowan, Utah, 200

Parsons, Elder, 13

Partridge, Edward, 158, 368

Partridge, Elinore, 334

Patrick County, Va., 22-23, 32, 35

Patten, David W., 368

Payne, William L., 261, 368

Pell, Edward, 138

Perpetual Emigrating Fund Company, 100, 103, 187

Peterson, Charles S., 377

Pettingile, E., 16

Phelps, William W., 94, 369

Philadelphia: anti-Rigdon tract from, 59-60; Caroline Smith's letter from,

48–50; Grant preaches in (1837): 18; Grant works with Kane in, 114–47 passim, Grant holds conference with apostles in, 45, Grant presides in, 45–67 passim; Grant in (1847): 76; Grant's letters from (1844–45): 51–52, 53–54, 63–64, 65–67, (1852): 123–26, 126–27, 136–40; Kane writes to Young from, 237; letters to *Herald* written in, 123, 124, 131; missionaries destined for, 45; William Smith's activities in, 43–58 passim, 63, 64–65; Woodruff in (1844): 57–58; mentioned, 149, 150, 155

Pittsburgh: apostles leave for, 46; Rigdon at, 57; Winchester returns from, 53, 54; mentioned, 62

Platte River, 76, 83, 114, 147

plurality of wives. *See* polygyny.

Polk, James K.: administration of, 113; agrees to enlist Mormons, 74–75, 334; biography of, 369

polygamy. *See* polygyny.

polygyny: as tool of Indian policy, 200–2; at Nauvoo, 42; Grant explains, to Kane, 118–19; Grant defends (1854), 216–17; in Grant family, 149, 215, 227, 257, 344; Jesus and, 199; Mormons admit to, 134; rumor of, in Philadelphia, 51–53; symbol of Mormonism, 51–53, 114, 149; Twelve attacked because of, 51–53; Young and, 3; mentioned, 94, 125, 156, 184, 266

Polysophical Society, 287

Pomological Society, 215

Pope of Rome, 239

Portage, N.Y., 17, 18

Portland, N.Y., 12

Potawatomi country, 73–76

Potomac River, 135

Potter, Mrs., 50

power of God: Grant's 1854 sermon on, 155–59

Pratt, Orson: attends conference in Philadelphia, 45–46; biography of, 369; in Boston, 50; in England, 271; philosophy of, 163–64; preaches funeral sermon, 64; mentioned, 67, 105

Pratt, Parley P.: answers anguish over temple, 72; arbitrates Grant-Taylor dispute, 76–77; biography of, 369; Grant given charge of livestock for, 25; helps organize Church in Ohio, 156; to ordain Grant, 63; mentioned, 66, 83, 94

Preaching: Grant's philosophy of, 25–27, 180, 191–92, 202–6; significance among Mormons, 338–39

Presbyterian Church: Grant holds meetings in, 32

Prophecy: Grant's 1854 sermon on, 166–70

prostitution: Grant's attacks, 234–36

Provo, Utah: Grant preaches in (1855), 212–15; mentioned, 187

Provo River, 251

Pulsipher, Zerah, 281, 282, 369

Punks, Susan, 15

Puritan New England, 95

Pursey, Elder, 15

Quakenasp Creek, 82

Quincy, Ill., 31, 37

Rappers, spirit, 155, 157, 158–59

Rawson, Brother and Sister, 50

Read, Christiana, 54

Read, Hannah, 54

Reid, Lazarus, 236

Reese, John, 103, 106, 369

Reeves, Brother, 15, 123

Reeves, Theda Grant, 5-6, 7, 26, 369-70

Reeves, William, 270, 370

Reformation: First Presidency calls for (1854): 177-78; Grant calls for (1855): 216-17; Grant starts (1856): 259-60; 341-42, 272; in Davis County, 259-65, 269-71, 294; in Salt Lake City, 265-69, 291-92; results of, 293-94; scope of, 271, 307, 326-27; mentioned, 322

Reorganized Church of Jesus Christ of Latter Day Saints: rise of, 149, 237

restoration: Grant's concept of, 165; sermons in behalf of, 15

Reve, Calob, 54

Revelation: Grant on nature of, 239-40, 247-51

Rich, Charles, C, 76, 370

Richards, Caroline, 50

Richards, Franklin D.: account of, of Reformation, 293-94; biography of, 370; visits dying Grant, 312, 316; mentioned, 145

Richards, Samuel W., 215, 370

Richards, Willard: at martyrdom, 47; biography of, 370; clerks for Young, 63; death of, 159, 176; helped by relief party, 94; meets with Grant (1847), 75; nomination of, for secretary, 140; sends news to Twelve, 48; mentioned, 37, 105, 324, 339

Richards, William, 46, 54

Richmond, Mo., 25

Rigdon, Sidney: biography of, 370; excommunicated, 57; Grant's pamphlet against, 58-60; Smith's thought on, 53; Young's advice on, 61-62 mentioned, 54, 284, 339

Riter, Levi Evans, 82, 370-71

Riter, Rebecca W., 82, 371

Roberts, B. H., 135, 333

Robins, Ebenezer, 45, 371

Robinson, Richard S., 101, 371

Robison, Elizabeth Squires, 107, 116, 122, 137, 226, 371

Robison, James Henry, 111, 115, 122, 125, 136, 371

Robison, Rosetta. See Grant.

Rockingham County, N.C., 24, 35

Rockwell, Orrin Porter, 47, 371

Rockwood, Albert P., 72, 75, 281, 282, 371

Romney, George, 220, 371-72

Roundy, Shadrack, 103, 372

Rousseau, Jean-Jacques, 335

runaway judges affair (1851-52): begins, 113-14

Russia, 168, 239

Sacrament: withdrawn during Reformation, 280

Safety Society: failure of, 17-18, 20. See also Kirtland, Ohio.

St. Louis: Grant in (1845): 71, (1850): 103, 107; Grant's letters from, 103-6, 106-7; letters from Young to, 75; Spencer dies in, 219; mentioned, 100, 115, 146, 326

Saints. See also Mormonism; Mormons.

Salt Lake City: Caroline buried in, 85; conditions in, 148, 173, 202; council of, petitioned, 190-91; Grant arrives in, 145, 229, 265, 289; Grant first mayor of, 111; Grant's homes in, 93, 257, 260, 275-76; Grant's grievances against, 173, 209-10; misrepresentation of, by missionaries, 178-80; Reformation spreads to, 265-71; Spiritualism in, 150-152; mentioned, 93-343 passim

Salt Lake County: Grant elected to represent, 217

Salt Lake Temple: ground broken for, 148

Salt Lake Valley: description of (1849): 95, 96–100; Mormons arrive in (1847): 3, 77, 85; ninth anniversary in, 244

Sanders, Ellis M., 138, 372

Sandy River, 83

Sanpete County, Utah, 187

Savanna, N.Y., 15, 17

Savonarola, Girolamo, 341

Schwortz, John, 54

Scipio, Utah, 202

Scotland: Mormons in, 231; Woodruff in (1845): 65

Scott Bible commentary, 252

Seneca Falls, N.Y., 15

Seventies: Grant attacks (1856): 281–83

Seventy, First Council of: Grant appointed to, 54, 72; Grant ordained to, 72; mentioned, 148, 155

Seventy, First Quorum of: Grant ordained to, 8–9

Shaver, Leonidas, 236, 372

Shaw, Mr., 12

Sherman's Corners, Pa., 7

Sherwood, Henry G., 372

Silver Lake: celebration at (1856): 244–47

Skinner, Mr., 47

Sledgehammer of Brigham: Grant called, 154, 218, 334

Smith, Asahel, Jr., 372

Smith, Caroline (daughter of William S.), 49–50, 71

Smith, Caroline Amanda Grant: death and burial of, 64; increasingly ill, 44, 57, 60; letter of, to Grant, 48–50; marries William Smith, 7; travels to Philadelphia, 44

Smith, Don Carlos, 13, 14, 19, 372

Smith, Emma Hale: animosity of, toward Twelve, 71; biography of, 372–73; Grant's sister dies in home of, 64; rumors about, in East, 49; urges Joseph to return to Nauvoo, 47

Smith, George A.: at Philadelphia conference, 45; biography of, 373; emigrating company of, 101; Grant mentions, in prayer, 246; mentioned, 67, 199, 326

Smith, Hyrum: biography of, 373; grave of, 257; mediums imitate, 158; murder of, 47–48, 60, 67; reports Grant's encounter with Clark's men, 25; spirit of, present, 265; mentioned, 66, 197, 245, 313, 324

Smith, John (1781–1854): 94, 373

Smith, John (1832–1911): 197, 373

Smith, John L., 94, 373

Smith, John P., 52, 373

Smith, Joseph, Jr.: biography of, 373; candidacy of, for President, 46; Caroline Smith buried in tomb of, 64; Church history and, 27; confounds Baptist minister, 180–81; Constitution and, 196–97; criticizes and defends Grant brothers, 44; cures Grant of dyspepsia, 206; defines Nauvoo, 31, 72; demeanor of, 17, 58, 147, 163, 205; Grant's loyalty to, 46–47, 335; grave of, 64, 257; Holy Ghost and, 249–50; imitation of, by mediums, 158; martyrdom of, 3, 47–48, 316, 321; meets Young, 3; millennial visions of, 335–36; murderers of, acquitted, 67; polygyny and, 52, 238; Rachel Grant sealed to, 215, 227; remembered, 65, 72, 265, 267; revelations of, 41–42, 156–57, 168–70; rumors concerning, 49; slavery and, 23; testimony of, 6,

198; thoughts of, on Rigdon, 53; mentioned, passim, *45*

Smith, Joseph, Sr., 4, 313

Smith, Lot, 373

Smith, Lucy Mack, 4, 50

Smith, Mary, 50

Smith, Roxcy Ann Grant, biography of, 373–74; mentioned,108, 122, 123, 125

Smith, Sylvester, 176, 374

Smith, William: biography of, 374; clashes with Winchester, 57; excommunication of, 65; Grant accuses, of adultery, 71; Grant calls, profligate, 238; marries Grant's sister, 7; marries second Grant sister, 108; mission to East, 45, 50; ordained patriarch, 64; wavering loyalty of, 43–44; wife admonishes, 48–50; mentioned, 58, 67, 238, 339

Smith, William R., 269–70, 374

Smith County, Va., 35

Smoot, Abraham O., 31, 103, 374

Snedaker, Johann, 101

Snedaker, John F., 101, 344, 374–75

Snow, Eliza R., 81, 84, 375

Snow, Erastus, 145, 375

Snow, Willard, 66, 75, 76, 82, 375

Snow, Zerubbabel, 133, 375

Social Hall, 148, 193, 202, 215

socialism: principles of, 98

South Pass, 83

Spanish Fork, Utah, 187

Sparks, Brother, 49

Spencer, Daniel, 76, 375

Spencer, Orson: biography of, 375–76; death of, 219

Spirit World: Grant's vision of, 313–15

Spiritual Wives. *See* polygyny.

Spiritualism: Grant attacks, 155, 157, 158–59

Sprague, L. L., 316

Springville, Utah, 187

Springwater, N.Y., 12, 13

Squires, Thomas, 261, 376

Staford, Mr., 32

Stanley, Harvey, 12, 376

Stark County, Ill., 31

Stenhouse, T. B. H., 272, 333–34, 376

Steptoe, Edward J., 190, 376

Steuben County, N.Y., 12, 18

Steward, Brother, 289

Stewart, David M., 316–17, 376

Stoddard, Solomon, 191, 376

Stoddard, Sylvester, B., 32, 37–38

Stokes County, N.C., 19, 23, 24

Strang, James J., 376

Stras, Mr., 34

Streeper, Wilkinson, 226, 376

Sugar Creek, Iowa, 73

Sullivan County, N.Y.: Grant labors in, 15–16, 17, 28; Grant's parents marry in, 5

Surry County, N.C.: Grant labors in, 24, 31, 38; Grant legends in, 329; Grant summarizes mission from, 35–38

Sweetwater River, 80, 81, 87

Taylor, Allen, 261, 376–77

Taylor, John: biography of, 377; Grant offends, 76–77; Grant prays for, 246; wounded at Carthage, 48; mentioned, 67, 83, 94, 100, 103

Taylor, Stephen W., 377

Taylor, Zachary, 113, 133, 134, 377

Tazewell, County, Va., 32, 35, 41

Index — 463

Teasdale, George, 377

Temple, J. T., 106

Temple Block: Grant's home near, 93; ground-breaking ceremony on, 148; wall around, 174; mentioned, 240, 294

Temple, Kirtland: compared to Nauvoo, 41; construction of, 11; manifestations in, 176, 264

Temple, Nauvoo: compared to Kirtland, 41; as emblem of Twelve's hegemony, 52; Grant collects funds for, 50, 64–68 passim; ordinances in, 72–73; Young seeks to finish, 60, 62

Temple rites, 42, 60, 72–73

Tennant, William, 337, 377

theocracy: in early Utah, 173, 211

Thomson, Deliah, 54

Thurston, George W., 244, 253, 377

Thurston, Sarah Ann. *See* Grant.

Thurston, Thomas J., 244, 253, 377

Tibbs, George M., 40

Times and Seasons (Church periodical), 35, 40, 61, 62

tithing: Grant orders, sent to city, 174–75; Grant to teach law of, 62

Tompkins, Silvan S.: model of commitment, 18

Tompson, Charles, 12

Toms River, N.J., 49, 121–22

Trees: Grant orders, planted, 210–11

"Truth for the Mormons" (first letter to the *New York Herald*), 131–32, 135, 333–34, 383–99

Turkey, 168

Turley, Theodore, 47–48, 378

Twelve, Quorum of: animosity between Smiths and, 71; attacks upon, 50–53; considers Richards's replacement, 173; directs exodus, 72–76; Grant's loyalty to, 50, 58; ordains Grant apostle, 173; preaching of, as scripture, 164; sends Grant east (1847): 75; mentioned, 146, 295

uniformity: Grant's 1853 sermon on, 151–54

Union, N.Y., 4

Union Hall, 193

Union Hotel, 193

United Order, 340

Urim and Thummin, 156

Utah Act (1850): 111, 233

Utah County, Utah, 187, 229, 258

Utah Territory: government established, 112

Utah War, 35, 327–28

Utopianism, 337. *See also* Millennialism.

Van Dyke, Caroline Ann. *See* Grant.

Virginia: conditions in, 23; Grant's missionary labors in, 19, 31–39; mentioned, 185, 190, 194

Wait, Anny, 13

Wait, Jabus, 14

Wait, Mary, 15

Wales: Mormons in, 231

Walton, Brother, 49

Wasatch Front, 200, 328

Washill, Va., 32

Washington, D.C.: Grant's 1847 mission to, 76; Grant's 1851-52 mission to, 114–20, 104–9; mentioned, 79, 149, 234, 236, 327

Washington, George, 194

Washington County, Va., 35

Wasson, Lorenzo D., 47

Waterloo, N.Y., 17

Watt, George D., 278

Watts, Isaac, 204

Wayne County, N.Y., 15, 17

Webb, Elizabeth Moyle, 378

Weber County, Utah, 174

Weber Valley, 244, 253

Webster, Daniel: biography of, 378; decides against runaways, 135; Grant visits, 117–20, 136

Weinal, John, 261

Welch, Lois Grant, 378

Wells, Daniel H.: administers to Grant, 312; biography of, 378; commands Nauvoo legion, 95, 322; helps with relief party, 94; oration of (1851): 113; mentioned, 95, 105, 120, 125, 221

Wesley, John, 203, 335

West Bountiful, Utah: Grant homesteads in, 193, 200, 215, 257, 291; farmhouse in, *195*, 344

Wheaten, Jane, 16

Wheaten, Miles, 16

Whitefield, George, 337, 378–79

Whitmer, Peter, Jr., 379

Whitney, Horace K., 45, 379

Whitney, Newell K.: biography of, 379; Grant's 1844 letter to, 53–54; mediums imitate, 158; mentioned, 105

Whittlesey, Elisha, 139–40

Wight, Lyman, 379

Wikoff, Mrs., 49

Willes, William: assists in Reformation, 258–64; biography of, 379; passim; mentioned, 308

Williams, Miss, 221

Williams, Thomas, 102

Willie, James Grey: biography of, 379; handcart company of, 299

Wilmington, Del., 49, 53

Wilson, Leonard, 13

Winchester, Benjamin: biography of, 379; Grant's missionary labors with, 18, 20; problems with, at Philadelphia, 44, 51–54, 57–58; mentioned, 339

Winter Quarters: apostles return to (1847): 82; Grant in party to locate, 74; Grant works to protect, 76; hardships in, 127; wards in, 75; mentioned, 78, 313

Winthrop, John, 211

Wiser, George, 54

wives, plurality of. *See* polygyny.

"Wolf Hunts," 62

women: Grant on role of, 297–99, 308–9; Smith's love of, 238

Wood, James G., 34–35, 380

Woodbury, Brother, 49

Woodruff, Phoebe, 67

Woodruff, Wilford: attends conference in Philadelphia, 45; attends ill Grant, 312, 316; biography of, 380; comments of, on Reformation, 271, 317, 326; describes Grant sermon (1855): 232; eulogizes Grant, 325–25; Grant constructs home near, 53; Grant's 1845 letter to, 65–67; Grant's relationship with, 270; in England, 65; leads emigrant party (1850): 105; meets other apostles in Boston, 50; records seventies meeting, 281–83; reports on Grant at Philadelphia, 57–58; toast to Grant (1852): 145; mentioned, 67, 200, 208

Woolley, Edwin D., 106, 380

"Word and Will of the Lord," 75, 89

Word of Wisdom, 286

Wrigley, Thomas, 115, 380

Wyoming: handcarts trapped in, 299
Wyoming County, N.Y., 11
Wythe County, Va., 32, 35

year without summer (1816): 4
Yolo County, Calif., 316–17
Young, Brigham: accusations against, 140–41, 150, 237–38; appoints emigration captains, 72, 76; as governor of Utah, 109, 111, 122; attempts of, to segregate Mormons and Gentiles, 212; becomes head of church, 3; biography of, 380; calls Grant to presidency, 173; catechism administered by, 179–80; characteristics of, 152–54, 200; conversion of, 7; death of Grant and, 315–16; directs gathering, 194; enters valley, 77; eulogizes Grant, 322–24; gives up horses to Grant, 82–83; Grant's letters to: (1844): 51–52, (1845): 63–64, (1847): 78–79, (1850): 103–6, (1851): 117–20, (1852): 126–27, 137–38, 139–40; Grant's loyalty to, 51–52, 149; honors Bernhisel, 215; illnesses of, 84, 290, 325; in East, 45, 48, 50; instructs Grant, 103; Kane's 1847 letter to, 327; leads advance party, 76; letter of, to Grant (1845): 61–63; millennial visions of, 336; ordained apostle, 8–9; ordains patriarchs, 94, 197; performs Grant marriage, 94; Perpetual Emigrating Fund Company and, 100, 109, 114; plans of, to stay in Illinois, 87; preaching of, 42, 94, 164, 205, 232, 265, 279–80; relationship of, with Grant, 3, 4, 150, 240, 339–40; sends Grant east, 100–1, 114; mentioned, passim
Young, Clara Decker, 85, 380
Young, Eliza R. Snow, 81, 84, 375
Young, John, Jr.: biography of, 380–81; in third hundred, 76, 79
Young, Joseph: biography of, 381; English mission of, 105; Seventies to support, 281–83; Reformation and, 258–65, 269
Young, Joseph Angell, 381
Young, Phineas, 78, 90, 380
Young Men's and Young Ladies' Society, 43

Zion: gathering of, 62, 100, 184, 194, 300–2; Grant's 1854 sermon on evil in, 188–91; Mormons leave, behind, 31; misrepresentation of, by missionaries, 178–80; spirit of, defined, 181–83
Zion's Camp, 7–8, 57, 339
Zion's Cooperative Mercantile Institution (ZCMI), 93, 344

Also available from
GREG KOFFORD BOOKS

Mormonism in Transition: A History of the Latter-day Saints, 1890–1930, 3rd ed.

Thomas G. Alexander

Paperback, ISBN: 978-1-58958-188-3

More than two decades after its original publication, Thomas G. Alexander's Mormonism in Transition still engages audiences with its insightful study of the pivotal, early years of the Churcah of Jesus Christ of Latter-day Saints. Serving as a vital read for both students and scholars of American religious and social history, Alexander's book explains and charts the Church's transformation over this 40-year period of both religious and American history.

For those familiar with the LDS Church in modern times, it is impossible to study Mormonism in Transition without pondering the enormous amount of changes the Church has been through since 1890. For those new to the study of Mormonism, this book will give them a clear understanding the challenges the Church went through to go from a persecuted and scorned society to the rapidly growing, respected community it is today.

Praise for Mormonism in Transition:

"A must read for any serious student of this 'peculiar people' and Western history." – STANLEY B. KIMBALL, *Journal of the West*

"Will be required reading for all historians of Mormonism for some time to come." – WILLIAM D. RUSSELL, *Journal of American History*

"This is by far the most important book on this crucial period in LDS history." – JAN SHIPPS, author of *Mormonism: The Story of a New Religious Tradition*

"A work of careful and prodigious scholarship." – LEONARD J. ARRINGTON, author of *Brigham Young: American Moses*

"Clearly fills a tremendous void in the history of Mormonism." – Klaus J. Hansen, author of *Mormonism and the American Experience*

The Annals of the Southern Mission: A Record of the History of the Settlement of Southern Utah

James Godson Bleak
Edited by Aaron McArthur and Reid L. Neilson

Hardcover, ISBN: 978-1-58958-652-9

James G. Bleak's *Annals of the Southern Mission* (1900–1907) number 2,266 loose and lined pages and represent the finest early history of Southern Utah stretching from its initial Mormon settlement in 1849 into the early years of the twentieth century.

Bleak submitted the first portion of the history, numbering over 500 pages, to the Church Historian's Office in April 1903. He submitted additional increments of the manuscript when he visited Salt Lake City, usually for general conferences. He delivered the final installment of his Annals to the Historian's Office in October 1907. The complete holograph manuscript has been in the continuous custody of the Church History Department (formerly the Church Historian's Office) ever since.

Carefully transcribed and annotated by Aaron McArthur and Reid L. Neilson, this important work provides a detailed historical, ecclesiastical, agricultural, governmental, and cultural record of Southern Utah in the latter half of the nineteenth century.

Praise for *The Annals of the Southern Mission*:

"Professional historians and lay readers will be inspired by this vivid account of the pioneer experiences mostly before statehood or modernization. Developing water systems, establishing schools, creating courts and laws, constructing civic and commercial building and homes, raising food and animals promoting the arts, and generating faith and community harmony in some forty villages in Southern Utah and nearby Nevada and Arizona are all captured by James G.. Bleak. We will all be indebted to Brandon Metcalf for the fine Introduction and to Aaron McArthur and Reid Nielson for their brilliant editing of this important and extensive document." —Douglas Alder, Professor Emeritus and Former President of Dixie College

Excavating Mormon Pasts: The New Historiography of the Last Half Century

Newell G. Bringhurst and
Lavina Fielding Anderson

Paperback, ISBN: 978-1-58958-115-9

Special Book Award - John Whitmer Historical Association

Mormonism was born less than 200 years ago, but in that short time it has developed into a dynamic world religious movement. With that growth has come the inevitable restructuring and reevaluation of its history and doctrine. Mormon and non-Mormon scholars alike have viewed Joseph Smith's religion as fertile soil for religious, historical and sociological studies. Many early attempts to either defend or defame the Church were at best sloppy and often dishonest. It has taken decades for Mormon scholarship to mature to its present state. The editors of this book have assembled 16 essays addressing the substantial number of published works in the field of Mormon studies from 1950 to the present. The contributors come from various segments of the Mormon tradition and fairly represent the broad intellectual spectrum of that tradition. Each essay focuses on a particular aspect of Mormonism (history, women's issues, polygamy, etc.), and each is careful to evenhandedly evaluate the strengths and weaknesses of the books under discussion. More importantly, each volume is placed in context with other, related works, giving the reader a panoramic view of contemporary research. Students of Mormonism will find this collection of historiographical essays an invaluable addition to their libraries.

Mormon Polygamous Families: Life in the Principle

Jessie L. Embry

Paperback, ISBN: 978-1-58958-098-5
Hardcover, ISBN: 978-1-58958-114-2

    Mormons and non-Mormons all have their views about how polygamy was practiced in the Church of Jesus Christ of Latter-day Saints during the late nineteenth and early twentieth centuries. Embry has examined the participants themselves in order to understand how men and women living a nineteenth-century Victorian lifestyle adapted to polygamy. Based on records and oral histories with husbands, wives, and children who lived in Mormon polygamous households, this study explores the diverse experiences of individual families and stereotypes about polygamy. The interviews are in some cases the only sources of primary information on how plural families were organized. In addition, children from monogamous families who grew up during the same period were interviewed to form a comparison group. When carefully examined, most of the stereotypes about polygamous marriages do not hold true. In this work it becomes clear that Mormon polygamous families were not much different from Mormon monogamous families and non-Mormon families of the same era. Embry offers a new perspective on the Mormon practice of polygamy that enables readers to gain better understanding of Mormonism historically.

Fire and Sword: A History of the Latter-day Saints in Northern Missouri, 1836-39

Leland Homer Gentry and Todd M. Compton

Hardcover, ISBN: 978-1-58958-103-6

Many Mormon dreams flourished in Missouri. So did many Mormon nightmares.

The Missouri period—especially from the summer of 1838 when Joseph took over vigorous, personal direction of this new Zion until the spring of 1839 when he escaped after five months of imprisonment—represents a moment of intense crisis in Mormon history. Representing the greatest extremes of devotion and violence, commitment and intolerance, physical suffering and terror—mobbings, battles, massacres, and political "knockdowns"—it shadowed the Mormon psyche for a century.

Leland Gentry was the first to step beyond this disturbing period as a one-sided symbol of religious persecution and move toward understanding it with careful documentation and evenhanded analysis. In Fire and Sword, Todd Compton collaborates with Gentry to update this foundational work with four decades of new scholarship, more insightful critical theory, and the wealth of resources that have become electronically available in the last few years.

Compton gives full credit to Leland Gentry's extraordinary achievement, particularly in documenting the existence of Danites and in attempting to tell the Missourians' side of the story; but he also goes far beyond it, gracefully drawing into the dialogue signal interpretations written since Gentry and introducing the raw urgency of personal writings, eyewitness journalists, and bemused politicians seesawing between human compassion and partisan harshness. In the lush Missouri landscape of the Mormon imagination where Adam and Eve had walked out of the garden and where Adam would return to preside over his posterity, the towering religious creativity of Joseph Smith and clash of religious stereotypes created a swift and traumatic frontier drama that changed the Church.

"Swell Suffering":
A Biography of Maurine Whipple

Veda Tebbs Hale

Paperback, ISBN: 978-1-58958-124-1
Hardcover, ISBN: 978-1-58958-122-7

Maurine Whipple, author of what some critics consider Mormonism's greatest novel, *The Giant Joshua,* is an enigma. Her prize-winning novel has never been out of print, and its portrayal of the founding of St. George draws on her own family history to produce its unforgettable and candid portrait of plural marriage's challenges. Yet Maurine's life is full of contradictions and unanswered questions. Veda Tebbs Hale, a personal friend of the paradoxical novelist, answers these questions with sympathy and tact, nailing each insight down with thorough research in Whipple's vast but under-utilized collected papers.

Praise for *"Swell Suffering"*:

"Hale achieves an admirable balance of compassion and objectivity toward an author who seemed fated to offend those who offered to love or befriend her. . . . Readers of this biography will be reminded that Whipple was a full peer of such Utah writers as Virginia Sorensen, Fawn Brodie, and Juanita Brooks, all of whom achieved national fame for their literary and historical works during the mid-twentieth century"
—Levi S. Peterson, author of *The Backslider* and *Juanita Brooks: Mormon Historian*

Villages on Wheels: A Social History of the Gathering to Zion

Stanley B. Kimball and Violet T. Kimball

ISBN: 978-1-58958-119-7

The enduring saga of Mormonism is its great trek across the plains, and understanding that trek was the life work of Stanley B. Kimball, master of Mormon trails. This final work, a collaboration he began and which was completed after his death in 2003 by his photographer-writer wife, Violet, explores that movement westward as a social history, with the Mormons moving as "villages on wheels."

Set in the broader context of transcontinental migration to Oregon and California, the Mormon trek spanned twenty-two years, moved approximately 54,700 individuals, many of them in family groups, and left about 7,000 graves at the trailside.

Like a true social history, this fascinating account in fourteen chapters explores both the routines of the trail—cooking, cleaning, laundry, dealing with bodily functions—and the dramatic moments: encountering Indians and stampeding buffalo, giving birth, losing loved ones to death, dealing with rage and injustice, but also offering succor, kindliness, and faith. Religious observances were simultaneously an important part of creating and maintaining group cohesiveness, but working them into the fabric of the grueling day-to-day routine resulted in adaptation, including a "sliding Sabbath." The role played by children and teens receives careful scrutiny; not only did children grow up quickly on the trail, but the gender boundaries guarding their "separate spheres" blurred under the erosion of concentrating on tasks that had to be done regardless of the age or sex of those available to do them. Unexpected attention is given to African Americans who were part of this westering experience, and Violet also gives due credit to the "four-legged heroes" who hauled the wagons westward.

From Above and Below:
The Mormon Embrace of Revolution, 1840–1940

Craig Livingston

Paperback, ISBN: 978-1-58958-621-5

**2014 Best International Book Award,
Mormon History Association**

Praise for *From Above and Below*:

"In this engaging study, Craig Livingston examines Mormon responses to political revolutions across the globe from the 1840s to the 1930s. Latter-day Saints saw utopian possibilities in revolutions from the European tumults of 1848 to the Mexican Revolution. Highlighting the often radical anti-capitalist and anti-imperialist rhetoric of Mormon leaders, Livingston demonstrates how Latter-day Saints interpreted revolutions through their unique theology and millennialism."
--Matthew J. Grow, author of *Liberty to the Downtrodden: Thomas L. Kane, Romantic Reformer*

"Craig Livingston's landmark book demonstrates how 21st-century Mormonism's arch-conservatism was preceded by its pro-revolutionary worldview that was dominant from the 1830s to the 1930s. Shown by current opinion-polling to be the most politically conservative religious group in the United States, contemporary Mormons are unaware that leaders of the LDS Church once praised radical liberalism and violent revolutionaries. By this pre-1936 Mormon view, 'The people would reduce privilege and exploitation in the crucible of revolution, then reforge society in a spiritual union of peace' before the Coming of Christ and His Millennium. With profound research in Mormon sources and in academic studies about various social revolutions and political upheavals, Livingston provides a nuanced examination of this little-known dimension of LDS thought which tenuously balanced pro-revolutionary enthusiasms with anti-mob sentiments."
--D. Michael Quinn, author of *Elder Statesman: A Biography of J. Reuben Clark*

A House for the Most High: The Story of the Original Nauvoo Temple

Matthew McBride

Hardcover, ISBN: 978-1-58958-016-9

This awe-inspiring book is a tribute to the perseverance of the human spirit. *A House for the Most High* is a groundbreaking work from beginning to end with its faithful and comprehensive documentation of the Nauvoo Temple's conception. The behind-the-scenes stories of those determined Saints involved in the great struggle to raise the sacred edifice bring a new appreciation to all readers. McBride's painstaking research now gives us access to valuable firsthand accounts that are drawn straight from the newspaper articles, private diaries, journals, and letters of the steadfast participants.

The opening of this volume gives the reader an extraordinary window into the early temple-building labors of the besieged Church of Jesus Christ of Latter-day Saints, the development of what would become temple-related doctrines in the decade prior to the Nauvoo era, and the 1839 advent of the Saints in Illinois. The main body of this fascinating history covers the significant years, starting from 1840, when this temple was first considered, to the temple's early destruction by a devastating natural disaster. A well-thought-out conclusion completes the epic by telling of the repurchase of the temple lot by the Church in 1937, the lot's excavation in 1962, and the grand announcement in 1999 that the temple would indeed be rebuilt. Also included are an astonishing appendix containing rare and fascinating eyewitness descriptions of the temple and a bibliography of all major source materials. Mormons and non-Mormons alike will discover, within the pages of this book, a true sense of wonder and gratitude for a determined people whose sole desire was to build a sacred and holy temple for the worship of their God.

Mormon and Maori

Marjorie Newton

Paperback, ISBN: 978-1-58958-639-0

**2015 Best International Book Award,
Mormon History Association**

Praise for *The Liberal Soul*:

"*Mormon and Maori* is the result of a labor of love that reflects not years but decades of diligent research. Indeed, in combination with Newton's earlier *Tiki and Temple*, it constitutes the most detailed discussion in print of the fascinating 160-year saga of accommodation and adjustment between Maori culture and Mormonism. Unflinchingly honest yet unfailingly compassionate, *Mormon and Maori* is a must-read for anyone interested in the extraordinary history of the LDS experience in New Zealand."
— Grant Underwood, Professor of History, Brigham Young University

"*Mormon and Maori* offers a substantial historical account that structures and organizes *te iwi* Māori's (The Māori people's) often complex relationship and attachment to an American religion. In this respect Newton's work should be considered groundbreaking."
— Gina Colvin, *Journal of Mormon History*

Jan Shipps: A Social and Intellectual Portrait:
How a Methodist Girl from Hueytown, Alabama, Became an Acclaimed Mormon Studies Scholar

Gordon Shepherd and Gary Shepherd

Paperback, ISBN: 978-1-58958-767-0
Hardcover, ISBN: 978-1-58958-768-7

How did Jo Ann Barnett—a Methodist girl born and raised in Hueytown, Alabama, during the Great Depression and World War II—come to be Jan Shipps, a renowned non-Mormon historian and scholar of The Church of Jesus Christ of Latter-day Saints? In Jan Shipps: A Social and Intellectual Portrait, authors Gordon Shepherd and Gary Shepherd tell the story of how Shipps not only became an important and trusted authority in a field that was predominantly made up of Mormon men, but also the crucial role she played in legitimizing Mormon Studies as a credible academic field of study.

Praise for *Jan Shipps: A Social and Intellectual Portrait*:

"The person and work of Jan Shipps comprise one of the ten most important factors enabling Mormon Studies to eclipse its parochial past. Authors Gordon and Gary Shepherd have adroitly marshalled the tools of history and social science to lay bare how this unlikely event came to be. This is important reading for any who hope to understand Shipps or the emergence of the field in which she worked. Important also for any scholar feeling that the deck in a competitive academy is stacked against them." —Phil Barlow, Neal A. Maxwell Fellow at the Neal A. Maxwell Institute for Religious Scholarship at Brigham Young University.

"Jan Shipps deserves and the Shepherds are to be thanked for this celebration of her celebrated career. The authors rightly insist this is not a thorough treatment of Jan's life but rather an account of her role in the rise Mormon Studies in the late-twentieth century. It was a watershed time and Jan was a creator of and catalyst to much of the best scholarship which flowed from it. As such, there is much to learn here about Mormonism itself and those who studied it during this period." —Kathleen Flake, Richard Lyman Bushman Professor of Mormon Studies, University of Virginia

Lot Smith: Mormon Pioneer and American Frontiersman

Carmen R. Smith and Talana S. Hooper

Paperback, ISBN: 978-1-58958-692-5
Hardcover, ISBN: 978-1-58958-720-5

Lot Smith: Mormon Pioneer and American Frontiersman is the comprehensive biography of Utah's 1857 war hero and one of Arizona's early settlement leaders. With over fifty years of combined research, mother and daughter co-authors Carmen R. Smith and Talana S. Hooper take on many of the myths and legends surrounding this lesser-known but significant historical figure within Mormonism.

Lot Smith recounts the Mormon frontiersman's adventures in the Mormon Battalion, the hazardous rescue of the Willie and Martin handcart companies, the Utah War, and the Mormon colonization of the Arizona Territory. True stories of tense relations with the Navajo and Hopi tribes, Mormon flight into Mexico during the US government's anti-polygamy crusades, narrow escapes from bandits and law enforcers, and even Western-style shoot-outs place *Lot Smith: Mormon Pioneer and American Frontiersman* into both Western Americana literature and Mormon biographical history.

Praise for *Textual Studies*:

"An excellent and effective example of a 'life-and-times' biography, this history of the legendary Lot Smith as an imposing figure in the Mormon settlement of the West provides a fresh and very interesting retelling of that story. In the hands of two family members, the treatment is understandably friendly but remarkably thorough and complete. We follow Smith not only through his remarkable role as leader of the guerrilla force that harassed and delayed the U.S. Army during the Utah War but also his involvement in such other adventures as the Mormon Battalion, the Handcart Rescue, service in the Union Army, extensive involvement in polygamy, and an ambitious sortie into Navajo country that led to his death. This is a fascinating book worthy of a truly fascinating nineteenth-century frontiersman." —Gene A. Sessions, professor of history at Weber State University and author of *Mormon Thunder: A Documentary History of Jedediah Morgan Grant*

Hearken, O Ye People: The Historical Setting of Joseph Smith's Ohio Revelations

Mark Lyman Staker

Hardcover, ISBN: 978-1-58958-113-5

2010 Best Book Award - John Whitmer Historical Association
2011 Best Book Award - Mormon History Association

More of Mormonism's canonized revelations originated in or near Kirtland than any other place. Yet many of the events connected with those revelations and their 1830s historical context have faded over time. Mark Staker reconstructs the cultural experiences by which Kirtland's Latter-day Saints made sense of the revelations Joseph Smith pronounced. This volume rebuilds that exciting decade using clues from numerous archives, privately held records, museum collections, and even the soil where early members planted corn and homes. From this vast array of sources he shapes a detailed narrative of weather, religious backgrounds, dialect differences, race relations, theological discussions, food preparation, frontier violence, astronomical phenomena, and myriad daily customs of nineteenth-century life. The result is a "from the ground up" experience that today's Latter-day Saints can all but walk into and touch.

Praise for *Hearken O Ye People*:

"I am not aware of a more deeply researched and richly contextualized study of any period of Mormon church history than Mark Staker's study of Mormons in Ohio. We learn about everything from the details of Alexander Campbell's views on priesthood authority to the road conditions and weather on the four Lamanite missionaries' journey from New York to Ohio. All the Ohio revelations and even the First Vision are made to pulse with new meaning. This book sets a new standard of in-depth research in Latter-day Saint history."
    -Richard Bushman, author of *Joseph Smith: Rough Stone Rolling*

"To be well-informed, any student of Latter-day Saint history and doctrine must now be acquainted with the remarkable research of Mark Staker on the important history of the church in the Kirtland, Ohio, area."
    -Neal A. Maxwell Institute, Brigham Young University

For the Cause of Righteousness: A Global History of Blacks and Mormonism, 1830-2013

Russell W. Stevenson

Paperback, ISBN: 978-1-58958-529-4

**2015 Best Book Award,
Mormon History Association**

"In Russell Stevenson's *For the Cause of Righteousness: A Global History of Blacks and Mormonism*, he extends the story of Mormonism's long-standing priesthood ban to the broader history of the Church's interaction with blacks. In so doing he introduces both relevant atmospherics and important new context. These should inform all future discussions of this surprisingly enduring subject."

— Lester E. Bush, author of "Mormonism's Negro Doctrine: An Historical Overview"

"Russell Stevenson has produced a terrific compilation. Invaluable as a historical resource, and as a troubling morality tale. The array of documents compellingly reveals the tragedy and inconsistency of racial attitudes, policies, and doctrines in the LDS tradition, and the need for eternal vigilance in negotiating a faith that must never be unmoored from humaneness."

— Terryl L. Givens, author of *Parley P. Pratt: The Apostle Paul of Mormonism* and *By the Hand of Mormon: The American Scripture that Launched a New World Religion*

"You might wonder what a White man could possibly say to two Black women about Black Mormon history. Surprisingly a whole lot! As people who consider ourselves well informed in African-American Mormon History, we found a wealth of new information in *For the Cause of Righteousness*. Russell Stevenson's well-researched exploration of Blacks and Mormonism is an informative read, not just for those interested in Black history, but American history as well."

— Tamu Smith and Zandra Vranes (a.k.a. Sistas in Zion), authors, *Diary of Two Mad Black Mormons*

The Trek East: Mormonism Meets Japan, 1901–1968

Shinji Takagi

Paperback, ISBN: 978-1-58958-560-7
Hardcover, ISBN: 978-1-58958-561-4

**2017 Best International Book Award,
Mormon History Association**

Praise for *The Trek East*:

"In *The Trek East*, Dr. Shinji Takagi has produced a masterful treatment of Mormonism's foundation in Japan. Takagi takes an approach that informs us of Mormonism in Japan in a manner that focuses on inputs and results, environmental conditions in Japan and cultural biases of a Mormonism informed by western assumptions."
— Meg Stout, *The Millennial Star*

"This is a wonderful book, full of historical knowledge on a lesser-known subject in LDS history. The author, who is Japanese, LDS and lives in Virginia, is deeply invested in the subject and carefully includes all sides of the history."
— Mike Whitmer, *Deseret News*

"A monumental work of scholarship.... I can't imagine that any future study of this period could hope to provide a more thorough and engrossing analytical study of the origins and growth of the Church in Japan. This remarkable contribution is unlikely ever to be supplanted."
— Van C. Gessel, *Journal of Mormon History*

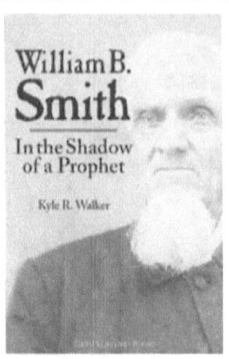

William B. Smith: In the Shadow of a Prophet

Kyle R. Walker

Paperback, ISBN: 978-1-58958-503-4

Younger brother of Joseph Smith, a member of the Quorum of the Twelve Apostles, and Church Patriarch for a time, William Smith had tumultuous yet devoted relationships with Joseph, his fellow members of the Twelve, and the LDS and RLDS (Community of Christ) churches. Walker's imposing biography examines not only William's complex life in detail, but also sheds additional light on the family dynamics of Joseph and Lucy Mack Smith, as well as the turbulent intersections between the LDS and RLDS churches. *William B. Smith: In the Shadow of a Prophet* is a vital contribution to Mormon history in both the LDS and RLDS traditions.

Praise for *William B. Smith*:

"Bullseye! Kyle Walker's biography of Joseph Smith Jr.'s lesser known younger brother William is right on target. It weaves a narrative that is searching, balanced, and comprehensive. Walker puts this former Mormon apostle solidly within a Smith family setting, and he hits the mark for anyone interested in Joseph Smith and his family. Walker's biography will become essential reading on leadership dynamics within Mormonism after Joseph Smith's death." — Mark Staker, author *Hearken, O Ye People: The Historical Setting of Joseph Smith's Ohio Revelations*

"This perceptive biography on William, the last remaining Smith brother, provides a thorough timeline of his life's journey and elucidates how his insatiable discontent eventually tempered the once irascible young man into a seasoned patriarch loved by those who knew him." — Erin B. Metcalfe, president (2014–15) John Whitmer Historical Association

"I suspect that this comprehensive treatment will serve as the definitive biography for years to come; it will certainly be difficult to improve upon." — Joe Steve Swick III, Association for Mormon Letters

www.ingramcontent.com/pod-product-compliance
Lightning Source LLC
Chambersburg PA
CBHW020235170426
43202CB00008B/89